Brzezany Memorial Book
(Berezhany, Ukraine)

Translation of
Brzezany, Narajow ve-ha-seviva; toldot kehilot she-nehrevu

Original Book Edited by:
Menachem Katz, Haifa, Brzezany-Narajow Societies in Israel and the United States

Originally published in Tel Aviv, 1978

JewishGen
מרכז עולמי לגנאלוגיה יהודית
The Global Home for Jewish Genealogy

A Publication of JewishGen
Edmond J. Safra Plaza, 36 Battery Place, New York, NY 10280
646.494.2972 | info@JewishGen.org | www.jewishgen.org

Brzezany Memorial Book (Berezhany, Ukraine)
Translation of *Brzezany, Narajow ve-ha-seviva; toldot kehilot she-nehrevu*

Copyright © 2024 by JewishGen. All rights reserved.
First Printing: December 2024, Kislev, 5785
Editor of Original Yizkor Book:
Menachem Katz, Haifa, Brzezany-Narajow Societies in Israel and the United States
Project Coordinator: Moshe Kutten
Project Coordinator Emerita: Ruth Yoseffa Erez
Cover Design: Rachel Kolokoff Hopper
Layout, formatting and indexing: Jonathan Wind

JewishGen Press is not responsible for inaccuracies or omissions in the original work and makes no representations regarding the accuracy of this translation. Digital images of the original book's contents can be seen online at the New York Public Library website or the Yiddish Book Center website.

Library of Congress Control Number (LCCN): 2024948942

ISBN: 978-1-962054-13-3 (hard cover: 682 pages, alk. paper)

About JewishGen.org

JewishGen, is a Genealogical Research Division of the Museum of Jewish Heritage - A Living Memorial to the Holocaust, serves as the global home for Jewish genealogy.

Featuring unparalleled access to 30+ million records, it offers unique search tools, along with opportunities for researchers to connect with others who share similar interests. Award winning resources such as the Family Finder, Discussion Groups, and ViewMate, are relied upon by thousands each day.

In addition, JewishGen's extensive informational, educational and historical offerings, such as the Jewish Communities Database, Yizkor Book translations, InfoFiles, Family Tree of the Jewish People, and KehilaLinks, provide critical insights, first-hand accounts, and context about Jewish communal and familial life throughout the world.

Offered as a free resource, JewishGen.org has facilitated thousands of family connections and success stories, and is currently engaged in an intensive expansion effort that will bring many more records, tools, and resources to its collections.

Please visit https://www.jewishgen.org/ to learn more.

Vice President for JewishGen: Avraham Groll

About the JewishGen Yizkor Book Project

Yizkor Books (Memorial Books) were traditionally written to memorialize the names of departed family and martyrs during holiday services in the synagogue (a practice that still exists in many synagogues today).

Over the centuries, as a result of countless persecutions and horrific atrocities committed against the Jews, Yizkor Books (Sefer Zikaron in Hebrew) were expanded to include more historical information, such as biographical sketches of famous personalities and descriptions of daily town life.

Following the Holocaust, the idea of remembrance and learning took on an urgent and crucial importance. Survivors of the Holocaust sought out other surviving residents of their former towns to memorialize and document the names and way of life of those who were ruthlessly murdered by the Nazis. These remembrances were documented in Yizkor Books, hundreds of which were published in the first decades after the Holocaust.

Most of these books were published privately, or through *Landsmanshaftn* (social organizations comprised of members originating from the same European town or region) that still existed, and were often distributed free of charge. The languages used to document these crucial histories and links to our past were mostly Yiddish and Hebrew. JewishGen has undertaken the sacred responsibility of translating these books into English so that the culture and way of life of these communities will be preserved and transmitted to future generations.

In 1986, a group of farsighted JewishGenners started a project to pool their efforts together in groups based upon their ancestors' towns and donate funds to translate the Yizkor books of their ancestral towns into English. As the translated material became available, it was made accessible for free at https://www.JewishGen.org/Yizkor . Hardcover copies can be purchased by visiting https://www.jewishgen.org/Yizkor/ybip.html (see below).

It is our hope that the translation of these books into English (and other languages) will assist the countless Jewish family researchers who are so desperately seeking to forge a connection with their heritage.

Director of JewishGen Yizkor Book Project: Lance Ackerfeld

About JewishGen Press

JewishGen Press (formerly the Yizkor Books-in-Print Project) is the publishing division of JewishGen.org, and provides a venue for the publication of non-fiction books pertaining to Jewish genealogy, history, culture, and heritage.

In addition to the Yizkor Book category, publications in the Other Non-Fiction category include Shoah memoirs and research, genealogical research, collections of genealogical and historical materials, biographies, diaries and letters, studies of Jewish experience and cultural life in the past, academic theses, and other books of interest to the Jewish community.

Please visit https://www.jewishgen.org/Yizkor/ybip.html to learn more.

Director of JewishGen Press: Joel Alpert
Managing Editor - Jessica Feinstein
Publications Manager - Susan Rosin

Notes to the Reader

The images in the original book were reproduced from photographs from the time of the first edition. These reproductions were already of poor quality, being pre-war and at least 30 or more years old. As a result, the images in the book are the best achievable.
A reader can view the original scans of the book on the websites listed below.

The original book can be seen online at the Yiddish Book Center website:

https://www.yiddishbookcenter.org/collections/yizkor-books/yzk-nybc313714/katz-menachem-bez-ez-ani-narayuv-veha-sevivah-microform-toldot-kehilot

OR

at the New York Public Library Digital Collections website:

https://digitalcollections.nypl.org/items/397056d0-5000-0133-8c6b-00505686a51c

To obtain a list of Shoah victims from **Brzezany (Berezhany, Ukraine),** the reader should access the Yad Vashem web site listed below; one can also search for specific family names using family name option. These lists are continually updated by Yad Vashem, so it is worthwhile to periodically search them.

There is more valuable information (including the Pages of Testimony, etc.) available on this website: https://yvng.yadvashem.org/

A list of all books available from JewishGen Press along with prices is available at: https://www.jewishgen.org/Yizkor/ybip.html

Cover Photo Credits

Cover Design by: Rachel Kolokoff Hopper

Front Cover:

The Great Synagogue in 1978 [page 227]

Front and Back Cover Background Photo: *Trees in Winter*, Rachel Kolokoff Hopper

Back Cover:

Upper Left: *Brzezany* [page 14]

Upper Right: *A Jewish soldier in the Austrian army (Mendel David and his son Itzkhak)* [page 33]

Middle Right: *On the bank of the river. The burnt flour mill is in the background.* [Page 89]

Bottom Right: *The orchestra in a comedy ball* [page 116]

Poem on Back Cover: *Remember by Moshe Bar David* [page 377]

Geopolitical Information

Map of Ukraine showing the location of **Berezhany** and **Narayiv**

Berezhany

Berezhany, Ukraine is located at 49°27' N 24°56' E 257 miles WSW of Kyyiv

	Town	District	Province	Country
Before WWI (c. 1900):	Brzeżany	Brzeżany	Galicia	Austrian Empire
Between the wars (c. 1930):	Brzeżany	Brzeżany	Tarnopol	Poland
After WWII (c. 1950):	Berezhany			Soviet Union
Today (c. 2000):	Berezhany			Ukraine

Alternate Names for the Town:

Berezhany [Rus, Ukr], Brzeżany [Pol], Brizan [Yid], Barzan, Berson, Berzhan, Brezan, Brzezhany, Bzezan, Bzhezhani, Bereschany, Berezany

Nearby Jewish Communities:

Narayiv 9 miles NW
Kozova 10 miles E
Stratin 11 miles W
Dunayev 12 miles NNW
Pomoryany 13 miles N
Rohatyn 14 miles W
Yezezhanka 15 miles NNE
Pidhaytsi 16 miles SE
Zboriv 18 miles NNE
Zavalov 18 miles SSE
Burshtyn 19 miles SW
Kozliv 20 miles ENE
Bilshivtsi 20 miles SSW
Kniahynychi 21 miles WSW
Ozerna 22 miles NE
Peremyshlyany 23 miles NW
Holohory 23 miles NNW
Zolotnyky 23 miles ESE
Burkaniv 23 miles ESE
Zhuriv 24 miles WSW

Bukachivtsi 24 miles SW
Zolochiv 24 miles N
Novi Strilyshcha 24 miles W
Vyshnivchyk 25 miles SE
Halych 25 miles SSW
Cherniv 25 miles WSW
Svirzh 26 miles WNW
Monastyryska 27 miles SSE
Khodoriv 28 miles W
Dolzhka 28 miles SW
Sasiv 29 miles N
Ustya-Zelene 29 miles S
Mariyampil 29 miles S
Voinyliv 29 miles SW
Yezupil' 30 miles SSW
Darakhov 30 miles ESE
Skvaryava 30 miles NNW
Ternopil 30 miles ENE
Zaliztsi 30 miles NE
Mikulintsy 30 miles E

Jewish Population in 1880: 4,712

Narayiv

Narayiv, Ukraine is located at 49°32' N 24°46' E and 263 miles WSW of Kyyiv

	Town	District	Province	Country
Before WWI (c. 1900):	Narajów	Brzeżany	Galicia	Austrian Empire
Between the wars (c. 1930):	Narajów	Brzeżany	Tarnopol	Poland
After WWII (c. 1950):	Narayev			Soviet Union
Today (c. 2000):	Narayiv			Ukraine

Alternate names for the town:

Narayiv [Ukr], Narajów [Pol], Nariav [Yid], Narayev [Rus], Naraiv, Narajów Miasto, Narayuv, Narajiw, Narajew

Nearby Jewish Communities:

Stratin 5 miles SSW
Dunayev 6 miles NNE
Berezhany 9 miles SE
Pomoryany 10 miles NE
Rohatyn 11 miles SW
Peremyshlyany 13 miles NW
Holohory 15 miles N
Yezezhanka 16 miles ENE
Novi Strilyshcha 16 miles W
Svirzh 17 miles WNW
Kniahynychi 17 miles SW
Kozova 19 miles ESE
Zolochiv 19 miles NNE
Burshtyn 19 miles SSW
Zboriv 19 miles ENE
Zhuriv 21 miles SW
Bobrka 22 miles WNW
Khodoriv 22 miles WSW
Hlyniany 23 miles NNW

Bukachivtsi 23 miles SSW
Skvaryava 23 miles N
Cherniv 23 miles SW
Bilshivtsi 24 miles S
Sasiv 24 miles NNE
Mykolayiv 25 miles NW
Vybranivka 25 miles W
Pidhaytsi 25 miles SE
Bilyi Kamin 26 miles N
Zavalov 26 miles SSE
Kozliv 26 miles E
Ozerna 26 miles ENE
Zvenyhorod 27 miles WNW
Berezdivtsi 28 miles WSW
Dolzhka 28 miles SSW
Halych 29 miles S
Zhuravno 29 miles SW
Voinyliv 30 miles SSW
Zhydachiv 30 miles WSW
Olesko 30 miles N

Jewish Population: 1,088 (in 1880), 775 (in 1921)

Translator's Forward

I became involved with Jewishgen's Yizkor Book project when I translated the Yizkor books from my father and father-in-law's hometowns. After those books, I just kept going. This work is a holy work that preserves the life and culture of the Jewish communities in Galicia.

I am thankful for the opportunity presented to me to be able to do my small part in making sure that the rich Jewish life in Europe would never be forgotten.

Moshe Kutten
Pennsylvania, USA

Table of Contents

The Synagogues in Brzezany

The Holocaust

Brzezany Memorial Book
(Berezhany, Ukraine)
49°27' / 24°56'

Translation of
Brzezany, Narajow ve-ha-seviva; toldot kehilot she-nehrevu

Edited by: Menachem Katz, Haifa, Brzezany-Narajow Societies in Israel and the United States

Published in 1978

———

Our sincere appreciation to Yad Vashem
for the submission of the necrology for placement on the JewishGen web site.

Acknowledgments

Project Coordinator

Moshe Kutten

Ruth Yoseffa Erez (emerita)

This is a translation from: *Brzezany, Narajow ve-ha-seviva; toldot kehilot she-nehrevu*
(Brzezany Memorial Book),
Brzezany-Narajow Societies in Israel and the United States, 1978 (501 pages, Hebrew, Yiddish, English).

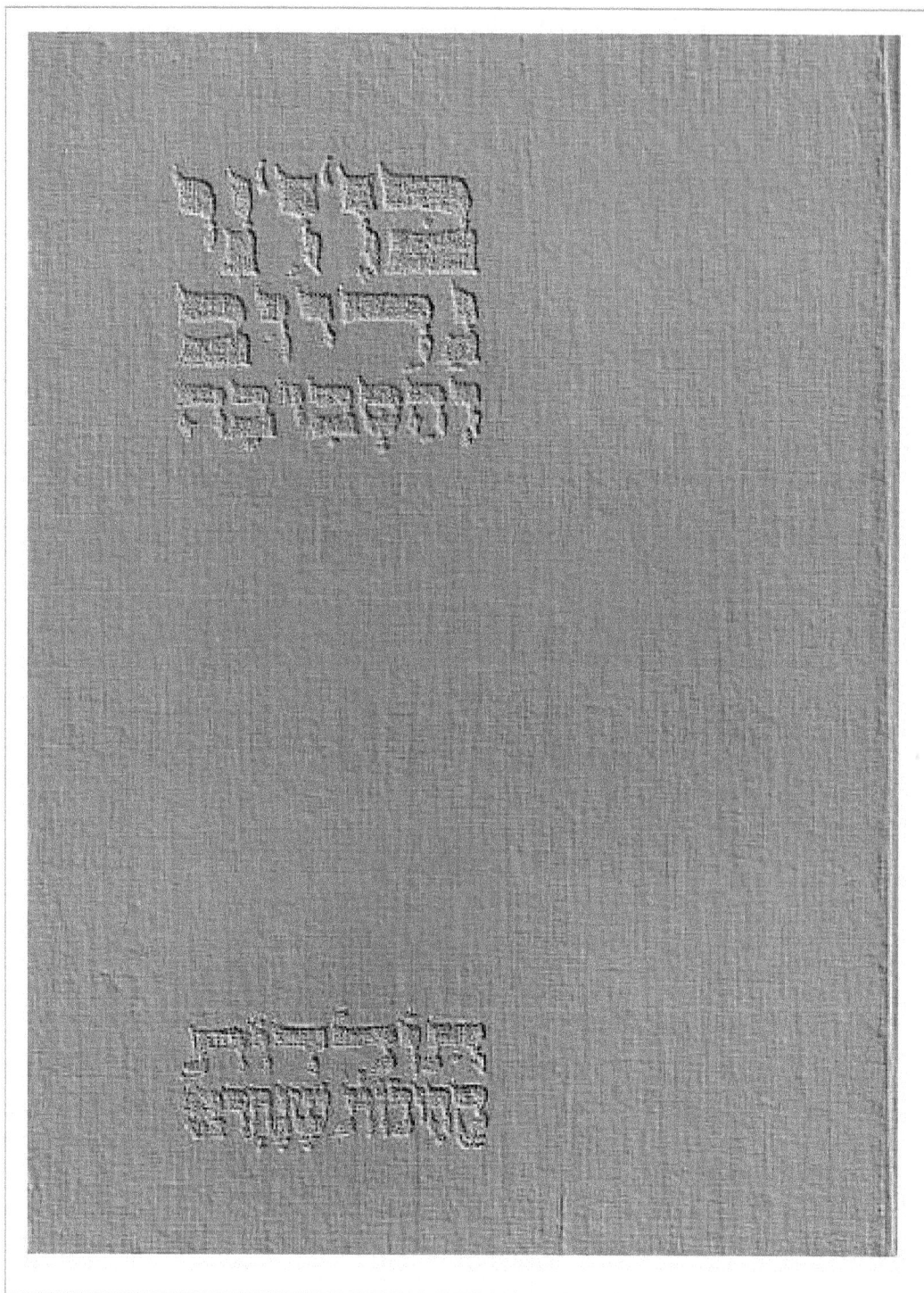

[Page 10]

Editor's Note

by Menachem Katz

[Same as English version]

[Page 11]

Introduction

One day, somebody will ask you: Who are you? Where did you come from? Who were your ancestors? What was their nature? What did they do? In other words, if you want to learn about your family's past, just read the book. You would find another world that is different from your world but close to your heart.

This book was written by people who devoted a substantial effort to collecting the material and brought it before the reader without adding or deducting anything.

We like to take the reader on a small tour of the city's streets and show him the *"Kheder"* where we studied. Our kindergarten and elementary school. We want to show the reader the big synagogue during the "Days of Awe," the home of a religious Jew on Friday night when they blessed over Shabbat candles and welcomed Shabbat with the words *"Shalom Aleichem"* ["Peace onto you"]…

We intend to show the community's leaders and the people's poor. To listen to a debate between Torah learners and the ordinary daily talk of the people. We will pass through the market and meet the merchants and their helpers, peddlers, porters, wagon owners, and artisans busy with their hard work. We would like you to see their life from different sides – in joy and, G-d forbid, in sorrow, on regular days and holidays, summer and winter. Only then will you be able to understand the secret of your past. You will learn where you suckled your wisdom and courage. You will know that you have not come from an empty space, that there is a tied connection between you and your past, and that there is no shame in that past. It was an arduous past, sometimes tragic. But your ancestors withstood that past honorably, and despite all the difficulties and the grueling struggle – they never surrendered!

Everything we have accomplished was thanks to their deeds, stubbornness, wisdom, and tradition. Your ancestors kept two basic commandments - at all times and under all conditions: "love of Israel" and "mutual aid" and therefore managed to maintain the religion and the unity of the people.

[Page 12]Blank[Page13]

The City and its Surroundings

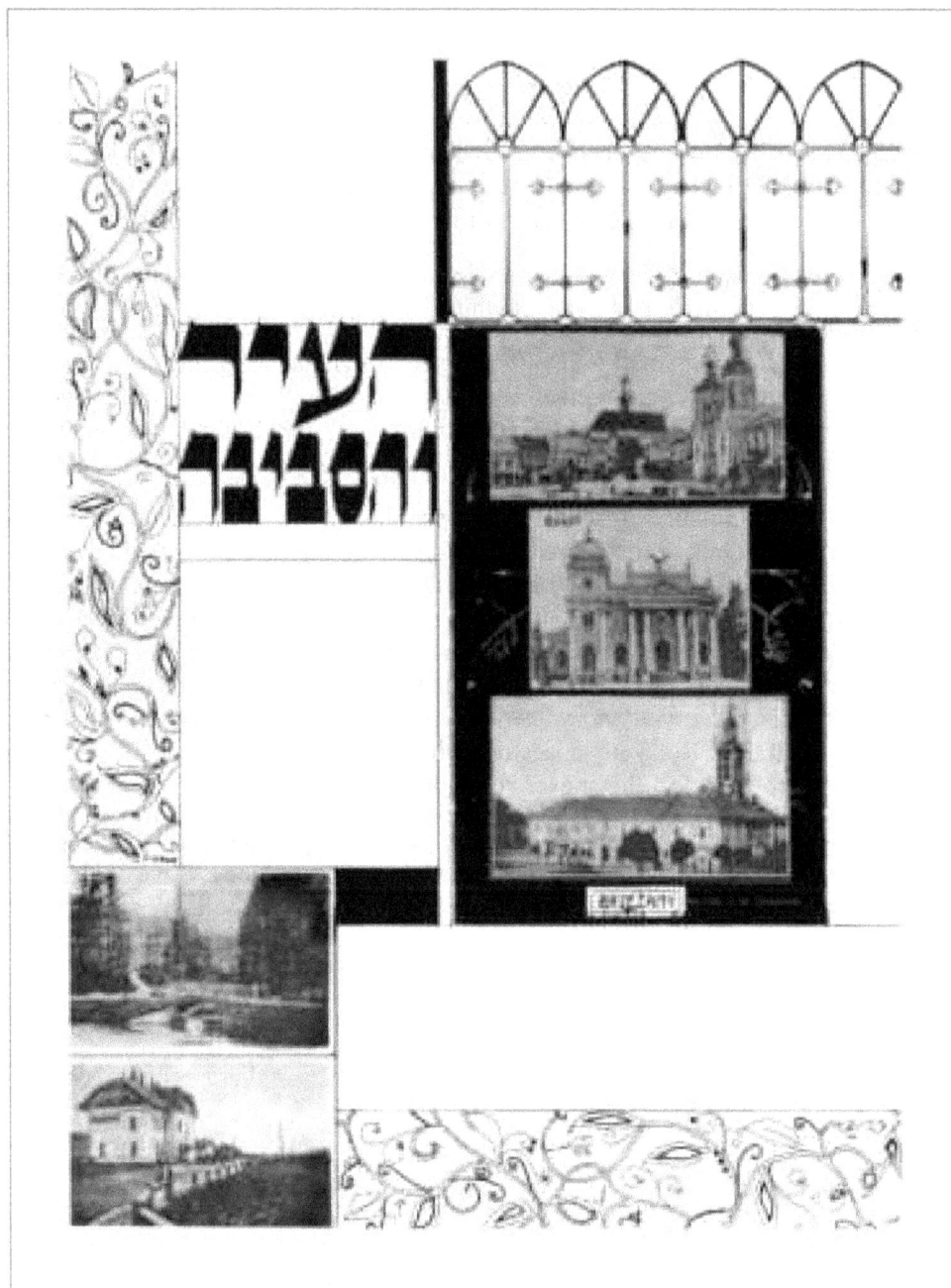

[Page 14]

The City's Surroundings

by Dr. Eliezer Shaklai[1]

Translated by Moshe Kutten

Edited by Jane S. Gabin

It's worthwhile to describe, in a few words, the city itself, which would make the understanding of the topic in question and the happening at a location and time.

The small town of Brzezany is situated in southeast Galicia, about 100 kilometers from the city of Lviv, in the triangle between the cities of Lviv, Stanislovov, and Tarnopol, hidden between trees and forests, close to the river Zlota–Lypa, at the edge of a lake in a low valley.

Seemingly, the town was like all other towns in that area, yet there was something unique about it that distinguished it from the rest: an incredible beauty and outstanding cleanliness. Brzezany was small in terms of its area or the number of its residents. Despite being small, the city was known in the world due to the Torah's great scholars and *Poskim* [deciders], who acquired a name for themselves beyond the limit of our town.

[Page 15]

The Area Around the City

A view of the lake from Keshtlovka Farm toward Storozisko Mountain

The lake lies on the city's northern side. Two huge forests - Zbiyezhinetz and Roriska - lie on two sides of the city, the southeastern side and the southwestern, both reaching the Carpathian Mountains.

Many types of trees grow in these forests: conifers such as pines, oaks, and cypresses, as well as fruit trees like cherry, walnut, and apple. Among the trees, meadows cover the ground like a multicolor carpet, seeded with many flowers and fruit bushes, including strawberry and raspberry.

Fields of grains and vegetable gardens spread around the city like a beautiful picture frame; the city's surroundings provide fruit and wood for heating and wood-based industries. There was fresh air and a pleasant place to spend time.

Four roads, running in four different directions from the center, connect it with the rest of the world; there is also another connection on the east side of the city's center. Brzezany boasts of -- the railway, passing in south-northern directions; the train station is about a kilometer from the city's center.

Thus, Brzezany is the central town of an entire region. Several villages with a population of one hundred thousand citizens are under its authority. Brzezany is a provincial city; several villages and towns (such as

Kozowa and Narajow) with a population of one hundred thousand are under its authority. These residents are tied to Brzezany municipally, economically, and culturally.

The city itself is divided into five sections: the center and four suburbs, which spread along the four main roads. In the north: Siolko; in the east: Khatky; to the south: Adamowka; and to the west: Miastczka.

A Look at the City

You can get an overall view of the city if you make an effort and climb to the highest point, in the northwestern corner of the city: Bernardines Mountain. On the top of the mountain stands the Bernardines' Monastery, a beautiful ancient building, big and long, with a bell tower. The monastery dominates the entire city, and the viewer is rewarded with an unforgettable view of the city. I loved the sounds of the bells. In them, I heard a whole chorus. It sounded divine and alluring. I loved climbing the mountain above the monastery and looking down at the entire city from above, with its streets, alleys, beautiful houses, flower gardens, and fruit trees. I could see the beautiful view, space toward infinity.

Usually, there were only just a few monks at the monastery. The place was quiet throughout most of the year. Only once each year, in the summer months on the holiday of "Holy Antony," the day of atonement in that monastery, tens of thousands of Christians came from near and faraway places to pray here for atonement for their sins.

The festivity began on the evening before the day of atonement. People gathered around the monastery, lit fires, sang, and danced throughout the night. It was a day that was all good. The Gentiles prayed for atonement for their sins – it was a market day for the Jews. It provided subsistence for several weeks. It was also a fun day for us, the children. The streets filled with people and merchants' stalls. People came from far away, whom we did not see throughout the year, with their goods: clothing, food, and even children's toys. We kept away from the *Kheder* and ran around in the streets until late hours.

[Page 16]

From the top of the mountain, one can see, stretching like a mirror, the long, broad, and magnificent lake framed east and west by mountains and hills. Two roads run along the length of the lake: on the east – the railroad, and on the west – the road leading to Lviv.

The lake was an essential resource for the residents, serving as a source of sustenance and relaxation.The lake provided fish during all months of the year. In the winter, people harvested ice blocks and preserved them for the summer months. A five-story flour mill took advantage of the difference in the water level between the lake and the valley below. The mill was destroyed during the First World War and was never rebuilt. For us, the youngsters, the lake served as a pleasant place for recreation. In the summer, we used to bathe in the lake and relax on its beach sands; in the winter, the lake served as a place for ice skating, and we spent long hours dancing on our skates there.

A high dam, one kilometer long and 20 meters wide, prevents the lake from shedding its waters into the town and flooding it. The water level was about 30 meters [100 meters in the English section] above the level of the market square. In some cases, most of which were in the spring, the lake overflowed its banks and endangered the city and its residents. I still recall the year 1912, toward the Passover holiday, when the lake water rose, and a substantial part of the city was covered by water. All the residents were ready to evacuate the city. During the summer days, the dam served as a place for social gatherings and a boardwalk for the youths.

The waters of Zlota Lypa River flow through the lake from north to south and leave the southern side of the lake as waterfalls, where they split into two branches, passing the city and recombining at the city exit.

East of the town, between the two forks of the river, stands a large stone structure, a remnant from the 16th century. It is a large building built from stones. A few Jewish families resided in it until the First World War. The fort also served as an elementary school for boys. A "*Capela*" – a small prayer house - stood in the fort's yard. A sign with the Tetragram was written in golden letters above the entrance. The *Capela* contained sarcophaguses with gravestones. Originally, the building served as a citadel for the Siekierski[?] family, the founders of the town. In this antiquated stronghold lived and were buried numerous generations of the Sieniawski family. The citadel, together with an immense fortune, was handed down from generation to generation. The last member of this renowned family was the famous Graf Pototski, whose palace was in a nearby village, Rai.

A municipal park was located on the western side of the fort. The park was big, well-maintained, and clean; now, it looks neglected. West of the park, the big and beautiful building of the Polish community center "Sokol" can be seen. Behind it, northward, stands a large but neglected building called "Reitschule." Close to this forsaken building is a wide-open field, which belonged to the fire brigade.

The dam in the closed state   The dam in the open state   The district committee's building

[Page 17]

From the city's center, we shift our gaze westward. This area is the most beautiful part of the city; glorious buildings, such as the district building (Starosetvo), and the buildings of the Savings and Loans Bank, post office, court and jail, the nearby municipal hospital, new high school, and others are located there. Villas with flower gardens and ornamental trees around them are there, too. Rayivska Street, leading to the neighboring village Rai and Graf Pototski's palace, winds there in the southwestern direction, amongst the gardens and the houses. Two cemeteries lie on the two sides of the road – the Jewish cemetery on the right side and the Christian on the left. Tall trees, hundreds of years old, grow along the entire length on both sides of the road, which served as a boardwalk for young couples.

The city center (and its surroundings) was the Jewish quarter - the center of Jewish life in our city. This was where the Jews lived and where their stores, houses of prayer, and community center were. The intensive life of the city's Jews concentrated there. It is, therefore, worthwhile to go into detail about the structure of that area.

The center of the town ran symmetrically. The streets stretch from east to west and from north to south. The central building in this area is the "Town Hall" (although the municipality's offices are not located in it). It is a big square building surrounded by a spacious yard. It is a two-story building with a tall tower housing a four-faced clock that can be seen from four directions. The clock always shows the exact time. The tower also bore the crest of Graf Pototski – a five-angled cross, with three branches on one side of the center and two on the other. According to legends, old Graf Pototski had six sons. This was symbolized in the original six-angled cross. However, after one of the sons converted to Judaism, the cross was flanked by only five branches.

The municipal building had two wide gates – one on the eastern side and the other on the western side. Many shops, most of which belonged to Jewish shopkeepers, were in the courtyard and surrounded the building and the square. The second floor of the building served as a high school. That school was transferred to our city from Zbarazh in 1805. Hundreds of students studied and graduated from the school, among them a substantial percentage of Jewish students. Two connected three-story houses are positioned around the central building, creating a frame-like structure.

A spacious square with a bell tower is situated between the building and the surrounding houses. Roads passing in the center of the square cut it into two parts. Around the square were the churches: the Greek-Catholic, behind it the Armenian, and south of them the Catholic. All of the churches are surrounded by associated buildings, and they are connected and support each other. The Greek-Catholic church is located between the houses. On two sides, north and east, were platforms that served as parking spaces for the horses and wagons belonging to the farmers. Part of this plot was set for the local drivers and porters. All the houses in the center of the town contained stores or bar rooms owned chiefly by Jews.

In the west stood the Greek Catholic Church with three tall towers. A well and a statute of the "Holy Mother" were situated in the front square of the church. A small garden on the south side of the church contained a small statue of the Polish king, Jan Sobieski.

Stalls and parking lots for the farmers' wagons and horses were located on the northern and eastern sides and close to the building. The farmers came to the city to do their shopping and other errands. Part of the parking lots

The church in the fort

The flour mills

The dam (Gorbla)

[Page 18]

was slated for the local wagoneers and porters (most of whom were Jewish). Shops or taverns owned by Jews were located in the houses in the center.

Another market, the "Nowy Rynek" (the new market), was located further north between the center and the lake. That market was smaller than the central market, less appealing, and neglected. Zbozuva Street connected the two markets. The Jewish community house was located on the east side of that street. It was built after the First World War thanks to Dr. Felk's (a physician) tenacity. It was a large and stable two-story building containing a large event hall and a few additional rooms. Two oak-wood gates were located on the side of the road, with a Star of David carved into the wood.

Around the commerce center, streets and allies lined with small and dilapidated houses stretched northward, eastward, and southward. That is where the poor people lived. The Great Synagogue stood on the southern side of that quarter – a grand renovated building from the last years of the past century. Two *Batei Midrash* and a few small Hassidic houses of prayers were located on the way to the Great Synagogue. The Jewish municipal ritual bathhouse, not-so-big hospital, and several other community-owned buildings were nearby.

Architect Menachem Katz describes the Great Synagogue and the rest of the houses of prayer in another chapter of this book.

[Page 19]

A 1755 map of the city and its fort from 1755

Translator's note:

1. Sections of the shortened version of the article in the English section, pages 8 - 9, were incorporated.

[Page 20]

The History of the Brzezany Jewish Community from the Establishment of the Town till the End of the 19th Century

By The Late Dr. N.M. Gelber

Translated by Moshe Kutten[1]

Edited by Jane S. Gabin

There is no evidence confirming when and how a Jewish community in our town began. Documents show, however, that in 1530, the year Brzezany received the status of a town, Jews already lived there, trading and taking an active part in its life. Little evidence exists about the life of Jews at this time other than a few tombstones, several hundred years old, and a cemetery in Zwiezyniec Forest, divided into Jewish and Christian sections. This cemetery was constructed for the victims of a pestilence plague that took the lives of most of the city inhabitants.

In 1530, based on the Magdeburg Law, the royal courtier Mikolaj of Sieniava [Sieniavski] permitted Sigismund I, King of Poland, to turn Brzezany, then a village, into a town. As a result of the need to establish fortified towns in this region, Sigismund was rather generous in granting such permits to the nobility. The permit or privilege to turn Brzezany into a town was granted to Mikolaj of Sieniava in the Sejm held on March 19th, 1530. The privilege states that he was allowed "to establish and create a town out of the village of Brzezany." In the same privilege, the town's inhabitants were granted permits "to display, buy, sell and trade merchandise and handle all types of businesses." The roles of the mayor and members of the council were positions of honor and were placed in the hands of wealthy artisans and merchants.

Brzezany included a large Armenian community, most or all of whom were merchants. The supplies for the Greek Catholic Church they erected were all drawn from their own storehouse. However, the Armenians could not compete with the local Jewish merchants and most had no choice but to leave the town. Only a few Armenian families stayed in Brzezany. The aforementioned church and the surrounding quarter called Ormianska to testify to the existence of a large Armenian community.

The story of the Armenian community in Brzezany serves as evidence of the existence of a Jewish community there. A document from 1638 mentions the election of a rabbi for three towns: Brzezany, Narajow, and Pszemyslany. It can be assumed that a Jewish community existed before this and that this was not the first rabbi to be elected in our town.

The history of our community resembles that of others in the region over various periods. Nothing worth mentioning is known. The law changed according to changes in the government. Before the Partition, Jews in Poland had complete freedom to manage their own community life and were completely autonomous concerning religion, rituals, and jurisdiction.

In those days, the leadership of the community was in the hands of several privileged families, the town's leadership. They elected the rabbi and fully controlled anything that had to do with the lives of Jews in our town. They collected taxes for the government, divided the tax load among the members of the community as they thought fit, and took care of the poor, education, and ritual. They determined issues of slaughtering, built the first synagogue, and helped build more. There were also smaller synagogues that were built through the contributions of individuals.

Coffins of Sieniawski family's princes, in the fort's church

[Page 21]

The organization of the Jewish community followed the Magdeburg Law. The Jews were defined as a special "Nation" in terms of community administration and had their own courts. They were subject to the mayor only in matters which had to do with the town in general. Thus, obligations such as the defense of the town were divided equally between Jews and Christians. Jews paid the owners of the town taxes for land and houses. A tax to the Catholic Church, paid regularly, was also demanded. In addition to the leaders, three more people were elected, who were called "good men."

The Jewish courts were run by *Dayanim* (Judges) and chaired by a rabbi. These courts handled all the conflicts between Jews. Their verdicts had to be approved by the community. Rabbis were elected by the community [council] and had to be approved by the owners of the town. The Jewish communities of Narajow and Pszemyslany were managed and controlled by the Brzezany community. The first rabbi, named Yehuda, is mentioned in 1638. Other early rabbis in Brzezany known to us are Rabbi Zvi Hirsch, son of Rabbi [Khaim] of Kolomyja, who served as a rabbi in Brzezany before 1680, the year he was appointed a rabbi in Drohobycz. He was replaced by Rabbi Itzhak Babad, who was married to the daughter of David Bar Itzhak from Zolkiew. Next was elected Rabbi Pinkhas-Mendel, son of Rabbi Asher Potoker. The rabbi mentioned after him was Rabbi Tuvia Yekhiel Mikhel Halperin, who served as a rabbi in Belz before coming to Brzezany in 1738. . He was the son of the Rabbi from Zbararzh, Rabbi Israel Halperin, and the grandson of Rabbi Avraham Halperin, who served as a Rabbi in Dubno.

The community life of Brzezany Jews centered around the synagogue. The first synagogue in Brzezany was built in the 17th century. The second was erected in 1718 near the town gate; its remnants can be seen there to this day. Near the synagogue, there was a school, public bath, hospital, and hostel for poor travelers. Sometime later, east of the synagogue, two *Batei Midrash* (religious schools) and two prayer houses were built for the *Hassidim* (disciples) of Rozlov and the *Hassidim* of Stratyn.

The town of Brzezany and its community grew stronger from year to year. From its establishment, the inhabitants of Brzezany were divided into 3 "Nations": 1) Poles and Ruthenians, who were called Christians, 2) Armenians, and 3) Jews. Every "Nation" had its own administration and judicial system. Early on in the history of Brzezany, the rights of Jews were limited. When the quarter known as Adamovka was established, the privilege granted in 1583 by the contemporary owner of Brzezany, Jadwiga of the Tarlow Sieniawski lineage, stated that bars in this part of town could not be leased to Jews. Also, Jews were not allowed to live in the market or purchase lots and houses from Christians. The purchase of real estate by Jews was subject to the approval of the mayor, who made sure that that property was previously owned by Jews or that no Christian wanted to buy that same property. These rules, however, remained theoretical since Jews bought houses in the market and the vicinity of the church as early as the beginning of the 17th century. This was made possible through special permits, which were issued in the palace accompanied by a recommendation of the Catholic priest.

By the end of the 17th century, 26 Jews lived by the market, 28 in the street leading from the Castle, and 27 in the street leading from the Adamovka Gate. As the town grew, so did our community. In 1570, the town included 260 inhabitants, of whom 4 families were Jewish. They were merchants and wine sellers. About 100 years later, in 1672, the traveler Urlikh von Wardokh [Werdum?] passed through Brzezany and described it. According to him, the town then included 500 families, of which 100 were Jewish. In 1682, 130 houses were owned by Christians, 10 by Armenians,

[Page 22]

and 55 by Jews.

In 1695, the fortified part of town included 183 citizen-owned houses, of which 75 belonged to Jews. The total number of houses in Brzezany at this time was 404, accommodating 3475 inhabitants. In 1762, there were 125 houses owned by Jews, of which 35 were by the market, 8 by the new market, 4 in the street leading from the Castle, and 3 near the Podhajce Gate. Despite the official rules limiting the purchase of market area property by Jews, by the end of the 18th century, almost all the houses in the market were owned by Jews, most used as hotels and bars.

The most prominent building in Brzezany was the Sieniawski Castle, which was built as a fortress. The members of this noble family, who were, as aforementioned, among the town's founders, took an active part in the life of the Polish State. Coming originally from Granova, in the region of the island Synsk, this family can be traced back to the 12th century. Mikolaj, the founder of Brzezany, played an important role in contemporary political life. He died in 1569 at the age of 77 and was buried in Brzezany.

In the 17th century, during the period of unrest and wars in Poland, Brzezany had its share in the general devastation as it was burned twice. During this period, Poland was invaded by the Swedes, the Russians, and the Tatars. In 1667, Jan Sobieski fought near Brzezany, and a memorial monument was erected in the market to honor him. This period of unrest lasted some 25 years into the 18th century. In the first half of the 18th century, Brzezany's ownership changed hands. From then on, it was owned by the Chertoryski family but ceased to be the dwelling place of the town's patrons. Its new owners only visited there occasionally. The daughter of Prince Chertoryski married Prince Lubomirski, and their daughter married Graf Potocki. This is also how Brzezany came to be owned by Stanislaw Potocki.

Jews made their living mostly as merchants and creditors. The main commerce was of corn, flour, wine, and leather. Most of the commerce outside the town was in Jewish hands. In addition, as of the end of the 17th century, all cattle and livestock businesses were in Jewish hands. Brzezany exported bulls to Silesia, and wheat to Danzig, and all this business was in the hands of a few affluent Jews. Small retail businesses gradually shifted into Jewish hands, and in 1695, there was no single Christian shop owner in town. Following the wars with the Kozaks in the middle of the 17th century, commerce with the East dwindled, and the Polish market was dominated by trade with the West, mainly Germany. These new routes were also largely Jewish. In 1762, there were 5 Jewish merchants in Brzezany who brought goods from Breslau. Their names were Itzhak Sukenik, Yehoshua Davidov, Herschko Sholimovitz, David Keikhinitski and Herschko Sokalski. It should be mentioned, however, that Brzezany Jews were not wealthy.

Following the complaints of some Christian inhabitants that the interest Jewish creditors charged was too high, in 1639, a rule was entered by Jews in the town chronicle stating that no Jew would charge interest greater than one schilling per Gulden. This, however, did not help much. Particularly severe punishments were imposed on Jews who bought stolen goods. The rules regarding this were particularly severe during the 18th century. In the middle of the 18th century, Jews from Zolochiv [Zloczow] bought stolen goods from Brzezany Jews. On December 16th, a verdict was issued, stating that each of the Brzezany Jews involved would receive 30 lashes on the bridge in front of the palace.

Jews were obliged to pay the poll tax. Documents specifying the poll taxes Jews paid in Brzezany in the 18th century are available, which enable us to estimate their numbers. In 1764, there were about 1000 Jews in Brzezany. The Frankist Movement in the mid-18th century left Brzezany unaffected, with one exception.

[Page 23]

The market square

The list of converts dated 1759, after the mass persecution of Frankists in Lviv, includes the name of a 32-year-old woman from Brzezany, Ludvika-Khana.

In 1740, lobbied by the "Council of Four Lands," the Region Convention was held in Brzezany. This must have been demanded by the government, which wished to regulate the collection of poll tax. This convention included 18 delegates from Zolkiew [Zolkwva], Brody, Khodorow, Yaniv [Janow], Lisky, Tysmenytsya [Tishmenitz], and Stryi. With the help of the Council of Four Lands, the convention in Brzezany reached final regulations regarding the poll tax. In the year 1762, the Jewish cemetery, which was constructed by the Jewish community outside the town's wall, was expanded.

In 1772, Brzezany became a part of the Habsburg Kingdom. This resulted in major changes in the lives of Jews there. During the Habsburg regime, the number of inhabitants in Brzezany reached 3000, half of whom were Jews. The Austrian administration introduced drastic changes, flooding the land and its Jews with new rules and regulations. This resulted in nothing but chaos. In time, the Austrian administrators understood that radical changes could not be made at once through rules and manipulations. Brzezany's fate was the same as that of the other towns in Galicia.

On December 6th, 1772, the first manipulation was introduced by Earl Fargan, who was in charge of the Jew's census. Rabbis and community leaders were required to present accurate reports about the state of the Jews in their respective communities, including community management, regulations, state of families, state of the property, occupations, and so forth.

With the diminishing of wine and alcohol production and retail, the economic state of Jews worsened. Their appeal to the government to cancel their taxes for 1772-73 due to their financial state was rejected. Compared to the taxes previously imposed by the Polish Government, the Austrian tax load was greater. During the Polish rule, Jews paid 30 Kreuzer poll tax per person. In the first year of Austrian rule, this was increased to a whole Florin and was enacted for children over one year old. In 1776, instead of the poll tax, the "Tolerance Tax" of 1 Florin per person was imposed, and to this, income tax and property tax in the same amount were added.

The Jewish management divided the tax load between the communities , and each community allocationdivided the allocated tax budon among individuals in the respective communities. Due to the heavy tax load, the community of Brzezany failed to keep up with its payments and owed the government increasing amounts of money. In 1780, the government ordered its administrators to foreclose on Jewish income due to unpaid bills. The community of Brzezany appealed to the government, asking to cancel their debt due to the poor financial situation of the town's Jews. In April 1780, instruction was given in Vienna to investigate the situation and postpone the foreclosure. This lasted till August 1784, when the tax load was reduced. In 1789, the Brzezany community owed 6,210 Florins for security tax, of which only 2,532 were paid. In 1790, the community owed 12,260 Florins for the "Tolerance Tax," of which 7,442 were paid. In response, the government in Vienna ordered their local administrators to deport all Brzezany Jews who failed to pay their taxes. Had this been enacted, a large number of families would have had to leave town, and that scared officials in Vienna, who canceled the deportation.

In 1785, administrative changes were made in Galicia, which was then divided into 18 regions. Brzezany was declared the capital of the 13th region, which included 8 additional towns.

[Page 24]

According to the 1789 census, the ten Jewish communities of the Brzezany Region included 2574 families.

In 1812, 6200 Jewish families were counted in the Brzezany region, with 24,760 individuals, and in Brzezany alone, 252 families with 1059 individuals.

The 1880 census counted 10,899 inhabitants in the town, divided as follows: Poles - 3749, Ruthenians - 2404, and Jews - 4712 (43.2% of the total population). In 1900, there were 11,443 inhabitants in Brzezany, of whom 4150 were Poles, 2605 Ruthenians, and 4395 Jews (38.4% of the total population). In the entire Brzezany Region, in 1900, there were 95,164 inhabitants, of whom 10,942 were Jews.

At the end of the 18th century, the economic state of Brzezany Jews was extremely difficult. In addition to their debts to the government, current taxes had to be paid, and the situation worsened rapidly. Very few did well, but most lived in great distress and despair, seeing no light at the end of the tunnel. Brzezany Jews were involved in several occupations. Among Jews, there were highly skilled artisans, mainly bakers and tailors. Many traded with yarn, wheat, barley, hay, and straw. Some traded with wood since the town was surrounded by forests. Most Jews in town were retailers.

In the 1820s, there were 18 merchants in town, of whom 17 were Jewish.

An attempt to alleviate the distress experienced by Jews was made at the beginning of the 19th century by Emperor Joseph II. He encouraged Jews to assume agricultural work by reducing the Tolerance Tax for Jewish farmers by 50% and eventually eliminating it altogether.

In 1785, as a result of the Jewish Rules and Regulations, thousands of Jewish families were left with no source of livelihood. On Aug. 16, 1785, the Emperor ordered his administrators to start settling the Jews in agriculture and farming. In the framework of a program to settle 1400 Jewish families from Galicia, the community of Brzezany had to designate 10 families, and in the greater Brzezany region â€" 69 families. After a while, 69 Jewish families settled in 49 farming plots. 10 Brzezany families settled in 5 farming plots. There were 5 settlers from Kozowa, 9 from Pidhaitsi [Podhitza], 7 from Bursztyn, 3 from Khodorow, 5 from Rozdvill [Rozdol], 4 from Steshalisk [Szczelisk], 8 from Bibrka [Bobrka], 12 from Rohatyn, and 6 from Peremyshlyany [Pszemyslany]. The costs of this project were the responsibility of the communities where the settling took place. In 1804 Graf Fuerstenbush announced that the region of Brzezany had filled its farm-settling quota.

By 1882, 40 Jewish families in the entire Brzezany region were still settled in agriculture, 24 were supported by the community, and 16 were self-supporting. In 1889, Jews owned 11.3% of the real estate in the region of Brzezany (5,487 hectares [13,558 acres]).

[Page 25]

In 1902, Jews owned 12% of the real estate in the region (5615 hectares [3,875 acres]).

In 1889, 19.5% of the forest land in the region was owned by Jews, and in 1902, 15.1%.

The Jewish population in Brzezany needed loan associations. The JCA [Jewish Colonization Association] began operating in Brzezany in 1906 and helped the Jewish population with interest-free loans. In 1908, the membership in the Brzezany association reached 371, compared to 190 in 1906. From the day of its establishment till Dec. 31, 1908, 753 loans for a total amount of 169,956 Crowns [Krones] were given. Loan association in the Schultse system operated in the Brzezany Region as well.

In the cultural and educational aspects, Jews experienced great difficulties as well. The Austrian Kingdom, as is well known, tried to "Germanize" the minorities within its territories, including the Jews, and to this end, established schools for Jews. Unlike in Bohemia and Moravia, this educational policy failed in Galicia, where parents refused to send their children to these schools. According to manipulation by Caesar Joseph II, as of 1789, such schools were established in Galicia, supervised by Hertz Homberg, and the teachers were brought from Bohemia and Moravia. One of the first 48 schools in Galicia was established in Brzezany, and in time, there were 100 such schools. A list from 1790 mentions a teacher named Wolf Reinenbakh, whose annual salary was 200 Florins. In 1802, teachers in Brzezany earned 900 Florins a year. Schools of this kind also operated in Rohatyn, with the teacher Shlomo Kornfeld, in Rozdol with the teacher Shimon Bland, and in Bubrka with the teacher Aharon Sharf. In most cases, the number of students has diminished over time. In 1806, 533 children studied in the Brzezany Region schools. The government decided to eliminate all the Jewish schools, and by an order of Caesar Frantz Joseph I, this decision was enforced that same year.

In 1805, the high school moved from Zbarazh to Brzezany. In 1858, there were 5 Jewish students in the high school, and their number increased from year to year, so in 1908, 186 out of the total of 825 students were Jewish.

Due to administrative changes, Brzezany became the capital of the region and the seat of the administration (Starostwo) and the Regional Council. There were also Government offices in Brzezany. Eight more towns, in addition to Brzezany, belonged to this region.

According to the Jewish Rules and Regulations, beginning from May 7th, 1789, a Regional Rabbi (*Kreiz-Rabiner*) was appointed in every region, while in other places, only religious teachers were allowed. Like the Leaders of the Community, the Rabbi was elected for 3 years, but unlike them, who were elected only by community members who were house owners, Rabbis were elected by all the Jews in the region.

The first Regional Rabbi in Brzezany was Rabbi Natanson. His duty was to supervise religious issues, manage birth, marriage, and death books in German, supervise cantors and others who held religious service positions, declare bans according to instructions of government officials, and take political oaths in the synagogues. The Brzezany Regional Rabbi, who also served as the rabbi in the town of Brzezany, earned 200 Florins annually and received a flat. Apart from this annual salary, he was paid for various services as well as for the registration of births, marriages, and deaths. The rabbi was exempt from community taxes.

[Page 26]

The Religious Teachers in other communities in the Brzezany Region also received annual salaries.

In 1821, the community of Brzezany appealed to the local government, stating that it had been brought to their knowledge that some measures had been taken to have the Jewish attire canceled. The community asked to resume their former attire for the following reasons: 1) The Jews were accustomed to it, 2) They were too poor to buy new clothes, and 3) Their overall situation was bad due to the high taxes. The local government did not succeed this time, and an order from Vienna instructed them not to force Jews to change their attire.

No significant changes were detected in the Brzezany community before 1848. As in the rest of Galicia, life took a routine course. In 1847, a convention of community leaders decided to petition the government regarding the dismal situation of the Jews. Since a collective petition was prohibited, it was decided that each of the larger communities would petition separately. Brzezany was not represented in this convention.

There were no serious responses in Brzezany to the 1848 events, where the abolishment of the impoverishing taxes was expected, as well as greater political and economic freedom. Yet, here, too, Jews, along with other communities, signed petitions to the Parliament, initiated by the teacher Reitman of Tarnopol.

The community of Brzezany did not collaborate with the political enterprise led by the Lvov community in 1853, striving to abolish the law from October 2, 1853, through which ownership privileges granted to Jews in 1848 were again limited.

Our community was controlled by several privileged families, such as Rappaport, Natanson, Fadenhecht, and Margaliot. In 1896, the community of Brzezany was headed by President Mordekhai Shwadron and his deputy, Meir Lieber. In 1902-12, the community was headed by Dr. Moshe Shenkar, the first Jewish lawyer in Brzezany. The community leadership in 1913 consisted of Mendel Bandler, Chairman and members of the board, Dr. Moshe Shenkar, Dr. Nathan Halperin, Joseph Neimann, Heinrich Sapir, Aba Shomer, and Rabbi Feivish Halperin who was elected to this position in 1911 after the death of the Great Rabbi Shalom Mordekhai Shwadron.

Little is known about our community's life in these years, for the community books were burnt by the Germans, and there are no traces of evidence. No evidence of the activity of the rabbis is available either, except that they participated in Regional Rabbinical conventions gathered by the government. In 1830, a rabbinical convention was summoned to declare a ban on those who challenged the meat and candle tax. Nineteen rabbis were summoned, including the Rabbi from Brzezany.

In this period, the *Maggid* [preacher] of Brody, Shlomo Kluger, was very influential in Brzezany and the surrounding towns. In 1843, Rabbi Shlomo Kluger left his community in Brody and accepted the invitation of the Brzezany community, who, in 1845, elected him the head of the rabbinical court. Despite the pleas of the Brody community leaders, the *Maggid* left Brody and moved to Brzezany. In the month of Adar 5605 (1845), a delegation from Brody arrived in Brzezany and took him back to their town. In Brzezany, he was received with great honor, especially by Rabbi Arie Leibush Natanson, father of the Lviv Rabbi, Rabbi Yosef Shaul Natanson, who had served as a rabbi in Brzezany before he was appointed a rabbi in Lviv. A few days after his first sermon in Brzezany,

[Page 27]

the *Maggid* caught typhus. He was sick for many years and, through this, understood that he should not have left Brody. He vowed to leave Brzezany and return to Brody as soon as he got better, and no pleading on behalf of Brzezany's prominent people changed his mind. He resided in Brody as a private person, refraining from intruding into the activities of Brody's new Teacher of Justice. His admirers, and especially Rabbi Yosef Natanson, supported him for the rest of his life.

Other facts known from this period are that in 1869, Jews were allowed to buy real estate, and Brzezany Jews asked to be allowed to buy lots, houses, estates, and land. The requests of some Brzezany Jews were acceded to: Shlomo Natanson, head of the Brzezany community and member of the Brody Chambre of Commerce, Baruch Fadenhecht, merchant, B. Rutenberg, and Ester Natanson. Shlomo Natanson also received 1869 the Civil Privilege (*Recht des Bürgers*) due to his status in the town administration and community.

In 1850 the first Chambers of Commerce and Industry were established in Galicia, one of them in Brody, which included the regions of Zloczow, Tarnopol, Czortkow, and Brzezany. The first president of the Brody Chamber of Commerce was Meir Kalir of Brody. Shlomo Natanson, the head of the Brzezany community, was elected its delegate to the Brody Chamber of Commerce.

Changes that took place at this time in the life of the state and its Jews were not felt in Brzezany, which was not a part of the Enlightenment Movement and did not introduce changes in education and social organizations as was the case with Tarnopol, Brody, and Zolkiew, which were actively involved in the Enlightenment Movement in Galicia. Single individuals who were influenced by the Enlightenment Movement were active in Brzezany, but they worked secretly, and there is no evidence of their influence on the town's youth.

The clock tower, 17th century. The high school on the 2nd floor
The photograph is from before World War I

Translator's Note:

1. Based on a translation that appeared in https://www.oocities.org/brzezany/

[Page 28]

From the End of the 19th Century until 1920

by Dr. E. Shaklai

Translated by Moshe Kutten

Edited by Jane S. Gabin

We do not have detailed information about the life of the Jews in that period. It was also hard to define the exact time when the influence of the Enlightenment Movement on the Jews in the city began. However, we know that it started in the second half of the 19th century.

We can only say for sure that even though the city was not an isolated island, the Enlightenment wave arrived late by tens of years compared to the other cities in the area, such as Lviv, Zolochiv, and Brody. On the other hand, Hassidism did affect Brzezany's Jews. It won many hearts. Several Hassidic currents left their mark on the city's Jews: Rozhin Hassidim (from the courts of Chortkov, Husiatyn, and Kopychyntsi), Belz, Stratyn, Zhydachiv, and others.

The number of *Mitnagdim* [people who oppose Hassidism] was large. There were also noncommitted house owners. We heard many stories about the wars between the various Hassidic courts and between the followers of one court to another - a real civil war between brothers in the same family. At the same time, we did not hear about any struggle between the *Mitnagdim* and Hassidim.

In the last years of the 19th century until the First World War, the two camps united in their fight against the influence of the Enlightenment Movement, which spread fast and captured the hearts of the youth.

Favorable conditions prevailed in our city that encouraged a fast spread. A high school existed in Brzezany, where our youth encountered students from other places who came to study in our school. The latter helped spread the enlightenment spirit. The university also opened its gates to anybody who wished to further their study, including Jews. Yeshiva students studied in secret - hiding (in the attic), where they made their first steps toward enlightenment. There were cases where the father caught his son reading and punished him severely.

The old R' Shtreizand told me that he was sitting, one day, in the attic holding a book. "Fortunately," his father found out and came up to him with a stick and beat him until he took the "*Dybbuk*" or the devil out of him. The beatings caused him to be sick for several months, but they helped "save" him from the devil's claws. His study friend continued his studies and "got hurt." He finished his studies at the university, becoming a lawyer and a "nonbeliever." That friend was Dr. Shenkar, who, over time, became the leader of our community.

Many youths who did not have the financial means to study in school had to acquire their knowledge from books without the help of a teacher. They came out of the "*Kheder*" and could not finish their studies. They studied and knew a lot but did not possess a graduation certificate. They could not secure a decent job, so they had to make a miserable living as private teachers. Some of them were Yekhezkel Goldberg (Khezkeli), Shaul Boneh, Peltz, Kipnis, and others.

The Enlightened in our city went in two distinct directions. Some students became perverted, abandoned their Jewish roots, and even converted. Others were assimilators who remained within the Jewish community. Many of them were not interested in Jewish affairs. Yet, some of the assimilators who remained

[Page 29]

Jewish in heart and soul, dedicated themselves to problems faced by the Jews, devoted from their free time to the advancement of the [enlightenment's] culture among the Jews, stood by the Jews in time of need, and searched for ways to resolve all the problems and hardships faced by the Jews in our city.

There are only some hints about the participation of the Jews in political life in that period. However, due to the general political situation in the area, we could clearly describe the political life of the Jews in that period until the Second World War.

The Polish-Ukrainian conflict flared up and even intensified. The competition for economic and cultural positions of a religious and national background commenced. That was one of the problems of the domestic policy of the Austrian government. The government supported the Ruthenians against the Poles and tried to introduce German as the spoken language. The Jews were not recognized as a separate nation and were counted as Poles, Ukrainians, or Germans. The Jews, both the Haredi and the Enlightened, split. Some supported the Poles (many Jews, such as Dr. Shenkar, participated actively in the Polish revolt and fought side by side with the Poles). A substantial number of the Haredi Jews and the Enlightened people supported the Austrian government. These were the officials, teachers, judges, and others. Two languages, Polish and German, competed with each other on the Jewish street. The intelligentsia mostly spoke Polish or German, and the masses spoke Yiddish and learned German. The dispute between the two camps intensified from one day to another, climaxing before the First World War during the election of the Austrian parliament (1907).

The Jews were already partially organized, and their candidate was the Zionist, Dr. Rappaport. Opposite him ran the Polish candidate, Dulema. Most assimilators and the Hassidim supported Dulemba, each for their own reasons. The Zionists (there was already a strong and organized Zionist movement in our city), in collaboration with the Ruthenian voters, fought for the Jewish candidate. Others wrote about that tough contest and its results. I would not repeat it. I would only want to emphasize the effect of the election on the Jews in our city. I am sure that even those who supported the Polish candidate, even if they did not admit it, were not at peace with their choice. This election pushed [the Jews], to a considerable extent, towards Jewish nationalism, and Zionism had won many hearts and followers.

The First World War erupted in 1914. A period that lasted about 6 years (although the War lasted only 4 years) commenced. That War brought with it far-reaching changes in communal life as well as in the individual. Following the War, a period began which was not only the continuation but also the result of the First World War. That period lasted less than two decades, but it was rich with critical and revolutionary events that directly induced the Second World War. For us, that period brought the destruction and total annihilation of Jewish life in our city. We, who survived, witnessed these events. We saw the turn of events and the deterioration of the political life in that period with our own eyes until what happened - happened.

Governments fell apart, and new governments replaced them. Regimes collapsed, and new ones were established in their place. A new kind of regime in Eastern Europe – the Communist regime, made an effort to widen its influence throughout the world, particularly in neighboring Poland. The economic crisis brought economic destruction to most of the countries. Its effect was also felt in our city. These were the indirect factors that affected our period and created it. For us, the revival of independent Poland was the most important and pronounced factor that changed our way of life. New Poland enacted new laws and issued new decrees, most of which were directed against us, and what they failed to enshrine in law, they practically brought into our lives.

[Page 30]

As in the rest of Poland, we Jews constituted a significant majority. The Jews constituted 30% of the population, and in terms of quality – the vast majority of the professional intelligentsia: Jews were lawyers, teachers, physicians, judges, and so forth. The trade was entirely in Jewish hands. Poland's government took all measures it had at its disposal, even if they were against the law, to change the situation to benefit the Poles.

We should not forget to mention one important factor, a familiar factor under a new cover – antisemitism, which intensified during that period to alarming proportions – up to pogroms. That was under the influence of the country located west of Poland, which made its mark on the steps taken by our government and the behavior of individuals toward the Jews. I will explain that by introducing facts in my continued description of the lives of the Jews in our city.

The city population, at that period, was about 14 thousand. The Poles were about half, 30% were Jews, and the rest were Ukrainians. The rule in the city was in the hands of a mayor and a committee of 8 members, elected by a 48-member council. The council members were elected in a secret democratic election. All the city residents eligible to vote participated in the election. The committee members were, according to an agreement, four Poles, two Jews, and two Ukrainians. The council consisted of 24 Poles, 16 Jews, and 8 Ukrainians.

The following were the Jewish members of the council in 1930:

Dr. Ravitz Yaakov – lawyer	Dr. Goldshlag Dr. – lawyer
Dr. Falk Bernard – a physician	Dr. Grossman Carol – lawyer
Horovitz David – high school teacher	Tadnier Wilhelm – judge
Rosenberg Leib – merchant	Lebel Moshe – merchant
Friedman Immanuel – merchant	Mitelman Ya'akov – merchant
Bihen Aharon – merchant	Reikhshtein Shlomo – merchant
Riger Oskar – merchant	Shtark Barukh – merchant
Bilig Shimon – tailor	Freier David – merchant

The following people were elected to the committee: Dr. Grossman and Riger Oskar.

The local authorities were liberal toward the Jews throughout all of those years. However, no Jew was accepted to work for the municipality except one – Dr. Pomerantz, who served as the municipal physician because there were no other candidates. The officials, Leon Lopater and Ogenia Kesselrovna, were remnants of before the war. Several Jews, all of them artisans, served as firefighters. All of them were volunteers.

[Page 31]

Members of the municipal council in 1930
The 16 Jews are concentrated on the right side

[Page 32]

The First World War. The Years 1914 – 1920

In July 1914, Austria declared war on Serbia. I was about 10 years old when I read an advertisement about the war declaration and general mobilization. Naively, I did not understand the magnitude of the disaster hidden in the wording of that ad. The enlistment began two days later, on the 9th of Av. Tens of thousands came to town from the neighboring villages with their escorts to enlist. Others came to shop. Among those who enlisted, there was a substantial percentage of Jewish youth. Twenty to thirty-five years olds were recruited first. A year later, all men ages 18 -50 were recruited.

Our city was situated not far from the Russian border and passed from one hand to another several times during the War. The front itself passed through the city twice, near the Zlota-Lypa River (for the first time in 1915 for several months and the second time in 1916 for the whole year). Many Jews left the city and escaped westward.

The remaining Jews witnessed the war operations, retreats, attacks, and

counter-attacks. The population suffered tremendously from those operations. The way of life of the residents totally changed. During the war, there was no Torah and no schooling. Also, when the father, the head of the family, was in the army, there was no income or upkeep. Everything got neglected and partially ruined. There was no trace of the days before the War. There was also no hope that things would change soon.

Besides the war activities, we suffered from attacks by neighboring peasants. They took advantage of the lack of rule in the city (between the retreat of one army and the entry of the other), came to town with axes and sacks for looting and robbery, broke into shops and apartments, and took everything, without interruption, that came into their hands.

Two big fires erupted during the war and burnt most of the houses in the city. The first was in 1915 when the Russians set the flour mill on fire on Saturday night after the "*Havdalah.*" I saw the Russians, with my own eyes, pouring kerosene into the wooden warehouse that bordered our house and setting it on fire.

The fire spread fast from north to south, engulfing houses in the city's center. A large part of the Jewish homes was burnt and destroyed.

The second fire occurred in the summer of 1918, the day before the holiday of "Shavuot," at noon. The fire erupted and engulfed most of the houses in the city at once. The following is how it happened:

Following the revolution in Russia and the peace treaty of Brest-Litovsk, at the end of 1917, hundreds of thousands of prisoners of war returned from Austria. Wretched, sick, and in tatters, they dragged themselves through the countryside. They died from the night's cold, hunger, and contagious diseases. The city residents tried to help them as much as they could. They erected kitchens, cooked light meals, and distributed the food among them. The government erected a few disinfection stations and

bathhouses outside the city close to the train station. The structures

were all covered with tar paper. On the day of the big fire, a hot water boiler exploded in one of the bathhouses. Flames took hold of all the structures. Black smoke covered the sky, and a strong wind pushed the smoke and pieces of burning tar paper from the east to the northwest. Before we had the time to comprehend how serious the situation was, the fire had broken out in many locations in the city's center and its suburbs.

[Page 33]

It was a hot day, and the wells dried up. The fire raged. Fires broke out in different places. People ran around like crazy. Tension intensified when the returning prisoners, who pretended to help, mingled among the people, purposely causing disorder and panic, and then began looting. That made it more difficult for people to fight the fire. Everyone remained in their place, guarding their apartments and property. People stood idly by the flames, which consumed their homes unhindered.

Help came from Lviv only after three days. Nothing remained for the helpers to do except to determine that three-quarters of the city – houses, warehouses, and properties – were already burnt, and the rest, whatever survived, was impossible to save for lack of proper tools. In the meantime, our people recouped, took the rescue operation into their own hands, and salvaged whatever they could.

Following the fire, the residents began to build up from the ruins with all the means available. They built temporary apartments, put in them the belongings they managed to salvage from the raging fire, and began everything from the ground up. We have already gotten used to these situations - standing and watching how the toil of years of work is destroyed, not shedding a tear, buckling up, rolling up our sleeves, and starting over until the next disaster.

The World War ended for a large part of the world's population, but for us, the war continued. The Poles and the Ukrainians fought for years over the ownership of Eastern Galitsia [Galicia?], and we, the Jews, were the scapegoats between them.

The Ukrainians, who ruled the eastern areas, seized power over the city. It is difficult to speak about a regime that was never elected. Every city and every district became the deciding and executing power on its own. Our youth, known for their sense of justice, welcomed the establishment of the Ukrainian state and tried to insert itself into that life. Some even joined the Ukrainian army and fought alongside them. We, in the youth movements, continued to meet for discussion and study Hebrew. We were only limited in the freedom of movement outside the city. The central regime promised to give autonomy to the Jews, but the officialdom and the military objected to that. They only gave the Jews the freedom to defend themselves. The Jewish "militia" was formed, and the [local authorities] gave it the weapons and a blue and white band for the sleeve. We were proud to receive that.

The economic situation was dismal. The limited commerce, which was until then in the hands of the Jews, fell out of their hands at once. The Ukrainians tried to take control of all aspects of life, although they were not ready or capable of doing so. They did not have the proper people with experience and knowledge in managing a state.

The life of that state was short. It was hard to say how the state would have developed if the Ukrainians remained in power. That time remained in my memory as a period with a sense of "today" without a "tomorrow," a foggy, insecure future, and an unpleasant episode in a life filled with the events of those days.

In the spring of 1919, the Poles received help from the outside and began attacking the Ukrainians. They slowly conquered one city after another and wiped out the young state before it had the time to fortify itself.

We suffered before from regime changes, but none of the past events can be compared to that period. The Polish army, under the command of General Jozef Haller, excelled in its brutality against the Jews during their campaign against the Ukrainians. They conducted pogroms and justified them by claiming that the Jews tended to side with the Ukrainians and hated the Poles. The Polish soldiers acquired a derogatory name for themselves "Haller'chiks," for their abuse and pogroms against the Jews: a pogrom in the city of Lviv, murderous beatings, chopping of beards, rapes, and hurried-up trials of innocent people.

A Jewish soldier in the Austrian army
(Mendel David and his son Itzkhak)

[Page 34]

Jews were caught daily for forced labor, to humiliate them in the eyes of the Gentiles, or just to take revenge. In addition, they were beaten during work. I recall a story that occurred in our city:

The monument of the Polish king Jan Sobieski was located in the center of the city. The Ukrainians took down the statue and threw it on the ground by its base. When the "Haller'chiks" entered the city, they caught

Jews, beat them, laid them down at the monument, and made a "staircase" from the bodies. One of the Jews was forced to take the statute, climb up on top of the people on the ground, and put the statue back in its place. That was one of the scenes that occurred daily, an addition to the dreadful economic situation of the Jews during more than five years of war.

The cultural life was halted. We did not have any meetings or gatherings, and the entire operation of the youth movement ceased. Fortunately, that situation did not last long. The army left the city, and power was transferred to civilian hands. That brought some relief, if not easement and betterment.

The experienced Jews began to reorganize their life. It was not easy. They encountered difficulties introduced by the Polish officialdom and difficulties due to monetary instability and irregular transportation (the need to travel by cart coupled with the lack of security on the roads). Nevertheless, everybody made an effort, gathered their strength, and began building their nest with the hope that, this time, it would be long-lived.

A year later, until the following summer, we breathed a sigh of relief. After all the impoverishment we had to endure, the regime decided to return to a more normal life. We overcame the difficulties we encountered, one step at a time. The youth also reorganized more vigorously and established the "HeKhalutz" youth movement. It also progressed one step forward when the first group of pioneers went out on a dangerous and circuitous way toward the future "Jewish State."

Against all our calculations and hopes for permanent peace, the Poles began with their new offensive eastward in their wish to expand their borders and annex the entire area of Ukraine. They reached the area near Kyiv. The Soviets organized themselves and opened with a counter-offensive, which took place during June, July, and August. The Soviets reached the Polish capital, Warsaw. During that operation, our city fell into the hands of the Soviets. They remained in it for four weeks. That period was etched in my memory as being different. This time, there were no attacks on the Jews, beatings, or forced labor. It was, however, a period of anarchy. All routine life stopped. The shops were closed, and there was no trade. The farmers did not bring their produce to the city, learning ceased, and the offices closed. There was no policing and nobody to complain to. In one word – "anarchy." It was like you owned everything and nothing. The army ran around to find food, which was nowhere to be found. The soldiers were torn and worn, dressed in tattered clothing, half civilian and half military. There was no robbery carried out by individuals since the regime confiscated everything for the common good. Everything in the hands of the Jews, whatever they managed to accumulate in the previous year, went to the state.

Gatherings were held outside in the center of the city, where enthusiastic speeches were given, describing the paradise on earth that we would experience soon. No more poor or rich people. Everybody is equal before the law.

Four weeks passed, leaving behind a strange dream and unpleasant results for us, the Jews.

[Page 35]

The Poles blamed us for collaborating with the Soviets. For that purpose, they tied the word "Jew" with the word "Communist." "Commune Jews," they called us, and that served as an excuse for them to abuse us at every opportunity. They conducted trials for innocent people, invited others for interrogation or to testify, and released them after profanities and beatings.

At last, the wars stopped. As a whole, those years were one big negative for us. Our men fell in battles, died from hunger and diseases, their property confiscated or destroyed, and the atmosphere around them was very hostile. Most of the Jews who left the city during the war never returned. Those who remained tried to rebuild their life without any hope for the future.

The Zamek [Castle] before WW I (built in the 16th century)

[Page 36]

The Community Committee

A decisive change occurred in the days of the renewed Polish rule following the First World War. The law decreed personal, secret, and democratic elections. Every Jew in town who reached the age of 18 could participate. The first elections were held in 1928, according to the laws, and 8 members were elected:

> Dr. Goldshlag – the head of the committee
> Lebel Moshe
> Riger Oscar
> Grossman Carol
> Rosenberg Leib
> Avraham-Yehuda Wilner
> Mitelman Ya'akov
> Tauber Hersh

They were the activists of the community in the city. Some of them were also elected to the municipal council.

According to the law, elections were held every four years. The following election year was 1932. Changes took place in those elections. For the first time, the craftsmen actively participated in the elections, and two of their representatives were elected: Dr. Pomerantz and Korn - the photographer. Another change: Barukh Shtark replaced Tauber, and Mitelman was replaced by Immanuel Friedman. The following people remained: Dr. Goldshlag – the head of the committee, Leib Rosenberg, Oscar Riger, and Avraham-Yehuda Vilner.

The last elections were held again four years later, in 1936. A vigorous battle commenced among several factors: the Zionist, unaffiliated house owners, and a personal candidate – the lawyer Somer David. Eight members were elected:

Dr. Klarer, a Zionist - head of the committee
Lawyer David Somer
Ginsberg David
Fogelman Shimshon
Dr. Grossman Carol
Ross Israel
Bernstein Leizer
Korn Ya'akov - photographer
Shvartz Moshe - a shoemaker

That committee served until the break of the Second World War. The activity of that committee ceased during the days of the Soviet regime and renewed only during the Natzi conquest. This administrative body automatically became the central part of the "Judenrat," representing the community toward the Nazi regime. That was the last committee. During its days, the community was annihilated, and its people perished.

[Page 37]

Towards the Change

I will start with the words told by R' Shalom Mordekhai Shvadron *ztz"l* when emissaries went to him and offered him to move from Buchach to our city to serve as a rabbi. He responded to them: "I am happy with this offer since Brzezany is acclaimed in its Jewish community, where world-renowned geniuses served in it as rabbis. There are house owners in the city [who can support a yeshiva] and great disciples-scholars. You can count on Rabbi Shvadron." Indeed, we had a large Yeshiva in the city. *Batie HaMidrash* were filled with god-fearing people knowledgeable of the Torah. The melodies of the Torah learners were not silenced even during the night. From our city, renowned scholars and rabbis went out to all corners of the world. It is enough to mention Rabbi Yosef-Shaul Natanson, a native of Brzezany, and later on the rabbi in Lviv, Rabbi Kluger, the Maggid from Brody, who served for some time in our city, Rabbi Schmelkes Itzkhak who moved to Przemyśl [Pshemishl], and Gaon Rabbi Shalom-Mordekhai Shvadron. [We should also mention] the rabbis: Rabbi Dr. Margaliot Shmuel Hirsh, the city rabbi of Firenze, a rabbi, and a researcher - Dr. Yehuda Bergman, the rabbi of the city of Berlin, Rabbi Meirson, the rabbi of Vienna, and Rabbi Berdovitz of Meidling. They were all natives of our city who learned the Torah and culture from the springs of the Torah's greats in our town.

Not only rabbis but even regular homeowners sat down day and night in *Batei HaMidrash*, debated a *Sugiya* ["A passage from the Talmud"], and studied a page of Gemarah with Tosafot and other commentaries.

The R' Avraham Tonis *z"l* once told me how his grandmother woke him and several other youths when she went early at dawn to open her grocery store with the following words: "Wake up lazy people! My husband, Moshe-Nathan, has been in the Beit HaMidrash for quite some time now. Wake up to study the Torah!"

My grandfather woke up early in the morning to give a Talmud lesson to the youths without getting paid. The Torah did not serve as an axe to grind for them. They did it in the name of the Heavens and the love of teaching the Torah.

The change came only in the second half of the 19th century when a few youths left the benches in the yeshiva and turned to general studies. They became lawyers, judges, teachers, physicians, and officials. In

1887, there were 14 lawyers in our city, and 12 of them were Jewish. In the beginning, their influence in the Jewish street was not felt. As aforementioned, some left Judaism or assimilated, while others did not forget their source, the knowledge they acquired in childhood, and remained involved with their heart and soul in Jewish culture and Jewish life. They affected the youth education in our town.

That was a period of awakening and organization and of looking for new ways in the nation's life as well as in culture and Hebrew literacy. Hebrew language monthly and weekly journals such as "HaMevaser" [The Heralder], "HeKhalutz" [The Pioneer], "HaMaggid" [The Preacher], and others. It is very difficult to describe the effect of that literature on the people of our city. The nation was resurrected. Not only the professional intelligentsia but also the homeowners were aroused and organized into a national movement. The Zionist Movement in all its factions, a Hebrew school, and youth movements were established.

[Page 38] Blank

[Page 39]

The Zionist Movement Chapter

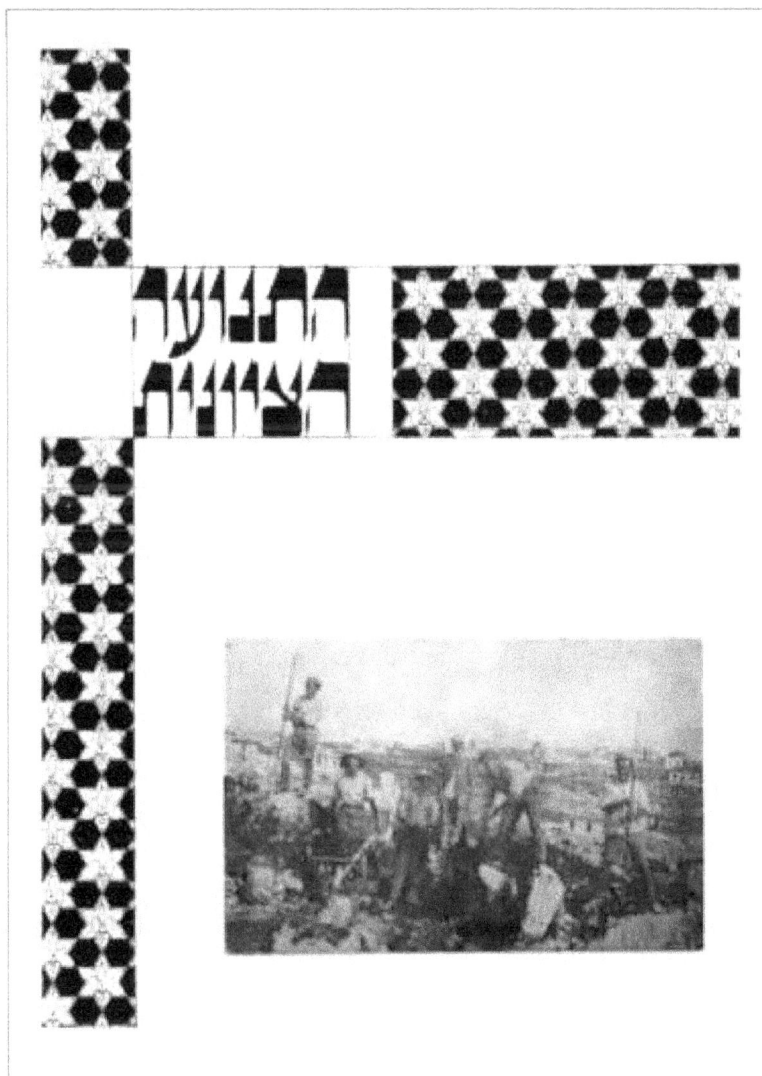

[Page 40]

The Zionist Movement

by Dr. Eliezer Shaklai

Translated by Moshe Kutten

Edited by Jane S. Gabin

We know about the Zionist Movement in our town only from 1893, when the Zionist association of "Bnei Tzion" [Literally –the Children of Zion] was founded. About one hundred members joined the organization upon its establishment. They were part of the intelligentsia in town, and most others were homeowners. Rabbi Leibush Landau and Dr. Gershon Zipper participated and gave speeches at the founding conference.

Shaul Meiblum was elected as the organization president, and Lebel as the secretary. In 1894, the number of members rose to one hundred and thirty. Shaul Meiblum, Leib Roza, and Kesil Zauer participated as Brzezany's representatives in the second conference of the "Bnei Tzion" movement, held in Stanisławow [today Ivano-Feankivsk] on June 26-27.

In 1897, our people participated in the elections for the First Zionist Congress. It was a momentous day for the city's Jews. When every one of the members approached the ballot booth, holding a [Zionist] Shekel, they felt that this was a political act of the highest importance and that by their vote, they were signing on establishing the state of Israel. Member Meiblum participated in the Congress.

Two years later, on 20 July 1899, a Zionist conference gathered in Lviv. Our member, Meiblum, participated in that conference as the Zionist representative from Brzezany. He gave a lecture, at that conference, about "The Organization in Galitsia." In 1899 there were 75 Zionist associations in Galitsia. One of them was in our town.

The organization had a reading and meeting room at the home of Yoskeh Pomerantz. An educated young man, diligent but sickly, named Egedran[Agderan?], the son of R' Moshe Egedran[Agderan?], the Talmud *melamed*. The members met there for reading, debate, and sometimes to listen to a lecture.

The Zionist Movement grew year to year. People from every walk of life, young and old, homeowners, officials, and Hebrew teachers, joined the movement. The latter helped in the dissemination of the Hebrew word and Zionism tremendously. The association invited lecturers who gave their lectures in a *Beit Midrash*. Not every *Beit Midrash* agreed to host such lecturers. The *gabbais* feared that the praying people, who objected to any political activity, would complain against them.

Among the first people who came to lecture in our city was Libel Toibish from Kolomyya, an educated man and a speaker par excellence. He gave a lecture in the "Built" *Beit HaMidrash* despite the objection of some of the praying people. Others came after him, and the crowd became accustomed to those lectures. In the winter of 1907, a Zionist preacher named Abramson arrived from Russia. He was a folk preacher, enthusiastic speaker, and a man of fine oratory. He resided in our city for about three weeks and gave speeches at gatherings. He had a big influence on the people of our town.

As aforementioned, the first president of the association was [Shaul] Meiblum. Yosef Ravitz was elected next, and Dr. Aharon Nagler after him.

The movement strengthened during the years between the two World Wars. It expanded its activity among the old-timers but also among the youth, who introduced new life and energy to the ranks of the old-timers.

[Page 41]

The Zionists became an imperative and decisive factor in the Jewish lives in our city. There were several ideological movements: General Zionists, which most old-timers belonged to, the Union, Mizrakhi, and Kherut. Some youth movements encompassed most of the young people in the city.

To advance and coordinate the activities, they elected a "Local Zionist Committee," which encompassed representatives from all movements. Member Karf, an old-timer, headed the committee. The following were the members: Dr. Goldshlag, Taler, Tonis, Reiner, and others. All of the institutions connected to the Jewish lives in the diaspora and Israel were part of the Zionist activities. These institutions included the K.K.L.-JNF, Keren HaYesod-UIA, assistance to *Hakhshara* and *Aliyah* (for local poor people), Hebrew school, kindergartens, local elections and elections to the Zionist Congress, Community House, orphanage, and more.

KKL activists in 1920

Standing from left to right in the first row: Lawyer Yosef Laber, Itzkhak Vinter, Moshe Segal, Tauba Rot-Tonis, Ya'akov Bumze, Rozia Shapira, Avraham Katz, Itzkhak Nadler
In the second row: Veizer, Eliyahu-David Rot, Rakhel Hibler, Ya'akov Shapira, Yona Kravitz, Leib Frid, Rozia Shapira [appeared twice, possibly an error], Tontzio Rutenberg, Bronia bik-Nadler, Rozia Likhtman, Moshe Reiss
In the third row: Moshe David (Bar David), Meir Taler, Regina Ast-Shomer, Dr. Shlomo Glazer, Mr. Kolker (from the KKL-JNF center in Lviv), Rotbaum, Tontzia Kohen
In the lower row: Zelig Segal, Feiga Velgar, Yosef Velgar, Mendel Tonis

[Page 42]

"Keren Kayemet Le'Israel" [Jewish National Fund]

The [blue] donation boxes of KKL on the wall by the picture of Herzl became the symbol for many Zionists in the year before the First World War. A few activists dedicated most of their time to this sacred work. We should mention the chairman for many years, Dr. Shlomo Glazer, secretary Tahler, Eliyahu-David Rot, and Menakhem Tonis. In Iyar 1927, the four people above were written into the Golden Book of the KKL by the jubilee committee. We celebrated the Jubilee of the organization that year. They received assistance from Zionists from all movements, but most were youths who performed the daily mundane work and collected donations for the KKL on every occasion.

The Golden Book registration certificate given to the members Dr. Shlomo Glazer, Meir Taler, Eliyahu-David Rot, and Menakhem Tonis as an appreciation for the activity on behalf of the KKL.

[Page 43]

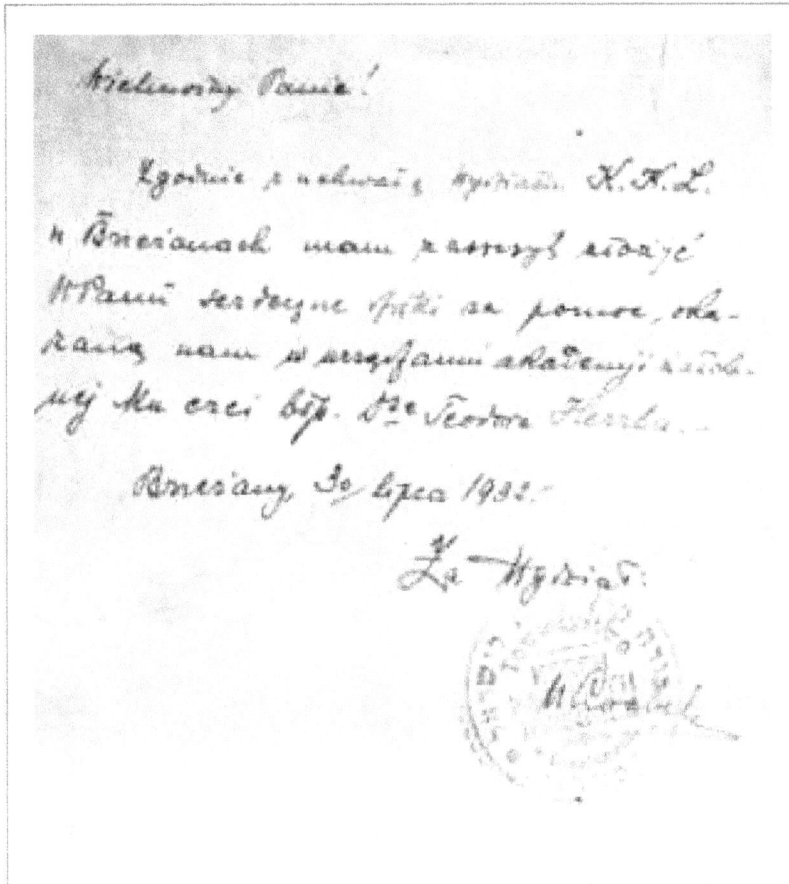

An appreciation letter given to Mr. Yehoshua Brik
For his activity in organizing the memorial for Dr. T. Herzl

KKL activists in 1928

Standing from left to right: Atlas, Mordekhai Kornbaum, Biterman, Mina Baner, Suzi Tonis,
Sheintzia Brik, Yoel Viethof, Mina Lakher, Shimon Bleikhberg, Tzeska Klarer
In the second row: Feibush Biterman, Erikh, Yehuda Peled, Samet, Reizer, Shlomo Libster, Sh.
Shapira, Itzkhak Nadelr, Frid, Panka Khayut, Miriam Nadler, Kohen
Sittng: Rozia Likhtman, Dr. Yosef Frid, Meir Taler, Natan Lebel, Dr. Klarer, Leib Frid, Mendel
Tonis, Avraham Katz, Shaul Noishiler

[Page 44]

"Keren HaYesod" [United Israel Appeal]

In our city, the organization was founded in 1932. Dr. Nagler was elected as the chairman, Moshe Tauber was the treasurer, and Moshe Bar-David was the administrator. A representative of Keren HaYesod solicited donations from the city Jews (hard and fatiguing work). He paid visits with our representatives to the wealthy Jews, and the local personnel completed the field work after he had already left the city. We acquired a distinguished name among Galitsia's donors due to our vigorous activity.

"Ezra" committee from 1931

Standing from left to right: Shaul Noishiler, Lakher, St. Riger, Ezra Reikhbakh
Sitting: Khaim Reiner, Nusika Hollander, Dr. Khaim Vilner –chairman, Dr. Lileh L. Reitman

[Page 45]

"Ezra" [Help]

The organization provided help for the poor preparing for *Hakhshara* [agricultural training] and *Aliyah* to Israel. Some youths could not afford to finance their *Aliyah*. "Ezra" people took care of them, headed by Dr. Vilner. We should note, with satisfaction, that none of the youths remained in the diaspora due to a lack of financial means for their *Aliyah*.

The activists of "Ezra" –1929

Standing from left to right: Moshe Bar-David (David), Ezra Reikhbakh, Mendel Tonis, Hersh Gliner, Lebel
[Sitting:] Ya'akov Shapira, Kuba Krokhtal, Yosef Vinter, Ze'ev Bomze, Itzkhak Kvertel

[Page 46]

"Tzeirei Zion" [Zion Youths]

This was a union of high school students from the lower to the upper classes organized in groups with students from other cities. They founded the "Union of High School Students" in Galitsia. In the entire province of Galitsia, there were about fourteen hundred high school students, thirty-two in our city among them.

The members divided themselves into various clubs: A club to study Hebrew, a club to study the geography of Eretz Israel, and a club to study Zionism. A Hebrew culture committee for spreading the Hebrew language and its literature was attached to the union. That committee nominated Dr. Mentza *z"l*, then a student at Brzezany high school, as the head of the committee. State conferences of "Tzeirei Tzion," which our representatives participated in, were held every six months. Dr. Zilbershtein was the head of the organization in Galitsia.

Union of Zionist University Graduates

These young men gathered for lectures, debates, and galas; however, their main effort was to assist other associations in giving lectures (on the history of Zionism and the geography of Eretz Israel). The activists were: Shomer, the Glazer brothers, Vilner, Halbertal, and others. Our representatives participated in the conference held in Lviv on 25-26 July [the year is not mentioned].

"HaShomer" [The Watchman]

A new generation rose in 1917 during the First World War, a period of curtailment, suffering, and poverty. That generation, all under 18, was full of vigor. It aspired to build a Jewish future in its homeland. The organizer was a young man who came back to the city from Vienna. He was an intelligent young man with organizational skills, a student of Meir Ya'ari.

His name was Moshe Frid, and he was a member of the "HaShomer" movement. Along with a few high school students, he founded the branch of the "HaShomer' Movement in our town. The movement was affiliated with the international scout movement with a Jewish character. The movement's slogan was "Pay Attention." The members were obligated to follow the ten commandments of the scouts, to establish a Jewish state in Eretz Israel. The image of the Jewish scout was a person of nature, a free person in a healthy body, with a Jewish heart, in his revived homeland.

Besides Moshe Frid, the founders were: Moshe Bergman, Zigmond Prash, Leib Glazer, Ya'akov Tzimerman, and others. There were several groups of young members and others of older members. Among those who were with me in the movement, I remember: Landesberg, Ravitz, Kaner, Alter, Bar-David, Segal, Haber, Noiman, Zinger, and others. Among the girls I remember were: Ester Pomerantz, Perla Glazer, Flam, Milkh sisters, Bliberg, and more. We spent the Shabbat in the forest, and during the winter, in the branch.

[Page 47]

Every group went out separately, meeting in the forest. There, we organized all sorts of games. During the evenings throughout the entire week, we met in the branch for a discussion, studied Hebrew, learned about the history of the settlement in Eretz Israel, and read books with Zionist content (the most demanded book was "Yizkor"). That youth movement grew and continued to educate to love Israel. That education took deep roots and bore fruit. In the following years, the movement branched off into youth movements of all political currents. The youth in these movements grew and was active continuously until the break of the Second World War. We, here in Israel, are all former members of those movements.

Union of Miriam's Girls' students

The girls were also organized in our city. An association called "Miriam" was founded in 1906 by Engineer Tishler from Buchach, then a high school student in our town. In the beginning, there were 25 girls. Among them were: the Milkh sisters, Gusta Rozenberg, Sabina Tirkisher, and Fridrika Morgen. In the second year, the number of members rose to forty. In the beginning, they met at the Milkh family home. Later on, they rented a room for the club's gathering. They studied Jewish history, Hebrew literature, and the history of Zionism. The lecturers were: Shefer, who lectured about Jewish history. Ze'ev Glazer taught modern Jewish literature, and Engineer Tishler lectured about the history of Zionism. The club activity was substantial, and the number of members continued to grow by the day. All the members were obligated to study Hebrew at the Hebrew school.

The Union of "HaShakar" (The Dawn)

A young teacher, Naphtali Zigel, came to our city in 5668 (1908). He came from the circle of the *Beit HaMidrash* youth. The association was organized under his leadership. He was elected as the secretary and conducted fruitful work.

A branch of the organization, "Settlement of Eretz Israel," headquartered in Vienna, also existed in our city.

"Poaley Tzion" [Worker of Zion"] Movement

The working youth was organized within the "Poaley Tzion" movement. In our city, [a branch of] that association was founded in 1904. The movement was headed then by Yosef Halbertal. The following were the activists in Brzezany: Mirberg, Zauberberg, Vitz, Meir, and others. Their activity was fairly modest. The members of that association were mostly sales associates and apprentices of craftsmen. The high school students and the academians assisted them with lectures and lessons about the history of Zionism and Israel's geography. Among the dedicated lecturers was Shlomo Glazer. The movement maintained a Hebrew and Yiddish library.

[Page 48]

"HeKhalutz" [the Pioneer]

Many who reached Eretz Israel during the period between the two wars were members of that movement. [A branch] was established in our city at the end of WWI, and its activity continued through the years until the outbreak of the Second World War. The people of the Third *Aliyah* enlisted from its ranks and together with other youth movements, prepared the youth for *Aliyah* and work and life in Israel. Its members organized the first group to make *Aliyah* –the group called "HaKoakh" [Power]. That group achieved their goal of making *Aliyah* through a way filled with obstacles. They were closely related to the "HaShomer" movement, and later on, the "HaShomer HaTzair" [The Young Watchman], who helped them with lectures and preparation for *Aliyah*. Among the first pioneers were: Bomze, Katz-Grad, Veintraub, Libling, Eigen, Korev, Moshe Glazer, Kalman, Ilan, Kravitz, Bergman, Feigenbaum, and others.

The HeKhalutz Branch in 1929

[Page 49]

First Group Makes Aliyah

by Moshe Glazer and Menakhem Katz-Grad

Translated by Moshe Kutten

Edited by Jane S. Gabin

In 1919, when the Ukrainian army fought with the Poles to establish a Ukrainian republic, the Jewish self-defense force in our town, founded upon the disintegration of the Austro-Hungarian Empire, began to defend against the Ukrainians who wished to abolish it. Many youths in the city prepared to join the Ukrainian warriors. However, others thought: "Why should we fight in the war of the Ukrainians?" Rumors began to arrive that the "HeKhalutz" [The Pioneer] movement was being organized to prepare and train the Jewish youth for making *Aliyah* to Eretz Israel. The thought of organizing our youth within "HeKhalutz" came up.

It was a sudden thought but not followed by quick action. Only when the Poles conquered Eastern Galitsia did we - the youth -get in touch with the Zionist center in Lviv. "HaShomer" Union in our city received accurate information about the "HeKhalutz" from the "HaShomer" center in Lviv, and from there, the news reached us. We began to slowly study the issues that the "HeKhalutz" organization faced, and the thought about making *Aliyah* began to take shape.

At the end of 1919, we began to act toward establishing a group to make *Aliyah*. The following youths joined the group: Shlomo Eigen, Yekhiel Brik, Ze'ev Bomze, Menakhem Katz-Grad, (Mekuzhni), Moshe Glazer, Veintraub, Sely Karb, and Yosef Kalman.

The members contacted A. Feigenbaum, the lessee of a farm in Martzelovka, to allow us to work there (Katz-Grand did not participate in that work session). We all went to work, and at that time, we only worked half days. In the winter of 1920, we stopped working there and gathered to discuss Eretz Israel and the work there. At the end of the winter, we began to work again on the in Martzelovka.

In 1920, we began to solicit information from the "HeKhalutz" center in Lviv to find out how to make *Aliyah*, get visas, and finance the expenses involved. The answers were straightforward: we needed to initiate, plan, and cover the trip expenses ourselves. We also had to plan what roads we needed to take. We turned to organize the plan in June 1920. We probably had a lot of energy, so without turning to the center, we decided to travel to Lviv, meet there with the HeKhalutz center (for Eastern Galitsia), and from there continue to Eretz Israel.

We received small sums from our parents but these were insufficient to cover even our travel expenses in Galitsia. We hired a cart (with two horses), and loaded our luggage and ourselves on the wagon. Our parents stood around us, and so did our friends, who accompanied and were jealous of us. Many tears were shed by the mothers. Blessings were said by everybody. We pretended to be heroes, told the waggoner to go, and we went on our way.

A few additional members joined us in Przemyśl [Pshemishel] on the way to Lviv. The center in Lviv probably provided them with the details and the time of our departure, and they decided to join. The people who joined us were: Avraham Katz, his sisters Shoshana and Tzipora, and Bela Fuks. We arrived safely in Lviv, without any delay or hindrances, even though it was a troublous period that presented many dangers for traveling Jews.

[Page 50]

In Lviv, we contacted the movement's center and were told to go to Krakow at our own expense. We stayed two days in Lviv. The people from Brzezany and Przemyśl, who lived in Lviv, welcomed us and provided us with food and lodging. We left Lviv and continued on the train to Krakow. Here, we were welcomed more warmly by the "HeKhalutz" people. They arranged lodging for us in the attic of a big building, probably a grain storage building, on the bank of the Vistula [Wisla] River. The "Joint" [JDC] provided food at a soup kitchen they established in the city, where we received a hot meal and bread for the rest of the day.

A few days later, we received instructions from Krakow's "Hekhalutz" about traveling to Bratislava. Upon arriving, we found out from the local Zionist Union that it was not easy to obtain visas to Eretz Israel there. But the Union arranged lodging for us in the building of the Jewish school, and we received food from the Joint. We went to the Joint's kitchen daily for lunch; we were also provided produce for the evening and morning meals, which we had to prepare ourselves.

While waiting for the visas, we asked the Zionist leadership in Bratislava to arrange work for us in the neighboring villages to avoid sitting idle. Soon, we got a job in a neighboring German village. Our members worked for several farmers in that village. In the beginning, they treated us suspiciously and were worried that we would not be able to do their work. However, our desire to prove them wrong and demonstrate that Jews know how to work worked in our favor. We worked hard, and our employers were satisfied. Many farmers came to see us working. More than once, we heard from them that there were no such diligent workers among Slovakia's Jews. The food provided to us was tasteful, but the work was arduous. We were too tired to go out. The "*Shiksas*" [gentile girls] wanted us to spend time with them (dance and go on trips), but we were too tired.

Two weeks later, when we found out that we would not be able to receive the visas for Eretz Israel in Bratislava, we were advised to travel to neighboring Vienna for that. After consulting with the Zionist Union, we decided to cross the border, which was very close by, illegally. We crossed on one of the Saturdays, and from there, we traveled a few kilometers by train to Vienna.

In Vienna, we met with Moshe Frid, a native of Brzezany (who studied at a university in Vienna at that time). We kept in touch with him through the mail while still in Bratislava. With his help, it was not difficult to find lodging in Vienna, and we resided in the ground apartment of the Caffe Hauptaleh, which was available for us in the fall. We also received food from the Joint. The walk to the Joint's kitchen was rather long, but we went every day for lunch and ate the other meals together at the apartment made from the food we received from the Joint. Two pioneers from Stanisław^Aw [today Ivano-Frankivsk], Dr. Porer and Gerstman, joined us in Vienna. We were idle for about six weeks as the British consulate was not in a hurry to provide Eretz Israel's visas. We tried to find ways to accelerate our *Aliyah* (Moshe Frid handled our case at the Eretz Israel's offices in Vienna, where he had some acquaintances. He was also in touch with the Zionist leadership in the city).

About 600 pioneers assembled in Vienna at that time (October 1920). As a result, it was not easy to secure a visa. We also needed money for the travel tickets from Vienna to Trieste, tickets for the ship, and visa fees. And we received money from the Joint and Brzezany natives who lived in Vienna. The most outstanding among them, who helped and encouraged us, were Moshe Izik, Moshe Ilan, and Moshe Frid.

Around mid-October, we received the visas and decided not to delay and depart immediately.

[Page 51]

We boarded the train leaving Vienna for Trieste. The road from Vienna was comfortable, and we arrived at the port city of Trieste two days later. We received comfortable train cars, and the staff treated us warmly.

We arrived on a gloomy and stormy day. The people from the Eretz Israeli office accepted us and led us to a building slated for "pioneers making *Aliyah*."

We bought tickets for a cargo ship. It paid for the trip only but not for the food. On the ship, we met many other pioneers from towns in Russia, Lithuania [Lita], Poland, and Galitsia, altogether about 300 people. We crowded over the deck "cover." The ship was dirty, and its captain was drunk, but the Italian sailors were friendly. We had to buy new food provisions in Trieste, but when we opened some of the biscuit boxes, we found worms. From Trieste, we sailed to Venice and docked there for three days, after which the ship sailed to Split. That destination was unveiled to us at the port when they woke us up at midnight. We had to vacate the cover due to the loading of cement sacks into the ship's hold. In the morning, when the loading ended, they put the cover back and allowed us back into our sleeping quarters. In Split, we stocked up on food we bought at the shops in the city. From there, the ship sailed to the port city of Brindisi, where we paused again to load as we had that night in Split.

From Brindisi, the ship sailed to the Balkan Peninsula, where goods were unloaded and loaded. That meant that they had to bother us time after time. The next big port was on the island of Corfu, where we docked for several days. The ship did not dock by a pier, so some of us went to the city on a boat to purchase food. From Corfu, we sailed to the island of Crete. They loaded baskets filled with grapes there. All the corridors to the sailors' cells were clogged with those baskets. It goes without saying that we tasted these grapes and, once in a while, threw the empty baskets into the sea. From Crete, the ship turned to Alexandria. On the way, the ship suddenly stopped. The sailors seemed confused, and it looked to them, and us, that smoke was coming up from the hold. The drunk captain ordered us to evacuate the cover and crowd into the coridors. The cold and the wind took their toll. We suffered terribly and asked for permission to come up to the deck. The captain did not allow us to do so. He ordered a wooden barricade erected on the stairs. He did not leave us a choice but to break it and climb up onto the deck. When the captain demanded the sailors oust us from the deck, they refused and laughed at him. Eighteen days later, we docked in Alexandria for two days. We disembarked and walked around the city. There were probably thieves on our ship because when we went to the market, we saw a peddler there who offered caps for sale. Yekhiel Brik noticed that the caps belonged to one of the passengers.

We sailed to Port Said two days later but stopped for only a few hours. We then sailed to Jaffa, where boats owned by Arabs, rented by the "Zionist Commission" (on behalf of the Jewish Agency), waited for us at sea. They waited about 3 kilometers from the shore since the shore was rocky and the sea was turbulent and rough. Policemen and officials were waiting for us at a place serving for the boats docking. After they checked our passports, they gathered us in a hut where they vaccinated us. We spent a few days quarantining in that hut. From there, we moved to the immigrant camp of the Zionist Commission, located on a sand hill in Tel Aviv (today the intersection of Allenby and Balfour Streets), where we resided in tents. The food was provided to us by the Zionist Commission through the kitchens of the party of "HaPoel Hatzair" [Young Worker] under the management of Khana Meizel, who was stationed in Nakhlat Benyamin Street. That street looked like a street in a [small] provincial town. The houses had one floor, surrounded by ornamental gardens without any shops.

Ze'ev Bomze and Seli Karb, Pioneers of HaShomer, on their way
to Eretz Israel. Vienna, 1920

[Page 52]

A few days later, Mendel Elkind and Yehuda Kopeliovitz (later Almog) visited us at the immigrant camp. Kopeliovitz was head of the "Third Aliya." and founded the "*Gdud* HaAvoda" and the "HeKhalutz" movement (together with Yosef Trumpeldor). They spent a few hours with us explaining the essence and goal of the "*Gdud*HaAvoda" [Work Brigade], named after Yosef Trumpeldor. They told us about the job slated for us: constructing and paving sections of the road between Tiberias' hot springs and Tiberias, and between Tiberias and Tabgha. These sections were part of the road from Tzemakh Junction [where the Arab village of Samakh was situated until 1948], through Tiberias, to Tabgha, and from there to Rosh Pinah. That road was constructed by Egyptian Arabs. After a whole day's discussion, we agreed to join the *Gdud* [battalion or brigade]. We sent a telegram, and the *Gdud* people came to take us, on the same day, to their camp located near Khamei Tveria, the hot springs in Tiberius. We traveled by train between Lydda and Haifa; from there, on a narrow gauge railway to Tzemakh. From Tzemakh, we sailed on the ship "Nordau" to Tiberias and from there by boat to the camp near the hot springs. We disembarked at the Kineret [Sea of Galilee] beach and arrived wearing festive khaki shirts.

We were given tents, four members to a tent, and the first meal was tasty. We began planning our lives and work at the Brigade. We should emphasize that our group members were very close to each other. Our commune lives continued until the people were sent to play various other roles and naturally separated.

It seemed that our work at the Tiberias' hot springs (the excavation of soil and transporting it for fill) satisfied "Akhdut HaAvoda" [Labor Union - Non-Marxist Zionist party]. Its people praised us and stated that they wished that "all the brigade members would work like you." A few weeks later, the *Gdud* was allocated another road section –from the Arab village Majdal to Tabgha. We worked during the rainy season opposite the *Gdud's* camp, erected on the beach of the Sea of Galilee (between Majdal and the citrus orchard of Sir Alfred Mond and Professor Warburg). In that section, the role of our group "Ko'akh" [Power] was to dig ditches on the side of the road that was being paved.

Members of the first group that made Aliyah, 1920

Standing from left to right: Yosef Kalman, S. Karb, Dov Katz
Sitting: Libling, M. Katz-Grad, Ze'ev Bomze

[Page 53]

The first group that made Aliya. Vienna, in 1924

We were exhausted at the end of each working day as we did not allow our members to rest during the workday. We used to urge each other: "Why aren't you working? We have not fulfilled the quota yet." There were cases when the members had to stop working due to blisters on their hands.

A few weeks later, we moved to work at a black stone quarry located on one of the hills northeast of the [Arab] village of Abu-Shusheh [depopulated in 1948] located close to the road about to be constructed. We blasted the big rocks with explosives. Not all of the members moved to the quarry. Some remained to dig ditches along the road and build the road shoulders. Our work satisfied the quarry experts, and we supplied more rocks than any other group.

Yosef Khaim Brenner *z"l* visited the *Gdud* on Hannukah, [and he initiated] Hebrew lessons. Despite our fatigue from the hard work, most of the members participated in these lessons. Close to the holiday of Purim, a decision was made to establish a new platoon to construct the railroad from Rosh HaAyin to Petakh Tikva. Rosh HaAyin was a station on the railroad between Lydda and Haifa. One of our members was among the founders of that new platoon.

During the following Passover, some group members were sent to the "Jeeps Platoon" (a Jewish work battalion of the British army). Some members from our group were among those. It seemed that sending some members to Rosh HaAyin and the Jeeps Platoon, on one side, and the absorption of other immigrants causing some members to join other groups, on the other side, weakened the connection among the members of the "Ko'akh Group." the natives of Brzezany, until its dissolution.

[Page 54]

"HaShomer HaTzair" [The Young Guard]

by Dr. Eliezer Shaklai

Translated by Moshe Kutten

Edited by Jane S. Gabin

All the Zionist activities, among them those of "HaShomer" [The Guard], which in our city was founded and was active during 1916 – 1920, ceased upon the entrance of the Polish army by a decree forbidding any political activity. In the winter of 1921 – 1922, a few friends, most of whom were high school students, met by chance - or perhaps not by chance. In a discussion at that meeting, we decided to establish a club of Jewish youths and to meet once a week. The objectives were to exchange opinions, have free discussions and lectures, and spend time together.

Even though we did not emphasize Zionism in our meetings, we felt that we continued the path of "HaShomer," and the subjects we chose for the lectures were all about Jewish issues or topics associated with Eretz Israel. The club was intimate and limited in numbers. We did not aspire to widen our activity or recruit additional members. The members were: Peled, Viser, Kampel, Frid, myself, and a girl student, Selka Tzeig.

Two additional students from our high school class in Pidhaytsi [Podhaitza] joined – Kestenbaum and Orenshtein (later Matzik Oren from Kibbutz Mizrah. Emissaries from the "HaKibbbutz HaArtzi" [The Socialist *Kibbutz* movement] appeared in many cities in Galitsia at that time. They organized the Socialist youth movement "HaShomer HaTzair" with a central leadership team in Lviv. When we heard about that movement, we decided join it at the following meeting . We contacted the leadership team in Lviv and received propaganda material with detailed instructions on organizing and expanding our activity; that gave us - the members of the club - a new direction and a clear objective for the future, to prepare ourselves for a new life, a commune life, in Eretz Israel. We knew then where we were going and what our goal was.

BILU[1] group on 5.16.1926

[Page 55]

A battalion of "HaShomer HaTzair" – 1929

We doubled our activity and dedicated most of our time to it. We changed the word "club" to "group" – the first group of "HaShomer HaTzair," and we called it "HaTkhiya" [The Revival]. Our activity was oriented in two directions. We met every evening to listen to lectures and study Hebrew, Israeli geography, and settlement history. On the other hand, we did not neglect the organizing work to expand our activity outside the group and establish a branch of "HaShomer HaTzair." We met with students from the younger classes of the high school and organized them under our leadership. We founded separate groups for girls and boys. Orenshtein led the first group of girls, and Peled headed the first group of boys. Over time, our branch grew and contained several other groups led by the rest of our group members.

Our next step was to find a meeting place for all of us. We rented the cellar from Yehuda Vilner (we did not have a lot of money). It was a small room, neglected and dark. We made it into a warm and pleasant place, full of life and singing. The lectures were usually held in the home of one of the group's members and, in the summer, outdoors. In the evenings, we gathered to listen to a lecture, and following that, we sang and danced until the late hours of the night when the neighbors kicked us out for disturbing their rest. In the summer, we went out for hikes in the area's forests. On those outings, several groups met at a preplanned location, where we lingered for games, singing, and dancing. We came back home late in the evenings.

Our branch grew by the day, and our influence was felt within the entire city. It was no longer possible to hide the existence of our movement from the regime, and it became dangerous to continue in this way. Because permits were already obtained in other areas, we decided to submit a request to the local authorities to approve our Zionist activity. Dr. Shlomo Glazer and Dr. Shomer signed the appeal as the people responsible for the movement.

[Page 56]

They advised us to obtain additional signatures from some of the city's prominent people to strengthen and accelerate the handling of our appeal. After some considerations and hesitations, Peled and I went to see Dr. Ravitz, a known lawyer favored by the regime for being non-Zionist, to ask him for his signature. When we read our petition to him, he responded as we had envisioned before the meeting. He admonished and cursed us and asked me whether it was in honor of my father that I was dealing with such nonsense. However, when he finished reading, he went to his desk and, to our surprise, signed the petition using clear letters and even added a few words of recommendation. Because of his signature, it became easier to obtain additional signatures from other city's prominent people. A few weeks later, we became a movement officially recognized by the regime.

The results of our work among the Jewish youths were fruitful, apparent, and favored. Following the destruction of the war years [1914-1918], our Jewish life was revived, renewed, and changed for the better. Our influence was felt in the street and at home. Hebrew songs and words were sung in the streets, and the blue box with the azure-white sign hung in every Jewish home. Zionism, which until then resided in the hearts of only a few, took hold and became practical and widely accepted. The slogan [of HaShomer HaTzair] – "Khazak ve'Ematz" [Be Strong and of Good Courage], and the anthem of the HaShomer movement - "We rise and sing," was heard in all corners of the city. Interest in what was happening in Eretz Israel strengthened by the day, including among the adults.

The youth brought a new life to the general Zionist activity in the city. We participated in all the activities and work associated with Zionism, such as KKL-JNF, "Keren HaYesod" [United Israel Appeal], and "Ezra" [Help]. We emptied the KKL-JNF boxes each month, collected donations at weddings and other joyous gatherings, and prepared the halls for lectures and other events, such as 20 Tamuz (usually the big synagogue). I vividly recall when we decorated the great synagogue in preparation for the public gathering that celebrated the opening of the Hebrew University in Jerusalem.

Other movements followed us and contributed their part, but we were the first. We invested substantial energy, faith, goodwill, and most of our free time in that work. More than once, I neglected my school studies in favor of "HaShomer" due to a trip, lecture, or urgent Zionist work.

"HaShomer HaTzair" branch in Brzezany

[Page 57]

The summer camp, the district of Brzezany-Ternopil, 5687 [1927]

The first summer camp

In the spring of 1923, our leadership decided to organize a summer camp among forests and fields for the youth from the area's cities in one of the neighboring villages. We were determined to realize that decision and rolled up our sleeves to fulfill it. As a first step, we contacted the rest of the surrounding area members to coordinate the preparations, select a location, and develop a detailed plan for each branch. Those preparations required a substantial amount of our time and effort. We did not have the experience or even an example we could have followed, and had to discuss every detail. We divided the work amongst ourselves, and each one of us dedicated ourselves to the project with our hearts and soul. Above all of these difficulties that we faced came the objections from the parents. They could not accept the plan and the unheard-of fact that boys and girls would be going to the same camp, living and spending time together for four weeks without the supervision of adults. They did not understand the pure spirit, aspirations, and roadmap of our youths. We visited with every single parent (ours and our students), persuaded, and made all sorts of promises to supervise, take care of, and responsibly handle everything – until we won their hearts, and they relented; indeed, we kept all our promises.

Besides our members, youths from Rohatyn, Pidhaitsi [Podhitza], and Kozova participated in that camp. That was the first time we met with youths from other locations. We had a unique plan for each day, and taking into account changes in the weather, we prepared alternative plans for rainy days. We woke up early in the morning. Following a run and exercise, we ate breakfast. After breakfast, we had a trip, lecture, or game. The noon hour was dedicated to resting. There was also a detailed program for the afternoons. The programs were conducted at regular hours. As in any other camp, kids played practical jokes, using all sorts of pranks, for everyone's enjoyment. That may have cost those who were pranked some precious sleeping time for both standing guard and taking revenge, but all such activities were done within the agreed-upon guidelines and under strict supervision. The camp succeeded beyond any expectation despite the lack of experience. It was an unforgettable affair for anybody who participated in it, and in its wake, know-how, experience, and tradition were gained for many years to come.

[Page 58]

The "Tkhiya" group

Kampel and Selka Tzeig left the branch in the beginning. Selka, for personal reasons, and Kampel for ideological reasons (his views moved more to the left). Mordekhai Orenshtein was forced to leave our school in the summer of 1923. The school management expelled him because of an offense they considered severe. The following is the story: Kampel prepared the homework for some non-Jewish students in our class and received 5 zloties from each one as a donation for KKL-JNF. When the school's management found out about it, they put him on trial and expelled him as a punishment. As a result, he transferred to the Hebrew high school in Lviv.

When we completed the matriculation exams in 1924, we had to plan our next steps and fulfill our main objective – making *Aliyah*. We had to consider whether we join the effort of building our homeland as *kibbutz* members. We passed the branch's leadership role to the younger generation, and they willingly accepted the burden of continuing the work that we started. Peled was the first to go to *Hakhshara* [an agricultural training for *Aliyah* candidates] at a farm. He stayed there until the fall months. He suffered from a crisis - he became lonely as he did not have any branch friends there. After mental and physical misgivings and hesitation, he decided to continue his studies in Prague and went to study medicine. But the young leadership team members did not forgive him for that and expelled him from the movement.

Kestenbaum and Rutenberg registered at the university after completing their matriculation exams and by doing so, turned their back on the movement. The young members considered that a betrayal and expelled them from the branch. Those who remained began to prepare themselves mentally and physically for *Aliyah*. We faced a long winter and used that time to establish a group and prepare its members for the mission ahead of us. That included studying Hebrew and discussing life at a *kibbutz*, with all the problems associated with that kind of life.

We went out for the *Hakhshara* in the spring of 1925. Viser and I, the last ones who remained from our original group, were among the first to go. We were accompanied by Shalom Tzimerman and Shpitzen and the female members – Fenster, Bomze, Selka Shapira, Yona Rizer, Rakhel Hibler, Regina Ast, and Khayut. The central leadership team chose the place of the *Hakhshara* for us at a large farm owned by a Jewish family named Albin. The farm was located far from the area's villages and had only a few houses, in which the permanent workers and their families, altogether about 30 people, resided throughout the year. There, we met people from similar *Aliyah* groups from other places, such as Drohobych, Borislav, Krakow, and other cities from Western Galitsia. All of these groups were slated to establish kibbutzim in the future.

Even before we started to work, already on the first day, we suffered a painful loss: one of our best members and the most beloved by all, Vizer became seriously ill, and his fever rose. We transported him immediately to the hospital in the neighboring city of Chortkiv [Chortkov], but he never returned. He died from tuberculosis. May his memory be blessed!

There is plenty to tell about the six months of communal life at the farm. There was substantial mental and physical training in preparation for real communal life, with all the good and the bad in it. We experienced many problems, and some were quite difficult. We assembled in the evenings, after a long work day, and brought them up for discussion. We argued and tried to tackle and solve them the best way we could; we succeeded. We removed many of them from our path, some of which were our doings.

[Page 59]

Altogether we were about 60 people. Our first act was to create a commune – each person brought clothing and personal items from home. We collected all of that into a single general storage; however, mentally, we were not ready for that, and each one of us felt connected to our own property. The same was true in the issue of work allocation. There were all sorts of jobs: in the field, kitchen, yard, jobs on rainy days, and more. There were also problems associated with the kitchen and food: how to prepare it, who would bring the food to our people working in the field. A daily problem was the rotation of the cooking duty. The cook of one day did not want to prepare the necessary ingredients for the next day. We resolved that problem by taking it upon myself to manage the kitchen for the entire month. The living conditions were adequate for the summer months. The attic of a huge cowshed was allocated to us as our quarters. We arranged ourselves easily on the two sides along the length of the attic, leaving a wide space in between for gatherings and dancing, which were always held on Friday nights and holidays and sometimes even during regular days. On the Eve of the Shavu'ot holiday, we danced until the morning. Apart from the cows beneath us, we did not disturb anybody. Some members wanted to show off their energy and did not stop dancing until they fell and fainted; we had to call a physician from the neighboring city in the morning to help them.

During our work in the field, we sang Hebrew and Hassidic songs, and the Gentiles, who worked with us, learned the melodies and even lyrics and helped us to sing. One can only imagine the response of the Jews in the area, who heard the melodies and sometimes even the lyrics (including those of the rabbi from Chrotkov) sung by Gentiles.

We went back home in the fall and waited for a notice from the leadership concerning the approval of our *Aliyah*. In the meantime, two group members dropped out – Shpitzen and myself. As far as myself - the truth was that I never found satisfaction in working in agriculture, for instance, walking the whole day behind the plow or pulling out sugar beets. I considered agricultural work slow, monotonous, and automatic. During the *Hakhshara*, I was always looking to work with my hands on something associated with thinking and being independent, such as carpentry, kitchen work, or work in the yard.

After completing the *Hakhshara*, I faced the need to make a decision! "Do I continue with the path I chose for myself and overcome difficulties, despite my inner resistance to working in agriculture, or should

I change direction and try my luck in continuing my studies?" I decided that, sooner or later, I would see myself outside of the movement and that it was better to decide about leaving now. With a heavy heart, I chose what I chose even though I didn't possess a strong inclination for studies, but I had to decide.

They expelled me from the movement as a traitor, just as they did for others. Those who did it turned to me a year later, and they, too, joined the ranks of medical students. Despite that, we remained connected in our hearts and souls to the "HaShomer HaTzair" Movement. Only a while later, people chose a movement [and party] close to their hearts.

The rest of the people in the group made *Aliyah*. Some of them reside today in the *kibbutzim* of "HaShomer HaTzair." Others transferred to the cities and continued to build their lives in their homeland.

Despite the departures, the movement in our city grew year after year. Before the Second World War, the branch consisted of hundreds of youths, some of whom made *Aliyah*, and they are in Israel with us.

Translator's footnote:

1. BILU is the acronym of the Hebrew words from the Book of Exodus: "Speak unto the children of Israel that they will go forward."

[Page 60]

Memories Chapter

by Batya Boneh-Prizand

Translated by Moshe Kutten

Edited by Jane S. Gabin

The memories written below are from more than 40 years ago and are taken from memory, therefore, they may contain inaccuracies or errors due to forgetfulness. Nonetheless, it is fitting that these memories be included in this book to shed light on a small corner of the life of the youth in our city during 1920-1930.

I absorbed the youth movement atmosphere, with all the good and the beautiful in it, from my early childhood. The branch of the "HaShomer" was once housed, for a while, in a rented room in my house, which stood at the edge of the city. I watched, listened, and even participated in the extensive activities of the branch members. Those were vibrant lives, full of content and appeal: singing and dances (Hebrew songs and folk dances, mainly the Hora), lively discussions and debates, parties, preparations for trips, and above all -- preparations for making *Aliyah* and farewell parties for people who were making *Aliyah*. That atmosphere enchanted and attracted me with an incomprehensible force. Perhaps I have already made the decision then to be like them and make *Aliyah* when I grow up.

Indeed, over time, making *Aliyah* became my life's aspiration, a divine dream that must be fulfilled. My work and all the activities of my youth served as means to achieve that goal. Naturally, when I was 12 years old and was offered membership in the girls' group of "HaShomer HaTzair," I immediately agreed.

The group was named "Shoshana" [Rose], and its first counselor was Pnina Bomze (Nir), who educated us with her passion and unmatched dedication until she made *Aliyah*. She is now a member of Merkhavia. Following her was counselor Selka Gross *z"l*. The members of the group were: Malka Bomze (Shutenberg), Pnina Bomze (Nir), Nuska Shtark, Ester Halperin, Rozia Barash, Rakhel Shapira, Henka Dorfman (Aharonson), Batya Prizand (Shtark), Nusia Hollander, Rokhatzia Habler, Gizia Gross, and Libka Shapira. Khanna Yeager joined a while later.

Joining the [youth movement's] branch and the period of my participation (1923 – 1932) was accompanied by great enthusiasm and a feeling of happiness and satisfaction from the way of life and aspiration. The movement shaped our characters and instilled universal human and national values that serve us throughout our lives.

There were three age groups in the movement. Each possessed its own goals and ways of doing work. The youngest was given goals of scouting education through hikes, sports, exercising, games, learning the Morse code and knots, and camping. The middle group's goals were national education and a systematic study of Jewish history (including tests), the history of Zionism, and the history of the Jewish settlement and geography of Eretz Israel. The oldest group's goals were socialistic education via lectures, guided reading, and preparation of papers on the entire socialistic literature (including Marx, Engels, Trotsky, Kautsky, and more), the history of the Hebraic labor movement, and additional topics in Psychology.

[Page 61]

The group was the smallest social cell, and several groups of boys and girls constituted a battalion. Folk evenings, holiday parties, trips, and summer camps were usually held under the format of a battalion and sometimes the entire branch. All the members studied Hebrew via lessons conducted by the older members or at a "Tarbut" [Culture] school in the city.

My first Hebrew teacher was a member of the oldest layer, Arye Peled, who taught the girls in my group the basics of the language through Hebrew songs ("BeMakhrashti" [In My Plow], "Yadainu LeTzad Mizrakh" [Our hands toward the East], and others). We sang, fluently, many Hebrew songs. One of the ways we spent our time at the branch was singing evenings. These evenings were incredible, and we sang Hebrew songs poured from our young mouths and hearts for hours. The singing transferred us on the wings of the imagination, to all the beauty and sublime – to the East – to Eretz Israel.

Conferences of the movement were held several times in Ternopil, the district city, and Lviv, the big city. The purpose was to conduct comprehensive discussions about the movement and *Aliyah*'s problems. At times, emissaries from Eretz Israel who came to these conferences visited our branch. They always brought new songs and a fresh and heavenly spirit from Eretz Israel. They even served as professional consultants for the needs of Eretz Israel.

The Zionist fulfillment, *Aliyah* to Eretz Israel to build it and be built in it via the commune life, and equality at a *kibbutz* were the top priorities among the members. The "*Hakhshara*" served as the training camp for commune life and physical labor. We heard and learned a lot about the need for a metamorphosis of the Jewish nation: from a people of merchants and scholars possessing diaspora characteristics to a people of workers who make a living from manual work and are free of slavery complexes. For several years, the big sawmill in Nadvorna at the foot of the Carpathian Mountains served as the place for the "*Hakhshara*."

The branch members collaborated with other Zionist movements in the city: "HaNoar HaTzioni" [The Zionist Youth], "Gordonia," and "HeKhalutz," mainly in collecting donations to "KKL-JNF" and "Ezra." I will never forget the three wealthy families (Lebel-Kurtzrok, Wanderer, and Goldshlag), who contributed generously, and mainly during the holiday of Purim when we came dressed in white *Keffiyehs* adorned by black *Agals* [a black cord, worn doubled, used to keep a keffiyeh in place] on the heads and white sheets arranged as clothing, like groups of Arabs. We were awarded generous donations for KKL-JNF. We note here that we liked the image of an Arab. It is possible that we learned to like those who would become our neighbors.

In 1928, the year the "*HaKibbutz* HaArtzi" was founded, the youth movement underwent a drastic change. Many of the branch's members left and turned to study at the universities. Other members joined other youth movements, mainly left-oriented youth movements. Almost all of them perished in the Holocaust. Only those who made *Aliyah* before [the Second World] War survived. We find them today in *kibbutzim* in Izrael Valley and the HaSharon area (Merkhavia, Sarid, Ein HaMifrtaz, HaMa'apil, and others) and Israel's cities and settlements.

May these lines serve as a memorial to dear friends and family members who did not reach Israel and perished in the Holocaust.

[Page 62]

"HaShomer HaTzair" (1926 – 1932)

by Dov Glazer, ~~Kibbutz~~ Gat

Translated by Moshe Kutten

Edited by Jane S. Gabin

My childhood scene and the first steps of my youth were in a remote Ukrainian village located about 30 kilometers away from Brzezany. I arrived in the town at the age of 12 with my brother, who is 2 years younger than me, to continue my elementary school studies, which were not available in the village, and mainly to fulfill my father's wish not to stay with the "peasants" and absorb some "*Yiddishkeit*." I totally fulfilled that wish. I studied with melameds [religion teachers], the Bible, and the Talmud until I was 18, when I became a Marxist and Epikoros [a heretic].

At my uncle's house, Ya'akov Bauer, where I lived for 8 years, I found an educated and advanced family with a Zionist tradition deep-rooted in Judaism and the Jewish nation. All the children of that family (5 sons and one daughter) acquired an education. The four elder sons have completed their studies and resided outside the house. My uncle was a scholar of Zionism and tradition. He was strict about his sons' education.

At that house, the educational spirit, which I admire until today, I saw for the first time - Herzl's famous picture and the blue cashbox of the KKL-JNF hung on the wall. There I learned what Judaism and the love of Eretz Israel are all about. The house was on Zbozuva Street near the "Nowy Rynek" [New Market Square]. The entire street was Jewish and was lined with small shops, tiny workshops of tailors, carpenters, shoemakers, and so forth. The stores of the rich were located at the city center around the "Rynek" [Market Square]. That market also served as the parking and shelter for wagons [who came to town] loaded with agricultural products of the villagers, who gathered here for the weekly fair.

All the Jewish cultural institutions were concentrated in that street: several houses of prayers (*Kloizes*), "Talmud Torah" [religious school], the *Kheder*, and "Yad Kharutzim" (the professional guild of the craftsmen). That was also where the Jewish "Community House," which contained a large library and a drama club, was located. My uncle's apartment was on the second floor. Below it was the branch of "HaShomer HaTzair," where the best of the Jewish working and studying youth were concentrated. Obviously, we did not remain indifferent to what was happening around us. The unique "HaShomer" folklore, boisterous "Hora" dancing on Shabbat, and romantic singing together attracted us. It did not take long, and despite the explicit objection at home, we joined the movement. We received a subtle hint from the "woman of the house," Pepka Shaklai (who was a member of HaShomer in the past and understood our feelings), that we could get the few pennies needed to register with "HaShomer."

We joined the "Eagle" group. In parallel to us was another group named "Tiger", and along with the girls' group, we formed the "Trumpeldor" battalion. Khaim Riner Z" L was the leader of our group. He was an exemplary counselor owning a solid image, athletic body, and a calm demeanor, rare among the Jews. He was always an optimist, with a slight smile and an image radiating onto his surroundings. We consider him a prodigy whom we loved and admired and were ready to follow him into fire. Thirsty and amazed, we listened to the group discussions about the "ten commandments" of the "*Shomrim*", which adorned one of the branch's walls with large letters. The reading chapters of our counselor of the "Yizkor" recitation for Trumpeldor and the HaShomer heroes, as well as the folklore chapters of the settlers' pioneers in Eretz Israel. We, the youngsters, ran exceptionally enthusiastically to the branch as we considered it our true home.

Under the joyful *Shomrim* atmosphere, we learn the whole doctrine – how to become a perfect human being, a proud Jew, and everything associated with the national life in Eretz Israel.

[Page 63]

"HaShomer HaTzair" – "Nesher" [Eagle] Group

When we joined the movement, the branch was at its peak popularity. It had strong leadership - the head, Arye Flick, with his impressive appearance, assisted by the leadership team, Reiner, Shekhter, and Selka Gross. The branch also had a battalion of graduates about to leave for the *Hakhshara* and *Aliyah*. We were in the middle layer (or B layer), which was later named "*Tzofim*" [Scouts]. The branch did not accept younger youths at the time since the young layer (layer A), which was called "Kfirim" [Young Lions], was formed a few years after members of our layer became counselors. If I am not mistaken, the branch consisted of 150 girls and boys from the best of the vigorous and alert youth in our city.

What attracted the Jewish youth from the *Kheder*, school, or football pitch to the branch? First and foremost was the Shomer'ic atmosphere. They were attracted by the romantic singing evenings, which spilled across the gray and desolate street, balls, scouting, Shabbat hiking to the great outdoors, and impressing ceremonial assemblies; the youths were also attracted by the skilled counselors who knew how to provide good education, comradeship, mutual aid, and national pride, which was degraded in the gentile schools; the traditional blessing *"Khazak Ve'Ematz"* [Be strong and of good courage], the scouting uniform with the picture of a lily on the tie, and the "ten commandments" [of the HaShomer Movement], constituted symbols for the youngsters that elevated their self-confidence and self-worth in a hostile environment. During those days, there was also substantial public support.

We called those years of the branch the "romantic period." The truth can be said that the generation of counselors did not stand the test of time. Most of them left the branch after the matriculation exams. Some turned to higher education studies, and others to their own private careers. That resulted in a severe crisis that led to the disintegration of whole groups; the number of members was reduced to 80 members, perhaps even less. The new leadership: Ozio Katz, Yitzkhak Feigenbaum (today, members of kibbutz Ein HaMifratz), Tulek and Hesio Noishiler, Esterkeh Halperin, and Bashka Prizand took on themselves to reorganize of the branch and prepare it for the future. The first elders, who belonged to the "Ein HaMifratz" and "Hamagshim" [in Hebrew – the Realizers], as well as a few pioneers from the HeKhalutz movement, went out for *Hakhshara*. We unified into larger groups, such as "Kokhav" [Star], and became the elder battalion. We began organizing new groups of younger youths from the classes of elementary school and also from lower high school classes. We called the new layer, consisting of 11-12 years olds - the "Kfirim" [Young Lions] layer.

Four members who completed the fifth high school class were sent to a counselor camp to train counselors for the new groups. The camp was organized by the movement's leadership and was held in the heart of the Carpathian Mountains in the mountain village "Zekla[?]." The following people participated in the camp: Meshulam Meser, Pekhter, Izio Zauberberg, and the writer of these lines. Zekla camp was one of the largest and most influential in the history of our movement. It was influenced by the appearance of the emissaries from Israel, like Rishard Weintraub and Eliezer HaCohen, as well as the stars of the movement leadership, like Shlomo Landkutch, Shmuel Shvartz, and others. They taught us, from mornings to nights, subjects that stood at the top of the agenda of the world in general and the Jewish world in particular: Eretz Israel, Zionism, Socialism, the history of the worker movement, youth movements, education, and psychology. These were subjects that established our ideological views (today, this program would be called "Brainwashing") and provided us with the power and courage to lead the second "golden period" of the branch during 1930 – 1932.

That period was stormy and full of upheavals. Despite the limitations on *Aliyah*, "White Paper," and the Riots of 1929, our movement in Galitzia grew to unimaginable dimensions. The reasons for that growth were clear: The world economic crises, the political situation and antisemitism in Poland, and unrest among the worker movements. These were problems that preoccupied us and provoked heated ideological debates. At the same time, we succeeded in absorbing the masses of youths.

[Page 64]

They huddled in the shade of the Shomer'ic branch, looking for encouragement to cope with their problems in the present and solutions for the future. Other youth unions popped out like mushrooms, and we had to compete for the soul of the child who could distinguish between left and right. During those years, we had the upper hand. HaShomer Hatzair's branch grew to 120 members, and its activity was also felt in the neighboring towns such as Nariov and Kozova. We were also the initiators of the conferences and the organizers of the unforgettable summer camps. For that, we need to thank the wonderful area of forests and other natural jewels that adorned our city and the neighboring villages.

Within that flourishing of the branch, distress and the feeling of a crisis approaching the Jewish world were felt. The youths were alert and sensitive to what was happening, which manifested itself in heated debates among the elders' ranks. "Leftism" began to show its first signs. We called it "Ideological fidgety," which heightened with the arrival of the "deserters", who slandered Eretz Israel. The fight for the soul of the branch was harsh and cruel. It is bordered with underground activities prevalent in revolutionary movements. Eliezer Peri Z" L was invited from Lviv in an effort to avoid a split and destruction of the branch. He expelled most of the leadership team and many members of the elder layer.

Those who were loyal to the movement recovered quickly. The leadership of the branch was transferred to younger hands. Today, these are the members of the *kibbutzim* Yad Mordekhai and HaMa'apil. We do not need to mention any names. They led the branch until the beginning of the annihilation period. When I came in April 1934, before making *Aliyah*, to say goodbye to the branch, I found it alert and vigorous, with extensive education activity, in all the layers. However, the atmosphere was already repressive and oppressive. On my walk from the train station, I already felt his steps and the investigative eyes of the man with no uniform. We knew that a disaster was approaching, but we could not have anticipated, even in our worst dreams, that it would become that horrific Holocaust.

"HaShomer HaTzair" "Kokhav" [Star] group, 1930

[Page 65]

"HaShomer HaTzair" [The Young Guard] – The Departure

by Z. Osrover

Translated by Moshe Kutten

Edited by Jane S. Gabin

One day, toward the end of October 1939, about a month after the entry of the Red Army into our city, I was called to the Komsomol's institution, where I received a *"Rezulatzia"* [Resolution], in which it was said that "the "HaShomer HaTzair," known as a movement that served the British imperialism, must be dissolved. It also said that I must transfer, within a week, all the property of the movement to their hands.

I did not have any illusion. I knew the day would come because the new regime could not tolerate Zionist activity. However, it was hard to come to terms with that decree. The hardest thing was to tell the branch members about it. Several days passed without any action on my part. I tried to delay the inevitable as long as possible. Since I had no other choice, I called the members of the branch sometime in November for a parting order. About three dozen members of all ages gathered in the movement's club on "Novi Rynok" Street at the house of Haselkorn. That club served us for about seven years (1932 – 1939), more than any other club in the branch's history.

We sat down for a long time in silence. Nobody said anything. Each member looked at a different corner of the room, which was very dear to us and would suddenly be taken away from us. It was so difficult to say goodbye to that corner, which unified us. We sat there deep in our thoughts about the not-so-long past, about the blessed activity of the branch over the past 20 years. In our minds, we saw the branch activities, that accompanied us over the years, were reality just yesterday, moving like a conveyor belt. No wonder we were so tied to that place.

And today, everything is in the past.

The activities were many. What was it that we did not do? Teaching knowledge in areas not covered in the school: studying the Hebrew language, the geography of Eretz Israel, the history of the Jewish nation, and the history of Zionism and Socialism. We also widened the horizons of culture and art. Who did not remember the literary trials and the public debates on global topics? We established a library, the second largest in the city, which served the branch members and tens of readers from the outside.

We formed a chorus, which was known for its quality. We also knew how to combine national cultural education with education for work. Tens of youngsters dedicated their Sundays to working in bookbinding or tiny carpentry workshops. We never neglected sports and scouting activities. We were educated to love nature. We organized summer camp every year, spending a whole month outdoors.

I will not forget those activities that benefited "Keren Kayemet" [JNF] or "Ezra" [Aid]. [I also remember] those meetings of the entire movement and those with other movements. There was almost no area in the city's Jewish public life where we were not involved. It is no wonder that when the time came to part from all of that, a feeling of loneliness enveloped me - a feeling of a horrible emptiness as if I was facing an abyss.

It was hard to look at the faces of the youngsters who sat down around me and waited for a word of encouragement. I felt their pain, but I could not find words of consolation. I could not and did not want to raise any false hopes. I knew that we would not be able to return to the past (at least not in the short term). I presented the reality as it was. I announced the parting from the movement's activities, but not the end of the road. We sang "Tekhezakna"[1] for the last time. At that time, the singing was more like a prayer than the singing of an anthem.

[Page 66]

We parted ways with the old slogan "Khazak Ve'Ematz" [Be strong and of good courage]. Indeed, we needed to be strong and courageous to withstand the horrific period ahead of us.

A week later, a small group of branch elders stole across the Lithuanian border, trying to find a way to Eretz Israel. We were able to fulfill that dream only after five years of wandering in Siberia, the prairies of Uzbekistan, and through destroyed Europe.

The youngsters who remained in the city never severed their connection with the movement. In the Spring of 1941, an emissary of those youngsters reached us in Vilnius [Vilna]. They asked for instructions concerning the continuation of their activity and passed the flag of the branch to us so that we could smuggle it to Eretz Israel. Most of those youngsters did not live to fulfill their dreams. They were murdered, along with the thousands of the city's Jews who were annihilated by the Nazis.

May their memory be blessed.

Translator's Note:

1. The popular name and the abbreviated and composed arrangement of "Birkat Am" [Nation's Blessing], a poem by Khaim Nakhman Bialik, was adopted as the anthem of the Israeli labor movement (from Wikipedia).

The History "HaMizrakhi" Movement in Brzezany
Tzeirei HaMizrakhi [Youth of HaMizrakhi] - HeKhalutz Mizrakhi [Mizrakhi Pioneer] - Bnie Akiva

Dov (Dow) Knohl

Translated by Moshe Kutten

Edited by Jane S. Gabin

The part of my review concerning the period between the two World Wars is familiar to me through my contacts with the activists and the events. However, unfortunately, there are no people left whom I could have gotten first-hand testimonies about the activity of religious Zionism in our city for the period before the First World War. I had, therefore, to rely on stories I heard in my childhood and on the news, which I managed to collect from books dealing with Zionism history.

When dealing with the religious Zionism during the period before the First World War, we need to take into account two facts related to the character of Galitsia's Jewry:

a. Galitsia's Jews excelled in their religious tolerance (except for some extreme minorities). They also advocated cooperation between the various circles in the Jewish communities and public affairs.

b. Some of the rabbis, who had a substantial influence on Galitsia Jewry, supported the activities benefiting the settlement in Eretz Israel and encouraged them. They also responded positively to the political actions activity that benefitted the Jewish Eretz Israel. They also supported the Zionist political policy in Galitsia, which was aimed to take the hegemony over the life of the Jews from the hands of the assimilated, who disregarded the needs of the Jewish masses and tried to present themselves as Austrian or Polish patriots.

It is, therefore, understandable why a substantial portion of the supporters of the Zionist activities were religious Jews. Most of the intelligentsia, which distanced itself from religion, tended to join the assimilated circles. Youth movements, which captured a central role in the Zionist movement's activity, just began to appear on the public stage after the First World War.

[Page 67]

Considering that two of the most eminent rabbis of the Brzezany community in that period had a sympathetic attitude toward the aspirations of the Zionist movement, we understand that this was the appropriate background for the religious Zionism activities in the city.

The rabbis in question were Rabbi Shalom-Mordekhai Shvadron and Rabbi Yitzkhak Schmelkes. The latter was a Torah great, a public figure, and the author of the book "Beit Yitzkhak." He served as a rabbi in Brzezany beginning 5625 (1865). Later on, he served as a rabbi in Przemysl [Pshemishel] and Lviv. He was a "lover of Zion." During his service in Przemysl, he joined a religious-Zionist association, published a public statement supporting the settlement in Eretz Israel, and supported settlement enterprises with his money. His brother, R' Mordekhai Schmelkes, was the chairman of the Zionist Association in Przemysl, and his son, also called R' Mordekhai, was the future Rabbi of Przemysl and the known leader in the "HaMizrakhi" movement.

Rabbi Gaon Sahlom-Mordekhai Shvadron, known by his nickname the MaHarShaM, was known in the Jewish world as a *"Posek"* [decider]. He was also a fan of the Zionist aspirations.

As a man with a great understanding of the public and world problems, with original views of Jewish thinking, he was a fan of the Jewish national revival. We know that among the teachers of "Tushiya" [Resourcefulness] Yeshiva, which he headed, there were enthusiastic "lovers of Zion" who respected the political activity of Dr. Herzl.

The branch of the "Bnie Akiva" in Brzezany – 1936

[Page 68]

Rabbi Shvadron also supported the program by Dr. Zelinger *z"l*, an activist of "HaMizrakhi" in Galitsia. The program envisioned the creation of a new type of national religious institution that would combine the studies of religious subjects with vocational training in its curriculum. A new association of "Tushiya" was established under the patronage of Rabbi Shvadron, who was tasked with advancing that idea.

My uncle, R' Moshe Toiber, a student at the MaHarShaM's Yeshiva, preserved the archive of that association.

The brother of the MaHarShaM, R' Yitzkhak Shvadron, a known industrialist in Zolochiv, who was a Zionist activist, and among the founders of the "Degel Yeshurun" [The Flag of the People of Israel] association that concentrated in it the best of the religious Jewry in the city.

It is also known that in the negotiation held by the religious Zionist activist, Dr. Aharon Markus *z"l* from Krakow, with the *Admo"r* of Chortkiv, Rabbi David-Moshe Friedman *z"l,* about bringing the religious Jews closer to Dr. Herzl's Political activities and support to the "Otzar HaHityashvut in Eretz Israel" [Eretz Israel Settlement Fund], the financial arm of the Zionist Union, it was suggested the Rabbi from Brzezany would participate in a committee consisting of prominent rabbis, tasked to prepare a platform for collaborative action.

Several prominent people who later went on to capture influential roles in the Zionist movement grew up, studied, or were active during their youth in Brzezany:

Rabbi Shmuel Tzvi Margaliot *ztz"l* and Rabbi Yehuda Bergman, whose details about their life will be brought up in another section of the book.

- Rabbi Yehoshua Feddenhekht [Peddenhecht?], a member of one of the prominent families in the city who exerted a lot of influence on the Jewish community life. He grew up and was active in Brzezany. He moved to Kolomiya later on. He joined the "Khovevei Tzion" [Lovers of Zion] movement in his youth, and with the establishment of the Zionist movement, he became enthusiastic about Dr. Herzl's ideas and dedicated his entire life to Zionist activity.

"HaMizrakhi," Brzezany, 5693- 1933

[Page 69]

A group of "Bnie Akiva," 1935

With the founding of the international "HaMizrakhi" movement, Feddenhekht was elected its formal representative in Galitsia. He visited many cities, managed the movement's propaganda, and organized many branches.

In light of that information, it is clear that there was a spiritual and organizational background in Brzezany for activity by religious Zionism.

In his book "The Zionist Movement in Galitsia," Dr. Gelber wrote that Brezezany's representative, Naftali Zigel, a known author and educator, participated in the 1908 Lviv conference of the youth movement "HaShakhar" [The Dawn], where the tendency to make *Aliyah* loomed.

In the 1907 and 1911 elections to the Austrian parliament, Dr. Shmuel Rapoport, an educated estate owner, a member of the Central Zionist Union Committee in Galitsia, and later, a prominent figure in the "HaMizrakhi movement, appeared as the candidate of the Zionist Party. He managed the elections' propaganda by emphasizing the religious aspect of the national revival. He received 1142 votes in 1907 and 1976 votes in 1911. Compared to the relative no. of votes received in other locations, that was considered a great achievement, particularly considering the election terror and forgeries the Polish parties conducted in collaboration with the assimilated parties. From the stories I heard in my youth, I knew that the religious Jews supported the Zionist party and that the "HaMizrakhi" activists were loyally active on its behalf.

The non-affiliated organization "Yeshuv Eretz Israel" [The settlement movement of Eretz Israel], founded by the *Admo"r* from Drohobitz, Rabbi Meir Khaim Shapira *ztz"l*, had many supporters in Brzezany.

The National-Zionist awakening that materialized in the Jewish communities in Galitsia at the end of the First World War as a result of the Balfour Declaration and the declaration by the heads of the allied winning countries in San Remo in 1920 (handing over the mandate over Eretz Israel to Britain, with the task of establishing a Jewish homeland), did not pass over Brzezany.

When the news arrived, advertisements were posted on the streets, calling the Jewish residents to gather at the large synagogue to celebrate that important event.

Many youngsters, among them a large group of religious youths headed by Rabbi Tzvi Grosvaks and Naftal Halperin *z"l*, who were the leaders of "Tzeirei HaMizrakhi" [Hamizrakhi Youths], went around and visited the Jewish homes, calling them to participate in the festive gathering. The large hall of the synagogue and the square in front of it were filled with a large crowd of men, women, and children, most of whom were religious Jews, who constituted the majority of the community.

Vigor Zionist life began to develop since then.

The branches of "HaMizrakhi" and "Tzeirei HaMizrakhi" engaged in cultural-religious activities, collected money for Zionist funds and organized agricultural *Hakhshara* near the city for the pioneers in the branch. They also supported the Zionist party in the election for the Polish Sejm and the Jewish community [council].

Even during the crisis that engulfed the Zionist movement as a whole, due to the economic troubles in Eretz Israel and the stoppage of the *Aliyah* that followed, the activists of "HaMizrakhi" and "Tzeirei HaMizrakhi" continued with their activities, even though there was no organized branch at that time.

Among the "Tzeirei HaMizrakhi" activists, Rabbi Tzvi Grosvaks should be specially noted. He married the daughter of the Rabbi from Narajiv [Naryov] and subsequently moved there. After the death of his father-in-law, he was nominated as the rabbi there. He organized an extensive activity of the "HaMizrakhi in Narajiv and also founded a branch of "Tzeirie HaMizrakhi" and the [religious youth movement] "Bnie Akiva."

[Page 70]

He took care of religious and Hebrew education, organized and conducted a broad cultural-spiritual activity, and organized a cooperative for weaving throw-rugs for local youths, including a group of "Bnie Akiva's" pioneers who train themselves in preparation for making *Aliyah* to Eretz Israel. He also founded a welfare fund to assist the city's merchants and craftsmen. With the help of the "JCA" [Jewish Colonization Association], he assisted Jewish farmers in establishing themselves in the neighboring villages.

Rabbi Grosvaks was an activist in the country's HaMizrakhi organization, participated in its conferences, and was elected its representative in the Zionist Congress. He perished in the Holocaust.

The bloody riots against the Jews in Eretz Israel in 5689 (1929) led to a reviving of the activity among the Jewish communities, aimed at strengthening and building the Jewish settlement in Eretz Israel. As a result, the Zionist and pioneering movements strengthened.

Subsequently, a large gathering was held at the community house in Brzezany, where expressions of solidarity with the Jewish settlers in Eretz Israel, who were at war with those who wanted to harm them, came to light. People were generous with monetary donations. Many donated expensive pieces of jewelry and announced they were joining the Zionist movement.

Many youths then joined the pioneering youth movements for making *Aliyah* to Eretz Israel.

That awakening pervaded the group of learners in the house of prayer of "Chortkov Hassidim." Some of them understood that the time had come to identify with the builders and defenders of Eretz Israel. A few of the regular learners in Chortkov's *Kloiz* (Shmuel Arazi, Ze'ev Kalman, Simkha Shekhter, and the writer of these lines) took it upon themselves to renew the activities of the branches of "HaMizrakhi" and "Tzeirei [youths] HaMizrakhi" in the city.

A few members of "HaMizrakhi" gathered for a discussion during the holiday of Sukkot, 5690 (October 1929), headed by R' Shimshon Fogelman and Ozer Rot (both made a with their families, participated in the building of the homeland and died here), and R' Mordekhai Knohl, and Eliyahu-David Rot, both of whom perished in the Holocaust. As a result of that discussion, the "HaMizrakhi" branch activity was revived. A club was arranged. Branches of the "Tzeirei HaMizrakhi" and "HeKhalutz [the pioneer] HaMizrakhi" were also formed. During those days, "HaMizrakhi" was the only adult organization affiliated with the Zionist Union with its own club. Social life was forged in that club, and cultural-religious activities were held. The branch played an active role in all of the financial, organizational, and political activities of the Zionist movement.

"HaMizrakhi" activists consider it an achievement when the "*Dayan*" [religious judge] R' Moshe Viner *z"l*, a known scholar and a teacher with a general education, who, later on, served as a member of the rabbinate in the city.

Special attention was paid to organizing religious youths with "Tzeirei HaMizrakhi" and "HeKhalutz HaMizrakhi," and to the spiritual activities among them. Besides the members mentioned above, the following members were active in this area: Sh. Halperin, Peplog *z"l*, Tzvi Lubiner, and others. A substantial number of members went out to a *Hakhshara* and, after receiving certificates, made *Aliyah* to Eretz Israel and stroke roots in it. The members, Sh. Arazi, Z. Klein, and Yosef Klein dedicated themselves to organizing the "Bnie Akiva" youth movement. Efforts were invested in deepening the educational activity. Work plans prepared for the organization of the branch's operation were later on accepted by the country leadership of "Bnie Akiva" as a basis for the work plan instituted country-wide. The branch's counselors were also active in the management of the summer camps of the movement and also served as counselors in them.

[Page 71]

The "Bnie Akiva" branch grew and expanded and was considered one of the city's largest and most established branches. It especially excelled in its action in the field of *Hakhshara* and pioneering *Aliyah*. Members of the branch were among the organizers of the *Hakhshara* groups in Kosiv [Kosov], Nariv [Nariov], and Pidhaitsi [Podhitsa]. Many of the branch's members went out for *Hakhshara*, and some made *Aliyah*. The letters joined "Kvutzat Avraham" [Grioup of Avraham], which first resided in Karkur and later on, settled in "Kfar Etzion." Shmuel Arazi will be notably memorialized in that respect. For many years, he contributed greatly to reinforcing the *kibbutz* direction in the education within "*Bnie* Akiva." He was among the founders of "Kfar Etzion," and in the end, was killed while defending the *kibbutz* during the 1948 Independence War.

With the *Aliyah* of the elder councilors, the younger layers took over the leadership of the branch until the break of the Second World War.

The influence of the branches of "HaMizrakhi," "Tzeirei HaMizrakhi," "HeKhalutz HaMizrakhi," and "Bnie Akiva" penetrated the various religious circles in the city, even those who were the opponents of the Zionist movement, and became an essential element in the life of the community.

The official activity lasted until the invasion of the Soviet and Nazi armies. However, even when the formal operation ceased, the members maintained connections among themselves. The activists among them continued to be active in community life, assisting the refugees arriving from the western parts of Poland and spiritual-religious work until the destruction of the community.

We will remember them. May their memory be bound in the life of the state of Israel.

Hakhshara Kibbutz, named after Sh. Mohiliver in Brzezany

[Page 72]

"HaNoar HaTzioni" [The Zionist Youth]

Lawyer M. Meiblum

Translated by Moshe Kutten

Edited by Jane S. Gabin

When I come to review the events related to the establishment of the "HaNoar HaTzioni" in Brzezany at the end of the 1920s, the streets of the city float in front of my eyes as do the lake, houses, and people, particularly my friends with whom I spend the years of my childhood, the period of my high school and higher education studies.

During those days of the 1920s, Zionist movements were expanding in the towns and cities of Poland. Heated debates between the Zionists and those who objected to Zionism ensued. There were also many debates among the Zionist factions about the righteousness of each faction's path.

I recall that in May 1929, some of us - about 10 Jewish youths, took the high school matriculation exams. For a short moment, it seemed to us that we faced unlimited possibilities. However, we quickly realized that this was just an illusion.

The engineering and medical departments in the universities closed their gates to the Jews. The departments that did open the gates every year were the law and philosophy departments.

That resulted in a substantial surplus of Jewish lawyers who, after graduating, could not find places to train for the experience. It was hard, even for teachers, to find jobs; idleness, frustration, and despair became prevalent.

That inauspicious situation constituted a fertile ground for the growth of the Zionist movements, which began earnestly among the Jews in Galitsia, particularly when many youths joined in masses and began to think about making *Aliyah* to Eretz Israel.

The branch of "HaNoar HaTzioni"

[Page 73]

The elder group of the "Hanoar HaTzioni"

Sitting from left to right: Bashka Halperin, Isidor Laufer, Khana Feld, Fritz Katz, Etka Katz-Spirshtein, Leibush Froindlikh
The girls in the middle: Rotshtein, Froindlikh, Amarant
Standing from left to right: Mundek Schmidt, Mundek Glazer, Zalman Gelber, Visyo Fenster, unknown, Lulek Katz

My father, *z"l*, was an enthusiastic Zionist and an activist of the "HaMizrakhi" movement. We often talked about Zionism, in all its factions, and the settlement in Eretz Israel, in all its own problems. Indeed, just after the high school matriculation exams, I decided to join the Zionist movement to make *Aliyah*, which necessitated getting a certificate for immigration. That required joining one of the Zionist factions, participating in *Hakhshara*, and waiting for our turn to make *Aliyah*.

Several Zionist youth movements were active in Brzezany at that time. Every ideological bloc formed its own youth movement to prepare the future generation for *Aliyah* and settlement through education and practical training.

The youth movements of "HaShomer HaTzair," "HeKhalutz," and "Trumpeldor-Beitar" were previously established by the various Zionist factions. However, at that time, the general Zionist movement did not understand the importance of the activity among the youth and, as a result, did not form a general Zionist youth movement. Only a short time before I finished my studies at the high school, a general Zionist was founded in eastern Galitsia by the name of "HaNoar HaTzioni." The movement announced then that there was no room for another flag over the blue-white one and that there was no need to add to the Zionist doctrine, on one side, various socialistic ideologies, which deviate in their cosmopolitan orientation from the natural national idea. On the other side, the militant revisionist faction was considered too extreme and divisive.

When I was in Lviv, I contacted Yitzkhak Steiger, the founder of the "Hanoar HaTzioni," who tasked me to organize the branch of the movement in Brzezany. I turned to some friends who graduated high school with me, but they did not want to join, and most of them remained and perished in the Holocaust. Bela Feld-Danieli was the first person to cooperate with me in establishing the first groups in the branch. We succeeded in organizing several layers, most from the students of the high school, and others joined later, such that youths from every circle of life were represented.

We faced many problems; the students were forbidden from belonging to any Zionist youth movement as long as they studied in state schools; we had to operate secretly, and it was not easy to find a proper location for our activities. It was essential for the place to be located in a pure Jewish neighborhood; we did not receive any financial support from the center, and our members were obliged to pay a monthly fee to cover the expenses. We did not have guidebooks and had to prepare them ourselves as plans for discussions and other cultural activities.

[Page 74]

The branch expanded quickly. We rented several rooms in the "National Jewish House," completed at that time. We gathered there for discussions, singing, and dancing in the afternoons and evenings. During Shabbat and holidays, we went hiking in the neighboring forests, sometimes in coordination with the branches from Ternopil, Rohatyn, Burshtyn, and other towns.

The youths who joined our ranks were imbued with Jewish and Zionist resolve and saw their future fulfilled in Eretz Israel. Unfortunately, only a few of us reached our homeland and thus survived the Holocaust.

I recall, even today, the debates about Zionism, *Aliyah*, and the way of life in Eretz Israel. We concluded that the best way is the "*kibbutz*" format. Debates ensued about the problems of a *kibbutz*, the commune life, and the integration into life in Eretz Israel. That was a beautiful period for me since I knew what I was doing was beneficial, which provided me with great satisfaction.

A year later, I moved to Lviv and, from there, made *Aliyah*. The branch leadership passed over to Shimon Bergman, Bela Feld, and Artek Klarer, all educated and skilled. They made our branch one of the best in the movement with their great vigor.

The "Hanoar HaTzioni" [The Zionist Youth] Branch

Bela Feld-Danieli

Translated by Moshe Kutten

Edited by Jane S. Gabin

The beginning of the movement was in eastern Galitsia in 1928. Immediately after that, it expanded throughout all parts of Poland. In western Galitsia, it was called "HaNoar HaMa'aravi" ["The Western Youth"] and in Congress Poland, - "HaShomer HaLeumi" ["The National Guard"].

A few years later, these factions united all under one roof with the name "HaNoar HaTzioni" ["The Zionist Youth"]. It found fertile ground for its ideas, even beyond the Polish borders. The movement encompassed tens of thousands of adolescents from elementary and high schools to universities, as well as working youths.

Brzezany was one town out of many in Galitsia, not unlike the others. The economic and social distress among the Polish Jews, and the antisemitism, brought upon various strange laws that further impoverished the Jewish masses. The "Numerus Clausus" did not allow the youths to study at higher education institutions. The high birthrate and the fact that the Polish industry was still in its infancy formed a bleak unemployment reality for the proud Jewish youth who aspired to greatness. The flames of the neighboring nations' nationalism reached Jewish youth, who established the "HaShomer HaTzair" youth movement in the first 1920; However, that movement deviated quickly from its initial ideas of being a broad framework for the entire Jewish youth. It became a socialistic-Zionist movement, closing its doors for those who did not abandon religion and tradition and those who did not believe in revolutions that encompass the whole world. The "HaNoar HaTzioni" movement was established from the bottom by the youths themselves and not by the adult leaders of the Zionist movement, according to their ideological orientations (parties). Only a while later did the "HaNoar HaTzioni" join the "General Zionists" party. At its core, it was a protest movement against the leftism of the "HaShomer" and against the apathy of the adults who lived in an illusion that they would have a satisfying future in the diaspora.

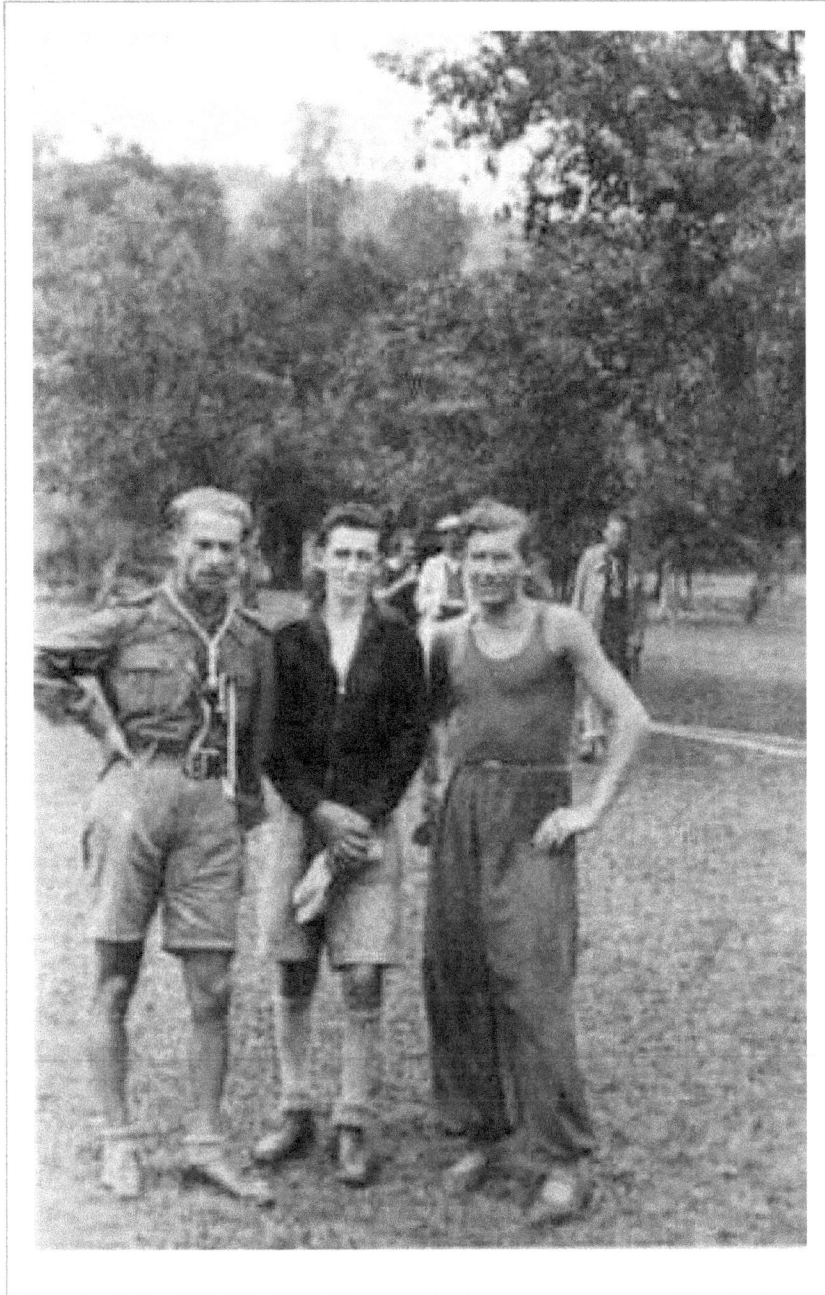

The leadership of the summer camp in Pivnitzna, August 1927:
Herman Katz (in uniform), Laibush Froindlikh, and Isidor Laufer

[Page 75]

A ceremonial assembly for the dedication of the flag for the "HaNoar HaTzioni" branch – 1933

We were a pioneering organization aspiring to establish *kibbutzim* and moshavim [cooperative agricultural communities of individual farms] in Eretz Israel. However, the movement was not against Aliyah individuals such as students or craftsmen. Although the identifying mark was embedded in the *Kibbutz* Movement and the pioneering spirit, many of our graduates elected their livelihood to come from private agriculture, free professions, trade, and industries.

Our branch in Brzezany was established in the same year the movement was founded, 1928. Our friend, Mendel Meiblum, today a lawyer in Haifa, brought the news to us. Together with him, we mobilized into action. The following people were among the founders: Dr. Yosef Frid, Shimon Bergman, the author of these lines, Avner Klarer, Reikhshtein, T. Veinshtein, T. Mirberg, Giler, N. Shvartz, Redlikh, Lehner, Polber, and Gusta Hertz-Shmushkin from Naryov (initiated the establishment of the branch in her town). Thanks to the vigorous actions of these founders, the branch strengthened and became a social center.

During the 1930s, under the leadership of the brothers Herman and Fritz Katz, Yitzkhak Laufer (Nagelberg), Leibush Froindlikh, and others, the branch developed, grew, and doubled in the number of members. The place at the community house was too small to contain everybody. We rented four rooms in the house of K. Erik on "Nowy Rynek," where the branch continued to operate until the break of the Second World War.

Many of our members perished in the Holocaust. Our member, Rozhka Meiblum, who survived the Holocaust, told about them and their lives in the ghetto, hideouts, among the partisans, and in the killing camps.

The branch of the "HaNoar HaTzioni" resembled a scouting youth movement in advocating a simple life, smoking-free life, trips to the surrounding forests, and participation in one of the many summer camps throughout Eastern and Western Galitsia and the Carpathian Mountains (including the high Tatar Mountains). The movement not only educated for Aliyah to Eretz Israel but also treated every young boy and girl as a human being to raise their human and moral values.

The movement strove to deepen the knowledge of its members in various areas of literature, science, history, and sociology. We put a particular emphasis on Jewish history and anything associated with Eretz Israel. The Zionist youth movement saved many youths from a life of idleness and vacuousness and recruited them to the struggle for the Zionist ideology. Special efforts were invested in teaching Hebrew. Thanks to that, when we made Aliyah, we felt equal to those who came before us, at least as far as language.

I can't complete this review of my memories without remembering our young members, who were killed in many unconventional ways in the Holocaust. I look at pictures sometimes that eternalized us together, and I am conscious about the loss of the best of friends and relatives and anguish that we must live without them.

[Page 76]

"Beita'r" Movement in Brzezany

Shimon Bleiberg, David Fas, and Shlomo Riger

Translated by Moshe Kutten

Edited by Jane S. Gabin

"Beita'r" branch's leaders with a group of girls

From left to right, standing: **D. Fas, Sh. Riger**
Sitting: **M. Mitelman, Sh. Bleiberg**

The branch of "Brit Yosef Trumpeldor" [Yosef Trumpeldor's Covenant], or as it was later called by its Hebrew acronym – "Beita'r," was organized in our city in 1929 by the members Ludvik Atlas, Shim'on Bleiberg, Solomon Braun, and Steshak Riger. Braun was also the first commander of the branch. The initiative for the organization came from our neighboring city of Rohatyn.

If we are not mistaken, it was the last Zionist youth movement branch established in Brzezany. Therefore, its capacity to recruit members during its first two years was limited but stable. The members who joined the branch came mainly from poor homes that struggled to make a living. Most of them did not have any skills or occupations. Some worked in the city, and others in the neighboring towns. We can say that their true occupation was the activity in "Beita'r's" branch. The "Beita'r" ideology unified them all and created a solid brotherhood that proved itself at times of need, unfortunately – too often. The branch always struggled with its finances since the membership fees were insufficient to cover the expenses. Because of that, we were forced to move from one place to another until we finally settled in the home of Mr. Fassel [?], a specious club on a central street. The winter days were the most demanding until we received free firewood from the sawmill at Potutory. Their support lasted several years.

We were enthusiastic and dedicated in hearts and souls to Ze'ev Jabotinsky's ideas – establishing a Jewish state in Eretz Israel and forming a Jewish legion to fulfill that dream. That was why we accepted the offer by the Polish military to establish a premilitary Jewish company. We knew who our "partners" were, and there were heated debates about that subject. However, the view that we needed to train ourselves militarily prevailed. Looking back, it seems that the latter was the correct choice. Undoubtedly, only such big ideas could have excited the imagination of the youths, whose knowledge of their nation's history was quite limited. However, they were aware of the problems and troubles of the Jews and sometimes experienced them themselves. An educational activity among them was called a "discussion," rather than teaching. That was conducted when a group of boys and girls of the same age gathered, most of the time - twice a week, for educational sessions under the guidance of the group leader. The main subject discussed in those gatherings was the pure Zionist idea, without the addition of any other ideology, regardless of how an exalted idea it represented. We thought the Zionist idea was sublime and meaningful enough to provide us with intellectual satisfaction. It seems that we have not erred. As proof, we note that even though the "Beita'r" branch consisted of poor youths who could have been influenced by promises of quick "salvation," none left us to join an opposing anti-Zionist organization. If we are not mistaken, we were the only movement in that respect. That directly resulted from our education toward adherence to the Zionist idea and moral obligations.

Our spiritual nourishment to warm our hearts and strengthen our ideological inspiration were our discussions about Jewish history, the history of Zionism based on the book by A. Bohm, Palestinography [homeland lessons], "Beita'r's" pamphlets, particularly the Yiddish booklet "*Di Beita'r Yungen Bavehgung*" [Beita'r Youth Movement],

[Page 77]

selections from the Yiddish literature, and, to the best of our ability, other topics associated with Jewish society.

We were very sensitive to the troubles of the Jewish people. They touched our hearts. I recall that we organized the boycott against Nazi Germany and German products and movies. In one case, the *Starosta* [district governor] himself threatened us to cease our "anti-state activities."

Most of the discussions were conducted in Yiddish. In that aspect, we seemed to be different from other organizations, where the dominant language was Polish. In our national instinct, we felt that Yiddish was the language of the Jewish people in the diaspora for a thousand years and a language that united us all. Another reason for our devotion to Yiddish was that most of us came from "*Amkha*" [simple people of the Jewish masses], who did not really need to use the state language. Two Yiddish newspapers had a substantial influence on us. In the beginning, it was the "Heint" [Today], and later on, "Der Moment" [The Moment], both published in Warsaw. We read those newspapers, and in actuality, we studied their entire content. To be precise, we received just a copy, which was passed from one person to another. You can guess what remained of the newspaper at the end of the day.

A few "Beita'r's" members took Hebrew curses in the local Jewish school. They knew to write and speak a little in Hebrew. We pronounced the following Hebrew words fluently: "*sikha*" [discussion], "*hakhshara*" [training], "*ezra*" [aid], "*akh*" [brother], "*kvutza*" [group], "*tzav*" [decree], "*makhoz*" [district], "*medina*" [state], "*galil*" [province], "*netzivut*" [commission], etc. Nevertheless, even though we were attached to Yiddish, the "cultural" language of some of the members, mainly the girls, was Polish.

We established a significant library, mainly in Polish, that served not only the members of "Beita'r" or the Revisionist Zionists but also regular people who could borrow a book every evening for pennies. Some borrowed books for free because they did not have a zloty for the monthly borrowing fee. It goes without saying that the library work, or for that matter, any other work, was done voluntarily. Today, it sounds unbelievable! This is the place to mention our friend, Mordekhai Mitelman, who administrated the library dedicatedly for many years.

A group of "Beita'r" members in uniforms with their weapons

[Page 78]

We also tried our hands at a dramatic activity (obviously, we did not intend to compete with the successful and accomplished drama club). The late Veisbeg encouraged us in that area. He was an educated man who had experience in dramatic direction. We vaguely recall a play in our community house, in which our member, Shalom Ginsberg, may G-d avenge his blood, played the main character.

The various Zionist youth movements collaborated in activities for KKL-JNF and "Ezra" [Aid]. We considered the work to benefit the JNF in the spirit of its slogan, *"Geulah Titnu LaAretz"* [Give redemption to the land – VaYikrah 25:24]. We ran around the town every month to empty the fund's [blue and white] boxes. We should not forget that most of the donors were families who were not wealthy. We also worked dedicatedly for the "Ezra" organization, headed for many years by Dr. Vilner. The methods used in soliciting donations were very original: from donation bowls on Yom Kippur Eve to contributions at family festivities. The "Ezra" organization supported poor pioneers by financing their *Aliyah* expenses. We considered it an important activity to collect money for that purpose. As far as we know, none of the "Beita'r' s" members who made *Aliyah* required assistance from "Ezra."

We did not lose in the competition for collecting money for the KKL-JNF. That was a worthy competition that yielded results. Over the years, including in our time, people ridiculed the rattling of the coins in the [Blue and white] box and the *"Shnor"* [begging for money]. We, on the other hand, considered that holy work. Selling the "Zionist Shekel" [certificate of membership in the Zionist Organization, given to every Jew who paid annual membership dues] was another competition. We took first place in selling the "Zionist Shekel" toward the 18th Zionist Congress, although we were the poorest organization. We took pride in winning that competition and regret the quarreling between us [the Revisionist Zionists] and the Zionist Union and the KKL-JNF [following the 18th Zionist Congress]. This is not the place to explain the reasons for that quarrel However, one thing was certain - the Zionist ideology was the essence of our lives. "Beita'r" comradeship prevailed in our branch. It was enough for somebody from another city to visit our club so that we make sure the visitor was taken care of. We had dear friends in the neighboring towns with whom we corresponded and met often, mainly at conferences. We loved those conferences where we listened attentively to the lecturers and conducted vigorous debates. Friendships and relations were developed at these conferences. The preparations, the gatherings, and the subsequent analysis provided subjects for discussions and material for endless deliberations and activities.

The desire to conquer the heart of every Jewish youth for "Beita'r's" ideology was tenacious. Whoever succeeded in organizing a new "Beita'r" branch in our surrounding areas should have been proud of fulfilling a commandment of the first order, as we considered it then. Great and active Beita'r branches were organized in that way in the villages of Lipitsa, Gorna, Kuzhni, and Bzhokhovitsa. We organized events there, such as conferences, visits, and parties to strengthen their branches. We can't omit to mention some of the projects of our branch, although it was not a strong branch. In one of the years, we organized a summer camp in Bzyaten. "Beita'r" members from several branches in the Ternopil District gathered there. We spent about three to four pleasant weeks immersing ourselves in beautiful nature. One of our organizational work records was the counselors' course in the Rurika forest near the village of Ulkhovtsa. Only the best of the Ternopil District's Beita'r members were allowed to participate in that course. The course was managed by counselors from Warsaw. At its completion, we organized one of the most impressive spectacles. We remember that evening, which left a big and pleasant impression on all of us, as a huge success.

The hunger for making *Aliyah* was enormous. It seemed that if the number of certificates available for the Brzezany branch would have been equal to the number of members, we would have probably closed the Beita'r branch and made *Aliyah* as a group. This is not the place to describe how hopeless our life in our city was. There was nothing we could have hoped for there. Beita'r members went to *Hakhshara kibbutzim*, often to faraway places such as Volhynia and various locations in Galitsia, mostly in sawmills.

[Page 79]

In a later period, we organized four *Hakhshara kibbutzim* in Brzezany itself, in the cellars and attic of the local community house. We recall the substantial effort required to find work for our pioneers. *Hakhshara kibbutzim* were also organized in Nartov, Kozova, and Bzovkhovitsa (in the last two years, only agricultural work).

We should note that the criterion for distributing the *Aliyah* certificates among the various movements was the number of pioneers in the *Hakhshara kibbutzim*. Looking back, we can surely say that the educational value of these camps was enormous. People learned to work in hard manual work! The joyous social life, economic distress, and lack of work or manual work while dreaming of a different and just life in Eretz Israel unified us and taught us an essential lesson. We understood the [Ravina's] song" "[Anu Banu Artza] LiVnot VeLehibanot Bah" ["We came to the land to build it and to be built"] literally, even though our opponents claimed that our movement was not sufficiently pioneering. We were sure in our righteousness. We believed in fulfilling the Zionist idea in the spirit of "Beita'r splendor" [in Hebrew Hadar-Jabotinsky's concept], based on which we were educated and tried to live. We took the expression "Beita'r splendor to mean a person who tries to live an orderly social life, is balanced, considerate of others, particularly in times of need, willing to scarify his comfort for the greater good, and tries to always give a thoughtful and serious response. Perhaps we did followwhat was demanded of us strictly, or perhaps we unknowingly distorted some concepts. However, we are sure that this education "penetrated our bones." For example, the issues of punctuality and fulfillment of obligations. That education sustained us for many years. Even though the political views of some of us may have changed over time, we kept our basic attitudes.

In these notes collected from memories, which may be inaccurate, we did not mention the names of our friends and brothers. They perished along with the rest of our city residents, including our families. We loved and appreciated all of them. Every time we meet with the survivors, we bring up, again and again, countless times, the memory of the good and innocent people who did not live to see the fulfillment of their dream. May these lines serve as the gravestone for their holy memory.

"Beita'r" branch in Brzezany

[Page 80]

Hebrew School

By Dr. Mentsakh, Eng. Tishler

Translated by Moshe Kutten

Edited by Jane S. Gabin

A unique and significant chapter in the history of the Jews of our town was the founding of a Hebrew School by the organization "Safa Brura" [Clear Language] in the month of Iyar 5664 (May 1903). That was a great and important event in the gray daily life of Brzezany's Jews. Zionists, homeowners, and just regular Jews, along with the children's parents, gathered on one of the weekdays to celebrate the opening of the school. Teacher Superman *z"l*, the chairman of Galitsia's teacher association, opened the ceremony with an enthusiastic speech. After him, teacher Abuhav, an educated, learned, and skilled speaker, spoke. Teacher Abuhav taught adults, and teacher Rakhovski taught youngsters.

The school "Safa Brura Group, Brzezany" was founded by Yehuda Zarvintzer and Zalman Zauer. Adolf Horn was elected president of the school. The teaching staff included: Abuhav, Cohen, Rakhovski, Naphtali Zigel, Dlugach, and Tzvi Scharfstein. The latter arrived in our city in 1907. Upon his arrival, the school's education level rose, new classes were established, and new students appeared. Under the management of teacher Tzvi Scharfstein, the school was repaired and improved, the number of students increased to more than a hundred, and the number of classes reached eleven.

Courses for high school students and lessons for adults were held. The school arranged special lessons for *Beit HaMidrash* students who were interested in modern Hebrew literature. In addition to Hebrew, the school taught [Hebrew] grammar, Bible, Jewish history, and modern Hebrew literature. Special courses for academics and teaching candidates were also arranged. The influence of the Hebrew School's teachers on our people was substantial.

The club "Ivriya" was revived. It existed before, but its activity was limited. A library and a reading hall were arranged in the club. Friends, students, and educated homeowners met there to listen, talk, read, and enjoy Hebrew culture. An "Oneg Shabbat" [literally Delight of Shabbat, Friday evening or Shabbat cultural gathering] was held there on Shabbat afternoon – a lecture about modern Hebrew literature followed by a lively debate that ended with public singing. The driving force behind those lectures was teacher Tzvi Scharfstein. The Glazer brothers, Shomer, Mentzakh, Halbertal, and others were also among the participants.

An important event in those days was the visit by the Hebrew author Reuven Brainin. A big ball was arranged in his honor, where hundreds of people participated, including the city's dignitaries. His lecture made a big impression, not forgotten for a long time. The author and participants did not forget the ball itself either.

The school experienced upheavals, ups, and downs, and even though it closed for a short period, it was an established fact until the eruption of the Second World War. It taught and educated our youth and spiritually prepared it for Aliyah.

During the First World War, teacher Feld organized and managed the school. He was a talented person, knowledgeable and educated. Like teacher Scharfstein in his time, he pushed for the teaching of the [Hebrew] language and planted in our hearts the love of the Hebrew word.

Thanks to the youth movements, participation in the studies was lively, a phenomenon that greatly influenced the Jewish street.

[Page 81]

Teacher Feld wrote Hebrew songs that were typical to those days and matched melodies for them. These songs expressed our feelings responding to events in the nation's life. I will mention two of his songs; the first song - "*Kuma ami, am hanetzakh, goy niflah, u'maleh raz*" [Rise my people, the eternal nation, magnificent and full of mystery"], and the second song – "*Shiru nah shir khadash, ami Israel hakat*" [Sing a new song, my tiny nation Israel]. The echo of these songs continued to resonate for many years after teacher Feld left our city (in 1921) and moved to Lviv to teach Hebrew at the high school there. That was an immense loss for us and caused an interruption in the school's operation. However, we did not forget Hebrew despite that interruption.

We continued to study, on our own, in private lessons, and as a compulsory duty at the youth movements. We advanced the language using all means available to us. Only in 1926 the school was reopened. Two teachers renewed the learning in the school: Yitzkhak Biterman and Avraham Halperin. The school program was revitalized a year and a half later when teacher Halperin left. The school brought a new principal, Mr. Komorovski, and Mr. Biterman served as the second teacher. A pedagogic committee was established, and it developed the curriculum for several classes. The high school teachers Horovitz, Shleikher, and Shekhter and the Hebrew teachers, Shlomo Redlikh, Komorovski, and Biterman were elected to the committee.

A second school was founded in 1929 by the Organization "Tarbut" [Culture]. The principal of the school was A. Mansfeld. Sara Gross and Biterman taught in that school.

Two hundred students studied in the two schools. In addition to the Hebrew language, these students acquired knowledge about Jewish history,

The Hebrew School with its executive committee

[Page 82]

Teacher Biterman with a mixed class

geography of Eretz Israel, the Bible, and modern Hebrew literature. All of these subjects were taught in Hebrew. The studies were on a high level.

The elected executive committee managed the school and took care of its needs. The following people were elected to the committee:

The chairman was Karp, his deputy was Immanuel Friedman, the secretary was - Khaim Reiner, the treasurer was – Dr. Vilner and the members were - Hirshhorn, Dr. Grossman, Moshe Lebel, Dr. Glazer, Dr. Shomer, Dr. Klarer, Natan Lebel (the son), M. Taler, Sh. Fogelman, Veisberg, Eliyahu-David Rot, Yitzkhak Nadelr, and Avraham Katz. Thanks to the school's management, who ensured the budget was secured, the school did not suffer from financial problems. The executive committee secured financial support from the Jewish community and the municipality.

The school was eliminated by the occupying Soviet regime!

The Hebrew-speaking people were eliminated by the Nazi occupiers!

The "Tarbut" school's extended executive committee

[Page 83]

The Management team of the school

Sitting from left to right: Teacher Mansfeld, Mr. Karp, and M. Fridman with one of the classes

Teachers H. Biterman (left) and Mansfeld with a group of girl students

Teacher Halperin with a class on a La"g Ba'Omer trip – May 1926

[Page 84]

"Mizrakhi" School

By Menakhem son of Shimon Katz

Translated by Moshe Kutten

Edited by Jane S. Gabin

Another Hebrew school was founded by the movement "Mizrakhi" and [its youth movement] "Bnei Akiva." The scope of that school was more far-reaching than the one for "Tarbut" Hebrew School (if one can call these individual classes a school). It did not have a permanent home. Every few years, those in charge would rent a building or a few rooms in different locations in the city where the studies were conducted.

Initially, the classes were taught in a house adjacent to the orphanage. Later on, two rooms were rented in the "Natzional Hoiz" [National House-People's Center]. When that location became too small, the upper floor of Widow Feieron's home on Koliyova (Train) Street was arranged where studies were held in three parallel classes until World War II. The teachers were city residents: Shmuel Arazi (Tanenbaum) *z"l* (killed in Kfar Etzion [1948]), Volf Reikhshtein (among the graduates of the seminar in Vienna), Mr. Shlezinger (from the neighboring city of Naryov), and others.

The management team consisted of elected people of the "Mizrakhi-Bnei Akiva" movement in the city. The team managed the school affairs voluntarily. The teachers received wages.

The studies were conducted every day in the afternoon hours, and on Sunday, classes were held in the mornings. The studies were more intensive and at a higher level than at the "Tarbut" school. In that school, mainly the basic concepts of the language for lower classes were taught, while in the "Mizrakhi" school, they taught higher levels of the Bible, grammar, and Hebrew literature aimed at the upper classes.

That institution was eliminated with the outbreak of the Second World War, and its students had the same fate as the rest of the six million Jews who were annihilated.

Kindergarten

A kindergarten under the management of Mrs. Felk-Reitman opened in the 1930s. The kindergarten was managed so successfully that within a short period, it was too small to contain all the children who wanted to be admitted. In the beginning, the kindergarten was located in the community house, and later on, when it grew, it moved to a dedicated building on Zhezhnitsa Street, In addition to general education, an emphasis was placed on instilling a Hebrew-Zionist education, in preparation for the Hebrew School.

Purim party at the kindergarten – 20 March, 1932

[Page 85]

Training course for men tailoring

קבֿרים · מלבֿישים · ונא חוב אנשים · טרדיים נבֿמלא · אתנ · יהוא · לשיב
לחיים · סקורים · עבֿדים · על · המדוה · עליח · עויד · הנס · הקבֿרי.
(נרום · סיסילים)

אויפרוף!

יאהרהונדערטלאנג האט מען אין דער יודישער וועלט נעזעהן און געשריבען
מעגען פראלעטאריזידואנצית און אומשיכטונג פֿין די יודישע מאסען, וועגען דער
ריכטיגקייט אינטערעדרגעהען פֿון בֿייעם פרנסות צו א לעבֿען פֿון מלאכה און
עהרלעכער ארבֿייט. ס'וועגען אטילו נאך אן אידעאלען וואם האבֿען געוואלט אין דער
גאיישער שװאַרצער ארבֿייט די אינגערדוע רמאה צי דער אידעיייסטבֿעטער
יודהן סראאנג. איצי אבֿער האט מ' א נער פֿון פתוער לינער יונענד האבֿעב
ספראלאם דיערע היטען און לעבֿען אוישער די שרעקליבֿסע בֿעדינגונגען און
די קמצי־הכשרה. שטעהטע די פלטעריש יודישע באפעלקסערונג אין דער דיים
און קוםם זיך צו גלייכגילטיג דורך מים בֿיטול צו ודייער אונערגעבֿונג.
דאם אין א גרוינע זינר וואָם בֿיר בֿעגעהן געגען אינדער בֿרודער און מער
בֿודישעלטער יונענד. מיר מאַרען נישט פֿערגעסען או דער שיבֿת־הגבֿלה
שטעלם נישט בלייז א בֿליח פֿון הגנע ארבֿיטונ מעגשאם. ניר אויך גלייב־
בֿימיג אייך דער, וואם פראלעטנרישם מאר דער דישער יודישער הכלם רעם
סיפת. פֿאלׄם גיעם יור. דעם אימפמור מים שטאַריעא מ'נטאקילן און גראמדען
רייכעם. דער חלוח וואם ארבֿיים און קבין וועניג דורך שוואַרעבֿאר און קלהסי־
רעלער ארבֿייטע, פֿליים און גייסטיג צולענערדים בֿום נייעם לעבֿען אין ארץ
ישראל. אוי מיזו דער לאראַנע סהיהרבֿער אין די די קורירה לאָם וואיל צו לידישוע.
אין עם בֿם ניטא די סיד פֿון די מלוטים צ־ א אנוע נר דלה. וואם מיר לעבֿעריו זיך קעגעו נ־
אם לעקרימעליתם זיים א לעבֿעטודיים א אלו..ה חבֿקהה און אונזער שמאמ. אוך גראאם די שליה
בֿעריהונג פֿון די הלוהם בֿעגוואס ויך די מיגע בֿעעלדעקמוירוז נאן אלוָני בֿי גיי מים ־יישע ארבֿייג.

זיי געפֿינגען זיך אין א שרעקליכען מאַטער-
יעלען מצב אזוי. אז עס פֿעהלט זיי לחם לאכל
ובגד ללבש אין פשום עו זין פֿין די ועראטער-

מיר בֿיוען מאבֿען א מלף או דעם און וראעלילבֿען מצב. הבֿטיק! איך ניטם מר. או דן
באלדעם פֿמרבֿיואדיגע בֿעל־רחמבֿוה האם קצו אן נטם בֿורטען ויי יודירע פֿודר ארבֿ־ןו
שטאַרטאם און שויברא ארבֿיים. הדם סיך אירף ורשן ניטנ אַו. אין אי די בֿיישע און ברעגמטים . אָבֿרס־יי
האם הילבֿען וין און אונרבֿרע אירינעדם או די ארבֿים פֿון ד' חלוַגם אל בֿורודיעשה.

נ·ו דינקס! און אייערע קינדער, בֿרורער און שוועםטער. וואַם
געמיבֿען זיך אין אנדערע קבֿוצים. אין טרפֿילט אייער מענטליכען
און יודישען חוב צו די חלוזים. און נעביצם זיך תמיד מיט
בֿייער ארבֿייט!

בֿעדדיעעגנג יענען ארבֿים חבֿרים בֿאגעגמען ביים סאלגבֿעדע ערער.
1. Plac Czackowa, Izabelówka 9,
2. Dr A. Feld, pl. Sokoła 1, Telefon Nr. 61,
3. Skład mąki p. Zldbogfa Tarnopolska 31.

מערון אדז.נ קאטטעדטעם

דר אריה פֿעלר   שלמה רעזליד   פּראַפֿ. מ. ראזענבערג

A call for support of the *Hakhshara Kibbutzim*

Hakhshara Kibbutzim

By Arch. Menakhem Katz

Translated by Moshe Kutten

Edited by Jane S. Gabin

With the establishment of the Hakhshara *Kibbutzim* in the 1920s, where groups of various youth movements prepared themselves for commune life and physical work in Eretz Israel, financial distress was apparent. Lack of work on one side and the indifference of the Jewish public to supply jobs to the pioneers on the other undermined the *kibbutz* movement.

Those groups of pioneers did not shy away from any work, starting with cleaning jobs, digging, cutting trees for heating in private homes, and ending with work at the sawmills. Despite the willingness of the youth to work in any job, the lack of jobs undermined the existence of the work camps. Zionist groups and some individuals woke up once and a while, and addressed the general public to provide places of work for the pioneers in the *kibbutzim*. The above proclamation [*Oifrouf* in Yiddish], published in our city, serves as a testimony to that struggle.

[Pages 86-87][1]

Between the Two World Wars

[Page 88]

The Economic Situation [1]

By Menakhem son of Shimon Katz

Translated by Moshe Kutten

Edited by Jane S. Gabin

The economic situation of Brzezany's Jews was hard for all generations and at all times. While a slight improvement occurred at the end of the 19th century, it benefited only a few people. For most Jews, the phrase "By the sweat on your face, you shall eat your bread" [Genesis 3:1] would apply. The truth is that there were some wealthy people, and there was a middle class, but the masses struggled, worked, and toiled to earn their bread.

Brzezany and its surroundings had no natural resources, industries, or mines. There were a handful of wealthy people, such as owners of estates, lumber dealers, processors of flour mills, bank owners, and distinguished owners of houses. These people were also the guides, direction indicators for community affairs' handling, and deciders in public affairs. In his story, "Hakhnasat Kalah" Bridal Canopy,"] Sh. Y. Agnon describes one of our city's wealthy and prominent families, the Rappaports. Many stories were told about that family.

I also have such a story, and it goes as follows: "The family had several daughters. The first married a great scholar from Russia from the famous Brotzky family. A short while after the wedding, he was stricken with depression, which lingered for the rest of his life. When his second daughter reached marriage age, the father set out again on a wagon to Russia to bring a groom for his second daughter. Families from the city and its surroundings were not wealthy or distinguished enough for him. On the way, the wagon owner's whip broke. When they reached a forest, the waggoner got off and entered the woods to find another whip. He stayed there a long time, and when he returned, he held a crooked whip. The wealthy man asked him angrily: 'For such a crooked whip,

The flour mill with the dam

[Page 89]

On the bank of the river. The burnt flour mill is in
the background.

you had to enter so deep into the forest? Couldn't find such a whip close to the road?' Using the words of the wealthy man, the waggoner replied rudely: 'And for such a crazy *"getsle"* ([or urchin, meaning] the wealthy man's first son-in-law), you had to travel so far to Russia? Couldn't you find such 'a bargain' by us?' "You are right," said the wealthy man. "The 'Finger of G-d' is showing me the way. That was a hint from the heavens," he said, turning around.

As a portion of the overall Jewish population in the city, the wealthy constituted just a small percentage. After them, in second place was the middle class. It consisted of lawyers, physicians, Jewish government officials (such as judges, schoolteachers, bankers, and railroad officials), and some established merchants. Although the number of middle-class people was also small, it was bigger than the upper class and not less important. They carried the burden. They were the majority of the leaders and public affairs activists. They were also our representatives with the authorities and the speakers on behalf of the community. Most of these people did their work dedicatedly, for the sake of it, voluntarily. They also headed welfare institutions.

They were accompanied by poor-class craftsmen or just kind-hearted people willing to help others. The latter worked modestly, devotedly, and gently, and they volunteered to help anonymously. The third class consisted of most of the craftsmen (a small portion was in a better situation), small merchants, workshop apprentices, store helpers, household workers (most of whom were women), all sorts of peddlers, market stall owners, wagon owners, porters, and other people who made a living doing any casual work. Most of the latter walked around in the market, bought produce (such as flax, poultry, eggs, butter, and cheese) from poor and small farmers, and sold the produce to merchants with a meager profit of a few pennies.

Craftsmen, like everybody in their class, worked hard. They started the workday at sunrise and worked all day without a break until sunset. That is, if they had work, which was not always available. Most of the craftsmen in our city were Jewish: tinsmiths, glazers, carpenters, bakers, shoemakers, painters, and more. During those days, they had already organized in "Yad Kharutzion" [literally "dedicated hand," the name of the Jewish craftsmen guild].

A dedicated corner in the market square was allocated for the waggoners and porters. They were the pugilists, the defenders at times of need, and the frontline in any assault or riot in the Jewish streets. Most of them married among themselves and were all relatives or blood relatives. During idle times, they sat down or stood around the wagons and talked to each other. They told each other about their life and consulted about things that bothered them.

One small story typifies those people. Among the waggoners, there was a Jew by the name of "Yukl." His nickname was "Firer" (the transporter [in Yiddish]) because his work was to transport garbage from the yards. He was a simple man with a short stature and a long and narrow beard who dreamt about being rich all his life. He always bought lotto tickets, and one time, he won. All of his three numbers matched, and he won a large sum. When people heard in the morning about it, big excitement enveloped the city: "Did you hear? R' Yukl is a rich man! He won the lotto." They were still talking when he appeared. The waggoners took him aside, sat him down on a wagon, gathered around him, and called him in a chorus: "Tell us! How did it happen?" He settled himself on his seat, "feeling like a wise rich man who knows how to play the game," took a deep breath, coughed, and began to say: "It was a wintery Friday night after dinner. I laid down to rest a bit after a week of hard work. I fell asleep, or perhaps I had not slept yet, and my aunt Yenta, may she rest in peace, appeared in front of me and approached me. I saw her as if she was alive, like in the old days when I brought her some food my mother had prepared.

[Page 90]

And she told me: 'Here are three kreuzers [Austrian pennies]. Go and buy yourself seven sandwiches.' I woke up and immediately understood the meaning of my dream. She brought me my salvation. "But Uncle Yukl," one waggoner from among the young ones interrupted impatiently, not wanting to wait for the end of the story, "In your dream, your aunt gave you only two numbers, three and seven. Where did you take the third number 22 from?" Uncle Yukl responded: "What is the problem? Three I had, seven I had, three times seven is twenty-two!"

'How is that?' interrupted that waggoner again, 'Three times seven is twenty-one, not twenty-two.' 'Wh---------at?' said Uncle Yukl And after thinking about this for a few minutes, he continued, 'It is possible that in arithmetic, you are right, but in life, with such wise calculations, you will never win.'

All the people in that class worked hard but still needed support, once in a while, in the form of a loan or financial assistance.

Quite a substantial portion were the poor people who had no income. Their entire livelihood was dependent on public support and welfare. Their situation was not easy, despite what was provided to them. Their state was expressed in a phrase of the "Birkat HaMazon" [Grace after meals]: "Lord our Gâ€'d, please do not make us dependent upon the gifts of mortal men nor upon their loans. "The poverty in those days was indescribable. The poor were hungry for a slice of bread. Some among the poor were ashamed to ask for a handout and were dying from hunger.

Therefore, it is easy to understand the reason for the massive Jewish emigration in the late 19th century and early 20th century when the gates were opened to the bigger world, to a country where all people are made equal, there is bread for everyone, work for all, labor shortage situation. That country was vast and rich and provided opportunities to earn one's living with dignity. Multitudes left to find their fortune in distant America, but even there, these people did not have easy lives. In the beginning, singles went, and later, the heads of families. The wives and the children stayed behind to allow the fathers to work peacefully and earn enough money to bring their families to America.

The market square – before 1914

[Page 91]

That emigration wave brought with it many tragedies. Some of the husbands who had emigrated disappeared. It is unknown, until today,+ what happened to them. They may have died (from an illness or hard work) or perhaps remarried without divorcing their first wives. It was difficult to know the truth during those days. They left a wife with all her children, who remained "Agunah" [a Jewish woman who cannot remarry according to Jewish religious law], destitute, with no means to make a living, and hopeless. During those days, there was no government welfare program, and the government did not aid their poor people. Without the mutual aid offered by the community, the Jewish poor could not have survived. Charitable Jews established welfare institutions. Compassionate people helped - one person brought bread, another – medication for the sick, and yet another – shoes or a dress to cover one's body. Thanks to that assistance and despite the harsh conditions, the children grew up, learned what they learned, and achieved whatever they achieved. They did not die from hunger and did not fall into bad ways.

The various wars that took place in the years 1914 – 1920 had a severe ill effect on the Jews of our town. Most men between the ages of 18 – 55 served in the army. A substantial portion of the Jews left the city and escaped westward. During the war years, the sources of livelihood were completely ruined. Most of the houses were burnt or destroyed by shells. The city served as a front for a whole year and transferred from hand to hand several times during the six years of war. The surrounding area's peasants took advantage of the opportunity every time the regime changed and looted and robbed Jewish properties. Jews who still had real estate sold it to survive, but the money they had received lost its value overnight.

When the wars ended, the city Jews tried to rehabilitate their lives. They tried to return to economic and spiritual equilibrium or even improve the situation to achieve organized lives. However, they were disappointed quickly and concluded that the opposite was true. There was no future for Jews and no hope for changing their situation. I will briefly describe the economic state of most Jewish families in our city.

[Page 92]

The Trade

Translated by Moshe Kutten

Edited by Jane S. Gabin

Merchants who returned home rebuilt their stores, each according to their ability. The young soldiers and the youth who grew up during the War and had no opportunity to acquire a trade now turned their attention to business. The number of merchants grew more than this economy could support. That resulted in vigorous competition. As if that was not enough, a new competitor rose, stronger and more dangerous, since the regime was on its side, and so was the law (or more accurately – distortion of the law, to take this essential occupation from the hands of the Jews). The competitors were the Poles and the Ukrainians, who introduced the elements of using physical force and propaganda, made available to them by the government, into the competition game. The introduction of these elements bore fruits. Some Jewish merchants liquidated their businesses and made Aliyah to Eretz Israel (Grabski's Aliyah)[2]). Unfortunately, not all those people succeeded (for known reasons, [a severe economic crisis in Eretz Israel]) and returned disgruntled and broken.

Under these conditions, trade became more complicated and less possible from one day to another. Under the initiatives of two merchants, a Pole called Shlosrek [?] and a Jew named Ya'akov Miteleman, the merchants organized themselves in a merchants' union. A gathering of merchants took place in our city on May 5th, 1922, where a committee of eleven members was elected. A union court and audit committee were also established. They decided to call for a gathering every two years to hold new elections. A year later, the union joined the Polish Guild of Eastern Poland.

The following people were elected to the first city committee:

> Yaakov Mitelman – Chairman
> Wagshal Hersh – his deputy
> Goldman Barukh – second deputy
> Baran Mauritzi – secretary
> Tzukerkandel – his deputy
> Taler Yehoshua – treasurer
> Reikhbakh Leib
> Horovitz Shlomo
> Rot Eliyahu-David
> Fuks Meir
> Roza Yeshayahu

Besides the objective under which the organization was founded, it had its own fund for short-term loans, tax consulting services, and consulting services for business accounting.

Upon the entrance of the Soviets, the trade was eliminated entirely and was never renewed.

[Page 93]

Academics in Government Positions

Translated by Moshe Kutten

Edited by Jane S. Gabin

Only a few Jews served in government positions, most of whom remained from the days of the Austrian regime.

Two Jewish judges served in the court: Tadnier and Hornik.

Three teachers taught at the high school: Dr. Shekhter, Horovitz, and Shleikher.

Two physicians: Dr. Pomerantz (who served as a municipal physician and at a clinic) and Dr. Bakhman (a military physician – not in Brzezani).

All these people (except Dr. Bakhman) were active in the city's public life.

Physicians

Translated by Moshe Kutten

Edited by Jane S. Gabin

During and right after the First World War, Dr. Felk was the only Jewish physician in the city. He remained active until the end of his life. Dedicated and responsible, he was very popular within the Jewish community. A few more Jewish physicians were added in the years between the two World Wars: Dr. Shomer, a beloved and respected physician by all people in the city. He was a Zionist and public activist who dedicated time from his free time to improving the lives of the Jews in the city. He treated poor patients for free. Dr. Pomerantz, who held government positions, practiced very little in a private clinic. He was the chairman of the Jewish drama club in the city. Dr. Kornberg stayed in Brzezany only a short time and then moved to another city.

A few more physicians became active during 1930 – 1940: Dr. Arye Feld, an alum of "HaShomer HaTzair" and an activist from his youth until his last day. Dedicated and skilled, he was the only radiologist in the entire area. Dr. Vagshall (Shaklai) wasvery active in Jewish life in the city. Some other physicians graduated abroad and did not have a permit to work in Poland. They began practicing as physicians only during the Russian conquest: Arye Falic, Lileh, Hibler, Landau, Dr. Moshe Frid, Yosef Meiblum, and Riner Khaim. They all left our city at the end of their studies. Meser and Veinshtein immigrated to South America before the War. Rozen, Vinter, and Likhtman studied abroad but have not graduated as of yet. Shekhter did not return to the city either when he completed his studies.

Two dentists worked in the city: Doctors Diness and Vondermeir. and a few dental technicians. They all had a license to operate a private clinic, earned their living honorably, and their situation was good. I also have to mention here Dr. Lebel, a children's physician. He was very active in the life of the Jews in the city.

Most of the physicians were also active during the Nazi regime until the elimination of the ghetto. Dr. Shomer and Dr. Arye Falik served in the Soviet military and survived the War. Dr. Vagshall survived the Holocaust.

[Page 94]

Pharmacists

Translated by Moshe Kutten

Edited by Jane S. Gabin

According to the law in those years (after the First World War), pharmacology required an academic degree. The law demanded three years of study in a university and one year of working in the profession. In pharmacology, like in medicine, "Numerus clausus" was imposed, so only a few were admitted. Our youth, who aspired to study for that profession without any limitation, went to study abroad. The degrees of these graduates were not recognized in Poland, and they could not secure work. They were allowed to work in their profession only during the days of the Soviet regime. Even those who graduated and secured a license could not find work. The Polish authorities avoided giving Jews permits for new pharmacies. Most of the pharmacies owned by the Jews remained from the days of the Austrian rule. That was just one of the economic obstacles enacted by the Poles against the Jews.

Brzezany had three pharmacies, two of which were owned by Jews. The first one was Pohoriles's, and the other was Goldman's. Two additional pharmacists, Magisters Orenshtein and Laufgang, had licenses.

Those who completed their studies abroad and did not receive a work license were: Glazer, Kh. Khaigenbuam, Noishiler, Tonis, Rubinshtein, Shvartz, and Oberlender. Some left Poland before the War to look for work overseas.

Lawyers

Translated by Moshe Kutten

Edited by Jane S. Gabin

Many lawyers made a living in our city due to the large number of court cases in the only district court in the area. At the end of the 19th century, twelve of fourteen lawyers were Jewish. They made a good living before the First World War, and most were involved in public affairs. After the War, their number grew to forty (besides the Polish and Ukrainian lawyers). That resulted in stiff competition, and some lawyers, particularly some of the young ones, had to work hard for their income.

That growth happened because, unlike other professions, there were no limitations on admitting Jewish students to the university in that profession. Everybody who completed their studies received a license without any difficulty. I will mention only some of them who remained in my memory: Ravitz, Nagler, Oberlender, Goldshlag, Landsberg, Milkh, Glazer, Vilner, Klarer, Finkelshtein, Grossman, Reikh, Lopater, Fridman, Reizman, Baigel, Riger, Noiman, Bleiberg, David, Salomon, Glikshtern, Nussbaum, Laber, Trauner, Binder, Erikh, and others.

Some of the lawyers, natives of Brzezany, who moved to other cities were: Freier, Leib Glazer, Brunek Fridman, Lifshitz, and others.

Many lawyers were prominent in their profession and were also dedicatedly involved in public affairs. They were very active and unforgettable.

Some lawyers were registered in the Golden Book of the KKL-JNF by the city Jews for their loyal and dedicated activism and work.

Most of them perished in the Holocaust.

[Page 95]

Engineers

Translated by Moshe Kutten

Edited by Jane S. Gabin

Only a few of our youths studied engineering since they knew they could not secure government or municipal positions. There were, however, a handful of Jewish engineers: Pinion Frid studied abroad and did not find work in his profession. He made Aliyah and worked as an engineer in the Haifa municipality. Merkur also graduated but could not secure a job until the Second World War. Landesberg converted to Christianity and was accepted for a government position. Noishiler, the youngest one, completed his studies with the outbreak of the Second World War.

The bridge on the Zlota Lypa River

Craftsmen

Translated by Moshe Kutten

Edited by Jane S. Gabin

The situation of the craftsmen did not improve after the First World War, and in many cases, it even worsened. Those who managed to learn a profession did not find work since the experienced craftsmen hardly made a living. There was no future for the working youths in our city. They joined youth movements hoping to make Aliyah to Eretz Israel. Unfortunately, the Aliyah was very limited in those days, and people had to wait a few years for an entrance permit. Those who made Aliyah were saved from the claws of the Nazis. I will never forget the youth we lost, filled with energy, goodwill, and creativity, who did not live to see their aspiration fulfilled. Only a few found refuge in South America.

Translator's notes:

1. Sections from the English version start on page 12.

2. A wave of Jewish Aliyah resulted from an anti-Jewish taxation policy by Grabski's government.

[Page 96]

World War II

By Dr. Eliezer Shaklai

Translated by Moshe Kutten

Edited by Jane S. Gabin

On the eve of the outbreak of WW II

During the period between the two World Wars, the economic situation of the Jews deteriorated. The Poles, and by us in Eastern Galitsia, also the Ukrainians, were determined to rob the Jews of their economic basis and the sources of their livelihood. They implemented their wish.

The Polish government supported them by enacting various laws the Jews could not withstand. On one side, it imposed high unjustifiable and unreasonable taxes that brought the Jews into bankruptcy, and on the other side did not allow the Jews to advance in the free professions (Numerus Clausus, Numerus Nullus). With some laws, the Polish government aimed at angering the Jews and taking revenge on them (for example, the elongated debate about ritual slaughtering). Under that environment of competition and warfare against the Jews, for the sake of it or not, the hatred by the non-Jewish population against the Jews strengthened, and the atmosphere became electrified more and more.

One tiny spark could have caused an enormous fire. Indeed, even before the War, there were some attacks, and several Jewish families were murdered.

The situation of the Jews in our province was extremely harsh. Most of the population was Ukrainian. The villagers (farmers) were Ukrainians, and a substantial portion of the city intelligentsia was also Ukrainians. The Polish government tried to "remedy" the situation by bringing Polish farmers from Mazovsha [Mazovian?] province – radical nationalists and antisemites who tried to suppress the national awakening of the Ukrainians that increased day by day. As a result of the external influence (Germany) and the internal influence (the radical Ukrainian intelligentsia), the interaction between the Poles and the Ukrainians escalated into fistfights, bloodshed, arsons, and murders. However, the real victims and the scapegoats in these battles were the Jews. They suffered beatings from both sides. Both the Poles and the Ukrainians used any opportunity to hurt the Jews first. Many Jewish families were harmed in property and lives. The political situation in the world should be added to the economic and social background of our city's Jews. The war atmosphere was felt in Poland as early as 1933 – since Hitler rose to power.

We all remember well Nuremberg's laws, the robbing of Jewish properties, Crystal Night, the expulsion of Jews from Germany and Austria, the closure of the borders for Jewish refugees, and the Evian Conference and its resolutions. All of that before the outbreak of the Second World War.

The beginning of the War

The war atmosphere was felt in our city a long time before the outbreak of the War, created by the many refugees who were expelled from Germany to Poland. The Germans sent them out beyond the border because they were former subjects of Germany. There were refugees from Austria and Germany in our city, too. We knew the War would eventually come, but when it did happen, it hit us hard and caused a real shock. We were not prepared for it, neither physically nor mentally.

[Page 97]

Though we heard on the radio and read in the newspapers about the approaching War, people lived their daily lives as if the news was not their concern. We were dreaming when the first siren woke us up. The choking atmosphere of War intensified. As early as the first day of the War, we realized how much we were unprepared. We were gripped by panic, and the enemy made use of it. Our people tried to enlist, but it was too late because the military warehouses had no uniforms, guns, or supplies.

"Go and stay home," they responded when we came to enlist. The confusion and lack of order increased by the hour. A siren could be heard every few minutes. We were taught that people should advise others about the approach of enemy planes by ringing bells, whistling, and yelling. The noise was so loud that people got confused and did not know what to do. The noise from sirens rose to the heavens, and people ran around without knowing where and why. Fortunately, during that period, we did not suffer from bombing, and there were no casualties.

The evacuation eastward, on loaded trucks and wagons, began as early as the first days of the War. High-level officials and military officers escaped after a few days in the direction of the Russian-Romanian border. As usual in these cases, the roads were clogged by people and vehicles, which resulted in many accidents. In addition, the bombing by the German air force caused many casualties. Many wounded people were left on the roads, and some reached our city. We assisted them as much as we could. We worked day and night without feeling tired. Everyone wanted to ease the situation somewhat, help, and participate in the campaign, although we knew that all was lost.

We also saw a lack of order in the supply of food. In our area, food was always in abundance. Our region was first in the export of butter, cheeses, eggs, and grains. But everything disappeared in the early days of the War. There was no bread, cheese, or eggs. A barter market commenced, and money lost its value.

Britain announced joining the War against Germany two days after its outbreak. A day later, we heard on the radio about France's decision to join the war against Germany. However, it was too late for us, the Jews. That could not have helped us at all.

It is hard to describe the days of the War - the retreat, panic, fear, sirens, lack of order, and most of all - hopelessness. There was nothing we could do. Along with the rest of the Polish army, part of our youth who served in the military became prisoners of War either by the Germans or the Russians. Some of our citizens managed to escape to the Romanian border. Two buses filled with men from our city went out eastward. Among the escapees were Dr. Vilner, Dr. Risman, and Judge Yosef Noiman, may he live long. Some of the escapees returned from the middle of the road. Some became captives of the Russians, and only a small portion managed to cross the border to Romania and save themselves.

On Sunday morning, 17 September 1939, we heard on the radio that the Soviets crossed the Polish border. The news was passed around very quickly. In the beginning, we did not believe it, but the rumor was confirmed at noon. Salvation would come from the East. We saw it as an opening for a rescue. The Soviet tanks entered our city on Wednesday, 20 September 1939, at 11 am. They came from the direction of Adamovka. They did not stop and continued on their way toward Rohatyn. A few Polish, Ukrainian, and Jewish residents gathered at the city hall to welcome the guests and greet them, but the Russians did not stop, even for a minute, and continued on their way without paying any attention to the delegation.

[Page 98]

The first impression of the Soviet Army invoked dismay – poverty was projected from their faces and uniforms. Since we did not know at the time that the entrance of the Soviet military would be temporary and that calamity would befall our city and our people, we felt relieved. We were sure that the big disaster was averted; we were saved from the Nazi regime.

The Soviet Rule

The army and the communist officials arrived after the first tanks passed. A revolution occurred in our lives overnight. A silent revolution, with no bloodshed, but a 180-degree change of direction nevertheless. It was like a fulfillment of the [Talmudic] phrase: "…upper ones down and lower ones up." They first released political prisoners from jail. They used these people to establish their regime. They also used them to execute all sorts of illegal tasks. They extracted from these prisoners all the information they needed – data about every person who could be relied on and who should be eliminated? The Soviets temporarily divided the positions among the local communists – some high-level authority positions, such as the mayor, and some low-level ones. The local communists recommended to the Soviets local unaffiliated people who could be trusted.

The local communists, who did not know the Soviet laws, did all the work of the Soviets: allocated grants, imposed taxes and customs on many merchants, confiscated a portion of their properties, and plundered their houses and furniture. Later on, Russian officials came and got rid of the local communists, took their positions, and slowly introduced the actual Soviet regime. In the first few days, people thought of returning to the routine life of the time before the War; the shopkeepers opened the shops, and artisans returned to work, each in his own profession, but the true reality became known quickly.

The Russians were good customers. They quickly bought everything there was to buy. The money lost its value; new merchandise was not available. The stores emptied and closed within a few days. It was difficult to find bread, let alone butter, eggs, and meat. The farmers did not sell vegetables for money. The farmer felt that he would not profit since the authorities demanded he hand over part of his produce and all this as a down payment. Since the demanding people were the local communists, most of whom were Jewish, the hatred toward local Jewish communists became a grudge and animosity toward all Jews.

The face of the city changed within a short time. The trade ceased, and the shops closed. The framers hardly paid a visit to the city. The search for a day's work, scarcity, and depression prevailed. In the meantime, the population continued to grow by the day - through the flow of refugees from Western Poland who managed to cross the border.

Russian officials and their families came from the East. Thousands of people came from neighboring cities like Zolochiv and Ternopil. They left their cities for fear or because they were forbidden to reside there. Some had the means to make a living, but others arrived penniless.

[Page 99]

The city population of thirteen thousand grew to thirty-five thousand people with about twelve thousand Jews (compared to three thousand local Jews). The main problem for the Jewish refugees was lodging. Some converted shops into apartments, others found a shelter at the large synagogue, and most resided with the non-Jewish population in the city suburbs after paying a fortune. Many fell sick due to the crowded conditions. They were not helped by the authorities. The local Jews made every effort to assist them, but because of the extreme poverty, their assistance was like a drop in the sea. A second problem faced by the Jewish refugees was getting food. As aforementioned, shops were closed, the farmers avoided selling their produce, and the prices soared. The locals blamed the refugees for that, and from their side, the refugees blamed the locals for being evil.

A committee to assist the refugees was established in secret because the Soviets forbade the existence of such associations, even for charitable purposes. Toward the end of the summer, my late father and two more Jews went on a secret mission to other cities to collect money for the refugees. Some donations were substantial, but [as the phrase in the Talmud says] "the handful does not satisfy the lion."

Over time, some refugees returned to the German side, but most of them found their place and livelihood in the city. Some others were taken out of their homes (among those who registered to return to Germany) and transported to Siberia along with some locals (Ukrainians, Poles, and Jews).

In 1939, elections were held in Eastern Galitsia. That was a referendum to determine the future of that region. One or two representatives from every city were elected to a conference that gathered in the city of Lviv. It was decided at that conference to ask "*Batyushka*" [Father] Stalin to accept the region under his patronage. They thanked Stalin for "freeing" them from Polish enslavement on that occasion.

That winter, they notified us of Stalin's agreement to have us join the big Soviet family. A command was then issued that every person should secure an identification certificate as a Soviet citizen. Whoever did not want such a certificate had to fill out a detailed form where they wanted to move to and indicate their local address. The Soviets sent to Siberia those who registered as refugees who wished to return westward, along with some of the people whose passport was stamped with a "paragraph" or clause (explanation below). However, an identification certificate only did not prevent a city resident from being moved to another location. Everybody had to work and try to find a permanent job, otherwise, the Soviets could have sent a person to work somewhere else (e.g., the coal mines in the Donbas region).

The Jewish population in the city was divided into several categories: 1) People who had free professions, such as lawyers, judges, teachers, and physicians. 2) Craftsmen such as shoemakers, locksmiths, carpenters, glazers, and painters. 3) Most people were merchants, business owners, peddlers, or people without any profession. The letters and some of those with free professions were forced to change their occupation and look for other work, sometimes physical. However, a radical change occurred for everybody. Physicians, pharmacists, teachers, and engineers became government employees who were not allowed to work privately. Craftsmen were organized in cooperatives. These cooperatives had a manager, accountant, secretary, and domestic workers. The lawyers joined a cooperative under a decree from above, where only a limited number of lawyers were accepted. Every accepted lawyer had to secure an agreement with the Communist Party. Most of the intelligentsia occupied positions as accountants, secretaries, or work organizers.

[Page 100]

Although there were plenty of places for work, many people remained unemployed. Some of the merchants tried to create jobs – they founded, with their own money, small factories in the form of cooperatives so that they could claim they had permanent jobs.

Every person had to carry an identification document containing details about the residence and work. Some had a "paragraph" or a marking on the ID, indicating that the person had a flaw or stain in his past or present. The ID was valid for a period of up to five years. People with a "paragraph" mentioned on their ID received their ID once a year or sometimes once a month. After the stated time limit, the person had to renew the certificate. Every person had a personal card at the NKVD [Soviet secret police]. The card contained details about the exact address, biography, biography of the parents and grandparents, and the family. When needed (nobody knew when that would happen and why), the card would be pulled out, and the individual would be invited to the NKVD, always after midnight, where he would be reminded of the "sins" of his youth (such as being a Zionist).

I am not able to describe in detail life under Soviet rule. I will only provide a short description of life during that period.

Life under Soviet rule was not easy. There were people who, by a command, had to appear once every week or two, after midnight, under a false name, to the NKVD to provide a detailed report about what they saw and heard at their residence or work from friends and acquaintances. Every place of work had several such people (snitches) that nobody knew about them. The supervisor had to carefully watch and tell his superiors about any deviation by any worker. The ultimate superiors were the *"Politruk"* [political ideology officer] nominated by the [Communist] party's secretary, *Prokoror* [prosecutor], or an NKVD official. Every place of work had a *Politruk* attached to it who was tasked with conducting ideology discussions, teaching the constitution and Stalin and Lenin's writings, and most importantly, investigating the attitude and loyalty of every worker, particularly of the management, to the new regime.

A "Red Corner" was allocated at every place of work – a "holy" place where the pictures of the "Big Four" - Marx, Engels, Lenin, and Stalin - hung. A worker assembly is gathered every week in every place of work to discuss work affairs, improvements, and praises or condemnations of workers. Workers had to arrive at work promptly on time. Lateness of three to five minutes or more resulted in an official condemnation at the worker assembly. After the third incident, the worker would be handed over to the court, facing a punishment of three to six months of forced labor and a deduction of 35% from the salary. A tardiness of twenty minutes or more was handed over to the court on the first offense. If a worker was late while serving the prior sentence, he would be sentenced to five to ten years in jail and deportation to Siberia.

The work itself was not that hard, but the responsibility was not only your own work but the work of others. You would be at fault if you knew about a "condemning" detail and did not report it in a timely manner to the supervisor, *Prokoror*, or NKVD. Under that atmosphere, people began to suspect and fear others. You never knew to whom you were talking, although you have known that person for a long time. Even if you were a friend of a specific individual until the War began, you did not know the nature of that person after the War. We got used to this life slowly and with difficulties. Social and cultural life ceased to exist. People met only at work or in gatherings under a cloud of suspicion and doubt. The synagogues were full of refugees, and public praying was done in secret,

[Page 101]

in private locations. Schools for children up to the age of 12 were opened for the entire population free of tuition. Initially, there was also a school where the teaching language was Yiddish, but it closed after the first academic year.

The library closed, and our books disappeared. It was forbidden to borrow books, and so were other areas of our cultural life. Nothing remained from the drama club or soccer team, let alone the activity of the youth movement. Our lives became similar to those of people in Russia. People were forbidden to think since thinking was done for them by their superiors and people in the "high places." Everything was done on command, according to a preplanned program, prepared and written in advance. An individual was just a tiny screw in a big machine. One should not have stood in the middle to think or ask. We learned to shut up.

The ruling language was Russian, and the secondary language was Ukrainian. Medical services were free for the entire population. There was one large polyclinic [providing general and specialist services] for the whole city and its surroundings. The hospital served everybody free of charge.

We were associated with the Ternopil District, and the district received instructions from Kyiv. Several physicians and nurses arrived from Russia, but there was a shortage of nurses nevertheless. We conducted courses for practical nurses at the hospital. Some practical nurses survived WW II since they enlisted in the Red Army at the beginning of the war (some reside today in Israel).

The court was at the hands of the Soviets, while the NKVD was in charge of security, and we all were under the supervision and management of the party headed by the first and second secretaries. Our communists could not join the party since the Soviets did not trust them, and to join, one had to be a "candidate" for five years. Some local communists were jailed immediately upon the arrival of the Soviet communists because their friends in the movement snitched on them that they were Trotskyists. We have not heard about or seen them since. Among the arrested people was one of our unaffiliated people, Dr. Pomerantz, but he was released after three months in jail.

As aforementioned, the economic situation was terrible. The salary was small, hardly sufficient to buy bread with some tiny extra. However, finding bread was difficult. Sometimes, the Soviets handed out sugar or another staple in the stores. The Soviets were against lines since a line meant "a shortage," and those existed only in the capitalist countries. The truth should be told that the Soviet regime wanted to prevent the formation of lines so that people would not waste their precious time. So, they would suddenly announce that a specific product is available in the stores. The result was an onslaught on the stores, and the inventory was gone within several minutes. There was not much of it in the store. Most of what had been supplied was hidden away and was later sold on the black market.

The artisans in their cooperatives worked mainly on repairs. There were almost no new works due to the shortage of raw materials. Some craftsmen had plenty of work – such as carpenters. There was sufficient wood in the warehouses, and they worked for the government to make furniture for schools and offices. We had forests in our area, but it was almost impossible to find wood for heating. The farmers did not want to work in the forest, and when they agreed, it was under pressure and threats. However, there was nothing to transport the wood from the forest to the city. Everything was run by the government, and in the summer, special offices were established to handle the wood supply, but it would usually not arrive on time. There was no cash in circulation. All payments were made through checks from the state bank. The governmentowned the pharmacies, and medicines were provided for free. However, it was almost impossible to get them due to shortages. We had to order the necessary medical instruments for the polyclinic and hospitals, but we never managed to buy the necessary equipment before the end of the year (because it was not available at the warehouse). Since we had to spend the money allocated in the budget for instruments before the end of the year,

[Page 102]

we bought what was available rather than what was needed.

Men between the ages of 18 and 50 were recruited. A substantial portion of our youth enlisted in the army (regular army) before the War and others during the first few days of the War. Some fell in battle, and some became prisoners of war. Only a relatively small portion survived.

In the winter of 1939, War broke out between Russia and Finland. That War lasted several months. Except for the gatherings, where the workers "demanded" that the government (on command from above) win over Finland, that War did not affect us. Nevertheless, we felt that something was wrong. We felt the tension and lack of trust between the Soviets and Germans. In the winter, a population exchange occurred between the Germans who resided in Soviet regions and the Soviets who lived in German areas. The Soviets got the people out of their homes during the most severe cold spell and transferred them beyond the border.

Formal holidays were celebrated twice a year – on the 1st of May and the 7th of November 7th – Revolution Day. The latter lasted three days: holiday's eve, the holiday itself, and the next day. During those days, candies and drinks were sold not far from the center of the celebration.

Under that atmosphere and regime, we spent a winter, summer, and additional winter. We got used to that life as though we were born with them – a life of fear and anxiety. The fear and danger increased with the type of job. The more important the position was, the more dangerous it was, and when something happened to you, you had neither a friend nor an ally. The opposite was true. Everybody distanced themselves from you to show the authorities that they did not have any association with you. One of the NKVD officials advised me, once after I had treated him - "If you don't want any trouble, don't tell anybody, including your wife. You must remain silent." Nevertheless, nobody knew if anybody wanted to take revenge and snitch on him.

On the 1st of May, a military parade took place as part of the holiday celebration. News that was heard on the radio was passed by word of mouth. It was reported that four German divisions entered Finland. We knew then that a War with Germany was unavoidable, that it was approaching, and we did not have the means to defend against it or to escape. We could not even store food for a time of need. We knew that we would be annihilated if the War was to break out. We did not believe that Russia could withstand a war.

And the War broke out! It erupted more forcefully, speedily, and cruelly than we anticipated. At that time, too, the War broke out suddenly. On the night of 22nd of June 1941, at 2:30 in the morning, German planes began bombing cities and airports and caused enormous destruction. It was the night between Saturday and Sunday. We heard what happened on the radio early in the morning. The initial news was disappointing. Despair and panic broke out as forcefully or greater than the first time.

Our city suffered mentally as well as losses of life and property. Part of our youth enlisted in the Soviet Army before the Germans conquered the city. Part of the Jewish population who were publicly active during the Soviet regime escaped on foot, trains, or wagons eastward to Russia. The majority stayed behind. The Germans advanced on all fronts. The retreat of the Soviets was more organized, with no yelling. The Soviets had a place to escape to.

Two airplanes approached on the 28th of June around 4:30 and 5:00 pm, lowered down, and encircled the city twice. We didn't think that they came to bomb the city. Before we had the chance to realize it, the planes dropped some regular and incendiary bombs.

[Page 103]

The first bombing demolished the Polish Workers' House. The rest of the bombs hit the Jewish quarter, the houses were decimated on Zbozuva Street, and there were many victims. Fires broke out in several other locations in the city. That was the first bombing attack, and it caused panic. People became confused and ran in the streets in different directions without order or plan. Only a few – mostly families of the victims, began to clear the ruins and search for survivors.

My parents' home was among the demolished houses. We succeeded in pulling out eight survivors in a few minutes. The hour was close to eight o'clock in the evening. The Soviet Army demanded that we leave the place and enter our homes by imposing a curfew from 8 p.m. to 5 a.m. We returned to the rescue work only at 5 a.m. After a substantial effort, we pulled out the bodies of my family members with other bodies. We covered them with sheets and brought them to the cemetery.

We dug the graves with our own hands and brought them to a Jewish burial. German planes circled above the entire time and dropped bombs on the Jewish quarter. There was a short break toward the evening, but the airplanes returned and continued to bomb more forcibly and vigorously, particularly the Jewish quarter, two hours later. People ran out to the fields surrounding the city. They suffered some hits, although nobody was killed there. There was total destruction in the city.

The Soviets left on the 30th of June, and a day later, on Tuesday, the 1st of July, the Germans entered our city. At first - motorcycles, then tanks. Our city was conquered without any resistance except for a short battle that commenced near the dam, where several Germans were killed.

[Pages 104-105]

Culture and Way of Life

[Page 106]

The Drama Club - "Yidishe Kunst" [Yiddish Art]

By Dr. Eliezer Shaklai

Translated by Moshe Kutten

Edited by Jane S. Gabin

We should consider the "Purim Spieler" [The Purim Players] as the beginning of the theater in our town. That play was shown once a year, during the holiday of Purim, for the amusement of the house owners. Real theater plays began only at the end of the 19th century with the expansion of the Enlightenment. At that time, troupes from larger cities came and played in front of a crowd. The first theater hall was at the home of Dr. Ravitz, where the plays were in Yiddish. A few years later, our townpeople founded a local troupe, and according to what was told, it was quite a successful one. The teachers of the Hebrew School also tried to bring plays in Hebrew to the stage. Since they could not find such plays, they translated plays from other languages into Hebrew. The school's students and adults from the youth movement participated in those plays. All the shows were directed by local people. Among others, Bialer, the brother-in-law of Shlomo Redlikh, was active in those shows.

Permanent troupes, which traveled from city to city, visited us from time to time. At that time, there were already two theater halls. One was the spacious and luxurious Polish theater, which contained a movie theater – "Sokol." The other was a smaller and more primitive - the Ruthenian theater – "Boyan." Shows of the playwrights [Avraham] Golfaden: "Di kishefmakhern" [The Witch], "Di tsvey Kuni-lemels" [The Fanatic or The two Kuni-Lemels], "Shulamith" [Shulamith or The Daughter of Jerusalem], and Bar Kokhba, and [Ya'akov] Gordin: "Got, Mentsh un Tayvl" [God, Man, and Devil], "Mirele Efrat" were staged. I still remember some of the songs that the players sang on stage. I remember one song that is famous even today - "Rozhinkes mit Mandlen" [Raisins and Almonds]. The song won many hearts and became a [Yiddish and Hebrew] folk song. I also remember Hebrew songs about Jerusalem, "Al Em Haderkh" [On the main road], and many more. Another Yiddish song that was etched in my memory was the swearing of the movement "Poalei Tzion" [Workers of Zion] - "Bir heiben di hendeh Gegen mizrakh, in shveren… bei…Tzion" [We raise our hands towards the east in oath...to Zion...].

We progressed in that direction during the period between the two World Wars.

The young son of Gutenplan's graduated from his instrument-playing studies in the conservatory and elevated his father's orchestra to a respectable level. As an honor and recognition, the father remained the orchestra's conductor. No competitors existed in those years. The orchestra, which also had piano teachers, acquired many students from among the youths in the city.

We also had a full-time cantor with a pleasant voice who was knowledgeable in his craft. He organized a chorus for the holidays and helped us to assemble one when needed.

There is only a little we can talk about the teaching or cultivation of music until the First World War. There were two famous families – Kurtz and Gutenplan – who appeared on festive occasions and also gave lessons on playing violin, clarinet, and other instruments. Most of the students came from high school.

Our youth shows were integrated with the drama club "Yideshe Kunst."

Our youth also learned to dance in private lessons. During the years before the [WW I] War, they did that in secret due to resistance by the parents. They used their knowledge on festive occasions (e.g. weddings) and organized dance evenings for their entertainment (a meeting place of boys and girls, hidden from the parents who objected to such encounters).

[Page 107]

The Musical-Dramatic Union
Yidishe Kunst [Jewish Art] in Brzezany

by Moshe Bar-David (Dawid)

Translated by Gloria Berkenstat Freund

The founding of the Musical-Dramatic Union, *Yidishe Kunst*, in Brzezany, was just a continuation of the cultural activity that had begun before the First World War but with new strengths. The composition of the cultural institutions was mixed, beginning with the former *Tseire- Zion* [Youth of Zion – socialist-Zionists] and *Poalei-Zion*[Workers of Zion – Marxist-Zionists], students, merchants, members of the middle class and young men, young girls – who were searching for an appropriate communal frame, in which to derive friendly pleasure. The Union did not have any political character; the members were from the various political leanings in the Jewish neighborhood, beginning with the General-Zionist, *Hitakhdut* [Association - Labor-Zionists], *Poalei-Zion,* Revisionists, *Mizrakhi* [religious Zionists], *HaShomer HaTsair* [Young Guard – Labor-Zionists] and the very left. Searching for various qualities and opinions created an atmosphere of community spirit and cultural worth for everyone interested, and they derived pleasure from it.

The first activity began in 1918. A group of young people came together in a private apartment of the Oks family, which lived in Shlomo Rajchsztajn's house on Lemberger Street. The Okses were a pious, religious family, and their daughter, an intelligent girl, donated a room and time for gatherings and rehearsals of the acting group. The composition of the group was also fortuitous. Remember who belonged to this group. First of all, some took part in the only youth organization, *HaShomer* [Watchmen], and a number of future *khalutzim* [pioneers who emigrated to *Eretz Yisroel*]: the brothers Moshe, Mikhael and Ya'akov Bergman, Moshe Frid, Hersh Landau, Zunya Frasz, Leib Glazer, the Flam sisters, Shtark, Ast and others.

A proclamation for the 15th anniversary of "*Yidishe Kunst*"

[Page 108]

It appears that during the time of war, a large number of the intelligentsia and so-called theater talents who could present a play were spread across the former Austrian monarchy, but there still were several talented young men to act as well as direct a theatrical piece. And if a performance did not stand at a high level, the amateur actors, as well as the theater audience, reacted with enthusiasm and were satisfied because, during the war years, we were starved for entertainment and cultural joy. We performed at the Ukrainian Bayan Room. A certain Aizenberg directed. Actors were Moshe Bergman, Polishuk (a student from Podhajce [Pidhaitsi]), Mordekhai Has, Meir Taler, Khanche Shapira, the Tirkesher[s], Shlomo Zoyberberg, Leible Mitelman, Khaim Gutshtein, Hersh Landau.

During the year, we produced two plays. One of them was *Basha di Yesoyma* [*Basha the Orphan*] by Jacob Gordin. It was at the time of Ukrainian rule. The conditions were not so good, bad theater wings, a lack of illumination, a heavy-to-move curtain, and other technically unsuitable props. However, we acted, and everyone felt enjoyment until after midnight.

The activities of the group ceased for a time when the Poles drove out the Ukrainian occupiers because we did not know who would remain the ruler of that part of eastern Galicia. Everyone took care of themselves and their family until the situation stabilized, and yet, their interest in culture did not end.

The management team of the drama club "*Yidishe Kunst*" in 1920

Sitting from right to left: Taler Meir, librarian, Redlikh Shlomo – cultural coordinator, Dr. Pomerantz Philip – chairman, Mitelman Leib – vice chairman, Has – a member of the Audit Committee
Standing from right to left: Lawyer Yosef Laber, a member of the Audit Committee, Magister Rutenberg Tontzio – secretary, Froindlikh Ben-Tzion – technical manager, David (Bar-David) Moshe – director, Shapira Ya'akov – treasurer, Froindlikh Ya'akov – administrator, religion teacher Taler – conductor, Vidhof Yoel – a member of the Audit Committee

[Page 109]

Conversely, the youth organization, *HaShomer*, became more active than previously.

They organized the *Khalutz* [pioneers preparing for emigration to Eretz Israel], and they took on intensive work. Young people were not bored even in the most difficult times. The thirst for spiritual and cultural values was always deep and strong among the young Jews.

In 1920-1922, the group grew and searched for a way to give the Jewish population in Brzazany a regularly organized cultural project that would be the center of Jewish camaraderie. We met in the apartment of Bernhard Leider, the dentist; [we] elected a club managing committee with a cultural lecturer, administrator, president, and secretary. We requested from the village elder and received legal permission for a musical-dramatic union, *Yidishe Kunst*.

In the beginning, the home of the Leider family was the living, pulsating center of the Union. Bernhard Leider was the make-up man for the actors, which was an important factor for them because they did not know the Torah of make-up. He did it with a great deal of ability, love, and great, healthy humor. Their daughter, Miskha, acted and also sang. [Leider's] wife offered the audience good things to eat, and they "acted."

For a certain time, the get-togethers and rehearsals were held at the Leider's home until a suitable premise was rented, provided with furniture, and a library was also transferred there, which once belonged to the *Tseire-Zion* Union before the [First] World War. The library consisted of Yiddish, Hebrew, German, and fewer Polish books. [There was] a good secular collection of books with Jewish-Zionist content as well as general, universal literature.

I want to pause here on the [subject of the] library because the library was an important component of the Union at that time. It supported the Union both communally and materially. Every subscriber who paid a security deposit and monthly dues for the borrowing of books made it possible to buy new books, supported the premises, and covered the remaining expenses. In time, the library strongly developed, taking in other subscribers. Non-Jews from Polish groups who were connected to the Polish Sokol Library came because our library could provide the best, the newest, and the most international books. In 1931, the library had over 3,000 books and also subscribed to six daily newspapers and periodicals in Yiddish, Polish, and Hebrew. It arranged literary lectures and presentations on art and literature.

A corner in the library of the drama club

[Page 110]

At first, the library was led by Meir Taler and Moshe David (Bar-David); later, they were joined by Yitzhak Nadler, Godel Biterman, and Yoelik Vidhof. Tantsa Rotenberg and Mendel Tonis contributed a great deal to the development of the library.

The library became a symbol of Jewish culture and sociability.

It is hard to remember chronologically when each play was performed, but I will try to keep a certain order.

In the years 1920-1921, we performed *Batlen* [Idler] or *Hochzeit far Shpas* [Wedding for a Joke] under the direction of Mates Thaler; participants: Mates Thaler, Miss Tirkisher, Zelig Sigel, Malka Moshel, Sana Vinter and so on.

Later, *Hertsele Meyukhes* [Hertsele the Aristocrat] took place, directed by Aizenberg, with Anshel Sigel, Zelig Sigel, Salka Reikh, Moshel, Sana Vinter, and so on.

[Also] in 1920-1921, *Der Yeshive-Bokher* [The Yeshiva Boy] of Yitzkhak Zlotorewski [was produced], directed by Aizenberg. Rejuvenation from the young, special scenery put together with the technical leadership of Moshe David (Bar David) and Khaim Gutshtein was part of the performance. The main roles were acted by Shlomo Pomerantz (he, later, was called Sala Pomer and also was called a Polish man-of-letters), Mendele Hekht, Benyamin Mitelman, Moshel, Anshel and Zelig Sigel, Gutsa Taksel, Rozka Flam and so on. Shlomo Pomerantz made an effort to be in his role á la the Polish artist, Aszwentowicz; he succeeded to a great extent.

A search for a better repertoire and a better director started in the era of 1922-1923, and we began to present the plays of Jacob Gordin. At that time, a very capable director named Veisberg arrived. He came from Staninsławów [Ivano-Frankivsk].

Veisberg already had many years of experience as a director of an amateur dramatic troupe, and he made constructive use of the experience with us, which helped a great deal to raise the level of the dramatic group.

In the years 1924-1926, many of Jacob Gordin's plays were produced under Veisberg's direction and with success. Among others, the so-called *Dankbare Dramen* [Grateful Dramas] allowed many actors to show their talent.

In [Jacob Gordin's] *Got, Mentsh un Tayvl* [God, Man, and Devil], Mendele Hekht, and Benyamin Mitelman, in the main roles, put together their creation with great success. Zelig Sigel, Miss Karten, and others also took part. Appearing in the prologue was Shlomo Veinshtein's brother, who had come on a visit from America and very much wanted to act in the prologue and did so very well. And when he left to return to America, he donated a considerable sum to the library.

[Page 111]

Der Vilder Mentsh [*The Wild Man*] by Jacob Gordin was produced with Mendele Hekht in the main role, and he acted so well that the scenes almost enraged the audience.

Mishka Leider took part in several performances, mostly in a main role, when there was something to sing as well as in dramatic roles.

Along with her husband, Rotman, she acted in [Leon] Kobrin's *Dorfsyung* [Village Youth], as well as with Gitel Zilber (Bar-David); with their naturalistic acting, they brought a new note to the dramatic acting. Veisberg directed. We performed two comedies by Moliere, *The Miser*, and *The Imaginary Invalid*, with B. Mitelman and Gusta Taksel.

Further on, with *Der Shtumer* [The Mute], under the leadership of Veisberg, we entered a more modern, literary, atmospheric, and unfamiliar mood, getting accustomed to living more psychologically in the roles and in the interpretations of a play. Meir Thaler and Shlomo Pomerantz gave the performance their stamp.

A new era, as well as a new mood, began with Peretz Hirshbein under the direction of Shlomo Redlikh. Peretz Hirshbein gave a different dramatic substance to the acting, and Shlomo Redlikh gave a new rendering from the director, as well as a different communal attitude and atmosphere in the club itself.

P. Hirshbein's *Di Grine Felder* [The Green Fields], with Sana Vinter in the main role, brought a fresh breeze of Jewish village life to the stage. Redlikh gave the actor the chance to be independent in the conception of the character of the person and situation in which he found himself, and the dramaturg had given him the play, less caricature, less pathos, freer in stage appearance as well as interesting staging. It was an entirely different conception, without any influence from other directors and previously seen performances – with its own face.

In 1928, Redlikh directed J[acob] Gordin's *Der Unbekanter* [*The Stranger*]. He infused the prologue with new strengths. The corrupt angel was played by Moshe David (Bar David) and the angel of love by Gitel Zilber with a new manner of acting. In the additional plot, Mordekhai was played by the "Turkish" Meir Thaler, Zelig Sigel, and so on.

Redlikh brought Mark Arenshtein's *Vilner Balebesl* [*Young Gentlemen of Vilna*] on the stage, with new ornamentation and with great success. Dovidl was played by Moshe David and Gitel Zilber, *Di Svester* [*The Sister*]. Those acting with them were Meir Shaler, Yosef Leber, Zelig Sigel, Salke Reikh, Sana Vinter, and many young members of the club. The rehearsals also were interesting and entertaining. With every rehearsal, those taking part enlivened their roles and also penetrated the essence of the drama and plot so that the atmosphere of a real theater studio and acting ensemble was created. There was also no lack of curious and humorous situations that gave charm and joy to this work.

Scenes from plays of the "Yiddishe Kunst"

[Page 112]

It was simply a spiritual, internal experience. They rehearsed with enthusiasm and had pleasure from it until performing.

During the same year, we performed Shenher's *Tayvls Vayb* [*Devil's Wife*] with Benyamin Mitelman, Zelig Sigel, and Etala Korten. It was a chamber play with three people and with good ensemble acting.

Searching for a new repertoire, Weisberg suggested [Abraham] Goldfaden's *Kishefmakhern* [*The Sorceress*]. Young, fresh singers were brought into the group. Nushka Holander, with her fine voice, played the orphan. With talent and with natural humor, Zelig Sigel enlivened his performance as Hotsmakh. Moshe Foygel was the true Bobe-Yakhna of Goldfaden. Etala Korten, as well as other new young performers, contributed to the success of the performance. A small, young Efraim Shmid showed himself to be a good singer. Sana Vinter, Y. Taub, Mikhael Bilig, and others contributed a great deal of freshness and charm to the performance.

Under Shlomo Redlikh's direction, we performed Peretz Hirshbein's *Di Nevole* [*The Infamy*], a realistic piece about another environment (milieu) that was not so well-known in our area.

Three people supported the entire performance; in addition to the people named. Moshe Foygel performed Abresh with a great deal of talent and feeling. Gitel Zilber, in the role of Rayzle, as well as Moshe Dawid, in the leading role of Mendl, brought a new tone and style of acting to the performance and also to the coming performances. It is hard to be objective

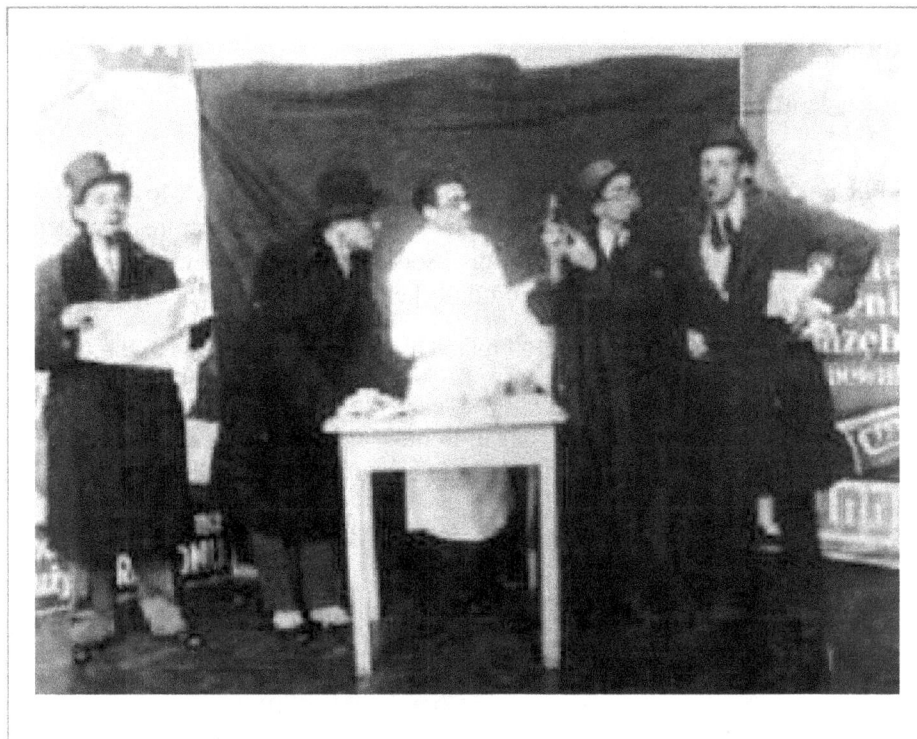

A comedy act with the following participants:

From left to right: David (Bar David) Moshe, Segal Moshe, Noiman, Tzeig Motek, Segal Antzel

[Page 113]

in evaluating their acting, so I will, indeed, be quiet. However, according to the evaluation and reaction of the theater audience after the performance, the performance was equated with a good, artistic, professional theater.

At the time, some voices said we should perform operettas. Lapater was the main initiator. He was stubborn and accomplished it. The performance involved a great deal of difficulty as well as large expenses because such an operetta as Goldfagen's *Shulamit* required appropriate costumes and an orchestra to accompany the piece, besides the need to cast the roles.

However, enough talented singers who did not disappoint and succeeded were found.

The main role, Shulamit, was played by Nushka Holander; performing with Holander were Arye Polak, Lipa Wagshal, and Bashka Citron. The rehearsal of the singers was given to the professional musician Nota Butenflan and his band. The rehearsals lasted a long time until the operetta was performed. Finally, everyone was enthusiastic about *Shulamit*. Later, we performed *Bar-Kokhba* with similar success, and there was nothing to be ashamed.

The main success was with the presentation of *Di Dray Matones* [*The Three Presents*] by Y.L. Peretz, dramatized by Hart, music by Khonf Walfstahl (1853-1924), special stage sets painted by Yehuda Feld, a member of our Union. The operetta, as I want to call it, was a musical mastery because it had an operatic character. It took a long time until we performed the play on the stage, and there were many difficulties. After long rehearsals, we brought it to the stage and with great success. In short, 40 people took part.

Dovidele Mihlshtok played "The Little Soul" and among others taking part were M. Bilig, M. Rozen, L. Wagshal, and Nushka Holander.

As the performance was a great success, we traveled to other cities and performed in Tarnopol as well as in Rohatyn.

The so-called light review and entertainment evenings were carried out by Moshe Sigl with a great deal of charm. For Chanukah and Purim, he produced review evenings with a repertoire of modern one-act plays, sketches, and timely [pieces], as well as folksongs. Sometimes, a local, critical song evoked a little resentment with the *kehile* [organized Jewish community] elite, but the audience had pleasure from it.

I want to remember that in 1925, Landesberg created a mandolin orchestra (in the club) that developed well and occasionally gave concerts.

At the beginning of 1929, Shlomo Redlikh began to thoroughly learn *Dem Dukus* [*The Duke*] by Alter Katsizne; it took a long time because a large number of people took part, and we needed a special place in which to hold rehearsals. We did so in a private

Scenes from plays of the "Yiddishe Kunst"

[Page 114]

apartment at Gitel Zilber's garret. The rehearsals provided an interesting, friendly, intimate atmosphere. The roles were divided into small groups according to the characters of the people, and they actually showed what they could do with a great deal of talent. Yoshe Leber played the "old duke" [and] Moshe Dawid the "pious convert." The "servant" [was] Meir Thaler, the "lessee," Sana Vinter, and Gitl Zilber, "his daughter." The other roles were also well cast.

Moshe Dawid, Ben-Tzion Freindlikh, and the two Haftel sisters prepared special costumes and the success was so great that it was talked about for a long time. We prepared to travel to the provinces with the play, but a fire destroyed the costumes and nothing became of [the plans].

The performance was the swan song of Shlomo Redlikh's directorship in our club. We have to thank him for being thedirector, as a cultural pedagogue, and as a good person who with his personality, brought a great deal of humanity and a warm, friendly atmosphere to our group.

Members of the Drama Club "Yiddish Kunst" During the farewell party
honoring Bar-David Moshe on his Aliyah, Brzezany, 3/3/1934

The lower row from right to left: Dudileh Mihlshtok, Tzeig Motek, Sara Taub, Philip Biterman,
S. Kasten, Mordekhai Rozentzveig, Vitriol, Vidhof Yoel, Sheintzia Brik, Taub, Moshe Pekhter,
......, Simkha Shekhter
Second row: Bernard Leider, Tontzio Rutenberg, Mendel Tonis, Meir Taler, Yitzkhak Nadler,
Binyamin Mitelman, Tirkelfeld Fuks, Moshe David (Bar-David), Bat Rivkah, Tova David, Leib
Mitelman, Zelig Segal, Betzalel Salomon, Yosef Laber, Moshe Segal
Third row: Vortzel, Moshe Podoshin, Polber, H. Frid, Fridel Oks, Reitman, Ostrover-Fishman
Hersh, Haftel Sonika, ..., Don Altshiler, Haber-Lufter, First, B. Feld, Morekhai Khayut, ...
Fourth row: Tzeig, Gviretz, Avraham Katz, Kravitz, Salomon, Dov Holander, ..., Feibush
Biterman, Shtern,..., Godel Biterman, Yosef Erlikh
Upper row: David Zeifert, Simkha Shvartz, Noiman, Breitel, Bilig, Yosef Shvartz-Cohen, ...
Tinter

[Page 115]

The honorary certificate given to Moshe Bar-David in appreciation of his fruitful activity with the drama club. The certificate was illustrated by Yehuda Feld.

[Page 116]

I took over the direction after Redlikh. My approach to the dramatic material was different from what it was before. First of all, young, fresh acting strength, [and I had] a conception of learning a piece thoroughly, which took on a special expression with a modern character, based on a prepared book of direction, previously thought through, [a set] playing time and the erection of a stage. [I required] easily transformed sets so that the production always ended early, not as before when the audience went home late, after midnight.

My first production was assisting in the work that Mates Thaler had begun and could not complete. The play was called *Toytshtrof* [Death Penalty]. The second independent performance was a Ukrainian play translated by Moshe Sigel, which he carried around for a long time and no one had dared to produce. The author was a woman, and the play carried the title *Di Legende fun der Alter Mil* [The Legend of the Old Mill]. Modernly prepared stage sets, so-called Reinhard sets, made it possible for the theater audience to go home early, at 10:30. It was a modern performance that was compared to the *VYKT* [*Varshever Yidisher Kunst Theater* – Warsaw Jewish Art Theater] performances that were seen in our province from time to time, with Janos and Zygmunt Turkow and Ida Kaminska. There was no lack of compliments. Then, I presented Yakov Prager's dramatic-poetic piece, *Der Nisoyen* [The Temptation]. The language was poetic, in verse, and many lines rhymed. It was not easy for the young actors to carry out and to keep the rhythm of the verses.

Soon, the hundreds of rehearsals gave perfection to the performances and ensemble, and it was a real a success. The rehearsals were themselves an experience. Everyone took part in them with enthusiasm and great interest [which led] to the success of the drama. It was a little difficult to build the mass scenes because almost all of those taking part were young, inexperienced

The orchestra in a comedy ball

The Drama Club's orchestra in the housewarming assembly for the Hebrew University in Jerusalem, 1st of April, 1925

[Page 117]

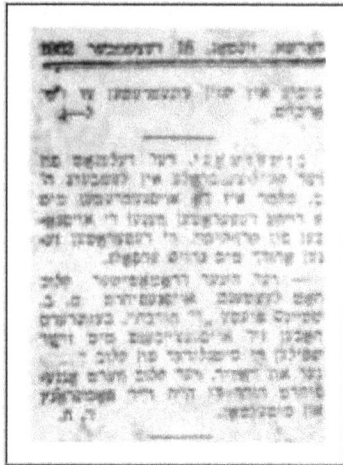

The play "Three Presents" by the members of the Drama Club "Yiddishe Kunst"

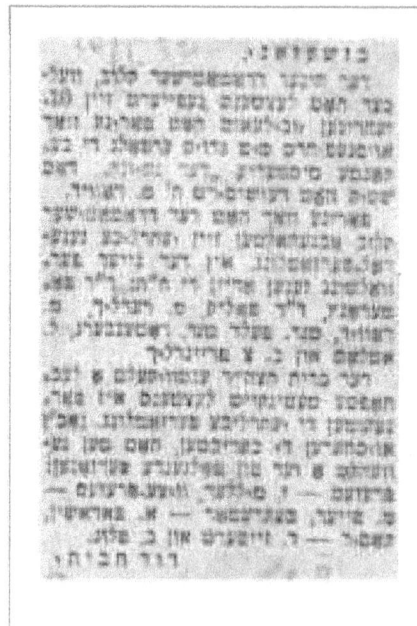

An address to the Drama Club's members to issue a 20th-anniversary pamphlet

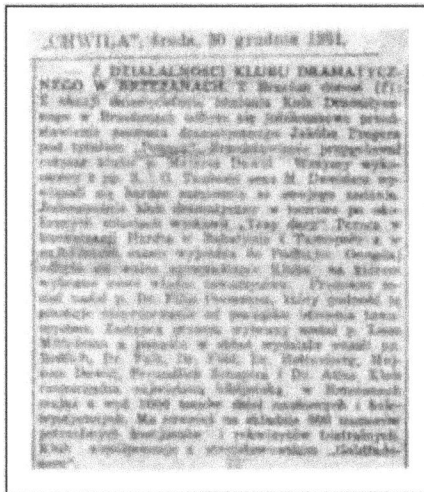

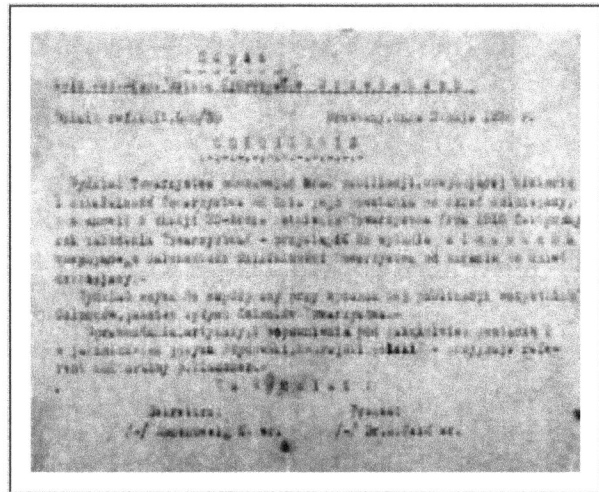

Excerpts from the Polish Yiddish newspapers about the Drama Club "Yiddishe Kunst"

[Page 118]

actors, and had never stood on the [floor]boards of the theater. However, after half a year of rehearsals, the drama was performed. Costumes were borrowed from the Stanislawów Dramatic "Goldfaden Union." The Scenery Was Painted by Yehuda Feld, and the technical direction was carried out by Ben-Tzion Freindlich. The main roles were played by Shimon Meiblum – the landowner, previously "Leibik the tailor." Dovidl, his son – Moshe Dawid andSurala Taub created the Daughter of the Landowner with a great deal of charm and feeling. Berka Holender, Merkur, and many young members of the Union contributed to the success of the performance.

In 1932, I led *Di Khurba* [The Destruction] by M.B. Stein in the newly built Jewish National House. The Scenery Was Painted by Yehuda Feld, and the technical direction was done by Ben-Tzion Freindlikh.

Twice, we presented the performance at the request of the audience that had not seen it but had heard about it. The income went to the Jewish orphans' home. They also sold the entry tickets. This time, those visiting the theater were those who rarely attended our performances, mostly Polish-speaking Jews from the professions, the intelligentsia, who bought theater tickets to support the orphanage. And

The management of the "Drama Club" in 1938

Sitting from right to left: Podoshin Moshe, Taler Meir, Dr. Feld, Dr. Wagshall (Shaklai), Vidhof Yoel
Standing from right to left: Biterman Godel, Feiering, Shekhter Simkah, Lebel, Rozentzveig Motek

[Page 119]

here they had an unexpected surprise. They did not know that the Dramatic Union could present such well-acted dramas. They compared the acting to the *Vilner Trupe* [Vilna Troupe], which adhered to Brener's conception of the presentation: light, color, and voice. In 1933-1934, I began a thorough study of Aaron Zeitlin's *Yosef Chaim Brener*. The conception was of light, color, and voice, with pure young actors. I wanted to create a production that we had not yet seen in our small city. I wanted to challenge myself with a daring that could be a success or a fiasco. My sudden departure for *Eretz Israel* ended the rehearsals and also my theatrical activity in the Union *Yidishe Kunst* [Jewish Art] in Brzezany. I believe that besides one try-out performance by Moshe Sigel and the later *Dray Matones*, the dramatic activity of the club ended.

The library was active until the Second World War and then disappeared with all of the Jews who lived and participated in the small cultural group whose trace remains sacred for all of those who remember them with love and sadness.

[Page 120]

A Purim Meal

by Moshe Bar David (David, Dawid)

Translated by Gloria Berkenstat Freund

A residential wing was built as a neighbor of the Rebbe, Rabbi Yudl's House of Prayer, next to the corridor passageway of the House of Prayer, where several neighbors lived. One not-too-large room served as a small synagogue for prayer as well as studying. The synagogue was called the *Potiker kloyzl* [small synagogue] after the name of a former rabbi Potiker, who years before had been the rabbi in our city. Two *minyanim* [prayer groups] of Jews prayed in the *kloyzl*. The worshippers supported the *kloyzl,* and the main contributor was a member of the middle class named Moshe Wanderer. He was the son-in-law of Markl's daughter Ryvtsa (Ryvka Dawid). He had married her daughter Frimtsa. Moshe Wanderer was a haberdasher and seller of fashion articles, a well-to-do Jew with a generous hand, a philanthropist, openly and covertly, a pious Jew who was capable of learning and with a modern approach to business. He earned well and presided over a beautiful home.

He was the only Jew in the city who, interpreting texts, tithed from his earnings for *tzedakah* [charity] and actually contributed. As he was rich from his profits, he tithed a great deal. He paid the tithe to the needy in the city as well as to the strangers who would visit the city. [He donated to] the Jewish hospital, to the security house, *Talmud Torah* [school for poor boys], the group providing aid to poor brides, to rabbis and to all the Jewish institutions as well as secret donations, and there was no lack of Jews in the city whose income was too small.

He would keep the tithed money separate, not mixed with other money, and when the months of Adar [March] and Nisan [March-April] arrived, he would take the rest of the money that was set aside as charity and distribute it at Purim at the meal and at Passover.

The Purim meal at [the house of] Moshe Wanderer was a renowned thing. Every Jew in the city knew that he could take part in the meal [there was] an open door. *Purim shpilers* [Purim actors] and Purim actor groups, who in the majority were needy young men, prepared their play thoroughly for months and visited the meal because they knew that from Moshe Wanderer, they would receive a good gift. Jews who also collected for themselves or for others would linger at the meal for a long time. The Wanderers' house stood in the middle of the Ringplatz. [It was] an old house that had been built a hundred years ago, a beautiful residence, with large, spacious rooms. [It was] the only house in which the ceilings were painted with artistic landscapes. On Purim evening, they opened the doors of the large dining room through the bedrooms and salon and thus created a long room illuminated by gas lamps, chandeliers, and colorful flasks

[Page 121]

to welcome a great number of guests to the white-covered tables with foods, whiskeys, fruits, candies, and various picante foods and invite them to enjoy the atmosphere and warmth.

On the side, around the walls, stood several kegs of Okocim beer, large bowls and pots of cooked beechnuts, kidney beans, chickpeas, nuts, and nontlen [honey and poppy seed or walnut confection] and *Hamantaschen* [triangular-shaped Purim pastries]. Every Jew who came to ask for a donation received at least one korona, which at that time was a very respectable coin. Less than a korona did not lay on the table and, if [a visitor] wanted to linger a little longer at the meal, he received something warm to eat and whiskey, a white roll, a *zrazy* (large meatball) with stuffed *kishka* [intestines], whiskey, beer and candy from the prepared table. The money lay on the table, only in silver, from one korona to five korona, and under the tablecloth lay the banknotes. Everyone carried out their Purim meal at home until around 10 o'clock. Then, all the relatives and their families would go to Uncle Moshe Wanderer and spend the time until midnight. My father, Mendele Dawid, and his family, my Uncle Berish Gros (Nauman) and his family, and the last and most beloved, my Uncle Shlomo Shapira and his large household (a dozen children) would go. In addition to all of those who were close and also distant relatives, there were also our Jewish neighbors [such as] Ahron Landau [and] good friends, who prayed in the convenient *kloyz*. Thus, the rooms were fully packed, and the tables were occupied. The orchestra of Nota Gutenplan (his wife was our cousin) entertained and their playing added charm and joy to the meal. *Purim-shpilers* in various bizarre masks began to arrive, entire groups each with its own program.

Pesakhia Grinberg with the *Yidisher Khasene* [Jewish wedding] was one of the most interesting spectacles, mainly Pesakhia as the *batkhn* [wedding jester] with various comic songs and rhymes and witticisms, puns that, years later, I found published in a small book by an American humorist named R[uvin] Granovski. Next was the *Goyishe Khasene* [Gentile wedding], which was organized by the Jewish porters. The *Yosef-shpil* [the Joseph Play – *Mekhires Yosef* – The Selling of Joseph] was performed by the journeymen who had thoroughly studied it for months. *Der Priziv* [The Military Draft] was a social-political satire. The main attraction was *Di Royberbandl* [The Robber Band] (taken from [Friedrich] Schiller's The Robbers – a mix of the folksy, terror-novel, *Rinaldo Rinaldino* – the Robber Captain – a mixture of Yiddish, Polish and *Deitchmerish* [words taken from modern German]), as well as the traditional Ahasuerus with Mordechai and Esther and Haman, with songs that were tragic-comic. All tried to act in the best possible way (exclusively men without women). In addition, came individual presenters with familiar

[Page 122]

and unfamiliar folksongs that evoked admiration and curiosity from the audience.

It was curious that over the course of an hour one of the *Purim shpilers*, almost undisguised, sang unfamiliar songs from another area that were unfamiliar in Galicia. It turned out that an unknown guest actor had come from the other side of the border – from Russia; therefore, no one knew him and his songs were different. After singing, he took the large amount of money that the middle-class men and the other guests had given him and left silently without saying a word. "Who are you? Where are you going?" No answers! Therefore, this was talked about in the city for a long time because he had not visited any other meals in the city.

Just before midnight came the masked students and academics who brought their costumes from Lvov (Lemberg) because at the end of Sabbath after Purim, they had organized a Purim masked ball. Other groups and unions, such as the Artisans' Union, *Yad Kharutzim* [Industrious Hands], would arrange masked balls during the week of Purim. The costumes would be the attraction and even the *Ne'ila* [final prayer recited on Yom Kippur] of the Purim meal. Mostly, the masks were worn completely covering the head so that the wearers would not be recognized. The masks were of animals, fantastic, exotic types; they spoke with animal-like voices, with cheerful, mischievous witticisms because Purim is Purim and one is permitted to do what one avoids for the entire year. Beginning with the "Purim Rabbi" to the reading of the *megile* [scroll of the Book of Esther] in *goyish* [not Jewish – a reference to language that is not Yiddish], that is a parody translated into Ukrainian (Ruthenian), which two nice, cheerful Jews, Yisroel Cajg and numerous helpers would read with a great deal of charm. A kaleidoscope of various bizarre, interesting figures passed through Moshe Wanderer's Purim meal in Brzezany. It was always a pleasant occurrence, also while remembering it. After the First World War, my Uncle Moshe again held Purim meals but not like before. At the time of the war, the material position of the Jews greatly changed and took a turn that shattered the Jewish way of life. However, Moshe Wanderer again gave charity in secret. His open hand and his Jewish heart were always ready to help.

In the 1930s, he made a trip to *Eretz Yisroel* and also planned to settle there permanently, but the Second World War disturbed all of his plans. He and his wife perished in the Shoah in 1943. Of blessed memory!

[Page 123]

Newspaper ad for a Purim ball organized by the
[craftsmen organization] "Yad Kharutzim" [Diligent
Hand]

Brzezany Strange Characters (Eccentrics)

by Moshe Bar-David (David, Dawid)

Translated by Gloria Berkenstat Freund

Every city has its local well-known types of people who have strange characters and they give the Jewish neighborhood their stamp and even a certain charm. The so-called "crazy ones" and fools. Comical and unfortunate people, each with his stupor, with his abnormality and his [difficult] life. Events and invented anecdotes always characterized these types, and they were woven into the way of life of the Jewish neighborhood. There were several such Jews in our city. Four types, each different from the others. Layzer Pif, Dudye Morgeh, Avrahamtze Khalemke, Hershele *Dzia Hop* [Grandfather Hop].

Layzer Pif

[Page 124]

Layzer Pif [Bang-bang]

A small, stocky body with a black-green beard, small *peyes* [side curls], a wide, shiny, fat nose with small mercurial, running eyes, sly and yet saying nothing. A black cap on his head from under which can be seen a once-black greasy *yarmulke* [skull cap]. He would speak fast and mumble, and it was hard to understand him.

He lived from donations, which he demanded with great insolence. Every week, mostly on Thursdays, he visited every shop and every house, and if they did not want to or could not give the demanded donation, he would play a trick and drop his greasy *yarmulke* into the barrel of water that usually stood at the entrance to the kitchen, or on *erev Pesakh* [the eve of Passover], covered with a white linen cover. In the street, he insolently ran after a passerby and demanded what he was due and did not stop until someone had to give him a few *groshn* [small coin]. He knew everyone's ancestry, knew exactly when a holiday fell on the calendar without having a calendar and he never erred.

Before the First World War, and for a certain time later, he would carry the flour that members of the middle class would buy for *Shabbos* [Sabbath] and he would be paid for this. Rascals and ordinary Jewish jokers would tease and menace him, calling after him with mocking names, Layzer Pif! Pif! And [they would] ask him questions that he would often answer. One question would anger him — if he knew Shaya the Beggar? Because before the First World War, he went through the country with Shaya the Beggar asking for donations. This was not suitable for him, for his honor. He was a local patriot; here, people knew him, and they knew who he was. He would boast of his occupations. Many occupations: once he was a *klezmer* [musician] – he would carry a large drum for the *klezmer* [band] to a non-Jewish wedding; he was a vagabond – wandered around the country, but do not remind him of Shaya; he was a porter – he carried the flour for *Shabbos*. He was a criminal – he was once arrested in an unfamiliar area without papers. He was the most popular character in the city. He never married. Walked fast, almost running, and grumbled under his breath, "Give me a kreutzer [Austrian coin]! Give me a kreutzer".

Dudye Morgeh

With a political trance. A Jew, a baker. It was doubtful that he could bake, but he had worked his whole life with the same baker, Mendl Flug. With a tangled, chestnut brown beard, rickety, twisted feet, always wrapped in superficial bandages, frighteningly short-sighted eyes. Dressed in old, flour-covered clothing and [speaking] a badly understood language. Did not always speak logically. His main theme was "voting." He would be a candidate for the city council; he would become [upgraded] to the *Pravent* (Parliament). *Pravent* was the main warehouse for material from the city hall. His unnatural relationship to voting and parliament arose after the Austrian times when elections to parliament took place. It was a widely held opinion that he had been normal then, and he had been beaten during the voting and became a little confused because of the blows, and "parliament" always troubled him. On *Shabbos*, he would

Dudye Morgeh

[Page 125]

go to pray dressed in clean and neat [clothing]. In general, he acted normal. However, if a "comrade" made a joke about him, they brought out the theme of "voting" and asked him to give a [campaign] speech. His speech was mixed with Yiddish-German and Polish. "A protest" against the city hall arrangements to destroy the bad fruit in the street stalls.

Dudye more or less gave his speech…murmuring unintelligible words and ending with, "As it burned, the beard did not drown." Rascals bothered him, but he had his means of support earned with honest work. On the eve of the outbreak of the First World War, Dudye went on a stroll in the woods. A gendarme met him and asked, "Who are you, and what are you doing?" [Dudye] did not know a great deal of Polish, but he had to answer. He said, "*Ick bin a royber* [I am a robber]." Being arrested and being brought to the city, they met a Jew who knew the gendarme very well. He asked him why he had stopped [Dudye]. [The gendarme] said that he is a *royber*. Dudye had meant that he was a *reyber* [grater] – he grated potatoes for Khaya…at her bakery. Dudye was a little confused but a pious and honest Jew.

Avrahamtse Khalemka

He grew up to be boorish, with a large, moving, meaty nose. His nose was his main characteristic. First, one saw his nose and then his face. A very simple young man with a bad expression, a blunt nasal voice, a little deaf with an ear trumpet. He was once an artisan but did not work very much and did not live from donations. He would travel far from the city and return dressed up after a time. In recent years, he suffered from want and Jews supported him. He would disguise himself on Purim, visit the houses, and receive Purim's money. Relatives in America would send him a few dollars, and thus, he carried on his life. His specialty was an acrobatic turn with his rear, and moving his large, fleshy nose, he made a racket, banging musically, which would evoke laughter from the audience. He had relatives in the city who would make sure he was clean and also had a little warm food. He perished with all of the Jews in the Shoah.

Avrahamtse Chalemka

Hershele *Dzia Hop*

[He was] a son of Moyna, the egg-seller, a middle-class family. [He became] a little half-witted through a childhood illness and from the mischief-makers. [He was] young and had a nice enough face; once studied in a *kheder* [religious primary school]; he knew how to pray and was very pious. He lived with his family and honestly earned his piece of bread. He had to carry water to the house owners; he did not want to bring [water] to everyone. One had to ask him for a long time. His reason was that they teased him with the cry of "Hershele *Dzia, Dzia Hop*." He would jump on the back of the person next to him, like a bull on a cow. In general, he carried on normally. He recited a great number of Psalms and was very pious. He made sure to pray on time. He perished like everyone in the Shoah.

[Page 126]

Z.K.S - The Jewish Athletes Club

by Dr. Eliezer Shaklai

Translated by Moshe Kutten

Edited by Jane S. Gabin

With the outbreak of the First World War, only a few Jews were involved in Sports. These were the students of the high school and a few from among the working youth. Anybody with a strong affinity for sports had no choice but to join the Polish club, "Sokol," where he was not looked upon favorably.

In 1921, a classmate, Vandmeir, turned to me with a proposal to organize a Jewish soccer team based on the example of the Polish team. We contacted several other friends and began to play soccer without shoes, proper uniforms, or a soccer field. At that time, we still did not have an executive committee or gatherings and did not even know the rules of the soccer game. Everything was amateurish, and anything we did know, we learned from the other teams' games.

Thanks to our stubbornness to solidify a Jewish team, we overcame the in-house and outside difficulties, starting with the parents' objections, who consider our games as "gentiles' behavior," and ending with the lack of sports equipment.

Despite all the difficulties, with the help of a large group of students from the high school, we founded a Jewish sports club in 1921 in the name of "Z.K.S. [Zydowski Klub Sportowy – The Jewish Sports Club] Brzezany."

The club was divided into two sections, Soccer and Track and Field.

We became a good team within a short period. In 1929, we participated in a tournament in our district and came in first place. That achievement awarded us recognition from the Polish Sports Association (L.O.Z.P.N), and we became associated with teams in the Polish second league.

The number of sports the fans grew and grew, and by 1930, our team had about 100 members who came from both the learning and working youth circles. In the same year, the Polish army organized a pre-military group within our club, training for the Polish military service (P. W.).

An executive committee was elected at the 1930 general assembly. The people elected to the committee were: chairman - Shimon Meiblum, his deputy – Yosef Laber, secretary – Leib Frid, and treasurer – Moshe Katz. The rest of the members were Shlomo Riger, Yosef Nebel, Shimon Bleiberg, and Yosef Lopater.

The coach of the team had the name Yerumovitz. With the help of his lobbying, we were awarded the right to use the municipal field for practices and games.

That activity ceased upon the entrance of the Soviets.

A group of soccer fans – 1930

[Page 127]

Z.K.S. in 1933

A group of gymnastic girls under the guidance of Y. Laufer (on the left) and G. Biterman (on the right)

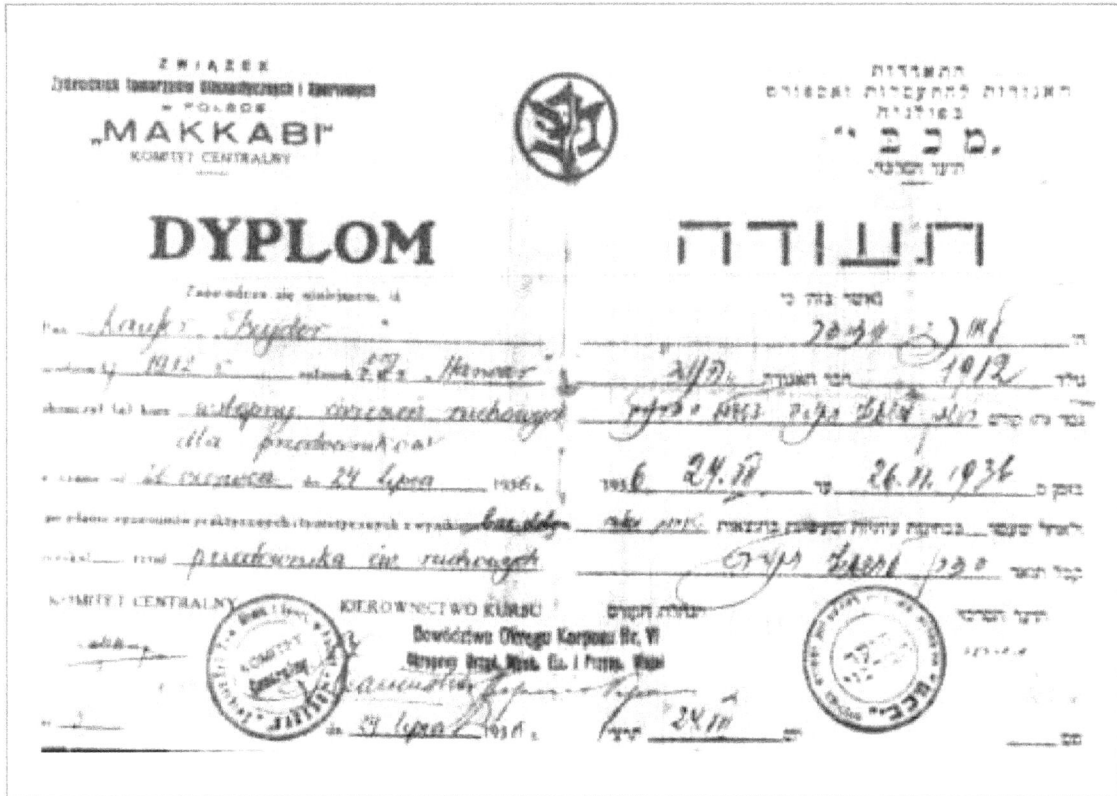

A coaching certificate given to Y. Laufer by [the sports organization] "Maccabi" in 1936. The certificate was approved by the Polish Sports Authority

[Page 128]

The Craftsmen organization "Yad Kharutzim" [Diligent Hand]

by Menakhem son of Shimon Katz

Translated by Moshe Kutten

Edited by Jane S. Gabin

The craftsmen in our town founded the organization "Yad Kharutzim" [Diligent Hand] on 20 October 1901. The objective was mutual aid, and they had a credit union. They also founded a synagogue on Shterzhatzka [?] Street (see the chapter on Brzezany synagogues in this book, page 250], where they held their gatherings. The organization ceased to operate for an extended period during the First World War, because of the cutback in production and the scattering of the members who escaped the city due to the war activities.

The organization renewed its operation only in 1928. The synagogue underwent a refurbishment, and the extent and quality of the activities grew. The cultural activities expanded during that period. Vocational courses for the working youth were organized, and financial and professional support to the members grew and expanded. The revenues of the organization revenues came mainly from membership fees, donations from wealthy members, and support from the community. The revenues from a Purim ball held once a year also benefited the organization.

Hirsh Shnaper was elected as the chairman during 1926 – 1932. Khaim Mariash was elected the secretary. The following members were elected as members of the executive committee:

Bilig Shimon, Berger Hirsh, Berger Shimon, Gutenplan Tola, Diamant Kasriel, Veintraub Yosef, Maler Oren, Feld Shalom-Mendel, Shtreizand Yosef, Shtern Zelig, and Rotin Ben-Tzion.

There were 86 members in the organization during the 1930s. They elected the dental technician Bernard Leider as their chairman. Thanks to his vigor, organizational skills, and sense of humor, the organization became a respectable institution with elevated professional ability and cultural level, and it competed with the counterpart non-Jewish organizations in the city. With the break of the Second World War, the organization dissolved like all other Jewish organizations.

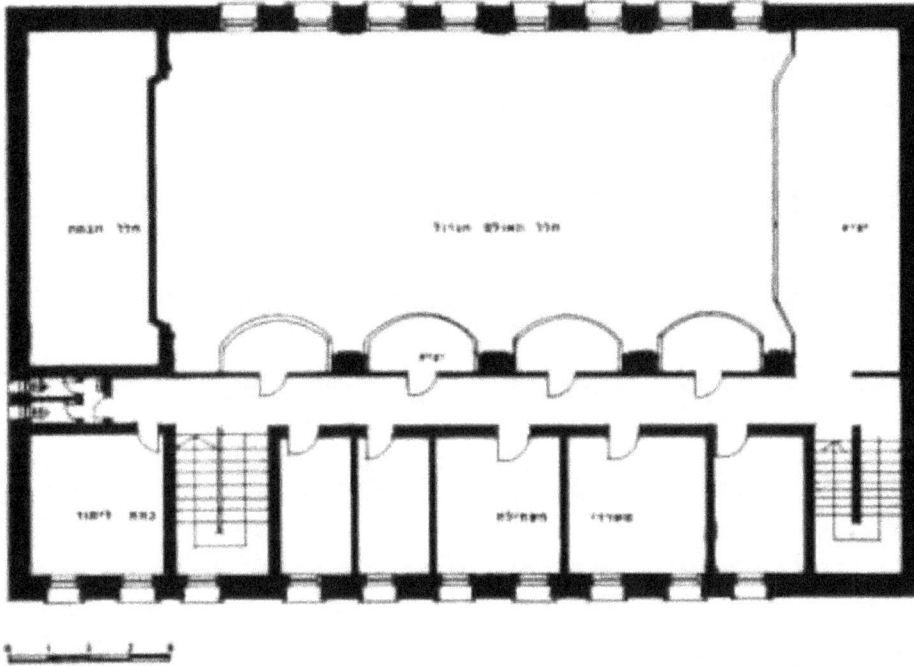

The People's House – Plan of the second floor

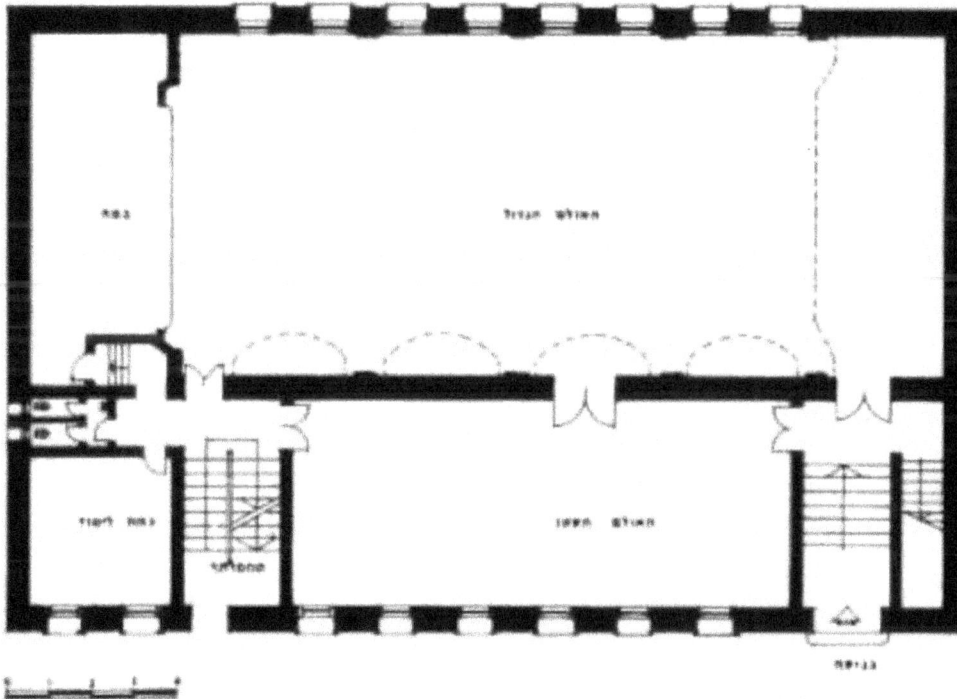

The People's House – plan of the first floor

[Page 129]

The People House – Natzional Hauz

by Menakhem son of Shimon Katz

Translated by Moshe Kutten

Edited by Jane S. Gabin

The People House [Community House] was an important cultural asset for the Brzezany community. The house, called "Natzional Hauz" [National House] by the residents, was located at the end of Zbozova Street, close to a small bridge over the river's branch. The name People House carries a hint about its purpose and importance.

For many years, the hearts of the people of the community and its leaders were filled with envy and sorrow about the fact that the Ukrainians and the Poles had their own cultural halls, which they rented to the Jewish residents when needed. Many years later, the idea of a community center came to fruition. It was the physician, Dr. B. Flick, a Jew with national pride, who made it his target, to which he aspired vigorously and continuously and urged everybody who could help him to reach it.

A public committee for building the house was established under the initiative of Dr. Flick, and he was chosen to be the chairman. Thanks to his inexhaustible energy, he lobbied his rich family in the US, and the plot for the house was purchased with a donation by the family.

Most of the funds for financing the construction of the house came from Dr. Flick's brother in the US and his own donation. The construction lasted long years due to the lack of an ongoing budget.

The house's luxurious inauguration, attended by a large crowd, was held on 4 January 1930. The house, which was devoted to public needs and utilization by the community, was registered as the property of the Jewish orphanage.

An impressive building was erected at the heart of the Jewish neighborhood. At the center of the building were the two halls: the main show hall with stands around it and a smaller hall adjacent to it. Spacious stairs on the southwestern side of the building led to a foyer and from there to the main hall. A door to the small hall opened from there as well. The stairs continued to the second floor, where the large stand and the individual booths were along the main hall. The corridor on top of the stairs that led to the booths on the east side also led to the series of offices on the west side, which served the community committee. An additional staircase serving all the floors (including the cellar that housed a series of storage rooms and the apartment of the house caretaker) was located on the side of the stage on the northwestern side of the building. On the side of that staircase was a study room that served the Hebrew school of the "HaPoel HaMizrakhi" movement.

The main hall and stage were adorned with decorative plaster cornices. The booths were sunken into the body of the corridor with exaggerated an elliptic protruding into the hall. Plaster columns with round slots separated them from the floor and rose to the ceiling. All the floors were made with oak parquet, and the entire finish was well-made using state-of-the-art materials.

The main hall, which could contain up to 400-500 people, was utilized mainly for shows, gatherings, and various public events. Weddings were also held there. The drama club also showed his numerous plays in the house, as well as troupes from outside of the city,

[Page 130]

ranging from the Vienna Operetta to tiny troupes. Public figures held gatherings here. Among others, the following people appeared in the People's House: [Ya'akov] Zrubavel, Dr. [Wolfgang] von Weisel, author Tversky, folk singer [Nakhum] Sternheim, and many more.

That ebullient and active center served the community from 1930 until the outbreak of the Second World War. During the war years of 1939 – 1941, the People's House was used for various purposes according to the Soviet regime's wishes. The Nazi oppressor used its halls to concentrate Jews before their expulsion to concentration camps. With the liberation of the city by the Red Army in 1944, after all the other city's public halls were destroyed, the People's Home became the only movie theater, and that was how I remember it, standing isolated and erect above a large plane, which was one filled with Jewish structures, purposely destroyed by the Nazis.

That People's Home was the only remnant of the Jewish neighborhood, standing like a gravestone and reminding passers-by that: "Jews once lived and worked here, and I, in my existence, memorialize them."

The Orphanage

by Menakhem son of Shimon Katz

Translated by Moshe Kutten

Edited by Jane S. Gabin

Many orphans remained in the city after the First World War without patronage or a roof over their heads. The streets served as the home, and the cellars were a place to sleep for many kids who ran around the city's alleys. Pity and sorrow filled all those who delved into the problem and thought about the future of those children.

The phrase "Save the orphans" was born. The ladies Rozia Reikh, Augusta Milkh, Henrika Goldberg, and others organized and established the "Organization of Jewish Women," which granted patronage to those street children. With the help of that organization, the children were placed in private homes, some for a fee and others for free.

In 1920, a reorganization occurred in the "organization of Jewish Women." As a result, the name was changed to the "Organization for Watching Over the Jewish Orphans."

Thanks to the substantial support from Brzezany *landsmen* in the USA and the initiative and backing by the family of Yitzkhak and Rozia Feld from Philadelphia, the organization purchased a house on Shterzhtzka Street and founded an orphanage there.

[Page 131]

Most of the work, organization, and support of the orphanage was done by volunteers - activists who dedicatedly devoted many years in the spirit of loving others to sustain the existence of the orphanage.

Dr. Tz. Reikh, Dr. P. Pomerantz, and Judge W. Tadnier served as chairmen and managers of the institution. The last chairman was the high school teacher Professor David Horovitz, a member of the municipal council. He was respected by all the population classes (he was sent to the killing camp in Belzec).

The management team of the orphanage included the following: Meshel Lebel – an industrialist, the pharmacists Henrik Pohoriles and Mark Kurtzman, Dr. S. Fridman, lawyer Shlomo Glazer, Mrs. Rozia

Reikh, Mrs. Ada Pomerantz, teacher Yoakhim Shleikher, and the merchants Leizer Bernshtien, Karol Altein, and Yehoshua-Mordekhai Taler.

Much effort and hard work for the benefit of the institution were invested by lawyer Bronislav Fridman, the manager of the sawmill, Y, Greif.

[Page 132]

Charity and Mutual Aid Institutes

by Dr. Eliezer ShaklaiMenakhem son of Shimon Katz

Translated by Moshe Kutten

Edited by Jane S. Gabin

Like in the rest of the Jewish cities, our city organized various charity and mutual aid institutions out of a collective sense of responsibility for the welfare of the entire community. The view of the generational Jewish tradition and Halakha were also factors. Due to a lack of documentary materials (which may be found in archives), I would only provide a few words on these organizations and the institutes that operated in the city during the last few years before the Second World War:

"Parnasat Aniyim" ["Livelihood for the Poor"] group

That accomplished group provided economic aid to the city's poor. That aid included cash, clothing, firewood (in the winter), and daily and Shabbat dishes. Among its other responsibilities was to ensure the supply of Kosher food to patients at the state hospital and inmates in jail. They also organized a Passover Seder for Jewish soldiers who served in the Polish army stationed in the city.

The group's operations were multifaceted thanks to the tireless energy of its chairman, who sacrificed himself for the public interest – Moshe Shpitzen (see the article about him, page 202).

It operated under the guidance of Rabbi Moshe for many years. Its members included the following people: Simkha Binem-Heler, Y. Khayut, Rabbi Khaim Halperin, Ya'akov Goldman, Laibish Rozenberg, Khaim Kahana, Yitzkhak Toiber, Leizer Berenshtien, and Y. Kornbaum.

"Parnasat Aniyim" group, Brzezany
(The order of sitting and standing people was assumed)

Sitting from left to right: S. B. Heler, Y. Khayut, Rabbi Moshe Shpitzen, Rabbi Khaim
Halperin, Y. Goldman, L.
Standing: Rozenberg. Kh. Kahana, Y. Toiber, L. Bernshtein, Y. Kornbaum

[Page 133]

Passover Seder for the Jewish soldiers in the 51st Battalion of the Polish Army, 1930

"Bikur Kholim" ["Visiting the Sick"] Society

People with a humanitarian sense belonged to that society. They volunteered to assist sick people in their time of need, particularly poor or lonely Jews who did not have anybody who could help them. The organization members visited sick people to encourage them and provide advice or financial or medical assistance when needed. A small hospital of the Jewish community (about ten beds) operated under their supervision and guidance. Poor or chronic patients who could not stay at home, due to their disease, stayed there.

"Gmilat Khesed" ["Bestowing Kindness"] Society

That society was a miniature financial institution that provided short-term, interest-free loans to anybody, particularly the needy. In some rare cases, they converted the loan to a grant.

"Tzedaka Ve'Khesed" ["Charity and Kindness"] Society

Like "Gmilat Khesed," this fund provided loans, but loans for longer periods and higher amounts. The society's objective was to provide substantial support to people whose financial situation had deteriorated.

Usually, these people kept their situation confidential. The organization followed the commandment of "Somekh Noflim" ["Supporting the Fallen"]. They succeeded in many cases to revive defunct businesses. Shalom Apel headed that organization.

"Malbish Arumim" ["Clothing the Naked"] Society

The head of that society was a prominent public figure, Dr. Ya'akov Ravitz. Due to his energetic and authoritative nature, he managed to interest many people who dedicated themselves to collecting clothing, mainly winter clothing, and distributing them among the city's poor. From time to time, they conducted operations to collect money. They would then buy new clothes and distribute them to the needy, including the orphanage children.

The Organization for Mutual Aid of the Jewish Academic Youth

The Organization for Mutual Aid was founded in July 1927 through the initiative of members Shimon Trauner and Zigmund Hess. The Objective of the Jewish Academic Youth Organization was to organize the Jewish youths in the city into a nonaffiliated movement and bring them closer to the rest of the youth by arranging meetings, lectures, and symposiums. The organization helped poor students with tuition and textbooks. Money was collected from membership fees, donations, and assistance from the Jewish community. The organization had about 80 members, including some who studied abroad. Zigmund Bleiberg headed the organization in the 1930s.

[Page 134]

Educational Institutes

by Menakhem son of Shimon Katz

Translated by Moshe Kutten

Edited by Jane S. Gabin

The high school stood out among the schools in the city – the elementary schools for boys and girls (in two separate buildings), a vocational school, and a female teacher seminary. The latter institution resided on the second floor of the town hall from the day of its establishment. A new large building was about to be inaugurated in the fall of 1914, but the events of the First World War prevented the holding of the start of the school year. During the First World War, the building served various military purposes. Only in 1925 was the building renovated and reoccupied. The luxurious and spacious building, with all its equipment and the gym, served many students between the two World Wars, including Jewish students.

During the Nazi conquest, the building became an office building, serving the district manager. After the Second World War, it became a school again under the Soviet regime; however, there were no Jewish students in it.

Anti-Semitism in the High School,
The Zvirski Affair

By Shlomo Doron–Dorfman

Translated by Moshe Kutten

Edited by Jane S. Gabin

The Polish linguistics teacher – Zvirski- taught me in the sixth class of the state high school in Brzezany. He was the dragon of all Jewish students. His contempt and hatred for the Jews drove him crazy. Since he was fundamentally corrupt, he began to demand "payments" from the parents of his Jewish students. He used Jewish intermediaries – conscienceless people – who were in touch with his wife and not directly with him.

I was a good student, including in Polish linguistics. I even served as a tutor (a senior student who provided lessons for weak students). Since my parents refused to pay a bribe for me, following my pleas and assurances that I was an excellent student, Zvirsky was cruel toward me and gave me an unjustified failing grade.

My resentment and my parents' anger led to trying to organize all the Jewish parents whose children were subjected to extortion; however, most parents were afraid to join, fearing that they would be prosecuted for collaborating in a crime. My parents insisted and hired a private investigator who researched the method of extortion and accumulated sufficient satisfactory pieces of evidence for the prosecutor to put the teacher on trial.

[Page 135]

I was forced to leave the city, and I moved to Lviv. I was accepted to the state high school there and scored excellent grades at the end of my studies, including in Polish linguistics. "Very Good" in Polish served as assistive evidence at the district court in Brzezany. Due to the large number of witnesses, most of whom were Brzezany residents, all three judges were transferred to Brzezany for that trial from the district court in Lviv. The prosecutor in Zvirski's trial was a Ukrainian named Boiko.

The trial lasted more than a year. Promises were given by the prosecutor to the parents of the involved children that no harm would come to them or their children due to testimony. Although legally, they were also criminals.

Zvirski hired two lawyers, both Jewish – Goldshlag and the late Lufter. Both were honest people who fulfilled their professional duty to the best of their ability. The entire Jewish press throughout Poland and the Polish press reported widely about the trial.

Zvirski and his wife were convicted in the trial and sentenced to one year in jail and a substantial fine. Zvirski's wife was pregnant, and hers was converted to a suspended sentence.

I met Zvirski again when I was an eighth-year student in Lviv, just before the matriculation exams. I went to see a movie one evening, and he was the pathetic cashier who sold me the ticket; he recognized me, smiled, and did not say anything but lowered his head in shame.

Upon emigrating to Eretz Israel, with my parents and brother, I registered at the teacher seminary "David Yelin" in Jerusalem. I have been serving as a teacher in Israel since I completed my studies at the seminary and the Hebrew University,

I served in the [British] Brigade during the Second World War. After the war, I stayed in Europe and worked on organizing the education system of the children - refugees of the Holocaust and transferring them from Italy to Israel.

The school I have been managing until today is called "Geulim" [Redeemed]. That name was taken from the name of one of the groups in the school for the Holocaust children that I managed in Italy.

That is my life, such a life – I am alive, a Brzezany native.

[Page 136]

Teachers State Seminary in Brzezany

Batya Boneh-Prizand

Translated by Moshe Kutten

Edited by Jane S. Gabin

I turn to write the review of the teachers' seminary in Brzezany, hesitantly because of the non-Jewish character of the subject. The reader would, no doubt, ask what teachers' seminary has to do with the memorialization of the Jewish community, which is the main objective of this book. However, because I educated and taught hundreds of Israel children at a state school in Israel, thanks to being a graduate of the seminary, and like me, two more graduates of that institution dedicatedly fulfilled their roles in the education field in Israel, the institution for training teachers in Brzezany is worthy of a its own article.

Not every city the size of Brzezany had a female teacher seminary, in addition to a coed high school. Therefore, many girls from nearby and faraway areas studied in Brzezany's seminary. It was not easy to be accepted. There was only a single Jewish student among the thirty students who began their studies every year.

Following a five-year program and success in the official matriculation examinations, the graduate received a diploma, authorizing her to teach in any state or private elementary school where the teaching language was Polish or Ukrainian.

The seminary combined theoretical and vocational characters, and the level of study was high. All the teachers had an academic education, and the teaching methods were quite advanced. An emphasis was placed on students' self-work and independence.

I will never forget my essay about the history of the Jewish nation in the history class of one of the upper classes. I lectured on that essay in class before the students and the teacher. The effect of the lecture on the students was immense, and I received special appreciation and an excellent grade in history. In the two upper classes, an emphasis was placed on pedagogic studies and training teachers in actual teaching work in the exemplary school located by the seminary.

A discussion about the lessons conducted by the students was held once a week, in which the teacher and the students analyzed the material. These discussions expanded our horizons and provided tremendous professional knowledge.

Studies in the seminary took place six days per week, while Sunday was a free day. We, the Jewish girls, five in total in the whole institute, suffered from being forced to go to school on Shabbat and Jewish holidays and conduct compulsory activities, some of which were forbidden according to Jewish law. As a daughter of a religious family, I had to hide these activities from my parents, particularly my father *z"l*, a G-d-fearing and pious man who was very strict in fulfilling the commandments.

We were released from our studies only during the Days of Awe, Rosh Hashana, and Yom Kippur - and the release required submission of a special request every year. However, the teachers were not considerate and did not give us any allowance. Besides these difficulties, the overall atmosphere at the seminar was positive, and the attendance of five Jewish female students did not result in any problems.

[Page 137]

Among the teachers who stood out in their education and their humanistic and educational approach toward the students were the principal and two additional teachers. On the other side, there were teachers who, despite trying to hide their hostile attitude toward the Jewish students, they did not succeed in that. The seminary management was strict about discipline and studying orderliness.

Despite all of that, the atmosphere at the seminary was not that of a monastery, and the students were involved in the life of the youth in town.

A ball with the participation of the seminary's girls and the high school's students was held once a year. Preparations for that event were lengthy and the program was diverse. Echoes from that ball continued to resonate long after the event and it became the topic of discussion among the youths.

Once a year, the seminary held a day trip with the participation of the elementary school's students, and it was a wonderful day in the life of the institution. I remember the charming nature location - a ravine among tall mountains, rich in water and vegetation, at the foot of an enormous railway bridge. We established a camp there, and teachers and students spent a long day playing games and sports. It was a day of joy and happiness.

Upon graduating from the seminary, and after the matriculation exams, I was hired as a teacher in a state elementary school in Khorostkiv, Kopychyntsi District. That was a rare occurrence in Poland, which restricted the acceptance of Jews to governmental positions.

Despite my successes, I felt like a foreign body at the seminary and also when I worked as a teacher. My aspiration was somewhere else. That is because I was a member of the "HaShomer HaTzair" ["Young Guard"] movement, and followed its objectives. I lived the life of the youth movements. The movement's principles gave me the mental fortitude to leave everything behind me and make Aliyah to Eretz Israel. I made Aliyah in 1932 and worked at a state school from 1936 until 1972. All that is thanks to the basic knowledge and professional training I received at the seminary.

Brzezany

by Tzvi Scharfstein

Translated by Moshe Kutten

Edited by Jane S. Gabin

In memory of [Prof.] Tzvi Scharfstein, who served as a teacher in Brzezany. This article was copied from his book "Haya Aviv BaAretz" [It was Spring in the Land], 1952, "Masada" Publisher.

I do not know who controlled it – but the rumor spread that I needed to leave Peremyshlyany [in Yiddish - Primishlan]. Two activists from the school "Safa Brura" ["Clear Language"] in neighboring Brzezany came to me and invited me to accept the management of their institute – I agreed. The change of place changed my situation for the better – I moved to a bigger city with a population of fifteen thousand Jews, Poles, and Ruthins. A third of the population were our brothers.

[Page 138]

There were two high schools in Brzezany, one for boys and the other for girls. Both schools contained large numbers of Jewish youths, some of whom were local and others from the neighboring town. Because, just as in the past, people migrated to different places of residence, Jewish youths began to migrate to locations of high schools and universities. Almost all Jewish high school students came from tradition-holders' homes, graduates of the "*Kheder*" who remembered their childhood roots, whether a little or a lot.

When I arrived to manage the Hebrew school in Brzezany, a delegation of upper high school classmates came and asked to arrange Hebrew evening lessons for them – and that was what I did. I also established morning lessons for the girls. About a hundred youths - boys and girls, came to study Hebrew – the best of the Jewish youth. Excitement was felt in the city. Hebrew talks could be heard when the youngsters strolled on the main street.

The students were divided into groups based on their knowledge. Some unique characters were found among the members of the upper course, a small group who read modern [Hebrew] literature.

One such character who stood out changed his name as early as then to Hebrew. He was the son of a good family from Buczacz [in Yiddish - Buchach], which the author S. Y. Agnon made famous in his literary creations. That student differed from his friends in appearance, views, and ways of life. In terms of his appearance – he grew a beard, which added an aura of maturity, seriousness, and a bit of strangeness since the combination of a high school uniform and a beard seemed strange. In terms of his way of life he was a follower of what can be called "natural life," and he avoided meat. He was nationalistic with all his soul and might and pedantic about his Hebrew speech. He read modern Hebrew literature and faithfully participated in Zionist activities. His attitude toward his friends and his sacrifice for their sake was paternal. He carried that ideological sense, not out of the recognition of a charity doer or for showing off, but out of simplicity and modesty and as something done anyway.

I have met many naturalists, vegetarians, and idealists in my life, and found that most lack a sense of humor. Their prominence was high in their own eyes, and they highlighted their seriousness and superiority over everyone. They assigned themselves the eminence of teachers and guides created to elevate their friends to their superior level. But he was not flawed by this. Although he was a vegetarian, he did not try to convert his friends. He used to visit me at home when he had free time to discuss literature, Zionism, and activities among the students. When he entered, purity entered, the room was filled with myrrh fragrance, and miraculously joy filled one's heart.

He studied with me for two years, and I became attached to him. After getting a graduation and matriculation certificate, he moved to Vienna to study medicine there. I threw him a farewell party before his departure. It was a modest party but a novelty and rare honor, nevertheless. His friends praised him, toasted in his honor, sang songs, danced, and dragged him into the dancing circle. He seemed to be happy. Since he left the city, the splendor of the group dimmed.

I received news about him from time to time. It was told about him that he neglected his studies and that he intensified his vegetarianism, turning to nature with a strangeness in his behavior. His studies lengthened. When he received the license to practice medicine, he returned to Brzezany and served as a physician there for a short while. Later on, he made Aliyah and settled in Eretz Israel.

[Page 139]

When I read Agnon's "Ore'akh Noteh Lalun" [A Guest for the Night], I found a few pages dedicated to a vegan physician whom the author found by chance after the First World War. He described the physician's great righteousness and generosity toward his poor patients and his frugal life and contentment with little. His good manners with people resulted in people beginning to disrespect him: "A sick person who can afford to pay calls a different physician, and one that cannot afford to pay calls this physician." And that physician came for visits and returned, even if not called. Not only that, but he also gave poor patients what he received from the villagers. The latter flocked to him as he accepted produce instead of payments: butter, eggs, vegetables, and fruits. A trace of the past remained in medicine: the more distanced the physician was from the people, the more prominent he became, and if he demanded an exuberant fee, he was called a physician-artist. Our doctor… did not practice any of those ways. He would meet a stranger, talk to him like he was his friend, and bring food for poor patients, and for that, people disrespected him.

Sometimes, I thought about home and wondered when I would see him again. It would be interesting to see the effects of grueling life and the time on him. The opportunity to see him again presented itself in the summer of 1948 when he came to see me in Jerusalem from his settlement.

When he sat down, I saw a skinny and wrinkled man standing before me; his speech was austere, and his eyes were filled with grief. The angel of laughter did not visit him anymore, and his voice lacked hope. I felt a pinch in my heart. I could not suppress my thoughts comparing the image of a young man with the radiance of an icon whose frequent smile filled my heart with joy, his warmth infected me with the joy of living, and his sense of humor created the illusion that life was easy. He went out to the world in a healthy body, happy, believing in his goodness - like an island of justice and peace. And now, when he reached the age of sixty, his experiences ravaged his island. From his talk, I could see that he battled with life and did not prevail because he could not add his voice to the chorus of deceits – and was left in the corner, lonely and neglected.

Did he stop believing in people? Does he continue to treat people kindly because he cannot change his character or because he still trusts the human race?

Who knows?

One day, I received a letter from a fellow in Russia who asked me to hire him as a teacher] in my school. "Do you remember me?" – he wrote – "Do you remember me standing in front of the yard's wicket at the "*Kheder Metukan*" [improved traditional Kheder] in Berdychiv [Berdichev] to prevent the children from entering their school? – I am sure you did not judge me on the scale of demerits and recognized my good intentions, and you do not hold a grudge against me. I want to leave Russia – no, I have to leave Russia. If you have me join your school, I will serve you loyally."

"Come, my friend, come!" I wrote to him. When he came, while I was writing the formal papers, I saw a young man with short stature, his eyes gleaming under the burden of his emotions, which warmed my heart. I said: "The bulky stick that you carried in your hand that you pounded with force on the cobblestones, and the face of terror that you put on did not conceal the tenderness of your temper and the grace of your ways. The weighty Marxist terms that you put forward, through efforts, did not cover your loyal Jewish feelings. I recognized you, Moshe. You are the son of Moshe. Moshe, who took pity on the tortured and broken.

[Page 140]

You have already stripped off your foreign attire, which does not suit you, and now appear in your natural image: A young Israeli from a good family who loves his people and speaks and enjoys the Hebrew language. Come, Lekhtman, and help me in my holy work."

He came and taught, and we became good friends. However, he carried a secret burden. He was called to serve Russia and the party (the "Seimists" party – non-Zionist Jewish Socialistic/Communist Party). A short while later, he left me, returned to Russia, and disappeared into the abyss. No memory remained of him except one: a photograph of three people - him, me, and Berl Loker, one of the leaders of "Poalei Tzion" in Galitsia and Bukovina in those days.

* * *

Reuven Brainin [journalist, author, editor, and Zionist thinker and activist] came to Galitsia in 1907 to lecture national students in Lviv and provincial cities. The student union invited him to promote the old language and its literature.

Brainin arrived at an opportune time. The national idea was gaining popularity in Galitsia, and the Hebrew schools were at their highest level and influence. The national sentiment was simmering in the hearts. No great Hebrew authors existed in Galitsia[1]. The Zionist, Hebraic Brainin, a man with exquisite etiquette, became a symbol of the revival. The generation's youths looked up to him and poured their love on him.

Brainin's banquet in Lviv became a substantial demonstration. Fifteen hundred men and women gathered in the hall, which was a big surprise. Nobody believed gathering such a massive crowd for a Hebrew literary lecture was possible. When Brainin appeared on the stage, he was showered with flowers. The cheer broke out: "Hooray! Long live Brainin." The author gave his lecture about the development of Hebrew literature and the significance of its authors, and the audience listened with beating hearts. During the banquet, the students handed him an expensive silver bouquet as a token of their admiration, and prominent speakers praised him. The rest of the cities were jealous of Lviv and invited Brainin. He passed through Stryi, Stanislawow [today Ivano-Frankivsk], and Drohobych. That was a victory lap.

I also invited him to come to Brzezany.

We paid him great respect when he came. We printed his picture – the one that showed his long hair flowing down the back of his neck, and his black tie spreading its wings left and right, the way of freedom and poetry. We distributed hundreds of copies of the picture. When Brainin passed on his way to the gathering hall, he could see his face peeking out from every lighted window with the word "Welcome" in bright letters.

We brought him to a homey Jewish inn that had no luxury. The inn owner, Roza, won the privilege of hosting the author by being a Torah learner, reader of research books, and loyal Zionist. When we brought Brainin there, he looked around and shook his head in disappointment. We praised the owner, but he insisted:

"Lodge me in a "European" hotel"

We fulfilled his wish and brought him to "Bristol," the city's only "luxurious" hotel. After a light meal, emissaries of the city associations and parties, came to congratulate him, each emissary with his short speech. It was a magnificent show. Brainin stood there as a king in his court. He listened attentively to the speeches

[Page 141]

and every blessing, and at the end, presented questions about the state of the city's Jews, the activity and development of every association and party. Humbly and submissively, the emissaries gave him a detailed report about their activities. When they encountered the insignificance of their actions, they began to stutter and buried their faces in the ground.

When the emissaries left, Brainin turned to me:

"Would you please accompany me to the pharmacy? like to buy cologne."

I brought him to the most "luxurious" pharmacy – whose owner was a Pole. The pharmacist handed him a cologne bottle, but Brainin shook his head.

"I want," – he said in a "Jewish-ide" German – "a French cologne. Perhaps you have 'Heliotrope Flowers'?"

"No sir," answered the pharmacist.

"How about 'Paris lilac'?"

"I am sorry, we do not have that one either."

Brainin named several other French perfumes, but the pharmacy carried none.

"There is probably no demand for good perfumes here," Brainin said.

"Why," the pharmacist was offended – the dames in the city know how to choose. We have good perfumes from Vienna and Warsaw."

"French perfumes are second to none. However, since I do not have a choice, please give me another good local one." Brainin shook his head disappointedly.

The gathering hall where Brainin gave the lecture was filled from end to end with people from all corners of the city: the enlightened and the one being enlightened, the professionally intelligent, the student, the yeshiva student, and the young woman who stretches out on the chaise longue to read love stories – they all came to hear the sublime and exalted – the words of the European Hebrew author. Brainin talked about the "Revival" in life and literature, about the Zionist idea, whose fulfillment is approaching, and the Hebrew language being revived, and the crowd was listening, holding its breath.

Brainin charmed the crowd with his noble image and manners. His face was cloaked with a veil of sadness, paleness, and concentration like a man pondering the world's purpose and the suffering of humans. He had tender hands, and their touch was soft and pleasant. In his lectures and discussions – like in his articles, he used to mention the names of the world's great authors and his meetings with them in the capacity of their confidant. His permanent apartment was in Berlin, but he was a frequent visitor in Paris, Saint Petersburg, Moscow, Brussels, Copenhagen, and everywhere a great creator resided. He introduced his listeners to the lounges of Georg Brandes, Maurice Maeterlinck, Max Nordau, and the rest of the prominent people. His flowery language was flowing and interspersed with catchphrases and proverbs that flashed for a moment. All these attributes elevated his image in the eyes of the audience.

The audience set there for an hour, riding on the clouds of the sweet dream. Zionism, which was nothing but a faraway dream or ornament – acquired a real shape. Here comes a man from the center of the world who speaks audaciously about the "Revival." The soul transcended, and when Brainin finished his lecture with his famous ending: "Long live the Hebrew people! Long live the Hebrew language," prolonged applause broke out and the walls trembled to the calling voice: "Hurray!"

[Page 142]

In the banquet held in his honor in the Ruthene Community House, the best of the Zionists blessed and praised Brainin. Then Roza, that innkeeper, stood and, with awe and reverence, praised Brainin: "You are the elect of God among us [Genesis 23:6]."

Brainin was moved, and his eyes moistened.

* * *

Among the people who welcomed Brainin was a graceful brunette girl with many talents and a sharp mind – Rakhel Dorfman. Her father was enlightened and saw his entire world in his talented daughter. Whenever he was free from his activities in his store, he sat her down by him and taught her a chapter from the Bible or its commentaries. She was my student, and I felt a special affection for her because of her pleasant manners and spiritual virtues. Originality was evident in her compositions. Brainin listened to her blessing and got excited. He talked to her and asked her to come to his hotel the next day before leaving town. She brought her compositions with her. Brainin read them and announced:

"A star."

He mentioned the girl in every place in Galitsia he lectured and prophesied greatness for her. He remembered her even after returning to Berlin and mentioned her in his letters.

I remembered that girls at times too. I thought about her and asked myself, "what happened to her, and where did she disappear?"

Forty-four years passed, and I did not hear about her or her fate. During one of the days in Sivan 5711 (1951), I got a call from a woman who spoke English:

"Can I talk to you in Hebrew?"

"Of course."

"My name is Dr. N. from Tel Aviv. Forty years ago, you were my teacher at the school in Brzezany. I arrived in New York and like to meet with you for a sentimental reason.""Yes, I would be happy to see you."

"When?"

"Now."

"I will come shortly."

Half an hour later, I opened the door for her. A woman with a delicate face and dark skin stood in front of me, and a thread of grief was drawn across her face. That was Rakhel Dorfman from the past.

She set down with me for about an hour and told me the history of her life in a soft voice. She studied in Vienna and received a doctorate in medicine. She married a wealthy merchant from Berlin and lived a pleasant life with him. However, they were forced to escape the Nazi oppressor. They reached Israel with their son and had to endure a miserable life of poverty.

She worked in simple and fatiguing jobs until she was finally able to return to her profession. But fate prevented her from doing so. She became ill and had to move to America to seek a cure for her illness.

She spoke softly, but disappointment roared from her voice.

"The prophecy of Brainin did not materialize," she said, "and I did not become an author. My heart does not even permit persistence in reading fine literature. Every time I recall meeting with the nobleman, Brainin, and remember his sweet talk – I feel a pinch in my heart."

Brainin's portrait is floating in front of her eyes, reminding her about fate and evoking nostalgia for youths that have passed, for talents that have been lost, and for dreams that blossomed in the dusty lap of life.

Author's Note:

1. There was an author by the name of Gershon Shofman in Lviv. However, he was mainly appreciated by people with fine literary tastes and was not popular with many people. Asher Barash was very young then, and so was Aganon.

[Page 143]

Khevra Kadisha [Burial Society] – "The Bed Carriers"

Translated by Moshe Kutten

Edited by Jane S. Gabin

"Khevra Kadisha" – the Burial Society - was founded in our city in 1837 under the name "*Nos'ey HaMitah*" ["The Bed Carriers"]. Its founders were Rabbi Naftali Hertz Halperin and Avraham Apel. In 1876, the association was recognized officially by the authorities in Lviv under the name "Tzdaka Va'Khesed" ["Charity and Grace"]. However, that name was not accepted by the members, and they continued to call it by the original name of "The Bed-Carriers" until its elimination during the Second World War.

All the association's activists were volunteers who fulfilled their roles dedicatedly and with great effort, fitting their mission of providing "true grace." Their job was particularly demanding during the rainy days and the harsh winters. Despite these conditions, there was hardly any turnover among the association's activists.

The *Tahara* [ritual purification], the funeral arrangements, and the burial were arranged immediately, if possible, free of charge. Money for the burial plot was imposed only on people who could afford it. The poor were brought to Jewish burials free of charge according toJewish tradition and Halakha.

In 1930, the following people were the association's activists: Chairman Ya'akov Mitelman, Deputy Chairman Shlomo Margolies, Secretary Kalman Altein, Treasurer Yosef Shtreizend, and members: Leib Bleishift, David Ginsburg, Meir Lifshitz, Efraim Veintraub, and Lezer Bernshtien. The association's comptrollers were Katriel Diamant and Ya'akov Shmeterlink.

In addition to their tasks associated with the organization, the members helped sick people, particularly the poor ones. They provided financial and spiritual assistance, organized bedside assistance at night, and any other needed help.

The association was active for many years, although its members changed once and again because somebody died, left, or made Aliyah to Eretz Israel. However, the spirit of volunteering and benevolence did not cease in all its transfigurations.

With the outbreak of the [Second] World War, the association continued to operate despite the substantial turnover of its members. With the Nazi conquest and the abandonment of most of the members, even at the beginning of the Holocaust, volunteers could not be found. An old-timer, R' David Ginsburg took it upon himself, through the assignment by the Judenrat, all of the tasks of the "Khevra Kadisha." He acted alone with dedication and limitless sacrifices, took care of all the burial arrangements, and, in the end, gave his life for true grace.

Khevra Kadisha with Rabbi Shraga-Feibish Halperin
(fourth from the right) at the entrance to the cemetery

[Page 144]

The Cemetery

by Dr. Eliezer Shaklai

Translated by Ruth Yoseffa Erez

The cemetery is part of the community. It serves as a live testimony to the history of the community from the beginning. It is as old as the community is.

The first Jewish settlers in our town bought a piece of land and sanctified it for a cemetery. They dug graves and put tombstones on them on which they engraved the name of the deceased and a summary of his life and achievements.

In between vegetable gardens and fields of grains, in the southwestern corner of the town, to the right of "Riska" street, on a hill surrounded by a stone wall – there was our cemetery. A wide gate stood at the entrance; on it was written: "Tzedakah (charity) saves from death." To the right of the gate stood the undertaker's apartment. Opposite it, to the left, there were the "Tahara" (purity) rooms.

In the cemetery, the old was mixed with the new. Right next to the entrance on the right side, there were a few middle-sized structures with tombstones inside them. Those were family graves of the rich and prominent Jews, called "*shtibalach*." Around them were hundreds of years old tombstones, deep in the ground, crooked and covered with grass and mold. The letters were erased by the rain, the wind, and the time. In between those tombs were bushes.

As we withdrew farther away from the cemetery entrance, the tombstones became straight and the writing was clear. That is where the new part began. There were tombstones from our time, big white stones with engraved letters, and familiar names.

There was a custom in the "Israeli house": mass visits to the cemetery in the month of Elul. During the early hours of the morning, many visitors came in. The cantor would eulogize and sing "el male rachamim," and the visitors would hand out donations to the poor. Of course, people would also visit the place during the year on memorial days and also just to "pour their hearts out" in this holy place.

[Page 145]

During WWI, the cemetery was harmed. For months, the front between the Austrian and the Russian armies was inside the town, and the Austrian army dug its trenches around the cemetery. From this action and from the artillery shells, the graves, the tombstones and part of the wall suffered heavy damage.

In the years between the two world wars, the Jewish community rehabilitated the cemetery. It was Baruch (Boozia) Stark who took the job upon him and fulfilled it completely. He cleaned the cemetery, rehabilitated the tombstones and, fixed the wall.

During the Soviet rule, all the activities of the Jewish community ceased to exist, including the supervision of the cemetery.

The Germans and their helpers utilized the cemetery and were responsible for thousands of victims, some in single graves and some in mass graves. They uprooted tombstones and used them to build roads and buildings and ruined the cemetery.

When we returned to the town with the Soviet Army in 1944, the few of us who stayed alive would visit the lonely and broken cemetery and commune with the memory of the holy victims. May those who dwell in it rest in peace.

Old tombstones in Brzezany's Jewish cemetery:

A tombstone from the beginning of the 19th century
(photocopied from the book ZYDZI W POLSCE ODROCZONEJ)
Old Tombstone from 1643 (Hebrew year of 5403)

[Page 146]

My Father's Home

by Dr. Eliezer Shaklai

Translated by Moshe Kutten

Edited by Jane S. Gabin

Our apartment was in a low house near Tarnoploska Street. We lived there with the parents of my mother, Moshe-Natan, and Roza (nee Kimel) Vilner. The young daughter, Ester, married my father, Hersh Wagshal, the older son of Zelig and Shindel (nee Bartfeld) Wagshal. We were three siblings - two daughters and I, the youngest.

I grew up and was educated in that house, on the street, and in the neighborhood. The neighbors and the children with whom I played left me with the feeling that my home was "my father's house." A patriarch-based regime prevailed at home. Life progressed according to the order of the generational tradition of laws and customs. The relations with the neighbors were hearty and friendly. People shared their worries and joys with each other. The closest family, with whom we stayed in friendly relations for our entire life, was the Bar-David family… The house got burnt, the street destroyed, and the property robbed, but the friendship remained until today!

Those years, home, neighborhood, and education, left not only memories but formed the foundations for our lives and values. They planted within us the love of the Torah, the understanding of knowledge in general, and the love of Israel. They fostered our attitude toward work and educated the human within us.

We suffered and were painfully hurt by the First World War. That period also left its mark on us. It taught us about life when the law gives way to power, and the only law that rules is "might is right."

My parents were a happy couple, an efficacious pairing between two people who loved each other, with virtues that complemented each other, and therefore, each one helped the other.

My father was a tall person, athletically built, with a symmetric face and blue eyes – a good-looking man in his exterior and mannerisms. He inspired respect, was quiet, restrained, spoke calmly and politely, and paid respect to everyone. He was modest and humble. He was a believer, wholeheartedly, without any hesitation, and without deviating from the honest way even by a hairsbreadth. His faith was not dependent on reward and punishment - it was an integral part of his being. He used to say: "You cannot cheat G-d since you are cheating yourself." He also used to say: "A person was created in the image of G-d, and there is no difference between one Jew to another, in anything associated with matters between one person to his friend."

He was very organized in his work and personal matters and was so in prayer, eating, and studying. An impressive experience was for anybody who stayed with us during Shabbat or a holiday. We felt "*Neshama Yeterah*" ["Additional Soul" - a popular Jewish belief that Jews are given an additional soul on Shabbat]. I would not expand here on Shabbat's and holidays. I will only say that Shabbat was completely holy, a day of rest. Yom Kippur was a completely restful day, the sukkah was a sukkah of peace, and the Seder night… Song of songs and praise for the holiday of spring.

My mother was a beautiful woman in her youth, but the hard life, work, and worries plowed wrinkles on her face…She was smart, practical, agile, had quick perception, good memory, and unique workability. She was not only helping my father, but he could also lean on her when needed. My father appreciated her, loved her, and felt more secure around her.

[Page 147]

She was a good person and a good woman. She was always willing to help others. My mother was full of vigor and tried to teach each of the children an occupation. She taught me to think fast and make a decision without hesitating. She said we should always try, otherwise, we would lose in advance.

Both of my parents were enslaved to work. They worked hard and sustained their family with dignity. They never complained and did not carry any resentment in their hearts. They only had their wishes. My father prayed that he would be able to spend his last two years before his death to dedicate himself to studying the Torah and holy worship. My mother wished to become free from worrying about sustaining her family so that she could devote herself wholly to helping others. She did that with all her heart, soul, and might.

The year my mother wished for approached its end. The Germans bombed our city. Our house was destroyed, and my mother perished there.

We dug her body out of the ruins. We performed the "*Tahara*" [ritual purification] ourselves, carried her body on our shoulders to the cemetery, dug the grave with our own hands, and I said "*Kadish*" under a barrage of bullets.

My father moved to live with us. Times were harsh. People suffered real hunger. My wife invested all efforts to feed our family and some of the refuses we hosted. She performed this task with dignity and talent. From then on, she became the foundation and center of the surviving family.

My father, who during the Soviet conquest, dedicatedly collected money for the refugees, became a "*Yoshev Ohalim*" [Genesis 24:27] [a person who devotes most of his time to studying the Torah]. We held public prayers in my room. My father dedicated the rest of his time to studying the Torah.

Before the holiday of Shavu'ot, he fell ill, and his fever rose. When his situation worsened, he called my brother-in-law (my wife's brother). He told him: "I am going to die. Know that I consider that a big privilege, as it would prevent me from witnessing the troubles of the Jews." He said his confession… The two years my father asked for ended.

It was forbidden for Jews to go out to the street that day. Distinguished guests came to visit the Gestapo. Despite the prohibition, the people of "Khevra *Kadish*a," headed by Ginsburg, appeared, performed the "*Ta'hara*," put the body on their shoulders, and upon stepping out, they recited: "Justice will march before him [Psalms 85;14]." Twenty people attended the funeral. On the alley from Adamovka Street leading to the high school, we met face-to-face with the Nazi entourage. We stopped, and they also stopped. We waited, and they signaled us to move. We passed quietly, and they waited, showing respect to the dead. Unbelievable.

During the "*Shiv'a*," people consoled me with the words: "He was lucky and had a great privilege. He lived his life in honor, died honorably, and his funeral was honorable.

His manners and memory will always be our guiding light.

[Page 148]

My Family's Story

by Pnina Shaklai

Translated by Moshe Kutten

Edited by Jane S. Gabin

I feel a duty and the need to write about my family history before everything is erased from my memory. I am the youngest and the only one who survived out of my entire large family.

My Parents

My father, Ya'akov, son of Avraham-Volf Bauer from Monasterzyska, and my mother, Matilda, daughter of Leizer-Hirsh Glazer from the village Podshumlantze, married and created a family in that village where their four sons were born. My father felt like a prisoner among the Gentiles. He was worried that his sons would learn from them and follow their ways. My father had a mental need to be among Jews and educate his children in the spirit of Judaism.

My parents' first steps in the strange city with a large family without an economic basis or support were atrocious. My father was a proud man who refused to get aid, even from his mother. My parents worked hard day and night and earned bread in toil. They traded in milk products, which was hard labor, with meager profit. When my father was asked once whether it is honorable for an educated person to work in such a dishonorable job, he answered: "That there was no dishonorable or hard work when one needs to earn a living and educate children." Over time, he acquired his place among the city's honorable people as a public activist. He was one of the founders of the Hebrew school. Two more children were born to them, a son and a daughter – their only daughter.

Before the First World War, they settled down, put aside some money, and enjoyed the children. The strict education, the enormous effort to teach the children despite the financial difficulties, ingraining in them Jewish awareness, and the Zionist atmosphere at home bore fruits. My two eldest brothers were active in the Zionist movement from a young age. They disseminated the Hebrew word vigorously and were engaged among the learning and working youth. They organized the youth, conducted lectures, and taught them the Hebrew language. It seemed that my parents finally reached peaceful waters.

But that was not what fate wanted. Life led my parents on a winding route with ups and downs. A life of calm and peace but became, in an instant, a stormy life filled with worries and struggles. That began before the First World War broke out. The elder sons were taken by the Russians as hostages, and the young ones enlisted and sent to the fronts. Toward the end of the war, my young brother also enlisted. The economic situation was not easy either. The entire property was robbed overnight. There were days when we were hungry for a piece of bread, and my parents reduced the household expenses to a minimum. Among the rest of the adverse and destructive phenomena that accompanied the war, the hatred toward Jews – antisemitism peaked with the arrival of Haller's Army. My brother Moshe became a victim of that hatred when he was tried in a military court. They blamed him for preparing for a terror act. Miraculously, it ended well. That trial cost my parents a lot of money, health, and nerves. With the end of the war, life returned to normal. My parents doubled their work efforts and efficiency to restock and cover the war's losses. Three of my brothers established families and continued with their public work. My younger brother and I continued our studies.

[Page 149]

Then disaster struck. My brother, Khaim, passed away, and my father fell sick with pneumonia with some complications. He slowly recovered but did not totally recuperate. He did not have the vigor he had before but continued to manage his businesses. His memory remained strong until his last day.

My father passed away in 1933, and my mother continued to live for another five years.

On the image of my parents

My father was a strong person in body and soul. He was good-looking, with symmetric facial features, fiery eyes, a high forehead, dignified, pleasant manners, full of vigor, strong will and argumentative ability, and quick decision-making. He was an educated man, learned, and a man of letters. He was a Zionist who was born Zionist. He understood that the Jews must have their own language, culture, and tradition. He loved people, cared about others, and sought justice.

My father built a family, took care of it, earned a living for it, and received pleasure from every one of his children, even if he did not always approve of their ways. He dedicated substantial effort, time, energy, and money to his children's education. At that time, the youth was busy searching for new ways, and many failed at the beginning of their ways. My father understood that the soul of a child should not be split up, and the sacred should not be mixed with the secular. A Jewish child should first receive a Jewish education, and only after that can general studies be added. I can testify wholeheartedly that my father succeeded in that. All of his children remained Jews in their hearts and souls, proud and loyal to the Torah.

My mother was my father's right-hand person, a devoted helpmate in the truest meaning of the word. Without my mother's help, my father could not have achieved what he did - not at work or with the children's education. She worked as hard as him, and often longer hours, to feed us and complement our income during the days of hunger. She experienced atrocious days, but she never complained. She willingly took the burden of managing the household and the children's education. She was a delicate soul. In the relationship between my father and the children, she was the "mother" - arbitrator, defense attorney, and protector. Often, she absorbed my father's anger directed at one of the children. She tended to poor families, distributed charity, and secretly provided shelter to them her entire life.

[Page 150]

I Remember Shabbat at Home

by Rivka Tomarkin-Shapira

Translated by Moshe Kutten

Edited by Jane S. Gabin

The preparations for Shabbat in our home began as early as Wednesday. The candlesticks, Father's wine cup, and the rest of the Shabbat table's items were polished. Shopping was done at the market: fish, poultry, and other Shabbat products. Food preparation started on Thursdays at dawn. My friends from the "HaNoar Tzioni" ["The Zionist Youth"] and "HaShomer HaTzair" ["The Young Guard"] were already waiting outside to confirm whose home's *"Bobnik"* [cake] was the best. In any case, the amount of food and delicacies was enough for the family and friends and for providing aid to the needy families. My grandmother, Sosha *z"l*, was in charge of that. She visited every poor and needy family daily, at their home, the sick at the Jewish hospital, and even the Jewish prisoners in jail. She always carried baskets filled with Kosher food. It was one of my duties, and the duty of all my young cousins, to help her ferry the baskets.

On Thursday evening, everybody was tired but happy that the work week was behind them. The only thing left was to polish and decorate the home, check the clothing, and polish the shoes. That was done between Friday morning and noon. At noon, the table was already set, covered with a white tablecloth, with the Shabbat candlesticks on it, the wall candlesticks were hung, *Khallot* covered on the table, and so were the wine, my father's cup, and a special cup for my brother as well as two small *Khallot*. Everything was ready to welcome Shabbat.

Father used to come home on Friday at noon time. He traveled to the neighboring villages on his business, but on Fridays, he made sure, G-d forbid, not to travel too far. He was a Hasidic and pious man. Upon his arrival, the house took on the atmosphere of Sabbath. In the evening, the whole family waited patiently for the return of Father from the synagogue. Despite belonging to the youth movements, none of the children dared to be absent from the Sabbath table.

Father used to bring "guests" to the Sabbath table, and we used to ask ourselves who would be the guest for the day. What would the guest look like? Would he behave and eat properly at the Sabbath table? Would he be a nice person, young or old? In most cases, our guests were needy people. Father was able to select the guest only during the holidays. Father used to bring Jewish soldiers stationed in the city, who received a short break for praying and the holiday meal at the request of his daughters.

Accompanied by our guests, everybody sat at the table. Right after the Kiddush, we all burst into Shabbat chants. Luckily, my father, mother, and most children had pleasant voices. Sabbath singing continued throughout the entire meal, during the breaks between one dish to another. It ended only after the dessert.

That Sabbath atmosphere, with the candles and the beautiful chants, lives in my heart until today. It guides me toward my children's education and in recreating a similar atmosphere in my home.

[Page 151]

Sabbath chants filled the home during the entire Sabbath. Upon arriving home at noon from the synagogue, Father erupted into singing, aided by the children's chorus, and the singing continued during the meal. After the heavy "*Chulent*," Father used to rest a bit and return to the synagogue to enjoy the Torah Daily Study. We, the children, dispersed' some went to the youth movement's branches, and some to the fields or forest. Mother would sometimes join us on a hike. When the time came to say farewell to the Sabbath, the entire family would gather at home again. Grandmother would sometimes come to us to listen to the [Sabbath conclusion] *Havdalah* blessing chanted by Father.

For many, their childhood was a happy period. It is a pity that the period had passed, and along with it, my father Mordekhai Leib, my mother Mina, my sisters Ruzha, Rakhel, and Shanka, and my young brother Hersh. May their memory be blessed.

Memories from my Parents' Home

by Tzipora Rozner

Translated by Moshe Kutten

Edited by Jane S. Gabin

The Fefer family was one of the ten families in the village of Wiezhbow in the Brzezany district. I was born in that village and spent my childhood and youth there in happiness and joy due to the warm family atmosphere that prevailed in my parent's home, and not the least thanks to the natural beauty and the view of the village and its surroundings. All the Jewish families worked in commerce and were quite successful. Most of the village's residents were Ukrainians who respected the Jews and trusted them, as the Jews provided them with all necessities. However, over time, with the growth of antisemitism in Poland, that attitude worsened, and the hatred toward the Jews intensified until it culminated with horrific pogroms against the Jews by the Ukrainians.

My father was an enthusiastic Zionist, and he educated us in the spirit of the love of Eretz Israel (We were five siblings – three sons and two daughters). My brother Moshe was the first to make *Aliyah* to Eretz Israel, and his letters served as a source of encouragement to the family in times of trouble when we began to suffer from our Ukrainian neighbors. Later on, my younger brother, Meir, went to Argentina to avoid recruitment to the Polish army. Many of the village's Jewish Jews did the same when they reached recruitment age (21).

[Page 152]

The economic situation of the village's Jews worsened during those years. The Gentiles continued to buy from the Jews but did not pay cash. As their debts grew –; so did their hatred. There were cases of theft and even cases of arson. We lost our entire property after a few cases of arson and robberies at my father's store, grain warehouse, and cow shed. The Ukrainians snitched on us to the authorities that we set fire to our property to claim insurance on a loss of property. The authorities always trusted the Gentiles, and justice was always on their side. Despite the suffering and troubles, life continued, and there was no lack of happiness, joy, and light.

I will not forget the wedding party of my sister. The entire crowd danced to the tunes of the cheerful "*Klei-Zmerim*" [musical band], and in the middle, my grandmother, a woman of about 100 years old. The Sabbaths and holidays were full of light. We hosted guests, refreshments and pastries were served, and singing and giddy cheers were heard.

All the family members hoped and wished to make *Aliyah*. With that hope in our hearts, we found the strength to live and overcome the hatred that enveloped us and choked us with a belt of pogroms and murders. The central pillar of the family was obviously my father, who was endowed with unique features and always knew how to influence the people around him with the goodness of his heart and his belief in humans and their actions. He was always generous. Even when we had already experienced shortages, he provided charity to the needy. I will not forget the wagons filled with food products (potatoes, oil, geese, raisins, and more) that left our yard on Passover Eves for distribution among the village's poor.

I made *Aliyah* in 1937 by invitation of my brother Moshe, who had already resided there, and with the great support of my younger brother Khaim. I did not know what was waiting for me in Eretz Israel. Since I was only 15 years old, I have been afraid of long trips and unknown land. The family members said farewell to me with mixed feelings, but we were careful not to cry. We all believed that we would meet again in Eretz Israel. But these were vain hopes because, in the meantime, the Second World War broke out. Our village passed first to the hands of the Soviets and later to the hands of the Germans!

I heard from a few survivors who arrived in Israel after the Holocaust about the tragic fate of my brother Khaim and my parents. They were cruelly murdered by their Ukrainian neighbors. I could not find any details about the fate of my sister and her family. They undoubtedly perished similarly. That was how these people, who were so dear to me - honest people who always believed that nobody would hurt them because they never hurt anybody, ended their lives.

[Page 153]

In Memory of My Father, Yossef Kalman, the Pioneer

by Israel Karmel (Kalman)

Translated by Moshe Kutten

Edited by Jane S. Gabin

From my father, Yosef-Tzvi *z"l*, son of Israel, son of Arye, I heard only a little about Brzezany. He told me about his town, not with longing but with respect. I heard more about Brzezany from my aunt, my father's sister and her husband, Shifra, and Ozer Rot *z"l*. In many aspects, my father was considered the "son of the land," and his years before his *Aliyah* were years of *Hakhshara* [preparation and training] for it.

My father was born in Brzezany in 1899 and received a traditional education. However, he paved his own route early at a young age. He abandoned religion, adhered to Zionist ideas, and prepared to study a profession. During the First World War, he studied mechanics at a vocational school in Vienna and worked for a Jewish wine cellar owner there. During a certain period, he hid to avoid being recruited into the army. He made *Aliyah* in 1920 with the first group of pioneers from the city. He joined the "Gdud HaAvodah" ["Work Battalion"] (see the article "First Group Makes *Aliyah*," page 49]. As part of it, he was among the founders of kibbutz Tel-Yosef. As a member of the "Work Battalion," he enlisted to work at the British military camp, aiming to take over the work from the Egyptian workers. Later, he moved to Jerusalem and worked in various jobs, mostly in quarrying (see the cover page for the Zionist Movement, page 39). He studied to be an electrician in the evenings at Lemel School. After completing the course (approximately in 1927), he became the electrician and generator operator at the Fast Hotel near the Jaffa Gate. Based on a recommendation from his friend and townsman, Benyamin Te'eni, my father moved to Haifa to work at the refinery, which began operating at that time. He married my mother and settled in the German Colony in Haifa. In 1937, my parents moved to Kiryat Motzkin. In 1938/9, my parents traveled to France for an operation on my mother and returned to Israel just before the Second World War.

The prolonged illness of my mother left its mark on my father's and family life. He moved to work in the water supply operation of Kiryat Motzkin municipality to be close to home. He worked on water wells' machinery and the maintenance of the pipes in the entire town. That was hard work that required working in shifts and even on Saturdays. The hard work and the economic distress did not lessen the emotional involvement in everything that happened in the country, the joy about achievements, worrying about the future, and the willingness to get involved in the national missions when needed. My father loved craftsmanship and respected manual work. Among all the Israeli public shortcomings, he was sorry to witness the decline in the value of work in our lives. It was symbolic that he passed away at my brother Arye's workshop (may he live long).

May the memory of my father be blessed.

[Page 155]

Figures and Personalities

אישים
ודמויות

[Page 156]

Rabbi Shalom Mordechai Hacohen Schwadron of Blessed Memory

by Dr. E. Shaklai

Based on the book by Rabbi Y. Bromberg

Translated by Moshe Kutten

Edited by Jane S. Gabin

The Schwadron family was known as one of the prominent families in Zolokhiv. The father of Rabbi Shalom-Mordekhai, Moshe, who was called R' Moshe Biyanover, was a scholar and a wealthy merchant, a recognized knowledgeable and learned man from among the followers of the *Tzaddik* Rabbi Meir'el of Przemysl [Pshemishell]. He used to set aside a tenth of his profits to charity. R' Shalom Mordekhai Hakohen grew up In that atmosphere of Torah and good manners.

He was considered a prodigy from childhood and a great unrelenting learner. He was a frequent visitor at the courts of *Admo"rim* and *Tzaddikim* [righteous]. The influence of those visits was considerable and became apparent in all his actions throughout his life. A story of the Rabbi testifies to that: He once fell seriously sick, and in his dream, he saw and heard how they judge him in the court of heaven whether to life or G-d forbid … and then one of the *Tzaddikim* said: "We need that youngster; he is destined to do great things for the nation of Israel on earth." Years later, he visited the Admo"r from Raizyn. Shalom Mordekhai recognized him as the advocate he dreamed about at the court of heaven!

He received his rabbinic ordination from some of the great generational rabbis at the young age of 15. The first rabbi to ordain him was Rabbi Shlomo Kluger from Brody. He married that year and remained with his father-in-law, who freed him from worrying about his livelihood, thus allowing him to continue his studies of the Torah. R' Shalom Mordekhai did not want to earn his living using religious knowledge and preferred to be a merchant. His parents, too, did not want him to become a rabbi. Therefore, he tried to be a merchant but was not successful. In 1866, he lost most of his wealth. That tipped the scales, and having no other choice, he agreed to serve as a rabbi in one of the cities. Over the years, he served as a rabbi in the cities of Potok, Yazlovets, and Buchach.

In 5642 [1881/2], emissaries from Brzezany came to R' Shalom Mordekhai to ask him to move to our city. He was happy with the offer and decided to accept it. As a great Hasid, he believed in the generation of *Tzaddikim* and in "*Urim and Thummim*[1]." He, therefore, decided to seek advice from both sources. He used to open the Bible, and the first words he read in the book directed his actions. He made his decision that time as well.

When he opened the Bible, he encountered the verse: "… and will teach you what to do" [Exodus 4:15]. He also received a rabbinical agreement [no rabbi's name is mentioned]. Based on that, he decided to accept the rabbinical position offer wholeheartedly.

He served as a rabbi in Brzezany for thirty years despite being offered more respected positions with higher salaries elsewhere. When they turned to him from the city of Kolomyy and a few years later from America, he refused to accept the offers and preferred to stay in Brzezany.

During those years, he acquired fame in the world. His was active well beyond the city limits. From all corners of the world, people turned to the Rabbi with questions about Jewish law, slaughtering, accreditation, Agunah dispensation [Heter], and more. He spent days and nights withstanding the pressure, dedicatedly and patiently investigating and finding the correct answers (he once received 115 letters in a single week). He tried to answer all the letters he had received in the shortest time.

[Page 157]

Gaon Rabbi Shalom Mordekhai Hacohen Schwadron

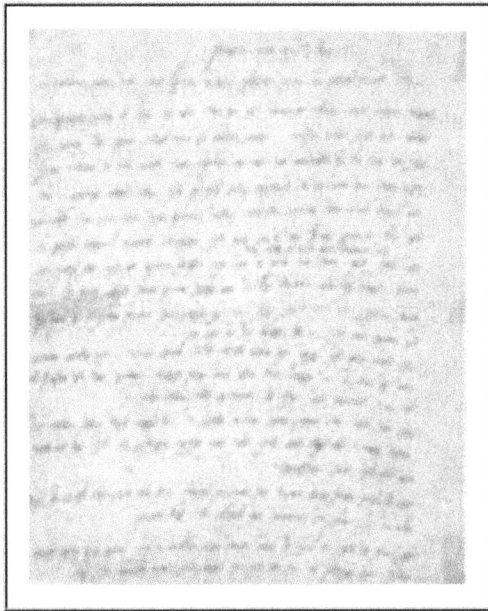

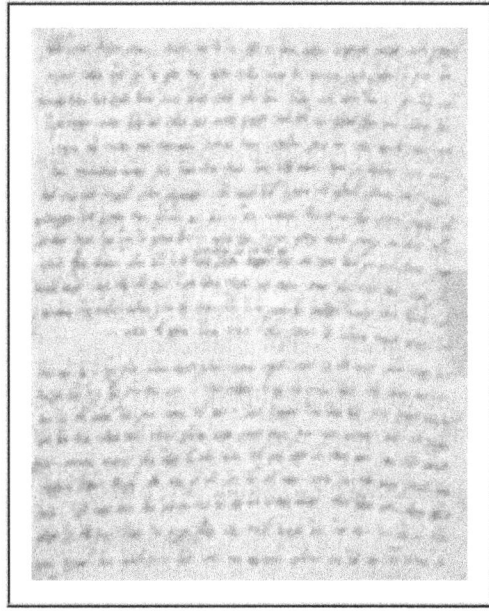

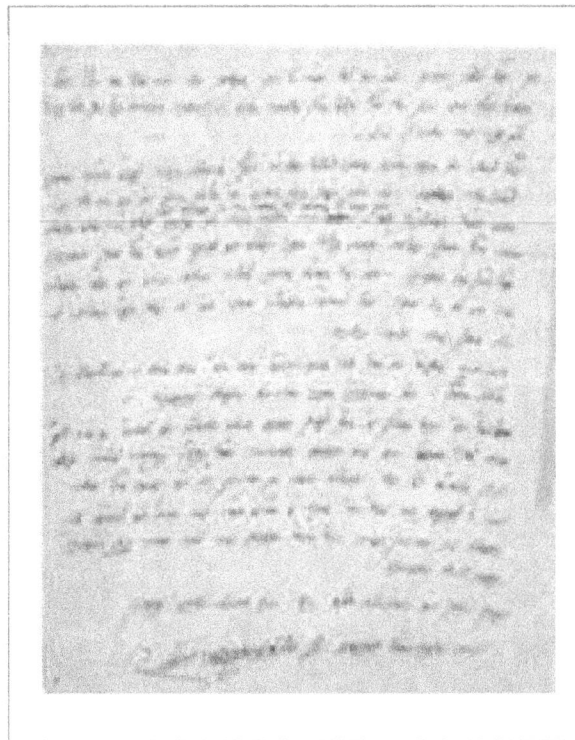

Return letter written by MAHARSHA"M

[Page 158]

One of the Rabbi's admirers and a close friend, R' Fishel Bomze, told me a story about such an answer. "I once reminded the Rabbi about a certain question. The Rabbi sat down and wrote an answer on 8 full pages, with references to support it. When he finished, he said: 'Listen, my son, you would probably go out of here and tell everybody that the Rabbi is a genius. So, for your information, I received a similar inquiry a few weeks ago. During the last few weeks, I read, researched, and clarified with others until I arrived at that answer. This is the fruit of several weeks of work."

He was considered an outstanding "answerer," one in a generation, second only to Rabbi Yosef Shaul Nathanson. Rabbi Nathanson said about him when he knew him and his knowledge: "I do not see, in our generation, a smarter scholar than him."

The wide world knew him from the books he wrote. His writings are considered of great importance by the scholars. I will mention some of them here:

- "Mishpat Shalom M'Shulkhan Arukh," 1871

- "Mishpat Shalom about 'Khoshen Mishpat'"

- "Responsa MAHARSHA"M " [10 volumes]

- "Analysis and Innovations on Shulkhan Arukh, Permits and Prohibitions

- "Darkei Shalom," 1929

- "MAHARSHA"M's "Analysis of the Mishnah," 1932

The following publications received much publicity:

- "Da'at Torah," 1891, about slaughtering laws

- "Gilui Da'at" about signs 61 – 69 of "Yoreh De'ah" and the Jewish laws of *Terefah*

These publications attracted a lot of attention. However, some great rabbis came out against it due to his tendency to ease in his rulings as much as possible.

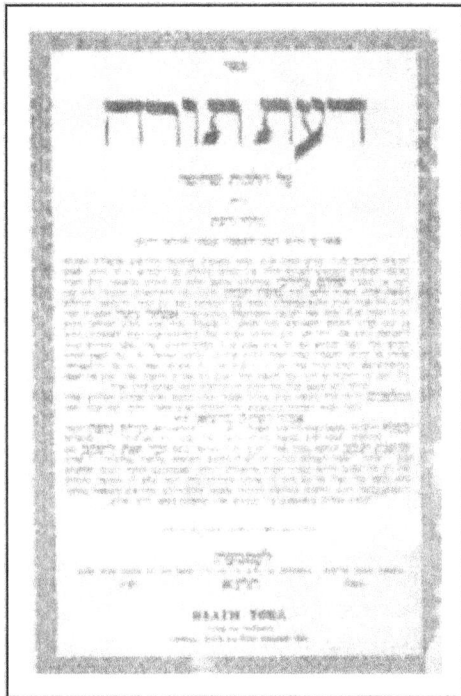

The cover of the book (4th volume) Responsa
MAHARSHA"M"

The cover of the book "Da'at Torah

[Page 159]

MAHARSHA"M's return postcard top Cairo

The following is another story I heard from Bomze. A question was asked of the Rabbi on Passover Eve about a turkey belonging to a poor Jew who fattened the bird a long time, especially for Passover. R' Shalom Mordekhai went into his room, immersed himself in books, lingered there for a long time, and finally made his decision: "There are some who claim that the turkey is *Terefah*, others claim that it is 'Kosher.' After much consideration, I decided to join the 'Kosher' *Posek*." The MAHARSHA"M tried his best to make it easy for people.

He was a knowledgeable person and also an independent and original researcher. He was an exceptional and eloquent preacher, leaving an enormous impression on his listeners. His words penetrated the heart and were never forgotten. He was also a great scholar in the Jewish *Aggadah*.

He was an exemplary rabbi and leader of the congregation in his pleasant manners and educational personality. He was careful not to cause pain to anybody and was sensitive to people's honors. When people came to ask him a question or seek advice (many came to him to hear his opinion about their personal affairs), he never had the person wait for an answer. He treated people with love and peace, even if they were not religious.

The MAHARSHA"M was also a public activist. He made great efforts in public affairs. He always found time to study, research, and express his opinion about crucial public issues. During all his years, he made an effort to improve education methods, mainly in elementary education in the *Khedders*. He tried to prepare a uniform multifaced curriculum and invited Dr. Yosef Zelinger, a known Haredi educator, for that purpose. However, he was forced to abandon his plan due to the resistance of Haredi circles.

MAHARSHA"M Hacohen established a Yeshiva in Brzezany by the name "Tushia" [Resourcefulness]. Many young, sharp, and knowledgeable scholars came from there and became rabbis in many towns throughout Galitsia and beyond. It was easy for rabbis who received their rabbinical certification from Rabbi R' Shalom Mordekhai Hacohen to find a rabbinical position. R' Shalom Mordekhai's certification was the best reference.

[Page 160]

MAHARSHA"M participated in rabbinical conferences and expressed his decisive opinion, which was approved by everybody. That's what happened in the gathering that took place in Lviv on the matter of the financial settlement of Rabbi Meir Ba'al Hanes's Kupa [fund]. There were disagreements and disputes, and people feared that they would lead to a crisis and rip. To avoid such a catastrophe, a man with a strong character and influence had to be found as the chairman of the gathering. They elected MAHARSHA"M Hacohen unanimously to that role, and he succeeded in managing the conference with a strong hand, good taste, and knowledge to everyone's satisfaction and brought it to a successful end.

[Author] Moshe Tzinovitz wrote about MAHARSHA"M in an article: "His behavior in his daily relations is without bias. Concerning Torah-based verdicts – the verdict for the poor is the same as for the rich. He never uses anybody. He always serves himself for as long as he can without relying on others. He is simple and humble in his behavior and does not impose his authority on others. He loves people and nature. Every morning he comes out his door and spreads seeds for birds and other animals." People, even those who were not his allies, knew and respected him. It was known that Gentiles who had a dispute with a Jew came to litigate in front of the Rabbi. He was also respected by the district court judges who consulted with him on complicated cases. He knew foreign languages (he knew German fluently)."

His home served as a central meeting house, open to all, to spiritual and Torah people alike who came to listen to him and learn Torah from him. He had the strength and will to overcome life's difficulties. He was amazingly organized. He arranged fixed working hours for himself and managed his lifestyle according to that arrangement. His schedule included learning Gemara, Shulkhan Arukh, and other *Poskim* [deciders]. He never missed his daily lessons, which contained 25 Bible chapters, one Mishna tractate, and 18 Gemera pages.

MAHARSHA"M was born in 5595 (1835) and died in 5671 (1911).

During his fruitful years, he became famous throughout the world. He acquired the name of a brilliant "answerer" and *Posek* greater than his generation's greats.

In the wide world, he was known as MAHARSHA"M Hacohen – the Rabbi from Brzezany.

Bibliography:

- A. Y. Bromberg – Sinai – 1952/1953, 32, pp. 295 – 299
- A. Feuchtwanger, "Khayei Yeshirim," 1965, pp. 94 – 97
- Encyclopedia Judaica, Volume 14, pp. 1484 – 1485.

The cover page of MAHARSHA"M's book, "Gilui Da'at"

Translator's Note:

1. According to the Avnion Dictionary [https://www.milononline.net] the stones in the high priest's breastplate - by which he knew the answer to the questions asked of God during important decisions; it can also be used as a nickname for someone who is trusted without a doubt - a person or an idea.

[Page 161]

Brzezany's Rabbis

by Rabbi Meir Wonder

Translated by Moshe Kutten

Edited by Jane S. Gabin

The importance of Brzezany was much beyond its geographical size. A place of honor was reserved for the city in the Torah world due to several phenomena that characterize it over other locations:

High-level witted learners concentrated in the city. Its rabbis were exalted geniuses, and many moved from it to the rabbinic position in Lviv or other Torah cities. From the early days, the city contained a higher level of Yeshivas for studying the *Seder Kodashim*[1], which was not studied much in those days. The rabbinical position was held for hundreds of years until the Holocaust by one family – Halperin. More than twenty of Brzezany's rabbis came out of that family, one after the other.

The fog is still substantial in arranging the rabbis in a correct chronological order, particularly in the early periods. We listed them more or less in the proper order based on the information available to us:

Rabbi Moshe Mordekhai Hacohen

He was the son of Rabbi Nathan Neteh *AB"D* [Head of the Rabbinical Court] of Ostroh [Ostraha]. He served as the *AB"D* in Brzezany and R" M [Rabbi who teaches at the Yeshiva]. The fruits of his innovations in his teachings at the Yeshiva were published in the book "Tzon Kedoshim," which he published together with Rabbi Avraham-Khaim Schorr. In the introduction, he writes about his Yeshiva: "We gathered great and extremely sharp people, and taught them the entire *Seder*." He moved to become the head of the Yeshiva in Lviv and died there on 21 Tishrei 5391 (1630).

Rabbi Moshe, son of Rabbi Avraham

He moved from Brzezany to serve as the *AB"D* in Lviv, where he died on 29 Av 5424 (1664). Grand praises were etched on his gravestone.

Rabbi Mordekhai Z"K from Premishle

He was the son of Rabbi Meir, *AB"D* Lviv who died in 1654, and the son-in-law of Rabbi Menakhem-Mendel Margaliot, *AB"D* Peremyshliany [Premishleh].

Rabbi Tzvi Hirsh [Kharif]

He was the son of Rabbi Khaim, the rabbi in Kolomyya (died in 1673), the son of Rabbi [Yehoshua-Heshil Kharif, the author of the book] "Meginei Shlomo." From Brzezany, rabbi Tzvi-Hirsh moved to become the rabbi in Drohobitz, Brody, and Lisky.

Rabbi Yitzkhak BABa"D

He was the son of Rabbi Yisaskhar Dov-Berish, an activist and leader of the Krakow community who was also called Krakover after his native city. Rabbi Yitzkhak moved from Brzezany to be the rabbi in Brody, where he died on 4 Tishrei 5465 [1704].

[Page 162]

Rabbi Menakhem Mendel son of Rabbi Asher [Potoker]

He was called Potoker, in tribute to his native city. His title is mentioned in his consent to the book "Dat Kutiel" in 5456 (1696). He was an *AB"D* and *Posek* in Brzezany. He died in Lviv on 3 Tevet 5477 [1716].

Rabbi Tuvia-Yekhiel-Mikhel Halperin

The first of Brzezany's rabbis from the Halperin family, who was known by that surname. His grandson, Rabbi Ya'akov-Shlomo Halperin, wrote in a pamphlet depicting the family tree of the family: "his name is the only information I could decipher." According to Rabbi Ya'akov-Shlomo, the family held the rabbinical position in Brzezany for many generations. He claimed that the first rabbi was the son of the Viennese Minister Rabbi Shimshon Wertheimer, who settled in Brzezany after he was expelled from Vienna. Rabbi Israel, *AB"D* Svirzh, Lviv, and Rzeszów [Reisha]. Rabbi Israel was the son of R' Avraham, *AB"D*, Kovel,

Rabbi Tuvia-Yekhiel-Mikhel was the son of and descendant of Rabbi Elkhanan, author of *Tosafot* [Talmud commentaries], and the Patriarch of the Halperin family. The latter was the son of Rabbi Yitzkhak, who was the son of Rabbi Shmuel from Vitry, who was the son of Rabbi Simkha Halperin, the author of "*Makhzor* Vitry[2]" and son of Rabbi Shmuel Halperin.

He was the son-in-law of Rabbi Yoel, *AB"D* Zavaliv (Zvolov) [could not be verified mk], and was also related to R' Leibush [?] and MAHARSHA" L [Rabbi Shlomo Luria (1510-1573)]. He served as Brzezany's rabbi for 52 years, from 5448 (1688) until his death on 21 Adar 5500 (1740).

[Rabbi] Yosef Khanina Halperin

He was the son of R' Tuvia. Some people spell his name as Khanania. He was born approximately in 5450 (1689/1690) and died on 22 Iyar 5524 [1764] (some say that he died on 11 Nisan 5530 (1770)).

Rabbi Yekhiel-Mikhel Halperin

He was the son of Rabbi Khanina. He was Berzezany's Rabbi and later *AB"D* of Skalat until he died in 5516 (1756). It was no wonder he served as a rabbi in Brzezany during his father's reign. It was a common practice that the local rabbi would have his son join as a "young rabbi" to assist him. In addition, we find in the literature that in addition to the Brzezany's rabbi, other rabbis served separately as the district rabbis.

Rabbi Avraham-Zerakh-Arye-Yehuda-Leib Halperin

He was the son of Rabbi Khanina, listed above. There is a certificate from 5544 (1784) where he is a signatory along with the members of his court. His consents appear in various books, published until 5570 (1809/10). He died on Saturday, 16 Tevet 5568 (1808).

Rabbi Khanina-Yosef Halperin

He was the son of Rabbi Avraham Zerakh. Before his rabbinical position in Brzezany, he was a rabbi in Skivisk [?]. In Brzezany, he served as the district rabbi. He corresponded in length about the *Halakha* with [Rabbi Efraim Zalman Margolioth, author of] "Beit Efraim." His consent from 5565 (1805) is known. He was buried in Lubartow.

Rabbi Tuvia-Yekhiel-Mikhel

The son of Rabbi Avraham Zerkah. His brother was Rabbi Elkhanan *AB"D* Peremyshlyany [Rabbi Khanina Yosef Halperin was also his brother]. He died on 20 Shvat5579 (1819).

[Page 163]

Rabbi Dov – Berish Halperin

He was the son of [Rabbi] Avraham-Moshe, *AB"D* Rohatyn, the son of Rabbi Tuvia. His sons-in-law were learned: Rabbi Arye Leibush, the father of Rabbi Yosef-Shaul Nathanzon, and Rabbi Tzvi-Hirsh Burstein, the father of Rabbi Pinkhas of Siret. One of his consents appeared in a book published in 5570 [1809/10]. He died in 13 Adar 5601 (1841).

R' Tzvi-Hirsh Halperin

He was the son of R' Tuvia. He was one of the students of "The Seer from Lublin" [Rabbi Ya'akov-Yitzkhak Halevi Horwitz]. He died on 27 Nisan 5588 (1828).

Rabbi Naftali Hertz Halperin

He was the son of R' Tuvia. The sources differ on whether he was the 15th or the 18th link in the Halperin rabbinical dynasty. He corresponded about the *Halakha* with one of the greatest Hasidic scholars of the generation - the author of the book "HaShoel Ve'HaMeshiv" [Asker and Answerer" by Rabbi Yosef-Shaul Nathanson].

After his death, a storm erupted about who would inherit his rabbinic seat. Written and verbal testimonies about that storm have been preserved until today. The author of the family tree mentioned above writes: "The rabbinical seat in the name only is not whole, since somebody from outside our family would be afraid to approach it." The Hasidic leaders harnessed themselves to the fight for electing the son of the deceased. The correspondence between them and the city's opponents is fascinating.

Rabbi Meshulam-Shraga-Feibush Halperin

He was the son of Rabbi Naftali. He married Khana, the daughter of Rabbi Asher Yeshaya Rubin. He was the son-in-law and the substitute of Rabbi Naftali [Tzvi] of Rupshitz. The community leadership refused to accept him as a rabbi since they wanted a Torah *Gaon* [genius], rather than a Hasidic *Admo"r* [honorific given to an outstanding Hasidic rabbi - rebbe]. It was written in his family tree that: "Although he did reach the teaching level of his ancestors, we were somewhat willing not to transfer the position to somebody outside of the family." His generation's *Tzadikim* fought for him unsuccessfully, and Rabbi Khaim [Halberstam] of Sanz promised that in the end, the rabbinic position would be returned to the Halperin family, as indeed happened. Rabbi Meshulam passed away in 19 Elul 5634 (1874). He became known for his book "Sfat Emet" [The Language of Truth].

R' Yosef Shaul Nathanson

He was the son of Rabbi Aryeh Leibush Nathanson. He was born in 5571 (1810) in Brzezany. In 17 Shvat 5617 (1857), he was nominated to be the *AB"D* in Lviv. He was a Torah great and was called by the name of his book,"HaShoel Ve'HaMeshiv" [The Asker and Answerer] (see an article in this book about the Nathanson family by Dr. Shaklai - page 170).

Rabbi Shlomo Kluger

He was a preacher, Rabbi, *AB"D* in Brody, and the author of 375 books. In 5605 (1845) he accepted the offer to be the rabbi in Brzezany. However, immediately upon his arrival, he became mortally ill. He attributed that to Rabbi Meir of Peremyshliany [Premishlian]'s objection to the move. He took it upon himself to return immediately to Brody when he recovered. Sh"Y Agnon says that the head of Brzezany's community forgave him for the downpayment they gave him, and he never returned.

[Page 164]

Rabbi Ze'ev Wolf Ya'akov Grizman

He was born in Rzeszow [Reisha] in 5600 (1840) to his father, Rabbi Shmuel, son of Rabbi Israel Ka"tz of Wielkie Oczy [Vilkutch]. He resided in Brzezany. He authored the book "Otzar Nekhmad" printed in Przemysl [Pshemishel] in 5636 (1875/6). He died in 5650 (1890) (see *Encyclopedia of Khakhmei Galitsia*, page 751).

Rabbi Yitzkhak Shemelkis

He was the son of Rabbi Khaim-Shmuel. He was called to be the Rabbi in Brzezany in about 5618 (1858) from his position at Zhuravno [Zuravna] after the city was without a rabbi for several years. In Brzezany, he served as the district rabbi for about 11 years. From there, he moved to Przemysl [Pshemishel] in 5629 (1869), where he was the rabbi for 24 years.

In 5653 (1893), he was elected as the rabbi of Lviv and served there until he died in 5666 (1906). He was considered a genius already when he served in Brzezany. He became a world-recognized expert, and Jews turned to him from the many corners of the Jewish world. A selection of the questions and his answers were published in four volumes while he was still alive. That selection was named "Beit Yitzkhak" [Yitzkhak's home], by which Rabbi Yitzkhak Shmelkis is known until today.

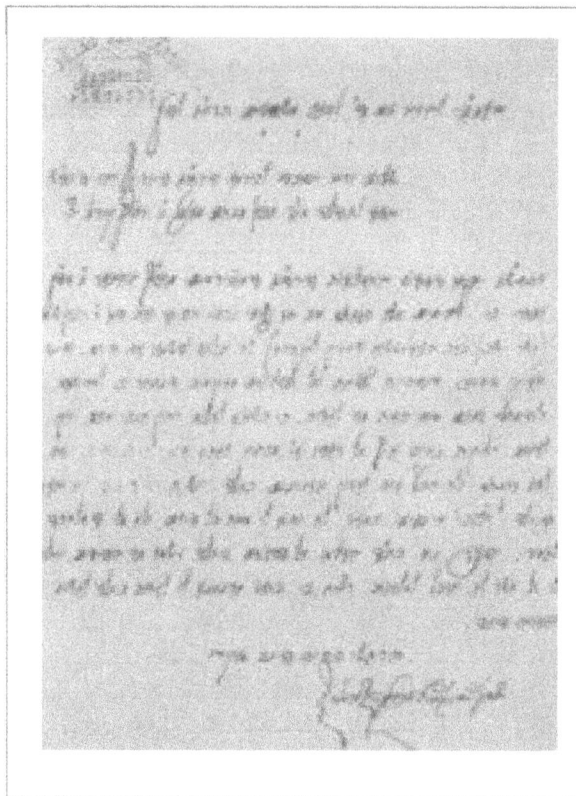

A letter of Rabbi Yitzkhak Shmelkis

Rabbi David Meir Feder

He is considered one of the Torah greats of his generation. He was the author of the book "SHU" T HaRaDa" M" [Responsa by the RaDa" M]. He was a follower of the HaSaraf [burning angle] from Sterlisk [Rabbi Uri from Sterlisk] and Rabbi from Olesk [Alesk] [Rabbi Khanoch Henich Dov Mayer?]. He previously served as the rabbi in Svirzh. Based on the recommendation by Rabbi Shlomo Kluger, he was appointed as a religious judge and *AB"D*. As there was no rabbi in the city at that time, he fulfilled that role as well, although he was not officially nominated. He lived in Przemysl [Pshemishel] in his old age, where he died in 5658 (1898).

Rabbi Shalom Mordekhai Hacohen Shvadron

He was known around the Jewish world as the MAHARSHA"M. He was a rabbi in Brzezany for more than 30 years (from 5640 (1879/80) until his death in 5671 (1911)). He established the Yeshiva "Da'at Torah' in Brzezany and brought over superior rabbis-teachers. After his death, his sons-in-law had some pretensions to be nominated to replace him. However, since none of them was at his level, the rabbinical position returned to the Halperin family.

Rabbi Moshe-Israel Feldman

He married the daughter of Rabbi Yitzkhak, the son of the MAHARSHA"M. He was nominated to be the *AB"D* in Brzezany. When he failed to be elected to the rabbinical position there, he moved to Dragomiresti [Dragmiresht] and became a rabbi there.

Rabbi Shimon Baba"d

He was the son of Rabbi Moshe, *AB"D* Mikulintsy [Mikolinitz]. He married Leah, the daughter of the MAHARSHA"M. He was a rabbi in Yanov (near Terebovlya [Trembowla]) for many years. In 5669 [1908/9], he was nominated as rabbi of Bozanov[?] and was named after the town since. After his father died, he settled in Brzezany and served as the *AB"D* until his death in 5695 (1935).

Rabbi Uri Halevi Eisen

He served as a rabbi in Strettin and Svirzh. He settled in Brzezany, hoping to be elected to become the rabbi there, replacing the MAHARSHA"M. When his hope was dashed, he moved to Bobrka [Bobrik] (in 1920), where he died on 22 Tevet 5696 [1936]. His wife and children perished in Belzec, may G-d avenge their blood (Bobrik Yizkor book page 33[3]).

Rabbi Uri Halevi Eisen

[Page 165]

Rabbi David Zilber

He was a rabbinical court judge during the period before the First World War and after it.

Rabbi Avraham-Zerakh-Aryeh [Halperin]

He was the son of [Rabbi] Meshulam Shraga. He was born (approximately) in 5608 (1847/8). He was an *Admo"r* in Brzezany for decades. He is known for his book "Imrei Yehuda." After the death of the MAHARSHA"M, the rabbinical position returned to him [as a member of the Halperin family]. He also groomed his son to become the rabbi after him. After the First World War, he settled in Lviv, where he died on 10 Adar A, 5689 (1929), and was buried in Brzezany, where his son Rabbi Aharon [Halperin] resided.

Rabbi Meshulam Feibush (Zeida) Halperin

He was the son of Rabbi Avraham-Zerakh. He was born in 5775 and served as a rabbi in Khododriv [Khodorov] replacing his father-in-law Rabbi Pinkhas [Khodorov] when he was called by his father to serve as a rabbi in Brzezany. After his father's death, he became the *Admo"r* for the Hasids, replacing his father. He served as a rabbi together with his son Rabbi Khaim [Halperin] until the Nazi conquest. In 5703 (1942) he escaped to the neighboring town – Kozova, and that's where he perished. May G-d avenge his blood.

Rabbi Uri Halevi Eisen

Rabbi Khaim Halperin

He was the son of rabbi Meshulam-Shraga (Zeida). He was born in Brzezany and served as a rabbi in the city with his father. Had a gentle soul and possessed a general education. He was active in charity associations. He was the last link in the dynasty of the Halperin rabbis that served in Brzezany. He perished with a large group of the city's residents in the quarries near the village of Olkhovitz [Vilkhovets?] a few days after Yom Kippur, 5702 (1941).

Rabbi Khaim Halperin

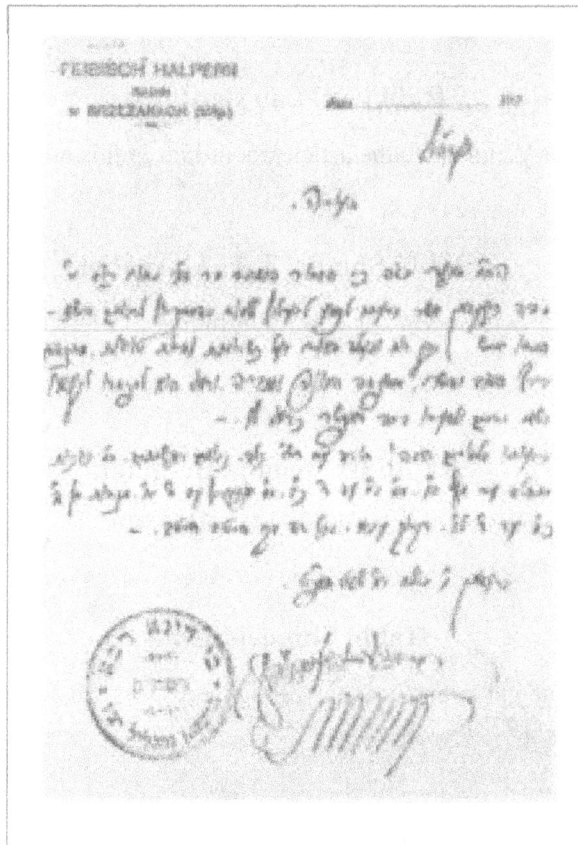

A recommendation letter
by Rabbi Shraga Feibush Halperin

[Page 166]

Rabbi Israel son of Rabbi Pinkhas Brandwein

He was born in Brzezany in 5635 [1874/5] to his father, the Admo" r from Stratyn, and replaced him there. He perished on Yom Kippur 5702 (1941) along with his daughter and his son, Rabbi Yehuda Tzvi and his children. May G-d avenge their blood.

Rabbi Pinkhas son of Ya'akov-Yosef Brandwein

He was the son of Ya'akov-Yosef, the grandson of Rabbi Mordekhai from Kremenets, the son of [Rabbi Yekhiel Mikel Rabinowitz], the maggid from Zolokhiv [Zlotzov]. He was called the Admor" r from Stratyn in Brzezany. He made *Aliya* in 5662 [1901/2], died in Eretz Israel, and was buried on the Mount of Olives on 27 Kislev 5676 [1915].

The following is a list of some of the prominent people who were born in Brzezany and moved to work in other places.

Rabbi Aharon son of Yehuda [Halevi]

Moved to Alksin [Alksinitz] and Brody (see the article about him in this book, page 172).

Rabbi Dr. Lau Berdowitz

The rabbi of Meiddling near Vienna (see the article about him in this book (page 179).

Rabbi Shmuel Tzvi Margaliot

He was the head of the *Beit HaMidrash* for education rabbis in Florence (see the article in the book, page 178)

Rabbi Dr. Yehuda Bergman

He was the rabbi of Berlin (see the article in this book, page 180)

Rabbi Shmuel Shapira

He was *Domet"z* [rabbinical judge and teacher of righteousness] in Dobromyl and *AB"D* Zolochive [Zlotzov] until he died in 5688 (1928).

Rabbi Yehuda-Leibaleh Roze'

He was the rabbi of Brzezany [natives] in Brooklyn, New York (see article in this book, page 181).

Rabbi Yehoshua Widerker

The leading student of the MAHARSHA"M in Brzezany. He was the rabbi in Neustadt [possibly the city called Prudnik, Poland], and from 5679 (1918/19), *AB"D* of Przemysl [Pshemishel] until he perished in the Holocaust.

R' Meir - *Sofer Sta"m*

It was known, in the middle of the 19th century, about R' Meir, a *Sofer Sta"m* [a person who writes Torah scrolls, tefillin, mezuzahs, and scrolls], a learned scholar and G-d fearing person in Brzezany who left his mark in the responsa literature.

Rabbi Yoel Ginsburg

He was born in Zhovkva [Zholkva, Zolkiew] to his father, the rabbi of Khodorov. In his youth, he served as the head of the Yeshiva of the MAHARSHA"M in Brzezany. He later served as the rabbi of Burshtyn. He was shot by the Germans in Bukachivtsi [Bokshevits]. May G-d avenge his blood.

[Page 167]

Rabbi Pinkhas-Moshe Burstein

He was born in Brzezany on 18 Kheshvan 5589 (1828) to his father, Rabbi Tzvi-Hirsh, and his mother, Vitel, the daughter of Rabbi Dov Halperin. He lived in Brzezany for many years and gradually became a more prominent Torah figure. He was the cousin of the author of the book "HaShoel Ve'HaMeshiv" [The Asker and Answerer," by Rabbi Yosef-Shaul Nathanson] from the city of Siret in Bukovina ("Encyclopedia shel Khakhmei Galitsia," page 471)

R' Joel Halperin

Rabbi Menakhem-Mendel Halperin

The son of Rabbi Meshulam (grandson of Rabbi Naftali Hertz). He was known to many by the name of Rabbi Mendeleh. He was an *Admo"r* in Brzezany, Dukla, and Wislo[?], He had Hasids of his own and managed his own court. His Hasids did not live in peace with the Hasids of Rabbi Avraham Zerakh Halperin. Rabbi Mendeleh was tall and skinny. He had dreamy eyes and a relaxed and pleasant character. His economic situation was not very good. He came, twice a year, from Dukla to Brzezany, where he had a synagogue. He benefited from the support of his Hasids. He died in Dukla while his family perished in Brzezany. May G-d avenge his blood.

R' Tzvi-Hirsh Halperin

Rabbi Moshe Winer

He was a rabbinical judge and a teacher in Brzezany, a unique and fascinating character. A great scholar with a broad general education and a modern approach to public affairs. He was a Zionist and a member of the "HaPoel HaMizrakhi." Brzezany's residents respected and favored him for his sincerity and honesty. Before the First World War, he was a teacher and secretary to a wealthy person in Bukovina, Mordekhai Koren, in Shopnitz near Chernivitsi [Tzernonvitz]. He consulted in matters related to families and businesses. In the early 1930s, he joined the rabbinical court in Brzezany. He perished on Yom Kippur 5702 (1941). May G-d avenge his blood.

Rabbi Alter Grosvaks

He was a Stratyn's Hasid, withshort stature, long beard, gay eyes, and fiery in nature, He moved heavens and earth during his prayers. He prayed with a loud voice. He was also a milk merchant. During the First

World War, he served in the Austrian Army. He used to say that he was inspired. He was told that he was destined to be a congregation leader. Since then, he abandoned civil life and dedicated himself to holy work. His behavior was like that of a rabbi, but a crowd of Hasids who believed in his powers were missing. Following the phrase "There is no prophet in his own town," the people of Brzezany did not believe in his virtues. He was forced to try his luck in other places. He moved to Yaroslav, where he lived until his death. His son, Rabbi Tzvi-Hirsh, was a rabbi in Narayiv [Naryov]. The people of that town talked about his greatness and work.

R' Joel Halperin

Translator's Notes:

1. From Wikipedia: *Seder Kodashim* is the fifth Seder in Mishan. The main subject of the Seder is the work of the sacrifices in the Temple and other matters related to this subject... The word that alludes to the Seder is "Khokhmat" [Wisdom], probably because its laws are more complex and wiser than others.

2. According to Sefaria.org, the original author of the "Vitry *Makhzor*" was Rabbi Simkha Halperin of Vitry. He lived in Vitry, France, at the time of Rash"i.

3. The original Hebrew version of Bobrka's Yizkor book appears on the website of the NY public library: https://digitalcollections.nypl.org/items/f6bd8080-5656-0133-8805-00505686d14e. The book is being translated and published on the Jewishgen.org
    website: https://www.jewishgen.org/Yizkor/bobrka/bobrka.html

The family of the Halperin Rabbis

by Moshe Bar-David

Translated by Moshe Kutten

Edited by Jane S. Gabin

The family of the Halperin rabbis was one of the oldest families in our town. The city's rabbis came from them for generations. The dynasty of Halperin rabbis began at the beginning of the seventeenth century, starting with the reign of Rabbi Yekhiel Mikhel, who sat on the rabbinical throne for fifty-two years – from 1688 until his death in 1740 (according to the family tree. His daughter Rachel, the wife of Rabbi [Aryeh Leib Lev Falk] of Hanover, Germany, is also mentioned in that tree. She died in 1775).

It is interesting to note that the prominent pedigree came from the women's side of the family. The wife of Rabbi Yekhiel Mikhel, Miryam, was the daughter of Rabbi Aba'leh[Avraham] of Belz. The latter was the son of the Rabbi from Buchach and Stryy [Rabbi Elkhanan Halperin]. On his mother's side, he was the grandson of the famous Rabbi Shlomo Luria [Rasha"l], from Ostroh [Ostrog] and Lublin, and a descendant of Rashi." Rabbi Luria was born in 5270 (1510) and died in 12 Kislev 5334 (1574).

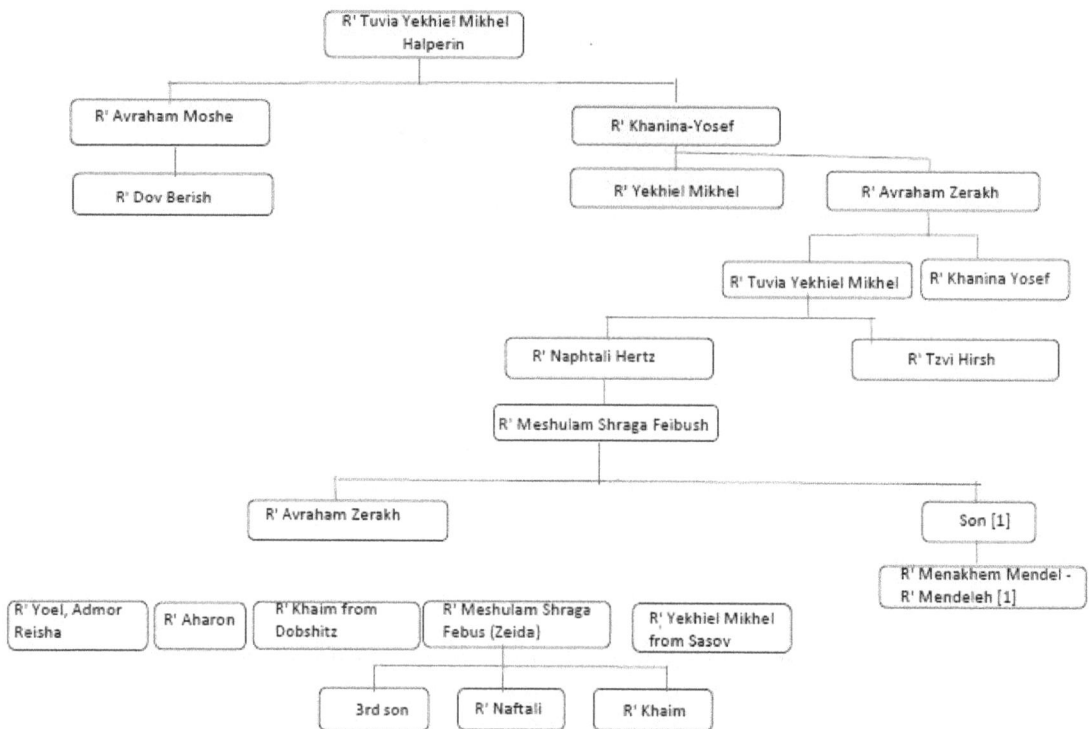

Family tree of the rabbis of the Halperin family

See also:

1. ***Translator's note:*** 1. According to the article on page 161, R' Mendeleh was R' Meshulam's son, not his grandson.

[Page 169]

The genealogy book of the Halperin Family

[Page 170]

The Nathanson Family
From Rabbi Bromberg's book "Rabbi Yosef Nathanson"

by Dr. Eliezer Shaklai

Translated by Moshe Kutten

Edited by Jane S. Gabin

The Nathanson family deserves that we dedicate an honorable place in the history of our city's people. It was a privileged family originating from Brody. The following ancestors are on their family tree: Khakham Tzvi [Rabbi Tzvi Hirsch ben Yaakov Ashkenazi] *ztz"l*, the B" H [?], the MaHarSh"A [Rabbi Shmuel Eliezer HaLevi Idles], the RaB"A [?], and up to RaSh"I [Rabbi Shlomo Yitzkhaki]. There were three brothers in Brody. The oldest was R' Yitzkhak, a rich person and a scholar. R' Yitzkhak had two sons, R' Arye Leibush and R' Yosef.

R' Leibush married the daughter of R' Dov Berish Halperin from Brzezany, and he became a city resident. R' Arye Leibush was a famous and knowledgeable scholar known throughout Galitsia, and authors turned to him to ask for a recommendation and approbation for their books. Besides his knowledge of the Torah, he had knowledge in many other fields. He was a great grammatologist and mathematician. He authored a commentary on Euclid's book that even [Rabbi Gershon Shaul Yom-Tov Lipman Halevi Heller Wallerstein, the author of the book] "Tosafot Yom Tov" could not follow. R' Leibush refused to accept a rabbinical ordination, but he willingly played various roles of a rabbi in our city. He was a preacher before the praying audience during the Days of Awe. He was one of the most dignified homeowners in our city. Without his approval, the community did not select a rabbi or take any other important decision.

R' Arye Leibush had two sons. The older one, Yosef Shaul, and the younger one, Zalman. R' Yosef Shaul moved to Lviv after his marriage. The young son remained with his father in Brzezany. R' Leibush died in 5,633 (1872/73) and was buried in our city. R' Zalman had a single son named Avraham, who married a woman descended from the Horovitz family of Barons from Vienna. They had a son named Meir, who was an exceptional learner.

Rabbi Yosef Shaul Nathanson

The *Gaon* Rabbi Yosef Nathanson was born in 5564 [1803/1804. according to Wikipedia, 1808], in Brzezany. The wise learner grew up in a house of Torah and charity. He excelled in his quick perception, exceptional memory, and diligence. He began issuing Torah commentary innovations at a young age while still residing at his father's home. After his marriage, he continued his studies while working with his father-in-law, Rabbi Yitzkhak Aharon Itinga. Together with his brother-in-law [Mordekhai Zeev Itinga], he insisted on allocating fixed time slots for Torah studies. Together with his brother-in-law, he published great and famous Torah assays. Their work, "Yam HaTalmud" ["The Sea of the Talmud"], should be especially noted. Prime importance is associated with three other works published by them: "Meir Einayim" ["An Eye-Opener"] about "Shulkhan Arukh," which presented an opinion concerning the Treifort of [animals'] lungs, "Ner Ma'aravi" ["Western Candle"] about the Jerusalem Talmud, and "Magen Giborim" ["Defender of Heroes"] about the Shulkhan Arukh way of life.

In middle age, R' Yosef Shaul became famous as the generation's greatest *Gaon* [genius]. He was knowledgeable in Halakha [Jewish Law], specializing in strict instructions. He was a great scholar and commentator of the Mishnah and a known teacher who practiced "Aliba de Hillkahtah" [study of a Halakha instruction that leads to a practical ruling, rather than studying the theoretical aspect only]. People turned to him with questions since he was considered the highest authority on issues of Jewish law and Torah's interpretation. He was known in the Torah world as "Ask and Answer."

[Page 171]

Rabbi Yosef Shaul lived and operated during a fascinating period in which many changes occurred in Jewish spiritual and social life. In that period, a big crisis took place in the acclaimed Lviv community with the death of the RABa" D [Rabbi Yaakov Meshulam Orenstein] (in 5599, [1939]). The Enlightened tried to reform the religious life of the Jews with the support of the Austrian authorities. They planned to make Lviv into a "modern progressive" city like Berlin and Vienna. They built a "temple" for themselves to pray according to the Enlightened style and also succeeded in nominating their preacher, Dr. Avraham Cohen, to the roles of Av Beit Din [ABD head of rabbinical court], and the Lviv district and city rabbi, roles that were held until them by the *Haredim*. The latter revolted against them, and a tremendous storm ensued, resulting in unpleasant acts. The two sides stood their ground and did not want to yield to the other side. That conflict lasted 18 years until the Enlightened relented and agreed to yield in favor of the *Haredim*. They agreed to let the roles of the rabbi and ABD be held by the [Ultra] Orthodox. They settled for their preacher practicing in their modern "temple."

R' Yosef Shaul was nominated for the role of ABD, with the agreement of both sides. The elderly Rabbi Nathan Ellinger, who served as the "Acting ABD," provided his agreement on behalf of the *Haredim*. *Gaon* R' Yosef Shaul began to serve in Lviv's rabbinical position in 5617 (1857). He served his community with honesty and justice, with the pureness of his heart, the depth of his mind, and his patience. The fighting spirits quieted down, and both sides faithfully served the community for the good of the public. R' Yosef Shaul did not neglect his Torah studies. During that period, he published the book "Shoel VeMeshiv" ["Ask and Answer"] containing all the Halakha areas included in "Shulkhan Arukh." We should note the fight between him and a good part of the Torah greats in Galitsia and the rest of the world concerning the baking of matzas using machines [which he allowed]. R' Yosef belonged to the "Mitnagdim" to the Hasidism camp [people opposing Hasidism]. However, he treated the greatest *Hasidim* Rebbes in reverence. He admired the Torah greats *Admo"rs* such as R' Khaim Halberstam of Sanz.

Rabbi Y. Sh. Nathanson served as the rabbi of Lviv during his last 18 years. He headed a Yeshiva, educated many students, and worked on public affairs without a monetary award. He also did not receive a salary from the community for his position as a rabbi. He was a man of peace and avoided conflicts and quarrels. He had a substantial influence on his surroundings with his bright personality, and everybody treated him with respect and admiration. Even the Enlightened people, his opponents, did not offend him since he treated them as a father among his rebellious children. He possessed a phenomenal memory and maintained an exemplary order. He was also a celebrated preacher. He proved to be a skilled author in either about Jewish law, in thinking, or sermonising,

He was very attached to his father, uncles, and grandfathers (on the two sides). He quoted them often in his books.

Gaon Rabbi Yosef Shaul Nathanson died in 5,635 [1875]. He was eulogized throughout the diaspora.

The "Khazan" [Cantor] *Beit Midrash* was built in our city to memorialize the Nathanson family with a dedication above the entrance gate:

"In memory of R' Arye Leibush and his son, Rabbi Shaul Nathanson."

[Page 172]

Rabbi Aharon Bar Yehuda HaLevi
(Author of moral books in the 18th century)

by Dr. Israel Mehlman

Translated by Moshe Kutten

Edited by Jane S. Gabin

A.

Berzan (Brzezany) was declared a city in 1530[1]. A Jewish settlement was established there as early as the 16th century[2], which played a role in the city's economy. The Jewish minority was successful in competing with the Armenian merchants.

From the beginning of the 17th century, several Berzan Jews began to show their strength and talent as learners and authors. The book "Tzon Kedoshim" [A flock of holy followers][3] that includes "*Tikunim*" [repairs] of Seder "Kaddashim" [fifth Seder of the Mishnah], had three partnering authors. One of them was R' Mordekhai Asher, who was probably an *Av Beit Din* [ABD – head of the rabbinical court] and a head of the yeshiva in the holy community of Berzan. Another author, a Torah great, R' Avraham Schorr, published his innovations during the years 5384 -5394 (1624 – 1634 or 1644) in Lublin and Krakow. The name of the book is "Torat Khaim" [Life Teaching], and tells in his own words: "Myself, and the famous *Gaon* our teacher and Rabbi, ABD, and head of the yeshiva in the holy community of Berzan, near Lviv, gathered the yeshiva that consisted great and sharp men and taught them the entire Seder Kaddashim, and repaired all the "thorns" and errors in the Seder and the Gemara, Rashi commentaries and "*Tosafot*" [medieval commentaries of the Talmud]"We explained them in detail for the benefit of many." The grandson of R' Avraham-Khaim Schorr, R' Khaim Hildesheimer, added his own views and published the book. That is how we know about the involvement of Berzan's exceptionally wise man from the 17th century in the "collective creation" of "Tzon Kedoshim."

Based on a gravestone in Lviv's cemetery, we found out that R' Menakhem Mendel Fatik [or Patik?], the son of Rabbi Asher[4], taught Torah and authored many essays[5]. He was an ABD and *Moreh Tzedek* (*Posek*) from Berzan; He also served as the leader of the community and ABD of the district on behalf of the Council of] Four Lands. He died in 5477 (1717). His many essays did not survive. They probably had not been published.

B.

R' Aharon bar Yehuda HaLevi was fortunate to have two of his moral books, "Khasdei Avot" and "Zot Torat Adam," written in rhymed prose, preserved as published books, probably the first works that survived from Berzan[6]. The second book was published in many editions, and some were translated to Yiddish for the benefit of women and uneducated masses. As far as the rest of his essays, such as "Toldot Eretz VeShamayim" [The History of Earth and Heavens], a poem and a commentary on the Haggadah, only sections embedded in his book "Kasdie Avot" were preserved. His work, the "Essay about the Torah," disappeared[7].

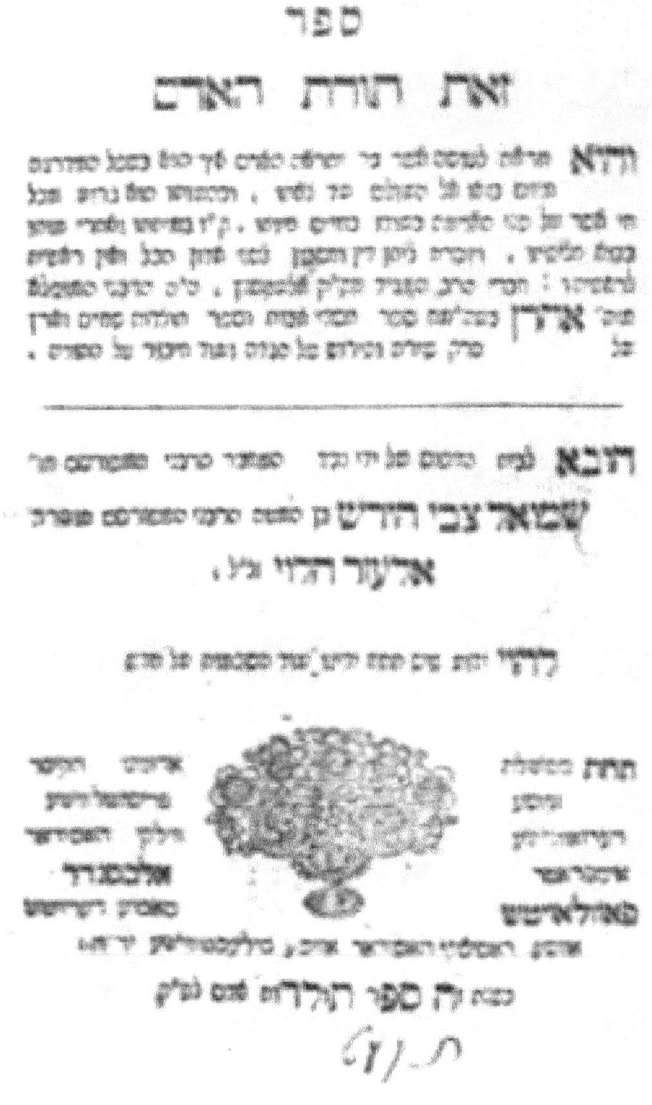

ספר

זאת תורת האדם

[Hebrew text of title page - several lines, partially legible]

The cover of the book "Zot Torat HaAdam"
by R' Aharon bar Yehuda HaLevi

[Page 173]

We know only a few details about R' Aharon's life, and it is difficult to determine whether he was born in Berzan or was just a city resident. He took a prominent place in public life and served as "*Magid Meisharim*" [preacher] and "*Moreh Tzedek*" [*Posek* – decider in Jewish law] in one of the important communities, Aleksinets[8]. Even before 5530 (1770), "he had a solid position in the *Kloiz Kadisha*" in the holy community of Brody[9]." The years he spent in the *kloiz*, studying and working, are also shrouded in fog. Incidentally, the whole affair of the wise men at "*Kloiz Kadisha*" was not thoroughly investigated. Even important chapters, such as the connections with Eretz Israel (where a few of the scholars made Aliyah), their diverse attitude to the first steps of the Hasidic movement, or their attitude toward the first buds of the Enlightenment Movement, were not exposed, and not sufficiently clarified. R' Aharon probably never left Brody and died in 5547 (1787)[10].

R' Aharon was a descendant of famous rabbis, including the Maharsha"l (R' Shlomo Luria)[11], among the Jewish greats of the 16th century.

His generation's Torah greats respected R' Aharon and praised him excessively. In the approbation to the book "Khasdie Avot," Rabbi Yitzkhak HaLevi Horovitz wrote about him: "ABD and head of the yeshiva of the holy community of Brody, was also accepted to the communities of Hamburg, Altona, and Wandsbek – all his actions are for heaven's sake." In another approbation to the book, he was named "One of the famous 'brightest lights'" from the *Kloiz Kadisha* in the holy community of the 'capital Brody' – the witty and the sharp, admirable, heals the soul and unparallel *Moreh Tzedek* [*Posek* decider] R' Aharon. Twelve of the *kloiz* scholars signed the approbation.

Thirty years after his death in 5579 [1818/9], R. Moshe Berizblum ABD of the holy community of Vishnevets commented after reading two or three pages of the book "Zot Torat HaAdam" that R' Aharon "heals the soul and refreshes it and puts it to sleep." He wrote that the language used in the book, "glows fresh and clean."

C.

The only book published while R' Aharon was alive was "Khasdei Avot," a commentary about the Ethics of the Fathers -Aharon Beharabi(?) and Yehuda HaLevi, a descended of the Maharsha"l [Rabbi Shlomo Luria]. It was published in the holy community of Zhovkva under the Government of Karl Stanislav Yadvil(?) [Stanislaw II August?], at the printer house of the son of Rabbi Khaim David Segal *z"l*.

R' Aharon indicated in the introduction to the book "VeKhasdo MeIto Lo Yamush" ["And His Grace would not Depart from Him"], 5527 (1767)[12], that many commentaries were issued about the Ethics of the Fathers, but he thought that there was room for additional innovations. His ancestors left much to research. Indeed, those who read the book find a tendency to discover something new in old essays, sometimes an idea, and other times – in formulation.

For example, his commentary about the opening phrase: "Kol Israel Yesh Lahem Khelek BaOlam Haba" ["Every Jew guaranteed a place in the next world."] His reasoning was that all the souls are one. They are like a tree that its branches are separated, but all of them have the same root."

[Page 174]

And for that reason, they would have a place in the next world, since together, they could fulfill all the 613 commandments written in the Torah (because they are all like one person)."

The phrase by Rabbi Yehuda HaNasi, at the head of the second chapter: "What is a straight path that a person breaks for him, to bring glory to its doers and glory to him from the man?" was explained by R' Aharon: "Studying Torah and fulfilling commandments, bring glory only to their people who do it from their maker. To bring glory from man, people need to straighten others and restore them from their evil ways. That way. a person would receive glory from the people who would not commit a sin again."

Explaining the phrase "more sitting, more wisdom," R' Aharon found an opportunity to criticize the traveling preachers and mock them: "There are people who travel from one city to another. They do not read and do not reread, and do not serve as students … They open their mouths without any control … they are never there to respond to questions … and after saying whatever these preachers want to say, they do not come back to the same city, and preach the same thing in another city. They never travel on the same roads because they bring nothing new. When they come to a village with a permanent rabbi, one can always tell that the traveling preachers lack knowledge. The local rabbi sits and learns, preaching time after time in the same location. That rabbi is sitting and thereby acquires wisdom." That is a direct criticism of a traveling preacher versus a permanent preacher.

On the cover page of the book, Rabbi Aharon promises to present "some collections from the Gemarah and *Tosafot*. However, he fulfills his promise very narrowly. He probably decided to allocate a chapter to the Halakha, not because of a mental need, but because he was attentive to his readers' opinion – the scholars, who would not accept moral teaching and attractive *Aggadah* tales until the author demonstrates his knowledge of the Halakhah. Lest they say: "Who is this one that wishes to be one of the authors and who preaches and scolds about acts done under the sun, and he just became known … without being versed in Gemarah and *Tosafot*."

R' Aharon apologizes at the end of the book for not fulfilling his promise with the following words: "Due to printing costs and the pressure by the printer to complete the book, I could not include the collections from the Gemarah and *Tosafot*."

On the last page, R' Aharon lists his moral scolding in an alphabetic order. On top of the list:

"You should prepare provisions / before the sunset and the dark night comes." That moral advice appears several times in the book.

D.

After R' Aharon's death, his second book was published. At first, it was just the book ending, which was a separate literary unit. A few years later, the entire 12-page book "Zot Torat HaAdam" was published in the holy community of Zholkova in a tiny format[14]. The year is not mentioned, but the cover claims that the book "was published under the rule of Emperor Frantz II." So we can only determine that it was published between 5552 (1792) (the year when Frantz II was crowned as the Roman Emperor) and 5566 (1806) (the year when he was named the Emperor of Austria Frantz I after Napoleon declared the end of the Rome Empire[15]).

[Page 175]

The complete book was published again in 5579 (1819) in a Russian town, probably Pavlivka [Poritzk]. It was published by the author's grandson, Rabbi Tzvi Hirsh, son of Rabbi Eliezer HaLevi ZTz" L, where the written text was found. Neither the author nor the people who wrote approbations for the book knew or mentioned that part of the book had already been published.

In the introduction, R' Aharon declares that "he wants to attract people who stay in the dark, to brighten their way, day and night, according to G-d's Torah and commandments." He claims that the moral level of the nation has deteriorated. Most of the masses abandon the study of the Torah, and they crave the pleasures and comforts of life. In his words: "They find delight in the pleasures of meat, fish, and other delicacies … in the afternoon, they nap, stroll, or do other idle things." He claims people "do not understand their fate and what will happen at the end of days."

To soften hearts and bring them back to repent, R' Aharon brings up the history and the essence of humans to show that they are "the worst of any animal on earth … and perhaps their alien hearts would yield … to worship and fear G-d." His doctrine seems austere and extreme, influenced by the book "Khovot HaLevavot" [Duties of the Hearts] of Rabbi Bakhya [ben Yosef ibn Paquda], whom he mentions. However, since his doctrine is not laid out as a method, it is adorned by parables, stories, and debates, and the language is flowery, it loses a lot from its strictness and severity.

In the center stands the human, who sins and fails in life, flung between an intense lust for life and a weak conscience, predicting the judgment to the Creator when the Day of Judgment comes. This is not an individual personality, just a regular human, or more specifically – a Jewish human. Such a motive wandered around in European nations, took the form of a debate, and shaped into a drama – in England, the Lowlands, and Germany[16]. Was that motive common in Eastern Europe? It is unknown whether R' Aharon, the learner and preacher, got it for that folklore story or drew everything, the shapes, and logic, only from Jewish sources?

When R' Aharon spreads periods and events from human life in front of the reader, he does not limit himself to general logic, does not take from folklore, but presents real pictures with a satirical tone.

The author discusses the childhood period in general terms: "Until the child comes out from just being alive to the period he starts talking, he is just a poor creature. He cannot observe and has an alien mouth … if he is hungry, he would not complain. He does not understand what is good or bad for him."

The author dedicates a few realistic lines to the studies in the Kheder, the customary punishments there, and the boy's rebelliousness. When the simple youth reaches Bar Mitzva age, his rebelliousness grows; he rebels against the rabbi, and there is "neither Torah nor Wisdom" in him, and then he reaches marriageable age. The author uses animating language when describing the tricks of the matchmakers and picturing the traditional Jewish wedding. The wedding is rich in food and drinks, and when the time comes for the groom to speak, he is an ignoramus and "does not have anything to say." His father saves him from embarrassment by ordering the "*Klezmer*" to play "so that the groom's bad words are not heard." Then, the cheerfulness that borders on promiscuity grows. "The men mix with the women, virgins, and married, all together with no shame. A man grabs his wife from among the dancing women and begins to dance with her in public… There is no oversight between the wrong and the proper until the next morning."

[Page 176]

"There is a moral lesson, from that too, for a man who has a daughter to marry her to a "*Talmid Khakham*" ["a student of sages"]. He weighs the opinion of some practical people who claim: "Why would you attach yourself to a "*Talmid Khakham*" and his Torah knowledge. What is it for you with the "*Talmid Khakham*'s*" distinguished lineage? They are all lying under their grave in the cemetery, while he does not have bread and clothing in his house? … [On the other hand, the man thinks for himself:] "It is possible that the "*Talmid Khakham*" would be accepted as a Rabbi of a town, preacher, or *posek*, and thus would be able to make a living."

The author criticizes those who hurry to "gather and accumulate wealth" after the wedding. "Who would take pity and forgive the person who did not care about his life in the next world and was busy living his material life … He would go alone and would not be able to take anything he collected with him … only Torah and good deeds could be carried over."

With some pity, the author draws a picture of the person at the end of his life and describes the other people's behavior toward him. In old age, "everything sweet becomes bitter… there isn't a medicine for every trouble" and death comes with extreme agony. "And the people responsible for the burial are sending emissaries to the wife and sons to take a deposit, a large sum of money, since the dyeing person never contributed anything."

After the burial, "the wife and the sons return home to eat and drink to heal their souls. They do not remember their father … They will only mention his name on the anniversary of his death … They enjoy their meals in all sorts of celebrations and forget him. They divide his fortune, and his wife marry someone else and forget about him."

The preacher-scolder author wakes up again and describes the torture of the sinner in the next world. The body and soul separate after death. The body is tossed up to be eaten by worms and maggots, and the soul has to pay for deeds and failures. If she had rebelled against G-d and his commandments in our world, she would have been sentenced to forgo severe tortures: She would have been hit with clubs and would have suffered blows and bruises. That soul is tossed, stepped on, and thrown to the dogs with the lesson: "Realize what you what you choose – this world or the next … and you will be paid for what you have done, good or bad."

A story is attached here, which highlights the aforementioned doctrine. It is a story about King Admon, ruling in Kirah, and his two friends, Brother Good and Brother Bad. Admon is the human. His kingdom is our planet, which is, in the story, being compared metaphorically to the Tents of Kedar ((Song of Songs 1:5) – like a temporary domicile. The two friends, Brother Good and Brother Bad, are the two inclinations that are trying to conquer the human heart. King Admon is enticed to follow his eyes and enjoy life's pleasures by Brother Bad. The latter promises the King that there will be no court and no judge at the end. Over time, the King realizes that there is somebody who watches over the world and expels his friend Brother Bad, the bad inclination, from his house. G-d forgives him and accepts him with mercy[17].

A short chapter is attached at the end - "A debate between the body and the soul"[18]. It concludes with three fables, all with a moral lesson attached. They had already been published several years before as part of the book: "Khasdei Avot." The author found it necessary to apologize for including the chapter again: "Since I have mentioned two Sayings of the Sages and saw a parallel in these fables, I chose to include them here even though they had been published before with Khasdei Avot, particularly since that this book is out of print."

[Page 177]

The second part of the book is a separate unit[19]. It has a different name and is written in a different style. While the first part is called "Sefer Toldot HaAdam" [Book of Human Life], the second part is called "Torat Adam VeKorotav" [Teaching and Life of the Human"]. The second part excels in its internal unity and the integrity of its structure. It is written in a flowery but clear language and in rhymed prose.

Yedidya [Literally -Friend of G-d], son of Elimelekh [literally G-d is King], talks about some adventures he encountered in this world. These are poetic and splendid variations of the stories and fables of the first part. Yedidia stands at a crossroads and is given a choice: One way leads to a place full of people with bad manners. They follow their eyes and hearts, fornicating, robbing, looting, and kidnapping women from their husbands. The other way leads to a place where people are righteous and honest, "Immersed in his thoughts, he approaches a large, joyful, and crowded city, "and its people are like Sodom and Gomorrah people." At the gate, he meets an old man "riding a red horse, and his sword drips blood." His name is Koshel [Failing]. The man invites Yedidia in and says: "I am just coming from the study house on my way home. I will make you a banquet at home."

When Yedidia reaches the age of thirteen, he receives a letter of reprimand from his father, Elimelekh, that contains advice to stay away from his friend Koshel and his counsel, to which he replies in the negative: "I could not accept your advice to leave, since parting from my friend will be difficult for me … How can I leave the pleasure house to the sad house of learners, and from good fun to dry bread … from milk and honey to poor meal … Therefore, I ask that you let go of me because I will never come back to you." Elimelekh tries two more times to return to get his son back on the right track, once using soft talk filled with love and the other using words of harsh rebuke accompanied by threats. When Yedidia reads the last letter, he feels cowardice, but he cannot pluck up his courage to leave Koshel, "his friend and benefactor."

A way out of this troubled situation came from an unexpected direction. Yedidia suddenly becomes critically ill , and his friend Koshel reveals his true villainous character. He leaves his friend and does not even come to visit him. In his agony, Yedidia writes to his father: "Here I am my father, cure me from my pains … and I will write my rabbi and teacher's words on my heart." The father takes pity on his son and sends him Raphael [literally G-D has healed, an archangel in Judaism]. These are the healing medicines

Elimelekh prescribes Yedidia: "First you should take this remorse fruits, caution weeds, agility flowers, modesty branch, and some holiness leaves, and faith roots. You should crush them in a repentance mortar … and boil it over the fire of the Torah … sweating the G-d fearing sweat." When Yedidia has recovered from his illness, he wallows in the dirt and cries. He abandons his wicked deeds, prays morning, noon, and evening, and goes to a house filled with books, sits down among the wise men, and thirstily absorbs their words.

The moral of the story, according to the author: "And you, my brothers and friends take a look at this fable … that is what happens to a man that goes after his stubbornness … when he falls ill …he repents …and G-d with his many mercies accepts those who repent[20]."

The two books of the Berzan man, R' Aharon, son of Yehuda HaLevi, who lived and operated in the 18th century, are worthy of attention. Even though R. Aharon was immersed in the world of opinions and beliefs of his contemporaries, a subtle tendency towards originality is noticeable in his writings, which are characterized by a keen moral feeling. At times, by observing folklore, at other times by his words. His perception, which is sometimes critical-satirical, should not be ignored either.

Original footnotes:

1. By King Zigmond I, Geographical Dictionary of the Polish Kingdom – Warsaw, 1890,

2. Horn: Horn: "The Jewish settlement movement in the cities of Red Ruthenia." P. 1640 (Bulletin of the Jewish Historical Institute, 1974).

3. Printed in Vanzbeck in 5489 (1729).

4. Baber: "Anshei Shem" [Famous people], Lviv 5,655 (.189.5)

5. It is unclear whether the essays were written by the son or his father, R' Asher.

6. According to his book "Khasdei Avot" [Ancestorial Graces], P. 2, Zhovkva [Zholkva], the city was called Berzan, and sometimes Brezan.

7. The three essays were mentioned in the opening of the book [by R' Aharon bar Yehuda HaLevi], "Zot Torat HaAdam" [That is the Teaching of Humanity], 5579 (1818/9).

8. According to the cover of the book "Khasdei Avot."

9. See note 8.

10. N. M. Gelber: The history of Brody"s Jews (Mother Cities in Israel), Jerusalem, 5,715 [1955], p. 77 (In error – Aleksandrov instead of Aleksinets).

11. On the cover of the book "Khasdei Avot."

12. The year 5527 (1766/7), obtained from the combination of the underlined letters, is uncertain because one of the approbations was given in 5531 (1771). It is difficult to decide between the dates.

13. Was not mentioned in the book "The Treasure of Poetry and Songs" by Israel Davidson [Philadelphia 1924 – 1938]. [There is no reference to this note in the article]

14. A list of all editions with some helpful critique notes appears in the article by R' Khaim Liberman: "The History of Hebrew Publishing in Poland and Russia. The book "Zot Torat Adam" was printed in "Alei Sefer," Jerusalem, 5,735 (1974/5).

15. The book, printed at Zhovkova Printer," was issued as a special edition (probably only one time) in Krakow in 5,689 (1929). Because of its small size, it was added as an addendum to other books (such as "Orakh Mishor" by R' Ya'akov Khagiz, or the book "Alpha Beita," in Yiddish translation with the name "Mashal and Melitzah" issued in several editions.

16. Jedermann - Every Man

17. The story about King Admon and his two friends was translated into Yiddish and published in Satu-Mareh in 5,697 (1937) under the name "Torat HaAdam."

18. That type of literature can be found in the old Hebrew literature.

19. Rabbi Khaim Liberman thinks that the second part, containing just a few pages, is a separate book (see note no. 14).

20. The whole book "Zot Torat HaAdam" was published in several additional editions, starting with the Sedilkov print 5,695 (1935) until the Kleinvardein print 5,689 (1929), see note 14.

[Page 178]

Rabbi, Dr. Margaliot Shmuel Zvi
Brzezany, 1 Khesvan 5,618, 1857 – Firnze [Florance], 12 Adar 5,682, 1922

by Dov Knohl

Translated by Moshe Kutten

Edited by Jane S. Gabin

Rabbi Shmuel Tzvi Margaliot

His father, R' Efraim Zalman, was a descendant of a distinguished rabbinical family and among the offsprings of Rabbi Zalman Margaliot from Brody, the author of many books and among the most prominent teachers of his generation. Shmuel Tzvi was a merchant and scholar who possessed some general education knowledge. His mother helped his father in his business, was versed in books, and was knowledgeable about the Bible.

He received his first knowledge of the Torah from his father and the city's best *melameds* [religion teachers]. Besides the Bible and Talmud, he also studied Polish and German. He also read research books by Jewish sages from the Middle Ages.

In 5638 [1877/8], he overcame the resistance of his parents and realized his desire to study at the Rabbinical College of Breslaw (at the beginning as an auditor because he did not have a matriculation certificate). A year later, he returned to the city, took the matriculation examination, and passed. He was then accepted as a full-time student at the Rabbinical College and also as a student at Breslaw University, where he studied philosophy and Semitic languages. He completed his studies Cum Laude in 5643 (1882/3) and was awarded a doctorate in Leipzig.

In 5645 (1884/5), he completed his studies at the Rabbinical College and was certificated to teach. Three months before his certification, he was invited to serve as a rabbi in the "Neveh Shalom" congregation in Hamburg, and in 5647 (1886/7), he was nominated as the rabbi of the Hesse-Nassau province, which included twenty small congregations, and he moved to Wittenberg.

In 5650 (1889/90), he accepted the offer of the Firenze community to serve as their rabbi. He served in this rabbinical position for thirty years until his last day. He was active in several areas there, and thanks to his dynamic personality, organizational skills, and educational efforts, he spiritually transformed the Italian Jewry, which had its center in Firenze. He considered his main objective to fight atheism and the reformist tendencies that had taken root among the Italian Jews and disseminate the knowledge of the Torah and Judaism in all circles against these tendencies, particularly among the youth. He succeeded in attracting the best among the young, who previously grew up in the spirit of total assimilation. He introduced a custom that every Bar Mitzva had to be tested with him personally before he was allowed to celebrate it at the synagogue.

The crown in his educational activity was the transfer of the rabbinical *Beit HaMidrash*, which was until then semi-paralyzed, from Rome to Firenze. The transfer occurred in 5659 [1898/9], and he revived it under his management. He made sure to attract a staff of young and promising scholars. With their help, the institution succeeded in graduating talented students who, later on, served as rabbis in the large Italian communities. He also established the journal *"Meeasef Rivista Israelitica,"* which, like other *Meassfim* [collectors] of its type, contained a lot of Judaica material. In addition, under Rabbi Margaliot's inspiration, the weekly "Israel" was also established. The weekly, under the editor Yehuda Menakhem Pachipichi, served as a mouthpiece for the young intelligentsia that arose thanks to the spiritual awakening under Rabbi's inspiration.

Other far-reaching activists included the forming of the international assistance committee for the benefit of the oppressed Russian Jews and the establishment of the corporation for the education of orphans in Firenze.

[Page 179]

He was a loyal Zionist and became active within the "HaMizrakhi" movement upon its founding. He participated in its various conferences and the Zionist Congresses as a representative of the movement's executive committee.

He published many articles in collections and other periodicals in Italian, German, and Hebrew collections. Among them, we should list "Mahadura Batra Yitzkhak's Fear" ("Eshkol," volume 5) and his editing on Shabbat Tractate (In the anniversary book for Rabbin Israel Levi – "Tif'eret Israel" ["The Splendor of Israel"]. Rabbi Margaliot also served as a consultant for the editorial committee of the Jewish Encyclopedia).

The Rabbi, Dr. Leo (Leib Hirsch) Bardowicz

by Menakhem son of Shimon Katz

Translated by Moshe Kutten

Edited by Jane S. Gabin

Leib Hirsch was born in the 1860s in Brzezany to his mother, Golda Rivka nee Faust. He went to a *kheder* as a child and studied as a youth at the Yeshiva of the Maharsha"m in the city. He showed interest in general studies and passed the matriculation examination as an extern. He went with his parents when they moved to Vienna, studied, and graduated from the rabbinical seminary in that city. As a progressive rabbi with vast Torah knowledge who learned from his prominent teachers in Brzezany, he published many books and articles about the Torah, Ramba"m, and Hebrew Grammar.

In 1885, he participated in a contest announced by the Teachers' College of the Judaic Sciences University in Berlin. He won the first prize for his article "The *Rambam's* rational commentary of the Torah."

He continuously published articles in the Jewish-German periodicals in Vienna, Berlin, Breslaw, Frankfurt-am-Main, and other cities.

He served as the rabbi of the Meidling congregation in Vienna for many years. He visited his native city and was a frequent visitor at the home of his prominent rabbi, the Maharsh"m.

He died in Vienna in the 1920s.

The following are some of his books [and publications] in German. They are all intertwined with Hebrew commentaries that he was so well versed in:

- *"Das allmähliche Ueberhandnehmen der matres lectionis im Bibeltexte und das rabbinische Verbot, die Defectiva plene zu sehreiben"* [The gradual prevalence of the matres lectionis in Bible texts and the rabbinical command to write the defective plene], *Monatsschrift für geschichte und Wissenschaft des Judenthums* [The Monthly Magazine of Science of Judaism], Breslaw, 1892

- *"Die Rational Schriftauslegung des Maimonides"* [The Rational Interpretation of Scripture by Maimonides], *Magazin für Wissenschaft des Judenthums* Neunzehnter, Jargang, 1892.

- *"Studien zur Geschichte der Orthographie des Althebräischen"* [Studies of the history of the orthography of ancient Hebrew], Frankfurt Am Main, M. Kaufman, 1894.

- *"Die Abfassungszeit der Baraita der 32 Normen für die Auslegung der heillgen Schrift"* [The time of the composition of the *Baraita* of the 32 rules for the interpretation of the Holy Scripture], Berlin, M. Poppelauer, 1913

[Page 180]

Rabbi Dr. Yehuda Bergman
Elul 5633 8.30.1874 – 26 Kheshvan 5715 11.22.1954

by Menakhem son of Shimon Katz

Translated by Moshe Kutten

Edited by Jane S. Gabin

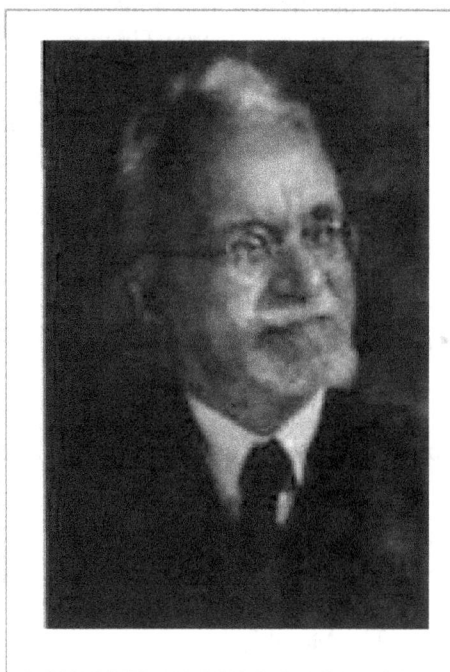

Rabbi Dr. Yehuda Bergman

The wise Rabbi Dr. Yehuda Bergman, who was active in Jewish sciences for more than fifty years, died in Jerusalem at 80. He published articles and books in Hebrew in a style that is difficult to associate with someone educated in Western Judaica. His youthful Torah studies in Brzezany enabled him to become a student in the first class of the rabbinical *Beit HaMidrash* in Vienna about 60 years ago. All the students of that first class, particularly those who came from Eastern Galitsia, occupied prominent positions in the Torah world and in life: Tzvi Peretz Khayut, Mikhael Berkovitz (the Hebrew translator and teacher of Herzl and the publisher of A. S. Liberman's writings), Y. L. Landau, Moshe Schorr and more. Bergman was the last survivor of that group. His activity in the Jewish public life in Germany, where he served as a rabbi for decades, and his involvement in the Jewish Torah life should be commemorated.

Bergman's writings were distinguished by their popular appeal without divorcing them from the scientific basis. His distinctive mark was knowing the subject matter thoroughly, although he did not boast about his knowledge, which flowed naturally.

His books published during his last years in Israel ("HaYahadut, Nishmata VeKhayeha" ["The Soul and Life of Judaism"], "HaAm VeRukho" ["The Nation and its Spirit"], "HaTzdaka BeIsrael" ["Charity in Israel"], and "The Jewish Folklore," were just like a signature for the series of books in German on similar subjects, where he provided encompassing reviews based on primary sources. These subjects were not just research topics for him. His enormous affinity to past Jewish life is apparent in his writings. He wanted to continue those ways of life, as much as possible, in the present. From that, he explained these ways of life and showed the grace and beauty in them.

Bergman was very active and published many articles in the German monthly magazine *Monatsschrift für geschichte und Wissenschaft des Judenthums* [Monthly Magazine for the History and Science of Judaism]. He published many articles on Jewish subjects, among them "Die Legenden der Juden" ["The Legends of the Jews"], in 1898. He was also active in Herzl's periodical during its first few years.

In Eretz Israel, he participated in the publishing of the quarterly magazine of folklore and ethnology – *Edut* ["Testimony"] starting from the first issue (Tamuz 5,707, 1946).

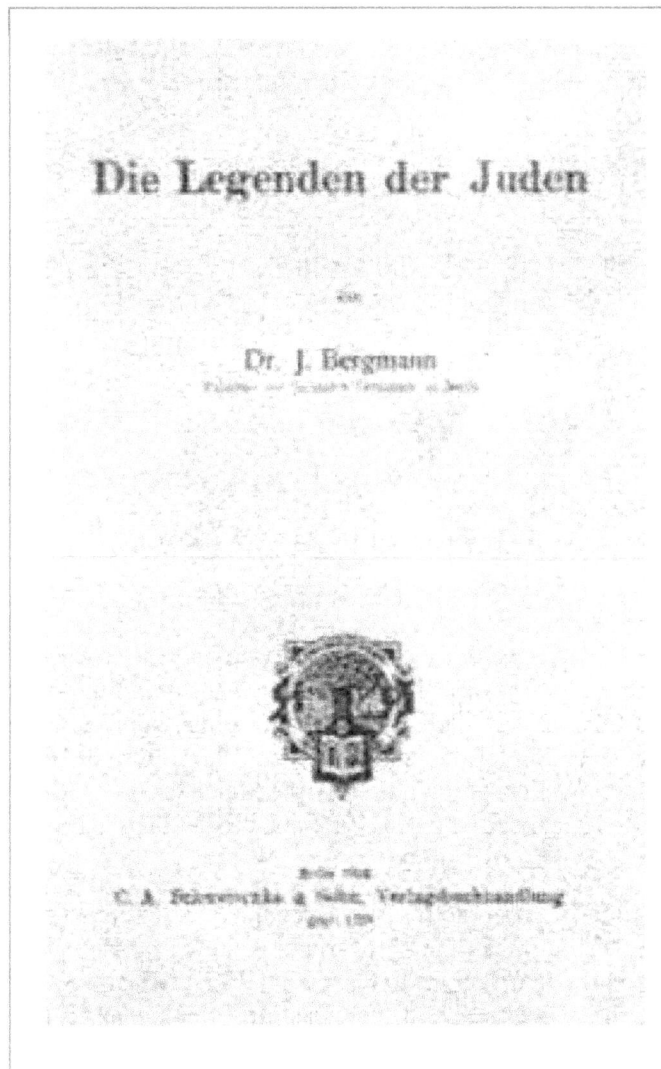

Rabbi Bergman's article
"Die Legenden Der Juden"

It was not common for a Rabbi serving in the Jewish community in Germany and participating in scientific periodicals to carry proudly the Zionist flag. However, Bergman did that like his friends – Khayut, Margaliot, Berkovitz, and Landau. It was not easy for a rabbi in the West to appear publicly in the name of the movement persecuted by the Western rabbis. However, that group of rabbis excelled in their courage and strong will.

Rabbi Yehuda Bergman did not follow the furrow perused by the leaders of the German communities at the big fateful hour when the German National Socialists took over until *Kristallnacht* in November 1938. Many of these leaders thought that a solution for the German Jews would be found within Germany. Rabbi Bergman, a Zionist who Joined the Zionist movement in the days of Theodore Herzl, objected to that opinion.

[Page 181]

In a speech in April 1933 at the great synagogue (Fasanen Str.) in Western Berlin, he urged his audience, the community members, to leave Germany and save themselves, even at the price of losing their property. With the increase in hopelessness and cases of suicides among the Jews in Germany, he encouraged them to make Aliyah, which was still possible during the period 1933-1938. He made Aliyah after serving as the congregation's rabbi for more than 25 years. He settled in Jerusalem and served there as the center for Jewish natives of Germany.

With his passing, this article was published in the newspaper, *Ha'aretz* and the following are its concluding sentences:

R' Yehuda Bergman passed away modestly, and it became known to the public only from the obituary notice. As in his life, so in his death.

Rabbi, Yehuda Leibaleh Roza

by Moshe Bar-David

Translated by Moshe Kutten

Edited by Jane S. Gabin

Many Brzezany Jews have been swept from Europe to America with every surge of immigrants. We do not know who came, but the first to organize Brzezany's natives in a *landsmanshaft* were Shtoknoff [?] and Katz. They usually concentrated in New York, and with the strengthening of their organization, they were looking for a social frame and a rabbi for the landsmen. They chose R' Leibaleh Roza, who still resided in Brzezany and had obtained a rabbinical ordination from the Maharsha"m and Rabbi Gedalya Shmelkis. He was respected in our city, was a scholar who secured a public standing, and was an enthusiastic religious Zionist.

Rabbi Leibaleh was born in Brzezany to his father, Khaim Tzvi Roza, a scholar and learned man. His grandfather belonged to the distinguished family of Rabbi Khaim Tzvi Messig, who was the Av Beit Din [ABD – the head of the rabbinical court] in his time, and the Rabbi of Gaon Rabbi Yosef Shaul Nathanson. The father of Rabbi Leibaleh Roza was one of the city's most distinguished and famous people. He was known as a scholar and an expert on "Yoreh De'a." He authored an in-depth essay (which exists in his handwriting) about the "Pri Megadim" of "Yoreh De'a." Rabbi Sh. Y. Nathanson mentioned him and wondered about his depth and knowledge. Rabbi Leibaleh studied from his father and Rabbi Yitzkhak Shmelkis *z"l* (The author of the book "Beit Yitzkhak"). As a Zionist, he wrote articles for the periodical

"Di Velt" ["The World"] and belonged to the HaMizrakhi movement. He corresponded with the HaMizrakhi leader, Rabbi Yitzkhak Ya'akov Reinis *z"l*.

[Page 182]

He preached the idea of education for Torah and work. He participated in trips with the Rabbi from Przemysl [Pshemishel], R' Gedalia Shmelkis, and the preacher from Kolomyia, R' Yitzkhak Weber, to promote that idea. He was a frequent visitor at the Maharsha"m and Rabbi Meizlis, who respected his learning and knowledge (including in books of general subjects). He was considered one of the candidates for the rabbinical position in Brzezany after the death of the Maharsha"m. However, the disagreement about that position between Rabbi Leibush Halperin and Rabbi Mendeleh Halperin (his nephew) deterred all the candidates.

With his acceptance of the offer of Brzezany people in the USA, he gave up on any opportunity in Brzezany. He moved to the USA and settled in New York as the Rabbi of the congregation of Brzezany natives. With their help, he established a synagogue at 180 Stanton Street called "Berzhaner Schul-Bnei Ya'akov." His home was opened to all Brzezany natives and anyone who came to ask for spiritual or material support. His home served as an address and a shelter for new immigrants to ease the feeling of being foreign in a new place. At first, the state of the R' Leibaleh's nine-member family was not so good. When an offer was extended to him to serve as a rabbi elsewhere, with wages higher than those he received from the Brzezany people, he refused. He used to say: "I was with them in my youth and would not leave them when I am old. The money and the honor are not the main things, but honesty and amiability for those who stuck by me, for good and bad, are the things that mattered. These people are like my children, and with them, I will stay until my death."

He served as a rabbi there for 38 years, and everybody respected and liked him due to his honesty and good heart. His wife, too, was active in the community, formed a charity fund, and assisted many needy who turned to her.

Rabbi Roza was elected president of "Kollel Khibat Yerushalayim" in 1941. He died on 12 February 1946. He left behind a branched family and a future generation of rabbis and scholars.

His daughter, Mrs. Rakhel Waxler, dedicated her life to public affairs and assistance to our people. Two of his sons are rabbis: Rabbi Dr. Moshe Roza, who served as a rabbi in New York and Pittsburgh for fifty years, and in parallel as a scholar in the Portuguese synagogue "Heikhal Sinai." The second son of Rabbi Avraham Roza was the president of the "New Zionists" organization in a Jewish center. Rabbi Dr. Noiman, a professor and president of the Drafsi[?] College and author of the "Jews in Spain" was a frequent visitor of Rabbi Leibaleh.

R' Leibaleh's grandchildren, the sons of his son, Rabbi Avraham Roza, are Rabbi David Roza, a rabbi in Cleveland, and Rabbi Imanuel Roza, a rabbi in Portland. The son of Rabbi Moshe Roza is Rabbi Herbert Roza, a rabbi in Flatbush. One daughter of Rabbi L[eibaleh]. R.[oza] is married to Rabbi Harry Shekhtman of Center Village in Palm Beach, Florida. Their son is Rabbi R. Shekhtman in Virginia. R' Leibaleh's second daughter was married to the Zionist scholar Dr. Halperin in Chicago. Their son was Rabbi Leo Libreikh, who served as the Rabbi in Trenton, New Jersey, and a professor at Gratz College in Philadelphia. Rabbi Felix Freifeld was related to R' Leibaleh's wife, and her brother was a philosophy professor in Vienna.

Rabbi Leibaleh left various essays about Talmudic subjects. These writings exist in a handwriting format and have not yet been published.

With the passing of Rabbi Leibaleh Roza, the congregation of Brzezany natives lost a spiritual leader who would be remembered for generations.

[Page 183]

The Prayer Master, Vava Ze'ev Direnfeld the Son of Moshe Shers

by Moshe Bar-David

Translated by Moshe Kutten

Edited by Jane S. Gabin

There are *Ba'alei Tefillah* [Prayer Master] who are respected only in their town, and there are those whose name precedes them in any location, even far away places. Such a *Ba'al Tefillah* was Vava from Kozova.

His family was among Brzezany residents for generations, and he grew up in the town and studied in the Yeshiva, where he received his rabbinical ordination from the Maharsha"m. When he got married, he moved to Kozova, a town near our Brzezany.

The *gabbaim* of Rabbi Yudel's *Beit HaMidrash* would invite him to serve as the "*Shli'akh Tzibur*" [leader of the congregation in prayers] because of his agreeable, clean, and tonal voice. The *gabbaim* would bring him from any location where he served as the head of a Yeshiva (Kozova, Buchach, and in 1918/19, they brought him from as far as Stanislawów).

Not every synagogue could afford the service of a distinguished *Ba'al Tefillah* like him. Only the homeowners of Rabbi Yudel's *Beit HaMidrash* could pay his price. They basically "owned" him.

I recall him serving as a *Shali'akh Tzibur* at Rabbi Yudel's synagogue before WW I. The synagogue was crowded since people came from other synagogues to enjoy his praying and majestic appearance. His prayers penetrated the hearts of his listeners, as people felt them coming from a deep and sincere religious feeling.

Not only Jews came to listen to the amazing *Ba'al Tefillah* on Yom Kippur. The Gentiles, too, came to enjoy his heavenly voice. They marveled at the prayers, although they did not understand their content.

He died in Vienna on 23 Nisan 5,690, 1930.

[Page 184]

Dr. Bernard Felk

by Dr. Eliezer Shaklai

Translated by Moshe Kutten

Edited by Jane S. Gabin

Dr. Bernard Felk

That time, I decided to arrive earlier than Dr. Felk. The time was 6 am, and I was already at the hospital, dressed in a white robe, preparing for surgery. On the prior evening, we decided to perform surgery on one of the wounded people early in the morning. After the arrival of the head nurse, Tz. Klarer, we did not wait long until Dr. Felk arrived, holding a package of his surgery tools from home. "Good morning!" he said, "there is a smell of ether in the air."

After the required preparations, we went to work, and at 8 am, we completed the surgery. Dr. Felk, a man of 82, breathed deeply, took off the robe, sat down with his eyes half shut, and sighed. "Tired?" I asked. "Not quite," he responded. "Do you feel weak after the surgery that lasted more than an hour?" "Not even that!" he answered.

After a break of a few long seconds, he breathed air into his chest through his open mouth and said: "Strange, I turned eighty-two today." "To a hundred of twenty!" I said, and he continued: "And I feel myself like a man of forty, full of vigor with a strong will to live. My ability at work is as good as it was at any time. Today, my youthful dreams and ambitions of many years are fulfilled. I was stubborn!"

In the meantime, the nurse prepared tea from the leaves of a plant without sugar (we did not have that), served us, and returned to the patient to watch over him until he recovered and woke up from the anesthesia.

Sighs of the sick could be heard from the adjacent room. It was suffocating in the room and warm, and we were tired, facing another long day of work.

After taking a few sips, Dr. Felk stood the cup, looked at me, lowered his stare, and continued: "Yes… I was stubborn… and this is my life story."

"I have a few memories from my childhood. One of them was the yelling argument between my parents about the older son (this is me). I do not remember the reason for the argument. But I do recall that my father *z"l* said: 'But he is stubborn. Where would that lead him in life?' I did not know then what the meaning of the word stubborn was, but I felt its implication throughout my life.

"My father was a tailor. He worked hard to make a living for his family. My mother helped him with the sewing and also managed the household. I decided to study. To fulfill my decision, I earned money by giving private lessons in high school and during my studies at the university. I graduated with honors. I had big ambitions. I believed in my abilities and dreamt of being a surgeon in a large Jewish hospital. That was why I accepted a job at a hospital.

"It was not easy for me. I had my own plans and did not want to give up. Not everything I dreamt about was possible. Today, I look at everything with different eyes. I did not understand then and fought with colleagues at work."

Then he stopped. "I did not achieve what I was looking for." He threw those words in the air as if he was talking to himself. "After a few years of work, I was forced to leave the hospital. It hurt me a lot.

"I married. Luckily, my wife helped me. We had two daughters. I began working in a private practice and earned nicely. I worked hard, but I was not satisfied. I did not feel gratified at that work.

[Page 185]

"I had the ambition to achieve more. Man shall not live on bread alone. Was I an honor chaser? I do not think so. I was restless. There was a demand and desire for action.

"Public work was the second endeavor where I tried my skills. I thought of taking the management of the community into my own hands – there was a wide field of action there. I approached the work with vigor and will. I did not spare my precious time or money. However, I did not consider that I was not alone in the community, and not everything I thought was good was also good in the eyes of others. Not many days passed before a conflict erupted between me and the rest of the elected people. I was stubborn and did not give up, but they ganged against me; I was alone and was forced out.

"Years passed, and the First World War was over. I saw our youth, how they progressed, and new horizons opened for them. I said to myself – the time has come to build a house for them. That time, I also decided to stick to my opinion until the end.

"I got money from my relatives in America. I bought a plot on my own initiative, organized the plans, and began building. I knew if I had to consult with others, the house would not be constructed. They resisted me there, too. All of a sudden, everyone became a construction expert. Everyone knew how, where, and what to build. They did not like the location, and all so more the plan! I did not give up that time. It cost me energy, health, and money, but I completed what I had started.

"The house – the 'People's House' exists and stands. But they took revenge on me. They called for a general assembly and elected a committee to manage the house without me, Dr. Felk. They took something dear to me, my 'dandled' child, and rudely drove me away. They told me – you completed the work; now you can leave. I left with a pain in my heart.

"I am at the end of my life now, and everything changed in my eighty-second year. They turned to me today, gave me my honor back, and gave me the possibility to act, do, and help. I am a member of the 'The

Committee of the Jews.' I got back to the People's House. It is all mine now. I am responsible for the health of the Jews in our city, and I manage the Jewish hospital.

"The conditions in which we live today are harsh and require effort, wisdom, and goodwill. I am ready to accept any task. If that is the reward for my ambitions of all those years, I am available to commit. I am not tired. This time, I would stay until the end."

"Well done!" I said, adding I am available to help you.

I got up, and I moved to help him wear his robe. He refused. "I am still young," he said. I looked at him from the side, the 82-year-old youngster. He was always dressed well. He was meticulous, a bit plump, with broad shoulders, average height, round face, wise burning eyes, short nose above thick lips, full of vigor.

One small bullet from the Gestapo put an end to his ambitions and plans. Dr. Felk fell on his way to the hospital. I was near him when he was hit. I admitted medical help, and he said to me – "continue in my way!"

"Yes, I will do that," I said, and at that moment, I thought – "he was stubborn all his life until his end. He died stubbornly."

His grave is in Litiatin Forests. May his memory be blessed.

[Page 186]

Dr. Khaim (Edmond) Vilner

by Moshe Bar-David

Translated by Moshe Kutten

Edited by Jane S. Gabin

Dr. Khaim Vilner

Dr. Khaim Vilner was the son of Avraham Yehuda and Cherna Vilner. He was born in Brzezany in 1892. He was one of the known and active figures in the Zionist and Jewish worlds in our city. As a child, he studied at a *Kheder* and later graduated from high school. He then continued to study law at the university. He settled in our city as a known lawyer. He joined "Poalei Tzion" ["Workers of Zion" – a Marxist-Zionist movement] in his youth and became, later on, the only person with an academic education who was active in that movement. He inherited a strong character from his father, who was also a public figure and acted for the good of the Jewish community, in the community committee, welfare for the poor, "Kimkha DePaskha" [Passover charity], and more.

After the First World War, Dr. Vilner began his Zionist activity as a member of the "General Zionists" movement. He was a member of the local "Zionist Committee" and a brilliant orator, giving speeches to Zionist gatherings. He served as the chairman of the "Ezra" ["Assistance"] charity organization. He had an open hand and a generous heart to help others. He preserved the pioneering character of the "Ezra" organization. When a pioneer was about to make *Aliyah* and needed financial assistance while the fund was insufficient to cover the costs, he handed him his own money so as not to delay the departure of the pioneer and thus lose his turn for an *Aliyah* certificate. Because of his steadfast masculine appearance and roaring voice, everybody liked him, old and young. He remained popular and did not look down on people because of his status and wealth. He was an enthusiastic fan of the Jewish theater and did not miss any Yiddish plays. He used to travel to Lviv to watch the shows by the "Vilna Band" or the "Vict" theater ["Warsaw Jewish Artistic Theater"].

Upon the outbreak of the Second World War, he escaped to Romania, from where he was deported to Russia, where he suffered from oppression by the authorities in faraway Siberia and from harsh financial hardship. At the end of the war, he returned to liberated Poland but did not find his family, his wife, and his daughter, who perished in the Holocaust.

He made *Aliyah* in 1950. In the beginning, his absorption in Israel was tough. He worked hard to make a living. However, he overcame and returned to his profession as a lawyer, dealing with German reparations. He died alone in Tel Aviv in 1958.

He left part of his estate to the Hebrew University in Jerusalem.

May his memory be blessed.

Dr. Aryeh Feld

by Dr. Eliezer Shaklai

Translated by Moshe Kutten

Edited by Jane S. Gabin

We Were Friends

I always tried to fulfill the sages' proverb "buy you a friend" through the years – on the school's bench, work, and daily life. I had many friends and some real buddies; among them, I connected with my body and soul. Dr. Aryeh Feld Z" L was my friend, buddy, and brother. We connected as friends, loving each other like David and Jonathan. Our love for each other was not affected by external or material factors.

From the day we met until the moment we parted ways (knowing that it was our last conversation), we went on our ways in the same direction, course, and objective with unified forces. He was always ready and willing to help. It was like that on the study bench throughout our entire life, until those critical moments during the Holocaust, when fate intervened and separated us.

[Page 187]

Dr. Aryeh Feld

Dr. Feld came from a family of five children. He received a traditional Jewish education in his father's home, which made a mark on all his future activities. I connected with that family and loved every one of them. They differed in their characters, but I had a tight relationship with all three brothers at different times and found common ground with all of them. We studied together and lived in the same room.

The second brother, Yehuda, did not complete his studies. A malignant disease put an end to his young life. I worked with my younger brother; he helped me tremendously with responsible and arduous work during the Soviet regime.

The parents were educated people and worked hard. They aspired to provide a solid basis for their children. I often visited that home. I loved to listen to the father's stories spiced up by jokes and phrases. Despite always being busy with his work, he found free moments to talk to me.

My friend, Aryeh Feld, who was a man with many skills who was educated, had a solid and stable character, and was reserved, quiet, self-assured, and friendly with people. He was dedicated and responsible, loved people and was loved by them, and gave respect and was respected. He went through several crises in his life, but nobody knew about them. He never told anybody when he faced a problem. He thought about it and often fought with himself until he arrived at a decision, and he always realized his decisions.

He was one of the members of "HaShomer HaTzair" ["Young Guard" – leftist youth movement], one of the founders and central pillar of that movement in our city. His wish in life, the dream of his youth, was to make Aliyah, and he aspired to achieve that goal until his last moment. He was a worker – active in anything related to Judaism, particularly the land of Israel. He established a family in our city and lived an exemplary family life. His fate had another opinion, and all his values were ruined with one sweep.

The Character of the Head of the Family

The Germans first caught Aryeh on the second Yom Kippur during an *Aktsia*. He sat with many others at the collection square and was the only one that [the Gestapo's] Miller [may his name and memory be blotted out] freed. He left the square with hesitant steps. Was he allowed to leave conscious-wise? He was walking and thinking and debating. Would he do good by his acquaintances in the square slated for the crematorium, getting out of there alone, back to life? It was not an easy decision for him to make! He experienced agonizing days and hours in self-deliberation – did he act appropriately? But then he realized that he had another role in life - his family was waiting for him at home. He must continue to live to protect them.

The Conscience of a Hero

It was different from the last time when he was led with his family and many others on their final way. I heard his confession from him two days earlier, in our last meeting, after which we parted ways with a handshake. A quiet and painful scream burst out from the depths of his heart: "I blame the entire world for our situation. Who would tell what we have experienced?" That scream penetrated my heart and shook me … I could no longer hold back and burst into tears … I gave vent to my tears, not to the words. I only shook his hand, and we parted ways. I still see him in my mind, marching toward the cemetery, holding the hands of his daughter, his wife by his side, supported by his other arm, and holding the son in her hand, covering his head with her dress. They are marching, step by step, to the cemetery toward the mass grave.

[Page 188]

The thoughts that bothered him so much during these days must have accompanied him on that long and tiresome road: who would tell the world, and who would believe what happened? They arrived at the mass grave. At first, they shot the children who fell into the pit. After them, the mother. His turn came. He approached – and stepped forward with his face to the pit. He threw a last look at his dear ones in the dark pit and waited for the bullet. But the bullet was late in coming; the seconds were long, but the bullet did not come!

Suddenly. the Gestapo order broke his heart like thunder: "Leave this place, leave the cemetery, and go back to the city! We still need your work. Go now, Jew! Your turn will come! Fast; do not just stand there! Bless your luck, Jew, and continue to carry your poisoned life until your turn comes … Go! Don't you hear the order? Ha, Ha, ha."

But he did not hear the order. Only the yelling and hellish lough of the Gestapo work.

"Do not judge your friend until you get to his place," said our sages *z"l*.

Shock-stricken, Feld obeyed the order, and with slow and stumbling steps, he lived in the cemetery. He was walking, but did he see the road? Did he understand and know where he was going? His being led him away from the cemetery. But at the same time, they freed him from the order. He became more aware of his surroundings. He recovered and began to think. He began to comprehend what happened. The farther away from the cemetery, the weaker the screams emanating from there, but they became more painful, and they gave him back the ability to judge. His heart was beating hard. His legs still carried him away, proceeding by the force of habit, but the pace was slow.

He stopped and thought: "Whom and what am I running away from? Where am I going? Who am I doing that for? Who did I leave my family with? Do I still have a purpose and a goal for my life? No."

He decided that it was not his way to leave. He returned to the cemetery. He ran; he was in a hurry to return in time for the mass grave to be still open. Everyone knew and felt that he was still with them. He did not abandon them, G-d forbids! He must show the murderers that no order would separate him from his family! There is one fate for everybody. He ran and finally achieved his goal! He was inside the mass grave together with his family and his brothers, the Jews.

I had a friend. I got him as a gift from the heavens, and there where he was taken to. May he rest in peace!

[Page 189]

Dr. Moshe Schumer

by Motek Rozentzveig

Translated by Moshe Kutten

Edited by Jane S. Gabin

Dr. Moshe Schumer

Dr. Schumer was a figure with noble virtues, rooted in the Hebrew culture, an energetic Zionist activist, and honest. As a result, he was loved and admired by all the population in Brzezany. He dedicated his life to the Zionist ideas and help for the needy.

He was born in Brzezany on 1/27/1890 to his parents, Ester and Aba Schumer. Upon the outbreak of the First World War, he went with his parents to Vienna, where he was accepted to "Vindobona" University [The old name of Vienna University was "Alma Mater Rudolphina Vindobonensis"] where he was active in all areas of the student life. He graduated medical school in 1921 and returned to Brzezany as a general practitioner. There, he became involved in all areas of public affairs. He served for many years as the chairman of Keren Kayemet [JNF-KKL] and, through that position, maintained a tight relationship with all the Zionist Youth movements in town. He was also active for many years at the Jewish orphanage. Although officially he was a member of the "General Zionists" [centrist Zionist movement], he did see it as a conflict of interest serving the representative of "HaShomer HaTzair" ["Young Guard" - leftist youth movement] and "HeKhalutz" ["The Pioneer" pioneering labor youth movement] toward the authorities.

He visited the summer camps of the "HeKhalutz." He also actively assisted the pioneers of the Hakhshara [Agricultural training] company in the movement in the city. He was the driving force in all national funds and contributed generously to anybody who turned to him for help.

He was registered at the Golden Book of the JNF-KKL when he reached 50. By all the Zionist movements in the city as a token of appreciation for his fruitful activity.

He treated anybody who turned to him and did not demand payment from the poor; on the contrary, he often helped to get the medicines for them.

The Second World War took him to Russia. He was recruited by the Soviets as a physician for the Soviet Army, and he passed the entire war on the front as a medical officer with the rank of Major.

He experienced a harsh mental crisis while serving in the Red Army. Somehow, the Russians discovered his Zionist past and began harassing him and restricting him. He was placed under continuous surveillance by the NKVD [The Soviet secret police], who made his life unbearable. Under that situation, he reached an atrocious state of mind. Only thanks to the encouragement from another Jewish physician who worked with him did he pull himself out of that crisis.

At the end of the Second World War, he returned to Brzezany. However, since he did not find anybody from his family, he continued to Germany, aiming to go to Israel. He stayed a long time in the refugee camps of UNRRA and practiced medicine there. That was when he met Regina Ast and finally established a family in the twilight of his life.

In 1948, he fulfilled his life dream – and finally made *Aliyah*. He settled in Hadera, where he worked as a physician for a short period for Israel's labor HMO and the Jewish Agency. He lived to enjoy the sun's brilliance in Israel.

He died on 5/10/1955

[Page 190]

Dr. Shlomo Glazer
On the Image of a Zionist Activist

by Dov Glazer

Translated by Moshe Kutten

Edited by Jane S. Gabin

Dr. Shlomo Glazer

The revolutionary period in the Jewish world - the transition between the nineteenth and twentieth centuries - gave birth to that man and made its mark on him. That period, which opened new horizons for the Jewish youth, also presented some tough problems to them: finding the right way and not getting lost on life's various roads. How to approach these problems, how to solve them, and the wisdom to distinguish between good and bad – all of that he learned in his father's home. Torah atmosphere prevailed at that home, progress, and Zionism. In that home, the roots of his personality were struck. Here is where he drew his wisdom and the "love of Israel." His father *z"l* knew how to connect all three in educating his children (he had five sons and a daughter). He considered the past (as the Torah and its greatness and wisdom as a basis for the entire Jewish nation); the present (the crossroad of "today" in search of new life), and the future (the future of the nation and his children). His motto in educating his children was: "[It is good to] grasp the one and not let go of the other" [Ecclesiastes 7:18]. He gave his children all the possibilities to advance in their new lives without neglecting the study of the Torah and the education to love the nation and the Jewish faith. That education bore fruit: "The sons hold the deeds of their father in their hands."

His initial work began in high school. He, several other students, and his elder brother organized themselves in a Zionist club. They studied Hebrew, Jewish, and Zionist history and utilized the knowledge they had acquired to teach others in Zionist circles by giving lectures and lessons and organizing "*Oneg Shabbat*" parties. That work continued until the outbreak of the First World War.

In 1915, he and his brothers were taken by the Russians as hostages to Russia. They returned home only in 1918, after the Bolshevik revolution.

Dr. Shlomo completed his law studies and continued his Zionist work, which he had temporarily ceased during those years. I came to know that modest and shy man while working for the Zionist cause. He always had a smile, liked gentle humor, respected old and young, was loved by people, and was friendly. He was always very busy. At home – he was establishing his family in the harsh conditions of the years after the First World War; in his professional work – he had a lot of work despite being a young lawyer. In all of those situations, he always found time for public work. He left speeches and honors for others while doing the actual work. In his Zionist work, he was unaffiliated. We saw him at all Zionist youth movements. We met with him at gatherings and went together to collect money for the JNF-KKL and "Keren HaYesod" ["United Israel Appeal"] or at the support activity for youth who were making *Aliyah*. He did his work perfectly, willing and alert.

A relative wrote about him: "Many of our city natives, spread throughout the country, surely have many memories related to the branch of "HaShomer HaTzair," which together with the "HeKhalutz" movement concentrated the best of the Jewish Zionist youth in the city. For many of us, it served as our second home. Within its walls, we were free from the troubles at home and from the pressure of the school's antisemitism.

We found innocence and friendship at the branch, like in a bird's nest. We grew up there without a feeling of inferiority, and we had a woven youth life full of content. That was where we dreamt about making *Aliyah* the Land of Israel.

[Page 191]

Everyone who raises the scene in front of their eyes of the "HaShomer HaTzair's" branch from its beginning until the days of its flourishing could not pass over to prominent figures: Dr. Schumer *z"l*, who died in Hadera, and lawyer Dr. Shlomo Glazer, who perished with most of his family in the Holocaust.

The members of the branch did not know these figures. They operated modestly behind the scenes. They were the "OPIEKA" ("patronage'), the committee responsible for the authority for the legal existence of the movement and the fulfillment of the by-laws. That was a heavy burden and tremendous responsibility. Not many people among the distinguished people of the intelligentsia were willing to be a guarantor for the passionate and rebellious youth. In particular, the atrocious period of the "Red Assimilation" must be noted. Many movement members left for ideological reasons and joined a rival camp, which was oppressed by the authorities. The threat of the closure of the branch was not late. Only because of the intervention and stability of these two figures did the authorities approve the continuous and stable existence of the branch. Thanks to them, we received permits for the summer camps ("colonies"), where we could maintain the life of a *Shomeric* Colony in the "bosom of nature," encompassing tens of branches from throughout the Ternopil district.

I did not know Dr. Schumer well. However, I frequently visited my relative, Dr. Melu ?] [Shlomo] Glazer's home. Despite the age difference, I was invited to his home as a friend. I particularly loved to come to his home because of the warm and friendly atmosphere he knew to induce in his family and guests. I felt equal among equals at his home. It was where I drew strength and belief in humans and the goodness of people.

He was an educated man with high virtues and reserved. He listened more than he talked and hid more than he revealed. He never preached morality to others because he believed that tests that people experience in life determine man's way. He did not like to stand out. He shied away from publicity and chose to be away from the limelight. From a distance of many years and periods, he remained in my memory as a simple, warm-hearted man, unformal, graceful, and fatherly. He understood the soul of the youth, as was expressed in his relations with his children and relatives. The house was full of fatherly love for his family.

He loved to stroll around with young people in an atmosphere of friendship and open heart. He behaved toward us joyfully and engaged in pleasant conversation. That joyful atmosphere could have become deep, and thoughtfuly serious in a moment while maintaining the feeling of being equal in his company.

That was the man, and that is how I will always remember him. May his memory be blessed.

[Page 192]

Ozer Rot – The Fulfilling Zionist

Translated by Moshe Kutten

Edited by Jane S. Gabin

Ozer Rot

By Menakhem Katz

Before I prepared to edit this book, my first thoughts turned to Ozer Rot, my teacher and rabbi *z"l*. The image of my teacher-friend accompanies me until today. I drew my initial Hebrew and religious knowledge from him, and I learned from him about the Land of Israel, building it, and its past and present heroes. His intellectual level was high. His knowledge of religious studies and his unexhausted vigor in his work for the pioneering-Zionist movement placed him on the first row of the movement leaders.

Ozer was a speaker par excellence who knew how to enthuse his listeners. He served as a *personal* example of fulfilling the pioneering idea of the Torah and work. That's how he acquired his name among his students and friends, and even his opponents. Whoever knew the warm-blooded Ozer respected his views even if they objected to them and knew that the views came from his heart and that all his motives were true and sincere.

I have decided on the article "The Fulfilling Zionist" because that was what he was.

When he died, I lost a relative, friend, and teacher. However, we all also lost a symbol of a dedicated and sincere Zionist, a symbol it would be hard to find elsewhere today.

As such, he is worthy to be remembered for generations. May his memory be blessed.

* * *

By Rivka Cohen-Rot

This is written on behalf of the daughters, sons-in-law, and grandchildren, who were loved so much by my parents and were their pride.

My father was born in a small town, Pomoriany, near Brzezany on 11 Tevet 5,656 (1896) to his father R' Nathan *z"l*, a ritual slaughterer and a Mohel, and his mother Bluma *z"l*.

He spent his childhood among the antisemites and violent Gentile children. Already in his childhood, he knew that he would need to better them in wisdom and physical strength. He says: "As a Jewish kid, he felt that I always needed to win against the big '*Shkutzim*' [derogatory term for hateful Gentile children]," and that was what happened. "Me, the little Jew, stood my ground against the big '*Shkutzim*' and won against them." That fact was the basis for his national Jewish views and the foundation for his strong character, required to withstand tough undertakings, not yield, be consistent, sincerely strive for justice, and deplore injustice.

Like many of his generation, he was educated in a *Kheder* and Yeshivot, for which we do not have any details. He served in the Austrian military in the First World War.

He arrived in Brzezany after WW I at the end of 1919, when the first pioneering groups began to organize to make *Aliyah*. Already then, he began to plan to make *Aliyah*. On 10 Kheshvan 5682 (1922), he married Shifra, the daughter of R' Israel and Khana Kalman (whose families lived in Brzezany for generations). He worked as a small merchant for a living, with my mother helping him. Her involvement enabled him to devote time to public affairs, to which he dedicated most of his time, strength, and vigor. As a national religious Jew on one side and a Chortkiv Hasid on the other, he was a member of "Tzeirei Mizrakhi" ["HaMizrakhi Youth"]. He participated in the leadership of the local branch and represented the movement in the district and province. He was also a representative of movement conferences and in the 12th and 13th Jewish Zionist Congresses (1921 and 1923 respectively, in Carlsbad-Karlovy Vary).

[Page 193]

Ozer Rot as a British guard (sitting fourth from right)

A group of Jewish guards guarding the airport in Kibbutz Afikim,
5699 – 1938. Rot is fourth from the right.

218 Brzezany Memorial Book

In addition to his regular job, our father worked in beekeeping to supplement his income. That occupation was his connection to nature. Everything connecting to nature and the natural landscape got him very excited. Beekeeping represented for him the attachment to the land, agriculture, and actually to his childhood in the village. His activity with "Tzeirei HaMizrakhi" led him to guide. He established the agricultural *Hakhshara* camp in Kosov, where he taught beekeeping to the members. The same members were among the founders of the "Avraham" group in Kfar Pines in 1934, and later, the group settled in Kfar Etzion in 1943.

As an educator, my father maintained a religious-national orientation. To realize that philosophy, he thought he must provide a personal example by educating his daughters according to that orientation. He, therefore, created the appropriate conditions that would complement the education at home. In parallel to enrolling us in the public Catholic Christian school, he made sure we also studied at the "Tarbut" ["Culture"] school (He was one of the activists in its founding and management). There, we studied Hebrew, the official language at the school, Zionism, etc. He also paid a *Melamed* to teach us reading in the *Sidur* and the prayers. When I entered the first class in school, he took me every Saturday to the branch of "Bnei Akiva" [religious youth movement], despite the objection by my mother and grandmother Z" l. He explained: "If I would not take her to 'Bnei Akiva', she would go tomorrow to "HaShomer HaTzair" [non-religious Marxist youth movement]. He valued the educational contribution of the youth movement in forging character and shaping our personality starting at a young age. In educating his children, he arranged for the three worlds to be merged – the general, religious, and national.

The stories told by my father, as they were etched in memory, concentrated around two subjects: 1) the relations between a people and the honoring of a father and mother;2) the Land of Israel, love of the nation and its land. Due to family and political reasons, he made *Aliyah* only in 1934. He joined a large group of Brzezany natives from the city. Like every new immigrant, he experienced a crisis that manifested itself in the decline of social and economic status. That lasted about half a year. Father, the joyful and smiley man who had a story for every situation, walked around in a serious and depressed mood. Since most of the Brzezany natives settled in Haifa, he, too, settled in that city. They constituted an economic and social support system for each other – that enabled him, like others from that city, to overcome crises and absorb the new reality.

For Father, the building of the Land of Israel and the Hebrew language were intertwined. He was already fluent in Hebrew in Brzezany. From the moment we got off the ship in Haifa, he did not allow us to speak Polish. He said: "In the land of Israel, we speak Hebrew. We no longer speak the language of the diaspora; we have just left with G-d's help." He even pushed aside Yiddish, even though he loved the language, and always pointed at its juiciness.

From the *Aliyah* until his death (28 Kislev 5723-1962), he resided and was active in Haifa. As a member of the "Hadar-HaCarmel Committee," he worked on constructing the first water system, which was hard physical work. He was also a member of the "HaMizrakhi" district office, the executive committee, party headquarters, and a representative of various conferences. In his activity, he concentrated on two important projects of the branch: 1) as a man of books, he volunteered to establish and manage the general and Torah-based library; 2) he was active in the charity fund and a member of the management team.

He self-taught and acquired his general education by increased reading. He was particularly interested in the relationships between people, Hebrew and general literature, and everything associated with Zionism and religious Zionism. He considered geography and Jewish history as complementary to the vast knowledge he had about Judaism.

[Page 194]

With the riots in 1936-1939, he volunteered for defense and guard duties, serving directly under Chief of Staff General Dori. We do not have details about his military duties. Everything we know is what we saw. He did hard physical work during the day, and at night, he trained in using weapons and guarded in various locations. He was sworn in as a "Gafir" [British mandate's auxiliary policeman] and as such, he guarded the first airport of the "Haganah" in 1938. He also served as a guard in other locations under the disguise of a fireman. Those roles allowed him to carry weapons approved by the English mandate authority – which, in turn, enabled him to hide additional weapons of the Haganah at home, despite the danger,

As a religious person, he despised using religion for personal benefit. When he was assigned guard duty on Shabbat, he tried to get a permit from the Rabbinate based on the principle of "Pikuakh Nefesh" [the preservation of human life overrides any other religious rule, including Shabbat rules]. Since he did not receive a clear-cut answer, he walked on foot to the guard location, endangering his life, and refused to be replaced by his non-religious friends. His concept was that "If there is a prohibition [of traveling by car], it should placed on everybody, since all of them were Jews. On this subject, he knew no compromises. He claimed that the problems of "the state in the making" must be solved by religiously-acceptable solutions equal to all.

The Jewish population in the Land of Israel experienced a severe economic crisis during the Second World War, which led to unemployment and dismissals. Among those who were dismissed were some of his closest friends. He offered to split his days of work with his friends. He worked only three days a week for several months and donated the other days to one of his best friends.

Despite the economic distress, my parents saw it as their utmost duty to provide their children with the broadest education possible.

At the end of WW II, my cousin David Goldshield *z"l*, the son of my father's sister, arrived in Israel. His parents perished in the Holocaust. He was only 16 and was sent to Mikveh Israel [agricultural boarding school] by the "Aliyat HaNoar." When he was not absorbed at that school, we took him in, and he grew up at our house like a son. David was killed near Jenin during the Independence War when he was only 19. That disaster had an enormous effect on my father. He joined and harnessed himself to the activity of the committee of grieving parents, "Yad LeVanim." He was instrumental in strengthening the committee and took part in its activity of memorializing the fallen.

The tragic events of the Holocaust were always on his mind. The loss of most of the nation did not let him rest. For that reason, he harnessed himself to the effort of establishing the *landsman-shaft* committee for Brzezany natives aimed to memorialize the fallen. As a secretary of the committee, he spurred and whipped to ensure the publishing of this memorial book. Unfortunately, he did not live to see the book published.

I mentioned that he was a thinker with original reasoning and a man of personal example. I will bring here a portion of the many letters he wrote to me: "You are reaching maturity and independence. I congratulate you and wish you that your way will not be paved with roses, thistles, thorns, and big rocks and that you will have the strength to overcome all of the obstacles and choose and pave the right way that fits you on which you will able to march safely with your head held high." Those words encapsulate his personality, his being, and way of my father's life. He was an "institution" not only for his children but for everyone whom he worked and acted with. When he was still full of vigor, he went on trips throughout the country, the whole width and length, swimming at sea in the summer and winter, always smiling, joyful, a man of humor and good words.

He died suddenly on 28 Kislev, 5723 [1962], when he was only 67.

[Page 195]

When we talk about my father *z"l*, it is impossible not to mention my mother, Shifra *z"l*. She was born on 7 Av 7/11/1892 and died on 4 Elul 5731 (1971).

She was a modest woman, very clever, practical, gentle, independent, and aspired to reach every objective alone without the help of others,

She helped Father loyally, modestly, and quietly. She worked hard at home and outside to help make a living. She was always by his side, enabling his activities while hiding behind the scenes. She was proud of his contributions to others. Our home was always open to friends, relatives, and Brzezany's natives. When the latter arrived in Haifa, they had a place to stay. It was never too small. Like having taken an active role in making a living, she had a role in our education and the direction of our studies: "Whatever I did not receive from my parents, I want my children to get." She excelled in her practical and artistic skills, which she did not have the opportunity to develop. She was sorry about that throughout her entire life. Mother was an" Inner King's Daughter," and that's how she remains in our memory.

Shlomo Redlikh

by Dr. Eliezer Shaklai

Translated by Moshe Kutten

Edited by Jane S. Gabin

Shlomo Redlikh

My neighbor, who was also a friend, was injured at work in his finger and came to me to dress the wound. Today, I think he came to me to talk. I wanted to treat him quickly because I knew he needed to return to work hurriedly. But he refused, saying that he had just come to speak to me. I understood him well. I, too, wished to meet him and pour my bitter heart out. I asked him to wait.

The German Army progressed eastward.

We are approaching annihilation, I said. I do not see any possibility to get out of this mess. Hi…r (may his name be blotted out) is ruling the whole world. He has already conquered Ukraine and is standing at the gates of Moscow. What will be the end? Do you think England will be able to withstand the pressure and hold on until America is ready to join the war? Besides that, isn't America busy with Japan? Everything was black in my eyes, without a glimmer of hope.

[Page 196]

"Why?" – he answered – "I see things differently. I can see now the defeat of Hi…r. Do you know where his demise will come from? – it will come from his win. He will be buried here. Here in the East. Here, in the snow, cold, mud, and the vast areas. They will defeat him. We will return to Zion. I already see our joyful day, the celebration after his defeat. Not everybody will indeed be there as the bride's parents, but the wedding will take place. I am sure that you will also be there. Remember!"

The clock showed five-fifty. "Go," – I said – "the gates are closing at 6, and Jews are not allowed to get out of their house!" He went, and I was left with my thoughts. Is it possible that this man is right? Perhaps he came to comfort.

Days passed, the summer ended, and every day brought a new victory for the enemy. Every victory resulted in brand-new troubles and decrees. Every trouble brought depression, bitterness, and spiritual and physical weakness. Winter 1941 arrived, and with it, a glimmer of hope. We secretly listened to the radio and read German newspapers. We read between the lines and found a partial comfort: H…r has paused. H…r cannot withstand general "cold" and general "mud." We met him again at the "Judenrat." And his face was filled with joy.

The winter passed, and with it – our hope. The 1942 offensive brought our enemy additional victories. The Germans conquered Crimea, penetrated the suburbs of Stalingrad, and stood in front of Moscow. They held most of Stalingrad, and the German Army crossed the Volga River. In the meantime, we moved to the ghetto. Many of us were not alive any longer – our people died from hunger, were killed in forced labor camps, and murdered in Belzec. The rest of us waited to die.

On one of the days, I met him accompanied by Ukrainians, who led him to work. His face was pale, his back bent, and he was weak and tired. I hinted at my question – "What will happen?" He answered with a small smile at the edge of his mouth. I understood …

A big turn took place in the winter of 1942/43. Hi…r suffered one defeat after the other. The Soviet Army conquered back one area after the other, city after city, and approached us from one day to the other,

The ghetto's residents disappeared by the day. We remained just a few. Hi…r was adamant to finish us all. There were victims every day. Every day, the Germans caught some of us and killed them. Every day – there were fewer people in the ghetto. A little comfort was the thought that Hi…r would eventually be defeated' however, who among us would live to see it?

On one of the February 1943 days, when I passed through the border of the ghetto, I heard his voice calling: "Wait, don't run away. Did you hear that Kyiv is in our hands? Did you hear what is happening in North Africa? You would live to see Hi…r's defeat. Another day, another month, and he would not last. Now I can see the voice of the people singing our victory song. I only want one thing from you. When salvation comes, and you will survive, then…"

[Page 197]

I did not see them, but I felt that they were coming and approaching. I did not say goodbye and continued on my way. My heart stopped beating, my face paled, and only my legs continued to carry me forward. I wore a band on my left arm, with a red Star of David and the word "Physician" written on it. I opened the door of a pharmacy located in front of me. I stood there catching my breath and waited. The moments lasted forever. One moment seemed like a whole year. One more moment and another, and another, and suddenly – shooting. "What happened? Was he killed?"

A few more long moments passed. I knew I could not stay in that location and needed to run away. When I opened the door, I met two Gestapo people. They recognized me and asked mockingly: "Are you going to determine the cause of death?" "No," I answered and went to where my friend lay to say goodbye. He lay there with his eyes half opened. Blood poured from his temples and colored the snow with a crimson stain.

I stood there for a short while and looked at him. His face did not change, but I saw his lips murmuring and whispering. I put my ears close to hear his last words. I heard his voice during his visit two years ago and again when we talked ten minutes ago: "Our joyful day will come. You will survive, and then, **don't forget me!**"

I kept his memory with me. **I did not forget him**, as I did with some others with whom I spent time together.

When I used to return to Brzezany during the breaks from studies, I and several other friends spent the evenings together and on trips outside the city. Among the regular people on these trips was this man, Shlomo Redlikh Z" L, a man who was older than us by many years but was young at heart, perhaps the youngest of all of us. He was full of vigor and love of life despite his physical pain and his worries, which he tried to hide from us. He was a bachelor. His friends had already grown children and even grandchildren. He distanced himself from his peers and remained young. He looked for and found his place among the young. His face and body testified to his years of physical suffering. Thin, bent, and with crooked fingers, he pulled his legs and breathed heavily. But in conversations, he was the opposite of that – young and fresh. He was educated, learned, and clever. He left the "*Beit HaMidrash*" to study general sciences. He disconnected from his past but, like many others like him, was unsuccessful in adapting to modern life and remained outside the fence. He was a Hebrew teacher par excellence, and I am not sure why he did not work in his profession. He was a gentle soul, sensitive to other people's suffering, had humor, was a storyteller, and knew to sing and joke. He understood the young soul, knew how to live with them, and understood when he needed to live alone with themselves.

We respected and loved him and learned from him life wisdom. His hobby was theater directing. In those moments, he forgot the entire world surrounding him, the worries and suffering, and found himself in a different world - all his. That was the only pleasure in his life, where he drew some satisfaction.

He experienced tremendous suffering during the Holocaust, but his spirit remained strong. He truly believed in Hi…r's defeat and Jewish salvation. His dream was eventually fulfilled. We will keep his request and **will not forget him**.

[Page 198]

Benyamin Te'eni

by Erica Ilan Te'eni

Translated by Moshe Kutten

Edited by Jane S. Gabin

Benyamin Te'eni

My father, Benyamin Te'eni, was born on 5/14/1900 to Aryeh and Henrieta Feigenbaum, who owned a farm near Brzezany. As a child, he grew up on the farm, in nature, but in Gentile surroundings. As a lonely child in a group of Gentile children, he developed the senses of self-defense and self-pride, which were apparent in his life as an adult.

When he reached the age of high school, he moved to Brzezany, where he studied at the high school and was involved in the life of student youth in the city. From among the many political currents that flooded our town after the First World War, he chose the Zionist movement. Since he viewed the Zionist idea as a way of life, he began to fulfill it in practice.

I heard about his young adulthood and first Zionist activity from his *landsman*, Moshe Bar David. "He was tall, good-looking with broad shoulders." That is how the story began. "It was in one of Saturday afternoons in 1918 when we went out on an 'activity' as members of the "HaShomer HaTzair" movement to the 'Roriska Forest,' to nature, to discuss the subject of Zionism and pioneering.

The discussion and the game we played progressed pleasantly until a group of "*Shkutzim*" [a derogatory term for Gentile children] appeared suddenly and began to harass us. Frightened due to the surprise and the size of the attacking group, we gathered around Benyamin. Without a hint of panic, he tried to convince the "*Shkutzim*," in a pleasant but firm language, to leave us alone. The "convincing" was not very effective, so Benyamin broke a branch from a tree and went alone to teach the "*Shkutzim*" a lesson about "the desired course of behavior" toward Jews. Not that many moments later, they ran away, yelling in pain. We completed our "action" safely and returned to the city.

"He was a 'leader in the making' who succeeded, early on, in gathering around him a large group of youths who flocked after him and listened to him without any complaint. His sturdy figure, good heartiness, and natural leadership instilled in us self-confidence, assurance in our way of life, physical safety, and feeling in our surroundings, which was missing so much during those days."

He first connected with the "HaShomer" movement and acted as a guide for the young generation. In 1919, he was among those who organized the first group of pioneers for *Aliyah*. When the date approached before completing high school, getting the matriculation certificate before making the *Aliyah* became problematic. However, the high school management considered his vigor and skills and granted him the certificate before the end of the year in order not to interfere with the date for his *Aliyah*. He made *Aliyah* in the same year, 1920, as a pioneer, together with two young men, Yosheh Haber and Libling.

[Page 199]

As his first step in Eretz Israel, he took then initiative to fulfill the principle of Hebraic work in the homeland. He first worked as an agriculturalist in Rosh Pina and Metula. While wandering around in the Galilee, he moved to Tiberias. He worked there as a carpenter and a guard in nearby Mitzpa and the surrounding areas. As the pioneering spirit never left him, he joined "Khavurat HaEmek" [a pioneering group of road pavers and public works workers] and worked in road construction. In 1922, he moved to Haifa with his friends to promote Hebraic work, where he worked until the dissolution of the workgroup.

At that time, he transferred to the public works department, where he managed the construction of various public buildings. In parallel, he completed his studies at the Technion [University].

His affinity for the public interest and his tremendous vigor brought him quickly to the management of public works. In 1925, he was elected a representative of Haifa workers to the "Hadar HaCramel Committee" [the municipal council for the Jewish section of Haifa]. In 1928, he was nominated to manage the water project of the committee, established as the "municipal authority of the city's Jewish population," which competed with the municipal council of the [British] Mandate. He demonstrated tremendous workability, skills, and expertise. Thanks to those attributes, he succeeded in establishing an exemplary water system, which successfully competed with other water systems in the city.

Besides his work activity, he was involved in other diversified public affairs activities. He was a member of the Judging team of the Magistrate court and of the "Histadrut labor union." He was also a member of the committee for housing disputes and other public committees.

With all of his public activities, he did not forget about his family and *landsmen*. Before 1937, he succeeded in receiving [*Aliyah*] certificates and brought his entire family from Europe to Eretz Israel. The Feigenbaum family was the first such family from Brzezany to make *Aliyah*. Before the Second World War, he visited his native city twice and convinced many people there to follow his steps and make *Aliyah*. With the increase in the number of people who made *Aliyah* during the 1930s, he did not neglect his *landsmen*. He invested precious time, despite his busy schedule, to help every immigrant from his native city. He advised, guided, and provided assistance. He handed real help to some by arranging for a job, others by writing a recommendation, and even by hiring for a job at the committee he managed.

He dedicated his vigor to the "HaPoel" [sports organization] and acted as an arbitrator in various opportunities. During the Second World War, with the formation of the Jewish Brigade, he devoted his time to the recruitment office. He was also active at the "Haganah," and fulfilled essential roles on its behalf in defense matters. Throughout his life, during calm days and in days of war, he believed in the path he chose for his life. He stood on guard, always self-assured in his way.

He was on a mission during his last day on 22 Shvat 5708, 2/2/1948. Despite warnings about sharpshooter shooting on the shore highway [between Haifa and Tel Aviv], he traveled with two of his friends to Tel Aviv to discuss the construction of security roads in Haifa. Opposite the [Arab] village of Tira, a bus hit their car purposely, a few shots were fired, and he was killed. He was brought to be buried at the military cemetery in Haifa.

* * *

Not only the members of the family who lost a father, husband, and relative, but the entire city of Haifa lost a leader. Our public lost an outstanding advisor and activist in public affairs, and his *landsmen* lost a loyal friend. These words here will serve as an eternal memorialization and recognition of his multi-faced activism and dedication to the needs of the individual and the public. May his memory be blessed.

The editor

[Page 200]

Yoshe (Yosef) Ast – The Book-Seller

by Moshe Bar-David

Translated by Joseph Schachter

The only Yiddish bookstore that sold both Hebrew and Yiddish books in our town was operated by the "bookseller," Yoshe Ast. He was not just any old bookseller who sold books to others without himself reading any of them, but to the contrary, he read them before he sold them. At one time, Yoshe Ast had been a grain merchant, and later, he began to deal with books. He was a devout Jew, well-grounded in [Torah] learning, and yet, he was also enlightened He loved Hebrew scholarly texts as well as modern Hebrew novels and good Yiddish literature. He read every book, knew all his customers, and knew what to offer them. He also had Holy Books [religious literature], tales of the Sages, and occasionally a rare manuscript. He knew a great deal and was familiar with the families of many previous generations who lived in the city, their pedigree, their rise and fall, and the complicated branches of the families, as well as a bit of local gossip. One could say that he was a living encyclopedia of the town. He was a friendly and upright person. The young people would happily patronize his bookshop and would listen to his talks about authors and their works, Rabbis and good Jews from the past and the present, a deep well-spring with much knowledge. His shop was in Yerucham Leber's house, and he lived on Bernardine Street near Shloimele Prisant's house. He had two children, a son Yehoshua (Shike) and a daughter Dvorke, both well-educated as teachers. Both, while living in Brzezan, were members of Zionist youth organizations in which they were actively engaged. In later years, they lived elsewhere, having taken educational posts in Congress Poland.

Yoshe Ast, who gave good advice to many Jews, was not able to find a solution when he himself really needed one. His honest and high moral stature presented him with a dilemma he couldn't overcome. When his son-in-law became enmeshed in business difficulties and involved his father-in-law as a witness – and since Yoshe felt he would have to testify under oath in court – which was against his principles, he was unable to bear the burden, he took it to heart, and several days before the trial he died of a heart-attack. The Jewish population was orphaned without a Yiddish bookseller, who for more than a generation, provided them with their needs of Yiddish and Hebrew books.

[Page 201]

Yekhiel Peltz

by Avraham KhaRa"P *z"l*

Translated by Moshe Kutten

Edited by Jane S. Gabin

Yekhiel Peltz studied at a *Kheder* as a child and later in *Beit HaMidrash*. He left the Torah studies with a few friends and went to Berlin to acquire knowledge and a profession. He did acquire knowledge but did not achieve his goal because of a lack of financial means, and returned home without an academic occupation. He married and then moved to Pidvolochysk [Podwoloczyska]. Since he did not do well there, he returned to his native city in the sense of the Talmudic phrase: "A change of place, a change of luck." In Brzezany, he made a living teaching. He taught the Bible and prepared students for the matriculation examination. He also helped university students with their doctoral theses. During those days, we both resided in the same apartment house.

A while later, when I got to know him, I became attached to him with intense love. I derived pleasure in meeting with him. My family, too, became very friendly with his family. It was very pleasant to conduct a discussion with him, even a casual one, since his discussions were like discussions among scholars.

He was an educated and learned man, deeply knowledgeable in many fields, particularly in the Bible, general history, Jewish history, and Jewish and general literature. Mr. Israel Fenster, a learned man, educated and exemplary Zionist, found comfort and satisfaction in his meeting with Mr. Peltz, and thus, a circle of three families was formed.

We had conducted meetings, particularly outdoors, in nature, on Shabbats and the summer holidays, where we listened thirstily to R' Yekhiel talks about various topics, starting with literature, Zionism, and Torah matters, and ending with politics and *Aliyah* to Eretz Israel. At the end of those picnics on Shabbat, we were always very thankful for the generous spiritual pleasure awarded to us.

[Page 202]

It is difficult for me to describe our farewell when we made *Aliyah* in 1934. I shook his hand and felt that he was devastated. He could not control himself because it was not him who was making *Aliyah*. He said: "If I could, I would have gone barefoot, days and nights to reach our homeland." Tears trickled down from his eyes. He did not escape from the fate of the rest of the Jews in the city. He tried to hide in a closet, where the murderous hand found him. No trace was left of his family.

May their souls be bundled in the bundle of life! May their memory be blessed!

Rabbi Moshe Shpizen's Doings

by By Avraham KhaRa"P *z"l*

Translated by Moshe Kutten

Edited by Jane S. Gabin

R' Moshe Shpitzen was a known and recognized figure in our city. He was recognized by the poor whom he helped and was respected by the wealthy, as he allowed them to fulfill the commandment - "…And the poor will live among you." He often reminded them of the commandment - "Be open-handed toward your fellow Israelites who are poor and needy in your land" [Deuteronomy 15:11]. He was a man who dedicated his entire life to helping others and demonstrated the "social aid" approach "on a small scale" without offices and officialdom. He provided aid to the poor in secret, with love, honesty, and respect. And all of that, on his own, only with his goodwill. He overcame many obstacles with the help of his loyal wife, Rakhel, who stood by him in everything he had done. It should be noted that Ya'akov Bomze, from the young layer, joined that effort in the last few years. May his memory be blessed!

R' Moshe was of average height but had a majestic appearance, a long beard, and bright, wise eyes that testified about his character, deeds, and honesty. He was agile, always in a hurry to go to work or return from it, carrying bags to allow a poor man to bless the Shabbat over a *challah* and praise his Creator. He worked in teaching Hebrew, arithmetic, and Yiddish. His wife sold leather in the store and, in the evenings, taught German. They both were happy with what they had and never complained toward the heavens.

His wife, Rakhel, the daughter of Moshe Apel, was modest and quiet, always wearing a smile on her lips, with a charitable heart and open arms, always ready to say a good word, and her face showed her good-heartedness.

Their assistance to the poor was manifested in several things: finding and supplying the needs of the needy for Shabbat, providing Kosher food to the sick at the hospital and the Jews at the jail, delivering wood for heating in the winter, and provisions for Passover. There were cases when his wife volunteered to wash the clothing for a sick and poor woman.

[Page 203]

It was quite a show to see them at work! Starting with the finding of Shabbat needs beginning in the early hours of Thursday, R' Shpitzen crisscrossed the city to gather *Challah*, fish, meat, and other provisions. When his bags were filled, he returned home to empty them and return for more rounds. He dragged his feet until close to the commencement of the Sabbath. Rakhel gathered the provisions and divided them into dishes according to the size of the needy families.

Whoever had not witnessed the food distribution on Holy Shabbat Eve by the *righteous* Rakhel does not know what fulfilling a commandment is! She welcomed those who came with the blessing "Shabbat Shalom," asking how they were, handing them the dishes, and accompanying them outside. That lasted until a late hour.

R' Moshe received the role of helping the sick from his father-in-law R' Yosheh Apel, who took care of that duty in the past and handed it to his son-in-law in his old age, knowing that he would fulfill the duty loyally. The Jewish hospital in our city was small and not well equipped. It lacked instruments, tools, and proper furniture. It could not afford to supply all the needs of the patients. That was where R' Moshe was active. He provided kosher food daily for the patients and even the Jewish patients at the municipal hospital, where the food was *Treifa* [not kosher].

The jail building happened to be located close to R' Moshe's home. When the jail management accepted a Jewish prisoner, they immediately notified him. Some prisoners were jailed for being Communists, and others were because of various offenses. But even the Communists did not want to give up on tasteful kosher food. The situation was more difficult before Passover. It required new dishes, pots, and bags. R' Moshe and his wife supplied kosher food and other provisions to prepare for the Passover *Seder*.

One work came on the other's heels. The winter was approaching. The poor could not afford to fix their houses, and they were not ready for the approaching intense cold. These people needed a supply of wood for heating and potatoes, the principal food in the winter. It was R' Moshe who took care of that. He spared no effort, dragging his feet from the wood merchant, forest merchant to the potatoes merchant, from one merchant to another, with a detailed list of every needy family. He talked, lobbied, explained the severity of the situation, turn to the Jewishness of the philanthropist until he received what he wanted. It may have taken a week, two weeks, and sometimes even longer, but in the end, we saw wagons loaded with wood and potato sacks going to the poor houses and dispensing their loads. Nobody knew who donated or received what except R' Moshe because he did not do it for the honor or his share in the next world. He did that for the pure intention of helping others and to ease the harsh life of the needy.

R' Moshe was an honest man with noble virtues who worshiped G-d with love. Many people turned to him and asked: "Your children are in Eretz Israel and would easily and gladly help you the make *Aliyah*. Why are you waiting?" R' Moshe responded: "Give me a person who would replace me here and accept my roles." He remained in the diaspora with his poor people.

The needs of the people were so numerous, especially before Passover. Besides food and drinks, people need a dress, shoes, paint to paint the walls white, cooking tools, and more. There was no money to buy these things. Some were ashamed to ask for help, and help had to be provided secretly. My father-in-law had a long list of "hidden" needy. Only he knew that they did not have a penny in their pocket. They were not ashamed of him, and he took care of them. He was their confidant.

A long time before the holiday of Purim, R' Moshe sat down at home until late hours and prepared the list of the needy. He wrote to our people in the United States and asked them to help. He narrated the miserable state of the poor in the city while emphasizing that the help must arrive in time for the holiday!

[Page 204]

He also turned to Rabbi Leibaleh Roza, the rabbi of the Brzezany people in New York, for his approval. With a heart full of hope, he waited … but was worried …who knows when the help would come?

And there, everything came together. The mailmen were running with letters, distributing them to the city poor, and R' Moshe stood on the side, and his joy was enormous. Many passed by him and hinted their thanks without words, only a turning of the head and a smile. He was waiting for that!

He was murdered in the Belzec killing camp, and his wife was murdered on 9 Sivan 5703 [6.12.1943] in the cemetery by the mass grave. May their memory be blessed!

I am writing these words with tears in my eyes. There is a phrase in the Talmud about *Shabbat Eruvin* saying that "whoever sheds tears after a *Tzadik*, G-d counts them and stores them in his archives." May my tears serve that holy purpose – the elevation of the souls of R' Moshe and Rahkel *z"l*!

Their decedents will carry their memory forever. May the people who inherit us learn the lesson after reading these lines, follow R' Moshe and his wife, dedicate themselves to public affairs, and thus, memorialize them, their doings, and holiness!

Rabbi Efraim Zalman Margaliot

by Avraham KhaRa"P

Translated by Moshe Kutten

Edited by Jane S. Gabin

His name suits him [Margaliot = gems in Hebrew], a dear man, a scholar, good virtues, teacher, and educator who educated two generations of students who carried his flag. He contributed his vast knowledge to the youths in our city. Due to his pleasant behavior and manners, he served as an example and a bright light for life.

More than eighty years have passed since a young man appeared at the gates of our city, dressed in ceremonial clothes with a top hat on his head. He came to us from Brody, a descendant of a famous family – Margaliot. Besides bringing some news, he brought teaching certificates from great rabbis and a few offers to serve as a city rabbi. He rejected those offers with some excuses. He claimed that a rabbi was like the High Priest. According to the [Jewish Law], he was not allowed to serve in that holy work if he was disabled (One eye of R' Zalman was defective). He also claimed that he did not want to use the Torah as his source of income.

He decided to try his luck in trade and went to England. However, since he lacked the proper attributes and approach for that work, he was unsuccessful and had to return to our city. He then had no choice but to dedicate himself to teaching. He hardly made a living until his children grew up and removed that burden from his shoulders. From that point on, he committed to studying the Torah for the sake of the Torah. However, he continued teaching. Assiduous Torah study became his main occupation. Torah learning filled his life. But he did not only study. He taught, educated, and guided those who came to listen to him about the Torah. He did it without receiving a wage. He taught for the sake of teaching and in honor of G-d.

[Page 205]

Those who woke up early would meet R' Zalman on his way to the *Beit HaMidrash* of R' Yudel. It was the closest place to his home. As early as 3 am, he was already humming his Talmud lesson. A few young Torah learners and some learned homeowners gathered around him. Then R' Zalman began his daily lesson for those hungry for knowledge and Torah. The lesson would end with the *Shakahrit* [morning] prayer. The people dispersed to go to work, and a new group gathered for another *Minyan*, and they went too. R' Zalman remained sitting, busy deciphering a *Sugiya* [theological question] and his entirety was in a different world. At 10 am, he stood up for a prayer at that same corner on the right side of the "*Bimah*," his regular place. That corner was not on the "East Side," G-d forbid because R' Zalman shied away from honor or prominence. He began to pray. People witnessed him in a trance while he prayed. With his eyes closed, without any movement, he united himself with his Creator.

He was a modest and humble man. He was shy and did not pay attention to his surroundings. He did not know what a political party meant. For him, all Jews were friends, and every one of them was a descendant of Avraham, Yitzkhak, and Ya'akov; he did not check the integrity of people, and he was careful not to hurt anybody's feelings nor insult their finances or honor. He loyally followed the phrase: "Who is respected? The one who respects others." When Shabbat came, he was all joy and prayer. Moysheleh Shu"v [ritual slaughterer and kosher inspector], R' Simkha Binim Heller, R' Yosi Streisand, Barukh Ast, Dudeleh "*HaKatan*" ["the small"], and others were sitting around him at one of the meals of Shabbat's "Three Meals" and singing "*Zmirot*" [Jewish hymns]. R' Zalman, too, sounded his voice. Whoever saw him in those moments knew he was in the world of imagination and legend.

He loved Eretz Israel, not less than he loved Israel. How great was his joy when, in 1920, the first group of pioneers made *Aliyah*! He was tremendously happy then. He always feared that – like our father Ya'akov toward his meeting with Esau, the right of his brother, who never left Eretz Israel, would win. At that time, the fact that Jews were returning to their homeland was a sign of the coming salvation. When his grandson Naphtali made *Aliyah* in 1935, he was filled with joy and with tearing eyes, he said: "At least, if I did not succeed, one of my descendants would fulfill our dream, to build and be built [in Eretz Israel]."

That was that man until his last day. He died at an old age at the beginning of the Second World War. His memory will protect us; his image and Torah will serve as our guiding light and as a guide for future generations.

[Page 206]

R' Leibush Perlmutter and R' Avraham Lokman

by Paulin Lokman

Translated by Moshe Kutten

Edited by Jane S. Gabin

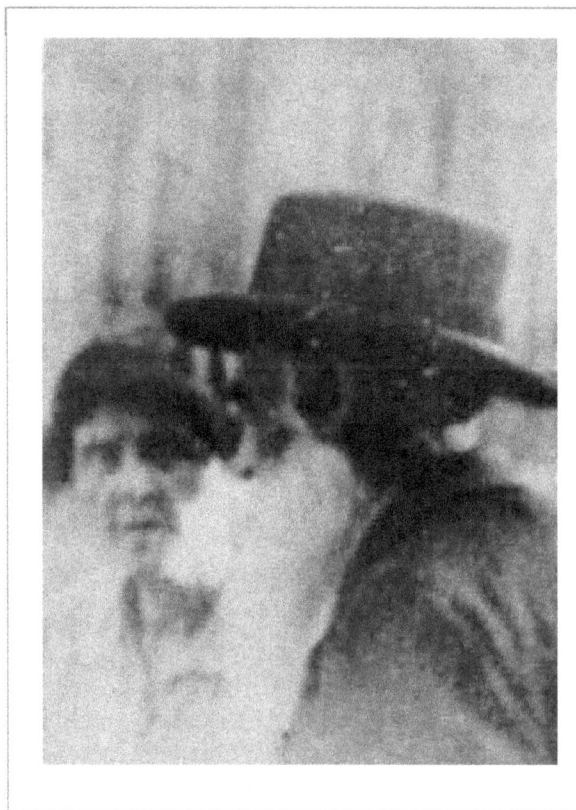

R' Leibush Perlmutter and his wife

A scholar and G-d-fearing man who respected people and was modest, were the attributes of R' Avraham Lokman, known in our town as R' Abish Shu'v.

I met him every day, passing by our house, and I always recalled the praises my father used to say about that R' Abish. "Good-hearted and honest" he used to say. "A scholar, not only in Torah matters. He was also knowledgeable of the world sciences and did not find any contradictions between them."

Those words were etched in my memory as a young man. I bring them here as an introduction to this article and as an appreciation for the memory of R' Abish, the public figure.

The Editor

Our little house on Nova[?] Street served our family for three generations. It was a modest house, and from the outside, it looked like the homes of our Polish neighbors, except for the light emanating from it early in the morning and late at night. The light was a sign that the father or grandfather was busystudying the Torah and reading other books from our extensive library in our home.

My grandfather *ztz"l*, Leibush Perlmutter the Shu"v [ritual slaughterer and kosher inspector], was a scholar and a *Hasid*, a remnant of the Jewish world that passed. He was immersed in the world of the Torah and Hassidism and almost oblivious to what happened in the world in the 20th century.

My father, *z"l*, was born in Kozova, a town near Brzezany, to his father, R' Yehoshua Lokman the Shu"v, known for his Torah scholarly and Hassidic nature. He was a shoot from the stock of the great rabbis of Belz Hassidim. My father was already famous in his childhood for his sharpness and education in the fields of the Torah and science. He continued to frequently visit the Belz's rabbis. He was known to have deep knowledge of mathematics and Astronomy. He married my mother, Gitel, the daughter of R' Leibush Perlmutter *z"l*, and took over the position of my grandfather *z"l* to the satisfaction of the public and the glory of the community.

My parents, Avraham and Gitel Lokman, were aware of the changes in the Jewish world through the new ideologies. Their main worry was to fight the foreign ideas according to the spirit of the Torah and tradition and to protect their four daughters, Brunia, Khana, Bela, and I, from what they considered the danger of foreign culture.

My mother was an exemplary helpmate. Together, my parents fulfilled the commandments of hospitality and benevolence. Our home was opened for guests and Jewish travelers from all over Poland who wandered around collecting donations for institutions and yeshivot. My mother provided these visitors with food and a place to sleep, while my father helped them collect donations from the community. When he found out that one of the visitors was also a scholar, the discussion about the Torah and *Halakha* continued until the late hour of the night and became a source of joy and satisfaction to my father.

I hope that these virtues and their intense faith helped them in their last days of June 1943, when they all perished before their time.

[Page 207]

Reb Shlomo Prisand

by Batya Bone Prisand

Donated by Michael Kreindler

Edited by Moshe Kutten

Reb Shlomo Prisand (1875-1941), who was known in our town by the diminutive Reb Shloimele, excelled in scrupulously observing the Mitzvahs, ignoring his own well-being and most material values of this world for the work of the Creator and life in Olam-Haba.

He was a distinguished scholar, a keen and proficient student of the Torah, Mishnah, Talmud, and Poskim. He was an educator admired by his pupils, some of whom were privileged to get to Israel and remember to this day their dedicated and humble teacher.

Reb Shlomo Prisand was born to a merchant family blessed with many children, a traditional Jewish family, whose sons continued in their father's footsteps as merchants. Only he, Reb Shloimele, yearned to study the Torah. He embraced the Torah with his entire spiritual being and spread (it) among others. Initially, he ran a private "Cheder" at his home near the outskirts of town, and many pupils flocked to him from far away. He soon acquired a reputation as a highly dedicated teacher who could explain and instill the Torah with his kind-hearted and patient manner, and many sons from the town's most prominent families came to study at his house. For many hours every day, the students learned the Torah from him and meticulously recited the verses of the *Mikra*, Talmud, and "*Tosafot*" (Addenda). Those who excelled among them were invited on Sabbath to recite their chapters in public.

After many years of carrying on his holy work at this home, Reb Shloimele began to teach and educate at the Talmud-Torah Institute in town, seeing in his work a holy mission to enlighten, enrich the knowledge, and teach decorum to his young students. But he was not fully content working only with children. Since he was unyielding about observing all the *Mitzvahs*, he was also active among adults, prodding and encouraging them to observe the *Mitzvah*s, give *tzedaka*, give anonymously, give for Pesach staples, help with donations for new brides, and above all, observe the sanctity of the Sabbath.

Reb Shlomo Prisand was a zealot when it came to observing the Sabbath, being strict not only with himself but also with others. Even before the arrival of the Sabbath, he would walk briskly in the commercial districts of town to remind store owners that Shabbat-Hamalka was waiting at their doorstep and they should hurry and finish their work. His scrawny figure was well known to the merchants who, upon seeing him, would rush to close their business, some out of respect for him and others out of shame and fear of sinning. Only after completing this public mission, during which he was once photographed unbeknownst to him, would he go to his home and prepare himself for the Sabbath. He would often bring with him a guest from the synagogue, and if he were fortunate enough to host a Torah scholar, the Sabbath would pass in reading and discussing passages and issues from the scriptures. Except for discussions of the Torah, Reb Shlomo Prisand did not talk on the Sabbath. On the other hand, he would sing *Zemirot* with Hassidic enthusiasm together with his family between courses at the Sabbath dinner table, Reb Shlomo was observing all Jewish holidays and all fasts, to the smallest detail. On the eve of Pesach, he would check every corner of the house to completely eradicate the *Chometz*. He would change all the dishes to a special Passover set that was maintained in the attic for the occasion. He even replaced the table-top (board) with a new one and covered it with a special tablecloth that was not used the rest of the year. The Matzos were of course *Matzah Shmura*.

Reb Shlomo Prisand

[Page 208]

He would never dip the Matzo in the soup or any liquid so that it would not form *Chometz*. On Yom Kippur Eve he would leave the house right after the meal and walk to the synagogue wearing his Keital and socks. He would not move from his place throughout the night and the following day of fasting, returning home only after the Neilah service, observing the scripture "It is a Sabbath of Solemn Rest to you, and you shall afflict yourselves ..." [Leviticus 16]. On Hannukah, Reb Shlomo would present a totally different image, and it was almost impossible to recognize this ascetic Jew, who would spend the rest of the year with the Lord's Torah. During the eight days of Hannukah, he would overflow with exuberance, play the dreidel and other games with his children, and tell them about the heroism of the Maccabees and Hanna, who sacrificed her children in the name of God.

Usually, he liked to tell Hassidic tales and did it with much skill and delight. His stories about the miracles and marvels done by the Baal Shem Tov and his students were a cause for memorable enjoyment and excitement to his listeners. I often thought to myself, where does this drawn and humble Jew draw the strength to withstand the trials of life and the growing current of many Jews who were abandoning their traditions? Undoubtedly, it was only his unshaken faith in his Creator that fortified him and guided him in the unwavering path of observing the *Mitzvahs*, from which he never deviated right or left.

It could be said about him that he conformed to the words in Joshua 1: "This book of Law shall not depart out of your mouth, but you shall meditate on it day and night..." Reb Shlomo Prisand was notable for perfection in all his deeds, and he never did anything with even a trace of conceit. He was unpretentious in all his ways and he was totally devoted to studying the Torah, doing good deeds, observing the *Mitzvahs*, and enlightening the eager to learn. He would defer his will only to his maker, and for he was admired and respected for that. The horrible Holocaust that flooded Europe also approached Reb Shlomo's town Still he was fortunate to have succumbed to natural causes. This fate that was denied by the rest of his family: his dedicated wife - Hava, his daughter – Hanna, and his son-in-,law Ezra Reichbach, with his two granddaughters, Rivkale and Zunia, were lost in the Holocaust after his death. His youngest son, Shimon, died in the Buchenwald Camp, and his two older sons, Michael and Feivish fell at the front during the First World War.

Only I was left since fate brought me to Israel in the early thirties - to the holy land about which my father, Reb Shlomo, dreamed and prayed all his life.

May these words serve as a memorial candle to my father, a righteous and honorable man who imparted the Torah to so many of our town's people.

[Page 209]

Reb Yosef Ben Meir Yehuda Streisand
In Remembrance of her Father

by Judith Kahn-Streisand

Donated by Michael Kreindler

Edited by Moshe Kutten

All who lived in our town knew that there were always people present in the *Beit Midrash* of Reb Yudel. Besides those who prayed there, many of the people of the city entered as they passed by the street to daven *Mincha* or *Maariv*. Some searched for a place to hide from the rain. Sometimes, the *Beit Midrash* provided a warm place and a roof over one's head on cold winter days, or a bench to sleep on if visiting from another town.

Among the local inhabitants who prayed there, one who especially stood out was Reb Yosef Streisand, *z"l*, not only because of his tall stature, and long beard, which added to his height, but also because of his holy spirit in the *Beit Midrash*. Even though he was a successful blue-collar worker who employed other workers, the *Beit Midrash* was very important to him. He was concerned with the conditions of the poor who prayed there, and he worried about their lack of material things. Thanks to his charitable nature, he succeeded in helping a poor, sick man who was in the hospital in our town. He was accustomed to going out on the streets and to the local stores to gather money to give to the family of the sick man so that they would not suffer while he was hospitalized.

Many small merchants traveled once a week to a nearby town for a flea market. Reb Yosef used to help them by giving them a loan to buy merchandise. After they sold their goods, they graciously returned the money at once.

Reb Yosef Streisand

When a speaker came to the *Beit Midrash*, Reb Yosef worried that the worshipers would leave before the end of the speech, so he gathered contributions beforehand. A large number of worshipers in Reb Yudel's *Beit Midrash* were very poor. Local people and strangers would gather there on Shabbat and Saturday night, and at the end of prayers, Yosef would stand by the door of the *Beit Midrash*, and personally arrange as Beitt he could, a home for each parishioner to go to for a hot meal. Because of his devotion and kind heart, he was always the last to leave, and he always had a guest or two in his own home. On Shabbat, he was accustomed to arranging *Minyanim* to read the Torah in his home, which was attached to the *Beit Midrash*.

Simchas Torah was a great and joyful day for him. He had great spirit when he stood with all his honor and beauty on the Bimah, inviting all the men to the *hakafot* with his strong, clear voice. This honor and position had been passed down to him from his father, Meir Yehuda Streisand *z"l*. He held this position until he left for Israel in 1936. He knew the names of all the worshipers and the names of their fathers, and he never confused them. When he invited the worshipers to the *hakafot*, he did not discriminate between poor people andthe rich people. He called upon those who sat along the Eastern wall, those who sat elsewhere, and even those who stood at the door. This irritated the rich parishioners, but he was not deterred because he was accustomed to treating everyone equally because he felt "all Jews are friends."

Simchat Torah was an entirely happy. Many people were accustomed to gathering in their homes, drinking beer, and eating sweets. In his home, he served a keg of beer and served good food. His guests were happy, and they ate, drank, and danced Chassidic dances. Reb Yosef danced with great enthusiasm on top of the table. Happiness with the Torah made a Jew's heart the happiest.

[Page 210]

During WWI, the Russians attempted to burn the *Beit Midrash*. Here, it is important to point out a heroic act by Reb Yosef. He climbed on the roof of the burning building and began to break up the shingles to prevent the spread of the fire to the rest of the *Beit Midrash*. The enemy saw him and shot at him, trying to kill him, but he hid until they left. He again went up on the roof, but this time, his clothing caught fire, so he quickly ran down to the river behind the building and put out the fire. He again returned to the roof to extinguish the fire, and this time he was successful. However, when he climbed down, he was completely black with soot, and he had burns on his body, but he was extremely happy that he had saved the building. His wife was unable to speak for two weeks because she was so hoarse from shouting and begging him to come down from the roof. People all over spoke of this heroic act, and one of the inhabitants of the city who had emigrated to the United States sent a letter praising Reb Yosef for saving the *Beit Midrash* from burning.

Besides his interest in the *Beit Midrash*, he worked with the Chevra Kadisha. If someone died in the city, the family came immediately to call him, and he would devote what little time he had to this duty. He would travel close or far away in heat, rain, or snow to do the *mitzvah* of kindness to the dead. He would travel by wagon if the place was in some distant village. Sometimes, the families would call him in the middle of the night, and he would go immediately to fulfill his obligation. He was never absent during the funeral, and he made sure that everything was done according to the Jewish Laws. One time, a deceased person who had been in the water for two weeks was brought to him from a neighboring community. Understandably, the appearance of the body was horrible, and the stench and deterioration were a dangerous health hazard. No one would come near the body, but Yosef prepared the body according to the law. He believed that a person performing a *mitzvah* would not be affected. Once, on a snowy day, Reb Yosef had to deliver a dead woman in a casket for burial, but the street was extremely slippery, and the casket was very heavy, so he got down on his knees and pushed the casket. Others soon came to help him, and they gave the woman a proper Jewish burial.

He also worked as a member of Yad Charutzim and *Shomrei Shabbat* (Keepers of the Sabbath), and he was one of the founders of *Kupat G'Milat Chasadim,* which was a charitable organization that provided loans to the righteous. Many stories about him seem to be fantasy, but they all are true. This working man who had a heart of gold sanctified his whole life to the Creator of the World and his creations and lived with complete faith throughout his life.

It is worthwhile to point out another event in his life. During WWI, the Russians would seize Jewish men for work camps. One Saturday night the Russians came to take Reb Yosef just as he began the Havdalah Service. He invited the soldiers to stay, and he conducted the service according to his customs. The soldiers respectfully sat through the ritual in silence. When he finished the prayers, he gave the soldiers food and drink, and the soldiers shook his hand, and left his home. My father called this "the miracle of *Havdala.*"

In 1936, he moved to Israel. He was a Zionist. He always had a JNF box in his home, and he donated to Karen HaYesod. While in Israel, he worked with the *Chevra Kadisha*, and with the synagogue where he prayed. The people of Kfar Saba knew and loved him. When he died in 1955, the local rabbi, in his eulogy, compared him to Jonathan the Shoemaker, who earned his bread all his life by the work of his hands with respect to the days of his death. May his memory be blessed!

[Page 211]

Michael Kara (Karon)

From "Gazit," Volume 21, Booklets 1 – 5

Translated by Moshe Kutten

Edited by Jane S. Gabin

Michael Kara was a typical bohemian figure – generous and a man of a broad culture, always immersed in his work, working from the morning until a late-night hour, and full of plans and ideas. He was an optimist in his character, filled with hope. He was always healthy (he was never sick). With all that, he was a sentimental person, very impulsive, loved the company of other artists, bubbly, and a lover of life. He wrote poems and songs. He died a week before his planned trip to the USA, where his artwork was to be presented in an exhibition.

He was born in Brzezany (Eastern Galicia). His father, Oscar Karon, was an officer in the Austro-Hungary military. In 1902, the family moved to Budapest, where the father worked at Mautner, a well-known company in the Austro-Hungary kingdom. Michael was one of six children, three of whom were artists: Professor Izhan Karon, an instructor at the National Art Academy in Budapest and the winner of the Kossuth prize[1]; Bartoledo Karon, a painter in Milan; and Michael Karon, who graduated from the regular high school in Brzezany. In 1903, he was accepted to the Art Academy in Budapest and studied sculpture and painting. Already in his first year of study, he participated in an exhibition at the academy with the painting he called "Self Portrait," despite the prohibition of doing so by the academy, and he won first prize for it. In Budapest, he worked at the atelier of the famous sculptor Zsigmond Kisfaludi Strubl. He won two scholarships from the Hungarian government to complement his studies in Italy (1910, 1911).

In 1912, he married Yehudit Shvartz, a theater student. In 1914, he and his brothers all enlisted in the Hungarian military. Michael graduated from an officer school with the rank of second lieutenant. In 1915, he received a temporary release from the army to erect a memorial for war-slain soldiers. He later fought on the Italian and Russian fronts. In 1916, he won first prize in a competition to sculpt the statue of the Hungarian politician Kalman Tisa. In 1918, he returned to serve in the Hungarian military as a lieutenant, where he was involved in Bela Kun's [Communist] coup d'etat. In 1919, he participated in the defense effort to repel the Romanian invasion of Hungary. After the Hungarian military lost that war, he was taken as a war prisoner but was released as a result of his wife's lobbying effort. She appeared before the Romanian commander and convinced him that an artist like her husband should not be jailed at a war prisoner camp.

With the retreat of the Romanian military, the family was moved to Transylvania and was housed in the famous antique castle-fort at Oradea. While there, Michael established an art school where some well-known Hungarian artists studied. In the meantime, his name preceded him - he was invited in 1920 to the Romanian royal court. There, in 1921, he sculpted a statute of the full image of King Ferdinand I, riding on a horse. He worked as an artist of the Romanian royal until 1925, and there he created silver reliefs and busts of the family members. In 1927, he published a binder with ten lithographs of images and scenes. In 1928, the family moved to Yugoslavia. Among his famous works during his stay there were reliefs at the train station and big wall paintings at the Workers House in Novi Sad (1934). In Yugoslavia, Kara became a fan of the Socialistic Zionism Movement under the influence of his son, who was a member of "HaShomer

HaTzair." He even gave a few lectures about the cultural and spiritual problems of the Jewish nation. In 1936, the family moved to Milan, where the brothers lived, because of the hatred of artists in Yugoslavia toward foreigners.

A stamp painted by M. Kara

[Page 212]

Since then, Michael has not stopped thinking about the problems associated with the spirituality of the Jewish nation. In Milan, he won the second-place prize in the Keren Kayemet LeIsrael [KKL-JNF] international competition for the cover of its sixth volume. In 1939, Michael escaped with his family to the Bargamo [Bergamo?] in [the Autonomous region of] South Tyrol. He returned to Milan about a year before the end of the war, lived there until 1947, and made a living by painting portraits. In 1947, his son, Khaim, who made Aliyah to Eretz Israel as a pioneer of "HaShomer HaTzair," got him an immigration certificate. Upon his arrival in Eretz Israel, he quickly assimilated with the population and art circles. His first work in Israel was a poster for "Sherut Ha' am" [National Service]. In 1949, Michael won prizes for painting the Independence Day Stamp of 5710 [1950] and the "Mo'adim LeSimkha" [High Holidays] Stamp of 5712 [1951]. In 1949, he had his first solo exhibition in Israel at a private gallery in Tel Aviv. At the same time, Kara also won the Dizingoff Prize for a sculpture showing the head of a child. In 1952, he won the first prize for the memorial for the defenders of Tel Aviv and the conquerors of Jaffa (the monument was erected at the Conquerors Park). In the same year, Kara won the City of Holon prize for the memorial of the slain soldiers of the War of Independence. In 1953, he and his son, Khaim Kara, won the first prize for the memorial monument for the fighters who died in battles fought over the breakthrough road to Jerusalem[2]. In 1953, Kara won the prize with his son, Khaim Kara, for the memorial monuments for the slain soldiers of the Independence War in Nesher and Kirat Ata. In 1954, Kara had a solo exhibition of his works in the Tel Aviv Museum. Altogether, Michael Kara won 14 prizes in Israel.

Kara, who was educated based on the academic concept of the 19th century, in its unique expression of the Budapest University, which was very famous at the time, showed his artistic talent already at a young age, demonstrated by his work, "Self Portrait," created by an eighteen-year-old youngster. He brought with him vast knowledge from the academic world and knew well how to use the foundation he acquired in his four years of studies. However, Kara did freeze in his tracks as he was blessed with a talent for sculpting and painting. He also possessed a personal creation fantasy in terms of space concepts and composing figures. He was an expert in several creative fields. He used his imagination, which released him from subjugating himself to a rigid academic formulation. Some of his paintings are done with a soaring fantasy, and others are made with strictness. The lithographs, drawings, and mainly the reliefs and the sculptures prove that he was a prominent artist who knew how to free himself from the academic molds and find his personal world. The influence of Cubism is apparent, particularly in forming stylistic images built on highlighted shapes and fluid rhythms. His artistic work, in all of these diversified fields, shows that he was a spiritual person and someone who loved poetry, spiritual melody, and restrained pathetic expression. Much of his mental philosophy and his attitude toward problems of society is expressed in his artistic work since he himself wished to discover the nation's spirit, the heroism in its pure form, and the humans in their personal soul exposures. He worked diligently on every detail. Every sculptured creation was accompanied by a series of drawings and outlines. He was strict with himself and his work, which he considered holy.

[Page 213]

A picture from Michael Kara

Translator's footnotes:

1. "Highest recognition award in Hungary for creation and cultivation of Hungarian culture. The award is named after the Hungarian leader, Layoush Kossuth" [from Wikipedia].

2. From Wikipedia: The proposal was won by Kara, who submitted a plan for a 12-meter-high rock-hewn statue, about 30 meters from the road, showing a young figure bursting out holding in one hand a hand grenade and with the other hand he supports a wounded friend who is kneeling next to him. The proposal was supposed to be carried out but was canceled due to the opposition of religious circles. Instead, a decade later, it was decided to erect an abstract monument (Naomi Henrik won the repeat competition and erected the monument).

The Actor Hersh Tonis

by Moshe Bar-David

From an Israeli broadcast

Translated by Moshe Kutten

Edited by Jane S. Gabin

Hersh Tonis was born in Brzezany approximately in 1920 to a distinguished family. He was an actor in the Yiddish theater in Vienna. In addition to shows in the metropolitan area, he appeared on shows in the Vienna suburbs, Czechoslovakia, and Hungary. During the Second World War, he escaped to the Soviet Union. He returned to Vienna after the war, where he died around 1962.

Leon Shpatzer
The Popular Singer[1]

by Moshe Bar-David

Translated by Moshe Kutten

Edited by Jane S. Gabin

Leon Shpatzer was born in Brzezany. His father was a caretaker in a synagogue, and his mother had a stall at the market. Leon studied shoemaking, but thanks to his pleasant voice, he joined a troupe of wandering singers and traveled throughout Galitsia and Romania. Upon becoming an adult, he wrote poems and even authored a few light plays. His songs "Doctor Tausik" and "Khurban Kishinev" ["Kishinev Destruction"] were particularly famous. He died in Bucharest approximately in 1917.

Author's Note:

1. Based on the article by Zalman Zilbertzveig: "Leksicon fon Yidedishen Teater" ["Lexicon for Yiddish Theater"], 1931, I/236.

[Page 214]

The *Melamed*, R' Yasha Fishlis
Yosef son of Fishel Shteinberg (1859 – 1940)

by Moshe Bar-David

Translated by Moshe Kutten

Edited by Jane S. Gabin

I remember my first *Melameds* favorably. I studied the Torah and Rashi with Getzaleh Halpern, a good-hearted and friendly Jew. When I was six years old, my father moved me to study Gemara with one of the best *Melameds* in the city, Yasha Fishlis. Initially, I had a hard time getting used to the new rabbi. R' Yasha was a tall and thin man with a black beard, long *Pe'ahs* [sidelocks], with gray hairs sticking out, here and there, from his beard. Even the students were different – older than me. I got quickly used to the new rabbi and the new atmosphere.

The House of the "*Kheder*" was located on Zygmuntowska Street, opposite the "*Beit HaMidrash* of the *Khazan*" [Cantor]. The house where the *Kheder* was situated stood in a big yard with only a single tree. The yard was surrounded by a tall wall.

The *Kheder* apartment contained two rooms. One room was used for a residence, and the other for a class and a kitchen. The students sat around the table with the Gemara books in front of them. The *Melamed* sat at the head of the table with agile eyes, watching the children. R' Yasha was amazingly dedicated to his role as a *melamed*. He cared that his pupils absorbed, understood, and knew the subjects he was teaching them. The *Melamed* was very strict about listening and quiet during the study. Woe to the pupil who did not listen and did other things during the lesson – the long arm of R' Yasha would reach him. The echo of the blow on the table, as a warning for that pupil, could be heard throughout the entire *Kheder*. During the breaks, the pupils were allowed to play in the yard or inside the *Kheder*. Studies took place mainly in the afternoon. Some students came to the *Kheder* directly from the state school and did not return home for lunch. Studies continue until the evening and, during the winter months, until the night. When the rabbi went to the synagogue for Minkha and Ma'ariv prayers, the students uploaded their energies with pranks.

R' Yasha treated his students with a hidden affection and taught without discriminating between the sons of wealthy people and the poor.

When he met one of his students many years later, he would show interest in the student's situation and family. At the end of the 1920s, R' Yasha abandoned teaching and settled with restive life and studying Torah. His children took care of him then.

Seven out of eight of his children perished in the Holocaust: Fishel, Tuvia, Ya'akov, Rakhel, Rivka, and Feiga [one additional name is missing in the original]. May their memory be blessed.

Only one son, Israel Shteinberg, married to the daughter of a Yeshiva head, Veveh Direnfeld, immigrated to Canada.

[Page 215]

Dr. Avraham Halbertal

by Moshe Bar-David

Translated by Moshe Kutten

Edited by Jane S. Gabin

Dr. Avraham Halbertal

Avraham was descended from the Hasidic Admor dynasty, known in Israel. Admor Rabbi Khaim of Sanz, the founder of the Hasidic dynasty, changed the family name from Halbershtat to Halbersham [should be Halbershtam or Halberstam]. The family of Avraham's grandfather changed their name, for some reason, from Halbersham [Halbershtam] to Halbertal.

All the family children studied Hebrew. The elder was a member of the committee of the Hebrew school "Safa Brura" ["Clear Language"]. Dr. Mitznakh z"l recalled Avraham in his memoirs. In 1907, he was invited to the home of Ya'akov Halbertal to teach Avraham and his sister Hebrew and to prepare Avraham for his Bar Mitzva. Already then, Avraham read the *Haftara* with the Sephardic pronunciation.

Avraham acquired his higher education in Vienna. First, he completed the higher school of trade. In 1915-1916 he served as an officer in the Austrian military. He then worked as an accountant for about thirteen years in large corporations on behalf of a prominent Viennese bank. At the same time, he studied and received his law doctorate. He continued to practice as a lawyer in various courts in Vienna. In 1937, he was sent to Bucharest to conduct a trial of a Viennese movie company. There he felt the influence of the Nazis. He returned to Vienna, hoping for a more accommodating political atmosphere for Jews. However, his hope proved to be an illusion.

In his journal, he wrote during those dark days, describing the fear of the Viennese Jews that their town, which used to be "a Mother City in Israel," changed its face overnight and became a cruel and "oppressive stepmother." Avraham described his experiences in his journal, written exhaustively. It was the testimony of an eyewitness who knew to observe events, understand them, and bring them skillfully into a written form.

During the years 1938-1939, he was incarcerated in Dachau Concentration Camp, where he suffered mental and physical tortures that left their mark on him for the rest of his life.

After many hardships, he finally arrived in Eretz Israel, on the Ship "Patria," "naked and penniless." In the beginning, he worked as an agricultural worker in Pardes Khana, and later on, thanks to his education and knowledge of English, he was accepted as an official at the offices of the British military. He worked there as a senior official in administrative and financial roles for about eight years. In 1948, he worked at the [supermarket corporation] "HaTzarkhan." After that, he worked in the Jewish Agency in Tel Aviv in the settlement absorption department. In 1961, he finally was able to meet his sisters in England.

After retiring from the Jewish Agency, Avraham worked in the regional council of Menashe. He worked there until he reached 70. Heart disease, which had its roots in the days when he was imprisoned in Dachau, progressed and worsened during his last few years. He spent his time at home, reading and listening to music. He especially dedicated himself to his hobby – cultivation and nurturing cactus plants. He suffered from his pains quietly and was careful not to burden anybody. May his memory be blessed.

[Page 216]Blank

[Page 217]

The Synagogues in Brzezany

By Menakhem Katz

Translated by Moshe Kutten

Edited by Jane S. Gabin

[Pages 218-219]

The map of the center of Brzezany and its synagogues

1. The Large Synagogue
2. The Beit HaMidarsh *Habaui* ["Built"]
3. The Stretiner *Kloiz*
4. The Rozlower *Kloiz*
5. The *Beit HaMidrash* of the "Khazan" [Cantor]
6. Tchorkower *Kloiz*
7. Beit HaMidrash of Rabbi Yudel
8. Potiker *Kloiz*
9. The synagogue "Yad Kharutzim"
10. The synagogue of Rabbi Mendeleh
11. Ya'ir (Jair) Synagogue

[Page 220]

Forward

by Menakhem Katz

Translated by Moshe Kutten

Edited by Jane S. Gabin

To my mother, from the home of Mendel David

Close to forty years passed from the outbreak of the Second World War, the day when the synagogues in Brzezany ceased to serve their worshipers.

As early as the first day of the war, an immense influx of refugees arrived, who flocked to our city and converted the houses of prayer into poor slums. A great outcry arose in our city. Despite all the lobbying, the city's leaders could not find a way to prevent the invasion of the refugees into the prayer houses. Tens of families, not only poor ones, settled in the synagogues temporarily but made it into their permanent homes, thereby sealing the fate of the synagogue to cease serving as a place for prayer. Only two synagogues - the Great Synagogue and the Synagogue of Rabbi Yudel - remained free of settlers and served the community for two additional years (1939 – 1941).

With the invasion of the Nazi oppressor, the destruction of the eleven synagogues of the city was complete. I want to memorialize those synagogues in the following articles. The pain about the destruction and the longing for what was dear to our hearts, which would never come back, motivated me to contribute, at least a little, to the memorialization of the legacy and the sacred and precious memory that has been destroyed. As an architect, I preserved the elevation silhouettes of the buildings and translated them into plans and descriptions. I used sources from the city's map, discussions with the worshipers, and books in Polish about Brzezany. I also relied on my memory and my extensive knowledge of the city.

[Page 221]

The Great Synagogue

by architect Menakhem son of Shimon Katz

Translated by Moshe Kutten

Edited by Jane S. Gabin

The Name

The "Great Synagogue" – is the name of the main synagogue in Brzezany.

Here, my mind wonders. Why wasn't the Great Synagogue called after somebody, as customary with the rest of the synagogues?

It is inconceivable that for generations (from the beginning of the 18ᵗʰ century), there was no philanthropist, rabbi, or *Tzadik* was found who was worthy of memorialization by calling the synagogue after him, particularly after the death of the last *Posek* [religious decider], Gaon Rabbi Mordekhai (the Maharsha"m), the eminent rabbi of the city for many years.

I searched the literature and made comparisons, and I think that because of the sizable measures of the building (23 x 21 some meters), rare for other synagogues in Galitsia, the community leaders did not want to change its name for prestige reasons since they felt that by doing that, they would diminish the value of the synagogue.

Thanks to the undisputed rule of the Polish princes' dynasty of the Sieniawski family during 1530 – 1726, Renaissance architecture was incarnated in all its glory in the city churches and testified to the tight connection between the construction style in the city and the construction of the civilized world in general, particularly in Italy. Thanks to the cultural relations of the Sieniawskis, exceptional builders were brought to the city from the outside. That level of construction affected the design of the Great Synagogue. As additional proof, we can point to the "Turie Zahav" ["Golden Columns"] synagogue in Lviv, which was designed by the Italian architect Paulo-Romano.

After a thorough review of Y. Finkerfeld's book "Synagogues in Italy from the Renaissance Period until Today[1]," I concluded that all the synagogues in Italy, at all stages of their development, did not reach the size of the Great Synagogue in Brzezany, except one – the Sephardic synagogue in Livorno. To my surprise and joy, I found an analogy between the two structures.

Livorno's synagogue - a bigger and more luxurious building, contained a unique feature that distinguishes it from the rest of Italy's synagogues – three arcades encircling the hall on three sides. The hall was nearly square-shaped (28.2 x 25.8 meters). The Great Synagogue in Brzezany was also nearly square-shaped, but its measures differ somewhat (23.2 x 21.1 meters).

The columns that form the arcades in Livorno were built on the first floor in Brzezany as support pillars with grates between them, forming the (poor) women's sections on the southern and northern sides and the main entrance to the hall on the western side. The rainbow shape of the curvature arcades' arcs in Livorno[2] was identical to the two-floor women's section arcs' curvatures in Brzezany. In both buildings, the measures of the flat wooden ceiling were larger than the customary measures.

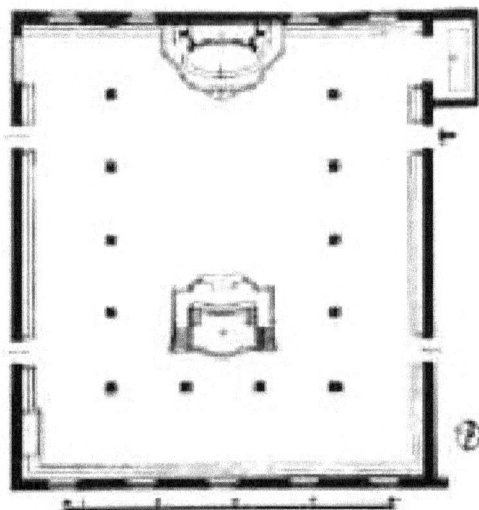

A diagram of the Sephardic Synagogue in Livorno
taken from Ya'akov Finkerfeld's book

[Page 222]

In both synagogues, the *Bimah* [the raised platform from which the Torah is read and prayer is led] was located in the center, the Holy Ark was placed at the short wall, and the benches encircled the hall from its three sides. The octagonal windows in Livorno took the shape of circles in Brzezany, but their location was identical. The metal grates separating the women's section in both synagogues reached only half the height and did not completely close the opening.

One hundred twenty-seven years separated the construction of the two buildings (the Livorno synagogue was built in 1591, and the one in Brzezany in 1718). Due to the similarity between the two plans, it is logical to assume that the Livorno synagogue served as an example of the one in Brzezany. The differences between them were in the degree of splendor, the shape of the front, and the marble pillars with arcs in Livorno. Also, the two-story women's sections in Livorno were on the second and third floors, while they were on the ground section, which was one floor above it in Brzezany. The extensive measures led to the name of "The Great Synagogue."

Other synagogues throughout Galitsia and Bohemia, including the large and palatial ones, were smaller than Brzezany's (approximately 21 x 23 meters, 483 square meters). For comparison, a few examples are listed below:

Rzeszów [Reisha] 16.52 x 13.00 (380 sm) (according to Grutta [synagogue listings])

Lutsk 21 x 19.2 (410 square meters) (according to "Boznice Drewniane" [by Kazimierz & Maria Pichotka], pg. 28)

"Turei Zahav" Synagogue in Lviv – about 200 m, Zhovkva [Zolkova] - 400 sm, Khodorov (the hall) – 100 sm (according to the book "HaUmanut HaYehudit" [The Jewish Craftsmanship], pg. 249).

Based on the theory presented here about the size of that building, I conclude that the community leaders refused to change the synagogue's name from "Great" to anything else.

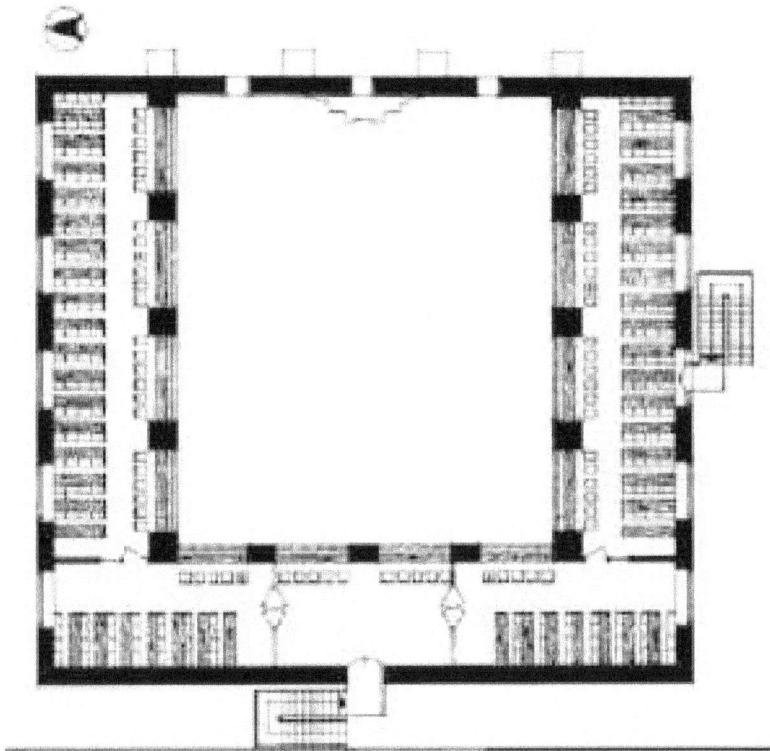

The plan for the women's section

[Page 223]

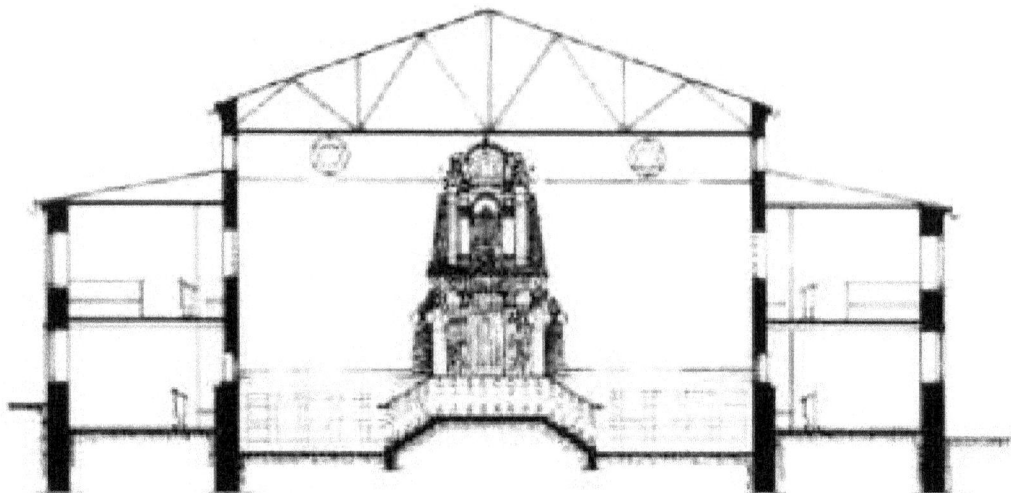

A width cross-section of the synagogue

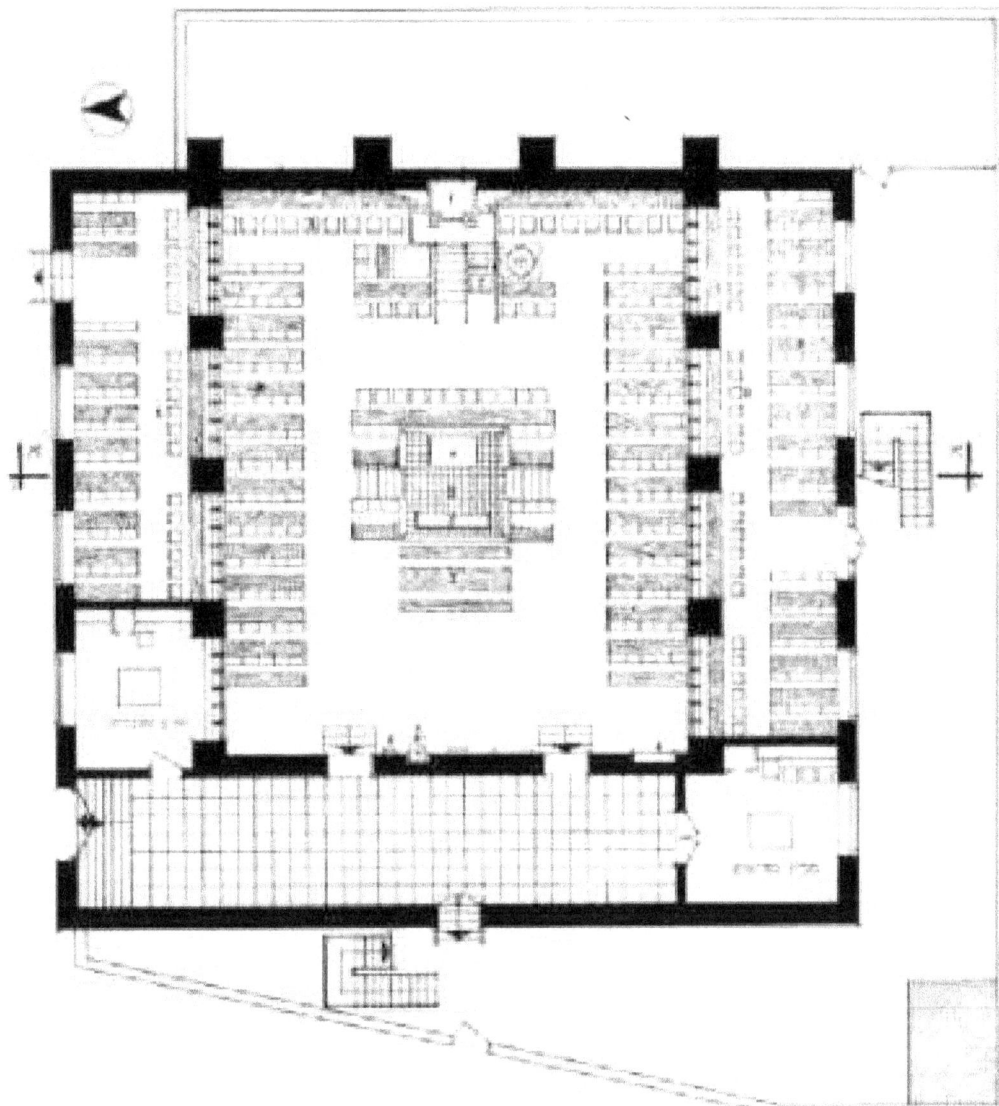

The hall plan

[Page 224]

The Synagogue and its Location

The Great Synagogue was built in 1718, and its name from those days was mentioned in the documents of the Roman Catholic community from 1762. The structure constituted a central building in the plaza, officially named "The Synagogue Plaza" during the Polish regime.

The synagogue constituted a frontal edge on the southern side of the plaza. It was surrounded by small houses of prayer and public Jewish institutions. In the east were the "*Beit HaMidrash* "HaBanui" [Built] (served the Stratyn Hasidim), the Jewish hospital, and the public ritual bath. In the West – the Rozlower *Kloiz*, the Jewish poor shelter, and several Jewish residential structures. The main entrance to the plaza was on the northern side, through a narrow street perpendicular to Zigmontovska Street. The positioning of the public buildings encircling the plaza testifies to the deliberate planning in constructing the plaza. It is not coincidental that the main building was positioned across the main entrance, and the rest of the structures constituted a frame for the plaza. The design was undoubtedly done by a professional architect with an urban sense, who planned the plaza according to the function of the synagogue. Other plazas in the city, such as the one in front of the Roman Catholic church, the one in front of the Greek Catholic, and other public buildings, were also similarly designed.

The construction and the Jewish ownership of the structures around the plaza indicate that Jews concentrated there for many generations. That was the cradle of the Jewish community in Brzezany. From there, the Jewish neighborhood spread northward and eastward. The synagogue and a group of structures appeared on the 1755 map of the city.

[A key for] The Plan of the Great Synagogue Plaza:

1.　　The Great Synagogue

2.　　The *Beit HaMidrash "Habanui"* [Built]

3.　　The Rozlower *Kloiz*

4.　　The *Beit HaMidrash* of the *"Khazan"* [Cantor]

5.　　The Jewish Hospital

6.　　The poor shelter house

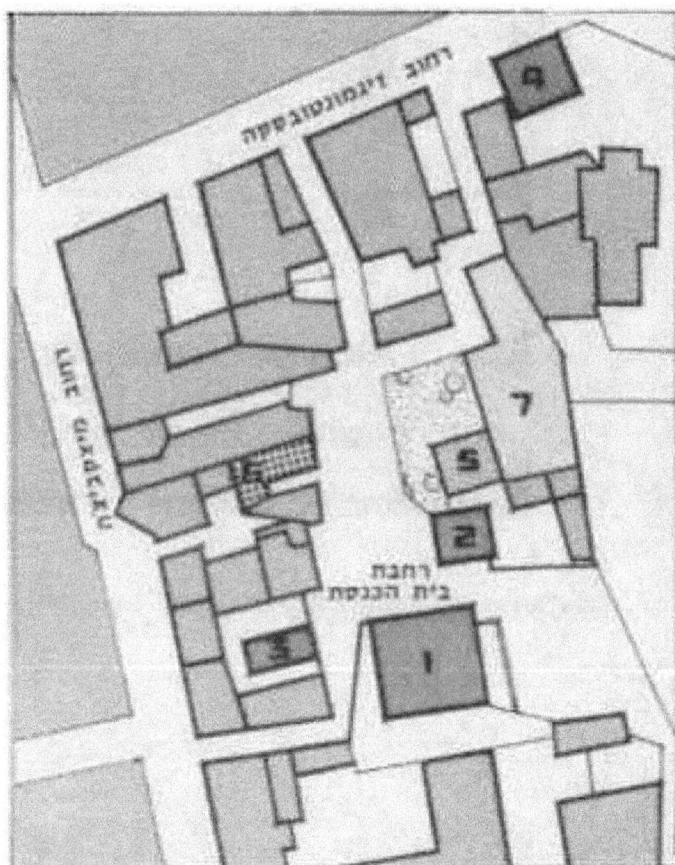

[Page 225]

The Description of the Synagogue

The Great Synagogue replaced an older 17th-century synagogue. The latter is mentioned in church archives (Lib. Instr. [?] from 1639, pg. 241). There are no additional details available on the old synagogue.

The square shape embodied an architectural space of a defined cube emanating from the specific design of that building, as mentioned above in the analogy to the synagogue in Livorno. According to the book by Metzishevski (1), the builders agreed to construct the pine-made flat ceiling using the method customary in the area. The breadth of the square hall was reduced by the three arcades that formed the women's sections on the two floors. Poor women, who could not afford to pay for the seats, used the northern and southern sides of the ground level free of charge. The three galleries on the upper floor were rented for a fee, the amount of which depended on the location of the seats.

I was deliberating over the shape and the construction method utilized in that structure since it was unusual compared to what was customary in that period. It was not a square with arches like the other synagogues in Galitsia. It did not have four central pillars and did not belong to the family of fort-like buildings like the one in Zhovkva [Zolkova] or Brody. However, there were some fort characteristics on the building's east side – four external pilasters that narrow toward the top. They served as support for the walls in the fort-like synagogues.

In summary, I conclude that the unique plan was copied from the Sephardic Synagogue in Livorno[2], where the arcades on the ground floor formed the women's sections on the sides, allowing for a long entrance hallway, from which two main gates opened toward the east side. The floor level of the praying hall was about two meters lower than the outside ground level.

There was a staircase between the level of the ground outside into the entrance hallway and an additional four stairs from the hallway level onto the praying hall.

Like in other cities in Galitsia, the governors of the Catholic cities did not allow the building of tall synagogues. These were the rigid laws of those days. Therefore, the structure here was not designed to rise above the Christian churches. It was built in the lowest topographic location [so, even with the two floors], and it was much lower than the nearby Christian church, which was positioned on the mountain slope.

The interior of the building, surrounded by the women's section on the ground level, was covered by grated oak dividers, and above them, open arcades in the shapes of arches separated by artesian metal grills. A *Bimah* rose in the center. People climbed up to it using three steps from the northern and the southern sides.

[Page 226]

The Holy Ark in the Great Synagogue

The *Bimah* was surrounded by an engraved wooden railing with four lamps in the corners. The canopy mentioned in Metzishevski's 1910 book was not there. Possibly, when the *Bimah* was revamped in 1886, the canopy was removed. The synagogue was completely renovated in 1880 by a city-native Jewish constructor, Shimon Meiblum. The concern for the preservation of the building was great. Before the Second World War, the walls were renovated. They were covered with a wooden oak coating, and all the seats were replaced. The entrance hallway, including the wooden entrance gates, was covered by oil wall painting. The old wall pictures and the engraved stucco were not renewed for lack of an appropriate artisan or perhaps for lack of budget. [The rest] of the walls were painted in bright colors. The ceiling was painted light blue with tiny golden stars. The holy ark on the east side was the dominant element in the prayer hall. It rose about a pedestal made of stone and marble. You went up to it on a staircase surrounded by metal grates. The baroque engravements of sea creatures, trees, flowers, fruits, and other ornaments attracted the eyes of the worshippers with their beauty and rich shapes. The dominant colors were green and gold, except for the white marble pillars.

[Page 227]

I will not dwell on the rest of the synagogue features, such as the standing and hanging copper lamps, but I would like to mention the western wall. It was decorated with swirl paintings and the following items concentrated around it: the eternal light, a crafted sink made of hammered-out copper with a towel rack near it, a memorial plaque for the benefactors and synagogue's *gabbais* [administrators], and a decorated recess where the *Matzah Shmurah* was hung.

In its exterior, the synagogue resembled a cubic monolithic structure. It was an architectural entity that projected strength and stability while at the same time demanding respect – an objective any builder aspires to when building a chateau.

The Great Synagogue in 1978

[Page 228]

The Folklore and Goal

In 1570, 40 years after the establishment of the town of Brzezany, there were only four Jewish families in it. It was the cradle of the Jewish community in the city. At the time, they could not gather enough people for a *Minyan*. One hundred years later, in 1674, a Belgian tourist, Ulrich Wardom, mentioned in his description of his trip that there were 100 families in the town. From the beginning of the Jewish settlement until one hundred later, this was the location of the public praying in the city. Unfortunately, we do not have details about when the first synagogue was built. Several sources mentioned that a synagogue existed where the Great Synagogue was later built.

We all understand the gatherings in the synagogue to pray, but that was not the only objective. Every house of prayer had something unique in it. One was not the same as the others. In our city, the main goal of the Great Synagogue was to represent the community toward the outside world - the gentile world that surrounded it. That was the main building by which the community identified themselves. Every house of prayer in town had a different character. The Great Synagogue was not the same as *Beit HaMidrash*, the *Beit HaMidrash* was not the same as the *Kloiz*, and the latter was not the same as any other house of prayer.

The law and court, punishment, holidays, birth, and death all revolved around that holy place. According to a [Latin] manuscript "Descriptio Status Ecclesiae" ["Description of the State of the Church"] from 1762, an iron "cage" was positioned at the synagogue. A Jew brought to trial and punished by a court (consisting of regime representatives and Jewish rabbinical judges) was brought to the "Pillar of Shame" inside the cage. His hands and legs were tied with iron chains. He stood there for everyone to see and fear. It was a sad sight of a Jew bound by chains, his soul tormented, and his sore body was displayed for all to see. His Jewish brothers passed by to enter the synagogue to pray and looked at the offender. All of that happened against the synagogue gates at the plaza.

Starting with the invasions by the Tatars and the Turks, the First World War until the days of the Nazi oppressor, the synagogue served as a shelter for refugees and shelter from pogroms and persecution, as the people considered the building a physical fort, and a mental sanctuary. The synagogue walls witnessed many hardships, troubles, suffering, and sighs over many generations, but it also experienced days of joy and glory.

Fitting its name, the Great Synagogue served for community gatherings, particularly on holidays. It was then crowded with worshippers and was too small to accommodate everybody. People stood in the passageway and entrance hallway, and the believers and their children filled every corner. A great deal of crowding prevailed everywhere. The air was stifling, filled with the scent of a mixture of fabric, furs, spices, and candles – the smell of the synagogue during the holidays. –. It is an indescribable and unique mixture: sweet and intoxicating, inducing a unique atmosphere of togetherness in which you feel and experience holiness, the power of the community in its gathering, and the power of faith throbbing within yourself. The crowding, smell, and the many voices with all their nuances and variations that surrounded the worshippers – did not prevent them from secluding themselves in prayer, covered with the praying shawl, and devoting themselves to G-d's worshiping.

[Page 229]

KADZIELNICZKA
O KSZTAŁCIE
PAPUGI.
Własność gminy żydow-
skiej w Brzeżanach.

Spice box for *Havdalah* – property of the Brzezany community

A completely different atmosphere prevailed in the Great Synagogue during Shabbat – calmness and majesty, exemplary order, and fresh air. Not all the seats were taken. Jews in Shabbat clothing sitting and listening pleasantly to the chorus, cantor, and Ba'al Tfilah [praying leader]. Only a few faces of old women were seen peeking out into the space of the main hall. Shabbat experience – comfort and tranquility prevailed everywhere.

The synagogue also served the community on state holiday gatherings during the Austrian and Polish regimes to show empathy toward the ruler. The Jews identified with the Polish holidays - Independence Day or the anniversary of the Polish Revolt. You haven't seen a staged show until you saw the Thanksgiving holiday at the synagogue.

The preparations began a few days before the holiday. The exterior of the synagogue was thoroughly cleaned. Dust was wiped, the windows cleaned, and the floors were oiled. Fragrant pine wreaths were hung among the galleries' arcades. The main gates were decorated with green branches and national flags. The copper lamps and candle holders were polished, and they shone with golden sparkles emanating in all directions. Everything looked new and specially prepared for the holiday. On the day of the holiday, the decorated gates were opened early in the morning. A special carpet was unrolled in front of the main entrance. The ceremony began at a predetermined time in coordination with the city's schools, the authorities, and the military.

Row after row of Jewish students from schools throughout the city flocked and marched to the synagogue plaza. Two Polish Army companies consisting of Jewish soldiers, with their commanders, followed the students. All of them were positioned on one side of the plaza. Opposite them stood the community representatives, in uniform, some wearing cylindrical hats. Behind them, the Jewish crowd. Stores were closed on that day, and people came to watch the regime representatives arriving at the synagogue.

The regime's representatives began to arrive. They walked in the gap between the students and the Jewish soldiers on one side and the Jewish crowd on the other, and so did the deputy mayor, several council members, "dolled-up" and decorated with medals, representatives of the Polish Army battalion, a representative of Prince Potocki (to whom most of the land around the city belonged), representatives of the fire department and professional guilds and other city dignitaries. They all passed on the avenue between the two sides of the plaza, with the community representatives waiting at the main gate shaking their hands, and everyone was accompanied inside by one of the community receptionists.

At the end of the representatives' procession, the students were followed by the Jewish soldiers, and the crowd began to move inside. A chorus stood on the stage headed by the synagogue's cantor and sang an appropriate thanksgiving song. The community representative (most of the time Dr. Pomerantz or Lawyer Grossman) would then deliver an emotional speech in which he blessed the dignitaries, president, government, and everybody else who could be blessed and express loyalty and best wishes. The chorus would then sing several songs and prayers appropriate for the circumstances. After the official ceremony, the crowd dispersed in a praise-worthy order, fitting a state event.

It was not only the staged show that took place in the synagogue's plaza. The plaza also witnessed Jewish holiday celebrations. The event that topped all other celebrations was the one that accompanied the joyful bringing of a new Torah scroll to the synagogue, donated by the philanthropist Dr. Flikh [Flick?]. Everything and anything occurred on that evening in the streets and the plaza: drum and trumpets orchestra,

[Page 230]

a parade led by a torchlight procession and a canopy under which Jews danced with the scroll. Topping everything was the singing of the youth and the parade with the rabbi, an impassioned march that moved through the city streets and gushed in a mighty stream into the plaza. The people danced and rejoiced as elation engulfed them. The gentiles fell silent in reverence and peeked from afar at the crowd celebrating their faith. Nobody dared to try to disturb the Jews in their joyous ecstasy, never seen before. The entire Jewish community was in the Synagogue Plaza. Everyone, from young to old, rejoiced and danced until after midnight.

And the day of the Balfour Declaration - was that a state holiday? No, and no! It was a celebration for the city's Zionists. The Synagogue was decorated, gatherings were held, a prayer of thanksgiving was organized, and numerous speeches were given. The gatherings were held in the plaza. Endless debates took place there. Boundless excitement befell the masses. That was spontaneously realized in the plaza.

Additional events were held at the Synagogue, including formal gatherings of the Zionist parties, meetings for the community elections and the Zionist Congresses, and propaganda for the elections of rabbis (both by their supporters and opponents).

And last, there were obituary ceremonies for dignitaries, activists, and city residents on their last way to the other world. Their funerals passed and paused here, in the plaza. Obituaries and speeches were delivered, and tears were shed in front of the synagogue gates and absorbed by the thick walls of the building. It was witnessed a great deal throughout the generations. Its secrets are impossible to decipher.

The Great Synagogue was the official home of the Jewish community. It was available for anybody within the community, with all its diversified sects and views, for social activities and prayers during sorrowful and joyful occasions.

The building stood strong and served its worshipers for two hundred and fifty years. Many turnarounds and changes occurred during those years. Still, the building always returned to serve its role until the Soviet conquest in 1941. With the entrance of the Red Army, the building served, for some time, as a shelter for the Jewish refugees from Western Poland. Over time, the refugees were removed by the authorities and they later converted the building into a wheat warehouse.

The Nazi oppressors did not change its function, and the building continues to serve as a warehouse until today.

[Page 231]

Klei Kodesh

The *Klei HaKodesh* [literally 'vessels of holiness'] of the synagogues in the city were numerous and splendid, particularly the ones in the Great Synagogue. Hundreds of objects, such as Torah Scroll crowns, trays, silver and copper candle holders, standing and hanging lamps, and multi-branched chandeliers, were donated from the 16th century until the 1930s. All, without exception, were lost during the Holocaust. A substantial part of these objects was buried underground by the activists of the Jewish communities. Among them were the *Klei HaKodesh* of Rabbi Yudel's synagogue, buried in the inner yard by the gabbai R' Shimshon Fogelman. The only surviving information are the pictures of the Torah Scroll and the spice box for the *Havdalah*, which were the property of the Jewish community, published in the book: "Zyddzi W Polsce Odrodzonej" ["Jews in Reborn Poland"][1]. The pictures of the other objects were identified by Moshe Bar-David as identical to those that exist in the synagogues and *Batei HaMidrash* in the city. These objects testify to the splendor of our community.

Klei Kodesh, like the ones in Brzezany's Synagogue
(from the collection of M. Bar-David)

***Sefer Torah* crown from the 17th century**
Property of the Brzezany Jewish Community

Translator's Notes:

1. Mauritzi Metzishevski – "Brzezany, Historical Monograph," 1910 (The National Library, Jerusalem, 36-1536:933.5 438).

2. Ya'akov Finkerfeld – "The Synagogues in Italy," diagram 23, pg. 37.

Translator's Note:

1. "Żydzi w Polsce odrodzonej: działalność społeczna, gospodarcza, oświatowa i kulturalna"["Jews in Poland Reborn, Social, Economic, Educational and Cultural Activities"], by Schiper, Ignacy, A. Tartakower; and A. Hafftaki, Warsaw, 1933.

[Page 232]

Rabbi Yudel's Synagogue

By Menakhem Katz

Translated by Moshe Kutten

Edited by Jane S. Gabin

The *Beit HaMidrash*, named after Rabbi Yudel, was located on the northern edge of the Jewish neighborhood on the crossroad of the roads from Ternopil and Lviv. Rabbi Yudel was a *Tzadik* who resided in the city. He died in 5568 (1808). The *Yahrzeit* [anniversary of passing] was observed annually by visiting the grave and a having *Mitzvah* meal.

According to the literature, there was no other house of prayer like it in the city. There were two types of synagogues in some Eastern European cities and towns: the first was called a synagogue, and the second was utilized not only for praying but also for public and private studying of the Torah. The latter was called "*Beit Midrash*." The "*Beit HaMidrash*," named after Rabbi Yudel, had other roles. Before we review them, I will describe the building's physical structure.

The main building of the "*Beit HaMidrash*" stood on the corner of the Tarnopolska and Lvovska streets on a spacious plot, surrounded by some auxiliary structures. The *Beit HaMidrash* was a square building like many other houses of prayer built in Poland in the 18th and 18th centuries. Unlike other synagogues with all sorts of arches, the ceiling of Rabbi Yudel's synagogue was flat and supported by wooden beams, as customary in other buildings in the city. The roof was covered with wooden shingles, which were replaced with a tin roof in the late years. The ceiling was made of plaster and decorated with spectacular pictures of the Four Beasts [from Prophet Daniel's vision of the four beasts].

When you entered the hall, opposite a simple and long wooden table, your eyes would meet a metal grate made by a tinsmith and decorated with heavy brass balls, which together formed the railing of the *Bimah* (raised stage - "Belemer" as the people in Yiddish called it). Above the *Bimah's* rail and through the thicket of rods and the hanging lamp chains, your eyes were attracted to the central part of the prayer hall – the eastern wall and the Holy Ark in its center. The Holy Ark, made of carved wood, was crafted by a Jewish artisan.

In 1936, the ceiling was replaced due to the risk of collapse. The decorations on the new ceiling were four plaster reliefs in the shape of a Star of David cast in the corners and a single Star of David relief in the center. Balls made of plaster were placed on the four sides of the ceiling between the Star of David's reliefs. A glass ball hanging from each of these balls contained an electrical lamp. Multi-branched copper menorahs on chains descended from the center of the Star of David reliefs. The menorahs were donated by the generous worshipper, Khaim Perlmutter. A thorough renovation was also performed in the same year. The floor and the windows were replaced, and many renovation projects were performed under the supervision of the *Gabbai*, Yitzkhak (Itzi), son of Menakhem David.

The building of the *Beit HaMidrash*, whose exterior was monolithic with a four-slope roof, was a collection of rooms with various purposes. The prayer hall, which measured a square of nine meters on each side, occupied most of the area. The *Bimah* was positioned in the middle. Attached to the western side of the prayer hall was a long entrance hallway, two and a half meters wide. The main entrance to it was on its southern side. On the opposite northern side of the hallway, an additional door led to a dim, long, narrow corridor, which connected a whole row of auxiliary rooms.

A wide double door led from the center of the entrance hallway to the prayer hall. On its northern edge, close to the exit door, stood a cabinet for Torah books *Psulim* [non-Kosher, invalid]. Above it was a *Gnizah* cabinet [for temporary storage of books designated for a burial].

[Page 233]

The Holy Ark was situated on the eastern wall. A canopy with a pseudo-classic frieze above two small columns formed an open space above the ceiling of the Holy Ark. Above the frieze were two lion figures with the Two Tablets of the Covenant. Behind them, on the two sides, were two large birds. The whole complex seemed to be made as a single piece – an engraved wooden structure whose spaces and protrusions, arranged in a rich configuration, complement its artistic appearance. Integrated into the holy Ark were the lights, shadows, and colors – red, green, blue, and gold - in a harmony that conveyed splendor.

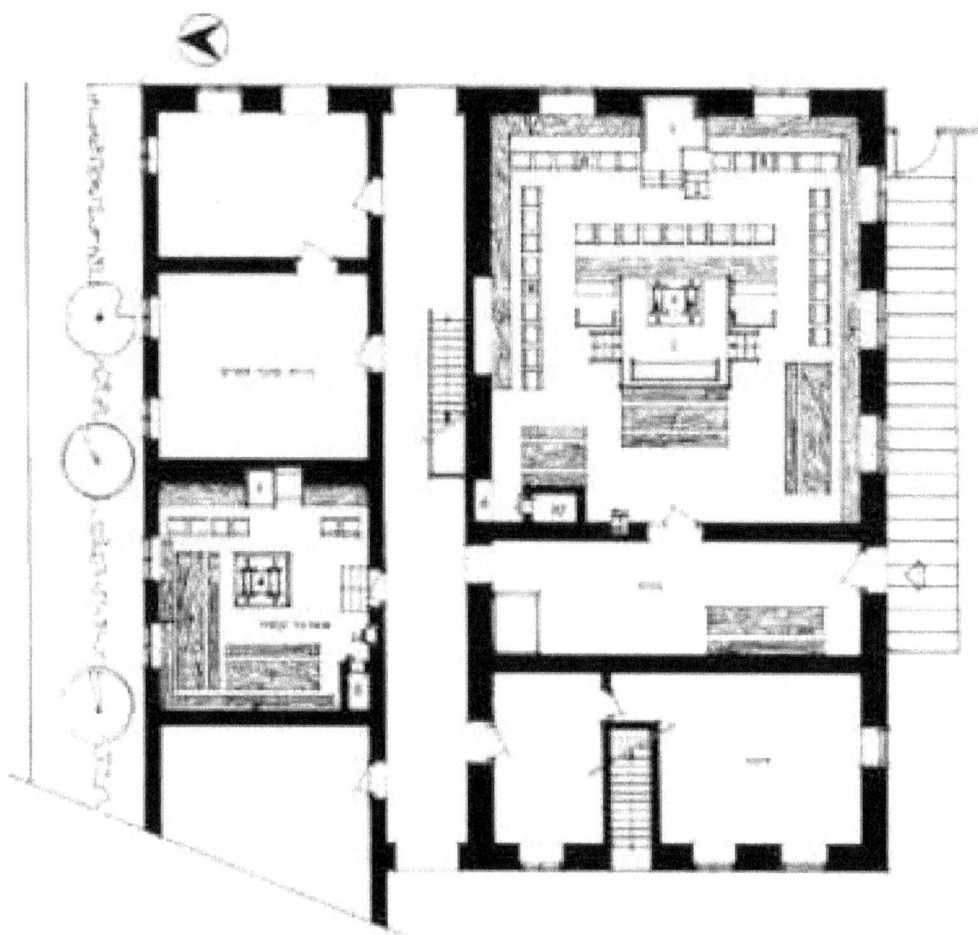

The Plan for Rabbi Yudel's *Beit HaMidrash*

[Page 234]

The artisan who created the Holy Ark was R' Meir-Hersh Shapira *z"l,* a pious and learned man, the *Mohel* of the town. I recall the admiration for that artisan I heard from my grandmother, who loved decorative objects. He created this masterpiece with his knives and rich imagination. Delicate leaves on thin copper wires, interwoven among pears, apples, and other fruits, rose and climbed on the side of the Ark. In the center of the Ark were two narrow doors made of delicate lace craft, with a small half-circle roof above to shield them.

Indeed. The Holy Ark was beautiful – a pure Jewish work of art. Reverence befell anybody who stood before it.

Two big windows topped by round arches were on the two sides of the Holy Ark. They cast an abundance of eastern light onto the prayer hall. Adjoining them was a half-circle hatch above the Holy Ark and a row of windows on the southern wall. There was no lack of light in the *Beit HaMidrash*, even on days without sun since its windows faced the south with a spacious entrance yard behind them.

Three stone stairs led to the *Bimah*, where a wide table stood on the east and a heavy oak bench on the west. On the left side of the table was a tall chair for the person overseeing the Torah reading – R' Mikhael Redlikh *z"l*.

Rows of "*Shtanders*" (prayer stands) were available for all seats, which encircled the *Bimah* from three sides. Long tables made of simple wood stood behind them. Close to the entrance, within an indentation, stood a cooper sink and a tap, and close to it, a towel hung on a roller.

An old clock, the eternal light, and a book cabinet were placed above the fireplace.

From the prayer hall through the entrance hall and into the dim corridor were two treacherous stairs that were obstructive to any stranger who did not know about them. A clay floor in the corridor led to a room of prayer, which was used as a "*Kheder*" called "*Potiker Kloiz*" for teaching little children.

Attached to the *Potiker Kloiz* on its east side was a two-room apartment for the "*Sofer St'm*" [scribe], and on the west side, three additional rooms, the apartment of my rabbi-teacher and *Kheder Melmamed*, R' Getzeleh Halperin and behind it, the apartment of the *Gabbai* [Torah reading administrator], R' Yosef Shtreizand. Behind the entrance hall were two additional rooms, and in the middle, a staircase leading to the outside and the women's section on the upper floor.

The women's section spread over the lower rooms. There were rows of benches with backs there and "*Shtanders*" (prayer stands), as in the men's section.

In addition to the main building, the "*Beit HaMidrash*" owned a spacious structure with a separate interior yard, which was leased to R' Yosef Shtreizand. With the entrance of the Nazi oppressor, R' Shimshon Fogelman buried in this structure in a deep pit (according to him), all the "*Klei HaKodesh*" [ritual objects] of the *Beit HaMidrash*.

In the yard, which was agriculturally cultivated, a row of ornamental trees shaded a row of sitting benches. A kiosk, which people in the town called "*de ginishe budkeh*" (the green kiosk), stood in the yard. The *Beit HaMidrash* also benefited from the lease it received from the renters of the auxiliary buildings.

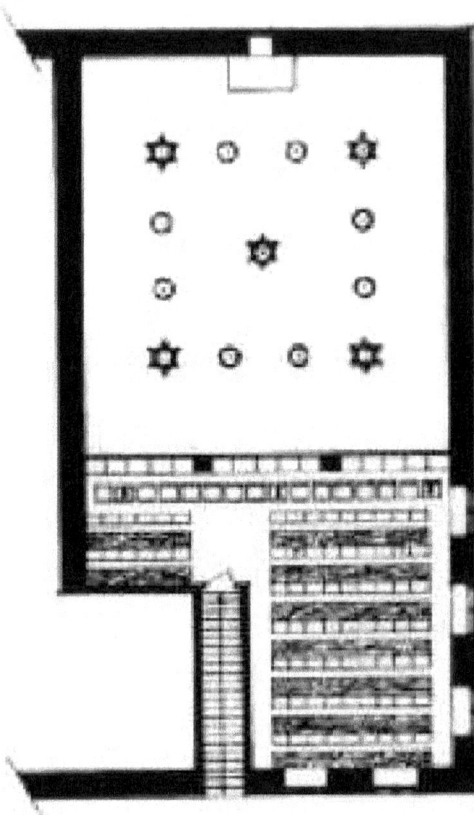

The plan of the women's section and the
decoration on the ceiling of the prayer hall

[Page 235]

Characters

The lifestyle of the *Beit HaMidrash* was reflected in its people. I cannot describe the entire crowd of homeowners, estimated to have been more than one hundred families, who were permanent members of the *Beit HaMidrash* and constituted most of the audience during the holidays. However, I will expand here on those whose personalities, roles, or appearance made their mark and shaped the character of the *Beit HaMidrash*.

First, I would mention some dignitaries:

Rabbi Moshe, the city rabbinical judge, possessed general education and inexhaustible knowledge of the Torah. For many years, Rabbi Moshe made a living from his real-estate business since he did not want to depend on public money. He also used to teach adults and the youth for free. His short stature, white beard, and slow and calculated moves invoked respect and appreciation from anybody he met, beginning with the children of the *Kheder* and ending with the community elders.

Behind him [in the hall of prayer], we should mention R' Efraim Zalman Margaliot, the grandson of the Rabbi from Brody and the author of the book "Yad Efreim" [The Hand of Efraim]. He was a *Talmid Khakham* [literally "a student of sages," an honorific for somebody who is versed in Jewish Torah, literature, and law], a pious and modest man. A separate article in the book [see page 204] is dedicated to him.

Near him sat R' Yosef Shaul Weichert, also a "*Talmid Khakaham*," one of few in town. He was very clever and had a majestic appearance. He served as a deciding arbitrator in feuds and negotiations.

We should also mention the *Gabbai*s, such as R' David-Meir Freier, a wealthy merchant with a majestic appearance, who was one of the Enlighted, but he also attended the *Beit HaMidrash* diligently. His golden glasses, calculated moves, and self-confidence did not prevent him from being a public servant and influential and respected *Gabbai*.

His neighbor on the east side seat was R' Shimshon Fogelman – the mighty synagogue administrator. He served as such for many years. He was a pious Jew who, in addition to his work, dedicated most of his free, and not so free, time to public activism as a *Gabbai*, initiator of charity events, and an enthusiastic Zionist. He was the one that enabled Zionist activities at the *Beit HaMidrash*. We should give him credit for all the gatherings, Zionist speeches, fundraising for the KKL-JNF, Keren HaYesod [United Israel Appeal], and other Zionist causes.

And who can forget the sturdy figure of R' Yosef Shtreizand? His nickname was Yosi Stoller (carpenter in Yiddish), according to his profession. He was a homeowner, a diligent *Gabbai*, a gatekeeper, and an administrator. He was a man of many actions when it came to charity organizations and served as the chairman of "*Khevre Kadisha*" [burial society]. His firm stance, energy, and public activism earned him respect as a man of action. He was imbued with the Zionist spirit and made *Aliyah* to Eretz Israel. He settled in Kfar Saba and continued to be one of the activists for the working religious public.

Every figure had its own characteristics – the dignified homeowners, people with unique nicknames, or others with a regular surnames, from the simple people to the local or passer-by poor people - and everyone was accommodated at the *Beit HaMidrash*.

In the corner, between the eternal light and the fireplace – was something that looked like a pile of tattered clothing or perhaps a folded blanket forgotten between the benches. That was the impression of anybody who was not a member of the *Beit HaMidrash*. However, that impression would evoke a smile

[Page 237]

on the face of every child and adult. For them, it was clear that the neglected pile was the sleeping figure of the hunchbacked scribe. The poor *Sofer St"m*, whose stature was not much taller than the prayer stand. The scribe was sitting there days and nights, during the hot summer days and the long winter nights, writing *Mezuzas* and *Tefillin*. The bench at the fireplace was his place of work. He sat there, worked, managed his business, and conducted whispered negotiations with his few clients who stopped there from time to time. This colorful figure had no home and no friends. The wooden bench, holy books, and the happenings at *Beit HaMidrash* were his only world.

Life in *Beit HaMidrash*

As aforementioned, in addition to the prayers, there were many roles for the *Beit HaMidrash*. First, I would like to mention that *Beit HaMidrash* was open day and night. Its gates were almost always open.

Before sunrise, on a bright sunny day, or during a snowstorm, one could observe the short and brisk steps of R' Gedalia Rozentzweig, the caretaker, hurrying to his place of work. He quickly reaches out with his hand over the upper door lintel, searching for the key in its hiding place, known to all the regular members. The key was always in its place. He takes the key down and puts it into the keyhole. However, before twisting it to unlock the door, he tries to see if the door has already been opened. Rare were the cases in which R' Gedalia had to unlock the door with the key. There was always somebody who came before him.

Who were the early risers? They were homeowners in a hurry to leave the city on their business with the sunset, people who studied the Torah and Mishnah, passers-by, those who carried packages from other towns, those who needed to say "*Kadish*" or on a *Yahrzeit* in a hurry for the first *Minyan* and just wondering poor, and "ragtag's and bobtails" who were always familiar with the customs at the *Beit HaMidrash*.

One scene of many that took place every day – before dawn, not quite a night anymore, but still not a day, within a bluish dim, penetrating through the windows, your eyes adapt to the grayish light, seeded by some lonely golden dots of candles here and there. Every candle has a figure close to it of a Jew covered with the Talit, whispering his prayers quickly. Another figure moves quickly, rolling up a sleeve and tying the *Tefillin* stripes on his arm. Somebody moves the prayer stand and takes out the *Klei HaKodesh*. In another corner, people whisper to each other. These are the poor who spent the whole night near the cooling fireplace. Everything moves slowly and mysteriously. Before the arrival of R' Gedalia, no palpable activity occurred in *Beit HaMidrash*. When his diminutive figure appears at the door, it is as if a spirit of new daily life blows through everything. He makes his first steps

[Page 237]

toward the *Bimah's* table and takes out a handful of candles locked in the cabinet below. The candles are quickly distributed among the people at the synagogue, and they are lit one after the other. He does not begin his daily work alone. His helpers are many, some willing and some are not, since they all need his favors, a poor person, or a dignified homeowner. One person needs another candle, the other an accommodation license and the third one forgot the key to his "*Shtander*" and is asking to lend him *Tefillin*. As he is hard of hearing, R' Gedalia divides the tasks without using many words. The fireplace and candles are lit, the sink is filled with water, the floor is swept, and the *Beit HaMidrash* is ready to receive its members.

With the arrival of the tenth person, they don't wait for another since the time is precious for the early risers. "Begin," hints one initiative person who is in a hurry. "Wait," answers his neighbor, "It is still dark outside." A hot debate arises occasionally, about whether it is permissible to begin the morning prayer or they should wait a short while. The minutes pass quickly, and the *Ba'al Tfila* [the prayer leader] approaches the lighted stand and begins. Almost immediately, the phrases start to flow from the prayer stand. From time to time, additional people who come "late" join the first *Minyan*.

After the end of the prayer, everyone is joyful, particularly the poor. Almost every morning, there is at least one homeowner who needs to fulfill the commandment of a "*Yahrtzeit.*" A mandatory custom is that the mourner sponsors a "*Tikkun*" [literally 'rectification,' breakfast after the morning prayer. Mourners are generous or not, but all dispense a small cup of wine among the attendees. Depending on the mourner's financial situation, cookies, beigels, or dry pastries are also provided. Standing, while folding the Tallit, the praying people grab a sip and light bite, and each hurry up on their way. For the poor people, that is the day's first meal, and they are waiting for it impatiently. They take as much as possible. R' Gedalia makes sure that the food is distributed equitably. That is why his standing among the poor people is so strong. During the economic crisis, R' Shimshon Fogelman established a custom, in which the mourners donate money instead of "*Tikkun's*" food. With that money, bread was bought and distributed to the needy according to a list prepared by the *Gabbai*s.

One *Minyan* after the other is held without a break throughout the morning. The *"Ba'al Tfila"* changes for each *Minyan*. Often, the number of *Minyans* reaches ten in one morning. The last *Minyan* concludes around 11 A.M.

Saturday afternoon – the prayer hall is full. A diversified crowd from all classes of the city population. The *Bimah* is surrounded by youths, and behind them, the homeowners, Hassidim, and Zionists of all shades of Hasidism and Zionism. At the center of the *Bimah* stands Rabbi Shores[?] – a professional preacher and a follower of "Agudat Israel" [the Haredi Jewish party]. Moral aphorisms with a political background spill from his mouth like blazing flames. The exuberant sermon fascinates the listeners – his supporters and the Zionist rivals. However, he peppers his remarks with incitement against Zionism, *Aliyah*, and the modern education of the youth.

At that point, after captivating the audience with words of Torah, admonition, and persuasion, the first statement of hatred against Zionism is heard, and the listening barrier is breached. A young and tall youth, Moshe Bergman, the leader of the Zionist youth movement in the city, vigorously utters the first dissent.

That call, presented as a question, forces the preacher to respond or embarrasses him, and he stops his enthusiastic speech. Questions and answers float in the air, and the voices of opponents and allies are heard. A debate between the speaker and the crowd ensues. *Beit HaMidrash* becomes a definite political stage that does not require the involvement of organizers. The questions and interjection calls are spontaneous,

[Page 238]

from the bottom of the hearts of the Zionist youths, fighting for the right to be Zionist among their people with all its shades of religious and secular views. That was a relevant debate between the young generation and the establishment consisting of homeowners, pious Hassidim, and just regular Jews. That was the atmosphere in the afternoon on Sabbath or a weekday (usually Sunday). That was just another folk episode at the *Beit HaMidrash* when the Zionists fought for free *Aliyah* from inside of the nation, and those layers became an inhibiting factor and a stumbling block to the Zionist effort.

Skipping over gatherings, religious-political speeches, state or community election gatherings, comedy shows, or simply small talks, I reach a story about a slightly strange night gathering. The space of the prayer hall was lit only by a few candles. A group of young men, before the age of enlistment, gathers and conducts their discussion in a whisper. They talk about this and that, just debating, exchanging political views, interjecting jokes, gossiping about the relations between a certain man and a woman, and so on. The discussion stops, and another figure joins them. A couple of young men leave the synagogue, just to return to it a short while later. Who are these young men who patiently spend the hours of the night with talks, torturing themselves not to sleep? People call them the "tortured." They deplete their strength by not eating or sleeping to lose weight below the minimum acceptable to the Austrian or Polish militaries.

Two figures whispering a secret to each other. One of them is a passer-by – a professional beggar who talks about his adventures and achievements to his friend, who is also a professional beggar. These people meet occasionally throughout the state, and Yudel's *Beit HaMidrash* is one of their regular stops. That is where the beggars meet and renew acquaintances, a tradition practiced for generations.

During the late period, a rule was introduced that forbade the Jews from begging. Instead, the community provided a uniform allowance and lodging to all foreign beggars to prevent them from going around in the streets. The bench by the fireplace served as a temporary stop for those who intended to stay in the city temporarily.

That corner was also where news was being told.

[Page 239]

What could you hear at that corner? You would learn about the movement of 'ragtag and bobtails' throughout the entire state and about the large amount of money collected by professional beggars. You could also hear who among the beggars owns a house in one town or another, and who is a dignified homeowner in his far-flung town at the edge of Poland, spending only the summer to beg for money as a profitable "profession." You could learn what preachers plan to come to town soon and even what has occurred in the synagogues at the sermons. You will hear about quarrels between rabbis at the courts of the *Admo"rs*, exaggerated stories, miracles performed by rabbis for their followers, and famous matchmakings between dignities and rabbis. News was told there, not only about the happenings within the Haredi world but also about the international prices of currencies in which the bench-sitters were experts. You would also listen to political debates on a reasonable level since knowledgeable and clever people are occasionally sucked into that debate corner. In summary – the table at the fireplace served as an updated means of communication those days.

A woman's plea

It was a bright summer morning. The prayer hall was awash with sunlight when two *Minyans* were immersed in a late morning prayer. I stood, along with the rest of the worshippers, not far from the Holy Ark with the calm of a youngster without worries, I delved into the holiness of the prayer. Suddenly, without seeing how and where from, a woman wrapped in black burst into the hall with her hands lifted, covered herself with her black transparent scarf, and, like floating in the air, stretched out in front of the Holy Ark.

"Is it a ghost or a dream I am dreaming? A woman in black in the men's section during the morning prayer? Impossible! Nevertheless, my eyes do not mislead me." Only a few seconds of passing thoughts behind me, and the figure removes the Holy Ark's "*Parokhet*" [curtain] and opens the doors. Her knees drop to the floor, she stretches her arms toward the open Ark, and a scream of terror emanates from her throat: "*Shema Israel*…My G-d, my G-d, help me; what was my sin before you? Please do not take my son from me - he is so young." And again: "*Shema Israel…*" combined with a scream, sob, and a cry of pain, echoing among the walls of the synagogue.

That episode lasted only a few seconds. After the first scream, and after the shocked and astonished crowd grasped what had just happened, two men hurried to the Holy Ark, lifted the woman, and locked the doors. She was the wife of Abba, the ritual slaughter, and it was not easy to lift her from the front of the Holy Ark. Words of persuasion and pleading were leveled at her to leave the place. Dignitaries intervened, but the woman persisted – and continued to extend her plea through pain and sorrow.

Long times passed before the worshippers convinced the sorrowful woman to leave the praying hall. The impression that episode left upon the small praying crowd and the echoes of the event continued to reverberate for a long time.

That scene of breaching the customs by a Jewish woman, the pious wife of the ritual slaughterer, symbolizes boundless fate in a divine force whose sanctuary and manifestation was the Holy Ark, and the approach to it was through the open doors of the Ark.

All of that occurred at the *Beit HaMidrash,* named after Rabbi Yudel, which served its worshippers for various purposes in the social and spiritual life of the town.

[Page 240]

The evening before *Yom Kippur*

The "Days of Awe" is an expression conveyed as a concept during the rest of the year. You express that concept as part of volubility and move on. During the month of Elul, it is not an expression or concept. During that month, the Days of Awe become a symbol, divine words that exert superhuman fear in you. They become days of preparation, days of asking for forgiveness and repentance, prayer, and fearing the day of atonement, the holy and divine day. Thoughts about that holy day would not leave you alone during the entire period approaching the critical prayers on *Yom Kippur.* The closer the big day, your pleas and prayers deepened. Prayers, asking for forgiveness, repentance, ritual immersion, confession and repentance, cleanliness of the body and soul - all of these are the preparations for that day.

The evening before one specific *Yom Kippur* at the *Beit HaMidrash,* one of many in generations, was etched in my memory.

The prayer hall at *Beit HaMidrash* is clean; its walls are gleaming from the whitewashing, and the copper objects shine, reflecting the sun rays that penetrate the space, inducing shining spots to dance on the white background of the walls like stars. It is late afternoon, and the entrance hall gates are wide open. The long table is covered with white paper, and all sorts of boxes and bowls are on it. There is a note on each one of them stating who would be benefiting from your donation. Tens of boxes for the fund of Rabbi Meir Ba'al HaNes. There are also boxes for the KKL-JNF and the elderly shelter in town – all arranged in a row and waiting for their donors.

The homeowners are flocking to the bowls. It is a custom to donate to charity and pay off debts at dusk between *Minkha* [afternoon prayer] and *Kol Nidrei* [a prayer recited before the evening prayer of *Yom Kippur* Eve.]. The worshippers are coming at a slow flow starting in the afternoon hours, walking along the length of the table, each man, and his donation. The metal coins strike the metal, and the return tone symbolizes the gratitude of the institution. The *Gabbai* sits at the head of the table and collects the year's debt payments from everybody. The long list of debts, oaths, obligations, and donations is getting smaller and smaller. That is the time to pay off the debts, and the Jewish hearts are open to charity since the time is running out, and it is going to be too late in a few hours. And thus, without any words of solicitation, the boxes are being filled with donations.

When you pass from the entrance hall into the praying hall – a holy spirit grips you. This is not the *Beit HaMidrash* of the regular days. These are not the same walls, not the same *Klei HaKodesh*, and not even the same people. These are different people – the Jews of the *Yom Kippur's* Eve. They look different from their daily looks. Every figure and every shadow familiar to you from the other days of the year are different on the evening of this holiday. People are different in their looks, behavior, cleanliness, and exultance before the big prayer.

And here is a picture, one of the few that may still be seen in a secluded alley in Mea-Shearim [old Jerusalem Haredi neighborhood] or Hasidic Williamsburg [in Brooklyn, New York]. The bent figure of R' Mikhael Redlikh, a very old G-d fearing man whom young and old paid respect to unreservedly, rose from his seat on the east and, with prudent steps, approached the *Bimah*. The wise man was frail as the years weighed heavily on him. However, when he approached the *Bimah* steps, he was suddenly granted youthful strength and with swift steps, he climbed onto the *Bimah*. Hinting with his arm, he called R' Gedalia, the caretaker. Without saying a word, R' Gedalia unrolled a small carpet on the *Bimah's* floor. With a slow bending motion, R' Michael got down on his knees

[Page 241]

and slowly tilted his body forward until the palms of his hands touched the carpet. The old man's slender body knelt on all fours, and his back arched upwards. With a quick hand, R' Gedalia pulled out a braided whip with long stripes and brought it down on the old man's back at a steady pace[1]. Raise and lower – raise and lower – the whip hit the back of R' Mikhael. Every hit yielded a dull echo. Occasionally, between one lash to another, you could hear R' Mikhael whisper: "Harder! Harder!" and R' Gedalia slightly increased the swing of the whip, only to retreat again in his following lash. The caretaker whipped forty lashes on the back of the old man.

The custom of flogging was over and done with. R' Mikhael rose on his feet, and his face brightened since his last preparation for *Yom Kippur's Kol Nidrei* prayer concluded. He was ready to worship his G-d on the Day of the Atonement.

A few other community elders passed under R' Gedalia's whip. And when the time for the "*Se'uda Mafseket*" [the last meal before *Yom Kippur's* fast] approached, the *Beit HaMidrash* emptied out. Only a few hundred *Yahrzeit* candles remained. They were made in white or dark shades of yellow colors and in shape, starting from a small tin box to sophisticated raided wax candles. They all made golden lights dance and, in the silence of their dance, waited for the crowd of *Kol Nidrei* prayers.

Translator's Note:

1. An old custom of *Melkot* (literally "lashes")is the tradition for all men to receive symbolic "lashes" on the eve of *Yom Kippur* to motivate themselves to repent.

[Pages 242]

The "Built" *Beit HaMidrash*

by Menakhem son of Shimon Katz

Translated by Moshe Kutten

Edited by Jane S. Gabin

A school stood close to the Great Synagogue. It was a structure made of dirt that contained two rooms. A Jewish *Melamed* or teacher lived in one of the rooms. The second room was like a synagogue. It means that it had the Holy Ark and a fireplace made of burnt bricks and covered with green enamel.

That is the description of *Beit HaMidrash* from the documents of the Roman-Catholic community in Brzezany from 1939. That meager structure was rebuilt from stone. That was the source of its name – "The 'Built' *Beit HaMidrash*."

That is also how I remember that unique architectural asset, a remnant of the 17th century, a member of the family of Galitsia's synagogues relying on four supporting pillars. It was built from plastered sandstone, which could only be seen on the rim and the doors' lintels.

Beit HaMidrash stood in the southeastern corner of the synagogue plaza, like kissing the northeastern corner of the Great Synagogue, leaving only a narrow pass between them.

The structure was square with nine "fields" of cross-like domes, the center one of which was supported by four heavy support pillars. Four arches connected the pillars, and eight additional arches connected the corners of the domes to the outside walls. The four support pillars, together with the twelve arches, formed a massive structure that provided the inner space of the building with a character of strength, evoking a feeling of security. It seems that this constructive aspect was not the only consideration that drove the builder (probably Jewish, as there were such builders in town at that time) to choose this design with four support pillars since our area did not have good building stones, but the Brzezany area was rich in forests, so it was much more logical to cover the hall space with a wooden ceiling. It seems that the emotional consideration of providing the worshippers with a sense of security was a considerable factor in the design of that *Beit HaMidrash*.

[Pages 243]

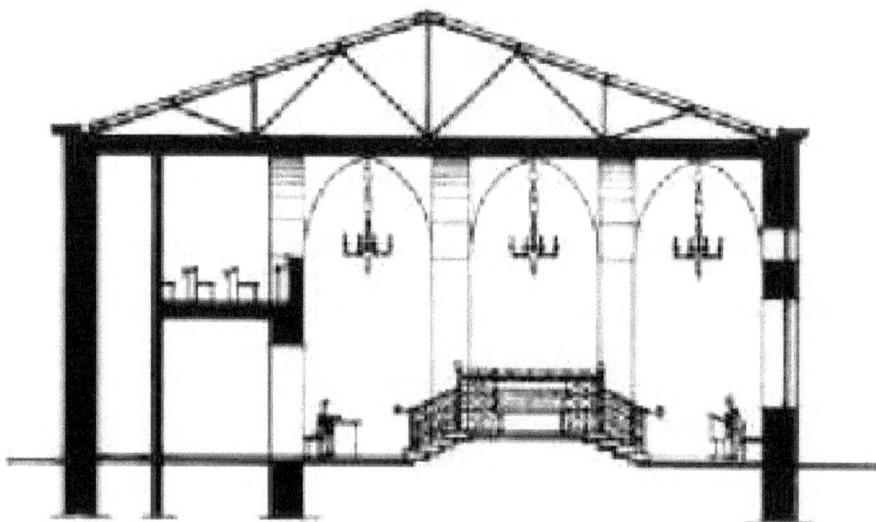

Cross section of the "Built" *Beit HaMidrash*

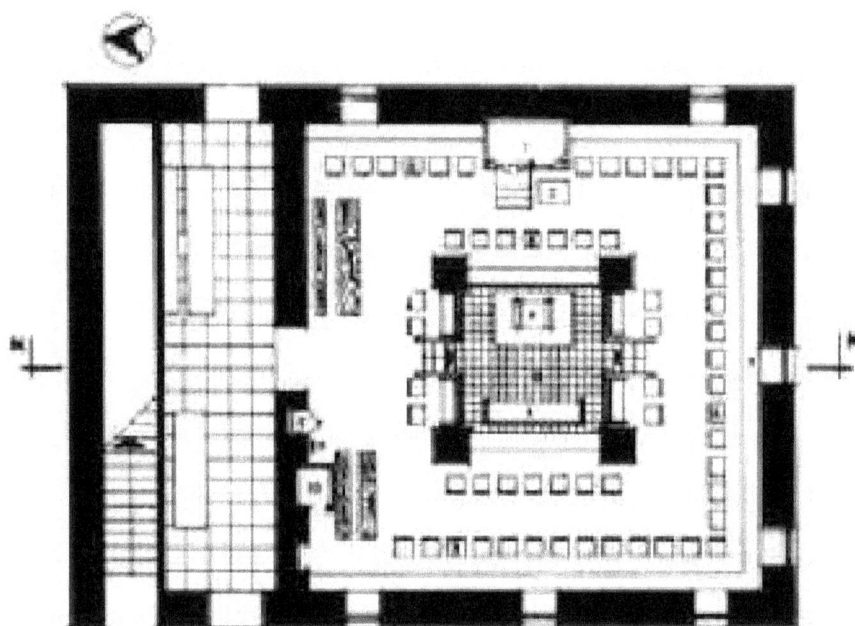

The plan of the "Built" *Beit HaMidrash*

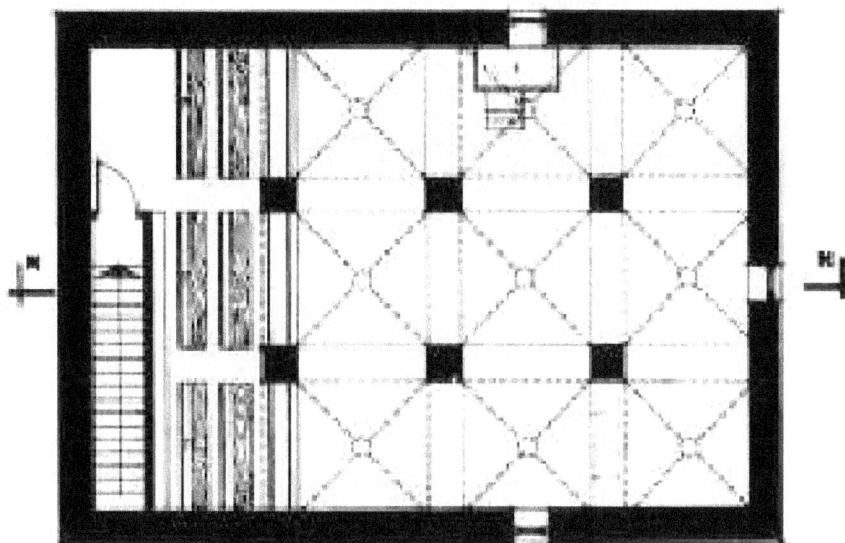

The plan for the ceiling and the women's section
of the "Built" *Beit HaMidrash*

On the side of the main entrance, another door led to a steep staircase rising up to the women's section, which occupied the area above the entrance hall on the second floor. The southern side of the women's section was open to the main hall, and only a short heavy metal railing made by a tinsmith separated the section and the main hall. The heavy construction of the domes was topped by a flat ceiling, and above it was a tin roof laid on top of a wooden grille as was customary for other structures in the city. Based on the construction of the arches, it is logical to assume the tin roof was added only recently and that originally, the synagogue could have served as a fort with a tall railing on the roof, as customary in the other fort-like synagogues in eastern Poland.

Stone staircases between the support pillars led onto the *Bimah* from its southern and northern sides. The Torah reading table stood on the *Bimah*. It was surrounded by an iron railing – the work of an artistic tinsmith. Muli-branched copper menorahs hung on an iron chain descended from the center of each dome. The large number of the menorahs was more than enough to light up the prayer hall. However, when gas lighting became available in the city, the "Built" *Beit HaMidrash* became the only synagogue lit by gas.

Most worshippers at the 'Built' *Beit HaMidrash* were middle-class and wealthy homeowners. Despite its name, people prayed in it only on Shabbat and holidays.

The gabbais of the *Beit HaMidrash* included Ya'akov Bauer, Mendel Fridman, Ya'akov Katz, Ya'akov Kaner, Ya'akov Shtern, and Eizner.

The building, except the furnishings, was preserved through the Soviet and Nazi conquest periods. When I left Brzezany, it served as a wheat warehouse for the Soviet supply authorities.

[Pages 244]

The "Cantor's" *Beit HaMidrash*

by Menakhem son of Shimon Katz

Translated by Moshe Kutten

Edited by Jane S. Gabin

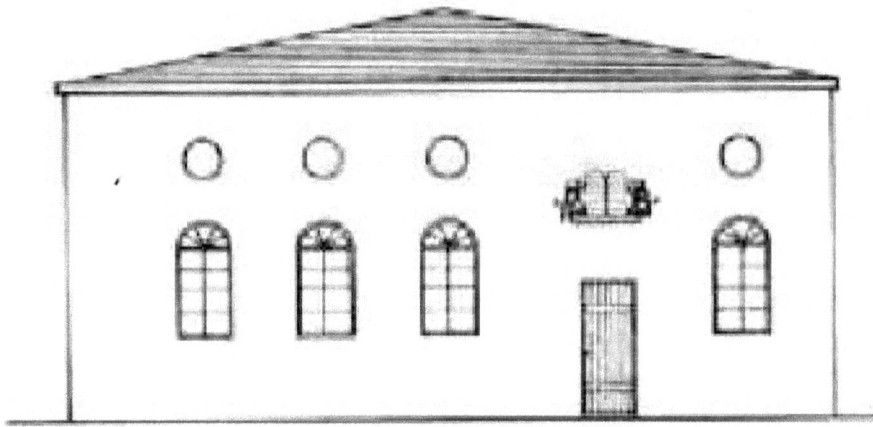

The southern front of the Cantor's *Beit HaMidrash*

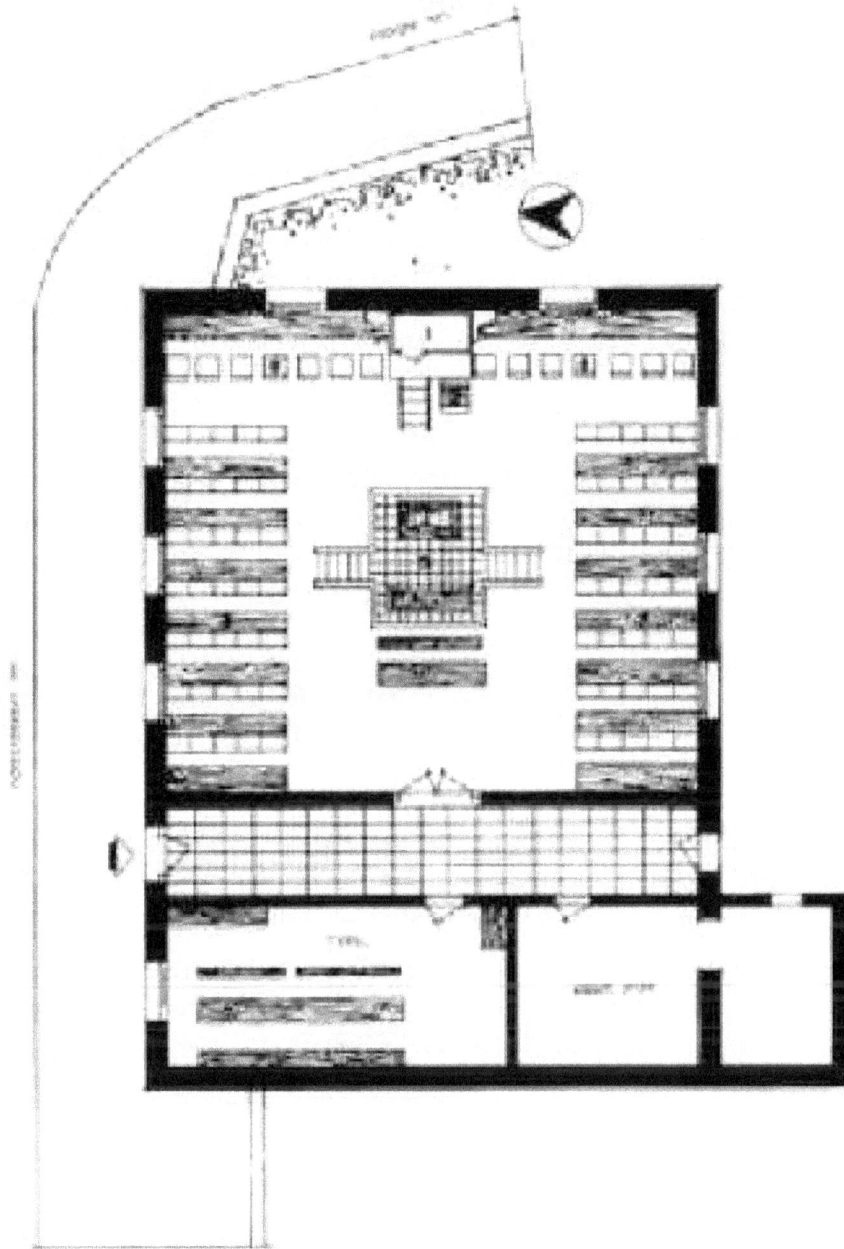

The plan of the "Cantor's" *Beit HaMidrash*

The *Beit HaMidrash* of the "*Khazan*" [cantor] stood on the corner of Zigmontovska and Shkolna Streets on the way to the city's two elementary schools. Nobody in the town called *Beit HaMidrash* with a different name, despite the fact that Rabbi Yosef Shaul Nathanson prayed, acted, and gave sermons there. The latter was a native of the city and the pre-eminent Rabbi of Lviv after he left Brzezany.

It was a square building without any additions. The narrow entrance hall had a wide door leading into the prayer hall, across the *Bimah* and the Holy Ark behind it. On the other side of the entrance hall were a large *Kheder* and the caretaker's apartment. The *Beit HaMidrash* was built in the middle of the 19th century and belonged to the family of square synagogues common to Galitsia. Its structure was functional and met the needs of its worshippers. The prayer hall was spacious because of the number of benches, the *Bimah*, and the furnishings. The hall reflected richness. Its furnishings were renovated in the 1930s, and the walls were covered in wood throughout. The new *Bimah*, surrounded by a curved railing, rose significantly high (about seven to ten stairs above the hall's floor). That was not common in the other synagogues in town. Perhaps that was done purposely because the "cantor," after whom the *Beit HaMidrash* was named, wanted to sound his prayer from a great height. The Holy Ark was similar to the one in the Great Synagogue. It was magnificent but smaller. The exterior was plastered, with a stone-made and oil-painted relief positioned above the entrance door. Two lions supporting the Covenant Tablets hinted about the purpose of the building. Large arched windows with colored glass emphasized more forcibly the purpose of the building.

Worshippers prayed only on Shabbat and holidays in that *Beit HaMidrash* and occasionally in afternoon and evening prayers. Despite that, the gates were open all day long, thanks to the "*Kheder*." One could hear the learning and teaching voices of the youngsters all day long.

Despite the heavy bombing that took place not far away from it, the *Beit HaMidrash* survived the Second World War. When I left the city in 1944, the structure was desolate and deserted.

[Pages 245]

The Old (Alte) Stratyner *Kloiz*

by Menakhem son of Shimon Katz

Translated by Moshe Kutten

Edited by Jane S. Gabin

After the fire at the old Stratyner *Kloiz* [small synagogue] on Belkherska Street in 1915, the worshippers moved, after the First World War, to that *Kloiz*. It stood in the yard of the "Built" *Beit HaMidrash* and was attached to it on the eastern side. The name "Alte" (old) moved with it.

The entrance into the *Kloiz's* small entrance hall was through the entrance hall of the "Built" *Beit HaMidrash* and through a narrow yard (that had no ceiling).

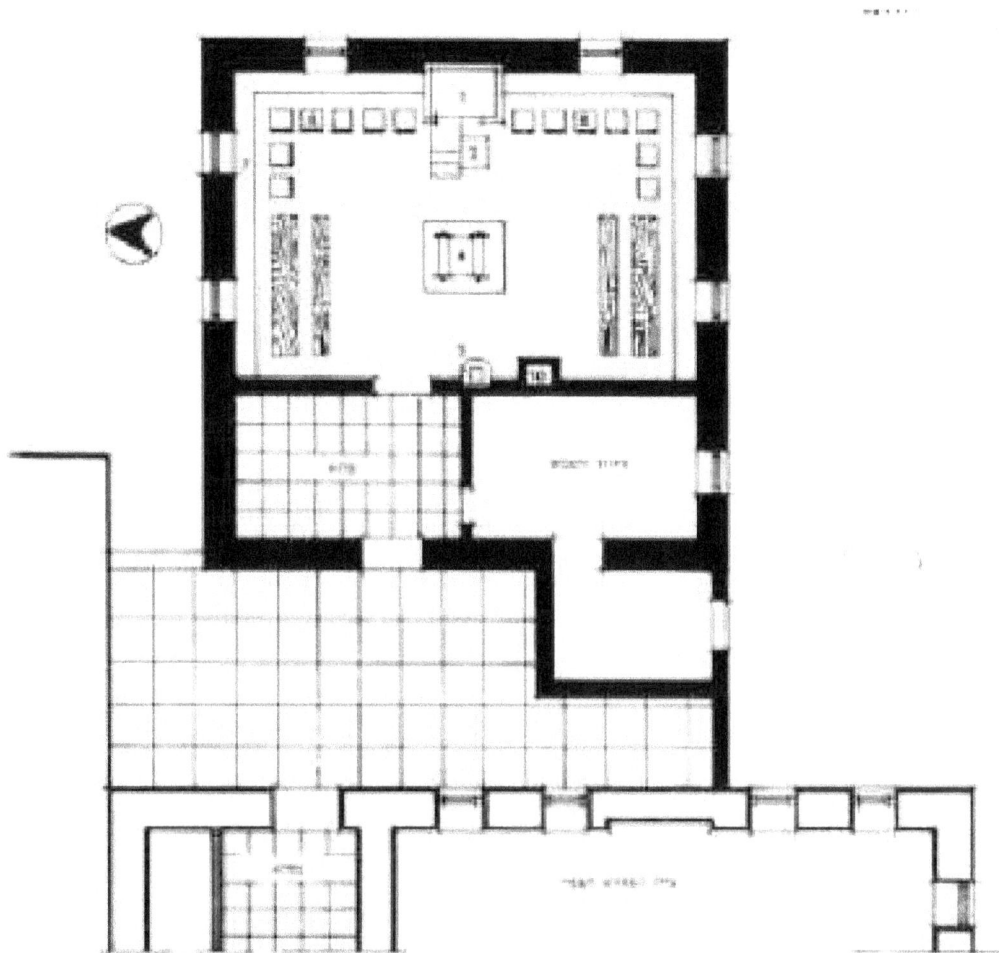

The plan for the Stratyner *Kloiz* with the caretaker's apartment

Like other houses of prayer that *Kloiz* throughout Galitsia, this synagogue consisted of a large prayer hall containing a Holy Ark, Torah reading table, and several "*Shtanders*" [stands] near the eastern wall, which served among other uses) the students of the "*Kheder*." It was managed by R' Shlomo Prisant.

Like the "Built" *Beit HaMidrash*, the building was made of plastered sandstone. Architecturally, the building did not have any special features, however, due to the stone details in the windows and the entrance from the yard with the door's lintel, it was apparent that it was built to serve as a house of prayer.

The prayers at the *Kloiz* were handled purely based on the customs of Stratyn Hasidim. Indeed, many of the people who prayed there were such Hasidim.

Among the latest *Gabbais* in the *Kloiz* were Alter Lufter and Yeshaia Tempel.

Like the *Beit HaMidrash*, the *Kloiz* remained standing, and in 1944, the Soviet supply authorities used the building as a wheat warehouse.

[Pages 246]

The *Kloiz* of the Chortkobver Hasidim

by Menakhem son of Shimon Katz

Translated by Moshe Kutten

Edited by Jane S. Gabin

The name "*Kloiz*" provides a hint about the Prayer House plan. That name defines a small structure that belonged to the family of small synagogues that were common in Galitsia.

The two-story house was built before the First World War by the followers of Rabbi David-Shlomo Friedman [According to the literature, the founder's name was David-Moshe Friedman], founder of the Chortkov [Today – Chortkiv] Hasidic Dynasty.

The first floor contained the prayer hall, and the second floor, the women's section. The building was burnt in the First World War. Chortkov Hasidim rebuilt the ground floor and established the prayer hall there.

It was a square structure about 9 x 9 meters. People entered it through an entrance corridor, which could be lifted to serve as a *Sukkah* during the holiday of Sukkot. The hall was furnished simply. The dominant piece of furniture was the Holy Ark, which rose to the ceiling.

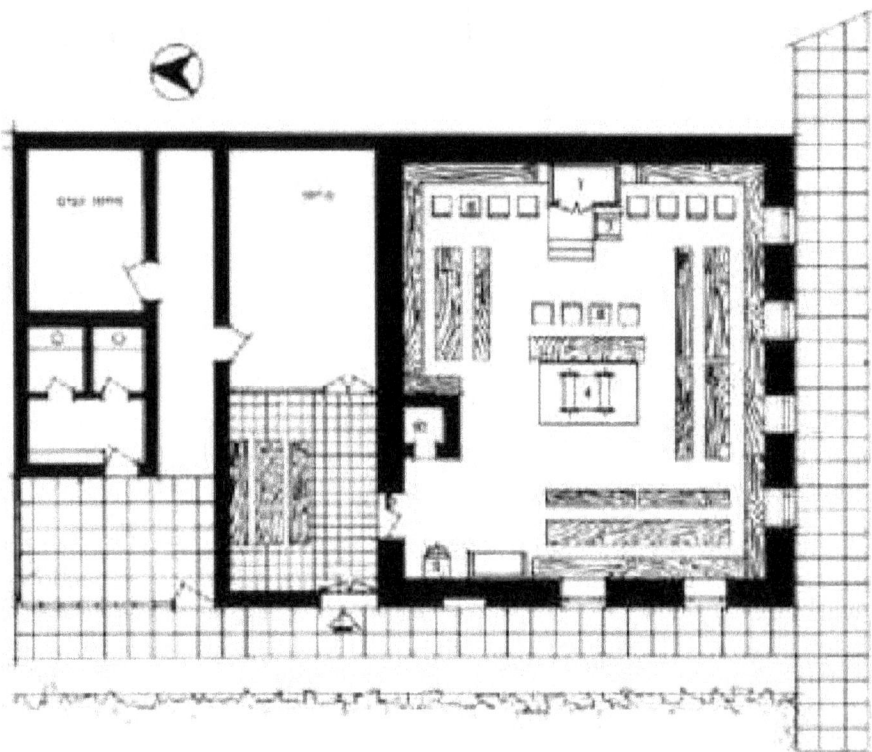

The plan for the *Kloiz* of Chortkov Hasidim

[Pages 247]

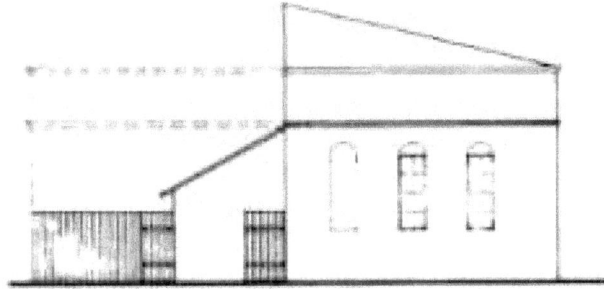

The western front of the *Kloiz*

The carving on the Ark included flowers, fruits, leaves, and stems, all strung and combined like embroidery. A complicated "wooden embroidery" of various plants enveloped the sides of the Ark and reached its top. Two lions, with two eagles on their sides, stood on the top of the Ark. There was no *Bimah* in that *Kloiz*, only a large table, covered with a colorful tablecloth, serving as a place for Torah reading.

Life at the *Kloiz*

by Dov Knohl

Translated by Moshe Kutten

Edited by Jane S. Gabin

Like the rest of the houses of prayer in the city, prayers took place on regular days, holidays, and Sabbaths according to tradition from time immemorial. However, the prayers in this *Kloiz* had a unique character. The prayer was marked by the utmost seriousness and the great devotion of the worshippers. At the same time, it was a quiet and concentrated prayer without unnecessary movements or raising voices. Looking at the worshippers, one could see old and young men, many of whom were standing, facing east with their *Talits* rolled down on their faces and their whole beings concentrated in the prayer. That was the prayer style of Chortkov Hasidim – inner enthusiasm arrested within the worshiper's heart.

The prayer's melody was jovial, sad, filled with longing and self-assurance. The *Kloiz* on Sabbaths and holidays did not resemble the one on weekdays. Although many worshippers prayed on weekdays, the *Kloiz* was too small to accommodate everyone on Sabbaths and holidays. Due to crowding, many prayed in the entrance hall and, in good weather, even outside in the spacious yard attached to the *Kloiz*.

The *Kloiz* was a center of Torah learning in the city, as the Yeshiva ceased its operation after the death of the Maharsha" m. In that period, between the two World Wars, it became the central location where high school-age boys and older young men concentrated all day long and studied. During the evening hours, older adults sat at the long tables at the end of their workday and dedicated their time to studying the Torah.

Among the learners were some young men who persisted in their studies throughout the day. Among them was a unique "studious" young man. A bright day or rainy day, summer, or winter - the *Kloiz*'s gate was wide open. Almost always, when you approached the building, you would hear the study melody rising and falling from afar. The voice echoed among the prayer hall walls, ceased for a moment, and then started again. The voice, which was coming from one of the corners, was of a young man, Zalman Shekhter *z"l*. He was a Torah scholar who was certified to teach by prominent Rabbis. He dedicated nights and days to his studies - a slender figure bent over the *Gemarah* and swaying in an even rhythm. When somebody entered the hall, he would raise his head, look at the person, and return to his study.

Another scene of life at the *Kloiz* was the Hasidic parties on Sabbaths, holidays, days of festivities, and anniversaries of the death of *Tzadikim* [righteous]. On those occasions, and particularly

[Pages 248]

in a *Kiddush* party following a Shabbat prayer or the party of the "Third Meal." Tens of Hasidim sat around a long table, enjoying a drink and singing Hasidic songs with great devotion. Suddenly, there was silence. One of the Hasidic elders or young scholars would talk about the weekly Torah portion, the essence of the holiday, or sayings of the *Tzadik* for whom the Memorial Day was celebrated. All the meal's participants would listen quietly and attentively.

In particular, the Hasidim liked to listen to R' Shmuel Adler *z"l*, the city's ritual slaughterer. His demeanor testified to the concentration of thought, moderation, and self-control. R' Shlomo told stories about the conduct of the *Tzadikim*, incorporating deep Hasidic ideas. He always began his story with: "I heard that story from my grandfather - who heard it from a Polish man who, in turn, heard it from an eyewitness…" He began his talk with a quiet voice, raising it gradually and lowering it again upon reaching a dramatic moment. The entire audience sat alert and attentively, absorbing R' Shlomo's talk.

Just as R' Shlomo ended his talk, R' Mendeleh, an aged man who knew many Hasidic melodies, began to sing, and the crowd followed him.

Those parties, some of which were short while others lasted several hours, were typical characteristics of life in the *Kloiz*.

Particularly known among the Jews were the "*Hakafot*" [literally "encircling" - dancing with and around the Torah scrolls] on the evening of the "*Simkhat Torah*" holiday and the prayer in "Ninth of Av" held by the Hasidim of Chortkov at the *Kloiz*.

A break was announced following the holiday prayer of the "*Simkhat Torah*" evening. Most of the worshippers went to the home of one of the *Gabbais* for a traditional holiday party. The young men gathered in another house for a more intimate party. Two hours later, people began to return to the *Kloiz*. In the meantime, the hall filled with women and girls, members of the youth movements, and other curious people who came to watch the *Hakafot* ceremony.

Following the prayer "Ata Horeta Lada'at" ["Unto thee it was shown that thou mightest know that the Lord, He is God"], sang with a festive melody, worshippers were invited to make "*Hakafot*" with Torah scrolls in their hands. After every round, the participants, accompanied by the congregation's elders, broke out with long and passionate dances. At the same time, most of the Hasidim sang devotedly and enthusiastically prayers and their melodies. They danced with their eyes closed endlessly encircling the scrolls without a break until they collapsed.

The Struggle for Zionist Influence

Although the *Admo"rs* of the Chrtokov dynasty excelled in loving the Jewish masses, they were among the leaders of "Agudat Israel" [anti-Zionist Haredic party.]. As such, the elders and some young men ensured that Zionist influence would not be reflected in the framework of the *Kloiz*. However, not everyone supported that view. Some worshippers demanded that the *Kloiz* would not differ from the other houses of prayer, where those who ascended to the Torah on holidays donated money to "Keren Kayemet Le'Israel" [KKL _JNF], and where notable events in the Zionist movement were held in the building. The people who led this struggle for Zionist influence were Mordekhai Knohl, Moshe Toiber, Arye Narol, Ozer Rot, and E. D. Rot.

[Pages 249]

Joining them was the young generation of youths, members of the Zionist youth movements. That struggle lasted many decades and was often stormy. It ended only during the last years before the Holocaust due to the news about the religious lives being established in the Jewish settlement movement in Eretz Israel, and principally because the Rabbi from Chortkov, who was forced to escape the Nazis from his place of residence in Vienna, arrived in Eretz Israel with the help of an Aliyah certificate secured for him by the Jewish agency. That also helped in securing donations for KKL-JNF and the Zionist movement [at the *Kloiz*].

The prominent figures

Like in any society, several people became prominent among the worshippers of the *Kloiz*, intentionally or unintentionally, due to their personality or way of life. Since they contributed to shaping life at the *Kloiz*, they should be mentioned and memorialized:

Admo"r Israel, son of Pinkhas Brandwein – grandson of the Stratyn family.
R' Shmuel Abelis Nebel [or Nevel] – a *Melamed* at the Maharsha"m's Yeshiva. A learner who dedicated his life to the Torah.
R' Naftali Gelber – served as a *Gabbai* for many years. Dedicated his fortune and efforts to constructing and renovating the *Kloiz*.
R' Yosef Noiman – a scholar and one of the dignitaries among the worshippers.
R' David-Hersh Haber – The "*Matmid*" [studios] who dedicated many years to studying Torah at the *Kloiz*.
R' Israel Tzeig – from among the leading speakers at the *Kloiz, Ba'al Koreh* [Torah reader], and public activists.
R' Tzvi Toiber – a scholar whose diligence in studying Torah and praying was exemplary.
R' Arye Narol – a modest scholar.
R' Mordekhai Knohl – studied Torah and served as an advocate for the Zionist idea at the *Kloiz* and follower of the "HaMizrakhi" [Zionist religious party].
R' Shreiber Yehoshua – a young learner from among the students of R' Meir Shapira *ztz"l* from Lublin, and a public activist who dedicated most of the day to studying Torah at the *Kloiz*.

[Pages 250]

The Synagogue - "Yad Kharutzim" ["Dilligent Hand"]

by Menakhem son of Shimon Katz

Translated by Moshe Kutten

Edited by Jane S. Gabin

A new synagogue was built on Strazacka Street. This synagogue was located opposite the Synagogue of R' Mendeleh. It was built by the Jewish craftsmen's guild in 1901 to serve as the prayer house for its members. It was a plastered brick building containing a prayer hall and an entrance hall, through which there was a shared entrance to the prayer hall and the women's section on the upper floor, a rare design feature in the town. Except for the shared entrance, the design was like the other latest houses of prayer in the city. In the 1930s, this synagogue served about 100 households, members of the guild, and a few homeowners who resided nearby.

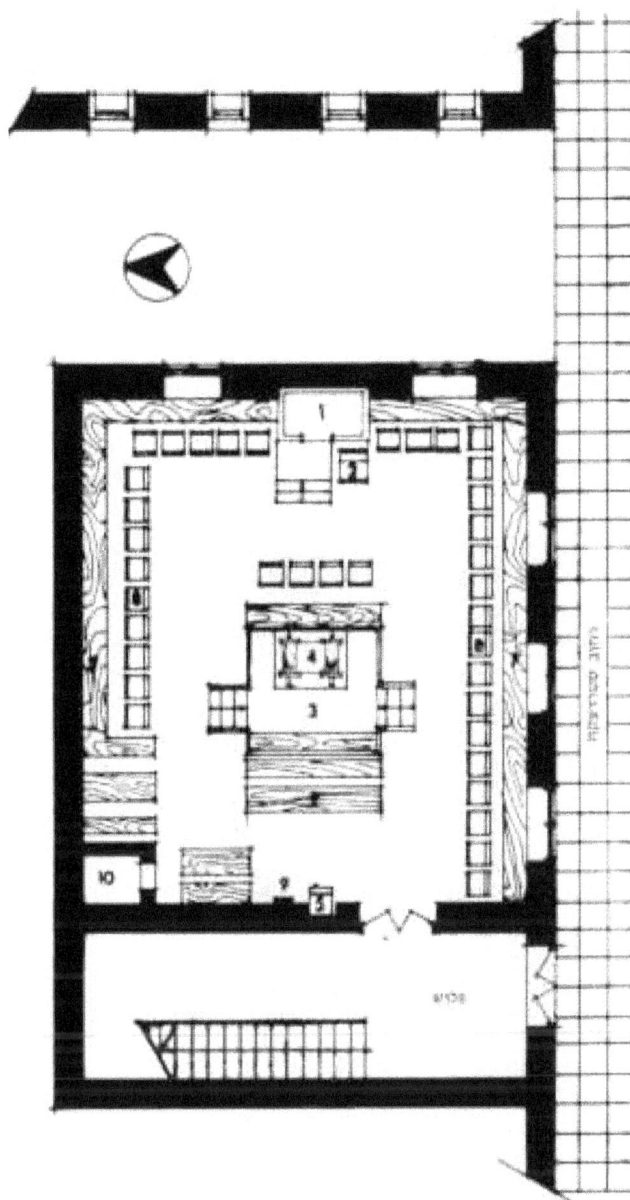

The plan of the first floor of "Yad Kharutzim" Synagogue

The members of the craftsmen's guild took care of the upkeep, cleanliness, and occasional renewal of all the objects. They made sure that it always looked like new.

The synagogue was burnt along with the rest of the buildings around it as a result of the Nazi heavy bombarding of the city on Shabbat evening, 18 July 1942. Its burnt skeleton collapsed over the years and was wiped off the face of the earth, as did its dedicated worshippers.

[Page 251]

Rabbi Mendeleh's Synagogue

by Dr. Eliezer Shaklai

Translated by Moshe Kutten

Edited by Jane S. Gabin

Rabbi Mendeleh Halperin was the city rabbi for many years until the outbreak of the Second World War. In fact, Rabbi Mendeleh resided in the city of Dukla, where he also served as a rabbi. He visited Brzezany about twice a year, where he had a spacious synagogue on Strazacka Street [opposite "Yad Kharutzim" Synagogue]. The synagogue building included an apartment for the rabbi, where he resided [when in town] and where he received his followers.

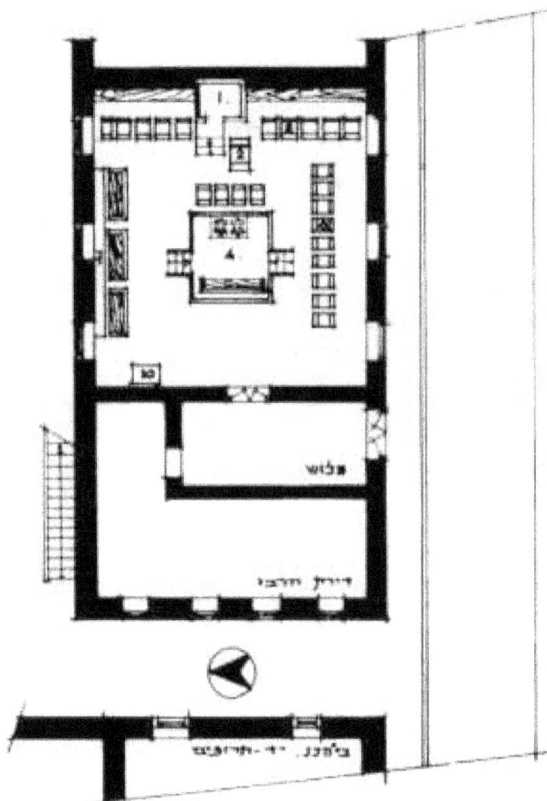

The plan for Rabbi Mendeleh's Synagogue

The plan for the synagogue was almost identical to the other houses of prayer, built in the later part of the 19th century. The difference in this synagogue was the rabbi's apartment and the entrance to the women's section [on the second floor], which was reached through a wooden staircase behind the building.

The synagogue was burnt together with the "Yad Kharutzim" Synagogue during the Nazi bombardment on Shabbat evening of 18 July 1941. Only these written words testify to the existence of the synagogue in the days past.

The Potiker *Kleizel*

by Menakhem son of Shimon Katz

Translated by Moshe Kutten

Edited by Jane S. Gabin

As mentioned in the article on page 232, a tiny room of prayer resided within the building of *Beit HaMidrash,* named after Rabbi Yudel. The room was named after Rabbi Asher Potiker, rabbi and teacher of Jewish law in Brzezany, who later served as the head of the rabbinical court in the district of Lviv.

The reason why I [the author] dedicated a separate chapter for that *Kleizel* was meant to separate it from the rest of the houses of prayer and to emphasize the distinct role of the "independent" [as the author was allowing himself to call them] synagogues.

Kleizel is a tiny place of prayer whose structure is included within another building. There were several others like it in the city.

In addition to being a room of prayer, where the worshippers prayed *Shakhrit* [morning prayer], *Minkha* [afternoon prayer], and *Ma'ariv* [evening prayer], the room also served as a *"Kheder"* where R' Getzaleh Halperin taught lessons throughout the whole day.

The accomplished and financial supporter of the *Kleizel* was the *Gabbai* R' Moshe Wonder, for whom one of his objectives in life was supporting the *Kleizel* and ensuring its existence.

With the destruction of [Yudel's] *Beit HaMidrash,* by the Nazi *Kreishauptmann,* damn him, the *Kleizel* was also destroyed, and only these words would serve as a testimony, in the future, about its existence.

[Pages 252]

Rozolover *Kloiz*

by Menakhem son of Shimon Katz

Translated by Moshe Kutten

Edited by Jane S. Gabin

The Rozolover *Kloiz* of the Rozolov Hasidim was located on the western side of the Great Synagogue in a long and narrow yard.

Like the rest of the houses of prayers in Galitzia, this *Kloiz* served the enthusiastic Hassidim who strictly observed their customs and contact with their rabbi.

We should note here that, like the Startyner *Kloiz* on the opposite side of the plaza, the architectural details of the window lintels and the entrance door reflected the public character of the building. The conclusion is that this structure was built specifically to serve as a house of prayer.

In addition, I would like to mention the colorful windows that decorated the *Kloiz*, thereby giving its space a special soft and pleasant light that created a unique atmosphere for the people in it.

Without its lintels, beautiful windows and floor, and its plaster peeling off, the *Kloiz* remained deserted and broken through when I left the town in 1944.

Ya'ir's [Jair] *Kloiz'le*

by Menakhem son of Shimon Katz

Translated by Moshe Kutten

Edited by Jane S. Gabin

On Tranopolska Street, no. 18, attached to a residential building, stood a small synagogue that people called "*Das Yores Kloizle*" [Yair's little *Kloiz*], a single plastered brick structure, with a tiled roof with three slopes, built only to serve as a house of prayer. The name "*Kloiz*" already hints at its small size. However, when examining the plan, you realize that it is an almost exact duplicate of the other synagogues, such as the Cantor's *Beit HaMidrash* or the Chortkover *Kloiz*, the only difference being the small measurements.

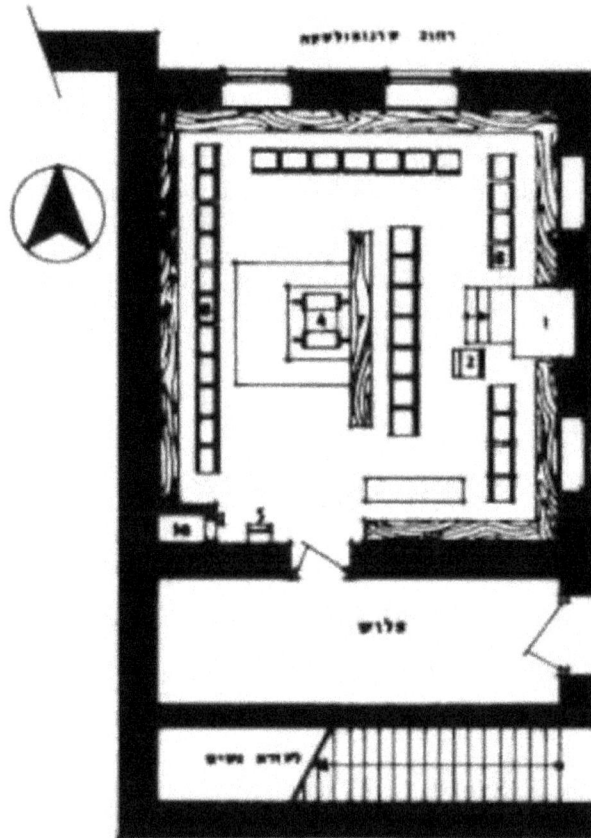

The plan of Ya'ir's synagogue

Distinctive characteristics of the *Kloiz* were its unusual cleanliness, a large number of lamps, and its exemplary order with all of the objects, thanks to the dedication of the *Kloiz's Gabbai*, R' Barukh Goldman, who devoted most of his free time to the *Kloiz*.

That house of prayer served its worshippers three times a day – *Shakharit* [morning prayer], *Minkha* [afternoon prayer], and *Ma'ariv* [evening prayer]. We should note that the *Kloiz* would open before the prayer and lock up at its end, which testifies to purposely enforced order.

In 1944, the *Kloiz* was broken into and robbed of all the beautiful objects. Only the bare skeleton remained as a sorrowful remnant of its glorious past.

[Pages 253]

Other Prayer Places in Town

by Menakhem son of Shimon Katz

Translated by Moshe Kutten

Edited by Jane S. Gabin

The *Kleizel* [small *Kloiz*] of the tailors was located at the end of the entrance hall of the Great Synagogue. We should especially note the abundance of tablecloths, *Parokhot* [Holy Ark curtains], and all sorts of velvet embroideries decorated with gold and silver [strings]. These were used to decorate the *Kleizel*. The tailors prayed there on Sabbaths and holidays.

The city's porters prayed in a room within the old *Talmud Torah* [Torah school] at the end of Strazacka Street. They called the room "**The Porters' Minyan**," where the porters and the local residents prayed on Sabbaths and holidays.

The last city rabbi, **Rabbi Faivush Halperin**, had his own *Minyan*. He organized a public prayer on Sabbaths and holidays in one of his apartment's rooms, where his followers and Hasidim devotedly prayed.

More than anywhere else in the city, young religious people were prominent in the **Minyan of HaPoel HaMizrakhi** [a religious Zionist party]. Because they did not have their own place, the Minyan moved around from one rented apartment to the other. They prayed regularly on Sabbath nights, Sabbaths, and holidays.

[Pages 254]

Legend

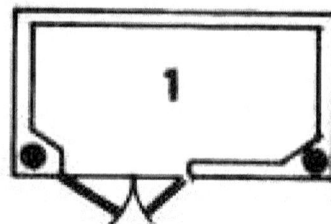

Holy Ark

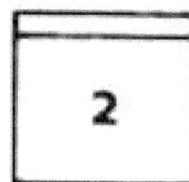

Prayer stand

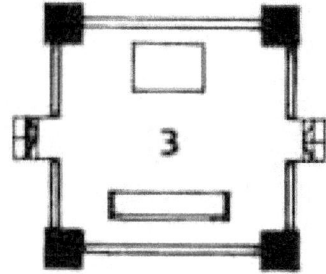

Bimah

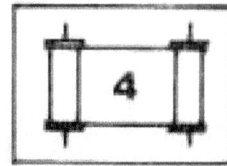

Table for the Torah reading

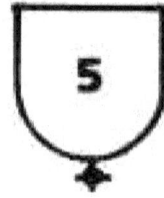

Sink

[Pages 255]

Eternal candle

Bench

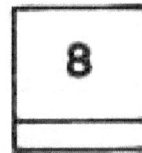

Private stand (*Shtander*)

Towel rack

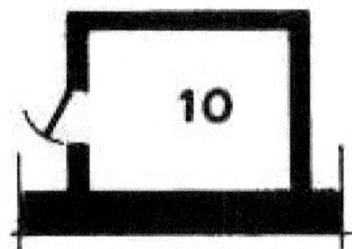

Fireplace

[Pages 256]Blank

[Page 257]

The Holocaust

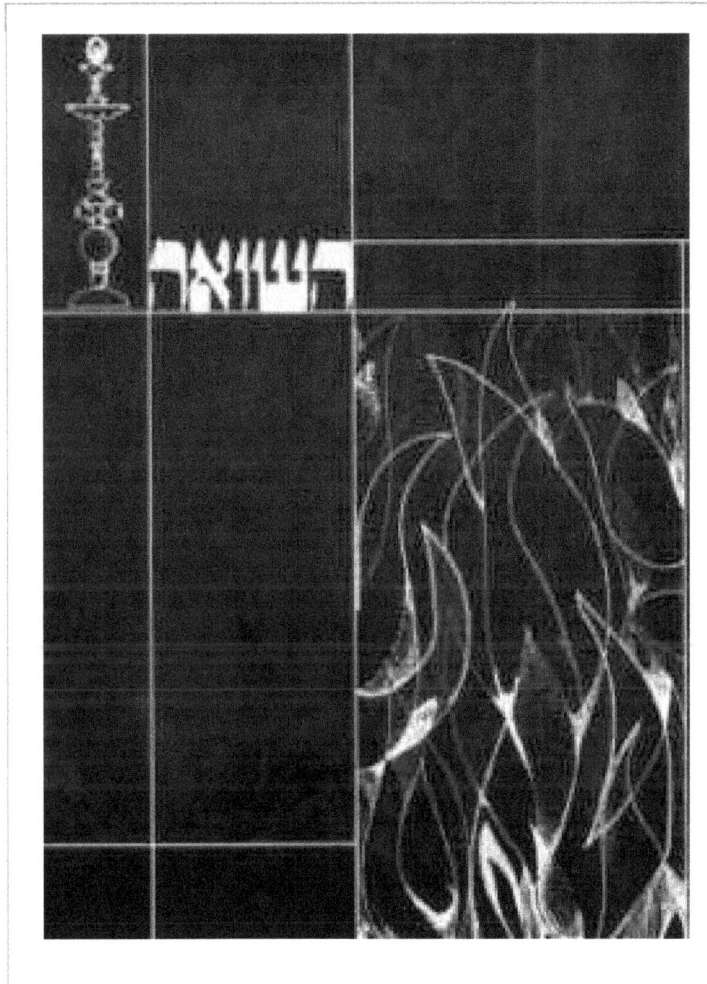

[Page 258]

[Page 259]

Translated by Ruth Yoseffa Erez

With awe and reverence, a feeling of responsibility, and knowledge of the task that I took upon myself, I approach the writing of this chapter. The most difficult chapter of my life, the last and final chapter in the life of the Jews in our town.

This is the story of twelve thousand Jews, the story of their suffering, their battle, and their death in our town Brzezany, during the three years of the Nazi occupation.

Before I approach the Holocaust chapter, I would like to answer in short words, to the extent that I can, the hurtful question: How did it happen?

It is a difficult question' it will take years and generations until researchers and historians in universities answer the question of who is to blame upon checking and reading the documents.

Neither you nor I are entitled to set a verdict on everything that happened at that period.

As for me, I am standing here today as a witness representing the Jews who found their death in our town, whether they were actually from our town or happened to arrive here as refugees, and this is where they died. God forbid that I judge or blame anyone in my testimony. I am only a witness, not a judge, and in this position as a witness, I must tell the truth, all the truth, and nothing but the truth.

[Page 260]

Time of Nazi rule

by Dr. Eliezer Shaklai

Translated by Ruth Yoseffa Erez

Edited by Moshe Kutten and Jane S. Gabin

The Germans entered our town with lots of splendor and with great force.

First came the motorcyclists and then soldiers on buses and trucks, followed by artillery.

There was a short battle by Zlota Lypa Lake in which a few Germans were killed, and the Soviet Army withdrew to the east. Throughout that day, the German troops passed by and surrounded a Soviet cavalry unit, preventing them from withdrawing.

On Wednesday, the battle started, and the German artillery corps was shooting all day long. They were shooting towards the Soviet Army to weaken them till shortly before the evening.

Towards the night, the Germans prepared an ambush inside the town. They knew that the Soviets would try to break through and run away eastward. During the night, a harsh face-to-face battle took place in town, in which many Soviet cavalry soldiers were killed.

On Thursday morning, we woke up, and before our eyes was a terrible sight: the Jewish part of the city was destroyed. Many burnt houses and hundreds of dead were scattered around town, and next to them were the corpses of horses. And there were blood stains all over, which were not erased for a long time, until the rain washed them away.

People, most of whom were women and children, were running among the dead, and each had essential matters to take care of - to look for food, get water, and find a relative or child that went missing. Some were trying to leave town, to flee before it was too late and before the sun rose and woke everyone.

The German town officer assigned a temporary Ukrainian body to govern the town. They received an order from the German officer to remove the dead and horses' corpses in one day. Of course, they took the Jews for this job. On top of this hard work, there were curses and whipping. The day claimed three more victims: just before evening, a German officer caught three Jews among the workers, whom he did not like for some reason. He made them enter the "Ritchula" by the public garden, and then he took out his gun and shot them. One of them was Chaim David Liblin, son of Idly (Idaly) "Kozovar," the second was Booksbaum, and the third a Jew from western Galicia. This event shocked all of us but also made everyone work faster, and by evening, they finished the job.

The news about the three dead Jews spread throughout the city, but our troubles were huge.

Even though the people received this news with bitter disappointment at that time, they did think that it was a sign of what was to come, of what would be done later on a much larger scale.

To the Ukrainians who helped the Germans watch over the Jews, this incident of killing Jews gave confidence and encouragement with the passion to make the lives of the Jews miserable. They saw that Jewish lives were meaningless, and they could be treated with no inhibitions and no mercy.

[Page 261]

Blood Libel

by Dr. Eliezer Shaklai

Translated by Moshe Kutten

Edited by Jane S. Gabin

A rumor was spread, as early as Friday, that twelve prisoners died in a closed cell in one of the jail's sections. A credible eyewitness, Dr. Bilinski, the head of the hospital, was called to the prison to determine the cause of death. He stated that the prisoners choked to death due to lack of air. We did not know, at the time, that the Ukrainians spread a rumor that the Jews were the ones who killed the prisoners and that the Jews were responsible for this scoundrel act.

The Sabbath passed in a relative quiet, but we felt disquiet in the air. We felt that something was approaching. On Sunday, the Ukrainian militia captured people – men and women, led them to the Christian cemetery, and told them to dig graves for the dead. Those people did not know that they were digging graves for themselves. When the digging ended, the Ukrainians pounced on the Jews. Some managed to escape, but the others were cruelly murdered with axes and hoes.

In the meantime, the neighboring villagers came in masses (it was Sunday) to pray at the city's churches. We did not know, and it did not occur to us, that they brought axes and knives with them, aiming to rob and murder. At the church, they received encouragement from their leaders during the prayer. The leaders repeated the libel rumor that the Jews had killed about thirty-nine Christians in the jail before the Soviets left the city.

The villagers dispersed through the entire city, and before we could comprehend what was going on, they cruelly murdered and injured hundreds of Jews. The Germans helped them in the slaughter or just stood by and looked. It was a pogrom like the ones during the days of Khmelnytskyi and Petliura – the mob killed and robbed without any intervention. Hundreds of Jews lost their lives and thousands of their property. Among those whom I remember are Wandermere Dzionek and the old Podoshen and his son. Many of the murders occurred in the city's suburbs while robbing and looting increased in the city center. Perhaps the fact that the [German military] city officer and many Germans were in the center affected the villagers, who were satisfied with only robbing there.

Most of the villagers left in the evening, taking the loot with them, while some of them remained in to complete the "job." They also buried the victims' bodies in the city park to cover their crimes.

Several weeks later, our people from the "Khevera Kadishe" [burial society], headed by Ginsberg, transferred two mass graves of about 250 bodies in the city park to our cemetery, except those who were buried at the Christian cemetery.

On Monday morning, the Jews were again reeling after the pogrom. The difference was that this time, the number of victims was more numerous than in the years past. In the morning, Dr. Klarer, the head of the community council elected before the war, with six other people, turned to the city's interim Ukrainian council and the German military officer to ask for help. In those days, there were still some people among the Ukrainian intelligentsia who were ashamed of what happened and objected to those barbaric views. The council promised to sway the masses so that they would not repeat that barbarian action. The city officer also promised to impose order in the city.

And the following is what the German order meant: Decrees against the Jews!

[Page 262]

    a. Night curfew only on the Jews. They should close all homes where Jews reside and should not leave the house after that hour.

    b. Every Jew had to wear a blue Star of David on a piece of fabric, twelve centimeters wide, on the right sleeve. It was seemingly a harmless decree. After all, the blue Star of David was not a derogatory symbol for a Jew. However, it was much more than a symbol. It was like an identification symbol, for people to recognize a Jew from afar that the Jew was outside of the law and therefore condemned to die. It was allowed to shoot a Jew on the spot without standing trial for that. From that day on, the identification symbol would accompany the Jew everywhere, on the street or at home.

    c. A Jew could not leave the city without a special permit.

    d. It was forbidden for a Jew to communicate freely with the wide world.

…etc…etc…

Some other decrees hurt less but limited personal freedom.

After the pogrom, emotions calmed down, and life returned slowly to "normal." We faced two crucial and urgent problems that required an immediate solution: easing the hunger in the city and finding work. During the first few weeks, the authorities were at the hands of the German city officer and his Ukrainian assistants - an interim council and a militia. They did not have knowledge or experience in management. They blocked all the roads into the city, and every villager had to undergo a thorough examination to prevent getting food and agricultural products into the city. Initially, the villagers themselves did not want to sell their produce to Jews. First, because of their tremendous hatred toward the Jews, but also because the Soviet currency lost its value when the regime changed from the Soviets to the Germans. However, over time, they began to experience a shortage of products that they could not get in the village, and they began to barter with the Jews.

The members of the Ukrainian council objected to that arrangement for their own reasons. Before the breakout of the war between Germany and Poland, the Germans promised the Ukrainians that they would recognize eastern Galitsia as an independent Ukrainian state. That would allow them to confiscate the Jewish property. They would become the owners of the produce of the villages, and by that, they would solve all these problems. They experienced great disappointment when, six weeks after the breakout of the war, Berlin announced the annexation of Eastern Galitsia as a province of the [Poland's General] Government. A substantial part of the Ukrainian nationalists turned their back on the Germans, but some remained loyal to the Germans for their own personal reasons – hoping to gain by doing that.

The relations between the villages and the city changed then. The farmers decided to take advantage of the food shortage in the city and demand valuables they had not dreamt about before for their produce, which was meager. The Jews did not have any other choice but to give anything for a piece of bread to sustain the body and soul. At the same time, the farmers also suffered from a shortage of food since the Soviets, before leaving the area, confiscated most of the crops, and the Germans that replaced them confiscated what remained of the crops. The hunger in the city grew day by day.

The second problem was work. The Germans demanded to provide people daily for various jobs, some hard jobs and others light, some in the town and others outside the city. However, besides fear and flogging, the workers have not received any material compensation for their efforts. The Jewish community council provided work that "paid" a single loaf of bread for a day's work. It was temporary work like fixing the railroad, working at the train station, fixing bridges, sanitation work for the Germans, transporting, unloading, and so forth. The community was obligated to provide

[Page 263]

suitable people to work according to their demands, even in the middle of the day. People sat by the community council office during the day and waited. All of that for a single loaf of bread.

There was another reason. We learned from the Soviets to stick to a permanent job for many reasons. Wages, even meager, allowed one to make a living, a job granted a work certificate (very important), and the main reason that there was an employer who could defend you. He would ensure that you would not be taken for another job in another location. All of these were good reasons during peacetime and all the more so at war with the German rule. However, most jobs were temporary for no [or little] wages.

The community office on Tranopolska, at the home of Dr. Vilner, was the address used by the Germans and the Ukrainians, whether it was a demand for people to do work, professional artisans, valuables, furniture, or just a dispatch. The community had to fulfill all requests on the same day and as fast as possible; otherwise, the Germans would have handled it themselves, aided by the Ukrainian militia, and would add flogging and cause enormous damages. Obviously, the Jews, for lack of any other choice, fulfilled every demand so that German intervention was not required. In the beginning, the requests were modest, but they grew in quantity and "quality" from one day to another as the appetite grew with time.

The community received a certain amount of bread daily, and Dr. Klarer himself distributed the bread among the people who worked that day. As aforementioned, there were all sorts of jobs within the community itself and outside of it. Many people asked to work to earn the loaf of bread.

The health situation of the Jews in the city was dire. There were hundreds of wounded people from as long as since the [German] bombing. The pogrom resulted in additional injured people. The municipal hospital did not admit them, as it was full of non-Jewish patients. Dr. Felk and I [Dr. E. Shaklai] turned to the head of the community and asked him to allow the opening of a Jewish hospital and clinic near the [municipal] hospital. We took it upon ourselves to supply the tools. We only requested assistance in providing us with the place, manpower, and, as much as possible, food for the patients. We opened a hospital and clinic in the Community House (National House). Hundreds of people received treatment free of charge. One of Dr. Klarer's daughters served as the head nurse.

With the approval of the German city officer, the hospital was approved as such for the Jewish population. In those days, only a few cases of contagious diseases were discovered. We anticipated that there would be harsh epidemics due to the severe hunger and overcrowding. We fought every case but did not succeed in stopping the spread. Epidemics occurred and spread among the Gentiles too but more intensely among the Jews. The epidemics and hunger assisted the Germans, in a major way, in annihilating the Jews in the ghetto and later in the forests.

The situation described above lasted about six weeks, with a few small surprises. We did not have a ruler. There was nobody to turn to, neither about the issue of regular places of work nor about matters related to daily life. Everything was temporary. People hoped that a civil German rule would bring relief and normalization to our lives. The change indeed came, but not in our favor. The temporary administration of the city officer and Ukrainian council transferred into the hands of civil Germans under the supervision of the Gestapo.

Galitsia became a province, part of the [Poland's General] Government, headed by [Hans] Frank[1]. Galitsia's governor resided in Krakow. The province was divided into districts.

[Page 264]

In the east Galitsia, there were three districts: The districts of Lvov [Lviv], Stanisławów [today Ivano-Frankivsk], and Tarnopol [Ternopil], every one of them with its own Landeshauptmann [district governor]. Every city was an administrative unit called *Kreis* headed by its own *Kreishauptmann* [city manager]. *Kreis* Brzezany was in the Ternopil district, and our *Kreishauptmann* was Asbach, and his deputy was Krieger. They were aided by the *Zonderdinst* [selected service militia] headed by Hazeh. That was a civil administration, but they were, like all other civil administrations in occupied Poland, under the supervision of the Gestapo. Our Gestapo unit was stationed in Ternopil, but they visited us frequently. The Gestapo supervisor of our city was Hermann. He was assisted by others. One of the assistants was Huber!

The "*Zonderdinst*" was responsible for the security of the city and its surroundings. The offices of the "*Kreishaumptmannshaft*" were located in the high school building. Departments for work, economy, health, water, electricity, and others operated in these offices. The Jews did not have any access to these offices. They were outside of the law. Initially, the *Kreishauptmann* chose to reside in Rohatyn since our city was in ruins. However, two weeks later, he decided to move to our city.

He dreamt of building a city for himself and according to his style in Brzezany – with Jewish work and money. Immediately upon his arrival, he ordered Dr. Klarer to appear before him and bring with him twenty-three additional people at five o'clock in the afternoon in the "*Starostvo*" [county administration] opposite the savings bank. I was among those twenty-three people. They notified me about half an hour before the meeting. When I refused to go, they sent me Dr. Pomerantz with an urgent order from the Gestapo, and we both arrived at the last moment. However, only twenty-two people showed up because Ya'akov Mitelman and Fas did not come. The *Kreishauptmann* demanded to apprehend and bring them over. All the excuses raised by Dr. Klarer to justify their absence were in vain.

I will never forget that meeting. Twenty-two distinguished Jews stood in a row. A fat and tall German in uniform sat before us, holding a "Ritpitche [?]." *Kreishauptmann* Asbach sat aside with several Germans. Dr. Klarer introduced everyone by name and profession. The Germans were not satisfied with the composition of the group targeted to become the "*Judenrat*." They thought that there were too many intelligent people in the group. Following a short speech filled with animosity and contempt, the Germans notified us that we were appointed to be the "*Judenrat*" who would be responsible collectively for the Jewish population toward the German authorities. Dr. Klarer was nominated to be the "*Obmann*" [chairman], with Ross as his deputy. They meant to say that for the action of a single Jew, the whole Jewish population, or a large portion of it, would be punished. A death sentence would be imposed for every deviation from the rules or resistance to fulfill orders from above. Upon finishing his speech, we were ordered to disperse. Only the "*Obmann*" and his deputy remained.

Everyone came from the meeting depressed. We went there free men, and came out the prisoners of the Gestapo. The following people were nominated to the "*Judenrat*": Dr. Shmuel Klarer, Israel Ross, Isar Shomer, Leizer Bernstein, Shimshon Fogelman, David-Meir Ginsberg, Freier, Dr. Bernard Felk, Dr. Philip Pomerantz, Dr. Shtark, Dr. Eliezer Vagshall, Dr. Grossman, Dr. Finkelstein, Magister Trauner, Magister Laber, teacher D. Horowitz, Ya'akov Mitelman, Feier, Benajmin Mitelman, Ludmerer, photographer Koren, lawyer David Somer, Israel Fas, and Simkha Shekhter.

We came out of there like we were sentenced to death. We did not talk to each other. I could not fall asleep that night, and I am sure that none of the others could either.

[Page 265]

Our people did neither elect us nor agree to the "*Judenrat*." It was ordered from above, and the selection was made based on Dr. Klarer and Ross. In those days, we did not know what the "*Judenrat*" was nor its power or ability.

Translator's Note:

1. "Hans Michael Frank was a German politician, war criminal, and lawyer who served as head of the General Government in Nazi-occupied Poland during the Second World War… After the war, Frank was found guilty of war crimes and crimes against humanity at the Nuremberg trials. He was sentenced to death and executed by hanging in October 1946. From Wikipedia.

The "*Judenrat*"

by Dr. Eliezer Shaklai

Translated by Moshe Kutten

Edited by Jane S. Gabin

The people on the street received the nomination with mixed feelings. Some people said that finally, there was somebody to turn to dignified people who are serious and clever, and therefore one can rely on them. "In these conditions", thought these people, "we cannot afford lawlessness." In these conditions, we need strong people who would know how to divide the burden among the entire population, every one according to their abilities - one person would be dealing with finances, the other working, etc. The main thing is to pass the war period, and a solution would present itself. On the other side, there were people on the *Judenrat* who were not suited to the role assigned to them, and the people did not elect them! We did not know then that the "Final Solution" was prepared for us and that everything the Germans did was to confuse us and use our energy to help them execute their plot until the bitter end.

We, the *Judenrat* people, divided among ourselves the handling of the Jewish population in the city; we had to take care of housing, economy, labor, health, law, security, and representation toward the outside. We did not know then that the relationship between the *Judenrat* and the Germans is one directional – orders from the top and nothing else. The people of the *Judenrat* had good thoughts and plans if only they had let us live. The Jews looked at the *Judenrat* as a scapegoat. They hoped that it would save them from being hit and tortured and that any request [by the Germans] could be divided among the entire Jewish population and fulfilled without the need for evasion. After all, the people in the *Judenrat* were Jews! In that way, it would be easier for the population as a whole to withstand the German requests. But that was not what happened. As we got into the messy mud, we all drowned in it – the *Judenrat* up front and the rest of the Jewish population followed it, and we could not get out of it. We only had one choice – fulfill the German requests or sacrifice ourselves to save others! Some sacrificed themselves! May their memory be blessed!

I once asked the *Obmann*:" Who gave you the permission to decide upon people's lives – some to live and others to die?"

He answered me:" You are a physician. If you have the following dilemma: cut off a healthy part of the body, a whole healthy organ, to save a person's life knowing well that the organ is healthy! Would you do it or not? There is still hope that in this way, we would be able to save some of our people, and therefore, we need to decide. What is the preferred way to proceed?"

In those days, it was difficult to say who was right. Only later on dis we see that everything had beenlost beforehand. We could not have saved anybody from the Gestapo's claws. We could only try the unknown to satisfy our conscience. We tried! In any case, there was nothing to lose. Faith solved the irritating problem and judged the "senders" and those who were sent. Everybody went on the same road.

We needed money, a lot of it, to satisfy the appetite of every German, whether it was the *Kreishauptmann*, his deputy, *Zonderdinst*, or the Gestapo's gendarme. We even have to pay hush money to the Ukrainian militia, hoping to avoid the malice of decrees. That continued to the end. We should not forget that a substantial part of the *Judenrat* people were executed by the Germans for not fulfilling their demands.

[Page 266]

We held a meeting a day after the meeting with the *Kreishauptmann*. Dr. Klarer notified us about the demand for a "contribution" of eight hundred thousand Zlotys that needed to be paid in two installments. We heard about such "contributions" from other cities. It was, therefore, not new but was very difficult to collect. We divided our work amongst ourselves. Part of the *Judenrat* divided the amount among individuals as they saw fit. Others went around to collect the money. Even though the amount seemed fantastic to us, we managed to collect the required amount. Some Jews fainted when they heard the sum each one of them would have to pay, but they paid because there was no other choice. We deposited the required amount in the *Kreishauptmann* account on time. However, that was just the beginning. There were additional equally crucial requirements. For example, there was a requirement to furnish the apartments and offices of the Germans who came to reside in our city. The Germans did not just want whatever came by chance. They wanted to select, and if they did not find what they were looking for, they ordered it, and we had to pay for it. It was not possible to refuse to fulfill their requests.

The *Judenrat* became the "great supplier." We supplied people to work, professionals, furniture, and various objects, including bedpans, and everything was provided according to the specified measures and the specific instructions. That was how we spent a few more weeks. Rosh Hashana arrived. People gathered in private apartments to pray, to "cry their hearts out" before the Creator, and to ask for mercy and salvation. During the same time, our [bitter] fate had been already inscribed, and it was even sealed: "Who is in the water and who by fire, and who in the plague and who in suffocation[1]." Eight additional days passed.

An order from the *Kreishauptmann* arrived at the *Judenrat* on the evening before Yom Kippur, 9 Tishrei, 5702 [30 September 1941]. The order stated that every Jew between the ages of 20 – and 55, led by the *Judenrat*, must appear, on the following day (Yom Kippur 10.1.1941), at the yard by the barracks at 10 am. The declared purpose of the gathering is registration. The notice was hung at the entrance and the window of the *Judenrat*'s office.

The bad news spread among the Jews in a flash. Questions sprouted immediately: "Why on Yom Kippur? Why on that particular hour? Why the yard by the barracks? What was behind this order"? We felt that something awful was prepared for us; otherwise, why tomorrow? What was the rash?… Who was the wise person to know and could answer whether we should go or not? Who should we ask, and who will answer?…

The *Judenrat* representative tried to inquire about the order. He went to the *Kreishauptmann* to ask him a few questions - what should people who had registered to work tomorrow at 7 am do? What should the physicians who work at the hospital tomorrow do? There was a lot of work at the hospital and there were many sick and injured people. The *Kreishauptmann* freed the physician from duty and ordered the Jews who had to go to work to appear at the "People House," where they would be registered. Except for that response, the representative was not told any information - not even a hint.

Restlessness gripped us. People turned around aimlessly. The faces of every one were gloomy. Everyone was pondering whether to go or not to go. What would tomorrow bring? Time crawled slowly, and the minutes were long. But life was running away, and you did not know how to hold on to them!

I did not know how many people prayed *Minkha* [afternoon prayer or tasted from the meal before the fast. We gathered slowly, with broken hearts, in our apartment for the "*Kol Nidrei*" [literally "All Vows – the prayer before *Minkha* on the evening before Yom Kippur]. We closed all the windows and sealed them to avoid the escape of any light or sound. We lit *Neshama* [memory] candles and put them in the corner, covered ourselves with *Talits*, opened the ark where the Torah scroll hid, and my father opened with the "*Al Da'at HaMkom*" ["With the consent of the Almighty"], and "*Kol Nidrei*" prayer

[Page 267]

That was not the first time I heard that prayer, but the prayer sounded different that time. It was an appeal and plea to the King of the Universe, a prayer coming out from the depths of our hearts. We were sure the petition would go straight to the throne, shake worlds, and argue with the Creator, the Lord: "Please do not leave us, send salvation to your persecuted people, and stand by us in our time of need! … etc…, etc…

We completed the prayer but did not finish to pray. Most of the people in the room remained covered with their *Talits*. Silence prevailed. Everyone continued to murmur a prayer - asking to be saved from the enemy. Suddenly, a horrifying voice- a cry, fragmented words, broke the silence: "Oy… Oy…" and the cry hushed, continued for a few more seconds, and stopped. I lifted my head – silence, not even a quiver in the room. I felt that I was among the dead. I saw the whiteness of the *Talits* standing motionless, in rows after rows, in a semi-dark room… the candles burn in a dark and monochromatic light. Suddenly, the flame of the candles rose, the light increased, the wax melted again, and then the flame decreased and faded. There was another effort to grow the flame, but the candles couldn't do it anymore, and they were dying.

"They are dying!" – I wanted to scream, but the words remained hanging in the air. They were left hanging and etched within me. I still remember that day. I still carry that picture, with the dying candles, in my heart. I only do not remember how long we remained in that state - minutes or hours.

The night ended. People gathered for the *Shakahrit* [morning] prayer at 5 o'clock in the morning. The prayers progressed slowly. After last night, we no longer had the strength to cry. We waited for the sentence with mixed feelings of hopelessness and hope.

At nine o'clock, the prayer ended. We removed the *Talits*, and one after the other left the apartment without saying anything. For many, that was the last confession – and the last way – their candles extinguished. I headed toward the *Judenrat* office. I found out that the Germans visited the people that went to work. The Germans asked everyone for their profession and sent them to work. The *Judenrat* people and all its officials were ready. The *Obmann* asked teacher Horowitz and me to stay at the office. The *Obmann* promised to remain connected and notify us as soon as possible about the happenings. They all went out, and we two stayed behind. We kept quiet, but my heart was beating hard, and I tried to control myself and my nerves. I stood by the open window and waited for the news! The long minutes continued…

At 10:15 am, the first people arrived from the barracks carrying the news. The Germans came at 10 am holding machine guns. They surrounded the yard, and one of them began the registration. He positioned the *Judenrat* and its officials separately from the crowd. They also separated people from various professions, such as teachers, merchants, and Hasidim. After the separation, they ordered the professionals to return to their work and the *Judenrat* to leave the yard. They taxed the *Judenrat* by calming the people and ensuring order and peace. The Germans organized the people who remained in the yard in rows, four people to a row, and moved them toward the jail under strict guard.

Panics befell the city. Women and children began to scream and cry, and then the Gendarme appeared in the streets and dispersed the crowd by shooting in the air. The people retreated and dispersed. When I saw the Gendarme members approaching, I escaped through the back door. I ran around the city and arrived at our house. When I opened the gate, I saw a German holding a gun aimed at me, standing about 10 meters away.

[Page 268]

I managed to throw myself on the ground before a burst of bullets passed above my head. I ran to a cellar in another street and hid there until the storm blew over. At the same time, my father and my wife stood by the window and waited for me. They saw me opening the gate and thought that I entered the yard. At the same moment, they heard a burst of gunshots. After a few minutes passed, and I did not enter the house, they were sure that I was killed. My wife began to cry and scream. My father turned to her and said: "My daughter, you should overcome your sorrow. That would be the fate of all the Jews. Please accept that sentence honorably. Be Strong! You are not the only one! When the noise outside subsided, I returned home. I was dazed and shocked by what happened. My father scolded me – "my son, be strong, don't be discouraged! You have to be resolute and calm in all conditions and situations." He took the Makhzor [Jewish prayer book] and continued his praying, secluding himself with the Creator. We did not hear a single additional word from him until the evening.

I returned to the *Judenrat*. We gathered, debated, and finally decided to ask for a meeting with the *Kreishauptmann*. The latter agreed to see Dr. Klarer and [his deputy] Ross. After the meeting, which lasted an hour, they returned and said that the *Kreishauptmann* demanded 5 kg. gold in exchange for the release of the people. In the morning, women, not necessarily from the *Judenrat*, went from house to house, collected gold pieces of jewelry, and brought them to Dr. Klarer. Our two messengers, Dr. Klarer and Ross, gave the entire collection to the *Kreishauptmann*. The day was Thursday. On the same morning, before the *Kreishauptmann* received the gold, Hazeh from the *Zonderdinst* released five people, among them the two sons of Fenster. Altogether, the number of people who were taken to jail reached 600-650 people.

On Friday morning, at 9 am, the Germans blocked the street leading to the jail. They took out the people and led them in trucks in the direction of the adjacent village, Ulkhovitz. Any trace of them was lost. We were told that they were sent to labor camps in Germany. A few weeks later, rumors spread that they were alive and that they wrote letters. However, farmers from surrounding villages told us that they saw from afar that they were brought [to a certain location], ordered to strip naked and run toward the mountain. When they began to run, the Germans shot them all and buried them in a mass grave. We did not believe and did not want to believe that they were murdered.

That was the first "*Aktsia*" [*Aktion* in German - rounding Jews to be murdered]. We waited for news from them for many weeks. The Germans, headed by the *Kreishauptmann*, promised us that they were alive in a labor camp. That continued until the second *Aktsia*, which put an end to any illusions. The bitter truth was revealed!

The German machine for annihilating the Jews worked fast and continuously without giving us time to think and act. Several days after the Yom Kippur *Aktsia*, the *Kreishauptmann* invited the *Obmann* and his deputy to appear before him. He treated them as if nothing happened, spoke to them arrogantly and angrily, and very clearly explained to them that he would not tolerate so many Jews in the city. He demanded that a substantial part of them be transferred to neighboring cities. Initially, he ordered that all the non-productive Jews must be transferred – meaning the weak, old, and sick. Only people who can work could stay in the city. He tasked the *Judenrat* with executing that mission and would consider *Judenrat* the responsible body. He stated that the transfer of two hundred people per week should be organized, and he should get the list and the note about the transfer every week. He was also assigned to the *Judenrat* the task of forming a Jewish militia - the Ordnungsdinst, to include twelve militiamen who would execute the orders from the *Kreishauptmann* to the *Judenrat*. He requested that the list of militiamen be made in one week. He had another order. He decided to change the appearance of the city, that is to rebuild it. For that purpose, the ruins that remained from the bombing and fire must be removed. It would also be necessary to destroy some of the standing houses that remained in the Jewish quarter. In that location, he would build a German-style modern city using Jewish money and labor. He warned the *Judenrat* that if they did not obey and execute his order, he would hand the problems to the hands of the Gestapo, and they would know how to handle them. That certainly would not be beneficial to the Jews.

Translator's Note:

1. Based on the *piyyut* (poem with melody) *U'Netanneh Tokef* ("Let us speak of the awesomeness"), sung as part of the *Mosaf* (additional service) prayer on Rosh HaShanah, and in many places and traditions on Yom Kippur.

[Page 269]

The Transfers Affair

by Dr. Eliezer Shaklai

Translated by Moshe Kutten

Edited by Jane S. Gabin

It was not easy for the *Judenrat* to fulfill all the requests of the *Kreishauptmann*. It was difficult to organize the transfers, taking out people from their homes during cold and rainy days and sending them to new locations when they were not physically and mentally ready to do so. It meant uprooting and throwing them onto a remote place, and there, without assistance, they would die of hunger, cold, and epidemics. But that was actually the Germans' intent. That was not just a local order [similar orders were issued in other cities]. The decision about the "Final Solution" (killing all the Jews without exception using all means and as soon as possible) was not yet made in those days. At that time, the local German authorities were tasked with the extermination of all those Jews who could not play a productive role for the Germans. They had to do it on their own and as fast as possible.

The *Judenrat* established a dedicated department with officials to prepare for and execute the mission of the transfers. However, they have never succeeded in reaching the quota presented by the *Kreishauptmann*. People ran away from their homes, and there was a need to use force to bring them to the concentration location. Many times, fistfights ensued. That, too, was an objective of the Germans - sowing discord within the Jewish population, inciting Jews against Jews, and sowing jealousy and hatred. They also succeeded in that objective. The Germans purposely did not intervene and left the despicable work at the hands of the Jews. That way, the Germans could claim that it was the fault of the *Judenrat* and its officials, and that's how it went. Every week or two, a transport of fifty to eighty people left the city on carts with their belongings, poverty, troubles, and tears. Accompanying them were sighs, cries, shouts, and curses!

The Jewish Militia – *Ordnungsdinst*

by Dr. Eliezer Shaklai

Translated by Moshe Kutten

Edited by Jane S. Gabin

The *Judenrat* also fulfilled the second request of the *Kreishauptmann* and handed him a list of twelve Jewish militiamen to help the *Judenrat* with the orders of German rule. The birth of the militia was difficult. I witnessed the debate where they discussed who should join and who should not. They were very careful in electing people to the Militia. The *Judenrat* decided to approve only those people who could stand the test, people you could count on their honesty and sense of justice -young men who came from dignified and respected families in the city. However, over time, something happened to these people or at least to some of them. I do not want to blame them; I am only stating that they did not stand the test! The opposite is true. The Germans succeeded in turning them into animals, some of them even predators. I will discuss the militia affair in another chapter. They had to withstand severe and unusual physical and mental pressure, not tailored to the strength of ordinary people, all the more so in difficult inhuman conditions under the whip and pressure. They cracked, and since they were not ready for that, they obviously failed!

[Page 270]

The Working Group for the *Kreishauptmann*

by Dr. Eliezer Shaklai

Translated by Moshe Kutten

Edited by Jane S. Gabin

The *Judenrat* also had to fulfill the third request, to provide people to work for the *Kreishauptmann*, people who would be available to him under the guard of his people, the "Zonderdinst" and its commander. These people would reside in a barracks, receive food from the *Judenrat*, and work from morning till evening. The Jewish "People House" was destined to become the barracks for these individuals. We moved the hospital and clinic that Dr. Felk and I had previously established at the "People House" to the house where the orphanage was located before the war. The barracks at the "People House" did not last long. The Gestapo visited that barracks and decided that the conditions where the workers were housed were "too good." The Gestapo claimed that the workers were housed in a clean and comfortable stone building located in the center of town. They gave the order to transfer the workers to a large stable located not far from the flour mill on the main road leading to Ternopil. They led the workers to work in the morning, under guard, and returned them [to the stable] in the evening. There were about forty people. Their situation was atrocious. Except for the beatings and hard work they received from the Germans, they did not have anybody to care for them. The *Judenrat* had many other problems and troubles, so they abandoned the workers and left them to their own devices!

I have already described the severe hunger. It grew even more severe from one day to another. Initially, the Ukrainian militia prevented the farmers from bringing food to the city. Later, the Germans followed them and demanded a regular quota of meat, grain, and vegetables from each village. The villagers had to divide their quota amongst themselves. Every farmer had to provide his share. The farmers were not in a hurry to fulfill those requests. The *Kreishauptmann* then sent the *Zonderdinsts* to take the requested quota by force. The *Zonderdinsts* fulfilled the mission enthusiastically. They [went into the first village and] wreaked havoc on the Gentiles. They destroyed anything that fell into their hands, ate and drank at the expense of the village until they got what they were looking for. They were then transferred to another village.

For the Jews, that was bad for two reasons. [The *Zonderdinsts*] used to visit the city during their free time and attack the passersby. They beat murderous blows and looted everything that fell into their hands. Their main victims were the people who worked in demolishing houses. These people did not have anywhere to escape.

The villagers, for their part, were afraid to sell their produce to the Jews because they were afraid that somebody would snitch on them. Because of that, prices of agricultural products, which were high to begin with, rose substantially even further. Along with hunger, epidemics such as typhoid fever, dysentery, and typhus broke out. Obviously, the hungry and the weak people fell sick and died first, if not from the disease itself, then from the inability to overcome and recover. That was how the hunger and the epidemics cut the lives short of many Jews in the city daily.

Several decrees were issued by the Germans as a result of the epidemics:

Decree A:

At the beginning of November, on a cold and rainy day, the *Kreishauptmann* gathered the entire *Judenrat* in his yard and let us wait for two hours. Then he came out and announced that every Jewish man and woman must, within twenty-four hours, shave the hair from the entire body and not just from the head and beard. He claimed that the Jews were to blame for the deceases and epidemics. He stated that if somebody was caught not obeying the order, the entire *Judenrat* would be punished. That is in addition to the death penalty imposed on the offender. The men received that decree favorably and fully obeyed. The problem was what to do with

[Page 271]

our women. The *Judenrat* representative turned to the *Kreishauptmann* with a hefty gift to rescind that paragraph of the decree. After raising the value of the gift, the *Kreishauptmann* agreed not to enforce it for women but did not agree to annul the decree altogether.

Decree B:

I was called to appear before the *Judenrat* as the physician responsible for the health of our city's Jews. There, the Gestapo man Hermann and one more person waited for me. They notified me that from that day forward, I would have to notify them about any case of infectious disease (the Ghetto has not been established yet). Dr. Felk did not work with me anymore. The following is a description of what happened to him at the beginning of December.

I was walking toward the hospital one morning, on Nowy Rynek [The New Market] Street, and suddenly I heard gunshots and saw a man falling on the ground. I approached and saw Dr. Felk lying on the ground, wounded in his neck, with blood pouring out of his wound. It turned out that Dr. Felk refused to bring the goose he bought from a villager in the market to Hazeh's home. Hazeh pulled out his pistol and shot Dr. Felk in the neck. I administered first aid and brought Dr. Felk to the Polish hospital, where he was treated by Dr. Bilinski. The wound was not critical, and Dr. Felk returned home after two weeks. He returned home but not to work, and I was left alone to serve at the Jewish hospital, as well as being responsible for the health of the Jewish population in our city toward the regime and the Gestapo.

My answer to the Gestapo was that I was doing everything at my disposal to prevent diseases and epidemics within the Jewish population. At the time, there was not even one case of infectious disease. I did not know, at the time, the purpose of that decree, but I felt that the request was not in our favor.

Before I left, the Gestapo people warned me not to take the request lightly and emphasized my personal responsibility.

That was how another month passed.

The *Aktion*[1] in Litatyn Forests – December 1941

by Dr. Eliezer Shaklai

Translated by Moshe Kutten

Edited by Jane S. Gabin

Eight days before Hanukkah, on 18 December, the *Kreishauptmann* invited the *Judenrat* to come see him. With anger and shouting, he notified them that he would not tolerate disrespect for his orders. The *Judenrat* did not transfer a sufficient number of Jews from the city to neighboring towns, and therefore, he had another request. In exactly seven days, during the night between the 15th and 16th of December (on the first candle of Hanukkah), the *Judenrat* must prepare a "transport" of a thousand Jews (not even a single person less) under the guard of the *Zonderdinst* and the Ukrainian militia, to the neighboring town of Pidhaitsi [Podhajce, Podhaitza], located about 32 kilometers away. The people will march on foot, in rows, four in a row! They would be allowed to take personal items with them, but not more than five kilograms each.

After what happened till then, we felt that the order was a hoax, another new contemptible plot. We suspected that a calamity was waiting for these people. Again, we had all sorts of questions! If he is sincere, why at night? Why in rows of four? Why on foot? Why on a specific and precise date? Why and why again? The whole order looked suspicious!

[Page 272]

The bad news spread very quickly throughout the city. People began to leave their homes, sleep outside the city, or with non-Jewish acquaintances for money or valuables. The *Judenrat*, for its part, proceeded in two directions. First, it quickly prepared the list of the people for the transport so that they could prepare for it was. On the other hand, it tried to find out, from the people close to the *Kreishauptmann*, what the real purpose behind the decree. The *Judenrat* did not trust the *Kreishauptmann* after the affair in Yom Kippur and looked for ways to get to the truth in some other ways. We reached the deputy *Kreishauptmann*, Krieger, through his secretary who received a gold ring with a big diamond for her mediacy.

Kieger promised to find out, for a large sum of money, about the order.

After his inquiry, he came back from the *Kreishauptmann* and promised to take the whole transport affair into his hands. He promised the *Judenrat*, with a word of honor, that the operation would only be a transport. He stated that he would personally make sure that nobody would be hurt. He could not change the date and the number (one thousand). He allowed the *Judenrat* to allocate twenty-five wagons for the sick, elderly, and children. Every person would be allowed to carry up to ten kilograms of personal items, and he would make sure to send the rest later with the help of the *Judenrat*. Krieger himself traveled to Pidhaitsi to instruct the *Judenrat* there to prepare space for a thousand Jews. He also requested that the *Judenrat* to prepare food for these people for several days.

After all these promises, the *Judenrat* calmed down and vigorously turned to prepare the people for the transport. However, the people slated for the transport were not affected by all the explanations of the *Judenrat*. They scattered to the edges and outside of the city. Left with no other choice, the *Judenrat*, its officials, and the Jewish militia began to lay siege to these people. When they were unsuccessful, the *Zonderdinst* and the Ukrainian militia joined them at midnight. They caught people as they encountered them, including those not on the list. Despite all the efforts, they managed to collect only about six hundred people, and the convoy left town at three o'clock in the morning. The convoy went out slowly toward Pidhaitsi on a wet and cold night. Accompanied the convoy were some *Judenrat* officials who helped in gathering the people. Altogether, the convoy consisted of about six hundred Jews.

At the head of the convoy was the Angel of Death, who was bringing his booty, accompanied by the angels of destruction, the *Zonderdinst*, and Ukrainians. They were holding flashlights "in honor of the first candle of Hanukkah."

At eight-thirty am, I met the *Zonderdinst* commander, Hazeh, at the *Judenrat* office, holding a list. He looked at the list and asked me: "Are you Dr. Felk?" "No," I answered. I managed to take a quick look at the list, and I saw the name of Dr. Felk among about twenty other names. Hazeh left the office in a hurry, and I understood that it had to do with the transport. In the meantime, Hazeh collected the people according to his list. Among them were: Dr. Felk's entire family, Lazar Segal, a woman called Berger, and others. They transported these people in a truck in the direction of the convoy. We sat depressed at the *Judenrat* office. We did not talk to each other. We felt this time that we were all guilty because we assisted in organizing the transport. We waited anxiously and impatiently for the news from Pidhaitsi that the convoy would arrive there safely. We knew that it would not happen before noon.

However, the news came early, long before the slated time. We did not have to wait until noon. The wagoneers came back with their wagons at ten thirty. We saw them from afar. And knew that they did not bring good news. Unfortunately, we were not mistaken. We fell into the trap again. We were rudely and shamelessly cheated.

[Page 273]

We heard the following story from the wagoneers: In the middle of the road, Near Litiatyn, in a place called Kribola (the "curve"), about 14 kilometers from Brzezany, the *Zonderdinst* stopped the convoy and ordered the people to get off the wagons. They then ordered the wagoneers to turn around and return to the city. They took the people toward the forest. After traveling back about five hundred meters, the wagoneers stopped. They waited a while, and then they heard shouts and crying voices from the direction of the forest. A short time later, they heard shots fired from a machine gun and some single shots. They then returned home. On their way back, they met a truck full of Jews traveling in the direction of the forest.

The whole situation then became clear to us. We began to believe the story about our people who were murdered in the forest, as was told to us by the villagers on Yom Kippur. We finally understood how the Germans deceived us with lies and how we were deceived. We understood there was nobody to talk to, request, or ask. There was no such thing as a promise, no word of truth, no honesty, no justice, and no judge. We needed to carry the load and hope for help from the heavens. We would not be able to stand against them on our own.

I heard the whole story in detail from an eyewitness a day later. He managed to hide in the forest and survived. When he appeared at the *Judenrat*, I saw him and talked to him; that was what he told me: When they arrived at the forest, Germans with machine guns were waiting for them. The Jews were beaten and given an order to strip naked quickly and gather all their belongings and clothing in piles. After that, everyone approached a pit dug ahead of time, and they were shot right there by the grave. After the "job" was completed, the Germans covered the pits with dirt. The Germans loaded the clothing and packages on trucks and left the forest. The eyewitness managed to hide behind a bush, and there he stayed the entire night, shivering from the cold and without clothes. He ran to the nearest village early in the following morning, where a farmer gave him some worn clothes and torn shoes. From there, he arrived at the city. I heard all of that from the eyewitness. He told me what happened to him from the moment he was taken by force until he arrived back in the city. He also saw how the Germans brought the people on the truck and joined them in the convoy people. Everyone was murdered. That was the second mass *Aktsia* [*Aktion* in German] in our city!

The following day, the *Kreishauptmann* called our representatives, Dr. Klarer and Ross, to quickly appear before him. Again, he received them with rage and shouts and, for the first time, with a whip. He beat them with the whip on their faces and wounded them. All of that was because of the unsuccessful and unorganized operation, where only about six hundred and fifty were taken instead of a thousand. That operation carved the fate of Dr. Klarer. His sentence was sealed then, although he continued to serve as *Obmann* of the *Judenrat*.

The date – end of 1941. Our balance sheet was immensely negative. More than 15% of the Jewish population lost their lives, and there was no hope that the future would improve for us. A limited consolation was the news that the German Army stopped its progress. On the contrary, it suffered heavy losses and, in many places, it was in retreat. With heavy hearts, no hope, and with warm requests to the King of the Universe, we received the new year – 1942...

Translator's Note:

1. *Aktion* (n German) or *Aktsia* (in Yiddish). A term used for any non-military campaign to further Nazi ideals of race, but most often referred to the assembly and deportation of Jewish concentration or death camps.

[Page 274]

Order to Jews to Give Away Furs

by Dr. Eliezer Shaklai

Translated by Moshe Kutten

Edited by Jane S. Gabin

It was an extremely cold winter but the Germans were not prepared for it. According to their plan, they were supposed to subdue the Soviets before the rains came. General "mud" and general "cold" stopped them near Leningrad and Moscow and in the south, not far from the Caucasus. The Germans suffered heavy losses on the fronts, and in many cases, the initiative passed into the hands of the Soviets. The Germans tried to make it easier for their army and sent them to the fronts with winter coats and furs. The German authorities turned to the Jewish population with an order to hand over all the furs within two weeks, with no exceptions!

Not handing over furs carried the death penalty. To ensure success, the *Kreishauptmann* requested from the *Judenrat* twelve people as hostages. The *Obmann* and two additional officials quickly prepared the list and handed it over to the Jewish militia with an order to capture the people and bring them directly to jail. They sent a copy of the list to the *Kreishauptmann*. The militia managed to capture only ten out of the twelve people. Two of the candidates escaped earlier and hid. The Germans did not want to give up and demanded to receive two other people, otherwise they threatened to hand over the matter to the Gestapo. Panic arose in the city. People were afraid of German retaliation. Nobody believed the twelve people would be alive after the fur collection operation. People hid or escaped outside of the city. All the searches for the missing people or "hunts" for two additional hostages were in vain. That game lasted about two weeks, and in the end, with the help of money and gifts, and after the Jews handed over almost 100% of the furs, the Germans freed the ten hostages.

However, additional decrees and troubles did not stop, and it did not take long for more to come.

The "Typhus" Aktions

by Dr. Eliezer Shaklai

Translated by Moshe Kutten

Edited by Jane S. Gabin

There were murderous operations by the Gestapo against the Jewish population due to infectious deceases, including "preventive" operations to prevent the spread of these diseases.

I have already mentioned that hunger and epidemics went hand in hand, and each caused a double dose. Instead of having twenty and up to thirty sick people per day, I had one hundred. The epidemics themselves wreaked havoc on us and killed many victims every day. My assistance to these people was minimal, more like encouragement, good words, and advice. I did not have any medicines, and in those days, whoever fell sick remained sick for days and weeks without the possibility of getting well and recovering. Surprisingly, the percentage of deaths, compared to the non-Jewish population, was smaller. This people's will to live and overcome was probably very strong.

I mentioned my meeting with the Gestapo, where they demanded to provide them with daily reports about people who were sick with typhus. Such a list was never provided to the Gestapo.

At the beginning of January, a Polish physician notified me that his acquaintance from a neighboring town told him about a visit by the Gestapo to the Jewish hospital there. In that visit

[Page 275]

the Gestapo exterminated all the patients along with the personnel, among them two physicians who worked there. With agreement by *Judenrat*, I notified all the patients and the personnel at the hospital to leave immediately so that nobody would remain there! Five people from among the hospital patients and personnel did not believe my warning and remained in the hospital secretly, against my order. Two days passed, and the Gestapo came to visit our city. Their first steps were in the direction of the hospital. They shot the five people they found there, among them the caretaker of the hospital, a lawyer in his profession working in Kertskov [?], called Bezen, who studied in the past in the city's high school.

That was the end of our hospital – the hospital of Dr. Felk *z"l*, who invested so much energy, will, and money. And he was no longer alive!

That was the first operation toward the exterminating of sick Jewish people. That continued until the liquidation of the ghetto. The Gestapo person responsible for the typhus operations in our city was Hermann. He visited the city often to exterminate the people who were sick with typhus. I, as a person responsible for the health of the Jewish population toward the Gestapo, notified Hermann officially that we did not have such sick people. Whenever Hermann turned to the *Judenrat*, he received my answer with some ransom money. After receiving whatever he received, he would go to the city accompanied by somebody from the *Judenrat*, most of the time Mitelman, or somebody from the Jewish militia, to fulfill the obligations toward his superiors, and killed on his way the people who were sick with typhus. His trips to the city always cost us some victims, not necessarily sick people, sometimes up to twenty people. In my opinion, he received hints from snitches among the Jewish militia people, besides his "*Volksdeutsche's*" assistants, who kept their eyes out and notified him about every suspicious case. When Hermann appeared in our city, people used to say that the first assistant to the Death Angel arrived. There was never a case when we got away with no victims, and the number of victims depended on his mood.

[Page 275]

Arbeitsamt - Employment Bureau

by Dr. Eliezer Shaklai

Translated by Moshe Kutten

Edited by Jane S. Gabin

The German Employment Bureau notified the Judenrat that every Jew must register with the bureau. Every Jew between the ages 18 and 55 had to fulfill a form through the Judenrat, with all the information: name, age, profession, occupation, and most importantly – the home address. A Jew could accept to work only through the Employment Bureau and with its approval. A work certificate was only valid for thirty days. Upon expiration, the worker had to extend it for another thirty days, and so on!

Our people, who learned a lesson from the past and remembered the previous registrations and their results, were not in a hurry to register. However, it was impossible to exist without work. Not having a choice, people with regular jobs began to find ways to obtain a work permit through an intermediary. And here, an affair and a new possibility to extort money from the Jews began again. The monthly permit cost money, and before the month was over, payment was due again. The resulting expenses didn't help when the day came, and they caught you! If they captured you with or without a permit, you would be at the hands of the German murderers, slated to be sent to a labor camp or an extermination camp. We learned about all of that over time but in the beginning, we did not know what the intention was behind the request, where it led, and whether that permit would be helpful or not.

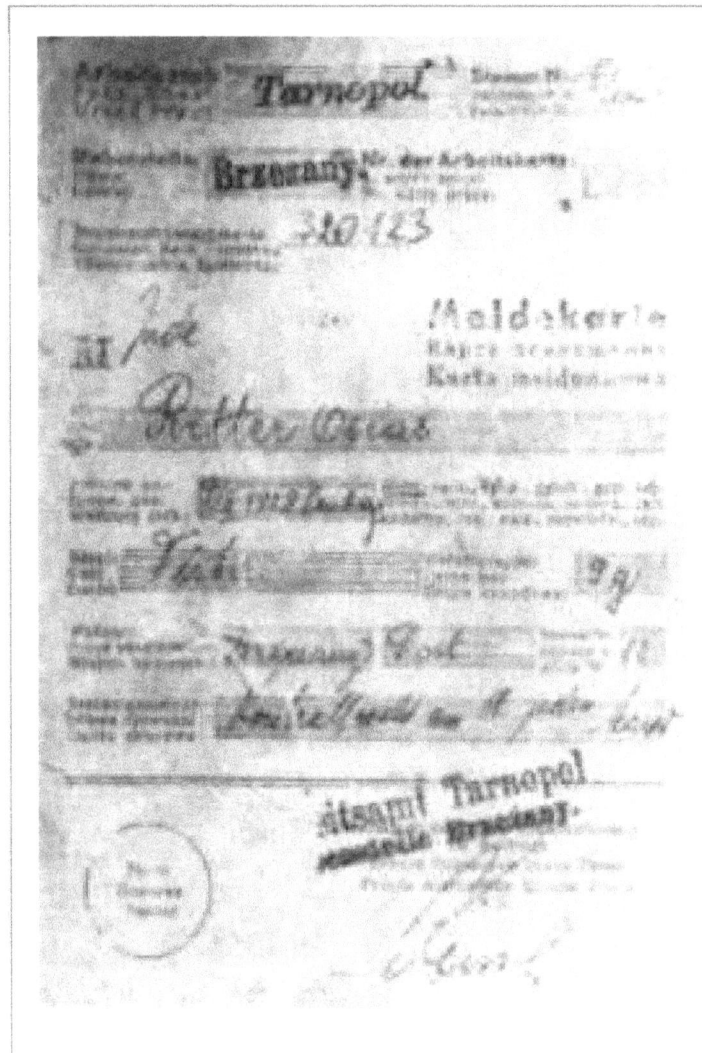

[Page 276]

The officials at the Employment Bureau knew well how to exploit our naiveness and distressful situation, invented new permits every now and then, seemingly safer for the permit holder, and obviously demanded more and more money for the "better" permits. They learned from the phrase: "A person would pay anything to save his soul." There were permits made of white tin, and people who received such a permit and paid the full price for it sewed it onto their clothes - a sign that the permit holder was employed in essential work for the state and should not be touched. As I said, that was another plot to extort more money from the Jews. They cheated us until the last moment and extracted money from us to the last cent. During an Aktsia, none of the permits were helpful, whether made of tin or not. Many people who owned and relied on their tin permits - ended up falling into the trap!

Labor Camps

by Dr. Eliezer Shaklai

Translated by Moshe Kutten

Edited by Jane S. Gabin

At the same time, the German Employment Bureau requested from the *Judenrat* sixty people slated to be sent to [forced] labor camps. That was the first time the Germans demanded from people for labor camps located far from our city. We had heard about these labor camps in Germany and Galitsia before. The labor camps where our people were last to go were around Ternopil. The people in these camps worked in quarries and on the roads leading to the front. They were responsible for keeping the roads in good condition.

The *Judenrat* prepared the list and notified these people to be ready on a specific date with winter clothing and personal effects. To calm down the people slated for the camp, the *Judenrat* notified them about the decision by the German Employment Bureau to exchange them with sixty other people in three months. No Jews would be able to evade this work. Sooner or later, everyone would be taken to the camp, and only then one could secure a working permit in another place. Our people did not believe in any promises, despite not exactly knowing what was waiting for them there, despite their identification with the people on the list, and the fact that they would be handled by the Gestapo if they did not come, only a few showed up.

More people who were not on the list were caught with the help of the Jewish militia. They were loaded on wagons and under a heavy guard, and without giving the mothers and the wives time to bring winter clothing and food for those people who were caught, the Germans transferred them to the labor camp.

That was the first transport. From that point until the liquidation of the ghetto, these transports did not cease. A transport left once or twice a month. That trouble, curse, and blow, not written in any book, was harsh for those sent and their families. They never returned from there. They died there under indescribable severe torture. Hundreds and thousands of our people died in those labor camps, which were work, torture, and death camps, as compared to the labor camps in Germany.

I will elaborate on these labor camps and everything connected to them. In this painful affair, the *Judenrat*, the Jewish militia, and everybody else who participated in organizing it failed. We heard much about the labor camps in Germany and the hard work and poor conditions there, but these were paradise compared

[Page 277]

to the labor camps in Eastern Galitsia. In Germany, people were employed in hard work in the factories or on farms. The employers were interested in receiving the maximum out of these laborers, supplying minimum conditions to survive. They needed the manpower since their people were on the fronts, and therefore, they took care of the workers. In Eastern Galitsia, on the other hand, the main employment for thousands of people was working on the roads. If they had provided these poor people with minimum living conditions, most would have survived the War and returned peacefully to their homes. However, for the Gestapo, Employment Bureau, and other German authorities, these camps were a profitable business, a one-in-a-lifetime opportunity to accumulate a fortune. They were interested in passing tens of thousands, not just a few thousand, people through these camps. For that purpose, they liquidated the people in the camps quickly and put in new ones to replace them. They earned a lot of money and gifts from every transport, and in addition, they robbed the things the people brought to the camp.

There were several labor camps. The first one is in Zboriv [Zborov], the second is in Kamionka, the third is in Holoboki Vialki [?], and others. In each of such camps there were six to eight hundred people.

Every camp contacted separately to the *Judenrat* with requests to prepare people on a predetermined date. Usually, they requested more than was required, and by paying ransom money, the *Judenrat* often succeeded in reducing the number to 1/3 of the original request. The Germans turned, in parallel, to several cities with the same request, which led to competition among the cities, who would contribute more money and send fewer people. On the agreed-upon date, the camp's representative (the deputy manager) would arrive accompanied by a Ukrainian militia to receive the people from the *Judenrat*. Very often, the *Judenrat* did not succeed in gathering enough people, and the Ukrainian militia, aided by the Jewish militia, would begin a "hunt" in the city after people. They did not rest until they fulfilled the quota. That process turned into a slave trade with the participation of the *Judenrat*. Whoever was caught and had enough ransom money paid the amount requested, and another Jew was captured instead. In the end, when the Jew lost all his money and was caught, he ended his life in the labor camp, as those who went before or after him.

There are no words to describe the "hunt" after people, the shouts, cries, beating, and curses, and the fights between one Jew and another and between the catcher and the caught. I will never forget how the Germans succeeded in transforming humans into animals. The "hunt," slave trade, and ransom money payments continued daily until the liquidation of the ghetto. As I said, the German Employment Bureau knew to exploit the situation through its intermediaries, who sold all sorts of permits as a defense against deportation to labor camps. They have done everything to extort the money from the Jew's pocket.

The person responsible for the workforce in the health department was Dr. Levrovski, a district physician at that time. He arranged permits for all the physicians and their families as state employees. These people were sent to the neighboring villages to take care of the health of the non-Jewish population and to try to prevent the spread of infectious diseases. They, too, had to renew and pay for their permits every month. Even that did not always help. There were physicians in every labor camp. Dr. Meiblum, the father-in-law of Leib Preis, and others came from our city. Their conditions at the camps were better, but their end was the same as the bitter end of all others.

The labor camps affair was one of the saddest, most painful, and most depressing affairs that left a black mark – a "Mark of Cain" on the forehead of all those who handled that problem. I am obligated to elaborate and give a full description of this issue.

People did not go to the camps of their own goodwill. The *Judenrat*, with the help of the [Jewish] militia, hunted people.

[Page 278]

The hunt began suddenly, usually in the middle of the night. The militia spread throughout the city and broke into apartments. Whoever they caught, they kept under a heavy guard until the transport to the camp. Mothers and wives, sisters, and children stood outside, cried, shouted, and begged for mercy. However, without ransom money, nothing helped, even the best nepotism - "only money talked." In the meantime, people were taken in and out, exchanged one with the other, and until they finished the bargaining, the wagons or the trucks arrived. The people who were caught would have been loaded quickly. Everyone received some food for the road and also beatings, kicks, and curses - when the person climbed onto the wagon or truck. The Germans ensured that the wagon or truck would be crowded with people pushing each other. The women, too, received a great deal of beatings from the Germans and the Ukrainians at the time of the departure. It was a farewell from afar because [the Germans and Ukrainians] did not allow the women to come closer. It was a farewell to have one more minute to see the beloved one and hear his voice, even from afar, for the last time.

Then the truck [or wagon] began to move, tearing apart the rope that tied sixty Jewish families. These people would not die together. The truck [or wagon] began to move, leaving emptiness and pain in the women's hearts. The women followed the truck and the dust cloud behind it with their eyes until they disappeared. The women dispersed and returned home, every woman with her own pain. There was no choice then. They had to continue living – becoming both mother and father for the children. They also had to send a package, through the *Judenrat*, to the son, father, husband, or brother, adding a few words of calm and encouragement. It was forbidden for Jews to use the postal service, and there was no address. Relatives were not able to approach or access the labor camp. Nobody was allowed to do so except the *Judenrat*'s contact person, who had a special permit from the camp commander, and even that was only on certain days. The contact person did not travel to the camp every week, and there were potentially a few factors affecting such a trip. First, the camp commander was the decider and the person who provided the permit. Even if you had such a permit, it was hard to find transportation. One could only travel on a wagon and, in the winter, on a sled. The villagers from the surrounding areas were not enthusiastic about traveling there despite the large sums of money paid for that trip. The distance to the camp was also a factor. With some camps, it would have been possible to leave in the morning and return on the same day. For other camps, the trip required lodging in the middle of the road in a village or a city. And last, the trip depended on the contact person, his character, and his goodwill.

Preparing a package requires time as well. People sent torn clothing and mainly food, such as bread, some honey, etc. But it was not easy to get food! And when everything was ready, one had to go to the *Judenrat*, meet the contact person, talk to him face to face, hand him some important information, and for G-d's sake, lest he forget to tell the husband, father, or brother…; one had to find out if he needed anything special? What did he look like? Where was he working? Maybe he would write a few words.

The women are standing by the *Judenrat* for long hours and waiting to catch a conversation with the contact person. He has not come yet; he is busy now; he is tired and not ready, or not able to even answer; he does not know himself when he will go. And so a day, two, or three days pass, until finally, good going, the contact person is going to the labor camp – on a wagon loaded with packages with tear-soaked letters.

So many thoughts, guesses, requests, and sighs accompany him on this trip. When would he arrive? Will he meet the people? What would he say to them? Will he not forget to say…? "Absit omen." And the thoughts are changing by the hour.

[Page 279]

They run together with the clock hours or even faster; they compete with the time. Now the thoughts are disturbing – when will the loved one be back? What will he say? What will be the news? They wait for hours by the *Judenrat*'s building in the cold, rain, and snow, and the hours last so long. They wait anxiously for the return of the contact person.

…And the package - there were cases when it did not arrive at its destination, as the person had already met his Creator. He was "lucky" and did not suffer much. In such a case, the contact person would not respond to the question by the deceased person's wife about how was her husband doing. The contact person would lower his eyes, and she would too, and then she would cover her face with her hands and burst into tears. She would move aside to allow the next in line to ask her question. For one woman, everything has already been said. Sometimes, the contact person would be so exhausted that he would settle for a general greeting and withdraw to his home until the following morning.

We return now to the people who were taken to the camp. When the truck just moved with the people who were caught, the German escorts and the Ukrainian militia began with their "treatment." Every address to the people was accompanied by murderous blows with a rifle or a whip. They warn the people not to try to escape since the group is responsible for every person. Tens would die if one escaped. Therefore, they all must watch each other. Money and valuables must be handed to the transport manager immediately. Seating is not allowed (there is no room). Talking is forbidden, and so is making signs to each other. That was how they traveled for hours until they arrived at the camp.

In the camp – as told by the contact person in the camps

They recognized the camp from afar! A large yard surrounded by a multi-layer barbwire fence with tall towers. In the yard – a long structure and several other smaller structures. The big gate opened when the truck or the wagon approached and immediately closed behind them, swallowing them alive. With that, their connection with the outside world ended. Inside the camp, they had been already waiting for them and prepared a "warm" reception. From then on, the fate of all of them was, for better or worse, in the hands of a few people. The first order was – come down! They were facing two rows of Germans and, beyond them, the Ukrainian militia. The camp commander and his deputy were at the head. The "welcome" everyone separately holding a whip. They greet everyone with a few heavy blows – on the face, head, and the rest of the body. Following each other oppressors with wooden or metal sticks. By the time they reach the end of the long row, they are bleeding.

[Page 280]

Making any sound was forbidden. Doing so would have resulted in additional blows. There were cases when the weak stayed in their place and never rose again.

The second order was to stand in a row and hand over all valuables. If somebody had reasonable clothes, they were forced to give them up. After the assembly, they had to run and enter the large wooden structure where the Jewish commander waited. He, with his entourage, was in charge of the inside of the building. Over time, these people learned cruelty from the Germans who supervised them. The symbol of that commander was a special stick he held in his hand. He often made use of that stick to over-validate his orders.

The inside of the wooden structure was long and dark, without a floor or ceiling. It might have been a stable once or was specially built for that purpose. The boards for the bunks were long – and the bunks were built in three or four tiers. Even in the center of the structure, bunks were constructed in tiers and made of boards. The building housed six hundred and often up to eight hundred people. Every person was allocated a limited, small, and narrow space, selected by the Jewish commander. The quality of that place depended on lack and sometimes on nepotism. The bunks deep inside were different from those near the entrance. The top bunks differed from the bottom ones. The top bunks required climbing, which was not easy to do after hard work at the end of a long day. The body was tired, and climbing involved a waste of energy. The air on the upper tier was also compressed and hard to breathe. Those on the bottom suffered from other disadvantages - all the dirt from the top bunks fell on them. The new recruits had to run towards the bunks, and each had to grab the allocated bunk. There was no time to waste. People were ordered to strip, and they had to pass a thorough examination to check that they did not hide any valuables in their clothes or shoes. The barber was already waiting to cut the hair from the entire body. That work had to be paid for by the people. Money brought to the camp had to be handed over to the Jewish commander. The commander and his helpers used force to ensure their orders were followed.

The camp commander was German, a Gestapo person, a wild animal, a cruel man who lacked human feelings, even not of a primitive person, a sadist who always tried to get himself into a drunk mode, thirsty for human blood, vengeful who knew his duty and objective: exterminate Jews and receive other Jews instead. He used all of the means available to him to achieve that goal. He himself lived outside of the camp. He used a deputy inside the camp who was similar in character and deeds. They had other Germans available to them who guarded the camp from their positions on top of the towers. The latter were equipped with machine guns. They were helped by a larger number of Ukrainians who helped guard the camps from the outside and inside. They brought the people to work, guarded them during the workday, and brought them back. They also traveled with the commander to catch new people and brought them to the camp.

[Page 281]

The interior of the building and all the arrangements, such as division of work, taking care of cleanliness, food distribution, and allocation of personal space, were in the hands of the Jews. It seemed as if the Jews had autonomy - a benefit. However, in reality, the Germans took advantage of the situation, as with the *Judenrat* in the ghetto. They caused conflicts between people by giving perks to some [and withholding them from others] and thus used those perks to make the people into snitches and have them watch over their friends. The Jewish commander and his helpers, the Jewish militia of the camp, had an easier life in the camp, and were more comfortable, with more food, less work, and even fewer beatings. They expected that by helping the Germans, they would be able to continue in that way until a miracle came – a day would come when they would be redeemed and saved from annihilation. Obviously, that was an illusion. Everyone went on the same road, some early and others later. The Germans took care to remove those among the Jews who collaborated with them to cover up their actions. The Germans always found people for that work, spineless people who, under the pressure of fear and feelings of superiority, became a good "medium" in the hands of the Germans, predators similar to those who gave the orders to them. Nevertheless, one word would be enough to sometimes undermine their conscience and make them face the truth. An appropriate strong person could bring their original image, at least in some cases.

Each camp had a chef and two people for manual work. There was also a stockkeeper, an accountant, and one or two physicians. The work of these people was lighter. They also ate better than the others, on the people's account. The food was less than the minimum required for survival. The German commander received fixed food portions according to the number of people. He took the majority for himself and sent it to Germany. The rest was divided among those who could do it. Only crumbs remained for the workers. If the workers continued to live, it was due to the packages they received from home. If these packages arrived late, the mortality among the people rose above average.

The food the workers received in the camps: Early in the morning, a slice of bread and black water ("coffee"), and in the evening, a watery soup and sometimes some potato crumbs.

The day in the camp began when the people were awakened at four o'clock, summer and winter. They had to be ready for the "call" in just a few minutes. It was quick because people slept in their clothing. Following the order by the Jewish commander, everybody had to go outside to the yard where each received his breakfast: bread and "coffee." One would drink the coffee or not, take the bread with him, and stand for the "call." The camp commander would pass through the rows, always holding his whip, and distributed blows according to his mood. Only then did the workers go out to work. They were divided into groups of thirty to forty people. The head of the group was a Jew responsible for his men, their number, and their work. Sometimes, as needed, they exchanged the groups for different types of work. They went out accompanied by the Ukrainian militia and some Germans. They walked in rows, four to a row, tired even before the start of the workday, broken, injured, with or without shoes, leaning on each other for support lest they fall or fall behind.

People who fell on the way received murderous beatings until they rose up. If the person did not recover quickly and catch up with the group, he was shot. It is hard to describe the torturous way to work and back. The situation was more difficult on rainy days, in the deep "Podolian" mud that stuck to the shoes and slowed the progress. People preferred to walk barefoot on those days. When they arrived at the workplace, tools were distributed among those who worked in the quarries or on the roads. They worked from sunrise to sunset under the watching eyes of the Germans and under the threat of their flapping whip.

[Page 282]

The workers used every opportunity to rest for a second, but if they were caught, it was very costly to them. The Jewish guard did everything in his power to ease the work for the people. He sometimes even helped by doing the work. He was responsible for making sure that the work would end on time. After sunset, they walked back to the camp – one big black shadow of people, almost lifeless, moving out of habit, pulling their legs. When they arrived at the camp, some gave up on the soup. They did not have the strength anymore to take the extra additional steps. They laid down on the hard boards, but even on the bunks, they could not rest. The lice, bugs, and insects began to suck their blood. They waited for the people the entire day and did not want to give up their blood portion. Others ate or drank the soup and did not even go to wash their hands. The lights were shut off at nine o'clock.

However, the day did not always end with going to sleep! It happened when the camp commander was in high spirits or, G-d forbid, the opposite, and he came to visit the camp. At his order, everyone had to appear in the yard, and the game would begin – a game of a man's life. The commander would choose a victim and order him to strip and lie down on a bench. Another prisoner, selected by the commander, received a stick in his hand, and he had to beat the victim twenty-five to forty times. If the blows were considered by the commander as too weak, a Ukrainian would take the stick and hit the victim. The game usually ended with the death of one, two, or even more people!

Worse than that was when the game turned into a punishment when somebody succeeded in escaping from the camp. That punishment was not the same everywhere and not in every case. They immediately organized the entire Ukrainian and Jewish militias to search after the escapee. Farmers from the neighboring villages in the search received a prize for any information about the escapee if he was caught. It wasn't difficult to recognize such a man according to his face, hands, or clothes marked with colors that stand out from a distance.

They would bring the caught escapee to the yard where the entire camp was waiting for him, for them to "watch and fear" [Deuteronomy 19:20]. He would kneel and ask for forgiveness from the commander. After a murderous beating, they hanged him in the yard for several days – as a warning to others.

A more severe punishment was when they gouged out his eyes and hanged him by his legs until he died from agony and hunger. If they did not catch the escapee, the punishment was as the commander saw fit. Sometimes, they demanded several people, often relatives of the escapee, from the *Judenrat* of the escapee's city. In other cases, they hung the mother instead of the escaped son. Some other times, they sentenced to death several people from the escapee's city. In more severe cases, they positioned the camp people in rows and took out every tenth person, up to sixty people. They placed them by a pit and shot them all. It all depended on the importance of the escapee and the commander's mood.

In those days, the camp commander forbade the *Judenrat* of that city to visit the camp. Neither packages nor letters from home could reach the prisoners, and the mortality among the people rose.

The first news about the harsh situation of our brothers reached us only days after they were taken to the forced labor camp. Some were killed on the way and during the reception held for them by the Germans when they arrived at the campyard. Others were severely injured. We received news about new victims daily. We had that whole inhuman tragedy played in front of our eyes. We had heard about these camps and the livse, for a long time. However, as long as it did not concern us, we pushed the stories out of our minds.

[Page 283]

We did not want to listen or believe until we began to feel everything on our skin.

A "labor camp" – two words which meant hunger, fear, torture, backbreaking hard work, beatings, and humiliation until salvation came at the hands of the angel of death. The forced labor camp was hell and suffering for the camp people and the ghetto people alike until the complete destruction of the ghetto in our city. The labor camp swallowed thousands of people without a trace. It was hell on earth, the record of slavery and humiliation, when a person loses his senses, stops thinking, and becomes a blind medium in the hand of Satan, who makes him into an animal and does whatever Satan wants him to do.

Methods of "Catching" People to Labor Camps

by Dr. Eliezer Shaklai

Translated by Moshe Kutten

Edited by Jane S. Gabin

In January 1942, the Germans held three more hunts of our people who were sent to labor camps. They used a different ploy every time, and if they did not manage to cheat our people, they caught them by force. After the first *Aktsia* to the labor camp, it was clear to us that any person who did not work in a regular and approved job by the German Employment Bureau was a candidate for the labor camp.

The Jews, being the People of the Book and quick learners, showed that they could also be good workers. At times of need, no work was too hard or impossible. Everyone was ready to do any job to continue living.

Most of the people succeeded, within a week, ining find work that was supposed to protect them. At least, that was what their employers and the Employment Bureau told them.

A second demand for sixty more people was received from the Gestapo in the middle of January. The *Judenrat* prepared the list and sent notices to the people via the Jewish militia to appear at a specific date, time, and location. These notices contained a threat that if they did not appear, the list would be handed over to the Gestapo. Only eight people from that list came. More than fifty people ran away from their homes, hid outside of the city, despite the intense cold, or at non-Jewish neighbors for money. The Germans came after notifying the *Judenrat* to retrieve the people promised to them. When they did not find the people, they became enraged. Without saying a word about their intention, they scattered throughout the city and, based on the information at the Employment Bureau, went to the formal locations that employed Jews. The Germans took every Jew they found, more than sixty people, loaded them on wagons, and left with the loot before the "hunt" was known to the *Judenrat*" or the wives of these people. That was how the Germans caught people who were not on the *Judenrat*'s list [and had a regular job], and the people on the list were saved temporarily.

After that *Aktsia*, we understood that even a place of work does not protect its workers. People thought once or twice, if at all, to go to work. They saw no use to do so. The opposite was true; during an *Aktsia*, it was more difficult, if not impossible, to run away from the place of work. The Germans also took advantage of that. The manager of the German Employment Bureau notified the *Judenrat* that he received complaints from many employers about the avoidance of coming to work by their Jewish workers. He stated that he would investigate the situation and punish the evaders by erasing their names from the formal worker list. Two days after that notice, he appeared along with his secretary in some

[Page 284]

places of work. He wrote down the names and addresses of each person who came to work. The employers quickly notified the rest of the workers. They came running and asked the manager to add them to the list of permanent workers. The manager of the Employment Bureau initially refused. However, the workers begged him and to appease him, gave him a double dose [of cash], and then he agreed to add all of them, about a hundred, to the list. How big was their surprise when they arrived home and found an invitation to appear in the morning of the following day in the Bureau, ready to be transported to the labor camp? The invitation was accompanied by a threat to hand over the evaders to the Gestapo!

At that time, everybody left their homes ahead of time and scattered outside of the city. Most of our city people, even those who were not invited, hid in safe hideouts until the storm passed over. The Germans did not give up. Early in the morning, when they did not find any people waiting for them, they began to hunt for people in their places of work. To their surprise, they did not discover people there either. They then turned to the *Judenrat* and, with the Jewish militia, searched the Jewish homes. They worked for the whole day and only managed to catch twenty people. The Germans added four people from the Jewish militia and sent them to the labor camp.

After that *Aktsia*, the German manager of the Labor Bureau, visited the *Judenrat* and informed them unequivocally that they needed to bring sixty people within four days, not even a single person less, otherwise the Germans would dismantle the *Judenrat* and Jewish militia, and send their people to the labor camp! That was a stark warning. The *Judenrat* understood that it did not have a choice. The militia received an order to do everything to bring sixty people on the requested date.

The militia knew better than the Germans where the Jews were hiding, the hiding place of everybody, and how to search, especially when it concerned themselves. They made all the efforts, stood the test, and provided the quota on time. From that day on, the *Judenrat* and the militia activities associated with the labor camps continued day and night. It did not cease until the liquidation of the ghetto.

A correction to my story: Not all the people of the *Judenrat* and Jewish militia participated in these activities.

Jewish Militiamen as a [German] "Tool" and as Human Beings

By Dr. Eliezer Shaklai

Translated by Moshe Kutten

Edited by Jane S. Gabin

The work at the *Judenrat* and the militia was divided. Only three or four people in the *Judenrat* dealt with the labor camps. The same was true in the militia. Most of the militia members were given less critical jobs, such as collecting money and objects for the Germans, bringing people to work for the Germans, watching over the people during the work and returning them, and other similar jobs. But even these militia members did not always sign on the negative page in the history of the Nazi conquest of our city. With these words, I am not defending them! I had the opportunity to watch them in their actions and talk and know them! They were all men of a weak character, exposed to the influence of the Gestapo. They might as well have been good partisans, freedom fighters, or even heroes if they had been influenced by a strong man who would have directed them in the opposite direction and saved them from deterioration and humiliation. Unfortunately, that strong hand never materialized. We lacked, among us, a strong man who fitted those days and situations and who could have influenced them.

[Page 285]

I will bring up some cases where I participated myself! I will describe them as they happened.

One day, Betinger, the Jewish militiamen, and I, the one responsible to the authorities for the health of the Jewish population, received an order from the Gestapo to visit several addresses they gave us to check people who, according to the information they received, were sick with typhus, in every place. I described our role, the reason for our mission, and what was waiting for them! I warned them about the approaching disaster. These people managed to escape within just a few moments. They jumped through the windows, escaped, and disappeared. Betinger heard everything and knew well what was waiting for him if the Gestapo would find out what happened. Despite that, he kept his silence.

Another case happened one evening. I sat down with the militia member Klarer, the son of Sender Klarer, at the buffet, situated in the first room of the militia, and drank tea. We heard shouts coming from the adjacent room. We did not pay attention to these shouts, as they were a regular occurrence in those days. Suddenly, the door to the adjacent room broke out, and a running man appeared, followed by two militia members who guarded him, running after him but did not manage to catch him. At the same moment, Klarer jumped in the direction of the escapee, tripped him, and began beating him. I approached Klarer and slapped him on his cheek (That was the first time in my life that I lifted my hand on another person). I slapped him so hard that he got confused, and so did the other two militia members. The young man took advantage of the confusion and ran away. A short while later, Klarer came to me and, with tears in his eyes, came to ask for forgiveness and said: "How far I've come that I've done what I've done? I can see that it is already in my blood. "Believe me," – he said – "I did not even think about what I was doing. I jumped instinctively. I do not believe I am not at fault. That would never happen again in my life." And that is how it was. – one firm slap in the face woke him up from his insensibility and he repented!

Another case happened in the fall of 1942. The Gestapo caught sixteen people sick with typhus in a hideout (it was a case of snitching). Following beatings and tortures, the Gestapo managed to extract a confession from them that I was the physician who took care of them. They killed them all and arrested me. They interrogated me for several hours and demanded that I provide them with a list of at least two hundred sick people. They stated that the list would be the only thing that would save me from torture and, perhaps, death. I did not cave in. The Gestapo commander then gave an order to four militia members, who were responsible for the militia (including Betinger) to pass through every room of every home in the ghetto and produce a detailed list of all the people sick with typhus. He was sure that they would fulfill his order with precision. I was ordered to accompany the militia members.

The Gestapo people went out and left me alone with the militiamen. Nobody in the room had any doubt about my fate. They only feared that several hundred people would go with me. When we were left alone, I turned to the four militiamen and explained unambiguously: "I am the person responsible for the health of the Ghetto Jews. As I have already told the Gestapo, there are no people sick with typhus in the ghetto! There is no need to search, and there is no value to any searches! Most of the people left the city anyway. You will not find any sick person!"

[Page 286]

"But we got an order from the Gestapo," said one of them. "And that was my order," he answered and looked directly into his eyes. "Whatever will happen to me will happen to you! You are Jews like me and not better than me. We all will have the same fate." They were silent. I also remained silent. Long minutes passed. We all sat down in the militia's room by the tables. Everyone sat in his own corner, each one with his own thoughts, each one knew what was waiting for him, each one did his own soul searching and calculated the sum total of his life to date.

The night lasted forever. We sat down in silence. Nobody rose or left us! We remained a unified group, bound by a common fate – waiting for tomorrow without hope. When the morning light reached us, I rose, and they rose too – we straightened up, I looked at my fate mates, separately at each one, and my eyes said to them – "Be strong!" We walked in the direction of the Gestapo, and each one knew that it was the final way in our lives. I marched up front, and behind me, the four militiamen. We entered.

I will talk about the end somewhere else. A miracle saved us from sure death. Even today, it is not clear to me how it happened.

I just wanted to tell you about the position taken by the four militiamen at a critical moment!

I will bring one more case:

On Friday, before the ghetto liquidation, people observed Hermann, the Gestapo man, conversing with Betinger. Based on Betinger's facial appearance, during the conversation, they understood that he received a crucial order. They notified me, so I immediately entered Betinger's room. I did not find him; I only saw his wife. I asked her what she knew about the latest order her husband received a short while ago from the Gestapo. In the beginning, she refused to answer; she hesitated. But when I explained to her that this was about the life and death of thousands of people – she relented and told me that her husband received an order to prepare twenty axes that day and to be prepared for that night.

I heard many other stories from eyewitnesses, but I will not bring them here. I only laid out those where I was an eyewitness. I brought them up for those who research the period and for the judges before they issue their sentences [about the militamen].

* * *

The *Judenrat* handed the Gestapo the sixty people slated for the labor camp and thus saved itself and the militiamen. As mentioned, it was the beginning of an action that continued until the liquidation of the ghetto.

In the meantime, the Gestapo surrounded the private labor camp of the Kreishauptmann, one day, loaded its people on trucks and brought them over to the general labor camp.

After that event, the *Kreishauptmann* demanded that the *Judenrat* provide, at his disposal, sixty other people for his private work. He did not give up on his plans to destroy the Jewish quarter and build instead an exemplary new city. He employed a young and skillful Jewish architect by the name of Lentz. He worked for the *Kreishauptmann* and prepared, under his command, prepared all the plans for the new city.

It was not easy to find people, in those days, who were ready to work in just a job. First, because it was hard physical work without appropriate tools. However, the main reason was the danger of being caught working at the general work camp. For the people who worked under the watch of *Zonderdinst*, there was no opportunity to get away or escape when the Gestapo appeared. The *Judenrat* searched for ways to convince the *Kreishauptmann* [to abandon his plan]. They gave him gifts, and that helped temporarily to postpone the order.

[Page 287]

At the beginning of February, the *Kreishauptmann* warned the *Judenrat* that if they did not complete the work – the destruction of the houses [in the Jewish quarter] – by the end of the month, he would hand the matter to the Gestapo and the *Judenrat* would bear the responsibility for that. Under the threat of a pogrom, the women of our city, with some older men, organized and completed the work! They worked every day, from morning until the evening. The children also helped them in that work. I do not know where the women got so much strength to withstand all the troubles and these works.

They finished the work on time, but the demands of the *Kreishauptmann* and the troubles caused by the Gestapo did not cease. Before they had the time to breathe a sigh of relief upon completing the destruction work, a new notice came from the Employment Bureau about a new registration of all the men at the Bureau. Our experienced people guessed ahead of time the intention of the Germans, and nobody appeared at the Bureau. The result, like in previous occurrences - a hunt of our people, threats toward the *Judenrat*, searches by the Jewish militia, and transporting the required number of people by the Gestapo to the labor camps.

Preparations for the "Final Solution" - Spring 1942

by Dr. Eliezer Shaklai

Translated by Moshe Kutten

Edited by Jane S. Gabin

It was the days of the end of February and the beginning of March. The weather was appropriate for that period of the year – rainy and sometimes snowing. Outside, mud combined with the snow, and inside the homes was cold and musty. Our situation has gone from bad to worse. Changes came with the coming of Spring, which, in the beginning, we did not know what they meant. They were severe and very dangerous. Only later on, we became aware that the purpose of every change was to accelerate the extermination of the Jews as fast as possible. It was the period when Hitler, damn him, and his entourage decided on the "Final Solution" – meaning the total extermination of all the Jews in the area under the Nazis' rule, without any exception.

People were nominated to realize that goal with complete authority to create the conditions and the means for total and complete extermination at a maximum speed. These people performed their work vigorously in complete secrecy and according to detailed plans. Among them were scientists, professors, engineers, physicians, and a large staff of workers. According to these plans, extermination camps were created, which, from the outside, looked like labor camps. Inside the camps were gas chambers for mass killing and crematoria to burn the many bodies.

The Nazis divided the areas under their rule into regions and established a dedicated extermination camp for each region. They brought the victims to these camps according to an accurate plan on predetermined dates based on detailed lists. The lists were prepared in advance and contained the number of Jews slated for extermination, which was performed daily. They brought them to the camps in trains, where the Jews underwent a selection and sorting (death or work). That operation was called "*Auszidlung*" – meaning "uprooting" - uprooting people from their place of residence and exterminating them. Every place where the Jews were liquidated was called "*Judenrein*," meaning "cleansed of Jews," and Jews would never step in that area.

[Page 288]

The Germans began those extermination operations in the west and expanded them quickly to areas in the east. Every region had its own plan, and the Gestapo people were responsible for realizing them. In this way, the lengthy fight between the German civil authorities and the Gestapo about the rule over the Jews was decided. The Gestapo had the upper hand. From that point on, any decision or execution was in the hands of the Gestapo. On the other hand, the civil authorities did not want to give up easily, on the treatment of the Jews, so also, we received orders from them, and we paid ransoms to both sides.

The load was too heavy. All the hopes for a quick ending of the war and changes in our favor did not materialize. The Germans prepared for the renewal of the battles on all fronts. For that purpose, they took care to fix the roads and railroads and maintain them in good condition for transports of army, supply, and heavy equipment going east – to the fronts. The people at the labor camps, responsible for maintaining the roads and the railroads during the year, were then assigned double the work. During the spring, the demands to recruit Jews grew enormously, and the Germans enacted new quotas and additional people. From his side, the *Kreishauptmann* increased his demands, and he published new orders daily and sent them to the *Judenrat*. He used to give the Jews all sorts of worthless permits, as they did not have the signature of the Gestapo. However, the Jews did not have a choice – follow the impossible orders and shut up – or pay the Gestapo for their signature by the signature of the *Kreishauptmann*. That created a situation where any certificate or permit became valid only when both sides signed.

Every one of these authorities had its own liaison. The liaison for the *Kreishauptmann* was the *Judenrat*, with Dr. Klarer and his deputy, Ross. They were the ones to receive the orders and the ones responsible for the execution. Although they did not always fulfill his requests, he never forgot and never gave up. He warned them again and again that he would take revenge on them. And he did!

Reorganization of the *Judenrat*

by Dr. Eliezer Shaklai

Translated by Moshe Kutten

Edited by Jane S. Gabin

During the same period, the tailor Bertzio Feld, the son of Meir, who produced clothes and uniforms for Krieger, the Kreishauptmann deputy, came to see me. He told me that the Kreishauptmann was not satisfied with the *Judenrat*, and it could turn against us. He claimed that the Germans intended to reorganize the *Judenrat* and nominate new people - "more disciplined" and "more responsible"! In other words, instill new life with more powerful and vigorous people. On that occasion, he asked me whether I would be willing to join the new *Judenrat* when established.

I understood from him that he took the role of reorganizating the *Judenrat* upon himslef. My answer was unequivocally negative. I explained to him that I was very busy with my work and that, as a physician, I bore a lot of responsibility. I also told him that he could not count on me because I did not fit the role. People like myself would not be useful for the *Judenrat*. On that occasion, I tried to explain to him the importance and responsibility of the role. I tried to convince him not to accept it and leave it for another person. I suggested that, despite the honor associated with it, I remain a simple tailor. I described to him the many difficulties

[Page 289]

he would face on his way, the challenging problems that did not have solutions, the huge responsibility well above his ability, and the dangers associated with that role – for him and the public!

My talk did not help, and eight days after our conversation, the changes came.

The Germans reduced the size of the *Judenrat* from twenty-four people to twelve. Dr. Klarer remained the *Obmann*. His deputy was Feld, and Ross was his associate. They added nine more people, most of whom came from the old *Judenrat*. From that time on, Feld became the driving force at the new *Judenrat* – until his demise.

Feld was a talented person who knew the German language sufficiently. He was a proud man, an honor seeker with great ambitions who did not know his place and behaved like the leader and dictator within the *Judenrat*. When Feld accepted the role, he had good intentions. He undoubtedly wished to help our people – as much as possible in those days, without breaking down while facing challenging problems. However, Feld was not the right person for the role! Indeed, he did not last long and failed! He was pushed aside slowly by the contact people with the Gestapo, who wanted to demonstrate their power and the importance of the Gestapo against the rule of the civil authorities.

Feld reorganized the Jewish militia. He nominated Betinger as the commander with three deputies (I need to comment here that it was Betinger who arrested Feld one day, long before the liquidation of the ghetto, and handed him to the Gestapo by their order). Except for Betinger, Feld nominated a few new loyal people to enforce his role and his power. People at the *Judenrat* feared and flattered him.

During those difficult days, I once entered the *Judenrat* (when the entrance was totally forbidden) since I had permission to enter that institution at any time and under any circumstances. I saw a big party there in honor of Mr. Feld! They celebrated his birthday. When I saw that, I could not stop myself and said to the people there while my eyes directed at Feld, "Are these your gods, Israel [Exodus 32:4]? Woe to you Jews who dance around the golden calf! Jewish blood is spilled in the streets, a fiery flame destroys the whole community, and at the same time, you are sitting down, eating and drinking, and celebrating without thinking that the flame will reach you soon!"

He never forgot these words I said and had a grudge against me until the end of his term as the deputy commander in the *Judenrat*.

The Gestapo had their own contact people. They wanted no deal with the *Judenrat* and selected individuals from the *Judenrat* or from the outside to serve as contact people between them and the Jews. Only these people had access to the Gestapo. All big, small, community-wide, or private matters were arranged through them. Our contact person was Benyamin Mitelman. Over time, the Gestapo added a second contact person, and his name was Safir. He came to reside in our city from Ternopil during Soviet rule because he had a note on his ID that prevented him from residing in a district city. He remained in Brzezany even after the Soviets retreated.

[The following sentence was assumed as the test in the original text is lacking] He worked at the hospital as a disinfector (nepotism of Dr. Levrovski).

In one of the evenings, we sat down over a cup of tea in my room at the hospital. In that discussion, Safir confessed to me that he had a good friend in Ternopil who served as the contact person there between the Gestapo and the Jews. That friend suggested that he become the contact person in our city. He proposed that it would help him, strengthen his position, and allow him to help others.

[Page 290]

As known, it was possible to accomplish a great deal with the Gestapo for money. We conversed into the night, and I presented the problem from all its sides and told him openly my opinion about that connection, which was directed only one way. In my opinion, we should not have any relation with Satan! It would not be beneficial for him or for the public. It was not good to approach them and be forced to appear before any demand from them and be obligated ahead of time to fulfill all the missions imposed on him and serve them with his eyes closed.

All my explanations did not convince him. The opportunity to earn money and to become a ruler overcame common sense, and he was nominated, a few days later, by the Gestapo to be the second contact person working parallel to Mitelman.

He was an easy-going person with good intentions and a working man who never forgot the financial side of handling the matters before him. He was a good and loyal friend, pleasant, with the will to help others. He was subjected to the influence of Mitelman, a man with a strong character who is sharper and more knowledgeable about things. They worked hand in hand, arranged all the matters, including financial issues, and connected between the Jews and the Gestapo until the end, upon the liquidation of the ghetto. However, when the Gestapo liquidated the ghetto, they also murdered these two people who served them loyally and faithfully for all this time.

Transferring the Jews
from the Villages to the City

by Dr. Eliezer Shaklai

Translated by Moshe Kutten

Edited by Jane S. Gabin

One of the most significant events of that period was the transfer of the Jewish families from the villages to the city. All the Jews who lived in the villages, except those who were there under the auspices of the Gestapo, received an order from the Gestapo to move to the city. Every permit from the Gestapo was valid only for a single month. At that time, the permit holder's family was allowed to be outside of the city, but only at his workplace and during work.

That law hurt the Jews, who always lived in the village, even before the conquest and the decrees. Some tried to secure work permits through lobbyists and remain connected with the villages. All the rest had no choice but to move to the city.

In the city, they faced the problem of housing, and the *Judenrat* was responsible for finding a place for them. The housing conditions were below the lowest minimum. The village's Jewish situation changed overnight from one extreme to another. Until then, they resided among the Jews-haters, Gentiles. They suffered from them, but they lived in their own place, and the hand of the Gestapo did not always reach them. Even when the Gestapo people came to the village, the Jews used to hide outside of the village in the fields, gardens, and forests until the Germans left. In the village, they were free of the troubles associated with the labor camps - one of the critical issues at that time. Also, the livelihood and food situation was better compared to the conditions of the city's Jews. All of that changed for the worse. The Germans decided to concentrate all the Jews in one area so that they could use the time when they needed it without much of an effort.

There was another problem, and it was the major one, which was on the agenda at the time – the ghetto problem. In our district, the Gestapo arranged ghettos in many locations. Our city's turn had arrived.

The Gestapo and the *Kreishauptmann* pressured us

[Page 291]

and wanted to put us in a closed area. The Germans wished to achieve that by the end of March. They searched for a place appropriate according to their goals – a small area that was narrow, stuffy, and without air, which could easily be surrounded and liquidated.

With unified forces, money, and presents, the *Judenrat* and the contact people with the Gestapo managed to delay the execution of that decree for six additional months. It was a big achievement for us, and despite costing a significant amount of money, brought us a big relief. First, we resided in our own apartments. Secondly, we were freer in our movement. We could escape outside the city when needed, meet with the Gentiles in the surroundings, and buy or barter for food.

Another reason for the delay in the establishment of the ghetto was the fact that the Jews were dispersed among the Gentiles. To establish the ghetto somewhere in the suburbs, they would have to move the non-Jewish population to the center to houses that were half ruined. The Gentiles objected to that, and we remained in our own apartments until Yom Kippur.

Two significant events happened to us in March. The first was an attack and kidnapping of people to labor camps. It was an unusual case since the kidnappers were not from our district and did not come during the regular time. They went in trucks to a city in their own district to capture people, and when they could not find any, they continued on their way until they arrived in our town. We found out about those circumstances later on. When they arrived in our city, they spread around without asking the *Kreishauptmann* or at least the *Judenrat*. They attacked every passerby, captured people, and loaded them up onto the trucks. That occurred during the afternoon hours, at a time when we usually did not have any kidnappings. When the people found out, a big panic ensued, and our people ran away to wherever their feet carried them.

The Germans succeeded in kidnapping about forty people, loaded them up on cars, and ran away. Only later on we found out the name of the camp the Germans took our people to. The connection with them totally stopped.

During that operation, I was on the way to a patient near "Novy Reinek." A Ukrainian who approached me hinted to me that I was being followed. Without looking backward, I entered a ruined house and jumped into the cellar with standing water. I hid behind a barrel that floated over the water at the end of the cellar. The Germans chased after me and lit the place with lanterns and spotlights. They shouted: "Get out, damn Jew," and shot a few bullets, but I did not respond. When they could not find me, they did not want to waste more time and took off. After a pause that lasted quite a long time, I again heard shouts and shots fired. I saw somebody falling into the water in the cellar. He was a boy, about fourteen years old, injured in his leg. I jumped toward him and dragged him quickly to my hideout. When the Germans arrived at the cellar opening, we were both already hiding behind the barrel. They shouted, shot, and waited for a response. When they did not hear any, they took off.

When it became dark outside, I got out and climbed onto the street. The neighborhood was quiet and peaceful. When I realized that the *aktsia* was over, I got the wounded boy outside, brought him to the clinic, and dressed his wound. Only then did I return home. They were worried about me at home. They knew that I was not kidnapped but did not understand what happened to me and where I had disappeared.

I told the reader about myself and presented a live picture of what happened in such cases. There were thousands of cases of that kind when the distance between death and life was only a few seconds and a bit of luck.

[The author mentioned two events in March, but only one was described].

[Page 292]

The Period of Passover 1942

by Dr. Eliezer Shaklai

Translated by Moshe Kutten

Edited by Jane S. Gabin

During the first days of April, our situation was so miserable that we forgot to celebrate the Jewish holidays and Shabbat. In the beginning, the Soviet authorities were the reason, and then – the Germans. Some religious Jews, mainly older adults, were devout in their religion. They avoided working on Shabbat and holidays and gathered to pray in private residences since all the synagogues were closed or occupied by refugees. However, most Jews were forced to work on Shabbat and holidays. Those who came to pray were just a few. We could not gather many people into a private apartment. It was dangerous. Those who did gather to pray were in a hurry to finish, just enough to fulfill one's obligation. They were sure that their good intention and the walk to the praying place were sufficient to grant them the fulfillment of the commandment of "praying in public." G-d would be satisfied with just a hint. They dispersed quickly after the prayer, not to raise suspicions. In all of these prayers, the traditional religious atmosphere was lacking.

Despite all of that, two days during the year were etched deep in our hearts. They were Yom Kippur and Passover. Mainly the Passover Eve - the first "*Seder*" of Passover! We did not celebrate these holidays the way we did in the days before the war, but the holiday feelings pulsated within us like during peace times. These two days signified the two most important milestones in the life of every Polish Jew, the transitions from the summer to the winter and from the winter to the summer. Through the generations in the diaspora, Yom Kippur was not just the holiest day for every Jew but also the day of soul searching, a day of thoughts and worries about the future - the approaching winter days. During that period, the days become shorter and colder, and the nights longer and darker. Winter clothes were taken out and started to be worn, windows and doors were closed, and the children did not go out to the street to play but came home directly from school. For many people, that period presented problems in making a living, and it also introduced a fear of diseases, rampant in that season. People lived with expectations for the following spring.

The opposite was during the holiday of Passover. The holiday spirit began as early as several weeks before. It was still cold then and rainy. But people did not pay attention to these obstacles. Everybody was busy preparing for the holiday in an atmosphere of nature renewal and awakening.

That was a family-oriented holiday, customary to celebrate together, and an opportunity for a family gathering. Relatives and acquaintances came for a visit and brought gifts for the children. On Passover Eve 5702 [1942], the holiday spirit was missing. Instead, it was an atmosphere of the evening before an *Aktsia*. We were sure, based on the information we had received, that the Gestapo was preparing a surprise and would arrange its own "*Seder*" for us.

We sat down, each in their own house, with the close family, with those still alive – under locks, bolts, and bars, guarding to avoid surprises. We sat down, reclining, at the table. We supported our heads with two hands, ready, not for a Passover filled with fables, but the reality! There was no wine or Matzas in that Passover, only plenty of troubles and blows. Every home suffered the loss of a family member. Everybody was broken and crushed like we were beaten by the ten plagues of Egypt. There was no blow written in the Torah that did not hit us. Every Jew was depressed. Some pious Jews celebrated the *Seder*, but I doubt they could concentrate.

[Page 293]

We were slaves, and we are slaves. We have not experienced such slavery since we became a nation. We recited - "Pour out his wrath on the other nations" [Passover Haggadah and Jeremiah 10:25] with a feeling of fear, lest new calamities approach. We recited "Next year in Jerusalem," but those words came out with no echo and without the feeling of hope since we were hopeless.

We ended with "*Khasal Sidur Pesakh*" ["The commemoration service of Passover has now been accomplished according to its order"], with the feeling that the evil people were going to liquidate us, and our nation, and the cry burst out of our mouths: "King of the universe! Put an end to the slaughtering."

That was our situation, and that was how we celebrated our holiday - Passover Eve 5702, 1st of April 1942. The eight days of Passover passed without any traumas or other unusual events, despite serious concerns, since Mitelman notified me before Passover that the Gestapo was preparing an *Aktsia*. It was supposed to include people above the age of sixty. I received a notice from the Judenrat circles in Ternopil that the *Aktsia* would take place in the coming days. Similar *Aktsia*s occurred in several locations throughout the district of Ternopil. I had to ensure my father would not be home during the *Aktsia*. The Gestapo planned that *Aktsia* for Passover, so time was short. I told our acquaintances and other people in the neighborhood. I rented a farmer and his wagon for the early morning hours. We woke up at midnight, left the city quietly, and brought my father to the neighboring town – Narajow. About twenty people rode with us. Others went to another city or looked for a hideout within our city. Days passed, and we waited for the *Aktsia*, day after day, and it did not come. Several weeks passed in fear until the Shavuot holiday. I knew that my father was away far from the grandchildren and suffering mentally and even more physically. Therefore, I decided to return my father home. The trip was dangerous since we did not have travel permits. The rest of the city Jews returned with us. Luckily, we did not meet any Germans on the road. My certificate protected me against the Ukrainian militia. To them, I explained that I came to take people sick with typhus. That was how we arrived home.

There were several new decrees in April. The order to transfer the Jews from villages to the city was renewed all the more forcefully, and new people came to live in the city daily after they were expelled from their villages.

During those days, we received the first worrisome news about the state of Western European Jews. The Poles brought them to us. They received them from their acquaintances who came from the West, letters they received from there, and eyewitnesses who tended to these people. According to the news, the Germans uprooted the Jews from their places of residence and transported them on trains to the Lublin district [where the Majdanek concentration camp was located]. [At that point,] it was not clear to us what the purpose of those transfers was. What would these people do in their new places, and how would they make a living? How would tens or hundreds of thousands of Jews survive in such a small place?! We did not get any answers to these questions. Everyone explained the meaning of those facts to themselves according to their character and spirit. Some who wanted to delude themselves believed that the Germans concentrated the Jews in dedicated districts, where they would supposedly enjoy a kind of autonomy or self-rule under the supervision of the Germans. Most of the people did not believe in those assumptions. We waited anxiously for additional information that would clarify the state of our brothers from the West.

The only consolation was that it was still far from us. Besides, we were already in the East, and that matter should not concern us. Nevertheless, talks about that news did not stop, and people continued to collect bits of information about that matter. The news we have received was limited. Eyewitnesses said that the Western Jews were not allowed to take any belongings with them,

[Page 294]

except for some personal items in small packages. They were prevented from carrying even the most needed items. They disappeared after they unloaded from the train, and nobody knew what happened to them. Every connection to these people was lost. There were many guesses and assumptions. That situation bothered us, and we could not let go of the thought that something very serious was happening there.

Hideouts – Bunkers

by Dr. Eliezer Shaklai

Translated by Moshe Kutten

Edited by Jane S. Gabin

The various guesses were worrisome, but in the meantime, our lives continued as usual. Every day brought new problems with it. However, our main problem in those days was the kidnapping of people to labor camps.

People looked for various ways to escape and hide from the searches. They learned from experience that there was no sure means against the kidnapping: no permits, no promises, no permanent job, and even money did not always help. The ransom was sometimes used to release a person who was caught; however, the money was not always helpful because the amount was too high for people to afford it. Therefore, people looked for other ways to escape during the kidnapping. Some ran away outside the city to the fields and forests.

Escapees were in danger of being caught during their escape, or somebody could snitch to win reward money or just due to malice or simply antisemitism. Sometimes, the searches for these people lasted days and nights. Then food became a problem - how and where to bring the food to the escapees without endangering them and how to find where they were hiding. In addition, the escapees did not know whether the Aktsia ended already and whether it was safe to return home. In fact, there were many cases when our people fell into a trap when they returned home, thinking that the Aktsia had already ended. Another way to escape was to hide at the home of a non-Jewish neighbor. That was an expensive way, as a lot of money was needed for the neighbor to hide a Jew. Not every neighbor agreed to have a Jew hiding in his home, and there was always the danger of snitching.

One cheaper and more convenient way remained, although not always safe - building a hideout in the house for one or two people who could hide there during an Aktsia.

In the beginning, that way was effective. The Germans entered the apartment and searched it superficially. If they did not find anybody, they moved to the next apartment. However, with time, the Germans learned to search thoroughly and find the people. It was needed to build a new and better hideout once in a while so that the Germans would not find it easily. It was more dangerous when the Jewish "Ordnungsdinst" joined the searches, who, The bunker had to be strong otherwise it could collapse and bury people alive. over time, learned all the tricks and knew where to find the hideouts. That situation created competition among the hideout builders. People dug out bunkers and improved them from time to time. They often invented better, more efficient, and larger bunkers to accommodate more people for longer periods. Over time, when the number of residents in the house grew, people had to build hideouts for five or even eight people.

The situation changed when we were enclosed within the ghetto and the hideout had to serve all residents and not just men at the age eligible to work. The number of people hiding in these hideouts reached sixty or even a hundred. The bunkers were built as whole structures, mostly underground. These structures were constructed from better materials – stone, bricks, cement, and steel.

[Page 295]

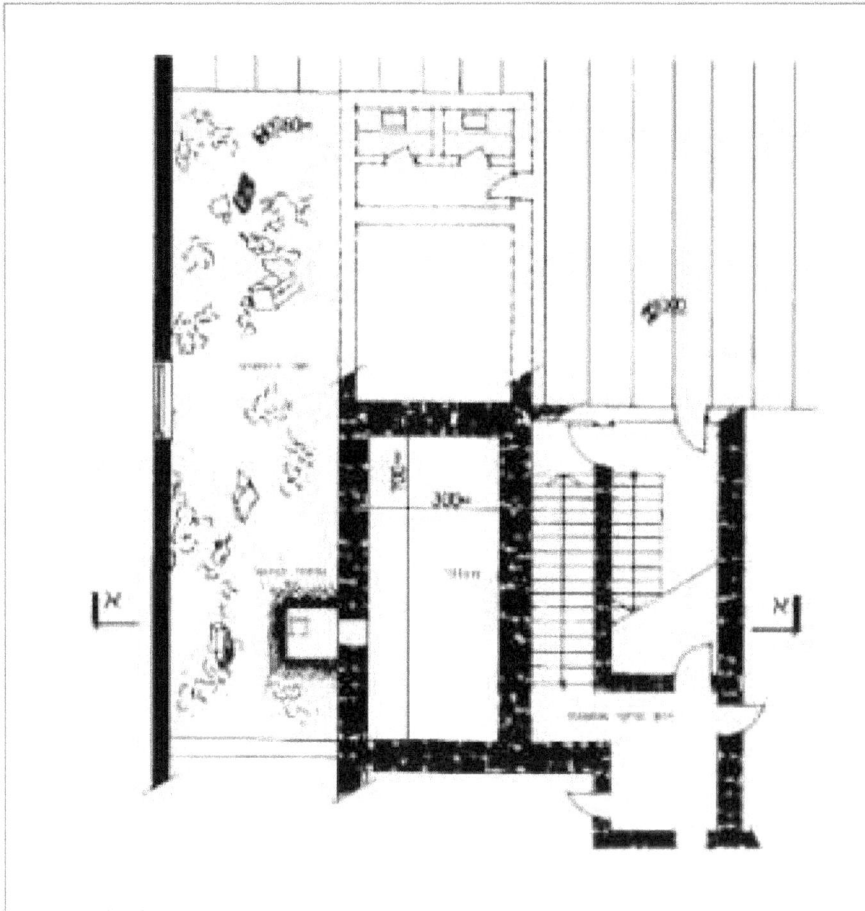

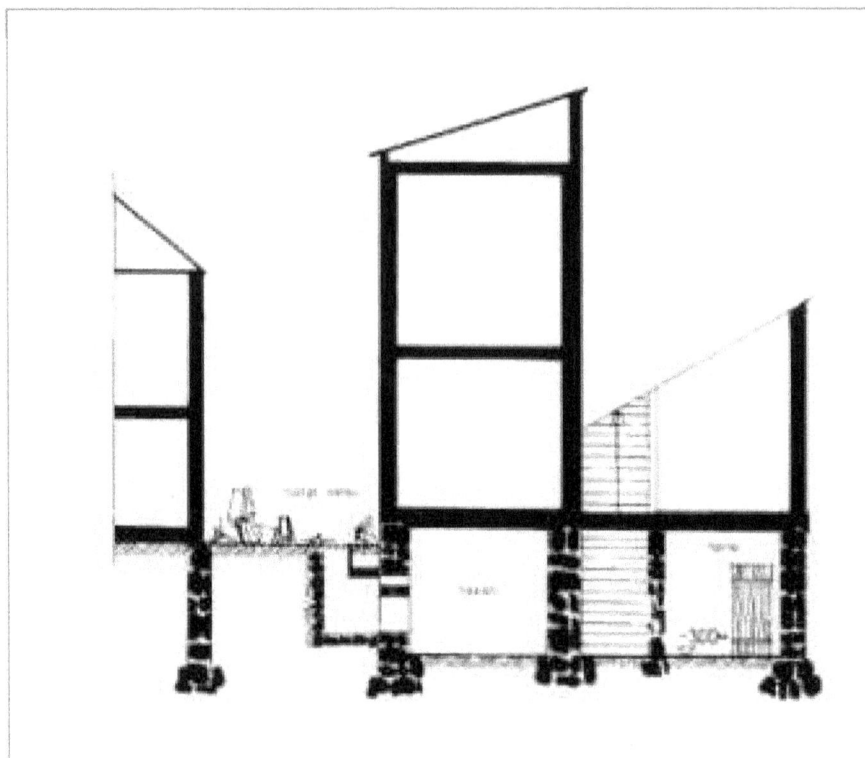

The plan for the bunker at the home of R. Froindlikhon Lvovska Street
where about thirty people were saved on Yom Kippur 1941

[Page 296]

We built the bunkers in complete secrecy and did not share this with anybody outside the house. Every house took care of itself and ensured the matter would not be publicized. It goes without saying that the construction was done at night after a hard workday. Women and children helped by taking the dirt outside the house and bringing in the building materials. We worked quickly and carefully. We hid when needed not to be discovered by the Germans or the Jewish militiamen during the construction. We feared the neighbors, even the Jews. The building of a bunker was almost like creating a masterpiece. Many obstacles had to be overcome, and it had to be done without any help from the outside. The bunker had to be strong; otherwise, it could collapse and bury people alive.

A difficulty we faced was the ventilation problem. We devoted many thoughts to finding a solution for exchanging the air that contained sixty to a hundred souls. We had to do it so nobody, particularly those who conducted searches, would find the openings. Sometimes, we managed to connect to the neighboring house's gutters. And other times to the street sewer.

Another challenging problem was how to hide the entrance to the bunker. The opening had to be as small as possible; however, it had to allow for quick entering and exiting when needed. It had to allow for a quick closing to evade the enemy and cover our tracks leading to the banker.

The bunkers were mainly built in the houses' cellars. They constructed the wall from stones, similar to other walls. It closed a significant portion of the cellar so that people would not notice the change and would not discern that the wall was a new construction. The entrance to that portion of the cellar was done by moving one stone. People who entered the cellar would shift the stone back with such accuracy that nobody could notice it. A dedicated mechanism was installed to allow locking from the inside. Sometimes, people constructed the entrance to the bunker from the kitchen, under the cooktop, which stood on small wheels.

When everybody entered the bunker, the cooktop was returned to its position, and the entrance was locked from the inside with the help of an iron rod. Nobody noticed any changes in the range that stood solidly in its place.

The walls in some houses reached eighty centimeters (about 31.5 inches). An entrance tunnel into the bunker was constructed through such a wall. A window lintel that could be moved from the inside served as the opening. When people entered the bunker through the tunnel, the lintel was returned to its place and closed from the inside. Nobody knew how and where the people disappeared. It was as if they were swallowed by the wall.

Sometimes, people built a bunker in one of the apartment's rooms, particularly in a windowless room in the middle. They plugged the entrance door with a plastered wall and painted the entire apartment. The entrance to the room was through the ceiling. All the tracks were covered by a volunteer who specialized in that work. The ventilation was achieved through a pipe inside the wall, which was connected to the chimney. Quiet inside that room was paramount, as every touch on the wall could transmit the noise, and that was enough for the Germans to find the bunker.

Some people established the bunker in a ruined house a short distance from the apartment. The entrance to the bunker was through an underground tunnel. Some people also constructed a bunker between two roofs. Another design was to build a double ceiling and leave space between the ceiling and the roof. The entry to that bunker was through the room below it. In such a room, people built a closet with a moving lintel that covered the entrance. People also built bunkers in the bathrooms. These bunkers were convenient, but the Germans found out, and that design was abandoned.

[Page 297]

In Polish small towns, the toilets were outhouses. It was a large hole in the ground, and above it - a wooden structure. A wooden seat – a board with a hole in it, was positioned above a hole in the ground. People dug another hole that closed from above. The entrance to that hole was from the first hole using a ladder. After the people entered the hole, the seat board was placed in its place and secured from the inside, and the ladder was removed. People sat quietly in the hole. Sometimes, one of the Germans or more came into the outhouse and did their business when people were inside. As long as they had not been discovered and survived, they tolerated it.

Over time, people learned to build two bunkers. People entered one to hide, and the other was left open to deceive the Germans. When Germans found the opened bunker, they thought that the people had already been taken away, and they would move to search in another place. In the beginning, that method was effective; however, over time, the Germans learned our tricks and searched in apartments where an open bunker was found.

In many locations, one of the residents volunteered to stay outside to watch. He would camouflage the entrance and cover all the tracks leading to the bunker. He would then hide in a small bunker or escape outside the city. If he had the misfortune of falling into the hands of the Germans, he would not disclose the location of the bunker and become a martyr by saving others.

There were some other types of hideouts; I would not be able to describe them all. The reality in those days taught us that a good bunker is one of the most crucial and safe means of survival. The main goal was to gain some time with the hope that time would cure whatever wasn't achieved by the brain. We devoted most of our time and strength to constructing the bunker and hoped it would save us.

At first, we used small bunkers to escape and hide during searches for the labor camps. These bunkers were comfortable and cheap, and there was no need to run to them through streets and alleys. The men who hid in them did not depend on others and did not fear snitching. When an alarm was sounded by the watch person or movement was detected in the street, it was possible to quickly hide without being caught.

We did not have an easy time with the rest of our daily life problems either. The difficulties in finding food worsened during April-May, and hunger increased. Finding some grains or potatoes was as hard as the parting of the Red Sea. The villagers demanded a fortune for just a limited amount of grain. When somebody managed to buy some grain seeds, he would roast them on the cooktop and grind them with a manual coffee grinder. People made pita bread from the flour, and everyone in the family received a single pita. Under these conditions, people were willing

[Page 298]

give a tithe to the poor or donate to the needy, who died slowly from hunger. Epidemics spread because the people were weakened by hunger and could not battle the diseases.

In June, a rumor spread that the Germans disconnected the *Judenrat*telephone line. That was our only way of communication with the neighboring areas and the district. Encoded messages were transferred from town to town in our district through that connection. With that connection, we warned each other about approaching danger from the Germans through news collected by the various *Judenrats*. The disconnection brought panic over the city. People gave that news different explanations. The optimists interpreted it leniently, and the pessimists with severity, meaning new harsh decrees were about to occur.

Indeed, on one occasion we all knew that the Germans were preparing a decisive act, and everybody prepared for what was to come. Some left the city or hid in the homes of non-Jewish neighbors. Others relied on their hideout and hid, waiting to see what the next day would bring. Two or three quiet days and people calmed down. People began to slowly return home, waited until midnight, and then lay down to sleep for a few hours, and so passed another two days. On the fifth night, when people just fell asleep, at around one or two o'clock after midnight, the sleeping people suddenly were awakened by shouts and noises of breaking into apartments through broken doors and windows. That was an onslaught by the Germans, assisted by the Ukrainian militia. It turned out that the attackers came in quietly and waited until everybody calmed down and fell asleep. When they received the order, they fanned out around the entire city, broke suddenly into Jewish apartments, and caught the people in their beds before they had the chance to recover and find a hideout.

In apartments where the Germans did not find men in the first search, they returned and searched again. When they did not find men again, they poured wrath on anything that stood in their way; on the children, women, furniture, and housewares. They broke, threw outside, and destroyed anything that fell into their hands. They yelled at and beat women, children, and old people with no exception. They left in the morning, taking with them the people caught during the night.

During the operation, the Germans held the people who were caught in the prison. They loaded them up on cars in the morning and left the city. The Germans did let the women and children approach the prisoners to say goodbye or bring them some clothes and food. They hit the women and children and expelled them from there. Hermann himself commanded that operation to teach the *Judenrat* and the Jew a lesson about what was waiting for them when they did not obey his orders.

Associated with these operations, the Gestapo reaffirmed an old decree – Mitelman and Safir received an order from the Gestapo to prepare a new list of all the city's Jews ages 14 and up. All the certificates issued until then were canceled. Without a new certificate, nobody can secure a job, whether regular or temporary.

We were familiar with these decrees for a long time and were not in a hurry to get the new certificates. However, when the German [Employment] Bureau terminated all Jewish jobs, people who had regular or important jobs did not have a choice but to turn to the contact people, pay handsomely, and receive new certificates. That story is not new to the reader. It was not new to the Germans and to us, the Jews. The Germans repeated the decree often to squeeze the money from the Jewish pocket and to keep us under constant stress.

[Page 299]

Women Leave for the Jagielnica Camp

by Dr. Eliezer Shaklai

Translated by Moshe Kutten

Edited by Jane S. Gabin

I have already mentioned our women. The burden of the housework was placed on their shoulders. In addition, they participated in all sorts of physical works. Some of the young women worked in cleaning houses and government offices. Others served as cooks in German kitchens or worked in temporary jobs. They were assigned by the *Judenrat* based on the demands of German or Ukrainian authorities. The women were notified through the Jewish militia when and where they had to appear for work, and they came with the tools needed for the specific job as long as there were no life-threatening consequences. The women worked for free. There were no wages associated with the work.

On one of the days of July, the *Judenrat* notified single women under the age of 35 to appear at a specific place at an early morning hour. About sixty young women came with their tools as usual. Without suspecting anything, they sat down on the ruins of the adjacent houses and waited in good faith for instructions. About an hour later, the people of the Jewish militia came, ordered them to leave the rugs and the tools, and took them to one of the apartments. They entered the apartment without fear or suspicion, but to their surprise, when everyone was inside, the militia surrounded the house, closed the windows and locked the doors, and notified them that they would be taken for agricultural work outside of the city. Panic ensued, accompanied by shouts and cries, but nothing helped. One or two women managed to escape by jumping from a window on the second floor (one of these women reached Israel). All others were loaded on trucks and brought over to [a forced labor camp near] Jagielnitsa, in the district of Chortkiv. They worked in collecting sugar beets. They remained in the camp until the fall and were freed. However, they had to wait for transportation to go back home. The transportation was late arriving. They were caught in an *Aktsia* and sent along with the rest of the people to the extermination camp.

Aktsia for Converted Jews

by Dr. Eliezer Shaklai

Translated by Moshe Kutten

Edited by Jane S. Gabin

At the end of July, Hermann suddenly appeared, accompanied by several Gestapo people. We sensed that they came for an important mission, to prepare or execute an *Aktsia*. Indeed, we were not mistaken. They stayed in the city for several days. Our people looked for ways to get out of the city or wait in their hideouts to see what would happen. At that time, the *Aktsia* was directed at converted Jews and Christians whose parents, up to the third generation, were Jews. There were about 20 such people in our area. The Germans caught them and brought them to Ternopil, where they were exterminated along with other "semi-Jews" like them. These people lived a calm life until then and considered the extermination of the Jews as a natural phenomenon that did not concern them. However, their time came, and they, too, fell victim to Nazism.

[Page 300]

Alternatives to Hideouts

by Dr. Eliezer Shaklai

Translated by Moshe Kutten

Edited by Jane S. Gabin

By that time, we had already received reliable news about what was happening to Western European Jews in the Lublin area. An extermination camp [Majdanek] existed there. Jews from all corners of Western Europe were brought to the camp where they were stripped naked, everything was taken from them, including clothes, and they were led directly to the gas chambers! The corpses were taken over to crematoriums to be burned. However, the Germans made soap from the fattish parts of the bodies and the ashes – organic chemical fertilizer. We knew the whole truth then!

We knew that the Germans decided to exterminate the Jews in all ways possible and as fast as possible. Everybody knew from that point on a death sentence was waiting for them. It was only a question of time. Only a miracle could save us from their hands.

There was only one goal then – gaining time!

After all, it was unbelievable and incomprehensible that the wide world would find out about these atrocities and remain silent! We believed there would be a response and that we should not lose hope. We needed to try all means, and salvation would come – hide, escape, and do anything to gain time! That was the need of the hour!

There were several methods of hiding from the Germans. I have already written about some of them and will mention some additional ones here. For us, it was a question of life and death.

It was possible to cross the border to Hungary. Compared to other European countries, the situation of the Hungarian Jews was good. In the beginning, some Jews who lived close to the Hungarian border managed to cross the border with the help of non-Jewish guides. However, over time, that crossing became dangerous. Gentiles in the area provided the Gestapo with information about the smuggling of Jews, and the border became more closed because of the stricter guarding. A short while later, the area's Gentiles organized themselves and conducted attacks on the smugglers, and they smuggled and robbed their belongings and clothing. In many cases, the guide himself was the snitch, and he and some of his friends were the murderers. Over time, that way ceased to be practical.

For us, there was another difficulty – we were far from the Hungarian border. We had discussed considerably about that way of saving ourselves considerably. Five young men went out to do so and were killed by the murderers. Among these young men were the two sons of the Fenster family.

Another way was to acquire a fake Aryan identification certificate and move to a new location using these papers in a place where nobody would recognize them. It was not an easy way since it was not sufficient to hold Aryan papers as one had to look as such and it also required a substantial knowledge of the Gentiles' customs. One had to follow the Christian religious rules, and even a single misstep could endanger the carrier of such papers and bring about a disaster. The Gentiles considered every person who came to live in a new area as Jewish people looking to save themselves, and many snitched on these people for money. People also snitched without any compensation and handed these people to the Gestapo. For men, that way was more dangerous because of the identification mark etched on their bodies. Many tried their luck this way, particularly women and children, and some succeeded.

Another way was finding a permanent shelter with Gentiles. Many tried that way, but only a few survived. Most fell victim to snitches by a neighbor or acquaintance of the homeowner. These snitches provided information to the Gestapo,

[Page 301]

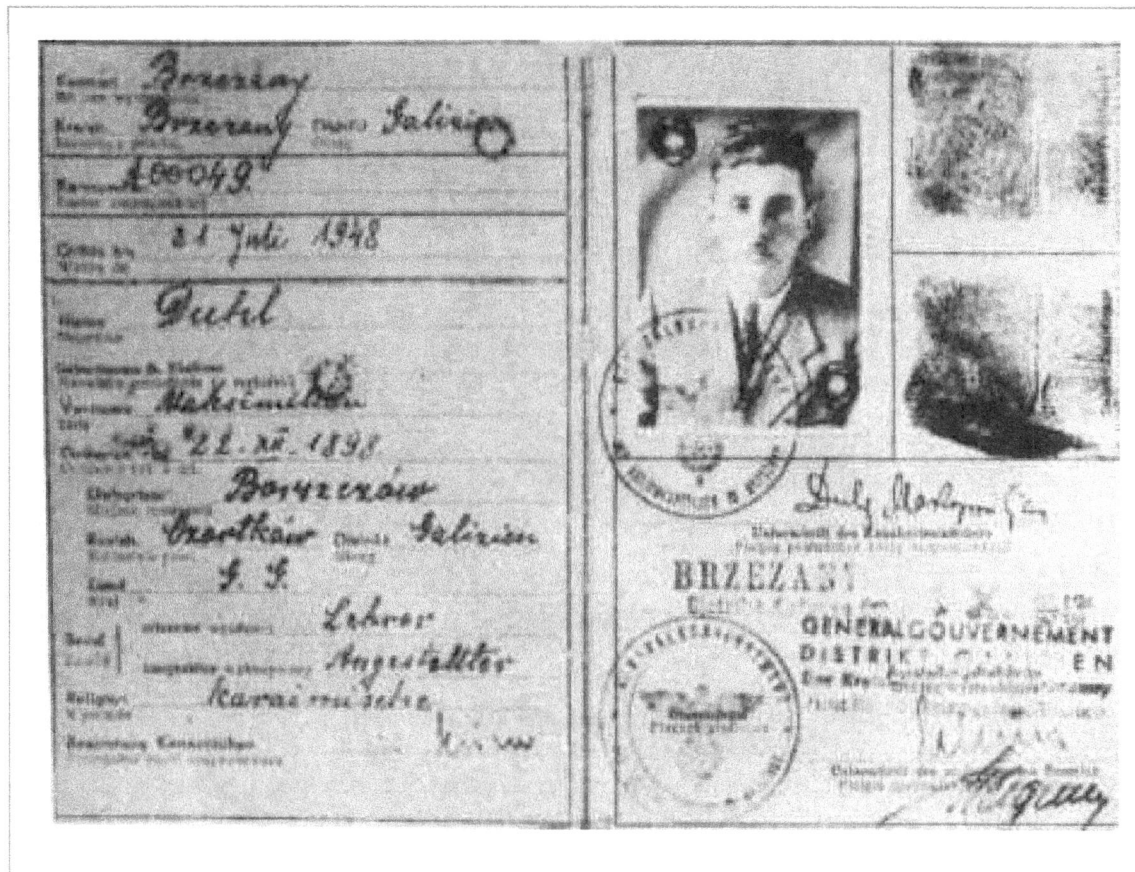

An identification certificate of M. Duhl, a Jew who lived in Brzezany under the disguise of a Karai

Which "handled" the homeowner and the Jews who hid in his home. In many cases, the Gentile person expelled the Jews from his home after he took all their money or handed them over to the Gestapo to receive the prize money for his act. In some other cases, the gentile murdered the Jews who hid in his house with his own hands and buried them outside the village.

In summary, only a tiny portion of those who hid in the Gentiles for money survived. Some Gentiles saved Jews and helped them with devotion, not to receive any compensation. These Gentiles were the "Righteous Among the Nations."

The simplest method, but not necessarily the best one because it was just a temporary solution, was to build a good hideout and receive food from a non-Jew acquaintance. Even if that possibility existed, it cost a tremendous amount of money because it was not easy to find a person who was willing to provide food. There was also the danger of snitching by the neighbors during the construction of the hideout. That danger grew after the "*Judenfrei*" [designation of an area as "cleansed" of Jews] when the Germans [and other] people in the area or gangs of hooligans watched and placed ambushes to catch the Jew on his way to receive the food from the supplier.

Our people tried their luck in many ways to gain time. Perhaps a miracle would happen. A miracle came to other nations, just not to the Jews. When salvation arrived, it was too late for us!

The News About Belzec

by Dr. Eliezer Shaklai

Translated by Moshe Kutten

Edited by Jane S. Gabin

At the end of Av or the beginning of Elul (August 1942), Poles brought sensational news from Lviv on what was happening there. The Gestapo surrounded the ghetto a few days earlier and, with the assistance of the Ukrainian militia and the "*Volksdeutsches*," went from one apartment to another and conducted searches. Those who were caught were brought to the train station. Those who resisted the elderly, sick, and the weak who could not board the train were killed on the spot by shooting. There was no home where they did not search, and nobody managed to escape. They filled up the train cars during the entire day. They closed the train cars in the evening, sealed them, and transported them directly to Belzec.

During a period of two weeks, thirty-five thousand people were caught and transported from Lviv to Belzec. Nobody from these people survived.

[Page 301]

Belzec! It was no longer just another small town in Eastern Poland. Belzec became a new concept, symbolizing mass killing – an extermination camp – a place etched in Jewish history in large letters of pure Jewish blood. That name passed from mouth to mouth as the symbol of death, killing, and extermination!

So, we, the Jews of Eastern Poland, had our own extermination camp - a killing factory where work was performed according to a detailed plan: an *Aktsia* that meant gathering the Jews in a collection place, with a train waiting at the train station – transporting the Jews, filling up the train cars, closing and sealing the cars – the train was leaving, and it would speed up and arrive at the camp, where the people would be unloaded, they beaten, stripped naked – and led directly to the gas chambers. Their bodies would be burnt, and before this would be finished their work, a new transport would arrive! People and machines didn't rest even for a moment. They gathered the raw human material and led it to the allocated location. G-d forbid to be late. Everything progressed according to the plan prepared ahead of time. Every city has an exact date. On that date, the number of people was set. The team worked accurately under the supervision of the Gestapo.

When we learned about what happened in Lviv, our contact people, Mitelman and Safir, traveled to the district city to search for true and credible information. They returned and validated the news with some additional information. There was only one consolation – the event that happened in Lviv happened, until then, only in big cities. They claimed that, for that moment, we did not need to fear. The Germans always try to numb our alertness; however, in the meantime, we heard about similar *Aktsias* in our district. From that, we understood and were sure that our turn would come. We did not know when it would happen but knew well that it was only a matter of time, perhaps only days! Every one of us knew what to expect. Deep in everyone's heart remained that spark of hope - the same hope that sustained us in our diaspora for two thousand years and gave us the strength to hold on during those days in all situations.

We continued to build bunkers and hideouts more vigorously, contacted Gentile acquaintances, searched for ways to escape when needed, and our contact people collected money to bribe the Gestapo people to postpone the death sentence as much as possible. The days passed quickly, and there was no day without an *Aktsia* in the neighboring cities or towns.

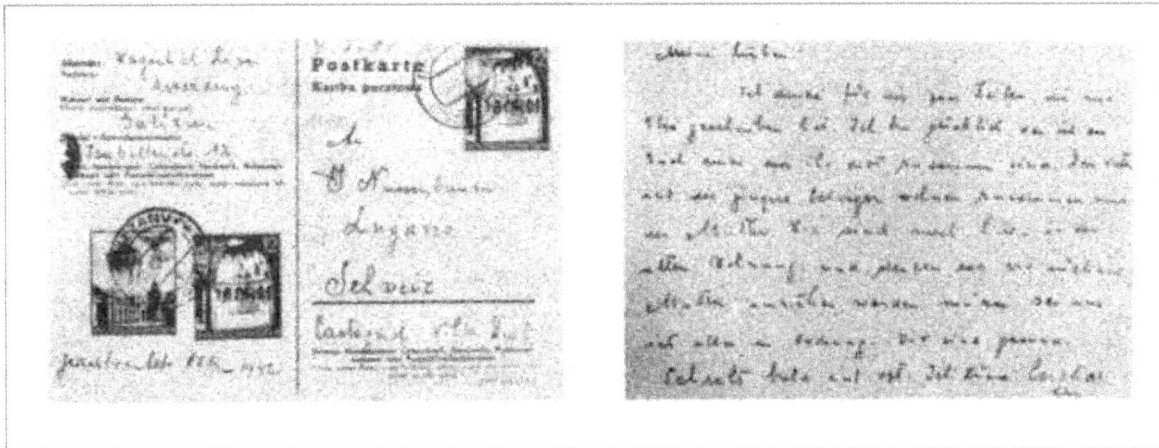

A postcard, sent by Dr. Shaklai to relatives in Switzerland with the news that the father and brother-in-law lived with the mother and that the rest of the family members were thinking about moving to live with the mother.
The postcard was sent at a time when the family in Switzerland knew that the mother was dead.

[Page 303]

The Days of Awe

by Dr. Eliezer Shaklai

Translated by Moshe Kutten

Edited by Jane S. Gabin

The Rosh HaShana [Jewish New Year] approached, and we knew well that a Jewish holiday is a date the Germans marked for an exceptional operation against the Jews. Yom Kippur came after the New Year, and we have not forgotten what happened on that holiday last year. And who knew what this year's Yom Kippur bring?

The *Aktsias* against the Jews during the Days of Awe were particularly cruel, and our turn was approaching. After Rosh HaShana passed without an *Aktsia*, our contact people decided to try their luck, once again, with the Gestapo, who were seemingly somewhat candid. Our people brought some appropriate gifts for that visit, whose purpose was to find out what was expected in that approaching holy day of Yom Kippur, and try to postpone the *Aktsia* until after the high holidays to gain time and give us the possibility to prepare for a passive struggle, find an efficient hideout, finalize the preparations in the bunkers, and simply live one additional day - maybe several days and maybe…

Yom Kippur of 5703 [1942]

by Dr. Eliezer Shaklai

Translated by Moshe Kutten

Edited by Jane S. Gabin

Our contact people returned with good news. I waited for them and talked to them. They were both satisfied and were sure they succeeded in their mission. The Gestapo people promised them, with their word of honor, that Yom Kippur would be a quiet day. That news calmed us down, and we allowed the solemn atmosphere of the holy holiday evening to envelop us. We decided to gather and pray in public, like in the previous year; however, we made arrangements not to be surprised, despite the promises of the Gestapo, since for them, promises are one thing, and an operation is another.

The pious people prayed the Yom Kippur's Minkha [afternoon] prayer, each one in their own home. (We met in public only for the "*Kol Nidrei*" ["All Vows"] prayer, which took place in one of the homes). We also arranged for it in our apartment. Many changes occurred during last year. Many people who participated with us in praying a year ago were no longer alive, among them my father Z" L. Those who came were also people who did not belong in this world. Everyone was holding a death sentence. Everyone had a single request from the "Master of the World" – "tear down our death sentence." About eighty people gathered in our apartment. We took a shower and changed clothes – and the holiday atmosphere enveloped us from the beginning of the gathering through the entire prayer.

That atmosphere fell upon us suddenly, as a "*Neshamah Yeterah*" ["Additional Soul"][1] penetrated us despite all the troubles, which did not ease. I felt the change in everyone's faces, in the way they looked and talked, in their wishes for the holidays, and in the quiet we met each other. We lighted the memorial candles, closed the windows and doors, opened the holy ark that held the Torah scroll, and opened with the words: "According to the opinion of G-d and the opinion of the public, ..."[2] and proceeded with the "*Kol Nidrei*" prayer.

[Page 304]

How different was the prayer at that time from all the previous prayers on the eve of Yom Kippur, even those from last year? Last year, we prayed with fear about what the following day would bring. Filled with hope for survival and life, we cried to the Master of the Universe: "Forgive us, reprieve us!"

That time, the prayer was different. It was a prayer that the soul required and the hour demanded. It was not just a regular prayer but a conversation with the Creator – perhaps he would be willing to entertain it. A bitter denunciation of the big and cruel free world was in that conversation. In that prayer of Job, we asserted our rightful claims against G-d and man, like an accusation of the last moment before extermination, before the execution of the death penalty – a confession aimed at removing everything that weighs on the heart, like the confession of a person in his last moments of his life, about to break free from the shackles of this world.

Everyone chanted their prayer by whispering quietly. One person cried, another just murmured by moving his lips, and others were immersed in their thoughts, far from the world's reality. In my life, I saw these moments of faith and sanctity in human life only once - on that eve of Yom Kippur during the prayer! The memorial candles were lit in the corner. We lighted them for ourselves and not for those who lost their lives because that day was no longer the day when the fate of a person was being decided since we stood there after the death sentence had already been given. In our prayer, we prepared ourselves for the big moment when the murderers would execute our sentence. However, everyone had that spark of hope in their heart, like a feeling that there was still hope as long you still have a soul.

We continued our prayer slowly. Each one had so much to say that we could have continued to pray until the light came in the morning. We would have continued if not for the warnings by the guards that we had to finish and disperse immediately, everyone to their own home, close to their hideout. We set the *Shakharit* [morning prayer] to begin at the crack of dawn so that we could finish it in the early hour of the morning and begin the Musaf[3] at 3 o'clock in the afternoon.

Most people left the apartment, and only some family members stayed behind (my wife and son stayed in a village at that time). We sat, each person in their own corner, immersed in our thoughts. We did not talk to each other. At one point, we all fell asleep from exhaustion. I also fell asleep and dreamt – or perhaps it was a daydream. In my dream, I saw my parents, although I knew in my dream that they were not alive. That scene remained etched in my heart, and I can see it as a live picture until today. I hear my mother saying: "My son, don't despair, and don't stand in the middle of the road. Try everything, do everything; otherwise, you will be lost!" In my father's eyes, I see the agreement with my mother's words as if to strengthen her words. His eyes are hinting: "I will be with you!"

These words were etched deep in my heart, and I have not disclosed them until today because I was afraid that I would lose them or that they would lose their power. During the most difficult moments throughout the Holocaust, at times of hardship, I thought about them and repeated them in my mind. They indeed helped me to overcome the obstacles I faced. They gave me the strength, courage, and faith to survive the perils I encountered on the way!

The morning had not lit yet, and the people gathered again for the *Shakharit* prayer. Some read Psalms poems all night long. Others sat down lonely and fearful that something unexpected would happen, and they wanted to be ready if… Usually, the German operations began on the third shift of the night. We had already passed that time, and there was no sign of the Germans. We began with the Shakahrit prayer. For most people, that was the last prayer in their life. I did not know why, but that prayer was different from the "*Kol Nidrei*" prayer of last night. We felt tension in people' they seemed restless,

[Page 305]

as if they were waiting for every moment, something crucial in their life. It was quiet outside, the pleasant coolness of a beautiful summer morning. It was one of the beautiful days of a Polish fall. People walked in the streets. The Jews were in a hurry. Those who completed the morning prayer ran home. Others had to go to their regular jobs since the holiday did not allow the Jews to take a break from their regular jobs. Others went outside to seek information.

It was calm in the streets. People did not feel the approaching storm. The time was already seven thirty in the morning, and we were about to finish the morning prayer when my brother-in-law *z"l* opened the door and quietly said, but with fearful and emotional words: "The Gestapo! The Gestapo is in the city!" They surrounded the city from all sides. Quiet descended, for a few seconds, and suddenly somebody shouted: "Belzec!"

That word affected all the people in the room like a bomb. They burst out and disappeared within one moment, leaving the Prayer books and Talitot behind them.

Suddenly the house emptied out and left deserted and sad. There was no prayer, no movement, and no people, only an emptiness and depressing quiet. You can hear your own heavy and restrained breath.

Five people remained in the room – two of my brothers-in-law, my sister-in-law, my sister *z"l*, and I.

Translator's Notes:

1. *Neshamah Yeterah* ("additional soul") is a popular belief that every Jew is given an additional soul from the entrance of each Sabbath until its termination.

2. "According to the opinion of G-d and the opinion of the public… we are allowed to pray with criminals," the words chanted by the prayer leader before the *Kol Nidrei* prayer on Yom Kippur. During the days of the Spanish Inquisition, Jews were forced to convert. Despite the danger, they gathered together in hidden cellars in Yom Kippur to accept the sanctity of the day and ask for mercy for being seen as criminals all year.

3. *Musaf* (Literally – additional) service is recited on Shabbat, major Jewish holidays, and at the beginning of each month.

The First *Aktsia* to Belzec

by Dr. Eliezer Shaklai

Translated by Moshe Kutten

Edited by Jane S. Gabin

As if by instinct, I turn my eyes toward the corner where the memorial candles stand and see that almost all went out because of a gust of wind as the escapees left the door open. I feel a squeeze in my heart, and cold sweat covers me. I consider that a hint. I run to the door and lock it to save whatever is possible to save. I move the cabinet located in the corner of the kitchen, hiding the entrance to the hideout. I lead my brothers-in-law, sister-in-law, and sister into the hideout. I move the cabinet back to its place, arrange the *Talitot* and prayer books, and sit by the window, through which I can see without being seen.

The sudden change and the new situation paralyze my movements. I act like a robot following my own commands. I look outside. I put one leg above the other and one hand into the other, like a closed circle inside my body. I try to freeze all body movements except for shallow breathing and my heartbeats. I do not know how I managed to put myself into that situation.

I sit like that for many hours. I hear the voices but do not respond – I sit like a fossil. Shouts of the Germans could be heard all around, and also children's cries and mothers begging for mercy. I see through the window how the Germans are leading people, beating them, shooting at them, and people falling down to the ground. Other people manage to escape. Disorder and confusion, crying, panic, shouts – all that I see but do not respond to.

All that passes before my eyes like a movie, a thriller. The pictures change fast, but the time stands frozen like me. My room is quiet. Nobody approaches the door. Nobody tries to open the door. The shouts and the shots are around my apartment. They take away everyone from my neighbor's rooms forever. After they leave, the quiet, like the cemetery, prevails in their apartments.

[Page 306]

I stayed in my place [at the window] frozen for many hours, without a movement, a thought, and without the feeling that I exist. I woke up from my frozen position only around midnight when my people in the hideout began to move the cabinet to get out. They thought I was caught early in the morning, and they stayed in the hideout by themselves. They saw shadows and flickering lights coming from the memorial candles and thought the house was on fire.

I jumped from my place at the window, approached the cabinet, and warned them not to come out as the *Aktsia* was still going on. I returned the cabinet to its place and again approached the windows. It was quiet in the street; only a heavy guard marched around, holding flashlights and weapons. I sat down at the window and slowly returned to my former state.

After midnight, I heard knocks at the door. They were quite gentle in the beginning, but when I did not answer, the knocks became stronger and stronger each time. I heard yelling to open the door. I recognized the voice of our house's caretaker. I did not open the door and did not respond to his knocks.

These knocks knocked me off balance. Cold, trembling, and restlessness took hold of me. The night was very long. The hours lasted forever, and I determined that a single hour at night lasted as long as a whole day. The hours passed slowly until the sunrise light penetrated through the window and lit the cold room, which seemed so foreign to me at those moments! My breathing accelerated, and fear sneaked into my heart. The street came alive - shouts, knocks, and shots were heard again like the prior day.

I hear knocking on the door. The caretaker says: There are Jews here! And after that, robust knocks and German shouting: "Open Jew!" The knockings got more robust, and when I did not respond, they broke the lock with an axe and busted the door. The Germans entered while the caretaker stayed outside. There were five Germans, and they were accompanied by a Jewish militiaman, the son of Sender Klarer.

The Germans turned to me and asked in amazement: "How did you get in a closed apartment sealed with a Gestapo stamp? Is it not that this apartment went through a thorough search, and all the Jews were taken out of it?" It was then that it occurred to me the reason why the Germans passed over on the door to my apartment at the same time when they searched all the apartments in my area. One of my patients, a Gestapo person, closed the door purposely and sealed it to save me.

In the meantime, they took me out of the apartment to the corridor, under the supervision of the [Jewish] militiaman, and the Gestapo people themselves searched the apartment and looted everything valuable. Klarer described to me the calamity caused by the Germans in the city. They caught his parents and his sister with her son, among the many others, and there is no way he can release them. There is also no way to escape since the city is hermetically surrounded. They led the people they caught to the city square, where several Judenrat people were already sitting. Many old and sick people were murdered by shooting.

A few minutes later, the Germans finished the search in my apartment. They did not find the hiding people. They took me down to the yard, the first stop on the way to the collection location in the square. At the same moment, two of the Gestapo men, who were treated by me (they put the stamp on my door), approached. They turned to the other Germans and requested to release me because I was a physician who worked in the German Hospital and was treating Germans. Their request did not help me. The Germans did not agree to release me and ordered me to move.

My patient, the Gestapo man, sent me a hint, and I understood what he meant. I quickly jumped and ran behind the wall that led to the staircase. I heard a shout behind me: "Stop!" and the shots, but by then I had already

[Page 307]

reached the staircase where I hid in a primitive hideout. A German passed, running near me, holding a drawn handgun. He shot several times in all directions, looked here and there, did not discover me, and left. I could not stay in that hideout because the caretaker knew the entire house and all the hideouts. Running outside of the house meant a danger of certain death. I also could not leave my relatives alone because the caretaker ambushed them, and they were lost without me. Therefore, I returned to my apartment and sat down in my place [near the window] with my apartment's door that was broken into.

Two hours passed, and the caretaker brought another German squad, among them a Jewish militiaman. When they asked me what I was doing there after the searches, I explained that I was a physician in the German hospital. They caught me when I returned from work and brought me to the collection square. However, Miller himself released me based on the request of the health department. The Jewish militiamen stood out for me and only demanded that I pay ransom money to the Germans. They were satisfied with what I gave them and left.

At noon, the caretaker brought yet another German squad. That time without a Jewish militiaman. They asked me again the same question: "What are you doing here in an apartment that was broken into after the apartment had been searched." I answered the same answer, "I am a physician, etc. … and that Miller released me when I was already in the collection square." One of the Germans, the squad commander, said: "You are telling the truth; open and I did not I was present when Miller released you. Sit down here quietly, and nothing will happen to you." In actuality, the German saw a physician being released in the collection square, but he was mistaken. It was Dr. Feld and not me.

I remained sitting in my place, as I was advised by the German, but the quiet was beyond my reach. The sun rose high, and its rays warmed up the room. It was stifling, but I was cold. I was trembling all over; cold sweat covered my entire body. I did not feel hungry despite the forty-hour fast. I felt like floating in a rubber boat in a stormy sea after my ship had sunk. Black clouds covered the sky, and my eyes were looking for a rescue point. Where would help arrive from?

That situation lasted until 2:30 pm. The caretaker did not give up. That time, he brought a person from the secret police, a Pole from our city. He explained to the policeman exactly where the hideout was and told him that many Jews hid there. The policeman entered, totally ignored me, and began to search. He moved from one room to another and returned to the kitchen (we had two kitchens). He opened the cabinets to find the entrance to the hideout (he knew that the entrance to the bunker was from the kitchen). In his searches that lasted two hours, he passed through the apartment several times and could not find the cabinet and the entrance. I saw tension and nervousness on his face when his friend came running suddenly and called him to go outside. They talked to each other and then disappeared. Through my window, I saw that the rest of the Germans disappeared and understood that the *Aktsia* ended. The truth of the matter was that it did not. The Germans just finished the searches and were mobilizing everybody to transport those who were caught from the collection square to the train station. I used those precious moments to release my people from the hideout, and they escaped from the house to outside the city.

I was left alone and felt relief. The tension that enveloped me for thirty-six hours slowly dissipated, but weakness overtook me. I felt like I did after a long illness when my fever finally dropped. My blood pressure dropped under the minimum. I have not eaten or drank a single drop of water for two days. I sat down and could not rise.

[Page 308]

I was close to a nervous breakdown. The door remained open, and I did not have the strength to stand up and close it. The night was cool, and the fresh air refreshed me a bit. I do not remember how I passed that night. I only recall that my neighbor, the photographer Ya'akov Korn, saw the broken open door, went in, and found me in a state of despair. He took me by force outside of the apartment, closed the door, fixed the lock, and brought me to the city, where he took me to the tavern. I received two large liquor glasses and a bagel. I drank and ate. My strength and alertness slowly returned, and I recuperated.

I stood up and walked out. My first steps took me in the direction of the Judenrat.

Testimonies of Eyewitnesses

by Dr. Eliezer Shaklai

Translated by Moshe Kutten

Edited by Jane S. Gabin

In the previous chapter, I described what I experienced during those forty-eight hours. In this chapter, I will try to detail the *Aktsia* from what I heard from eyewitnesses - from the people who boarded the train cars, jumped, and returned to the city.

Since an hour had passed beyond the time that the Germans used to begin their operations, our people did not suspect anything when they observed military trucks loaded with soldiers traveling to the city square and stopping there. Following these soldiers, the Gestapo came in private cars, and they, too, stopped at the city square. Some curious people approached the scene. The Gestapo got out of the vehicles and gave the soldiers signs, and they dispersed. At that moment, the Jews began to suspect the worst, and they left in a hurry. Some tried to escape outside of the city, others to their own homes, but the escapees did not run far when the Gestapo, who were calm until then, changed their skin and became predators and attacked the people to catch them. Only a few succeeded in escaping, but most of the people were captured by the murderers.

In the meantime, the German soldiers in the trucks managed to surround the city from all sides. Panic ensued within one minute. It was too late to escape by then. Those who had hideouts tried to sneak away and reach them. Others ran around to try to find an opening between the guards. The latter were the first to fall into the hands of the murderers.

The Germans collected everyone in the city square. The Gestapo divided its troops into several squads. Some encircled the city and stood with their weapons drawn, ready for action. The others dispersed and broke into houses to search for people. Many who were in the middle of praying were still covered with their *Talitot* at the time, as they had not heard about the *Aktsia*. They were caught and brought to the collection location at the city square. In the meantime, an enforcement for the Germans arrived. It was the Ukrainian militia, along with the *Volksdeutsches*, who played a considerable role in the searches. The Germans also demanded that the *Judenrat* and the Jewish militia make themselves available to them.

During the *Aktsia's* first hours, they effortlessly caught the Jews. Many were caught when they were praying, and they were led to the city square. The Jews walked calmly and proudly, with their heads held high, while they muttered

[Page 309]

their prayers and accepted the verdict from the heavens. After all, one can not escape the will of the Creator.

When they reached the city square, they were ordered to sit down. They were forbidden to stand up or to talk. The punishment for every offense was a murderous beating or a shot. Following the men, the Germans led the mothers with their children to the city square. The children cried, and the mothers asked for mercy, but to no avail. The Germans pulled, pushed, and beat them without mercy until the mothers and children were brought to the collection location. They, too, sat down, murmuring the day's prayer with choking voices, tears, and groans. The mothers complained to the Master of the Universe: "Why?!" They pled: "Help the little children, for you if not for us."

The city square was filling up slowly. People were still being brought in, but less and less every time. At that stage, there were pauses in dragging people to the city square. The operation commander, Miller himself, the Gestapo commander of the entire district, was getting irritated. He ordered the *Judenrat* and the Jewish militia to participate in the operation against the Jews accompanying the Germans, to hurry up and discover all the hideouts, and to complete the mission quickly. He threatened they would join the people in the collection square if they did not cooperate. A Jewish militiaman now joined every five-person German squad in addition to the Ukrainians and the *Volksdeutsches*. Those people were going around in the streets accompanied by bandits, robbers, looters, scoundrels, and mere Jewish haters. They followed the Germans as if to find Jews, but their main goal was looting and theft. The Germans conducted the first search, looking for Jews and valuables. The horde followed to complete the work – breaking, destroying, breaking the windows, and taking whatever fell into their hands.

For the Germans, that is not the first *Aktsia*. They already learned where and how to search. They knocked on the wall to see whether there was an echo of an inner room. Sometimes, the Germans broke the wall with axes, checking the ceiling, floor, and built-in closets. They also moved all the furniture. They were executing their mission expertly, faithfully, and meticulously.

What did the people hidden in their hideouts do during those terrifying moments? Are there words to describe the situation and suffering of these people and what they were experiencing? Can we depict the long moments from the time they heard how the Germans break in the door, then the shout: "Get out, Jew," and the knocks during the searches when they heard the approaching knocks holding their breath, a cold sweat covered the body, and they trembled from fear and the cold. Their nerves were stretched to the maximum. The three and four-year-olds understood the danger, so they kept silent. Little children received sleeping drugs. It happened that the dose was too small, and the child woke up. The mother had to hold the child and press the mouth forcibly onto the breast or shut the child's mouth with a hand until the child stopped breathing. There were cases when the dose of sleeping drugs was too high. Combined with the poor ventilation conditions, the child fell asleep and would not wake up. The mother had to hold the dead child in her arms.

It is easy to understand that one cry of a child could attract the Germans to the hideout, and all the people in it would be lost. There were cases when the mother chose to stay outside with the child so as not to endanger the others.

If the hiding people got lucky, and the Germans did not find them in the first search, it did not mean that they were safe. Sometimes, a single German remained quietly in an ambush at the apartment to see if he could hear an echo of a cry, talk, or movement, which would allow him to discover the hideout. Usually, the searches did not end in a single search. As aforementioned, following the Germans came the bandits and the *Volksdeutsches*. Following them, another German squad.

[Page 310]

That continued until the end of the *Aktsia*. There were cases when the people in the bunker were sure that the *Aktsia* had ended, left the bunker to go outside, and were immediately caught.

All of that happened when the Germans did find the hideout. However, if G-d forbid, the Germans found the entrance, they would open it, stand on the side, and send the Jewish militiaman to pull out the Jews from the hideout because the German heroes were afraid to go into the bunker. The outcome then depended on the character and the Jewish militiaman's goodwill. If he had the courage, he would divide the people into two groups, young and old. He would then leave the young ones in the hideout and pull out only the old ones. He knew well what would be his fate if the Germans would find out about what he did. The Germans asked him if that was all, shot a few shots inside the bunker, waited to see if there was any response, took the people whom the militiaman pulled out, and brought them to the collection location.

There were cases when an old grandmother or grandfather, or both, sacrificed themselves and became martyrs to save the rest of their family. They stayed at the apartment outside of the hideout. We heard from several cases where the Germans found one or two people in the apartment and were satisfied with them and did not conduct additional searches. These people had to possess a strong character so as not to reveal their hideout location under beatings and threats. Indeed, when the Germans encountered these grandmothers and grandfathers, they could not get a word out of them, only their souls, which they gave up willingly. What was the feeling of people who sit and wait for the angel of death? What did they experience in those long minutes before they were caught? Who could understand what their heart was saying? These people were heroes.

When the Germans found bedridden people, they tried their best to bring them to the collection square. Each of the Germans was obligated to deliver a certain number of live Jews to the city square; therefore, they tried to drag people who were half-dead to the collection square. Those who could not be brought to the collection point were killed on the spot with horrific cruelty and the sadism of predatory animals (I was told that by Jewish militiamen eyewitnesses, who were present and saw it with their own eyes). For the murderers, killing by a gunshot was not sufficient. They stood across from their victims and looked into their eyes with satisfaction until the victims' souls left them. They accompanied the torments of the dying victims with the laughter of people who were enjoying themselves and sometimes added some kicks in the leg of the dying people after they expired.

For the people in the hideouts, on one side, time seemed like it was standing still; on the other side, it seemed to be passing fast as it looked like days, weeks, and even years had passed. Every minute in the bunker seemed longer than a year in freedom. However, the *Aktsia* had just begun, and everything that happened occurred in the morning hours. It is impossible to know the limit of human strength and the ability to endure suffering before they are caught.

The Germans fought a war of extermination and nerves against us. When they were unsuccessful in discovering us, they tried to break our resistance and strength to withstand the war of nerves. We prevailed, and they did not win that war.

The time moved slowly, in no comparison with the regular time in the collection square. However, the Germans increased their effort and worked vigorously with all their might. They would have willingly delayed

[Page 311]

the sunset so that they could complete the work in the daylight, but the sun was setting.

[In the meantime] the *Aktsia* was quickly expanding, taking the form of fighting, destruction, and cruelty. The Germans and their collaborators continue to search, destroy, beak, burst in, and bring people to the city square, the collection location. Here, the people were sitting, cramped and crowded, unable to move, stand up, or even turn. From afar, the people looked like a single block, one big black stain, with hundreds of heads close to each other. The black stain was expanding, becoming bigger and bigger. They kept adding heads, albeit slowly, not as fast as in the morning when the flow was unceasing. Black stain, mute and motionless. No voices were heard, and the people were silent due to fear, exhaustion, or indifference. The square became an arena. Those who were sentenced to death were sitting in the middle, and not too far around them, curious Gentiles stood and watched the miserable people for long hours.

Miller, the Gestapo commander in our district – supervised the whole operation. Based on his shouts and the look on his face, it was clear that he was not satisfied with the operation's progress. He had hoped to complete it by noon. Several hours later, the Germans were far from reaching the required quota.

In the meantime, the sun was about to set. For the Germans, the sun was setting too quickly, but for the Jews, the sunset was too slow. For those who sat in the square, that day was the most arduous and the longest in their lives. Nobody complained about discomfort or pain. They did not even feel the fasting, as if they were no longer a part of this world. Only one thing that bothered them now - how long would it take until the end of their suffering, until they arrived at their final destination, to Belzec?

They no longer prayed; neither the *Minkha* [afternoon prayer] nor the *Ne'ilah* [Yom Kippur's closing prayer]. After all, the gates to the heavens were closed. They also completed their *Viduy* [confession] prayer several times. Only the troubles were endless.

The night brought with it the dew and the cold. At first, the people felt relief after the hot and long day. Now, they began to tremble from the cold. They moved now, taking advantage of the darkness. They straightened their backs, breathed deep, and turned their heads. Miller felt it, so he ordered his people to transfer the prisoners to the train station. Trucks arrived. An order to stand up was given. It was not easy to stand up after the prolonged sitting, in the conditions they sat, after a day of fasting, without a drop of water for twenty-six hours. People helped each other, stood up, straightened their backs, leaned on each other, and moved forward.

The Germans loaded the young ones onto tracks and led the elderly, weak, and women with their children on foot under heavy guard. The young ones had the privilege of traveling on track to prevent any attempts to escape on the way. The elderly, weak, and women with children would not have the strength and the will to escape. The block of several hundred heads moved slowly under the moonlight and the lights of the flickering flashlights. A shot could be heard from time to time when somebody tried to escape.

Following them, the *Volksdeutsches* and bandits marched slowly. It was not enough for them to delight their hearts and eyes by watching the troubles and suffering of the Jews. They wanted to continue to witness the "show" until the end. They were worse than the jackals.

They finally arrived at the train station, but the train was late, or perhaps they were too early. Several people tried to escape. Some were hit by German bullets and dropped dead, and others were caught by the *Volksdeutsches* and the bandits, and it was pointless to tell what they did to them until they expired.

No caption: A picture of the artist Michel Kara?

[Page 312]

The hour was late when the train arrived. The doors to the train cars opened quickly. The Germans gathered the people and pushed them forcibly into the train cars. They did not care if anybody was wounded, bruised, had a broken hand or ribs, or even killed. On the contrary, that was done purposely to make the trip more bothersome. When they finished their work, they closed the doors from the outside. They covered all the windows with barbwires and boards fastened with nails. They secured the train cars hermetically from all sides to prevent any attempt at an escape, and by doing that, they blocked the flow of fresh air for the poor people inside.

The commander was angry, seethed, and shouted out of shame because they had only achieved half the quota that day. What would he tell his supervisors? The train left, but the Germans stayed in the city since they had to reach the predetermined quota assigned to them. At 2 am, they received an order to get ready for another *Aktsia* at at 5 am.

That time, the operation was more nerve-wracking, crueler, and faster. The Gestapo, who were reprimanded, tried their best to achieve their goals. They warned the *Judenrat* and the Jewish militia that they would join the transport if they would not help in reaching the required number of Jews. The Gestapo told the people in the collection square that they would release the person and his family that would disclose to them the location of the hideouts of their acquaintances and neighbors. They tried to convince or force people with terror and false promises. I heard many stories about that subject. Were there people who broke and complied with the Gestapo's demands? How many people believed that they could save themselves in that way? I cannot say for sure. There were a few who found that snitching did not help them. Nobody was released from being caught by the Germans except those who freed themselves from the train on the way to Belzec.

The *Aktsia* on the second day ended at about 5 pm. On that day, the Germans succeeded in gathering more Jews than on the previous day. The reasons for their success probably lay in the snitching of several people and the increased effort by the Germans, but mainly because of the exhaustion of the people in the hideouts. The operation itself was a repeat of the previous day. The Germans used the identical collection location at the city square, the same torturous way, and possibly the same train and cars. After thirty and a few more hours, the Germans completed their work but did not leave the city.

The murderers and their collaborators gathered to celebrate the successful end to the murder of the Jews, dined, gave praises, and summarized the two formidable but fruitful work days. That cost us additional victims. Some people thought that the Gestapo had already left the city. They came out of their hideouts and were caught immediately by the *Volksdeutsches* and the bandits, who roamed around in Jewish homes to loot and rob. They handed these captured people to the Gestapo, who, as a "dessert," took them out of the city and shot them to death.

In the meantime, the train made its way to Belzec.

It was dark in the train cars, suffocating, stinking, crowding, and lacking fresh air for breathing. People lay on top of each other, crying, shouting, and trying to free themselves from the weight of their neighbors, trying to find their hands and legs in that crowd and catch some air to breathe.

[Page 313]

Slowly, everybody calmed down; the people were trying to help each other. Somebody lit a match, the people opened their eyes, a light ray in the dark. They saw a crack at the top. Once, there was a small window there. They needed to open it! Several youths approached and began to work. After all, there was nothing to lose. They tried their strength. One of the youths climbed on the shoulder of another and hit the wall with his fist once or twice, and indeed, the board moved. A few more firm knocks, and the board fell down. A flow of fresh air burst into the train car. New lives are awakening; now, they tried to loosen the rest of the boards from the hatch. After they achieved that, they encountered a new problem – how do they open the door? It was almost impossible to reach the door latch from the hatch. One of the youths pushed himself through the hatch, and two youths held him. These are critical moments, to life or death!

The youth freed the barbwire around the hatch and removed it. He was exhausted and could not continue. He caught the hatch's side panels with his hands and tried to lift the door latch with his leg. It was not easy. He tried again and failed. His hands were falling asleep, becoming weak. Suddenly, the train car jumped up on the rail tracks, and the latch moved! Another pull with the leg, and the latch opened. The youth held the door with all his remaining strength to prevent it from locking again. In the meantime, the people inside moved the door from the inside, and it was now wide open.

An Opening to Life

by Dr. Eliezer Shaklai

Translated by Moshe Kutten

Edited by Jane S. Gabin

Who dared to jump from the train to freedom? Courage was required, but also a lot of luck. The Germans were positioned on the roofs. There were one or two Germans situated on train cars, holding machine guns. However, the people inside the train cars did not have much to lose. The first one jumped, then the second, and the third. Twelve people jumped through the open door. They did not get hurt except for scratches and bruises from the fall on the ground. They returned to the city. Most people on the train were afraid to jump or incapable of doing so. They knew their end. There was no place they could return to. They would not be able to withstand another such day: the searches, bunker, and worst of all, the sitting in the city square waiting for the redeeming angel – the death angel. These people were broken. There was no hope for them. They were unwilling to receive any help or proof. They went to face death with their eyes open.

Those who jumped from the train returned to the city secretly, hiding from the militia and the Gestapo, and began everything all over again…

[Page 314]

The Destruction after the *Aktsia*

by Dr. Eliezer Shaklai

Translated by Moshe Kutten

Edited by Jane S. Gabin

Several hundred to two thousand people [were taken in the *Aktsia*]. From the *Judenrat*, they took Dr. Klarer, Shomer, Freier, and the teacher, David, with their families. My brother-in-law, Ya'akov Bomze, was also among the victims. He was one of the people who could but refused to jump from the train.

At the *Judenrat*, I found out that Mitelman was nominated by the Gestapo as the head [*Obmann*] of the *Judenrat*, replacing Dr. Klarer. They threw out Bertzio Feld from the *Judenrat*. That was probably their response for not appearing on Yom Kippur with the rest of the people of the *Judenrat* at the collection location. The Gestapo wanted, even before that, to remove him as the representative and messenger of the *Kreishauptmann*. They added a few more people to the new *Judenrat* to replace the people who were killed.

Commotion prevailed in the *Judenrat*. The noise was deafening, and the work was plenty. First, it was necessary to bury all the victims who were shot at home or in the streets. The *Judenrat* also needed to provide men to clean the streets after the pogrom and destruction. There were also all sorts of demands coming from the Germans. The latter knew how to take advantage of situations when Jews were depressed by not letting them recuperate and take a deep breath. On the contrary. They oppressed the Jews at times when they were humiliated, not to let them raise their heads - to rise up and recover.

I ran away from the *Judenrat* and went down to the street. I do not have the words to describe what I saw there. The people who survived were still under the last few days' effect. They were all running. The people spoke quietly, more with hand movements than by their mouths. A husband was looking for his wife, a woman – her husband, children – their parents, and parents – their children. People stood by the ruined hideout, empty and open, black and dark. They looked inside, called, and yelled. They went inside, searched, did not find anybody, and went out. Whoever left the hideout would never come back. The bunker was silenced. There wasn't even an echo to the calls. It was deserted, humiliated. It did not succeed in fulfilling its mission. It failed the test. It could not be relied on any longer. There was destruction around the bunker and destruction in the streets. Anything breakable was broken, and the rest was thrown outside to the street. The souls of the survivors were also destroyed, like the whole area for those who survived.

On my way, I met an acquaintance. I worked with him in the clinic during the Soviet regime. He was one of the people who jumped from the train and returned to the city, ready for a new struggle. He told me how they opened the train car's door and jumped out. He told me who stood near him, what they were talking about, and who refused to jump. He provided me with all the details, from the moment he was captured until he jumped. He gave me a full report because he felt he needed to "pour out his heart." He wanted to tell me what he had experienced to ease his heart. I listened to his story until somebody else asked him a question, and he began to tell his story from the beginning.

I left them and walked toward the "Riska" [Street]. Mrs. Ross-Mandelberg, the owner of the tavern, came toward me. She approached me, dancing with laughter and song. She sang the song of a bereaved mother, looking for her children: "Where are you, my children? Far, far away from me." We heard that song once in a show. That woman lost her mother and two children on Yom Kippur. I saw from a distance that the tragedy hit her hard. She approached me and looked at me as if for the first time in her life. She suddenly hugged me and burst into bitter tears.

[Page 315]

That was beyond my powers. I released myself from her arms slowly. During the entire time, I did not find even one word of comfort to say to her. What can possibly comfort her? We stayed standing for a long moment. She murmured all the time: "Where are my children? Where are they?" She looked at my tearing eyes and walked away. I also went on my way, and perhaps I ran, escaping.

A short while later, I reached the hospital. I entered, and everybody looked at me. I told my nurses that I was unable to work that day. The nurse told me: "Go take a rest. You look exhausted." I was unsure how I looked at them and what they thought about me when they saw me in that state. I left the hospital. I was not in a place where I could rest. I went to the village to see my wife and son.

I was tired and sleepy; I dragged my legs slowly, and the road seemed long. I decided to stop by the side of the road for a short rest. I saw a large rock not far away, among the grain fields. I approached and sat on it. The sun rose to the top of the sky and radiated plenty of heat. I was drenched in sweat. I took off my coat and discovered I still wore holiday clothes.

It was good to sit there and rest. Silence prevailed around. The air was fresh, and the sky bright. I heard the singing and laughing voices of the farmers. What a difference, I thought, between a Jew, who was a prey all over the world, and the Gentile, the citizen, who settles his land and cultivates it? The inner calm, there is nobody around me, freedom, and no interruption. There were no Germans, bloodshed, shouts, and no destruction. A peaceful atmosphere was around. One was allowed to breathe whatever he wished. And one was allowed to live. I slowly freed myself from the pressure and stress I was under throughout the last sixty hours. The calm and refreshing environment helped me to regain my mental balance and to digest the things I heard about and repeat, word by word, the thrilling story I heard from the person who jumped from the train.

I asked myself: "Who was right? Was it the man who jumped from the train to continue his arduous struggle for survival? Or perhaps my brother-in-law and others who stayed on the train, thinking that there was no escape from death, no hope for salvation, and no use in continuing with the struggle for survival. I do not know the answers to these questions. Would I, a person who was not captured, was not present in the collection square, and did not jump from the train, have been able to undergo the same tension again?

I arrived at my family's place in the village in the early evening. I told them what I went through and what I heard and listened to what they had experienced during the last three days.

In the evening, when conversing with my wife. I told her: "You know, I thought a lot in the last two days. I do not see any use in the struggle to survive. There is no hope for salvation because we will all go in the same way: Hideout, search, transfer to the collection point, the train, and Belzec. Wouldn't it be better if we end our life quietly, in our apartment, at once?" My wife answered: "I am willing to swallow the poison, and so do you. However, who will give the poison to our son?" I remained silent. "You are right," I thought." We do not have the permission to decide about his life!" I remembered my parents and what they said: "You should not lose hope. One must continue with the struggle, no matter what!"

I woke up the following early dawn and returned to reality, my work, and my struggle to save my family. A lot of work accumulated for me at the hospital. In the evening, I went to visit my patients in the city.

[Page 316]

The Road to the Total Extermination - and the Struggle Against it

by Dr. Eliezer Shaklai

Translated by Moshe Kutten

Edited by Jane S. Gabin

After the destruction caused by the Germans on Yom Kippur and completed on the following day by the Volksdeutsches and the bandits, the latter received an order from the Gestapo to collect the Jewish property. That was the "inheritance" that fell into their lot – apartments and properties after the extermination of thousands of Jews as in the verse: "Have you not murdered a man and seized his property? [1 Kings 21:19]."

Many months before the *Aktsia*, the German and Ukrainian newspapers warned the non-Jewish population not to approach the Jews, contact them, and buy or barter with them. They claimed that the Jews were infected with all kinds of diseases, and any contact with them involved a health risk and even a risk of death for those who bought merchandise from them. However, after the *Aktsia*, the Germans were not unafraid to enter the Jewish homes, examine every object, large or small, sort the objects, arrange them, and determine what to send to Germany and what to leave in the city and distribute among the Volksdeutsches' hordes.

I passed by them and saw their work. I saw how they loaded furniture, tools, and other items on the wagons. It was a "legal robbery" under the sun, and nobody protested against that evil injustice. I did not have any affection for these objects, but each reminded me of the person who used to own the object. The Germans did not only exterminate the people but destroyed every memory of them, even their belongings. It was like a total obliteration from the face of the earth.

After they emptied an apartment, they closed it and sealed its doors with a wax seal. These apartments became *Judenrein*, and every non-Jew could receive it under the approval of the local authorities.

The Jews repaired the rest of the apartments as much as they could afford the repair. They closed the windows with tins, board, and any other material that allowed protection from the winter's wind, rain, and cold.

The fall had begun, and the nights became very cold. People did not rest even after they repaired the apartment and plugged the cracks. They all continued vigorously to run around, arrange, and repair here and there. A big change was apparent in them. They became more serious, and their hair grayed. The destruction could be seen on the face of every Jew. Something broke in them and could not be fixed. Even time could not heal it! Although people were ready for more calamities and knew that an additional *Aktsia* was coming, they feared it. The fear did not allow for any rest during the day or at night. A thought is not the same as an action in the same way that fear is not the same as an actual trauma. What I wanted to say was that the destruction we experienced in those "days of Awe" also destroyed the people who survived it. Although they returned to their daily work, they were devastated, in body and soul, carrying the certainty that the *Aktsia* was the first but not the last. Additional *Aktsia*s would come until the entire Jewish population would be exterminated.

Quite a few people did not recover and remained heartbroken, losing the will to live, melancholily walking around like shadows. Those were mainly the people who lost a part of their families and remained alone, without a helping hand, with no encouragement, and without the strength and will to continue with the struggle, like those on the train who refused to jump. These people were neglected in their appearance and stood out in their indifference. They were the first victims of the second *Aktsia*.

Eight days passed, and another persecution was imposed on us.

[Page 317]

The Ghetto

by Dr. Eliezer Shaklai

Translated by Moshe Kutten

Edited by Jane S. Gabin

To definitively determine a small place, surrounded by a fence, the location of the ghetto for the remnants of the city's Jews, Miller, the head of the Gestapo, gathered the *Kreishauptmann* and his people and others from the local authorities. The group went around the city's length and widthwise, discussed every detail, and negotiated. In the end, they could not find a better place than the half-ruined houses in the city center, with several adjacent streets. That was once the Jewish quarter before the war. It was now mostly ruined, and the housing possibilities were few. It was impossible to put into that small and ruined quarter all of the Jews that were still alive. Miller joked that the Jews would be able to enjoy a sweating bathhouse [sauna] 24 hours a day. He issued an order that all Jews must relocate into that quarter within 24 hours and that the area would be marked and fenced around. That would be the Jewish ghetto, and from it, only those who had work permits outside of the ghetto would be allowed to get out. Non-Jews were forbidden from getting into the ghetto.

Since the place we got was too small to house all the Jews in the city, our contact people began to lobby vigorously with the authorities, with the help of gifts and bribes, to enlarge the ghetto by adding some houses from the outside of the allocated place. It was not easy, but we achieved a few changes that worked in our favor: we secured a few more houses and received a three-day extension. There was another decree, according to which it was only allowed to bring belongings weighing less than 25 kilograms. According to the new rule, there were no limitations as long as the transfer would last less than three days. The authority also gave up on the part of the order to wall the ghetto and surround it with a barbwire fence. It was agreed that the closing of the ghetto would be implemented in stages. That was a crucial achievement for us. The ghetto was not only a cramped, narrow, and dark place to reside in but also a jail-like place. We were all placed in "jail" at once, closed up and under the strict supervision of the Germans. The eyes of the Germans were on us during the days. They could capture us at any time without any effort and without the need to search, as we were all concentrated in a single area without the ability to escape when there was an *Aktsia*. We were all dependent on the Gestapo for good or for evil.

The housing conditions were inhumane; up to twenty people crowded in the same room. There was no room for furniture, not even beds. People slept on the floor. When they managed to put a bed in the room, several people slept on it. A table was placed in the house very rarely. In those conditions, it was hard to think about minimal cleanliness. As a result, pandemics erupted in the ghetto, which infected many people in the winter. At least one hundred sick people were in the ghetto on any given day, and sometimes two hundred. There was no way to prevent the spread of a disease from one person to another because of the crowdedness. The sick slept in the hideouts, in dark and wet corners, on the ground, without substantive human treatment. There were no medicines nor food except drinking water given to the sick without any limitation. Many people, particularly those older than sixty, died from these diseases. Young ones also died, and those who recuperated did not completely recover. They remained frail and thin. There was no wonder since they did not receive the required food portions for these diseases to help them recuperate. There was also no fresh air since they hid from the Gestapo in hideouts. And if there were still many patients who survived, it was thanks to the will to overcome the disease, which also helped them overcome any other difficulties associated with the disease.

[Page 318]

Brzezany – the plan for the ghetto and camp

[Page 319]

There was no possibility to buy food at the ghetto. The authorities agreed to allow the Jews to leave the ghetto and go to the "*Nowy Rynek*" [the new market square] for half an hour, from 12:00 pm to 2:30 pm, to buy food. However, the market was mostly empty, and there was almost nothing to buy. The little food that reached the ghetto was brought over by the people who left to work outside or by those who risked their lives to leave the ghetto secretly to shop and return through all kinds of breaches in the fence. The latter sold the food in the ghetto for a retail price.

The other problem was that in the ghetto, we were left without hideouts, without the possibility to hide in a bunker when needed. Building a bunker big enough to house forty to sixty people was a project that required time, workers, construction materials, and know-how in building bunkers. However, the time was short, and the area was too small to build a bunker for so many people.

There were also tiny but repeated problems in daily life. People accustomed to a comfortable life had to give up that life at once. It was not achieved easily. As much as possible, the *Judenrat* tried to distribute apartments and rooms based on the needs of the families. They did not always overcome the difficulties in doing so. Obviously, the *Judenrat* did not forget to provide the best apartments and rooms to "respectable people" (nepotism) of those days.

The move into the ghetto was slated to take three days and two nights. Until then, it was allowed to take out anything transportable from the previous apartment. It is exceedingly difficult for me to paint for the readers that horrible and degrading picture. People ran in all directions, to their former residences and back to the ghetto, carrying sacks, furniture, wooden boards, etc. Everybody was working, children too. People moved wardrobes, tables, chairs, and clothing on small loaded hand-carts. Everything was done in disorder. People did not put their belongings into their new apartments or rooms. There was no time for that. They threw everything in the middle of the street. A small child was positioned at the pile to guard that nothing would be taken or lost. A side observer would have thought that a fire had broken out in the city, and people were making the utmost effort to save their belongings from the fire. It seemed like the people took valuables out of the burning homes. Indeed, that is what it was. Everything was valuable in those days, even a small board, a broken tool, or a torn rag.

The three days of the move passed without any disturbances. The Germans did that on purpose to imbue the feeling among the Jews that they moved into a sanctuary, which would be their home for the future and would not think about their previous residences or about escaping from the ghetto. The Germans knew that the move would cause the Jews to suffer and oppress them. Fights among the Jews broke out due to trespassing between neighbors who shared an apartment or room. The Germans and the other Gentile citizens enjoyed and laughed at seeing those scenes. They observed scenes the like of which happened in the Middle Ages when Jews lived in ghettos.

[Page 320]

Some Gentile families moved from the areas around the ghetto, following the phrase: "It is beneath our honor to be with you." Those Gentiles received hefty compensations: nice new apartments and a move paid by the *Judenrat*.

The move ended at the conclusion of the three days. However, the work around the move and the results it caused lasted for days and weeks. There was a need to put the belongings in the rooms and arrange them. Due to lack of space, people needed to put some belongings in the corridor, the yard, and every possible corner, and after all that – leave some of the belongings in the street. A few families were allowed (for a hefty sum) to reside outside of the ghetto, on the condition that they move to smaller apartments close to the ghetto. That permission was revoked a month later. The families who took advantage of that had to move twice, causing double work and suffering. In addition, most of the rooms and apartments had been distributed, and the housing situation of those families became extremely difficult.

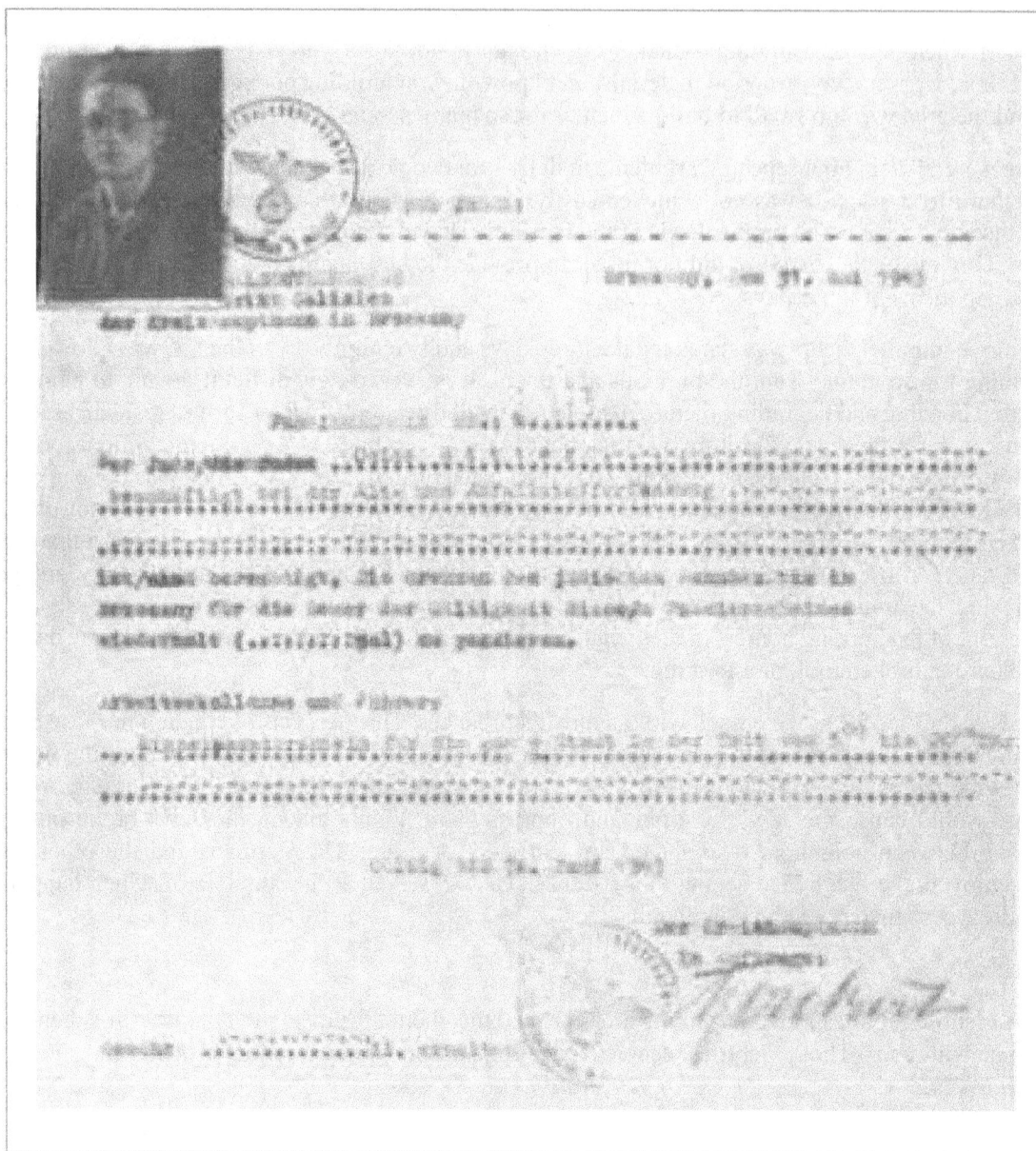

Exit certificate from the ghetto for the Jew, Osias Ritter

[Page 321]

In those days, the Gestapo completed the first round of *Aktsias* to Belzec. The Gestapo caught as many Jews as it could find in the small towns. They then took the Jews from those towns and announced them to be "*Judenrein.*" The captured Jews were sent to bigger cities. Our *Judenrat* also received an order to make two large apartment buildings available for the Jews expelled from the small towns. There was no room for the Jews who resided in these buildings, so they were divided among the other ghetto residents. With that, the crowdedness in the ghetto increased and became unbearable. Probably, the Gestapo planned that ahead of time! That time, even the optimists among us, who believed that the *Aktsia* on Yom Kippur was a one-time operation and that our situation would improve, realized they were mistaken. They finally understood that the Germans plan their operations ahead of time, as was the view held by the pessimists among us for quite some time.

Not even a month since the Yom Kippur *Aktsia* passed when news arrived about the second round of *Aktsias* that began in Ternopil. We received bad news daily about what was happening in farther away areas, other locations, and other cities in our district. [This round] had the same operations, disappointments, and number of victims, if not more.

[The Germans used] the same methods and means: searches, Jews were being caught, they were led to a collection square, train, Belzec, murders in gas chambers, burning of the bodies in crematoria, and the circle turned, and the whole story kept repeating. The Machines work continuously. The trains transport and bring "Raw Material," and the [murder] factory processes it!

Now, people are trying to arrange, as quickly as possible, hideouts for as many people as possible in a short time. People worked days and nights digging, carrying out dirt, and preparing construction materials. However, all that effort was insufficient to complete proper hideouts, where people could hide during an *Aktsia*. People set guard duty during the day, and especially at night, to receive an early warning of an approaching calamity. Perhaps that warning would enable hiding or timely escape outside of the ghetto.

The Second *Aktsia* to Belzec

by Dr. Eliezer Shaklai

Translated by Moshe Kutten

Edited by Jane S. Gabin

This time, the Germans did not give us a long break. On the 31st of October, the Germans arrived in total quiet in unlit cars and approached the ghetto carefully. The number of the murderers and collaborators was the same as in the last operation. The first thing the Germans did was to position guards in key positions around the ghetto. By the time we found out what was going on, the ghetto was already encircled.

People among us who did not construct or did not finish constructing a hideout tried to escape outside of the ghetto. After all, they did not have any other choice. Most of them were killed by German shots. This time, the Germans did not chase after the escapees and did not try to capture them. They fired indiscriminately and without warning in all directions. This time, there were more shot victims than the first *Aktsia*. The guarding around the ghetto was stricter and more efficient using a smaller number of people, which succeeded in closing the ghetto hermetically. Nobody came in, and nobody came out. The *Aktsia* itself was delayed until the morning hours. The Germans were afraid to go into the ghetto in the dark during the night.

[Page 322]

There is no need to describe the second *Aktsia* since it was a repeat of its predecessor, only more organized, faster, efficient, and crueler. Using the same forces, the Germans and their collaborators managed to execute in several hours what they could hardly achieve during the two days of the previous operation. Several reasons contributed to the faster speed and more numerous victims: Many people who survived the last *Aktsia* had not recovered from the calamity of Yom Kippur. These people did not resist their arrest this time; they just fell into the hands of the murderers. Another reason was that the Germans learned and specialized in the art of the search: where to search, how to find the hideout, and how to quickly open it. An additional reason was that we were not yet prepared for that *Aktsia*. As aforementioned, the construction of the hideouts has not yet been completed. The hideouts were also more superficial than in the last operation. The Germans captured more than twenty people in many of the discovered hideouts, and some contained about sixty people.

The change in this operation, which was much shorter, faster, and more organized, was that it started in the early hours of the morning, while the ghetto had been already surrounded at midnight. The searches began at once from all sides and at the same time in most apartments. A second and third wave of searches followed the first one. The Germans progressed fast, according to their order and plan, broke into doors and windows, shouted, destroyed walls, lifted boards from the floor, and searched the cellars and every place they found suspicious. Like last time, they did not spare the furniture and other belongings. They purposely broke everything and threw the fragments outside. They killed the elderly and the sick on the spot and did not bother at all to take them to the collection location. They only took the captured people who could walk to that location. The same show took place, but this time, the audience consisted of farmers from the neighboring villages to whom the Germans wanted to show off their power and heroism so that the farmers couldlearn a lesson. This time, there were beatings to improve and diversify, and screaming to the point of madness to scare the Jews and hurry up themselves. They hoped and were successful in finishing the *Aktsia* under daylight. They completed the transport of the people to the train station in the afternoon.

The Germans completed the loading, closed and sealed the train cars, and inspected the train. The locomotive whistled, and the train moved forward toward Belzec.

After the train left the city, our people went to work, broke the doors, jumped out, escaped, and tried their luck again by returning to the ghetto. Indeed, that was what happened. The doors of one train car after another broke, and the people jumped out while the train was traveling at its maximum speed. Our people learned how to jump from a speeding train and helped each other during the jump. One of the people stood on the side and watched the outside into the darkness. He would give signs to two people who stood on the two sides of the door to notify them whether the road was safe and that there were no trees, rocks, or telephone poles ahead. Based on the second sign, the two people helped the person who waited to jump at the right moment. I do not know how many people jumped from the train and how many jumpers survived. However, throughout the night, about one hundred people returned to the ghetto, among them many wounded people who required care or orthopedic treatment.

I took care of the wounded, and they told me what happened to them from the moment they were captured until they returned to the ghetto. Each had a unique experience that can never be forgotten. Every jump was a thriller, an unforgettable adventure. Among the jumpers were five people for whom it was the second time to jump, escape, and live to wait for the third *Aktsia*!

[Page 323]

Those who jumped successfully walked along the railroad tracks and helped the wounded to return home or hide on the way home. The returnees told me a story about a waggoner from our city who helped people jump from the train. When he saw that the people in the adjacent train car could not open the door from the inside, he jumped over to that train car while the train was moving, holding a small ax, and opened the door for them. The Germans caught him in the act and shot him with a burst of bullets. That waggoner sacrificed his life to free others and save them.

Many more heroes acted quietly and with sacrifice, whose stories would never be told and would not be praised as heroes.

The people who jumped returned to the ghetto and sneaked into their apartments very cautiously to avoid being discovered by the Germans. The latter would, most certainly, execute them. They also feared the Jewish militia who could reveal their secret.

On the following day after the second destruction, whose dimensions were no less severe than the first destruction, the survivors began building new hideouts, that time at a much greater speed, to be ready for the third round we all knew would come.

The shock after the second destruction was enormous, as was its effect on the survivors. However, this effect did not last long. People recovered quickly and got themselves into the mood for the third round's eve to be ready more efficiently to escape, hide, and jump from the train if needed. People wanted to live!

Towards the Winter

by Dr. Eliezer Shaklai

Translated by Moshe Kutten

Edited by Jane S. Gabin

The second *Aktsia* took place in the fall of 1942. The Germans were then at the top of their success on almost all fronts. They ruled most of the European areas. Rommel's corps arrived at El-Alamein in North-West Egypt. In Russia, the Germans ruled areas from Leningrad [today Saint Petersburg] in the North, Moscow in the center, and Stalingrad [today Volgograd] in the south. They reached the Volga River and even penetrated the Caucasus Mountains. Every day brought them a new victory. Despite all that, we felt that the Germans were nervous and restless. We had the feeling that we faced crucial events in the coming days. Maybe the Germans were afraid of the approaching Russian winter.

Thoughts about the harsh winter gave rise to new hopes. Our people were awakened instinctively, filled with a new will to live, and were ready to battle with spirit. Indeed, we felt that our win was not that far. We believed in the approaching salvation, and our people tried with all the means at their disposal to save their lives. Those courageous people left the city with Aryan papers despite knowing the difficulties they might be facing.

However, on the other hand, there was nothing to lose. One may only succeed. Indeed, it was possible to succeed in that mission. Those who could afford it searched for permanent hideouts outside the city 'till the storm blew over.' They looked to hide the entire family, part of it, one or more children with the Gentiles in the neighboring areas. Sometimes, people divide their family as follows: the father and one child with a farmer in a particular village, and the mother with another child with another farmer. Those who did not possess the financial ability to hide outside the city invested all their might, vigor, wisdom, and knowledge in building hideouts. We did everything we could to gain time. We thought that the Third Reich was facing a disintegration despite the latest win.

[Page 324]

The truth was that in the following days, there was a turnaround on all fronts. In November, H…er, may his name and memory be blotted out, suffered one defeat after another. On the 2nd of November, the British began their counterattack in El-Alamein and did not stop until they expelled the Germans and the Italians from North Africa. The Americans successfully landed in North Africa, and their army progressed speedily. On the 22nd of November, the Soviet Army began its most forceful counterattack in Stalingrad. That attack was later spread to all fronts. Under that atmosphere, our will to live and celebrate H…er's defeat strengthened. At that time, we did not know that H…er would not collapse, even if he would be forced to retreat all the way to his capital, Berlin. We could not anticipate that he would withstand those defeats and that his people would continue to believe in him and obey his orders until the last moment. The Germans did not break and did not surrender easily. The Allies had to dislodge them one step at a time and fought with them for two additional years. We could not foresee that, and we all lived in illusions that encouraged us to overcome the superhuman difficulties.

Several *Aktsia*s took place in our district in November. We also did not experience a total calm. There were some kidnappings in the labor camps despite the approaching winter. It was executed by the Jewish militia and the *Judenrat*. Besides those kidnaps, we faced daily problems, like the problem of getting food. The farmers experienced excess produce that year and would willingly barter with us. However, it was hard to meet and organize the exchange. The main problem was how to bring the food products into the ghetto. As I have already mentioned, there were several ways to do so. For money, a substantial part of our professional people received a permit from the Germans to cross into the Aryan side and work for the Gentile population. These people included gold and silversmiths, photographers, locksmiths, glaziers, and more. These Jewish professionals received agricultural products illegally instead of wages for their work. They brought the products into the ghetto, also illegally. Some people made a living by buying food products outside and bringing them illegally into the ghetto. Both Jews and non-Jews were involved in that, which resulted in price gouging. The difficulties associated with these daily issues were dwarfed by the most difficult problems: the pandemics, which spread towards the winter and intensified with the move to the ghetto, and the counter activities of Hermann, which cost us many victims.

My Fight for the Typhus Sick

by Dr. Eliezer Shaklai

Translated by Moshe Kutten

Edited by Jane S. Gabin

On one of the evenings in November 1942, I found out at the *Judenrat* about the death of the lawyer Finkelshtein. I went to comfort the bereaved and, on that occasion, to pray and say *Kaddish* in memory of my Father *z"l*. We held two prayers a day in my room until October. On those occasions, I said *Kaddish* first, in memory of my mother and then my father. When we moved to the ghetto, that arrangement ceased because it was not possible. Once in a while, I tried to find out where people were praying so that I could join the *Minyan* and fulfill the *Kaddish* commandment.

On that evening in November, I served as the cantor, and I prayed the *Shmona Esrei* prayer with devotion. Two militia leaders broke in at that moment, approached me directly, and handed me a notice from the Gestapo to appear before them in the militia room, under a threat that if they did not bring me there within five minutes, they would be killed. They told me the reason for the notice! Somebody snitched about Jews hiding in a bunker. Based on that snitch, Hermann found the bunker with sixteen people sick with typhus in it.

[Page 325]

He squeezed a confession from them before they were tortured to death that I was the physician who took care of them. They shot them in the bunker, and they were waiting for me then!

I felt at that moment as if I saw my father *z"l* in his full stature, standing before me, looking at me, and saying: "My son, they call you, and you need to go! Don't be afraid, and don't break. I will be with you!"

The interrogation in the militia room lasted two and a half hours or longer. They used all the means they usually use in such cases (except beating) to bring me to a nervous breakdown and admission of guilt. I found out during the interrogation that they knew many things, even cases that I was sure remained a total secret. One of their complaints against me was that I accepted Jewish patients at the hospital under false names and treated them there on account of the German government. The truth is that I treated such patients in the hospital. However, they were admitted to the hospital by the head nurse after she had received a sum of money as a gift for her monastery. I treated them at the hospital as Aryan patients. We (myself and the patient) knew the truth, but we never discussed that. It turned out that the caretaker of the hospital followed these patients and notified the Gestapo. The Gestapo tried to capture these patients, and for that purpose, they often conducted sudden searches but never succeeded. They needed substantive evidence to accuse me and also the entire hospital management. That was why they wanted me to admit my fault and to serve as the state witness against the management!

How did it happen that the Gestapo never caught a Jewish patient at the hospital? The story goes as follows. A German engineer who worked on the war front left his wife in our city. She was a beautiful woman, full of vigor. She had many lovers, among them Hermann, the Gestapo man. He notified her on the phone every time he planned to visit our city. She resided in the apartment of Dr. Bilnksi [is it Bilinski?], the manager of the municipal hospital, and they shared the phone with the engineer's wife. Bilinki [Bilinski?] family members tracked every telephone call (they spied on behalf of the Poles). They notified me every time about Hermann'splanned visit of Hermann, so I always knew ahead of time about what was to happen. When I received the warning, I took all the Jewish patients out of the hospital and got out of there myself until Hermann left the hospital. It was only a coincidence, but that saved the lives of the patients and mine and continued as long as I worked at the hospital. However, after that incident, we acted more cautiously and kept clear of the caretaker.

I am returning to the main topic of this article.

I have already written about the order by the Gestapo to our militia concerning the searches for Jewish sick in the ghetto during the night, and the sleepless night I spent with the militiamen in the militia room. I will now return to my visit at Hermann's office, accompanied by the four militiamen, following an order by the Gestapo. We went to the Gestapo headquarters in the early hours of the morning, where two Gestapo people (who were treated by me) tried to convince me, at the last moment, to change my testimony, to admit my guilt, and to snitch about one hundred Jewish sick people as a "human ransom" to save my life. I did not respond to them and directly approached the office door. After a soft knock and without waiting for an answer, I opened the door, and we all entered Hermann's room. He lay on the bed in his full uniform. His eyes were closed; he was probably asleep. A loaded handgun was placed on the nightstand to his right. I set my eyes on the gun, and a thought came to me to kill the murderer. That episode lasted only a few seconds since Hermann opened his eyes and suddenly saw us standing before him. Perhaps he noticed my gaze in the direction of the gun. He was totally baffled and began to shout at us: "What?! What are you doing… here?!" I answered him that he had invited us

[the end of the article appears on top of page 328]

[Page 328]

to address the issue of the sick people in the ghetto. Long seconds passed when he made an effort to concentrate. He suddenly turned to the militiamen and asked them how many sick people did they find in the ghetto. When they answered that they had found none, he finally woke up, jumped from the bed, turned to me, and said:" You get out from here." With the whip he was holding, he began to lash the militiamen. We escaped the room in a hurry. Our people, who followed the event from afar, told me that after we escaped his room, Hermann got out, almost running, jumped on his jeep, and left the city. The rest of the Gestapo people, who waited outside, stood on the side, surprised at the strange and incomprehensible behavior of their boss, like a person who got bitten by a snake. They looked after him until he disappeared.

These last ten hours etched a deep groove in my soul. After I survived the calamities of Yom Kippur, I was strong and did not break, but I was tired of the tension that suddenly stopped in the way it did. We, myself and the four militiamen, returned to the militia room and felt as if we had been resurrected. There [the other militiamen] prepared for us, those the survivors of certain death, black coffee. I drank, rested, gathered my strength, and returned to my work at the hospital and to my patients at the ghetto from which sixteen people who were killed by the Gestapo were missing.

1942 Hannukah's *Aktsia*

by Dr. Eliezer Shaklai

Translated by Moshe Kutten

Edited by Jane S. Gabin

The month of November passed us *ex gratia* since who would pay attention to some shots or a few deaths? After all, those things occurred daily. Important was the fact that we did not have an *Aktsia*, and our oppressor had not begun with the third round. The break allowed us to build hideouts. At the same time, we tried to find connections with the world outside the ghetto, in the city, or in the villages with the villagers.

The days passed too slowly compared to our troubles but too fast compared to readying the hideouts for Doomsday. We reached the month of December. On one side, we received good news from the fronts about the retreat by the Germans and the numerous defeats they suffered. On the other side, we heard about the new *Aktsias*. We ceased counting the *Aktsias* and could not categorize them as the third or fourth rounds. We looked at our situation with open eyes, with a shred of hope. We knew that they intended to annihilate us very quickly. We faced a calamity with hope in our hearts. We were waiting for the H…er's defeat and our salvation. It was our partial consolation – seeing with our own eyes the beginning of the Nazis' defeat.

We thought, and we were not mistaken, that an *Aktsia* would be conducted in December – the "Hannukah's *Aktsia*." Instead of miracles and wonders, calamities engulfed us. Like its predecessors, the *Aktsia* began in the morning. This time, it lasted until the late evening hours. The Germans were satisfied with fewer people since there were fewer sick people and elderly in the rooms. Most of them had died already from hunger and pandemics or were shot by the Gestapo in all sorts of operations. Our bunkers withstood the test this time.

The people who were caught decided again to escape from the train cars, no matter what, and return to the city. They were ready to take the risk of dying on the way back and not give up trying to jump from the train cars. Like their predecessors, many of the jumpers were wounded, and I treated them. I worked very hard due to the large number of cases since the rest of the physicians resided in the neighboring villages.

The *Aktsia* itself was an exact duplicate of its predecessor. We lost several hundreds of people again.

[Page 329]

The number of Jews in the ghetto was reduced every month, every week, and every day. Another *Aktsia* to Belzec took place in those days. That was the last *Aktsia* in which our people were sent to Belzec. It was a short, cold, and hard winter day. The Germans were forced to begin the *Aktsia* under the moonlight to be able to capture a sufficient number of people to fill the train cars. Despite their cruelty, their success was only partial, and they had to settle for much fewer people than they had hoped for. Our people made the last effort. Almost all jumped from the train. On one hand, it was easier to survive the jump because of the soft snow. However, it was more difficult because of the cold and because the snow hid the rocks. Therefore, we had many more people who were victims of the cold and people who were injured by falling on rocks. According to the estimate of the jumpers, only about five to ten percent of the people remained on the train. As mentioned, that was the last train that transported our people to Belzec[1].

I do not know the reason for the halting of the *Aktsias* to Belzec. There were probably reasons for it. The Gestapo people who spoke openly about the pending liquidation of the ghetto and its residents told me in private conversations that the *Aktsias* were halted temporarily. They admitted that a change had taken place but did not know to tell me why and until what time.

Translator's Note:

1. According to the Holocaust Encyclopedia
    (https://encyclopedia.ushmm.org/content/en/article/belzec), Belzec was the first of the Operation
    Reinhard camps to close in December 1942. By the time deportations to the killing center halted,
    German authorities had murdered approximately 434,500 Jews at the site.

Our Situation in the Ghetto
and our Struggle leading up to the Ghetto Liquidation

by Dr. Eliezer Shaklai

Translated by Moshe Kutten

Edited by Jane S. Gabin

That was how 1942 ended. It was an atrocious year for us, a year with many victims. We were left with just a small number of Jews waiting for their extermination. Many locations around us had been declared *Judenrein* ["Clean of Jews"]. Despite the many troubles, a change for the better was felt; the Germans were in retreat on all fronts. It gave us hope.

Most people who survived in the ghetto were young or a bit older. The elderly and the sick had been either caught, killed, or died in the pandemics and were no longer a burden to the ghetto. Most of the people who survived were professionals. They were allowed to work outside. Many other people officially continued to reside outside the ghetto, such as physicians and other professionals, whose work was essential even at night. These people had connections with the external non-Jewish world. They tried to find hideouts in the villages because people were willing to give everything they had to save themselves. The rest of the people relied on their bunkers and a miracle. Although one was not supposed to rely on miracles, it was a different matter without any other alternative!

After the last *Aktsia*, there was a break until Passover. However, there was never total calm. Small local *Aktsias* took place, and our oppressors killed people once in a while. All of that bore a local character. These activities were carried out by the Gestapo and the local *gendarmerie*. Every so often, the oppressors conducted searches in a single house or a few houses. They searched for certain people for whom we did not know what their "crime" was. When they found them, they brought them over to the cemetery and killed them there on the spot. Alternatively, they were brought to the prison, where they joined other captured people. The oppressors then took the whole group and shot them into a pit prepared in advance.

[The article continues on page 326 in the original Hebrew book]

[Page 326]

The Gestapo and the local *gendarmerie* put an emphasis on searches for people who left the ghetto illegally, hid with the Gentiles, or mixed with the general population using Aryan papers. They found some of them every day with the help of snitches. The Germans were unable to capture these people on their own without the assistance of the snitches. They could not distinguish between a Jew and a Gentile. Furthermore, they could not search in the villages because they did not have the time, ability, and sufficient workforce.

It is worthwhile to note that, in our area, none of the Gentiles were punished when Jews were found hiding with them. We, therefore, suspected that the hosting Gentiles themselves provided the information about the Jews they were hosting and received money for that information. They received money and jewelry from two sides: from the Jews for shelter and from the Gestapo for information.

In some cases, they bragged to other villagers about their wisdom and heroism, about how they took advantage of both the Jewish victims and the Gestapo.

The month of January passed as I have described. We had already got used to that life. The closest family cried over the individual, and the rest of the people breathed a sigh of relief every day that passed without an *Aktsia*. At the beginning of February 1943, the *Judenrat* got an order to bring in all Jews who resided outside of the ghetto, particularly from the surrounding villages. The licenses of all kinds expired on the 15th of February without exception. I was the only person allowed to be anywhere in the district 24 hours a day. However, my official residence was inside the ghetto. Those who returned to the ghetto, or more correctly, those who entered the ghetto for the first time, found it difficult to adjust to the conditions. They suffered much more than the people who resided in the ghetto for some time. The housing situation was much more complicated than before. There were no hideouts ready for those people. Fortunately for them, there were no more *Aktsias* to Belzec, and the closest *Aktsia* would be local and take place after several months.

The latest order was a clear hint to us that we were facing the liquidation of the ghetto. It was expected to happen shortly, perhaps before the end of February. The Gestapo talked about it in the open. They knew that we were all in their hands because there was no place to escape. The Germans kept a close eye on us inside the ghetto and around it during the day and particularly at night. The *Volksdeutsches* took it upon themselves to do the guarding role. They acted as assistants to the Gestapo and the *gendarmerie*. They were ready for another *Aktsia* but had to wait for an order from above. It was not dependent on the local or the district Gestapo since it was a state-wide operation. It was not clear how it happened, but the liquidation of the ghetto was postponed for another three months.

There were several assumptions as to the reason. People talked about an exchange deal between the Germans and the Americans. The Germans requested vehicles and other accessories of war for the remaining Jews. The Americans did not agree to that kind of a deal. As told, the negotiations lasted a long time. In the end, the Germans received a negative answer.

Another assumption was that some of the German government officials requested to leave some Jewish professionals until the end of the war. Yet another assumption was that the Germans feared an American-Russian reprisal and waited to see their response [to the mass murdering of Jews]. When the response never came, the Germans completed their mission without interruption.

[Page 327]

We did not know the reason for the postponement and how long it would be until the final *Aktsia*. We waited day by day, evening by evening, and night by night for that operation.

Everything written here is a true and accurate description of the situation.

We did not have even one minute of rest, neither during the day nor at night, from the day the people gathered in the ghetto until the "*Judenrein*" *Aktsia*. It ruined our nerves. People who went to work did not know if they would live to return home. In the evening, when they returned, they went directly to the bunker or the hideout. That's where everybody gathered, ready for any sign that they had to get into the hideout [and close the opening]. We entered the hideout and got out of it countless times for anything suspicious. The elderly and slow-moving people sat in the shelter, most of the time, not to impede others. We did not take off our outdoor clothes and remained dressed for days and weeks. Everyone carried hacking tools in case there was a need for them. Everyone had a bit of food with them, and some food was hidden in the bunker for an emergency.

Every house had a commander, and all obeyed his orders. Strict twenty-four hours a day guard duty was organized, particularly at night. Every house selected an observation point, where one person or two sat, guarding without a break, and watched to see whether there was any movement on the roads. The guards performed their duty faithfully. They observed well and carefully listened to pick up every sound. They maintained contact with the house commander and reported on anything that aroused their suspicion. Such news passed quickly from one house to another. We were always on constant alert and unrelenting tension, even on Sundays, despite knowing that the Germans would not give up their weekend's rest.

It is difficult to describe the electrified atmosphere of those days and more difficult for people who were not there to comprhend. Every slight movement, every passing car, aroused tension in us. We spent most of our time in the underground hideouts rather than in our apartment. The apartment only served as a corridor to the bunker.

We got used to thinking that we were facing total annihilation; we seemed to have come to terms with the situation. However, we could not get used to the unbearably long period of tension.

The Germans knew to take advantage of our situation. They purposely spread rumors and all sorts of fake news to confuse us. They told stories about apparent reliefs that were about to be given to us and, at the same time, spread opposite stories about an *Aktsia* and ghetto liquidation. They raided individual houses and conducted long searches that lasted a day or two.

They murdered the people they found outside of the ghetto on the spot, in front of the area's Gentiles. Sometimes, the Germans brought the captured person to the cemetery to present him in front of the Jews so they could see what was waiting for them if they tried to escape.

Among those who were killed on the spot were the two daughters of Mr. Altman, caught by the gendarme and shot in a farmer's yard. The parents paid the farmer to bring the bodies to the city [for burial]. The two children of the watchmaker Pomerantz were caught at the house of a Gentile outside of the ghetto. The oppressors brought the entire family to the cemetery, where the children and their mother were killed. Pomerantz himself was permitted to return to the ghetto, as he was a professional the Germans needed. He refused to receive that permission and the order from the Germans, and he was [killed and] buried together with the rest of his family.

No caption: A picture by the artist, Michel Kara?

I recall that on one of the afternoons, we heard the sound of several shots. I went down to the street to investigate the reason for the shots and ran in the direction where the shot echoes were heard. On the way, I met a Jewish person

[Page 330]

and I asked him for the reason for the shooting. He answered: "It was nothing. They just shot three Jews." I said to him: "What do you mean? They killed three Jews, and you consider that nothing?" He responded: "They found them outside of the ghetto, brought them here, and shot them on the pile of trash." So! I thought to myself. How far have we come? The killing of three of our brothers does not make any impression on us any longer, as if that was a natural event. On my way home, I met two of the gendarme's people. They asked me mockingly whether I was going to conduct an examination on the bodies to determine the cause of death. Yes! Our lives became worthless in the eyes of G-d and man, and not only that – our lives became worthless in our own eyes!

The "Milk" *Aktsia* and Others

by Dr. Eliezer Shaklai

Translated by Moshe Kutten

Edited by Jane S. Gabin

Twelve women got out of the ghetto in March 1943 and passed to the other side by the market, "Noye Rynek." They went out at twelve noon to do food shopping, mainly milk, according to the Gestapo's permission and license. At noon, a few people passed through the market because no merchandise was left. On the same day, the *Gendarmerie* waited for them on the other side and took the women with them. The Judenrat people turned to the *Gendarmerie* to clarify the reason for the arrest, but the *Gendarmerie* refused to accept them for discussion, claiming it was their noon rest hour. They told the Judenrat people to return at four o'clock in the afternoon. The Judenrat people were not particularly alarmed since their relationship with the police was usually good. The people of the Judenrat were sure that they would manage to get the women out of there by the evening. However, at two o'clock in the afternoon, the relatives of the women who waited by the Gendarme's office said they saw the women being transported outside the city.

[Page 331]

The *Gendarmerie* brought them to the Jewish cemetery, ordered them to strip naked, and shot them.

Lawyer Fridman's wife and the daughter of Lufter, the glazer, were among these women.

Some additional local operations and searches took place in March. They surrounded the house on the corner from the market to Adamovka (Block Rosenberg). During the three-day siege, they did not allow anybody to enter or get out of the house. They conducted searches and destroyed whatever they could but could not find the bunkers, which our people constructed and named "Stalingrad." They caught a resident of the house, but he did not reveal the secret of the bunker, and they shot and killed him. A similar operation but on a larger scale, a real *Aktsia*, happened at the beginning of April.

The Last *Aktsia* Before the Ghetto Liquidation

by Dr. Eliezer Shaklai

Translated by Moshe Kutten

Edited by Jane S. Gabin

This *Aktsia* was conducted quietly by the Gestapo together with the *Gendarmerie*, with increased forces. The oppressors did not surround the ghetto. It was not necessary since we were surrounded all the time anyway, and it was impossible to escape from the ghetto during the operation. The Gestapo walked around in the ghetto and conducted searches, every time in a different location. They entered a house, got out, and entered again. Whoever was found in a bed was shot on the spot. The Germans found several hideouts, got the people out, and took them to the jailhouse. This time, they conducted the searches without the Jewish militia. However, some militiamen did walk around with them.

Our people entered the hideouts immediately at the start of the *Aktsia*. They remained there (those who were not caught) for three days without eating. Even though they had some food, they could only a little bit due to tension. The tension grew by the hour. The Germans entered the houses, checked, knocked, shouted, got out, and

returned to the same house. We heard shots once in a while. We saw people being led to the jail. I saw all of that from my observation point, where I sat, maintaining a connection to the people in the bunker. I passed them news about the movements of the Germans in our area. It was the atmosphere of the end of the struggle, with the feeling of the "Approaching End" along with the growing tension and the endless *Aktsia*. We did not know when the *Aktsia* would end or whether it would continue until they exterminated us all and declared the city "*Judenrein.*"

On the evening of the third day, I saw from my observation point that the Germans led the people from the jail in the direction of the cemetery. A short while later, we heard shots. When the shooting ended, people breathed a sigh of relief, and some took out food and dined after a fast that lasted three days. I looked at these people, saw their facial expressions, and thought: "Humans are only flesh and blood, weak creatures, egoistic and egocentric, forgetting easily things that don't concern them directly." The Germans killed several hundred Jews, but we survived, and it was possible to breathe a sigh of relief. Indeed, that was still not the end. They did not finish us; we were still alive and would fight for our survival!

[Page 332]

About three hundred people were captured in that *Aktsia*. Hermann and his helpers came to the jail toward the end of the *Aktsia*, took out the people, and gathered them in the jail's yard. In the yard, Hermann conducted a "selection." He divided the people into two parts, some to the right and the others to the left, those who were slated for forced hard labor and the others condemned to die. The Germans loaded the eighty-nine men whom Hermann liked onto trucks, and they were transported to the labor camp in Kamionka. Among these people was Miorka Taler, who was the only one who survived out of all the people captured in the *Aktsia*. He later wrote about that *Aktsia* and his life at the Kamionka labor camp; he died in Canada. The rest of the people, men, women, and children, were taken to the cemetery, where they were ordered to strip naked and were shot at the open pit one by one. The Germans annihilated them all. The bodies fell into the pit on top of each other. In many cases, the victims were still alive and, in some cases, fully conscious.

Our people told me that they planned to sneak into the cemetery to investigate whether they could help those who were still alive in the mass grave. They pulled out one woman, wounded in the chest by a bullet, which penetrated her chest on the left side above the heart, causing an internal hemorrhage. They also pulled out a twelve-year-old child, seriously wounded in his face. The bullet passed through his two cheeks and wounded his tongue. I contacted Dr. Bilinski, and he admitted the wounded, performed the required surgeries, and brought them over for my treatment at the ghetto.

Passover came in April. At that time, the holiday was not used for timing an *Aktsia* – in that case, the liquidation of *Aktsia* as part of our district "*Judenrein*" plan. For us also, there was no importance as to whether the *Aktsia* would be before, during, or after the holiday. At that time, the future and also the past did not belong to us any longer (seemingly). Was it hopelessness? I don't know, but that was the reality. Only time, day, and hours were the factors that determined how long we would live. We would spend the days of the holiday, if we still lived, like the regular days and nights – in the bunkers. Only a few people brought up memories from days gone by, but in their hearts, everyone hoped for a miracle. We were still not in the collection square, where everything was forbidden except breathing and thinking – thoughts in the shadow of the gallows. We were still allowed to think and believe in a miracle. However, there was no time to think. We were tense all the time, living in the shadow of the gallows.

We also forgot to do another thing in those days – sleep. During the time slated for sleeping, we worked on improving and fixing the bunker! We worked fast, in a state of a dream. It would be difficult for me to go back in my thoughts to those days and their atmosphere. It was not similar to the state of a person sitting in jail and waiting for the execution of his death sentence, even if the waiting period was long.

Our situation was also not similar to the state of a critically ill person, clearly feeling that his end was near. We were full of life and vigor, the will to live - today and tomorrow. Although we lost our past, the future was hidden; it was not shown on the horizon, it was far. To live! Live even the miserable life in the shadow of death, but still hoping that the rope would cut off, even if it was already tied around our necks.

A handful of people met at the *Judenrat* in the twilight evening. We talked, told the others about our experiences, and even told jokes - "self-mocking humor," joking about ourselves in the shadow of the gallows. We parted ways with the words: "Same time tomorrow if we live."

Those were our lives in those days.

[Page 333]

The Orphan Girls and the Locked Gate

by Dr. Eliezer Shaklai

Translated by Moshe Kutten

Edited by Jane S. Gabin

I would bring up another picture – a short story that characterized those days:

One evening, I returned from the municipal hospital after a meeting and discussion with Dr. Bilinski. I asked him and received from him a dose of poison (cyanide) for myself and my family to use at a time of distress (it was a highly sought-after commodity, which could not be obtained in the ghetto). I left with a calm heart with my secret weapon in my pocket (poison for an emergency use). I first thought of stopping by the *Judenrat*, as I did every day, to hear the daily news, and only then would return to my wife and son. I walked and thought about our tomorrow. It was easier to foresee the future or, more correctly, the days of the future when you have a choice as to what way to choose if you would ever face the final decision. I continued to walk home, and thousands of thoughts passed through my mind about how to avoid using the poison and survive.

When I crossed the ghetto, I saw a militiaman from afar running and approaching me and yelling: "Stop! Stand!" I also heard a shivered scream of a boy or a girl, a high-pitched, heart-piercing voice accompanied by a knock on the gate: "Open! Open!" I turned around and saw a small girl, holding her little sister in her arms, falling over the closed gate, knocking on it, and begging: "Please open the gate for me." Her facial expression and speech were like that of a frightened person upon seeing a predator animal approaching with its opened jaw, preparing to devour its victim. Jumping once, I was ahead of the militiaman just as he stretched his arm to catch the girl. "Keep your hand away," I yelled. With a quick movement, I held his stretched arm and stopped him: "I was the first," he said, "the girls are mine. First come, first served." I said: "Think about what you are doing. What do you want from the little girls? What did they do to you?" He looked at me angrily, dropped his arm, and lowered his head. He stood in silence, trying to catch his breath. A minute later, he said: "Hermann was the one who ordered the militiamen to bring him a victim within ten minutes – as a ransom for their lives." "Take me," I told him. "You caught me, so let us go to the *Judenrat* together, but leave the girls here." "No," he said, "I did not catch you. You win this time." With tearing eyes from anger or fear, he turned around and left. I remained at the gate with the two orphan girls. They had been going around the ghetto for several weeks already. One of the girls was eight, and the other a year and a half old. Their parents came from a village with the girls by the Gestapo's order. Their father was captured and sent to a forced labor camp a short while later. The mother, a hero, was left to take care of the girls. She worked for the Germans on behalf of the *Judenrat*, three days a week, for a loaf of bread. Once a week, she used to sneak outside of the ghetto to go to her former village to barter valuables for food for her children. The eight-year-old child was left to watch over her little sister until the mother returned.

On one of those trips, the mother did not return. I often met the orphan girls on the street, where the older girl held the little one in her arms. Merciful Jews helped them and made sure they would not die from hunger. When I met them, they stood in front of the closed gate of their bunker. I took out two candies I received at the hospital for my son. I handed one to the little one and the other to the older one. The little one put the candy in her mouth and calmed down, and the older one put hers in her pocket and said as if she was talking to herself: "I do not need it; I will hold on to the candy for the little one so that she would not cry in the bunker."

No caption: A picture by the artist, Michel Kara?

[Page 334]

In the meantime, things calmed down. The darkness enveloped the ghetto, replacing the setting sun's rays of fire. It was time for me to leave, but I could not leave the orphan girls in the street. I knocked on the gate, but [the people inside the bunker] did not answer, although I knew that they heard the entire conversation and knew that the orphan girls, who resided in their bunker, were the ones waiting at the gate.

I knocked gently for the second time. After that, I called the name of the house leader and threatened: "If you do not take the orphan girls inside, I will open the gate by force, with the help of the militia." By the force of the threat, the gate was opened a pinky width, and through the narrow gap, the people put out an arm and got the two sisters inside. The gate was closed behind them.

I skipped my visit to the *Judenrat* due to the delay. On my way home, I stopped by the militia room, where the light was seen, and joyful voices could be heard. I wanted to find out the reason for that festive atmosphere. I found out that the order issued by Hermann was only a joke. After he had given the order, he left town, and the captured people were allowed to return home. Forty militia men celebrated and toasted a drink in honor of one of them, the hero of the evening who decided to sacrifice himself and did not bring a ransom. That was the man I fought with for the orphan girls. When he saw me, he lowered his head and remained silent. I was silent too but thought in my mind that he was really a hero. He conquered his anger in one moment, which was probably the most difficult in his life!

The Gestapo's Divide and Conquer Method

by Dr. Eliezer Shaklai

Translated by Moshe Kutten

Edited by Jane S. Gabin

Passover has arrived. We did not celebrate the "*Seder*" this time. We spent that evening, like all other evenings, in the hideout. We conducted entering and exiting practices into and out of the bunker. I had only a short period to think from one practice to another.

The eight days of Passover passed like the rest days and nights of that period. Several victims, news about liquidations of communities and the "*Judenrein*" operation in the area, news from the fronts, kidnaps to forced labor camps, deaths from a pandemic, and more.

During the same period, the Gestapo invited the Jewish militia, selected a group of twelve militiamen from them, and put them in jail. The Germans selected those militiamen who were the closest and most loyal to the Gestapo. They told the arrested militiamen that they were accused of storing weapons and organizing sabotage and attack operations against the Germans. According to the Gestapo, they received information about it from the ghetto's Jews. It was a lie. No Jew informed or got in touch with the Gestapo people. The actual reason for putting the militiamen in jail was to perform "brainwashing" on the militiamen, make them into loyal dogs who would participate in the liquidation of the ghetto, and sow division and hatred between the militiamen and the people of the ghetto, which the Germans needed to occur in the last few days before the final annihilation. They succeeded. The militiamen who went through the brainwashing in the jail believed that they fell victim to snitching by the people in the ghetto to take revenge on them.

From their side, the *Judenrat* made all of the effort to take them out of prison unhurt. Indeed, [it seemed that] they succeeded since the militiamen were freed after two weeks in jail. I doubt that the release was a result of the *Judenrat's* effort. In my opinion, when the Gestapo were convinced that their plot to generate hate in the militiamen's hearts toward the people in the ghetto succeeded, they freed them.

[Page 335]

The snitching story penetrated deep into the hearts of the militiamen, and they took revenge the first opportunity they had – they greatly assisted in the liquidation of the ghetto!

The month of May arrived. The Soviets began their attacks on all fronts, and they progressed fast. On the other hand, the British and the Americans conquered North Africa and landed in Sicily. People raised the possibility of a second front in Western Europe, France, or Italy. We began to see with our own eyes the defeat of H…r (May his name and memory be blotted out). However, progress was too slow, and we searched for ways to gain time. Time was the most valuable commodity for us then.

The Barracks

by Dr. Eliezer Shaklai

Translated by Moshe Kutten

Edited by Jane S. Gabin

At that time, we received a new offer. Our contact people notified us of the agreement by the Gestapo to establish in our city a barracks to house two hundred professional men. Those people would remain there even after the city was announced as "*Judenrein*." The proposal was that these men would reside in one structure under the guard of the Germans. They would work for the Reich under the supervision of a German manager. I do not know who was the originator of that proposal, whether it came from our contact people who turned it to the Gestapo and proposed it or the Gestapo itself contacted our contact people and agreed to maintain such a barracks after the ghetto liquidation, similar to other cities.

An entrance fee to the barracks was quite high. Despite that, the number of interested people grew and passed over the nominal number of two hundred within a few days. The quota was increased to three hundred under the lobbying by our contact people, and a short while later, it reached up to four hundred. The Gestapo and the contact people nominated me to the barracks physician, but I elected to remain in my place of work at the municipal hospital (luckily). The Germans selected the former house of Dr. Felk Z" L as the barracks. They surrounded the house with barbwire and made it into a real prison with an iron gate and a heavy guard from all sides, as with the forced labor camp. Based on all calculations, there would be no safer place than in the barracks after the ghetto liquidation.

The Germans constructed the barracks in May, and some people moved right in to reside there. Most of those who registered and paid the entrance fee moved in until the end of May. From that point on the people in the barracks were under tight supervision. It became a confined place slated for only four hundred professional men. The Germans did not allow even a single woman to enter.

The house was recognizable from afar as a prison surrounded by barbwire and constant guards at the gate. I was never inside the rooms of that barracks, but I received a description from Menakhem Katz, the only man who was there and survived.

During May, the Germans liquidated one ghetto after the other in our district and declared those places as "*Judenrein*." Our city remained almost the last one. There are only a few places left in our district. According to the pace of these operations, we could tell for sure what day the liquidation *Aktsia* would take place in our city. The Germans no longer hid their plans since they knew that we could not escape anywhere,

[Page 336]

and that we were supervised tightly. We were surrounded from all sides, and we were followed day and night to observe what we were doing in the ghetto. There was special supervision on the roads. The Germans caught everybody who exited the ghetto without a permit. That was how we spent the last days as "legal" Jews and "legal" Judaism in our city!

The Last Dance

by Dr. Eliezer Shaklai

Translated by Moshe Kutten

Edited by Jane S. Gabin

I was asked to visit a patient a few days before the ghetto liquidation. I promised to come in late in the evening. The ghetto was enveloped by darkness and complete silence. The ghetto people listened, trying to penetrate the darkness with their glances. I was familiar with all the Ghetto paths. I knew every house, walkway, apartment, and every resident. I approached the door carefully so as not to frighten the people. Without knocking, I opened the door and got in.

It was dark in the room. There was nobody in the room. I heard echoes of music. Was it music from a record in the adjacent room? Music - in the ghetto? Maybe I was mistaken? I approached the door to the room. I stood there and listened. Yes! A melody of an old song. I found courage and opened the door. I saw a long and dark room in front of me. The hanging flashlight illuminated the room with a dark light. It was hard to see anything. There was no furniture in the room. A gramophone with a record turning on it was placed on a small crate in a corner. A 'shadow' of a person was standing beside it.

Hugging young couples sang and danced with closed eyes; turning around in a circle, they passed by me with clasped hands and arms, attached like a single body. They did not see me and did not hear me coming; they only danced to the rhythm of an old dance melody.

Standing and looking at them, I opened my eyes wide. The people in front of me were like from another world. They did not know that this was their last dance! They invested in it their remaining life aspirations, will, strength, and vigor – the essence of their lives!

With my eyes closed in pain, I walked away and disappeared into the darkness. I took in my heart the picture of the dancing youths. That youth, full of grace and a vibrant life, the youth of beauty, desire, and the right to live!

That precious picture of the dancing youth was etched in my heart forever. The darkness engulfed me, but only the melody stuck with me and accompanied me wherever I went. With that tune, I heard the words of the angel of death: "You are mine! You will not be able to avoid me!"

[Page 337]

The Last *Aktsia* - the Ghetto Liquidation. "*Judenrein*"

by Dr. Eliezer Shaklai

Translated by Moshe Kutten

Edited by Jane S. Gabin

At the beginning of June 1943, several *Aktsias* were conducted daily in our district. The objective of the *Aktsias* was to cleanse areas of Jews and make them "*Judenrein*." Only a few cities remained, waiting for their fateful day and competing with each other as to who would be the last. We were waiting for the last *Aktsia*, and when it was not coming, new calculations were made to predict how much time was left to live. Another day, two days, or a few hours.

From a mental point of view, we were ready for that end. However, the more we approached that day, the stronger the will and desire to live became. We tried to "earn" another hour. That hour may sometimes be critical to saving lives. We took advantage of all the possibilities!

One such possibility came when Ukrainian acquaintances notified me they were looking for a Jewish physician to join them with his family in the forest. These were the Ukrainian nationalists (The Banderovites – [Bandera's people]) who were fighting for an independent Ukraine. These nationalists settled in forests and conducted attacks on the Germans and, during the Soviet rule, on the Soviets. They killed Poles and Jews at every opportunity. Ukrainian physicians did not want to give up on their free life in the city. Therefore, they turned to Jewish physicians and promised them and their families salvation. I contacted the [Ukrainian] headquarters, and luckily, the opening was already filled.

After the war, it turned out that the Ukrainians killed the family members of the Jewish physicians and kept them in atrocious conditions until they killed them. Only a few of these physicians managed to escape during the battles between Ukrainians and the Soviets and return to the city. Their situation was worse since the Soviets considered them fighters on the side of their enemies, and because the Banderovites looked after them, they regarded them as defectors from active duty who could hand their enemies their secrets.

Two physicians, Dr. Laber and his wife (nee Rozen), managed to escape our city. They hid by us for eight days, and we barely got them across the border to Poland.

Every one of us tried his luck by staying with acquaintances for a short while or a long period by paying or for free, but we pinned our hopes on the barracks. If a strong nucleus of four hundred people would survive, their relatives could hide with the Gentiles for a short time or long. The main objective was to gain the required time!

The Shavuot holiday fell on the eighth and ninth of June. We stopped thinking about the holiday itself a long time ago. What was important were the dates and days devoted by the Germans to *Aktsias* and other calamities. When those days passed, we breathed a sigh of relief. We gained two days and perhaps a few days. According to our calculations, the Germans had to start an *Aktsia* on June 10. When calm prevailed on the morning of June 11, we had to recalculate: June 12 fell on Saturday, and the 13th fell on Sunday. The 14th and 15th fell on the Gentiles' Shavuot holiday, and it was not conceivable that the Germans would start an *Aktsia* on Saturday and then break for three days to continue it after the holiday. Therefore, the people who claimed that the operation would begin on Wednesday next week, meaning June 16, had to be right. However, calculations were one thing, and reality was another. As always, the Germans acted in contrast to our calculation.

[Page 338]

On Friday afternoon, the pharmacist notified me that he saw Hermann, the Gestapo man from afar, talking to Betinger. Based on Betinger's response, he concluded that it was a crucial order handed to Betinger by Hermann. I turned my walk toward the barracks to Betinger's apartment. It is important to note that all four hundred Jews who registered to reside there were already in the barracks starting on June 1st, except me. I was the only one who could be outside of the barracks, even during the night. Although I did not find Betinger at home, I met his wife there. After some negotiations, she told me about Hermann's order: to prepare axes and to be ready for Saturday morning, June 12.

I notified the *Judenrat* and the people in the ghetto immediately. The *Judenrat* people tried to verify my version. They had their own intelligence sources. According to those sources, no operation was expected before the 16th. Despite that, we decided to be cautious and not to believe the Germans. Unfortunately, only part of us did that!

Everyone utilized the time to fix, prepare, and research. I decided to leave the ghetto and transfer my wife and son to the hospital where I worked. It was not a problem for me, but I had a problem with my son, who was not quite five years old. The head nurse promised me many times to help me when needed. [At the time] I did not believe her. I thought about constructing a bunker near the hospital for my family. I turned with that matter to the caretaker. I promised him a large sum, but after consulting with his wife, he refused to help. He redoubled his vigilance toward me from that point on. Therefore, I gave up on building a bunker. In the meantime, I just wanted to gain some time until after the *Aktsia*. The head nurse helped me to move my wife into the hospital and hide her there. She also helped me to take out my son from the ghetto, transfer him to the hospital, and hide him with my wife. We obviously kept the whole thing secret from the caretaker.

Before I left my room where we resided, I warned again the house residents. That house was called the "Physicians Block," where the physicians, their families, and relatives lived. I told them that I was leaving the place with my son and wife and escaping to outside the ghetto. I said goodbye to my friend, physician Dr. Feld. We shook hands. He was the last person with whom I exchanged words. We parted ways as eternal friends. He also left the ghetto that evening after our discussion.

On Saturday morning, after I finished my work, I decided to visit the ghetto and the *Judenrat*, as well as some of my patients, and to hear about the situation there. I was cautious not to take the main road a Whoever hides a Jewnd used a side trail. I saw from afar the members of the German gendarmerie riding their horses. I hid until they passed and returned to the hospital. From there, I called the pharmacy (located in the city outside the ghetto), where the pharmacists Goldman and Tonis worked. From them, I heard that a "wedding" had, indeed, begun early in the morning, accompanied by a powerful "orchestra." They told me there were already "invited guests" there, and then the phone call was interrupted.

I remained at the hospital and continued my regular work. On Sunday morning, I visited the patients at the hospital, as usual. When I finished the visit, I asked the head nurse to go to the city and report to me; when she returned, about the Saturday operation. I specially asked her to pass near the barracks and find out whether the people there went to work or remained in their apartments. I could not guess whether anything happened to them. However, once again, the Germans succeeded in lying to us!

[Page 339]

The head nurse returned two hours later and told me about the operation and the notices in German, Polish, and Ukrainian in reference to Saturday. In those notices, it said: "Our city Brzezany from now on cleansed of Jews – *Judenrein*. Whoever hides a Jew or helps a Jew will be punished." The head nurse also passed by the barracks as I asked her. She said that nobody was there, no guarding, and the gate was broken and open.

That meant that they also exterminated the people in the barracks.

On 9 Sivan 5703, 12 June 1943, Brzezany's Judaism was exterminated.

After the ghetto liquidation

by Dr. Eliezer Shaklai

Translated by Moshe Kutten

Edited by Jane S. Gabin

In my meeting with the head nurse at the hospital where I worked, the nurse told me that early in the morning of the day after I left the hospital, Hermann, the Gestapo man, came to "meet" with me (The caretaker snitched about me. He called the Gestapo that I was hiding at the hospital). However, at that time, Hermann was late. The meeting between us was postponed by twenty-three years. It was held in the court in the city of Stuttgart, Germany, in a trial of the Gestapo people about their operations in our area during the conquest. I delivered my testimony against them, and especially against him in that trial. Hermann was sentenced to ten years of jail time. He died in jail.

The "Black Shabbat" was just the beginning of the Nazi operations. The persecution and searches for Jews and Jewish properties continued until the liberation by the Soviets more than a year later. We had actually not totally liberated. I will bring here some of the things known to me about that arduous period, whatever happened to the remaining Jews in the city from the beginning of the *Judenrein operation*, as I heard from eyewitnesses.

At the time of the ghetto liquidation, more than two thousand Jews were alive (many fewer, according to the Germans). On Black Shabbat, which was the first liquidation operation, the Germans succeeded in capturing about six hundred and fifty people in the ghetto and about three hundred and fifty Jews in the barracks, together with about a thousand people. After capturing them, they brought them to the cemetery, where a deep and long mass grave, dug previously by Polish workers, was ready.

[Page 340]

An eyewitness, a Polish judge, told me that he stood on the roof of his house from the morning until the evening and, using his binoculars, looked at the murder of Jews in the cemetery.

Every Jew brought over to the cemetery stripped naked and put their clothes on a pile. Naked and barefoot, they approached the edge of the mass grave facing the pit, with their back to the German [executioner]. The Germans shot them. They jumped or were pushed into the pit.

That *Aktsia* lasted until the evening.

On Saturday evening, the Germans took a break for three days. They renewed their searches only on Wednesday of that week. The *Volksdeutsches* and the bandits arranged for themselves their own holiday during these break days – a holiday of plunder and looting of the properties of the murdered Jews. They also conducted searches after bunkers, where more Jews remained. They were experts in that work. They destroyed everything to the ground in searches for Jews or valuables.

On the second Saturday after the first *Aktsia*, Polish workers dug additional graves in the Jewish cemetery. A Polish eyewitness, who was among the diggers, told me a story that shook him and his friends: the Poles covered the mass grave of the Shabbat murder operation's victims with dirt two times: On Shabbat after the murder, and on Monday morning because the bodies were not completely covered. The diggers added additional dirt on the grave, containing about a thousand bodies, on Tuesday. While covering the grave, they noticed tremors and vibrations in the dirt level above the mass grave. They fearfully stepped away slowly from that place and observed to see what would happen. A few minutes later, a sort of explosion took place. The ground opened, and bodies were thrown up forcefully far from the mass grave.

The diggers considered it a sign that the ground was also shocked, that it objected to these atrocities and did not want to participate in covering these atrocities up. It was as if the ground opened her mouth toward the heavens and announced that it would not be a partner for these acts.

Searches for the Jews in the ghetto and around it continued in earnest, almost without a break, for another two weeks. During these searches, many more Jews were found, among them my sister and my friend, Dr. Arye Feld, and his family. May their memory be blessed.

According to a story by an eyewitness, the Germans brought the Feld family to the cemetery, where they shot his wife and two children first. They released him since they needed his expertise. He was the only roentgen specialist in the area. He went down to the city and reached as far as the Polish church on Raiska Street. Then he suddenly stopped, hesitated for a second, and began to run back toward the cemetery, and there he died near his family.

During the *Aktsias* and more at the extermination camps, there were cases in which the Germans captured whole families and broke them apart. They separated a man and his wife, mother and daughter, and father and son. Every one of the family members continued on their own way, some to die and others to another fate. A barrage of cruel beating forced the people to accept the punishment of separation without an appeal, say goodbye to each other, or respond in any way if they did not want to miserably die on the spot under the beating sticks.

Meir Taler told me about another case. It was in the yard of the prison in our city when the Gestapo conducted a "selection" to the right and left. They selected between people slated for a forced labor camp and those who were later brought to the cemetery to die. Hermann conducted the "selection." When a family passed in front of him, he broke it apart at once - the father to the camp and his wife to the cemetery. The husband tried to catch his wife but failed.

[Page 341]

He was pulled by the flow of the miserable people under the barrage of beating, and he found himself in the labor camp in Kamionka. For the rest of his days, he did not forgive himself for that moment of weakness when he did not choose to go to the cemetery with his wife. He found some consolation [when he found the bodies] at a mass grave of the forced labor camp.

In their searches for Jews, during the two weeks after the ghetto liquidation, the Germans were helped in that despicable work by the Jewish militiamen who were uniquely selected for that purpose (these were the twelve militiamen whom the Germans had subjected them to brainwashing several weeks earlier). They were placed under strict supervision by the Gestapo.

The end of these militiamen was the same as the end of the rest of the Jews, and perhaps even more bitter! The Germans not only killed them but took revenge on them before their death. After the two weeks of searches, the Germans gathered the twelve militiamen, tied them under beating with barbwires, and pulled them to the cemetery. They submitted them to murderous blows until they killed them so that there would be no eyewitness testimony for their savage acts. That was the end of the people who served their German masters like loyal dogs who were ready to execute any order without an appeal.

At the end of the searches, the Germans notified the non-Jewish population about the heavy punishment (up and including the death sentence), which would be imposed on those who would provide any assistance to the remaining Jews in our area.

During the period of the thirteen months that the Germans still stayed in our area, they succeeded in discovering many more Jews, most of them due to snitching by the Gentile neighbors or by the person who hid the Jews in his home. It turned out to be the truth because, in our entire area, no Gentile was punished. Neither a financial nor physical punishment was imposed even though Jews were found in their home.

The farmer that hid us told us, all the time, about the new victims of snitching. Among those whom the farmer remembered by name were the following: Hesio Redlikh and his wife, Klara (nee Preis), the Podhortzer family (one child survived and remained with relatives), and many more that he did not remember. The state of the people who escaped to the forest was more arduous. They hid in the forest or field during the day, and in the evenings, they came out from their hideouts to find food, but the area Gentiles ambushed them, arrested them, took away anything they had, and handed them to the Gestapo for money. It was hard to find, even for money. The villagers were afraid of any contact with the Jews. Thus, a situation was developed where the Jews died from hunger, even when the Germans could not put their hands on them. Many Jews in the forest died from disease, without any help, or from malnutrition or exhaustion when they were forced to leave their hideouts and walk around in the forest in the mud and cold. The situation worsened during the winter. Our people suffered from the intense winter cold, which was especially harsh that year. The snow was particularly harmful because it allowed the discovery of their footsteps. Many were caught because of the traces in the snow.

Our estimate was that about two hundred and fifty to three hundred Jews survived that winter when the Soviet attack was approaching our district for the first time. Many of them would be free if it wasn't for the fact that this attack was repulsed. The Soviet retreat caused the death of most of these people, and salvation came only four months later in the summer, in the second attack, when only thirty or forty Jews remained.

[Page 342]

The Soviets Rule Again

by Dr. Eliezer Shaklai

Translated by Moshe Kutten

Edited by Jane S. Gabin

In the period after the "*Judenrein*" *Aktsia*, we found shelter with several farmers in a bunker we dug ourselves. We stayed in the underground bunker one additional day after the liberation. The liberation news found us at the very last minute. Our situation was dire. We were all "skin and bones." People who saw us did not believe that we would be able to recover and live.

We left the bunker at night. After everyone left, I returned to the bunker to see it and say goodbye for the last time. All of a sudden, the bunker was empty. It really frightened me. I saw a black "grave" in front of me, dark and wet. Was it possible that we spent eight months there? We left [the village] around two o'clock at night. We intended to walk the whole distance to the city. Only some of us succeeded in walking the entire distance on our own power. My brother-in-law, sister-in-law, and their son Mark remained exhausted in the middle. The Soviet Army found them in the evening and brought them to the city. We reached our destination after eight hours of walking (sixteen kilometers). Torn and worn and dressed in rags, we entered the city thirteen months after leaving it during the ghetto liquidation. Thirty-five Jews returned with us. That's what remained from a Jewish population of about twelve thousand at the time of the Nazi conquest!

We formed as one big family. We all lived in one area, far from the ghetto and the place we lived in during the Nazi rule. We did not enter the ghetto. We did not even look at it from afar. It was beyond our strength. Our only wish was to be as far as possible from that place of horrors, where our lives and the lives of our dear ones were ruined. We also wanted to be far from the evil population who assisted in the murder of Jews.

I have previously described our lives under Soviet rule in the chapter "The Soviet Rule" [page 98]. This time, things changed a lot for the worse.

After all, we have endured, our situation as a small group of surviving Jews was much worse than in the early [Soviet rule] period. The official and unofficial antisemitism affected all aspects of our lives. It must be noted that there was still a state of war. That in itself gave the authorities an excuse for strict treatment toward the population, which was under the Nazi rule, and especially toward the Jews who survived. The fact that these Jews were not annihilated by the Nazis made them suspicious in the eyes of the Soviet rule.

A confidential circular was sent to the party secretariat. According to this circular, it was forbidden to nominate a Jew to any responsible or managerial role. I asked my Jewish Communist friends for the reason for it, and they did not answer. I asked the non-Jewish Communists the same question, and they explained to me that these steps were not aimed, G-d forbid, against the Jews. On the contrary, in their opinion, they were aimed at protecting the Jews from the wrath of the Gentiles. The Soviet authorities feared reprisals by the Jews against the non-Jewish population. If the Jews reached ruling positions, even local and temporary, a murderous response from the Ukrainians could be evoked, and they would eliminate the small group of surviving Jews. Another reason was to bring us closer to the non-Jewish population, which absorbed feelings of hate and distrust toward the Soviets.

In the meantime, the Jews were the victims again. The Soviets treated us with disfavor and distrust. The fact that we survived the Holocaust called for another investigation.

[Page 343]

Not once dis the Soviets call me to the NKVD or the KGB and ask questions. They interrogated me for hours. One of the questions that they kept asking was: "How did it happen that everyone was killed, and you and several other Jews survived? It must be because you cooperated with the Germans." They could not forgive me for staying alive after the death sentence was issued against me.

In those days, I had difficulties understanding the approach of the Soviets toward the Jews. However, over the years, I understood and assessed correctly their attitude and approach toward us.

I encountered that negative attitude in all of the institutions in the city. They were hostile to us, which also endangered our lives, particularly coming from part of the Ukrainian population, which established ambushes to capture Jews and kill them.

Leaving the city was life-threatening for a Jew. The population in the city could not tolerate us either. They got accustomed to living without Jews, and it was hard for them to come to terms with the fact that Jews lived among them again, even though the number of Jews was small, and it was just a temporary situation. For them, our stay among them was unnecessary and unwanted. There were several reasons for that. One of the reasons was the fact that we were eyewitnesses to their horrible acts during the Nazi regime, which many of them took an active part in. Some were forced to return some of the loot they robbed from the Jewish properties. But the main reason was their hatred of Jews. [The old antisemitism] and the hatred that the Germans planted in their hearts began to spring up and grow on their own power. The dimensions of that hatred grew daily, widened, and deepened.

The two sides – the Jews and the Gentiles – waited anxiously for the moment when they would separate from each other forever. For us, the Jews, it was clear that we would not be able to find our place among the murderers. Also, every step in these places reminded us of the horrible past, and we longed for the moment when we would be able to leave our native country, the former Polish land. They, the Gentiles, waited for the day we departed and left the remaining real-estate assets in various corners of the city for them.

Life in the city was soaked with sadness. The people were depressed, the stores closed, and darkness prevailed in the streets. Most of the town was in ruins and uncleaned, evoking fear and unpleasant memories. Only about five thousand people remained in the city, compared to 1941 when the city population was thirty-six thousand. The phrase "Once the Tzadik leaves, the beauty and the glory of the city have departed" [Rashi commentary on Genesis 28;10] fits the situation. That was our city without the Jews. The Polish and even the Ukrainian intelligentsia escaped westward with the German Army.

In those days, a night curfew was enforced. It was forbidden to go out after eight in the evening. After that time, it was forbidden to go out to the street. That also hurt our mood. We spent the evenings, each one at their own home. The essence of our life was an "expectation." We waited for the end of the war. We hoped that we would be able to move out from there then. We lived transient and temporary lives, waiting for the day we could leave the city.

One day, we found out that an agreement was signed between Soviet Russia and Poland about an exchange of citizens in both directions. Even though we remembered what happened with the previous list during the first Soviet rule, it ended with the transfer of the registered people to Siberia. Nevertheless, we decided to register for a transfer to Poland, no matter what, despite the risk. The Soviet authorities did not want to forgive us for that step and looked for ways to delay us, blame us for all sorts of offenses we did not do, and punish us. That was one more additional reason for the negative attitude and oppression against us.

That was how the summer went. The days of the spring arrived. During these months, the Soviet, British, and the rest of the armies advanced on all fronts, and the cessation of hostilities was approaching.

[Page 344]

In the meantime, a few more people returned to the city. Young people who served in the Red Army and those who ran away to Russia at the beginning of the war. The young people - full of vigor and will to build new lives, decided to establish families, and we arranged wedding parties for them. Those were the few joyful occasions we experienced. They were double joys: the joy of the wedding and the greater joy that we lived to see the revival of our nation. The nation resurrected! We all met during the public prayer on holidays and Shabbat. We arrange for the prayers to be held at a private home. From all the houses of prayers that were in our city, only the Great Synagogue remained. The Soviets made it into a grain warehouse!

The End of the War

by Dr. Eliezer Shaklai

Translated by Moshe Kutten

Edited by Jane S. Gabin

On the ninth of May 1945, 26 Iyar 5705, we were notified that all war hostilities ended. The entire free world celebrated the victory over H…r (may his name and memory be blotted out). That victory was not ours, and neither was the joy. We only hoped that we could move out of there.

I Leave Town

by Dr. Eliezer Shaklai

Translated by Moshe Kutten

Edited by Jane S. Gabin

I leave my native city, where I had spent half of my life, where I had buried my parents, my dear ones, and my childhood and youth dreams in secret. I escape it like a thief, through allies and side streets to avoid undesirable encounters. The last day is filled with worries, events, and moments critical to my future. I try my best to overcome all the difficulties and complete my regular work, avoiding drawing the attention of my superiors to "my plots" and, at the same time, not being late for the train, which waits for me at a distance of 16 kilometers from the city. I make my way to the train on foot. I am hurrying. These are the late hours of the afternoon. The sun is setting westward, radiating its red rays in the abundance of light and warmth, enveloping the city. I stop. I send my thoughts and glance at the city for the last time. My eyes are photographing it, etching its image in my memory. During these seconds, I am trying to bring up my past in my native city and hug it with my glance for the last time. My parents, my dear ones, and the city people - I promise I will never forget you. I swear on that.

[Page 345]

The Final Way

By Menakhem son of Shim'on Katz[1]

To my father, Eliyahu David Roth

Translated by Moshe Kutten

Edited by Jane S. Gabin

[Page 346]

A documentary description of the liquidation of the forced labor camp in Brzezany.

As the sole survivor of the German "*Wehrmacht*" labor camp in Brzezany and as a witness to the annihilation of the last of my city's people, I found it my holy duty to describe and memorialize the last hours of my brothers in this chapter.

Town's View

[Page 347]

In the winter of 1942-43, a few dozen Jews in Brzezany were "protected" by the German Army - the *Wehrmacht*, and employed in the service of the German war effort. Their main task was cleaning guns, collecting war material and items plundered from Jews (rags and metals), classifying them, maintaining them, and providing general services to several officers of the local *Wehrmacht* headquarters. This group had a unique status. In addition to the white band with a blue Star of David, they wore a *W* tag on their chest with a *Wehrmacht* stamp on it, which entitled them to a special privilege: they could travel freely outside the ghetto during the day. To be free, to move about among the other second-rate citizens of the "General Government Protectorate," was a privilege, a small gap into Nazi Europe, a shred of security, a conscious illusion of the hope of being rescued.

To possess a *W* tag was the dream of every Jew in town. The magic tag proved to be worthwhile. Their owners were not snatched for the work camps in Kamionka, Tarnopol, and the like, and those who were, found themselves released through the intervention of the army and put back into their jobs. This single fact increased the illusion of security.

Rumors, whispers, guesses, and promises Jews made to each other created a legend, the legend that the "*W* Jew" status could not be violated by the Gestapo because its bearer was vital to the war effort. "*W* Jews" would not be murdered; they were needed, they were vital, and they would live.

To live, to live at least as a second-class citizen, to live while the rest of the Jewish people were being exterminated day after day, to live and wait for the war to end, for salvation, for resurrection – no words could describe it. This will to stay alive and generate super-human strength, which the mind of an ordinary person could not perceive. It could drive one into anything: to sacrifice property, forego one's pride, and put aside reason and logic. People of a hopefully required trade, and the affluent tried any possible tactic to obtain the magic tag – even paying a fortune for it.

The cunning Gestapo knew that the "*W* tag" could serve its vile objectives, and as of the winter of 1942-43, the much-desired camp was constructed outside the ghetto boundaries.

The house of the late Dr. Falik, who, together with his family, lost his life for being proud of his nationality, and two adjoining houses, which together formed a fortress-like structure, were selected to accommodate the "*Wehrmacht* Jews'" camp.

The buildings formed a fortified court, which opened toward Tarnopolska Street. On that side was a tall iron fence and a massive iron gate. To the north, the houses bordered a stream; to the west, a street; and to the east, an empty lot with the ruins of the Reb Yiddle Synagogue. The choice of location was not incidental, but rather a well-planned scheme for creating a detention camp that was easy to guard. The place had the appearance of a residential camp, and except for the sole entrance, which was staffed by a Jewish *Ordnungsdienst* guard, no signs of the Nazi regime were to be found. During the day, the camp was almost empty since, except for a few women who were busy cooking,

[Page 348]

all its inhabitants were working outside. At dusk, they gathered inside, and this, too, varied according to the general mood in the ghetto.

People whose trades were needed by the local *Wehrmacht* headquarters, gatherers of war supplies, and others who managed, through bribes or connections with the *Judenrat*, to get permits to live there inhabited the camp. It was quite common that only men, or one of a family, lived in the camp, while the rest of the family lived in the ghetto. For this reason, when the atmosphere in the ghetto was relatively safe, people tended to stay there overnight.

At the beginning of the summer of 1943, when the extermination of Brzezany's Jews was approaching, Gestapo soldiers consented, through *Wehrmacht* people, to admit into the "camp of the fortunate" a few more Jews who pleaded to get in.

This was a trick by which a few more Jews were trapped in the cage so that on the day of extermination – the *Judenfrei* – would already be gathered in the "protected" camp, and there would be no need to look for them in hiding places and bunkers in the ghetto.

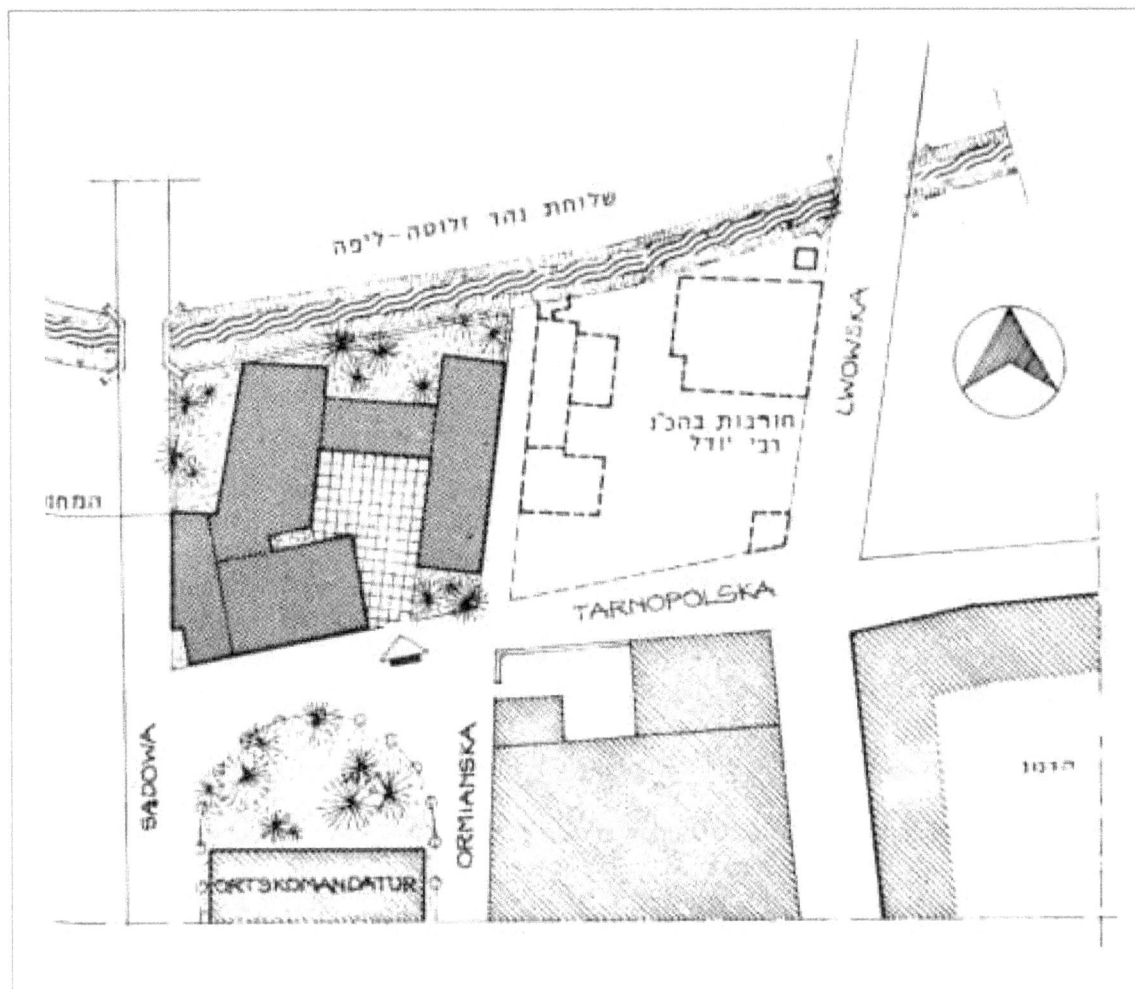

The Camp map

[Page 349]

About two weeks before the extermination day, my father, E. D. Roth, a beverage specialist, got a permit to spend nights at the camp, without being entitled to wear the "*W* tag."

It was Friday around dusk, Sabbath Eve following *Shavuoth* (Pentecost) of 1943. The atmosphere was tense. Rumors about the extermination of the Pszemyslany and Podhajce Jewish communities were alternately proved and disproved. People were running around for news. Was the end truly imminent? That it was a matter of days was quite clear, but still, everyone looked for a sign of hope, a miracle that might take place. Despair and hope, illusion and the bitter truth, a lie about some chance to be rescued, were the only topics of discussion during these last moments. As if trapped in a cage or surrounded by the fire with no outlet, shadows of stooped, terrorized figures were wordlessly slipping away along the alleys; each running to a place that seemed safer. Here and there, in small groups, people whispered in each other's ears, sharing a secret, which would never be retold.

I also stood with my father, mother, and two of our neighbors at the gate to our yard, trying to figure out what to do. A sentence here, an idea there, a meaningful gaze, silence, and over again, but time did not stand still. The sun's last rays cast long shadows, but the despair was longer. The neighbors left; time was pressing. What should we do? The last words exchanged between us were: "Should we go to sleep at the camp or not? That was the third night I had to sleep at the camp. Should I say goodbye to my mother and father and go to the camp, or should I go to the bunker I had outside the ghetto, where I slept all these years? My father was desperate, my mother was in favor of going to the camp, and my father agreed, but then hesitated and changed his mind. The light was getting dimmer and dimmer, the zero hour was approaching, and the decision was made – a few last warm kisses, and turning my head back for the last time, seeing my mother disappearing in the shadow of the hallway, we, my father and myself, stooped and hesitantly sneaked into the camp.

I was one of the last few who walked through the iron gate into the camp's court at Dr. Falik's house. The gate closed; no one walked in, no one walked out. This last Sabbath Eve did not look like any Sabbath Eve. No sign of Sabbath, no trace of a Sabbath atmosphere, no trace of anything human – it was all over.

The camp was full, about 350 people. People who knew each other and lived together for many years. That night they seemed like strangers: stooped, silent, buried within themselves, as if they were mute from birth as if they could not stand each other's presence.

Intolerant toward others, intolerant toward themselves, unending despair numbed all feelings. Silence – they were silent externally, toward their environment, yet their insides ached and cried out for help, revolt, revenge, ceaselessly bursting within themselves, turning spiritual suffering into physical pain. Overwhelmed by pain, people walked from room to room, seeking advice, and making plans. To escape, to hide, to sneak away at the last moment. Escape – but how? Where? To the forest? To a gentile acquaintance who was not trustworthy? What would they do? How would they pay? How would they get food in a hostile environment? How would they survive in the ocean of hatred awaiting them on the other side of the locked iron gate?

[Page 350]

And again, they withdrew into their thoughts or ran over to a friend who occupied a bunk across the room and whispered their thoughts into his ears. Whispered, because everything was secret. They did not want others to steal and use their plans, their ideas about and how to live, how to escape, how to get hold of a shred of hope for survival. Another reason for the whispering: traitors who could inform the *Judenrat* of people's plans and ruin them.

That evening, a few people advocated an uprising: breaking the iron gate and scattering through the windows. To run away and be free, even for a few hours before the imminent end. That was the wish. People talked to each other, whispered, gave advice, and reconsidered weighty questions: What about my wife in the ghetto? What about my wife who is in hiding? What about the children who now stay with this and that person? How is it going to be in the forest? Will I manage? And silence. The silence of depression and hopelessness characterized this morbid evening. At the last moment of life, my mates did not find the strength to instigate an uprising that night, just as they had not in the preceding two years of persecution.

The absence of active leadership, which could have established more partisan troops, was the reason for our failure to fight the enormous, sophisticated mechanism contrived by the monstrous Nazis.

Even though no clear information was available, no one would have announced an *Aktion* ahead of time, a feeling that the end imminently prevailed and felt everyone's heart. The dim light of a kerosene lamp, helplessness, and mental and physical fatigue made most people curl up in their bunks with their clothes on and retire early in the evening. Most did not sleep, but only lay silent, each wrapped in his thoughts and pain. Every once in a while, the silence was interrupted by a loud cry, which was nothing but a deep, heartbreaking groan, followed by a boundless stillness and no response.

Occasionally someone would climb down from his bunk for a short, hushed conversation with a friend or look through the window into the darkness of the night and quickly return to his place.

A few times during that night, the iron gate opened. Some of the *Ordnungsdienst* people returned from the ghetto, and those who were not asleep tried to get some news out of people whom they knew. But there was no news. By ten o'clock it was completely dark, the last night of the camp. Some, those who could, slept placidly, and others quietly suffered their last hellish night on earth. Before dawn people began to climb down from their bunks and wander around for news. Had anything happened in the darkness of the last hours? Stillness and pale sun rays announced the first Sabbath after *Shavuoth* of 1943.

Everybody waited for the gate to open so that they could leave the camp at the end of the tormenting, long night. But on this day the gate remained closed, following an order the camp commander had received that night from the Gestapo.

[Page 351]

The news spread in the camp with the speed of lightning. Everything was topsy-turvy. The clear, cloudless sky of that Saturday (12 June 1943), the fragrance of blossoming gardens, and the joyful twitting of birds, all failed to lift the gloomy atmosphere. The streets around the camp were still deserted, and no living soul could be seen or heard. "It's still early," explained the optimists, while the realists kept quiet and the pessimists uttered: "This is the end."

Restless, unwashed, unshaven, straight out of bed, people wandered around, not uttering a word, avoiding eye contact, and passing each other in the narrow passages between the bunks. Occasionally someone would walk swiftly across the yard to other wings of the camp for news; perhaps the damned *Judenrat* members knew something.

It was still early. The stillness and emptiness enveloping the building, the streets, and the adjacent, yet invisible, ghetto increased the tension.

Suddenly, around eight o'clock, an open Gestapo car emerged with a shriek onto Tarnopolska Street, manned by four soldiers in green uniforms. It was followed intermittently by other such cars full of soldiers in various uniforms. A car would appear and disappear, leaving behind the same morbid stillness as if nothing had happened.

With the vehicles going in the direction of the Gestapo headquarters at Sondova Street, it was clear to all that the *Aktion* was imminent and would be carried out with notorious German precision. The tension increased, and so did the silence, as people withdrew deeper into themselves.

No one came into or left the camp except for a few *Ordnungsdienst* people, who went to the ghetto "on duty," which was mostly to collect information.

Around half past eight, it was confirmed that an *Aktion* was taking place in the ghetto, but what kind? Was it a "regular" or a "final" one, a "*Judenfrei*?" Nobody knew. Nobody wanted to predict the near future. Occasionally, people would gather in small groups to discuss the situation, trying to delude each other.

Perhaps it was only a "regular *Aktion*:" Those who would be captured would be captured; the rest would stay particularly the camp inhabitants.

And perhaps it was a "final *Aktion*," but the camp inhabitants would stay alive for a while longer, and in the meantime, maybe the war would end. Nothing was known, and the end was still hovering in the air.

And then, around ten o'clock, a few distant shots were heard from the ghetto. Everybody froze, for their meaning was known to all.

[Page 352]

Several hundred yards away, an anonymous Jewish soul ceased to exist. Someone I knew had breathed his or her last breath while shot by a German murderer. I felt as if my blood had stopped circulating. The first shot that day was crueler than the pogrom and killing that followed, a clear sign of the horror, which was beginning in the ghetto. Petrified, I leaned against a doorframe, unconnected thoughts flashing through my mind.

What should I do? The only thought that insistently recurred in my mind, and in the minds of the others who were with me was: "Escape!" Run away at any cost, anywhere, without thinking of the immediate consequences. But how? In a moment or two, another, a brighter solution would surface; a shred of hope, a chance to be rescued, and a subconscious voice that would guide me.

But no!

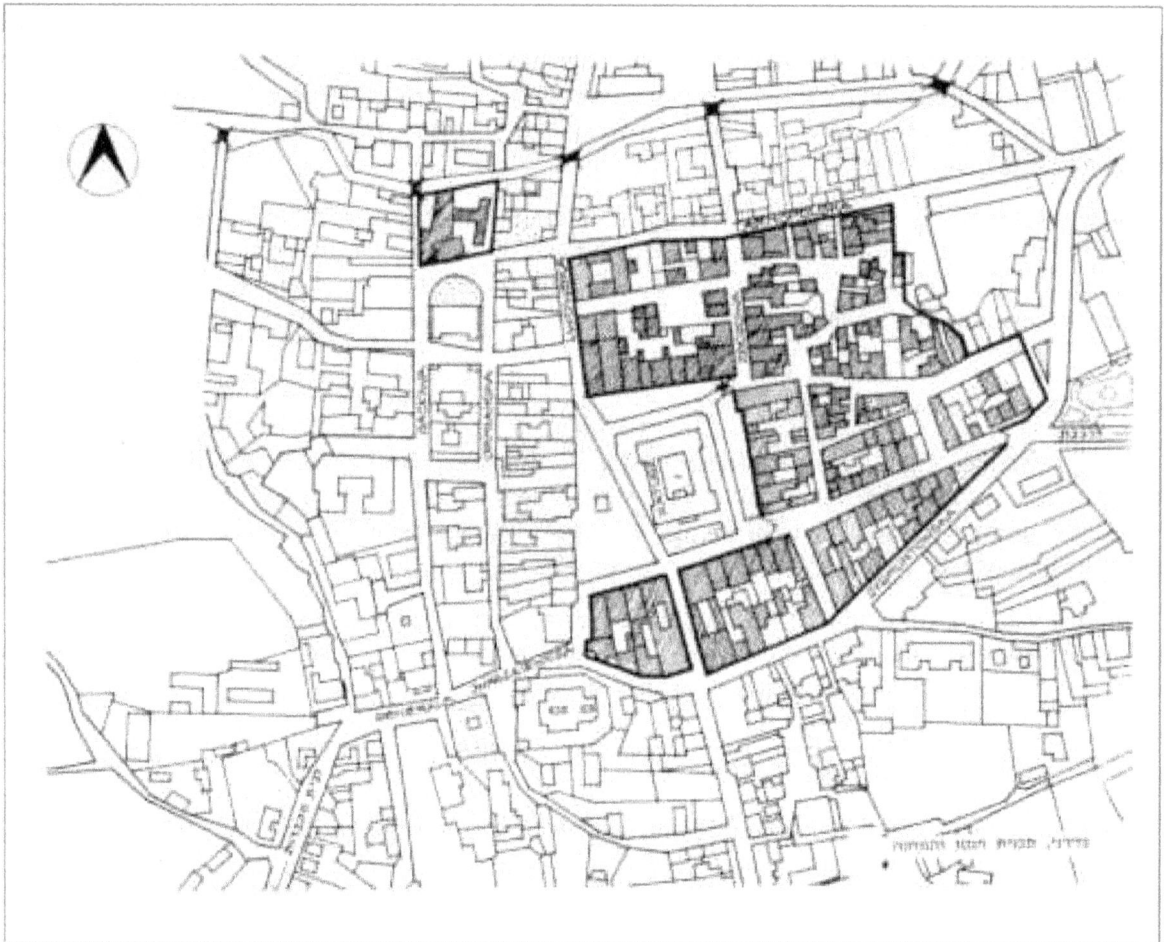

Brzezany map, Ghetto, and Camp marked in black

[Page 353]

No logical thinking could lead to a possible, reasonable rescue. Perhaps one of my friends or relatives would come up with something. But why think of a relative when my father was the closest? Yes, my father was there with me.

I went over to him, looked him in the eyes, and a barely audible whisper uttered a single word … father! He looked at me, firmly held my shoulder with his muscular hand, and remained silent. He could not utter even one word of solace, for he had none.

We knew each other all too well to tell lies for consolation. His hand tightened over my shoulder, and I took it for an answer: Be strong. A gentle push and a release of grip ended our next-to-last meeting. We both looked through the window toward the ghetto, where my mother and sisters were hiding in a bunker and buried our silence even deeper, for we could see a cloud of smoke swirling and rising from a burning ghetto building.

Reassured for a moment by a fatherly touch, yet desperate, my thoughts drifted through the endless conversations I had had with him. "Be strong and maintain your dignity." That was the motto in our home. And now… what dignity? What strength?

A flash of bright thought – to be strong means to be fully aware of the present. At the speed of lightning, I began to contrive a scheme of escape. Another followed one thought – a scheme began to form and seemed to turn into reality. The spirit of juvenile rebelliousness was still with me. My conscience and lust for life screamed from within – do something, follow your spontaneously worked-out scheme. Do something quickly, and you will be saved.

And indeed, with the instantaneous drive and the scheme I had in mind, I quickly moved toward the window to check a certain detail, and instinctively jumped backward, into a shadow cast by the wall at the side of the window.

Instead of the detail, I wished to check, I saw the muzzle of a machine gun located on top of the ruins of the Reb Yiddle Synagogue, and a soldier in a green uniform aiming it at me.

My scheme dissolved and cruel reality manifested itself. We were surrounded. The Gestapo and its supporting forces surrounded the camp and manned all its corners with armed guards.

The situation became clear in an instant – this was the end. The news that the camp was surrounded spread at once among its inhabitants. Then everybody was silent again, and only a few understandably tried to find out whether the rumors were true. Here and there, someone approached the window, trying to take a look at the guards through a slit between the window frame and the half-open wing. Some went up to the attic, and from there, through some slits, had a clear view of their executioners, who were idle by their guns, fooling around and smoking cigarettes, showing no trace of concern regarding the upcoming slaughter. These German soldiers seemed rather content to be guarding a camp with some 350 Jews locked in it.

At about 11:00 a.m., there was a burst of fire from a distant machine gun. Everyone froze. In the room I shared with my death-mates, one could hear a fly crossing the room. Our dulled senses sharpened, and our ears

[Page 354]

seemed to grow longer and wider to better perceive indistinct, distant echoes of the shooting. Bursts of fire followed each other, some longer and some shorter, becoming more and more frequent. Nobody moved. Petrified, we, the Holocaust victims, either sat, stood, or lay on our bunks, waiting for the end. Descriptions of death and the last waves of life ran through my mind. What was it like? How could life end on such a beautiful summer day? Was it at all possible to die under the bright sun amid spring blossom? I? So strong, young, healthy, I would die in a few hours, just as my soul mates were dying out there, not very far, in the town's cemetery?

Yes, everybody knew, and there was no trace of doubt that those shots signaled a major slaughter taking place in the cemetery. This was the final *Aktion* in the ghetto. No one dared to interrupt the silence of the first death wave of that Saturday.

At this stage, the machine guns blasted continuously for half an hour and then gradually dwindled into less frequent short bursts until they stopped. A few moments later, we felt a release of tremendous tension.

Here and there, one could see someone stealthily moving his hand or shifting position. The eternal silence had not yet taken hold of the living crowd.

The first shock of the first death infliction of that day was over. People resumed their whispering and moving about the place. Then the silence was replaced by agitation. People went restlessly from room to room, unsuccessfully trying to communicate with each other.

Close to noontime, Raful Freundlich, a friend of my father, returned from the camp's west wing with the news that some people had killed themselves by taking drugs: Fogel, the pharmacist, his wife, and Dr. Trauner. This news did not make a particular impression but led to mild arguments. Most remained indifferent. Some supported the act and overtly envied them for having the drugs and the courage to take charge of the last stage of their lives.

I was standing at the door of my room when suddenly the figure of my father appeared before my eyes as he returned from a talk with Benjamin Mitelman, the *Judenrat* leader. His face was frozen. His large, strong body seemed to me at that moment like the body of a giant. He stood in front of me, erect and somewhat pensive. With the slightest movement of his hand, he signaled me to move to a quiet corner in the hallway. With no further questions, I stepped back and he followed me. I sensed he had something important to say to me.

He was silent. We stood facing each other for a few seconds. Very very slowly, and without blinking he turned his gaze toward the window facing the ghetto, through which swirls of smoke were still visible. Quietly and with unshakable strength, he said: "It is all over."

He put his hand on my shoulder and continued: "Look, son, toward the burning ghetto. Mother and my other children are probably gone, and as for myself, I have nothing to do here without them. I am about to finish in a few seconds.

"As for you, I only want to remind you of your promise.

Take it perhaps…" More he could not utter and it seemed to me that a tear appeared in his eye.

[Page 355]

He did not cry. He put his hand in his pocket, pulling out his black wallet with some documents and money. He released the chain of his watch slowly as if trying to gain time. His hand glided down my back, vertebra by vertebra, and then he calmly handed me the wallet and watch.

I took them, put them on the nearest bunk, and remained silent. My father grabbed my right hand, pressed it tightly in a painful way, and an unwavering voice repeated: "Remember your promise, keep your dignity… and be strong."

These were the last words I heard him say.

He abruptly released my hand and held my body tightly against his. We stayed that way for a few seconds and released each other abruptly. Before I could utter a word, he stepped back and disappeared behind the door of the next room. The door closed quickly, and I doubt if my cry "Father!" reached him.

I stood where I was for a few minutes without noticing that some people were standing around watching me silently. Naturally, I wanted to open the door, but the hand of Raful, my father's friend, held me back.

"Not now," he said. "Come with me."

[Page 356]

We went together to the hallway. Raful, who had always been very fond of me, did not say a word. We stood together before the balcony facing the yard, lost in thought. I was thinking of my father, and probably so was Raful, for he was a close friend of my father until the last minute.

A second wave of machine-gun fire jolted us. I do not remember how long we stood there, but no more than five or ten minutes. The machine guns rattled in the distance. Somebody opened the door and Raful and I walked into the adjacent room, where, on one of the lower bunks, my father's body was lying.

He looked calm, as if asleep lying on his side. His head was slightly tilted down and the only sign of lifelessness was a black phlegm spot on the floor he spit out in his quick dying.

I glanced at my dead father for the last time, and rapidly turned back and walked out of the room.

The shooting intensified, the intervals getting shorter and shorter. Occasionally people would freeze as they heard the bursts, but they grew accustomed to the noise which was heard everywhere in the camp. The utter silence, which characterized the first wave of shooting, disappeared. People talked with each other, trying to interpret the echoes, noises, and sounds in their own ways.

While I was standing in the hallway, my father's body, wrapped in a blanket, was carried downstairs. I watched him silently and respectfully, and so did the others around me.

At that very moment, a *Judenrat* man by the name of Srul Rus went up the stairs. Formerly an affluent man, he was a hypocrite and a traitor who thought that all the restrictions and calamities were intended for people other than himself and his family. When he passed by the corpse, he provocatively said to the good-willed, benevolent people: "What a fool – why did he do that?"

These words made my blood boil, and spontaneously, without thinking twice, and as I was standing higher than he did, I spat a mouthful of saliva on him. Astounded, sweating, and with an increasingly reddening face, the detestable *Judenrat* representative did not understand how such a thing could happen to him, and who would dare do that to him, the "community representative." He approached me furiously, wanting to seize me, but this time his status was of no help. The people who were standing around did not let him come near me.

There was a bitter, short argument between him, the others, and me. Although he was older, I told him he was dumb and brainless. He wanted to protect his dignity by saying that those in the camp are safe while an *Aktion* was taking place in the ghetto. People around me answered him each in his own way and convinced him to leave the place before my insult took the form of revenge. He immediately disappeared into the adjacent wing.

With no sense of remorse, or shedding of tears, which did not surface in my eyes, or the eyes of any of my companions that day, I sneaked silently to the attic. I figured I could spend some time alone there. I knew I did not have much time, but what should I do with the time I did have?

Cautiously I walked with a bent back between the attic's joists, and in the stifling darkness of the scalding hot tin, I sat down with my head between my hands, leaning on my knees, and let my gloomy thoughts ramble.

Suddenly, unaware of the passing time, I woke up. Somebody hastily passed by me, and in the darkness probably did not see me and pushed me unintentionally. I lifted my eyes and looked around.

[Page 357]

Srul Rus Statues, perhaps mummies or demons? Who are all these? Real human figures or shadows from the other world? At first, I was not quite aware of what was going on, because I had just returned to reality from a world of thoughts. A few beams of light, broken into all the colors of the rainbow, filtered through small holes in the tin roof, each taking its own course, flickering between dust motes and throwing colored spots on the figures who stood by the slits and holes and through them peeped out to the street. Dim light, colored rays in clouds of fine dust, crossed the attic in all directions, on human figures leaning in various postures over slits in the roof – that was my environment. A ray flooded the face of someone, a bright spot on someone else's, floating eyes, not carried by anything moved slowly, as if trying to get through the point of light in the roof. A man with both hands raised, holding two beams, appeared as if crucified, and another clung with one eye on the sloping tin, his hands hanging down as if he were dead. In a corner, someone lay, shrunk to fit the small space, his head toward the slit which let in a beam of bright sunlight. His face was blanched and his red sleepless eyes had a dark frame. The contrast of light and shade made him look like a creature from the world of terror.

I was wide awake, but the attic did not look any different, and the figures did not dissolve or disappear. The moment-before-death reality did not change. A figure moved lazily as if pushed by a ray or an indecipherable force. This was not the gait or movement of someone who was in control of his senses. It was the residue of human energy left in a body devoid of initiative, energy, or the will to live.

The misery of the last two years and the tension of the last day filled people's capacity for suffering. Almost every face conveyed indifference and reluctance to struggle for life. Only a few maintained their vitality and continued to struggle, talking when they could find a tired ear, which would listen.

As I was sitting rolled up on a beam, I vaguely heard something being said repeatedly. I concentrated and figured out what was going on. "Come down, come down." Illusion turned into reality. We were ordered to go down to the yard – and then where? In no time, I skipped toward the stairs leading from the attic down to my room. People moved toward the yard very slowly. Here and there someone seemed to run to the attic to hide, but very soon I saw them coming back. People ran terrorized between the bunks; some went down and back to their rooms but found no way out.

I searched for a familiar face, someone with whom to exchange a last word. I stood at the top of the stairs, by the balcony facing the yard, and watched the slow stream of friends climbing down the stairs. "Raful! Raful!" I yelled to my father's friend, who appeared at the door. He was suffering from severe stomachache and bent forward with his hands tucked under his belt. He came close to me and stopped. His face was frozen, but still, he responded: "Yes?"

"Raful, what should I do?" I asked desperately.

"You should go down to the yard with everyone else or hide in the building. One way or the other, you have nothing to lose, my boy." Slowly, saying no more, he turned and climbed down the steep staircase. Every step on the wooden board seemed like a hammer stroke on my brain and heart. My blood circulation accelerated, my heartbeat was fast, and my brain began to work rather intensively.

[Page 358]

Hide? Where? In the attic? In the basement, although I did not know where it was. In a hiding place, I overheard someone say that existed in the camp. No! None was a good solution. I decided to wait inside and be the last to leave. Maybe somehow, I would manage to hide from the murderers. I had no idea where or how I would implement my scheme, but still, I followed my resolve to wait, to be the last person in the building.

I opened the door and walked to the balcony facing the yard. I gripped the iron railing as if I was about to bend it. I held my breath for a moment and tightened my grip even more. "Be strong!" I remembered.

The yard filled up. People were coming out of all the building's wings and lined up in groups of four, following the order of some unseen person. Foursome after foursome stood in magnificent order and with hardly any noise. I recognized the faces. Friends, neighbors, acquaintances, and others all came out of the building and lined up. I was alone on the balcony, viewing this death parade, caring about nothing.

The yard was full, and I saw Gestapo soldiers pushing and kicking people, squeezing in more and more people in groups of four. Then came the last group, consisting of *Judenrat* members, some of whom had thought *Aktion* and forced labor were for others and believed they could be saved by serving the Germans. Others knew very well they would eventually share the fate of their people, but still organized the community the way they did. That was their fatal mistake.

And then, from the wing in front of me, the last *Judenrat* Chairman came down, Benjamin Mitelman, the man who had known, and had told my father, how the Nazi murderer, Hermann, playing with his gun during a meeting had said to him: "The last bullet shot from this gun will be dedicated to you, my friend."

The chairman was followed by his wife and their two children, other *Judenrat* members, and last arrived the *Ordnungsdienst* people in their blue uniforms. All – with no exception – good, stupid, and villains. Jewish fate is equal, regardless of looks or position.

The last groups of four were squeezed in. On the order of Gestapo officers, some of whom were standing on a platform by the main entrance to the Falik house, both wings of the iron gate opened wide. Two lines of murderers in green uniforms and Ukrainians in dark blue ones streamed to the sides of the Jews. Gestapo people who stood by the entrance turned into the buildings to look for anyone who might be hiding, and then I saw murderer Hubert climbing up the stairs, waving his gun and shouting: "Down! Go!"

Having no choice, I went down to the yard. I was the last person in the line. A few seconds later, my uncle, Iche David, and his son appeared and stood next to me. As I was standing, petrified, I noticed the grill over a sewer opening near my feet. I pulled out the money I had on me and threw it in. In a few minutes, a few more groups of four were gathered and the file was complete.

The armed murderers arranged themselves around us, and the order to move was given. The file moved slowly through the gate. At the beginning of Tarnopolska Street stood a few Gestapo officers, as if blocking the way into that street. The file continued into Ormianska Street.

[Page 359]

"To the cemetery," people whispered to each other. "Do not speak, hold your hands up!" shouted some of the murderers. For a short while some of the people held their hands above their heads, but most of the crowd did not obey the order. Here and there, people exchanged some last words between them. We went up Ormianska Street, and the last hope that perhaps we would go to the railroad station through the marketplace faded out. On every street corner, like Miasteczko and Sondova, there was a vehicle with machine guns ready to shoot.

Not far behind them, you could see small groups of citizens, "brave" Ukrainians and Poles who did not want to miss this parade. In every gentile house I saw, at windows, on balconies, and in yards, the indifferent faces of people, nonchalantly watching us in our last march. All kinds of faces, most arrogant, and they seemed amazed to find out that we were still alive.

When we arrived at Generala-Ivashkivicha Street and turned up the hill, I said goodbye to the last shred of hope I had of being taken to the railroad station. The only route ahead of us at this point was the one leading to the town's cemetery.

Sondova Street

[Page 360]

The file seemed to be shaking as it turned. A kind of wave of motion, shivering, a tendency toward scattering streamed through the file. I imagined that here, at the spacious square in front of the Farna Catholic Church, with its trees, gardens, and alleys, everybody would scatter and escape in all directions. I was deeply disappointed when the whispering and agitation quieted down and nothing happened.

The file kept marching, and there was no help. I passed by my house and glanced for the last time at my grandfather's home: the high wall and three stories of windows empty of those who, in the past, had welcomed me with a smile each time I came to visit. But the tenants were gathered in the yard and I clearly saw their amazement as they saw me. Only one neighbor hesitantly waved to me and then turned away. Holding my head straight up, I passed by them, looking at them coldly with no trace of emotion.

From there to the cemetery there was only one more turn, to the right, with two last houses on the right, the fence of the priest's garden on the left, and then a section with no houses, leading directly to the cemetery's gate.

The sight of the tenants of the house where I lived, the inheritors of our belongings, diverted my thoughts for a moment, and I forgot where I was heading, but only for a moment. The file turned right. In the face of what would be a humiliating death, people became agitated. Endless thoughts galloped through my mind, changing constantly in response to my environment.

Most of the people were silent and ignored the murderers' shouted orders to raise their hands. Only those who walked next to soldiers, and were periodically hit by their guns, raised their hands, which, after a short while, naturally returned to their normal position.

A few words, short phrases, or questions were heard here and there.

"Father, father, look around, how beautiful the spring and the sun are and I have to die now," said the 12-year-old daughter of Benjamin Mitelman, the *Judenrat*'s chairman.

The girl continued to march but received no answer from her father, who only held her hand, and the hand of his young son, and with everyone else they proceeded toward the open gate of death.

My uncle, Iche David, who marched next to me, whispered chapters from the Psalms most of the way. As the cemetery gate became visible, he lifted his hands and continued loudly *"Ein k'Eloheinu, Ein k'Adoneinu…"* [There is no one like our God, no one like our Lord], and part of the crowd joined him.

Unrestrained singing burst forth to the clear, cloudless sky, and was carried with the light wind to the open spaces of blossoming fields. The crowd chanted its last request, the only encouragement they could have, which confidently led to God.

The murderers remained silent for a moment, alarmed by the mass ecstasy, which again seemed about to break the chain of armed guards and scatter in the fields. And at last, the ultimate riot, the natural and only resistance came, albeit too late and too small, but there it was.

Hearing a few shots, which somehow sounded soft against the loud singing, I turned back. To the left, up a slope, and a few yards from the edge of the road, by the priest's garden fence, the first victim of this last group was shot dead. A bullet went through the head of a short man, one of the Viennese refugees, who had served the *Wehrmacht* as a driver and mechanic. The sight of his brain spewed over the dark soil and his rolled-up body made me turn my head in the opposite direction, to the right, toward the down-sloping fields.

[Page 361]

The figures of two brothers, Velvel and Shaye Klein, expert rope makers, broke off from the group and ran down the slope, but after a few yards, they too were shot dead. At that moment, two more figures, those of the Taller brothers, strong drivers, collapsed while running, quite far from the marching file. Then I noticed another figure running away, with a good chance of success, toward the edge of the field and the first peasant house. A few more steps and a plaited fence would have concealed and saved him, but no … a short distance from the first house a machine gun bullet reached him and he collapsed.

These hunters of escaping Jews raced against time, distance, and the number of attempts. Tensely, I watched the terrifying mass murder scene, which began before we passed the cemetery gate. The guards became unusually nervous and over the heads of those who were in file, tried to shoot a few people who were escaping toward the downhill slope. Then, they distanced themselves from the file so they could better aim their weapons. There was shooting and the rattle of machine guns placed on fences and the roof of a gunpowder warehouse in the distance.

The last rows of the file, including mine, reached some 20 meters into the open field. My mind was fully aware of what was going on and did not stop making plans and contriving schemes even for a second, and then I saw the picture of my bitter end which was only a few moments away. I did not lose even a fraction of a second. I looked at the left side of the file, up the slope. The field was empty. Nobody chose the uphill slope, which was not very steep, as a direction for escape.

I looked again downhill, and far away from me, at the beginning of the file about to reach the cemetery gate, I saw the tall figure of Nathan Katz, my father's brother, detach itself from the crowd and quickly hop over the furrows of a potato field down the hill. My breath stopped. Will he succeed? Yes! Yes! He did, he got further and further away very fast in long leaps, he was already in the middle of the field, and in a second he would be behind the fence on the slope. My heart seemed to have stopped beating. It seemed as if I were with him. I watched his amazing movements. Hope and fear alternated and I followed his figure until a few meters before the fence, and all of a sudden, his body leaped to a height which, to my mind, was impossible. An unusually courageous leap, which, to this very day seems to me beyond human capacity, one last leap and he landed at the bottom of the fence. He was the seventh to have the courage and the strength to challenge the death, which awaited them at the open pit on the other side of the cemetery wall.

"These are the last minutes of your short life. A few weeks ago, you turned 18, and now you have to die," I thought. "No!" Everything in me rebelled.

"To die? OK, but not with such disgrace over the pit."

The innumerable arguments I had had with my friends and acquaintances about survival flashed through my mind for a fraction of a second. It's all over. This is the end.

Face it in your own way, the way you thought more than once, and act according to your promise. Remember what your father said to you a few hours ago. Live up to your promise not to die over the open pit and wait for the murderer's bullet.

[Page 362]

"Be strong!" my father's last words kindled a super-human strength in me. I looked for the last time at the downhill slope. Nobody was running at that moment.

"I am running away!" I screamed toward my cousin, who marched beside me. Without listening to his reply, I switched over to the left-hand side of the file, to the side going uphill. I forced one of the guards out of my way and quickly leaped into the potato field. The clods of earth were aligned in deep furrows, and since I was strong, I leaped over them quickly. Despite my desire and natural instinct to disappear as fast as possible, in a straight line, I did not do so.

My cool, well-calculated plan did not desert me. I ran forward, as fast as a young man could, in diagonal leaps. A leap and a step to the right, a leap and a step to the left, and straight forward again.

After 20 or 30 meters, I noticed clouds of dust popping up around me. At first, I thought these were birds who were flying away, frightened by my fast movements, but a moment later I grasped their significance – machine gun bursts that were aimed at me. I increased my leaps to the left and the right to make it impossible for the murderers to aim their viewfinders in a straight line toward me.

The deep furrows and the potato plants made my escape very hard, and after 50 meters, I stumbled over something and fell for a second. At that critical moment, one of the hundreds of bullets aimed at me hit me. I did not feel it at that moment, and luckily it hit only my muscle and left the bones intact. Instantaneously, as I fell in a fraction of a second, so did I get up and continue with my diagonal leaps. They kept shooting, and I continued running with all my might up the hill toward my first destination, a field of tall wheat.

My luck, fate, and courage helped me when my life was very close to its end. Within seconds, I reached the edge of the wheat field and dropped. The bullets went on reaping the wheat, but I advanced, crawling along the field.

After a few moments, the murderers lost their target and the shooting stopped. Perspiring heavily and with foam around my mouth I continued crawling on all fours, hidden by the wheat. I advanced toward the edge of the plot and looked for another wheat field to which I could proceed and fool the murderers who would most probably try to chase me. Leaping to an upright position, I crossed potato and low wheat fields and crawled through the tall crops. In that way, I crossed dozens of plots and approached a road leading to the village called Rai (Garden of Eden, in Polish).

Hell was much closer to me at that moment. Exhausted I dropped into one of the tall wheat plots, and crawled along it some dozens of yards and then decided to rest and see what would happen. I covered myself with wheat and lay down.

My mind was hard at work, I was excessively fatigued, my leg began to ache and my sense of security was not strong. I had the feeling I would be chased but decided not to reveal myself. I lay hiding in the wheat and waited. Every second seemed like an hour, every minute seemed a whole year, endless, an eternity.

[Page 363]

What was going to happen? What should I do? Every thought led to others, and my reason kept whispering, "Stay in hiding." Slowly and cautiously, I crawled to the adjacent plot, and then to a third, and then I rested again.

Rai's town gate was very close to me, and since I suspected it was guarded, I decided to wait inside the field till evening to avoid crossing the road in daylight.

I made myself comfortable and lay down, but remained alert. I counted the minutes. Time went slowly, and ceaseless shooting was heard from a short distance away.

Twenty minutes went by, and I heard voices getting closer and closer to where I was lying. My hope that I was saved vanished, but still, I decided not to reveal myself and to wait. Slowly, I covered myself with wheat, lay flat on the ground, and looked up. The voices were getting closer. I said to myself: "I am being chased - they are looking for me." So I remained lying on the ground, expecting a bullet. My blood froze. I felt the two murderers getting closer to me from both sides of the plot, which was no wider than 12 to 15 yards. I was inside it, between them. About 10 yards before they reached me, I heard one say to the other in Polish: "A few more yards, and he should be here." My young nervous system did not fail me. I kept lying and waiting. Perhaps they would miss me. I waited for my killers with open eyes. They came very close to me, and I saw them clearly passing by. One was tall with a dark blue uniform and a gun, and the other, in a green uniform, was holding an automatic weapon, ready to fire.

They passed by without noticing me and went on. When I was unable to hear them, I cautiously crawled back in the direction they had come from.

Now, there was a chance I might be saved. The chase had failed. I switched to crawling on all fours, far away in the opposite direction, and stopped to lie down with mixed feelings but a slightly better sense of safety.

The sun was still high. Time passed very slowly, and the echo of the continual shooting gnawed at my nerves. Gloomy thoughts plagued me, and I could not get rid of them. The wound began to be very annoying, particularly because I did not know what it was like or how bad it was. I lay flat on the ground for about an hour, and my sense of security grew stronger.

The song of death rising from the nearby cemetery was tormenting and stayed with me for a long time. Lying down, it seemed to me that dusk was nearing. I looked at my father's watch – it was five past five. The sun was pretty far from the horizon, and occasional shooting was heard.

I had been saved once again. Till the next time, I thought. At this moment, I understood that my struggle for survival had begun once again. I turned on my side for the first time after an hour of lying motionless on my back. I tied a kerchief around my wounded leg and kept lying there, waiting for the darkness.

[Page 364]

Around five thirty, on Saturday following *Shavuoth*, 9 Sivan, the 12 of June 1943, the shooting finally stopped.

On this Saturday night, the last of my town mates were killed. All members of the Brzezany Jewish community fell victim to the villainy of the Nazi monster.

That was the end, but the earth refused to accept them. It was not their place. For forty years now, I have been carrying the image of those pure souls in my heart. I salute all the people who passed the test of life, and in their death, they maintained their Jewish and human integrity.

Let their death serve as a warning for generations to come. Blessed be their memory.

Translator's Note:

1. This is an edited version of the translation that appeared on https://www.oocities.org/brzezany/

[Page 365]

The Will of the Pohoriles Family

By Peleg-Marianska

Translated by Moshe Kutten

Edited by Jane S. Gabin

The will of the Pohoriles family, in its Polish original form, is kept in the archive of "Yad Vashem" in Jerusalem. Only sections of the will are brought here along with the review by Mrs. Peleg-Marianska and with the kind permission from "Yad Vashem."

The Editor

The Pohoriles family:

Emanuel Pohoriles, an agronomist, Ternopol District
Roza Pohoriles, the daughter of Herman and Regina Freudenthal, was born in 1891 in Aleksandrovka village, Skala province.
Hulda Pohoriles, the daughter of Emanuel and Roza Pohoriles, was born in Lviv in 1920.

The entire family perished in Brzezany. May G-d avenge their blood.

A unique correspondence containing six letters was assembled in this article dedicated to the history of the Pohoriles family's Holocaust years. Three of the letters were written in April 1943, in Eastern Galitsia's town of Brzezany, by members of the Pohoriles family: the father Emanuel, mother Roza, and 23-year-old daughter Hulda.

These letters are the farewell compositions of people condemned to death. They all died in June 1943, three months after the date of the letters, during the final liquidation of the town's Jews. A copy of Emanuel's handwritten original will, signed by the three family members, is attached to the letters.

Another two letters, added to this collection, were written by a family friend, the Polish engineer Tzebinski, in 1946. He kept the material and sent it to their relatives in Israel after the War, as requested by the deceased. The sixth letter is an acknowledgment and thank-you to Mr. Tzerbinski by a family relative, Dr. Shvager, in Tel Aviv, for receiving that precious patrimony.

The letters of the Pohoriles family members excel in their shocking accuracy of the description of the slaughter waiting for them. Following the period of oppression and murders they had witnessed, they are heading toward their death with their eyes open, without a shadow of hope.

And here are some sections from these letters, translated from Polish:

From the mother's letter:

"...Now we are no longer waiting for a miracle. Four to five million people, we included, are dying. I am haunted by horror and avoid talking about it. I try to control my nerves, but I am so fearful from that moment. G-d would ensure that all three of us, or maybe the two of us, die together ... Be healthy... I say farewell with kisses to you. I thought that we would be able to see you again, but that will not happen..."
Yours, Rozalka."

Teraz już cudu nie czekamy. Poszło 4—5 milionów ludzi i my między nimi. Zgroza przejmuje mnie, kiedy o tem zaczynam myśleć. Unikam tych tematów. Nerwy hamuję jak mogę. Ale tego momentu strasznie, strasznie się boję. Daj Boże, byśmy wszyscy 3 albo obie padły równocześnie. Bądźcie zdrowi. Żegnam Was jeszcze raz i całuję długo, mocno, myślałam, że może przecież jeszcze Was zobaczę. Stało się inaczej.

Wasza Rozalka

A copy of the section from the letter from Rozalka (Roza) in Polish

[Page 366]

From the father's letter:

"…Do not forget… when the time comes for the negotiations about the peace, do not forget the millions who fell victim to the executioners. Do everything to take revenge for their... pure blood… These letters will be kept by noble people who helped us a lot and requested nothing in return. They will tell you when we were murdered and where we were buried…"

Pamiętajcie, gdy przyjdzie czas pertraktacji pokojowych, nie zapominajcie wówczas o Waszych braciach i siostrach, o tych milionach ludzi, którzy zginęli z rąk tych oprawców i róbcie wówczas, co w waszej mocy będzie, by pomścić niewinnie przelaną krew.
List ten pozostawiamy u jednych godnych ludzi, których tu poznaliśmy i którzy bezinteresownie dużo dobrego nam zrobili i którzy będą mogli Wam podać kiedy nas zamordowano i gdzie leżymy.
Bądźcie zdrowi i miejcie się dobrze. Całuję Was wszystkich serdecznie.

(—) Manek.

Brz. 12/4 943.

A copy of the section from the letter written by Manek (Emanuel) in Polish

From the letter of the daughter:

"…We now stand in front of the gates of death and wait for it fully conscious, with no hope for rescue and mercy. Our will is strong to live and to get out of this horrific situation, to laugh at the whole world under the sunlight…and to live…to live. "We do not have poison because it is difficult to get it here, so there is no choice but to go by ourselves to our funeral, strip naked, stand face to face with our grave, and receive the bullet in our heads. It seems that I would go alone since Mother cannot march. They will 'finish' her at home, and the labor camp will wait for Father…"

"We are waiting for 'it' during Passover when you pour your holiday wine – Here it would be the warm red blood…All of you be healthy, enjoy yourself, love, and don't bother yourself with nonsense. Today, I would also know how to live, but I understand it is too late. Now I know that everything is vanity…and spring is so wonderful compared to our horrific death."

Teraz my sami stoimy u wrót smierci, nas samych czeka smierć, gorsza niż tamtych wszystkich. bo z pełną swiadomoscią tego, co nas czeka. I nie ma ratunku, nie ma zmiłowania. Tak bardzoby się teraz chciało życ — przeżyć ten koszmarny okres i życ dalej, smiać się do słońca, do całego swiata i żyć, żyć. My trucizny nie mamy, bo o nią dzis bardzo trudno, dlatego też nie mamy innego wyboru, jak iść na własny pogrzeb, rozebrać się do naga, stanąć twarzą do grobu i dostać kulę w tył głowy, pójdę pewno sama, bo mamusia nie może chodzic, więc zafatwią się z nią w domu, a Tatuś ma jeszcze obóz przed sobą, Spodziewamy sie tego na swięta Wielkanocne — a przypuszczalnie będzie to już akcja likwidacyjna. Widzicie więc, że wtedy kiedy u Was z okazji swiąt lało się wino, u nas lała się czerwona, gorąca krew ludzka.

A copy of the section from the letter written by Hulda in Polish

A copy of the section from the letter written by Hulda in Polish

[Page 367]

Special attention should be given to the Will of Emanuel Pohoriles, which contains a detailed list of the family's property. This is a typical list in its character and form. As an owner of an agricultural farm, the deceased counted accurately all the details. Among the details are the number and "private" names of the horses and the quantities of crops in measures customary to Polish villages, every tool, and agricultural machinery. All of that is listed with the indication of the monetary value at the time of the confiscation by the Soviet and German authorities. In the end, the deceased asked to divide the anticipated compensation between the engineer Tzerbinski and his relative in Israel.

The Will was written three months before the final *Aktsia* and testifies to the deep belief of the condemned to death in honesty and justice that will come after the War. Obviously, there is real meaning attached to that document, but it also constitutes a precious human document.

Tzerbinski's letter contains information about the progress of the *Aktsia* in Brzezany in June 1943 and details about the fate of the Pohoriles family. According to the Tzerbinski testimony, all three were killed when their bunker, where they were hiding, was discovered. At that moment, Emanuel Pohoriles shot at the Germans, and after that, he shot his wife and daughter and then killed himself. The family's burial is in a mass grave, marked by Tzerbinksi, in a prominent location in Brzezany.

This bundle of letters, which was kept until the end of the War, was sent to Israel and handed over to "Yad Vashem" by the relatives of the Pohoriles family. It would serve as historical material and, at the same time, as a memorial for three among the million.

Memories from the Ghetto

By Dr. Shimon Redlikh

Translated by Moshe Kutten

Edited by Jane S. Gabin

Our family resided at the edge of the Ghetto on Train Street, at the house of the Arauner family. The men worked in jobs provided by the Germans. Some of them worked in jobs of particular importance. These people were the owners of the letter W. The women, too, worked in various jobs.

Like in every house in the ghetto, hideouts (bunkers) were constructed in that house. The hideout, constructed before the *Judenrein*,

[Page 368]

saved the lives of several people. It was constructed as a double roof in the corner of the attic. It consisted of a limited space between two tin walls with a door located on the inner wall, which could be detected from the outside when closed.

About 40 people, almost all the house residents, entered the hideout on the evening of the *Judenrein Aktsia*. My father *z"l*, Shlomo Redlikh, who was among the barracks' people, was convinced by his barracks friends that the Germans were about to conduct an inspection and that he had to be there. That was the last time we saw him. He was murdered a day later when the barrack's people were the first to be eliminated by the Germans.

On the day of the *Aktsia*, we heard the voices of those people who were taken out from their hideouts and led outside of the ghetto. There were three children and several elderly in the hideout, among them my grandfather, Fishel Bomze *z"l*, and his wife, Rivka Bomze (nee Shvartz) *z"l*. Since the hideout was small, people lay next to each other for three days. The food ran out, and the *Aktsia* lasted a few days. After a week, people began to exit the hideout to look for ways to be saved.

Only eight people remained in the hideout after two weeks: the owner of the house, Mrs. Trauner, her sister, Fishel Bomze and his wife, my mother Khana Redlikh, myself, and grandmother Flug and her nine-year-old grandson, whose parents left him with the grandmother to try to save themselves. Mother and Grandmother discussed what to do. In the end, it was decided to turn to a friend of the family, a Polish blacksmith, Stanislav Kadugni, who owed my grandfather a lot of money. When we looked through cracks in the windowsill, we saw that he had passed near the house several times. My mother and grandfather went out to that Gentile's home, several kilometers from the ghetto. My mother told us about that visit: "Grandfather knocked on his window, and the gentile immediately opened the door and got us in. We told him about what happened to us and cried. We asked him to help us with food. The gentile said he would help as much as he could. He gave us a pail of water, a few loaves of bread, and a sack of charcoal to prepare hot food." My mother and grandfather agreed with Kadugni that they would come to him every two weeks on Tuesdays, in the middle of the night, to take food and water. These night trips became a routine.

During the following few weeks, Poles and Ukrainians entered the house below us, breaking walls and looking for properties and bargains. The house remained empty and half-ruined while we were hiding in the attic like ghosts inside the empty and destroyed ghetto.

Two months passed from the day we entered the hideouts when Mrs. Trauner fell seriously ill. She was dying for two days, witnessed by two children, eight and nine years old. After her death, my mother and grandfather tied her body and lowered her down to the cellar. Her sister, Mrs. Trauner, left the hideout the following day. We were left with six people in the hideouts. Three more months passed.

On one of the days, we heard people who arrived at the house and came to fix the apartments. That lasted for several weeks. One night, my mother and grandfather went down and saw that everything was ready to accept new tenants. A question was asked then: how would they be able to go out and bring food, and in general, should they continue to live in a house populated by people? They consulted with Kadugni, and he stated that he could not provide shelter for us. In January 1944, when Mother and Grandfather wanted to leave on their regular night trip to bring food, they found, to their horror, that the door to the attic that led to the staircase was locked. They returned to the hideout and sat down. They spent the whole day trying to find a solution. Grandfather woke up the following day and opened the door with an ax. Our former apartment was located across from that door, from where a woman came out in panic. She promised not to snitch to the Germans but requested that everybody vacate the attic within a day or two.

[Page 369]

In the evening before the *Judenrein,* my mother's sister and her husband escaped to the village of Rai, and where they found a shelter with a Ukrainian woman farmer. That woman came to our friend Kadugni, and by that, the connection between the two parts of the family was maintained. When our house was reoccupied, Mother and Grandfather did not go to Kadugni, so my aunt began to worry, and she sent the Gentile woman every evening to find out what happened to us. The day following the meeting with the new woman resident in our former apartment, Grandfather went out in the middle of the day, and when he arrived at Kadugni, he found the Gentile woman farmer sitting there. Grandfather cried and begged the woman to save us. In the end, she agreed to take all six of us to her village. Kadugni did not let Grandfather return to the ghetto during the day. When my mother saw that her father did not come back in the evening, she decided to come down with me from the attic. We left the attic and stood in the house corridor by the window, where we could look outside. We waited there for about an hour, and when it became dark, we suddenly heard the steps of Grandfather. He said: "G-d is great. The Gentile woman agreed to take us today and the rest of the people tomorrow." My mother took my hand and went out of the house. The Ukrainian woman farmer and Kadugni's eighteen-year-old son stood on the sidewalk near the house. We had to cross the lit street, where we could have been discovered and handed over to the Germans. The young man walked in front of us so that he could slip away in a moment of danger. The woman farmer walked about five steps behind us. While crossing the street, the youngster whispered to my mother: "Pray to G-d, pray to G-d." When we crossed the street into the darker side, the woman farmer took me on her back (I could hardly stand on my feet from lying down and not walking), and she also held my mother's hand. We walked like that for six kilometers in the snow that reached a depth of about a half meter (about 19.7 inches). We left at 6 in the evening and arrived at 5 in the morning. My mother tripped and fell several times, but she rose and continued to walk. We both grabbed snow and drank it thirstily since there was a shortage of drinking water at the hideout during the last few days. The Gentile woman went out to the ghetto again on the following day to bring over the rest of the hideout residents to her home. However, young boys discovered them on the way to Kadugni's house and handed them to the Germans. They were undoubtedly beaten and tortured but did not tell the Germans about us.

We spent the next six months, until the summer of 1944, sheltered by the Ukrainian Gentile woman, whose name was Tanka Kontzevitz. Her husband was taken to forced labor camps in Germany, and she remained with her two children, a son, 6 years old, and a daughter, 10. We helped to sustain her by asking a Polish woman friend to hand over various items we had left with her in the past.

In the winter, we hid in a narrow storage shack, where only a single bed was placed. In the summer, we moved to a small attic above a cowshed. Gentiles and even Germans entered the woman's home often, and we feared that we were going to be discovered every moment. Our hopes grew toward the summer when we heard the voices of the approaching front from the east. However, it was then that the dangers rose. The woman farmer decided, several times, to expel us, but with tears and shouts, we convinced her every time not to realize her threat.

In July 1944, we finally received the news about the liberation of the city and its surroundings by the Soviet Army. We returned to Brzezany, which was empty of Jews. We stayed there for about a year, and in the summer of 1945, we moved to Poland under the repatriation campaign of Polish citizens.

[Page 370]

Forced Labor Camp Kamionka

By Meir Tuller

Translated by Gloria Berkenstat Freund

Edited by Jane S. Gabin

For the sake of knowing, each of us needs to be informed not only about the crematoriums (Auschwitz, Majdanek, Treblinka, Bergen-Belsen, Belzec, and all of the others) and not only about the ghettos and mass graves at the municipal cemeteries. All Jews all over the world must also know and remember the hundreds of thousands of Jews tormented to death in the Nazi forced labor camps that existed in eastern, Lesser Poland and, principally, how the German murderers reigned over and tortured Jews.

Three of the innumerable such forced labor camps where hundreds of young men were taken from out of the city and area and where they perished were: 1) Gawrielubka (Tarnopol camp), 2) Borki Wielkie and 3) Kamionka (train station – Bugdnubka). I will here relate how the drudgery looked and the death in the forced labor camp Kamionka.

After all of my experiences and fateful trials in the ghetto, hunger, and death *aktsias* [actions, usually deportations], I was, yes, really the only Berezhany camp Jew who survived. A witness who, by a miracle, personally endured over and over again and survived the great tragedy that took place in the forced labor camp Kamionka, only one from among the hundreds. Places of hell, as if cut off from the world, fenced in by electric barbed wire, tormented and starved to death, approximately 10,000 Jewish men from eastern Galicia, including a very considerable number of fellow townspeople.

During a smaller death *aktsia*, during a selection – instead of going to a *shmaltz grub* [a pit of chicken fat, an indication of something good], I entered the camp itself. On the 2nd of April 1943, I and 300 Jewish men, women, and children were caught and arrested. Standing in a suffocating throng 90 in our cell, we barely made it through the night. On the 3rd of April 1943, very early, all 300 of the captured Jewish victims were led out of the three cells into the prison courtyard where the Gestapo *Sturmführer* [German paramilitary rank] Herman, may his name be erased, carried out a selection.

"Who should live and who should die" was only dependent on the direction of his finger. The consequence was that 200 men, women, and children were instantly taken away to the cemetery, and the remaining 89 men were loaded on two open trucks to Kamionka.

The work there consisted of breaking stones, pouring tar, digging, repairing, and keeping constant the material stream that led from Tarnopol to Kiev through Podwo³oczyska for military purposes.

[Page 371]

Nearing the area of the Kamionka camp, we met a group of exhausted people, half barefooted, their feet bloody, wounded, and swollen; their clothing was torn, dragging themselves with tired steps – in rows and singing (!). Their expressions were miserable and resigned, with frozen noses and ears. With empty bread sacks and thin mess kits hanging, they walked as if at a funeral to their camp grave and were ordered to sing a song with the last strength of their almost exhaled souls.

This was the first image, the first greeting of our coming days.

Arriving before the camp gate, soaked by the rain, we were ordered to place everything we had with us on a pile; thus each of us remained penniless. To my good fortune, Yosek Majblum, who was the camp doctor, saw me there. He covered his face in pain wanting. He asked, "How did you come here?" At that time, I did not yet understand how painful his question was. However, he immediately consoled me and assured me he would help me if he could. At the time and in those conditions, such a promise was a rarity.

The camp was located near the main street 10 miles [16 kilometers] from Podwo³oczyska [Pidvolochysk]. It was very high uphill, and we had to bring buckets of water from the wells in the valley. Therefore, there always was a lack of water in the camp. The camp consisted of a long chain of horse and cattle stalls in a former Polish farmyard. In addition to the camp managing committee, the number of prisoners was always 700 people (men).

In order to explain to us immediately what kind of area we were located in and how we had to act, they took our clothes from us to "delouse." While we were standing completely naked, as guests, we were honored with 25 lashes, but if any of us fainted from the pain, pails of water were ready for the "lazybones" to revive them in order to finish with the other 25 concentration camp inmates. Cleaned clothing was distributed as was appropriate for a collective: a shirt, a pair of pants, and a jacket for every man. Yours, not yours; there was no mine or yours in a camp.

Beaten physically and troubled spiritually, we were taken to our apartments of clay-covered cattle stalls with small windows and wooden bunks arranged one on top of the other. Everything was smeared with tar, a kind of strong tar that killed all sorts of insects. No linen and no covers; under the head - a slanting, suitable little board. This was prepared for 60 of our group. This was our residence, our place of rest.

[Page 372]

Everyone slept in their clothing because there was no heat, and we were not permitted to use any light because of the danger of fire. We lived under these conditions and, as previously mentioned, there was a lack of water. But we immediately received the club for dirty ears or, God forbid, for a louse. And this actually happened very often.

This is my account of the first day in the Kamionka camp. On the first day, after the welcome, in taking over the dwellings, we were considered as regular residents, and the internal camp management, which consisted of only "our Jewish brothers," ruled over us. They were harnessed to the brutal work of more quickly reaching the "final solution," to be free of Jews, with another spoon of soup or another potato, and with the false assurances that we would remain alive.

In my time there, the management of the camp belonged to "Kalts" – the commandant, a Jew from Germany who had escaped to Poland to save himself.

> Cukerman – the vice commandant, an academic from Tarnopol.
> Ellowicz – the barracks commandant, a refugee from Radom.
> Kranc – police commandant, also a German refugee. <
> Rotman – the council writer [secretary?], a refugee from Western Galicia.
> A chief cook and an undercook to run the kitchen.
> Twenty brigades to urge on the workers.
> Twenty-five militia men, simply bloodsuckers.
> As well as an overseer of provisions, a manager of the workshop division, a doctor, and a clinician.

They all devotedly carried out all of the orders from the Gestapo, believing the promise that they would be protected. However, the Germans, with their feeling of justice, treated "all Jews equally" and also paid them the same "death wages" as the ghetto Jews and as the *Judenrat* [Jewish Council]. The second day in the camp began *paskudna* [nasty] very early for the freshly arrived under the new leadership. At four in the morning, they shaved our hair off our heads. Everyone received a yellow *Magen David* [Shield – Star – of David] on the front and shoulder of their jackets. Everyone received a bread bag, a mess kit, and a spoon. Then a little bit of black coffee was passed out from the kitchen. At six o'clock, we stood with all of the other camp inmates, 700 in number, and waited for the Gestapo chief.

A tall German arrived wearing a long, leather coat with a riding whip (of the same color leather); he listened to the report, looked over the horde of slaves, and commanded:

March to work singing!!!

[Page 373]

After a walk of seven to 10 kilometers [a little over four to a little over six miles], we arrived at the workplace – everyone received tools, someone a pickax, a spade, a hammer to break stones, or a wheelbarrow. Every brigade of 10 men also received a designated order, how much and where to work that day.

Tormented for eight hours with deadly sweat, having absorbed a number [of blows] from rubber sticks from the brigadier, we crawled home singing. We had to stand in rows in the camp for a long time to receive the daily food distribution that consisted of one liter [about one quart] of soup (in which one had to search with a candle to find a diced vegetable), 20 grams of bread [about three-quarters of an ounce] (always moldy) and 10 grams of butter or 40 grams [about one and half ounces] of marmalade.

Thus, it was repeated day after day. This was what the daily life of the Jewish prisoner looked like. If he did not appear at the roll call because of a certain illness, he was healed immediately with a bullet. Two prisoners were specially designated as the *khevre kadishe* [burial society] specialized in the burial of the worthless [meant ironically] element. Standing in reverence, they carried out the "worthless one" so that everyone could see. The bundle of bones was laid down in the wood cabinet, covered with several shovels of dirt, and done. From December 1941 to May 1943, approximately 9,000 "parasites" were disposed of under the wood cabinet, I was secretly told by the writer Rotman.

We did not officially receive any mail, newspapers, or other information about what was happening in the world. We would ourselves learn [what was happening] according to the military traffic on the street or from secrets grabbed from the air. As a supplement to the picture of daily, normal camp life, extraordinary events occurred that remain deeply engraved in my memory, and I will tell about several of them.

A Father and a Son Together in a Camp

By Moshe Bar David

Translated by Gloria Berkenstat Freund

Edited by Moshe Kutten and Jane S. Gabin

They were together in a camp for an entire year. Suddenly, the son escaped. Because of this, the father had to endure a real hell. A reduction in food, heavy labor, whippings at every opportunity, slept not on a plank bed but in the passageway where everyone had to step over him in order to go by. Several days later, a Ukrainian policeman brought the son back to the camp with his hands in chains. We prepared for a terrible scene … "for our benefit."

[Page 374]

As in all other camps, gallows (a tall pole from which a rope hung down from an iron scaffold) was erected in the middle of our [camp] courtyard as a means of terror for bad behavior. There was no doubt that we would be witnesses to a frightening ceremony. In the morning, we all stood for rollcall, deadly pale in terrible trouble. The shackled "criminal" (Frajzinger was his name) stood under the gallows and waited for the "Angel of Death." He [the "Angel"] came closer with a sarcastic smile, raised his head toward the rope, made a motion with his leather *fajtshe* (whip) pointing to the gallows, and ordered us to shout "Hoorah" during the ceremony!

At the last moment, the shackled one fell to the feet of the man from the Gestapo and asked him to change the sentence because of his father. An unbelievable miracle occurred! "Give him 25 lashes," the murderer ordered. All of us felt as if we had become frozen, but only for a short time. The young soul, exhausted, from fear and suffering, died at the 18th lashing. The emblem *chai* [life] had no effect, and the call to God did not help.

Two Brothers in the Camp

Only two young brothers from the murdered Halperin family of Trembowla [now Terebovla, Ukraine] remained alive. One was caught immediately and taken to the Kamionki camp, where he was lucky to become the bootblack in the cleaning stable of the Gestapo *Hauptsturmführer* [paramilitary rank equivalent to captain]. The other brother remained alone; he was lucky to become the bootblack in the cleaning stable of the *Judenrat* [Jewish Council] in Trembowla; they should help him to be with his brother in the camp. During a *lapanke* [*akstie* – usually a deportation], he was taken into a group of slaves in the camp militia.

He actually wore the hangman's uniform with a rubber club, but he was given guard duty. Every morning before the roll call, he would stand at the door of the barracks, where Jewish believers had sneaked in to grab a holy blessing, and he would protect them so that, God forbid, there would be no evil eye because every gathering of even three people would threaten death.

*[Translator's note: there is a typographical error in the text. Text is repeated and/or missing. The text has been translated as it appears, including the errors.]

His brother, the boot-polisher, would sneak in when the murderer was not in the house – to the radio - and would often bring news to us in the camp, which we would always interpret as being good. This strengthened us and helped us persevere.

Four weeks before the total liquidation (by shooting) of the camp, I really succeeded in getting help from Dr. Yosef Majblum to escape from the camp. Understand, it was through a daring plan and through unbelievable miracles. (But this is a chapter in itself.)

[Page 375]

How fortunate I was when after the liberation, being in Czortków [Chortkiv] as a bookkeeper while delivering the balance of my work, I met the two Halperin brothers. We all cried together with joy. And they told me the end of the Kamionki affair. The boot polisher overheard the noise and conversation of the drunk members of the Gestapo and immediately ran to the camp and shouted that the end was sealed for that night. Only approximately 100 men were able and dared to storm the armed camp guards and escape to the surrounding forests. They assured me that my brothers-in-law, Shlomo Zauberberg and Itshe Gros, and his son, Pesakh, were among those who escaped. I was excited and hoped, perhaps… but all or almost all who escaped fell as victims of the wild forest epidemic that reigned in the forest at that time.

Those remaining in the camp were all shot the same night.

Passover in the Camp – 1943

Brzezany's wagon driver with the name, Rajbsztajn, would always bring bricks from brickyards to the houses being built; his son-in-law and Pinya Mehler's son, both prisoners from a year earlier, worked at the Av Barukh group. They would go to Jewish houses as well as those that were bombed and burned in the surrounding cities and villages and take the materials away for military purposes.

We already lay tired on the plank beds, the Universe our questions? a desolate night like all of our nights (no "why is this night different" [reference to the Four Questions asked on Passover]). They suddenly came into our barracks with matzos in their hands. They had probably found a living Jewish family somewhere near their work.

They crumbled the matzos into small pieces and distributed a piece to each of us. Agitated, with a wild voice, he shouted: Let us ask the Master of the Universe our questions.

A hearty moan and cry broke out. The feelings and thoughts of everyone passed like a hurricane, a whirlwind without control. The *Haggadah* was pouring out our bitter hearts without words – our tears and death sweat which ran like wine; the matzo was the substance and symbol of an exodus from the camp!

Our hope then for [the Exodus] were the bitter herbs!

[Page 376]

The Provision of Clothing in Camp Kamionka

Right after Passover 1943, an auto with used clothing, pants, jackets, dresses, underwear, long fur-lined coats, *talitot* [prayer shawls], and various children's garments came to the camp. Everything was dirty, wrinkled, and useful only as rags. These were the remnants from the cleaned-out Jewish homes. According to their method, the Nazis would always carry out a murder *aktsia* [action, usually a deportation] during a Jewish holiday. The Jews were taken to the crematoria, or later, when they lost their shame, [the Germans] murdered them daily at the local cemetery. And then they sold the most valuable things to German families for small change; the less valuable household items were sold to the *Volksdeutchen* [ethnic Germans] by weight (50 kilos [110 pounds] for 2 *zlotes*], and the real rags were brought to the camp for the half-naked and half-dead camp Jews.

The rags had to be delivered before the division. Until the disinfection, the entire pile was thrown up in the attic of the supply barracks, The ladders were taken away so that, God forbid, no one should climb up and steal a bit of treasure. Still the prisoners, with torn fringes on their half-naked bodies, made a living ladder, climbed one on another's shoulders and laughed at the "thou shalt not steal!" What was stolen [from the attic] was taken from many as well as the provisions for an entire week as a punishment.

This is just a minimal picture of camp life and the various abandoned legends of which the world, in general, was not informed, but hundreds of thousands of Jews suffered inhumanely and actually were tortured until a bullet freed them. These camp Jews drank up the bitter cup of Nazi poison to the very bottom.

It is hard to believe that a human life could endure this. As is evident, human suffering brings out inhuman strength!

May both remain for the ages! The one who reminds us and the one who remembers, of blessed memory!

[Page 377]

Remember

by Moshe Bar David

Translated by Gloria Berkenstat Freund

Edited by Moshe Kutten and Jane S. Gabin

There was a *shtetl* [town], clean and neat
Near the golden linden,
Life exterminated – ruins remaining
Memories that demand – an echo that shouts.

White birch trees encircle
The hilly valleys and dirt roads,
Soothing – tree-lined paths quietly consoled
At the shores of a silver river.

Meadows and fields turned green
Around orchards full of fragrant branches,
Intoxicated the earth and nighttime air
Waited for the serfs – summer harvest.

Moonlit night – winter cold
Legends were spun
Around generations-old castles
Holy Mother's water well.

Water cans draw crystal water
Sleds go in white snow
And deep thoughts awaken in minds
And hearts ache with regret.

Street of Jewish houses – brick
Small cottages, shingled, clay
Locked, bolted doors and gates –
Of houses from the past.

Young people longing, dreaming of the future,
Pure, dear young pain,
Familiar with the fences
Of every house and every stone.

Window eyes look blue
Cast with lamplight,
Announce the late hour
And remain alone with you.

Remained alone, but not unfamiliar
With what had gone away into the void
Carrying the sacrifice on bloody hands
Extinguished candles full of fear.

No headstone, no coffin
Not given a Jewish burial
May their memory be sacred
A torch in the dark night.

[Page 378]

About the Community's Memorialization

by Elisha

(Principal of Ramba"m school in Hadera)

Translated by Gloria Berkenstat Freund

Edited by Jane S. Gabin

The historical memory of the nation of Israel preserves in it all those events and outbreaks that it experienced since it came into being, which threatened to annihilate it from the world. The phrase "Remember (*Zakhor*) what Amalek did to you on your journey after you left Egypt" still echoes in the ears of every Jewish person.

A prophetic order is joining the historical memory: "When I passed by you and saw you wallowing in your blood, I said to you: "Live despite your blood." Yea, I said to you: "Live despite your blood (Ezekiel

16:7)". Together, they preserve the Jewish nation with all its troubles

It is, therefore, natural for our nation that we preserve in our memory the greatest calamity – the calamity of our century – the Holocaust of the European Jewry, caused by the Nation of Israel's greatest oppressors. And that is so we can examine our way so that our nation would never suffer such a Holocaust again.

But not only the Holocaust we are ordered to remember but also the heroism. There is no greater heroism than the heroism of the thousands of Jews who marched toward their death, singing the partisans' song with the phrase: "We will survive" echoing behind them, and the heroism of the thousands of Jews who continued to live and hope for new lives in Eretz Israel.

Every 27 of Sivan, the nation of Israel communes itself with our six million siblings who were annihilated by defiled hands. In our school, we go beyond that commune.

Every year, we dedicate a whole week in the 9th grade to study and delve deeper into the chapters on the Holocaust and heroism. As part of that study week, representatives of the Brzezany community, remnants of that magnificent Zionist Jewry, visit our school for some years now and tell our students about the life and death of the Brzezany community, one of many.

When the idea that schools adopt the memory of communities that were destroyed in the Holocaust came up, we adopted the Brzezany community. The adoption ceremony was held in the school about two years ago.

The city of Brzezany was wiped out.

The Brzezany community – only remnants remained from it. These remnants added a brick to the nation-building in our holy homeland.

Brzezany will not disappear or be erased from our nation's historical memory. It will continue to live and exist in the hearts of its remnants and in the hearts of the students of the Ramba"m school in Hadera. It would become, like other wiped-out Jewish communities, a torch lighting the way of the nation in its homeland.

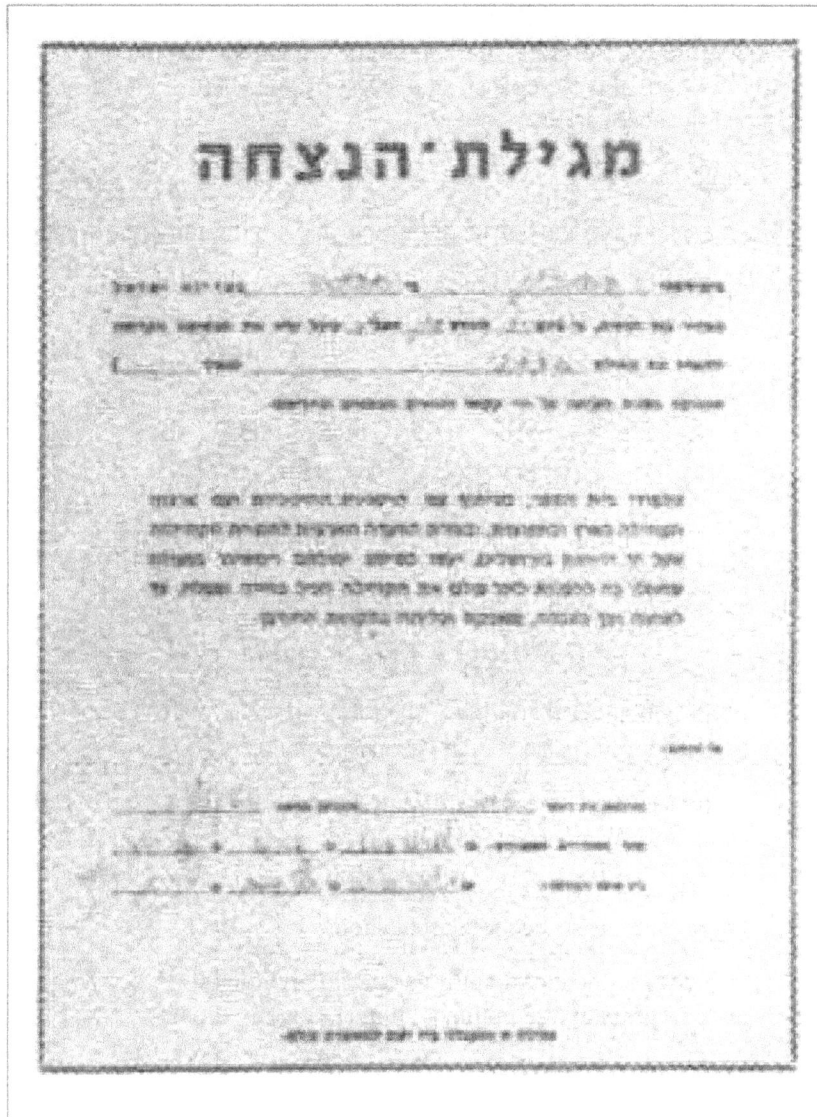

The memorialization scroll of the Brzezany Community by the Ramba"m School

[Translation of the Scroll]

The Memorialization Scroll

The school: Ramba'm, in Hadera, State of Israel, ceremonially declares here that on Date: [unreadable] it took it upon itself to memorialize the Community: Brzezany in the Country: Ukraine, which was destroyed in the Holocaust by the defiled Nazi hordes and their followers.

The school's students, in collaboration with the educational authorities, the community organizations in Israel, and the diaspora, and with the help of the State Committee for the Memorialization of the Communities at the "Yad

Vashem" in Jerusalem, will do their best to continue their activity they have already begun to memorialize the community mentioned above and its life, and activities until the Holocaust, and its suffering, battle, and destruction during the Holocaust period.

Signed by:

Signatures of school officials, the Committee, and Community representatives

That scroll was accepted at "Yad Vashem" for eternal preservation

[Page 379]

Remember [*Zakhor*]!

by Dr. Eliezer Shaklai

Translated by Moshe Kutten

Edited by Jane S. Gabin

I will remember the blood spilled forever,
I will never forget; I will always remember.

In my ear, the voices are still thundering:
Mother's moaning, begging, baby crying.

The German roars: "Jew, go out!"
In my head, is still echoing that shout.

The days of the ghetto until its end, in my mind, they scream,
they accompany me in the daytime and in my dreams.

How houses are destroyed, how the ghetto is burning,
how they take out the people from the places they are hiding.

How hundreds and thousands toward death they are led,
sights like that - you can never forget.

I will not forget him, escaping from the rows,
made me swear when he arose:

If you live, if you survive,
swear that you tell my words to those who are alive.

They kill us Jews, there is no way out,
and nobody lends us their hand, they all flout.

Satan himself rose against us Jews
to wipe our memory by the crematorium fire's misuse.

But when the bodies burn, not everything torches,
there is still a spark among the ashes.

A spark of hope in our eternal existence,
that the Jewish nation will rise from that spark with persistence.

The day will come – Israel will rise – and celebrate a victory,
and when the time comes, will light a candle of memory.

A memorial candle for all the victims is lit
For those who were burnt in the crematoria, tortured, or murdered.

When I die, do not honor me with flowers,
exalted words, or eulogy showers.

My ashes and those of my siblings in the homeland you bury,
and the word "Remember" in your hearts you carry.

Tell the future generations who come to the memorial,
so that will learn and understand the tutorial.

That people without a homeland – a nation nobody will consider,
contempt and ridicule they will suffer like a prosecuted leper.

Only people in their homeland will live safely,
and will garner recognition, honor, and glory.

"Remember!"

[Pages 382-408]

Brzezany's Martyrs List

Last name	First name	Gender	Father's first name	Mother's first name	Spouse's first name	Remarks	Page
	Andzia		Yeshayahu	Roza			404
	Ganke		Yeshayahu	Roza			404
	Roza	Female					404
	Roza	Female			Yeshayahu		404
ADLER	Kive		Shlomo				382
ADLER	Pepka		Shlomo				382
ADLER	Shlomo	Male				Profession: Ritual Slaughterer	382
ADLER		Male			Shlomo		382
ADLER		Male	Shlomo				382
AKSELROD	Beile			Rivka			382
AKSELROD	Elkana	Male			Etel		382
AKSELROD	Etel	Female			Elkana		382
AKSELROD	Frimtzia			Rivka			382
AKSELROD	Kuna			Rivka			382
AKSELROD	Noakh	Male					383
AKSELROD	Rivka	Female					382
AKSELROD	Rozia	Male	Elkana	Etel			382

AKSELROD	Shalom	Male	Elkana	Etel			382
AKSELROD		Male			Noakh		383
AKSELROD		Male	Noakh				383
AKSELROD		Male			Yoel		382
AKSELROD		Male	Yoel				382
AKSELROD	Yoel	Male					382
AKSELROD	Zysl			Rivka			382
ALTEIN	Kalman	Male					382
ALTEIN	Khana	Female		Mina			382
ALTEIN	Mina	Female					382
ALTEIN		Male			Kalman		382
ALTEIN		Male	Kalman				382
ALTEIN		Male	Kalman				382
ALTEIN		Male				Profession: Tailor	382
ALTEIN		Male					382
ALTER	Shlomit	Female					382
ALTER		Male			Yosef		382
ALTER	Vultzio						382
ALTER	Yosef	Male					382
ALTMAN	Feiga	Female	Khaim	Roza			382
ALTMAN	Khaim	Male			Roza		382
ALTMAN	Rakhel	Female	Khaim	Roza			382

ALTMAN	Roza	Female			Khaim		382
ALTMAN	Sheindl	Female	Khaim	Roza			382
ALTSHILER	David	Male			Khana		382
ALTSHILER	Don	Male					382
ALTSHILER	Khana	Female			David		382
ALTSHILER	Khava	Female					382
ALTSHILER		Male	David	Khana			382
ALTSHILER		Male			Don		382
AMARANT	Brunia	Female	Yosef	Klara			382
AMARANT	Dora	Female	Yosef	Klara			382
AMARANT	Klara	Female			Yosef		382
AMARANT	Sima	Female	Yosef	Klara			382
AMARANT	Yosef	Male			Klara		382
ANGEL							383
APEL	Avraham	Male					383
APEL	Elka		Yehuda				383
APEL		Male			Avraham		383
APEL		Male	Avraham				383
APEL		Male	Avraham				383
APEL		Male	Avraham				383
APEL	Yehuda	Male					383
ARENBERG	Dasio			Yekhit			383

ARENBERG	Rita	Female		Yekhit			383
ARENBERG	Yakhit	Female					383
ARTMAN	David	Male	Yisaskhar	Minka			383
ARTMAN	Itamar	Male	Yisaskhar	Minka			383
ARTMAN	Minka	Female			Yisaskhar		383
ARTMAN	Yisaskhar	Male			Minka		383
AST	Barukh	Male			Khaia		383
AST	Fela		Barukh	Khaia			383
AST	Khaia	Female			Barukh		383
AST	Moshe	Male			Roza		383
AST	Roza	Female			Yosef		383
AST	Roza	Female			Moshe		383
AST		Male			Yehoshua		383
AST	Yaakov	Male	Barukh	Khaia			383
AST	Yehoshua	Male					383
AST	Yosef	Male			Roza		383
ATLAS		Male				Profession: Photographer	382
ATLAS		Male					382
ATLAS		Male					382
ATLAS		Male					382
ATLAS		Male					382
ATLAS		Male					382

AUFRIKHTIG	Beltzie		Yaakov	Hudel			382
AUFRIKHTIG	Hudel	Female			Yaakov		382
AUFRIKHTIG	Moshe	Male	Yaakov	Hudel			382
AUFRIKHTIG	Yaakov	Male			Hudel		382
AUFRIKHTIG	Zlata	Female	Yaakov	Hudel			382
BANER	Dov	Male	Yosef	Golda			385
BANER	Golda	Female			Yosef		385
BANER	Khanokh	Male					385
BANER	Mina	Female	Yosef	Golda			385
BANER	Shula	Female	Khanokh				385
BANER		Male			Khanokh		385
BANER	Yosef	Male			Golda		385
BARADOVITZ		Male			Volf	Died in the USSR	385
BARADOVITZ		Male	Volf			Died in the USSR	385
BARADOVITZ		Male	Volf			Died in the USSR	385
BARADOVITZ		Male	Volf			Died in the USSR	385
BARADOVITZ	Volf	Male				Died in the USSR	385
BARAN	Adela	Female			Mauritzi		385
BARAN	Bela	Female	Mauritzi	Adela			385
BARAN	Mauritzi	Male			Adela		385

BARAN		Male			Yosef		385
BARAN	Yosef	Male					385
BARASH	Rozeshka	Female					385
BARASH		Male					385
BARASH		Male					385
BARASH		Male					385
BART		Male					385
BAUER		Male	Yaakov				386
BAUM	Khana	Female			Volf		384
BAUM	Volf	Male			Khana		384
BAUMGARTEN							384
BAUMGARTEN		Male					384
BAUMGARTEN		Male					384
BEIGEL		Male					384
BEIGEL		Male					384
BER	Ester	Female			Fishel		385
BER	Faivel	Male					385
BER	Fishel	Male			Ester		385
BER	Khana	Female					385
BER	Shulamit	Female		Khana			385
BER		Male			Faivel		385
BER	Yosef	Male	Fishel	Ester			385

BER	Zalman	Male		Khana			385
BER	Zalman	Male	Fishel	Ester			385
BERGER	Avromtzi	Male			Khana		385
BERGER	Etel	Female			Hersh		385
BERGER	Gitel		Hersh	Etel			385
BERGER	Hersh	Male			Etel		385
BERGER	Khana	Female			Avrumtzi		385
BERGER	Khanokh	Male					385
BERGER	Kuku		Moshe				385
BERGER	Moshe	Male					385
BERGER	Moti	Male					385
BERGER	Nakhman	Male	Hersh	Etel			385
BERGER	Seima		Hersh	Etel			385
BERGER	Shimon	Male	Hersh	Etel			385
BERGER		Male			Khanokh		385
BERGER		Male			Moshe		385
BERGER		Male			Yoel		385
BERGER		Male			Moti		385
BERGER	Yoel	Male					385
BERGER	Zalman	Male	Moshe				385
BERGMAN	Edit	Female			Moshe		385
BERGMAN	Mikhael	Male			Nusia		385

BERGMAN	Mina	Female	Shmuel	Risia			385
BERGMAN	Moshe	Male			Edit		385
BERGMAN	Nosia	Female			Mikhael		385
BERGMAN	Risia	Female			Shmuel Halevi		385
BERGMAN	Shmuel	Male			Risia		385
BERMAN		Male					385
BERMAN		Male					385
BETINGER		Male					384
BETINGER		Male					384
BETINGER		Male					384
BEZEN	Breina	Female			Eli		384
BEZEN	Eli	Male			Breina		384
BEZEN	Gusta	Female					384
BEZEN	Khaim	Male	Eli	Breina			384
BEZEN	Khartush						384
BEZEN	Milosh						384
BEZEN	Perel	Female	Eli	Breina			384
BEZEN		Male					384
BEZEN		Male					384
BEZEN		Male					384
BEZEN		Male					384
BEZEN		Male					384

BEZEN		Male					384
BEZEN		Male					384
BIHN	Aharon	Male					384
BIHN		Male			Aharon		384
BIK	Brunia	Female			Oziasch		384
BIK	Dzunia		Uziasch	Brunia			384
BIK	Osziasz	Male			Bronia		384
BILIG	Artur	Male	Mikhael	Sonia			384
BILIG	Hunie	Female			Moshe		384
BILIG	Khaia	Female			Shimon		384
BILIG	Mikhael	Male			Sonia		384
BILIG	Moshe	Male			Honia		384
BILIG	Reizia	Female			Yosef		384
BILIG	Shimon	Male			Khaia Sara		384
BILIG	Sonia	Female			Mikhael		384
BILIG	Yosef	Male			Reizia		384
BILINSKI		Male				Profession: Shoemaker	384
BILINSKI		Male					384
BILINSKI		Male					384
BILINSKI		Male					384
BINDER	Mina	Female					384
BINDER	Rina	Female					384

BINDER	Saba	Female					384
BINDER		Male			Saba		384
BINDER		Male	Saba				384
BITERMAN	Dov	Male	Zeinvel	Mintzia			384
BITERMAN	Feibish	Male			Zuzi		384
BITERMAN	Mintzia	Female			Zeinvel		384
BITERMAN	Shimon	Male	Zeinvel	Mintzia			384
BITERMAN		Male			Yitzkhak		384
BITERMAN		Male	Yitzkhak				384
BITERMAN	Yitzkhak	Male					384
BITERMAN	Zeinvel	Male			Mintzia		384
BITERMAN	Zuzi	Female			Feibish		384
BLANK	Kuca		Yosef	Malka			385
BLANK	Leibish						385
BLANK	Malka	Female			Yosef		385
BLANK	Rela		Yosef	Malka			385
BLANK	Shabtai	Male					385
BLANK		Male			Shabtai		385
BLANK	Vitzia						385
BLANK	Yona						385
BLANK	Yosef	Male			Malka		385
BLAUFELD	Meir	Male					384

BLAUFELD		Male			Meir		384
BLAUFELD		Male	Meir				384
BLAUFELD		Male					384
BLAUFELD		Male					384
BLAUFELD		Male					384
BLEIBERG	Hela		Leon	Rakhel			384
BLEIBERG	Leon	Male			Rakhel		384
BLEIBERG	Rakhel	Female			Leon		384
BLEIBERG	Rozia		Leon	Rakhel			384
BLEIBERG	Tzila	Female					384
BLEIBERG	Visia	Female			Zigmund		384
BLEIBERG	Zigmund	Male	Leon	Rakhel			384
BLEIBERG	Zigmund	Male			Visia		384
BLEIER	Pinkhas	Male					384
BLEIER	Tonne		Pinkhas				384
BLEIER		Male			Pinkhas		384
BLEIKH	Beril	Male			Zysl		384
BLEIKH	Dov	Male	Volf	Shprintza			384
BLEIKH	Fenka		Beril	Zysl			384
BLEIKH	Frida	Female	Volf	Shprintza			384
BLEIKH	Hirsh	Male	Mendel	Perla			384
BLEIKH	Mendel	Male			Perla		384

BLEIKH	Nosika		Mendel	Perla			384
BLEIKH	Perla	Female			Mendel		384
BLEIKH	Rozia		Volf	Shprintza			384
BLEIKH	Shimon	Male	Volf	Shprintza			384
BLEIKH	Shprintza	Female			Volf		384
BLEIKH	Tonka		Beril	Zysl			384
BLEIKH	Volf	Male			Shprintza		384
BLEIKH	Yaakov	Male	Volf	Shprintza			384
BLEIKH	Yaakov	Male	Mendel	Perla			384
BLEIKH	Zysl	Female			Beril		384
BLEISHTIFT	Gitia	Female			Yosef		384
BLEISHTIFT	Leib	Male					384
BLEISHTIFT		Male			Leib		384
BLEISHTIFT		Male	Leib				384
BLEISHTIFT		Male					384
BLEISHTIFT		Male					384
BLEISHTIFT	Yaakov	Male	Yosef	Gitia			384
BLEISHTIFT	Yosef	Male			Gitia		384
BLITZ	Barukh	Male			Pnina		384
BLITZ	Khaia	Female	Barukh	Pnina			384
BLITZ	Pnina	Female			Barukh		384
BLITZ	Sara	Female	Barukh	Pnina			384

BOGNER	Avraham	Male			Rivka	384
BOGNER	Rivka	Female			Avraham	384
BOGNER		Male	Avraham	Rivka		384
BRADSHPIZ	Frimtze	Female				385
BRANDVEIN		Male			Yisrael	385
BRANDVEIN		Male	Yisrael			385
BRANDVEIN		Male	Yisrael			385
BRANDVEIN	Yisrael	Male				385
BRANSHTEIN	Arie	Male			Selka	385
BRANSHTEIN	Berl	Male			Rivka	385
BRANSHTEIN	Leizer	Male				385
BRANSHTEIN	Perel	Female			Yisrael	385
BRANSHTEIN	Rivka	Female			Berl	385
BRANSHTEIN	Selka	Female			Arie	385
BRANSHTEIN		Male			Leizer	385
BRANSHTEIN		Male	Leizer			385
BRANSHTEIN		Male	Leizer			385
BRANSHTEIN		Male	Leizer			385
BRANSHTEIN		Male	Leizer			385
BRANSHTEIN	Yisrael	Male			Perel	385
BRATER	David	Male				385
BRATER	Poldek	Male	David			385

BRATER		Male			David		385
BRATER		Male	David				385
BRAUN		Male	Mordekhai			Profession: Fireman	385
BREITEL	Ester	Female		Meita			385
BREITEL	Meita	Female					385
BREITER	Berta	Female	Faivel	Perel			385
BREITER	Faivel	Male			Perel		385
BREITER	Perel	Female			Faivel		385
BREITFELD	Barukh	Male			Ita		385
BREITFELD	Feibish		Barukh	Ita			385
BREITFELD	Ita	Female			Barukh		385
BREITFELD	Sara	Female	Barukh	Ita			385
BREITLING	Yetka						385
BRENER	Shimon	Male					385
BRIF		Male			Yaakov Meir		385
BRIF		Male	Yaakov				385
BRIF		Male	Yaakov				385
BRIF		Male	Yaakov				385
BRIF	Yaakov	Male					385
BRIK	Cyna	Female			Daniel		385
BRIK	Daniel	Male			Cyna		385

BRIK	Daniel	Male					385
BRIK	Sheintzia		Daniel	Cyna			385
BRIK	Tuvia	Male					385
BRIK		Male			Tuvia		385
BRONER	Frida	Female			Volf		385
BRONER	Henri	Male	Volf	Frida			385
BRONER	Pepka	Female	S				385
BRONER		Male		Pepka			385
BRONER	Volf	Male			Frida		385
BUKSBAUM	Reizl	Female					384
BUKSBAUM		Male			Reizl	Profession: Shoemaker	384
BUKSBAUM		Male		Reizl			384
BUMZE						In Berezhany during the war. From Sienkow	384
BUMZE	Fishel	Male			Rivka		384
BUMZE	Rivka	Female			Fishel		384
BUMZE	Yaakov	Male			Zlata		384
BUMZE	Zlata	Female			Yaakov		384
CHACHKES	Bluma	Female			Khaim		403
CHACHKES	Ester	Female	Khaim	Bluma			403
CHACHKES	Khaim	Male			Bluma		403
DANZIGER	Herman	Male					388

DAVID	Elza	Female	Khanokh	Reizl			388
DAVID	Elza	Female	Mendel	Mina			388
DAVID	Ester	Female			Itzia Yitzkhak		388
DAVID	Itzia	Male			Ester		388
DAVID	Mania		Itzia	Ester			388
DAVID	Mendel	Male			Mina		388
DAVID	Mina	Female			Mendel		388
DAVID	Moniyo	Male	Itzi	Ester			388
DAVID	Reizl	Female			Khanokh		388
DAVID	Rubi		Khanokh	Reizl			388
DAVID	Selka	Female			Sumar		388
DAVID	Serka	Female				Maiden name: HABER. From Bobrka	388
DAVID	Somar	Male			Selka	Profession: Lawyer	388
DAVID	Yaakov	Male	Mendel	Mina			388
DAVID	Yosef	Male	Mendel	Mina			388
DIAMANT	Katriel						388
DINES	Artek		Yitzkhak	Ester			388
DINES	Ester	Female			Yitzkhak		388
DINES	Yitzkhak	Male			Ester		388
DORFMAN	Beila	Female			Leib		388

DORFMAN	Bluma	Female			Muka		388
DORFMAN	David	Male	Yaakov	Malka			388
DORFMAN	Duvtzi		Muka	Bluma			388
DORFMAN	Frida	Female	Yaakov	Malka			388
DORFMAN	Fridka		Muka	Bluma			388
DORFMAN	Leib	Male			Beile		388
DORFMAN	Leizer	Male	Yaakov	Malka			388
DORFMAN	Lusy		Muka	Bluma			388
DORFMAN	Malka	Female			Yaakov		388
DORFMAN	Mikhael	Male	Yaakov	Malka			388
DORFMAN	Moke	Male			Bluma		388
DORFMAN	Shoshana	Female	Yaakov	Malka			388
DORFMAN	Shraga	Male	Muka	Bluma			388
DORFMAN	Shraga	Male	Yaakov	Malka			388
DORFMAN	Tova	Female	Yaakov	Malka			388
DORFMAN	Tova	Female	Muka	Bluma			388
DORFMAN		Male			Leizer		388
DORFMAN		Male					388
DORFMAN	Yaakov	Male				Profession: Lawyer	388
DORFMAN	Yaakov	Male			Malka		388
DRUKER		Male					388
DRUKER		Male					388

DURST	Beti			Gitel			388
DURST	Gitel	Female					388
DURST	Izio			Gitel			388
DURST	Khaim	Male			Mania		388
DURST	Liber	Male				From Teniow	388
DURST	Mania	Female			Khaim		388
DURST	Monoi			Gitel			388
DURST	Natan	Male	Khaim	Mania			388
DURST	Nunio		Khaim	Mania			388
DURST	Risia		Khaim	Mania			388
DURST		Male			Gitel		388
DURST	Zeev	Male		Gitel			388
DZIALOVSKI	Karla	Female			Leib		388
DZIALOVSKI	Leib	Male			Karla		388
EIGEN	David	Male					382
EIGEN	Ester	Female	David				382
EIGEN	Leib	Male	Volf	Sushia		From Buszcze	382
EIGEN	Levi	Male	Volf	Sushia		From Buszcze	382
EIGEN	Moshe	Male	Volf	Sushia		From Buszcze	382
EIGEN	Shlomo	Male					382
EIGEN	Soshia	Female			Volf	Maiden name: HILFER	382
EIGEN	Tauba	Female			Yosef		382

EIGEN	Tova	Female	David				382
EIGEN	Tzipora	Female	Volf	Sushia		From Buszcze	382
EIGEN		Male					382
EIGEN		Male					382
EIGEN		Male			David		382
EIGEN		Male	Yosef	Tauba			382
EIGEN		Male	Yosef	Tauba			382
EIGEN		Male	Yosef	Tauba			382
EIGEN		Male	Yosef	Tauba			382
EIGEN		Male	Yosef	Tauba			382
EIGEN		Male			Shlomo		382
EIGEN		Male	Shlomo				382
EIGEN	Volf	Male			Sushia	From Buszcze	382
EIGEN	Yitzkhak	Male	Volf	Sushia		From Buszcze	382
EIGEN	Yosef	Male			Tauba		382
EINSHTOS	Daniel	Male					382
EINSHTOS		Male			Daniel		382
EIZEN	Khana	Female					382
EIZEN	Leib	Male		Khana			382
EIZNER	Gershon	Male					382
EKHOITZ	Bluma	Female					383
EKHOITZ	Khana	Female		Bluma			383

EKHOITZ	Malka	Female		Bluma			383
EKHOITZ	Moshe	Male		Bluma			383
EKHOITZ	Rivka	Female		Bluma			383
EKHOIZ	Khanokh	Male					383
EKHOIZ	Rakhel	Female					383
EKHOIZ		Male			Khanokh		383
EKHOIZ		Male			Rakhel		383
ENTIN	Avraham	Male			Khana	Profession: Metalworker	399
ENTIN	Khana	Female			Avraham		399
ENTIN		Male	Avraham	Khana	-		399
ENTIN		Male	Avraham	Khana			399
ENTIN		Male	Avraham	Khana			399
EPSHTEIN	Moshe	Male			Yeta		383
EPSHTEIN	Yeta	Female			Moshe Isser		383
ERIKH	Elkana	Male			Sara		383
ERIKH	Hirsh	Male	Elkana	Sara			383
ERIKH	Hirsh	Male					383
ERIKH	Khana	Female	Elkana	Sara			383
ERIKH	Leib	Male	Moshe				383
ERIKH	Meir	Male			Tova		383
ERIKH	Mendel	Male	Elkana	Sara			383

ERIKH	Metel		Elkana	Sara			383
ERIKH	Mordekhai	Male	Moshe				383
ERIKH	Moshe	Male					383
ERIKH	Pola	Female			Yehuda Leib		383
ERIKH	Rivka	Female					383
ERIKH	Sara	Female			Elkana -		383
ERIKH	Tova	Female			Meir		383
ERIKH		Male	Yehuda	Pola			383
ERIKH		Male	Meir	Tova			383
ERIKH		Male	Meir	Tova			383
ERIKH		Male			Moshe		383
ERIKH	Yehuda	Male			Pola		383
ERIKH	Yeti		Elkana	Sara			383
ERIKH	Yosef	Male	Elkana	Sara			383
ERLIKH	Neshka	Female					383
ERLIKH	Shaul	Male					383
ERLIKH		Male	Yosef				383
ERLIKH		Male				Profession: Clerk	383
ERLIKH		Male					383
ERLIKH		Male			Shaul		383
ERLIKH		Male	Shaul				383

ERLIKH		Male			Nashke		383
ERLIKH	Yosef	Male					383
FALIK	Bernard	Male					400
FALIK	Bina	Female			Moshe Yosef		400
FALIK	Dolek	Male					400
FALIK	Eliahu	Male			Genya		400
FALIK	Genya	Female			Eliahu		400
FALIK	Koba						400
FALIK	Moshe	Male			Bina		400
FALIK		Male					400
FALIK		Male					400
FALIK		Male			Bernard		400
FARB	Emilia	Female					400
FARB	Valeria	Female		Emilia			400
FAS	Dov	Male	Tzvi	Rakhel			400
FAS	Mania	Female			Yisrael		400
FAS	Meir	Male	Tzvi	Rakhel			400
FAS	Rakhel	Female			Tzvi		400
FAS	Rivka	Female	Yisrael	Mania			400
FAS	Tzvi	Male			Rakhel		400
FAS	Yisrael	Male			Mania		400
FAS	Yokheved	Female	Tzvi	Rakhel			400

FAS	Zeev	Male	Yisrael	Mania			400
FECHTER							401
FEDER	Boma						400
FEDER		Male					400
FEIER	Beniamin	Male			Berta		400
FEIER	Berta	Female			Beniamin		400
FEIER	Dolek	Male	Beniamin	Berta			400
FEIER	Durka		Beniamin	Berta			400
FEIERING	Adela	Female			Max		400
FEIERING	Max	Male			Adela		400
FEIERING		Male	Max	Adela			400
FEIERING		Male					400
FEIERING	Yosef	Male					400
FEIGENBAUM		Male					400
FELD	Arie	Male			Sara		401
FELD	Barukh	Male	Arie	Sara			401
FELD	Berta	Female			Yehuda		401
FELD	Bertzia	Male			Zahava		401
FELD	Bluma	Female			Yitzkhak		401
FELD	Dvora	Female			Yisrael		401
FELD	Ela	Female			Lipa		401
FELD	Eliezer	Male	Mikhael	Frida			401

FELD	Feibish	Male					401
FELD	Fentza		Arie	Sara			401
FELD	Frida	Female			Mikhael Leib		401
FELD	Golda	Female	Yitzkhak	Bluma			401
FELD	Khaim	Male	Yisrael	Dvora			401
FELD	Khana	Female	Shalom	Miriam			401
FELD	Leibish	Male	Yisrael	Dvora			401
FELD	Lipa	Male			Ela		401
FELD	Meir	Male					401
FELD	Mikhael	Male			Frida		401
FELD	Miriam	Female			Shalom Mendel		401
FELD	Moshe	Male	Arie	Sara			401
FELD	Moshe	Male	Yisrael	Dvora			401
FELD	Sara	Female			Arie		401
FELD	Shalom	Male			Miriam		401
FELD	Tzvi	Male	Yisrael	Dvora			401
FELD	Tzvi	Male	Mikhael	Frida			401
FELD		Male			Meir		401
FELD		Male			Feibish		401
FELD		Male	Feibish				401
FELD	Yehuda	Male			Berta		401

FELD	Yisrael	Male	Bertzia	Zahava			401
FELD	Yisrael	Male			Dvora		401
FELD	Yitzkhak	Male			Bluma		401
FELD	Zahava	Female			Bertzia		401
FELD	Zelig	Male					401
FELD KOK	Golda	Female			Yaakov		401
FELD KOK	Yaakov	Male			Golda		401
FENSTER	Izio		Yisrael	Tuntzia			401
FENSTER	Tuntzia	Female			Yisrael		401
FENSTER		Male					401
FENSTER		Male					401
FENSTER		Male					401
FENSTER		Male					401
FENSTER	Visin		Yisrael	Tuntzia			401
FERSHING		Male					402
FERSHING		Male				Profession: Seamstress	402
FERSHING		Male					402
FERSHING		Male					402
FERSHING		Male					402
FINK		Male					400
FINK		Male					400
FINK		Male					400

FINK		Male					400
FINK	Yekhiel	Male					400
FINKELSHTEIN	Artek		Nisan	Helena			400
FINKELSHTEIN	Helena	Female			Nisan		400
FINKELSHTEIN	Liba	Female					400
FINKELSHTEIN	Lunk	Male		Liba			400
FINKELSHTEIN	Menakhem	Male	Yosef				400
FINKELSHTEIN	Nisan	Male			Helena	Profession: Lawyer	400
FINKELSHTEIN	Silvia	Female	Nisan	Helena			400
FINKELSHTEIN	Yosef	Male					400
FIRST		Male					401
FIRST		Male					401
FIRST		Male					401
FISHER	David	Male			Khana		401
FISHER	Khana	Female			David		401
FLAM	Moshe	Male					401
FLAM	Pepka						401
FLEDERMAUS	Alter	Male					401
FLEDERMAUS	Lea	Female					401
FLEDERMAUS		Male			Alter Yaakov		401
FLEDERMAUS		Male			Yisrael		401

FLEDERMAUS	Yisrael	Male					401
FLESHNER		Male					401
FLUG	Mendel	Male			Zysl		401
FLUG		Male	Mendel	Zysl			401
FLUG		Male	Mendel	Zysl			401
FLUG	Zysl	Female			Mendel		401
FOGEL	Adela	Female			Yaakov		400
FOGEL	Berish						400
FOGEL	Dvora	Female			Feibish		400
FOGEL	Feibish	Male			Dvora		400
FOGEL	Gize		Shlomo				400
FOGEL	Hinda	Female					400
FOGEL	Rina	Female	Feibish	Dvora			400
FOGEL	Rina	Female	Shlomo				400
FOGEL	Shlomo	Male					400
FOGEL		Male			Shlomo		400
FOGEL		Male				Profession: Fuel store	400
FOGEL		Male				Profession: Fuel store	400
FOGEL	Yaakov	Male			Adela		400
FOGELMAN	Moshe	Male	Shimshon	Hentzia			400
FREIER	David	Male					402

FREIER		Male			David Meir		402
FREIFOGEL	David	Male			Teske		402
FREIFOGEL	Teska	Female			David		402
FRESHEL	Barukh	Male			Genya		402
FRESHEL	David	Male	Barukh	Genya			402
FRESHEL	Genya	Female			Barukh Meir		402
FRESHEL	Imak		Barukh	Genya			402
FRID	Gusta						402
FRID	Khaia	Female			Yitzkhak		402
FRID	Leitzia	Female					402
FRID	Mendel	Male		Leitzia			402
FRID	Mikhael	Male					402
FRID		Male			Mikhael		402
FRID		Male	Mikhael				402
FRID		Male		Leitzia			402
FRID		Male		Leitzia			402
FRID	Yitzkhak	Male			Khaia		402
FRIDLENDER	Moshe	Male			Rakhel		402
FRIDLENDER	Rakhel	Female			Moshe		402
FRIDLENDER	Rut	Female	Moshe	Rakhel			402
FRIDLENDER	Shmuel	Male	Moshe	Rakhel			402
FRIDMAN	Barukh	Male					402

FRIDMAN	Mendel	Male			Zysl		402
FRIDMAN	Moshe	Male					402
FRIDMAN	Shlomo	Male					402
FRIDMAN	Zysl	Female			Mendel		402
FRISH	Ida	Female			Leizer		402
FRISH	Leizer	Male			Ida		402
FRISH	Mina	Female	Leizer	Ida			402
FROIND		Male					401
FROIND		Male					401
FROINDLIKH	Hinda		Rafael	Rivka			401
FROINDLIKH	Izio		Rafael	Rivka			401
FROINDLIKH	Rafael	Male			Rivka		401
FROINDLIKH	Rivka	Female			Rafael		401
FROINDLIKH	Rozia		Rafael	Rivka			401
FROINDLIKH	Sara	Female					401
FROSH	Adela	Female					402
FROSH	Beniamin	Male			Mina		402
FROSH	Eliezer	Male			Ida		402
FROSH	Ida	Female			Eliezer		402
FROSH	Khana	Female					402
FROSH	Lusia		Beniamin	Mina			402
FROSH	Mina	Female	Eliezer	Ida			402

FROSH	Mina	Female			Beniamin		402
FROSH	Ozio		Beniamin	Mina			402
FROSH	Zuniu		Beniamin	Mina			402
FROSH FRUKHT	Frida	Female					402
FRUENLICH	Dvosia	Female					401
FRUENLICH	Lubke			Dvusia			401
FRUKHT	Dvora	Female			Volf		401
FRUKHT	Ester	Female	Sukher	Ruzia			402
FRUKHT	Frida	Female					402
FRUKHT	Henia	Female					401
FRUKHT	Izik	Male					401
FRUKHT	Khana	Female			Leon		401
FRUKHT	Lea	Female					401
FRUKHT	Leon	Male			Khana		401
FRUKHT	Mendel	Male					401
FRUKHT	Moshe	Male					402
FRUKHT	Nakhman	Male					402
FRUKHT	Rozia	Female			Sukher		402
FRUKHT	Shlomo	Male		Henia			401
FRUKHT	Sokher	Male			Rozia		402
FRUKHT		Male			Lea		401
FRUKHT		Male			Nakhman		402

FRUKHT	Volf	Male			Dvora	401
FRUKHT	Yaakov	Male	Leon	Khana		401
FRUKHT	Yitzkhak	Male	Nakhman			402
FUKS	Feiga	Female			Yisrael	400
FUKS	Khona					400
FUKS		Male				400
FUKS	Yisrael	Male			Feiga	400
FUKS	Yosef	Male	Yisrael	Feiga		400
GALINER	Herman	Male				387
GALINER	Mikhael	Male	Herman			387
GALINER		Male			Herman	387
GELBER	Matel		Yosef			387
GELBER	Motl	Male	Yosef			387
GELBER	Natan	Male	Yosef			387
GELBER	Nunio		Uziasch			387
GELBER	Osziasz	Male				387
GELBER	Otek		Uziasch			387
GELBER	Reiza		Yosef			387
GELBER		Male			Oziasch	387
GELBER		Male			Yosef	387
GELBER	Yosef	Male				387
GELBER	Zalman	Male	Yosef			387

GENZEL							387
GERSTLER		Male					387
GEVIRTZ		Male					386
GEVIRTZ		Male					386
GEVIRTZ		Male					386
GEVIRTZ		Male					386
GEVIRTZ		Male					386
GEVIRTZ		Male					386
GINSBERG	David	Male			Mina		386
GINSBERG	Khava	Female	Shimon	Sara			386
GINSBERG	Mina	Female			David		386
GINSBERG	Rozka		David	Mina			386
GINSBERG	Sara	Female			Shimon		386
GINSBERG	Shalom	Male					386
GINSBERG	Shimon	Male			Sara		386
GINSBERG	Tzila	Female	David	Mina			386
GINSBERG		Male			Shalom		386
GLANTZ	Beniu		Leizer	Rivka			387
GLANTZ	Leizer	Male			Rivka		387
GLANTZ	Lurke		Leizer	Rivka			387
GLANTZ	Rafael	Male	Leizer	Rivka			387
GLANTZ	Rivka	Female			Leizer		387

GLANTZ		Male				Profession: Matchmaker	387
GLANTZ		Male					387
GLAZER	Ester	Female			Leib		387
GLAZER	Hadasa	Female	Volf	Pnina			386
GLAZER	Irit	Female	Leib	Ester			387
GLAZER	Leib	Male			Ester		387
GLAZER	Mundek	Male	Shlomo	Roza			386
GLAZER	Pnina	Female			Volf		386
GLAZER	Risia	Female					387
GLAZER	Roza	Female			Shlomo		386
GLAZER	Shlomo	Male			Roza	Profession: Lawyer	386
GLAZER		Male		Risia			387
GLAZER	Volf	Male			Pnina		386
GLIKER	Bektzia	Male					387
GLIKER		Male			Baktzia		387
GLIKER		Male	Bektzia				387
GLIKER		Male	Bektzia				387
GLIKSHTERN	Szainka	Female					387
GLIKSHTERN		Male			Szainka	Profession: Lawyer	387
GOLDBERG	Aharon	Male	Hertzel	Shoshana			386
GOLDBERG	Hersh	Male					386

GOLDBERG	Hertzel	Male			Shoshana		386
GOLDBERG	Shoshana	Female			Hertzel		386
GOLDBERG	Tania	Female					386
GOLDBERG		Male			Tania		386
GOLDBERG		Male			Yekhezkel		386
GOLDBERG		Male			Hersh		386
GOLDBERG	Yekhezkel	Male					386
GOLDBLAT	Berta	Female			Yona		386
GOLDBLAT	Fila		Yona	Berta			386
GOLDBLAT	Malka	Female	Yona	Berta			386
GOLDBLAT	Yona	Male			Berta		386
GOLDHABER		Female			Yosef		386
GOLDHABER	Leib	Male					386
GOLDHABER		Male			Leib		386
GOLDHABER	Yosef	Male					386
GOLDHAMER	Yehuda	Male					386
GOLDHAMER	Yosef	Male					386
GOLDMAN	Avraham	Male	Leon	Pepi			386
GOLDMAN	Bank	Male					386
GOLDMAN	Barukh	Male			Khaia		386
GOLDMAN	Emil	Male				Profession: Pharmacist	386
GOLDMAN	Fishel		Yaakov				386

GOLDMAN	Gina					386
GOLDMAN	Hersh	Male	Yaakov			386
GOLDMAN	Khaia	Female	Yaakov			386
GOLDMAN	Khaia	Female			Barukh	386
GOLDMAN	Khana	Female	Yaakov			386
GOLDMAN	Khana	Female	Leon	Pepi		386
GOLDMAN	Leon	Male			Pepi	386
GOLDMAN	Morris	Male				386
GOLDMAN	Pepi	Female			Leon Leib	386
GOLDMAN	Rozika					386
GOLDMAN	Shlomo	Male	Leon	Pepi		386
GOLDMAN	Tzila	Female	Yaakov			386
GOLDMAN		Male			Banek	386
GOLDMAN		Male			Yaakov	386
GOLDMAN		Male			Emil	386
GOLDMAN	Yaakov	Male				386
GOLDSHLAG	Emilia	Female			Pesakh	386
GOLDSHLAG	Pesakh	Male			Emilia	386
GOLDSHLAG	Yozef	Male	Pesakh	Emilia		386
GOLDSHTEIN		Male				386
GOLDSHTEIN		Male				386
GOLDSHTEIN		Male				386

GOTSHTEIN	Gitel	Female			Leib		386
GOTSHTEIN	Leib	Male			Gitel		386
GOTSHTEIN	Noshe		Leib	Gitel			386
GOTSHTEIN	Roza	Female	Leib	Gitel			386
GOTSHTEIN	Tzirel	Female					386
GOTSHTEIN		Male			Tzirel	Profession: Tailor	386
GOTVORT	David	Male			Khaia		386
GOTVORT	Feige		David	Khaia			386
GOTVORT	Frimtzia	Female			Shimon		386
GOTVORT	Ire	Male					386
GOTVORT	Khaia	Female			David		386
GOTVORT	Kreindel	Female	David	Khaia			386
GOTVORT	Kreindel	Female			Yitzkhak		386
GOTVORT	Shimon	Male			Frimtzia		386
GOTVORT		Male			Ire		386
GOTVORT	Yitzkhak	Male			Kreindel		386
GRAD	Etal	Female			Hirsh Tzvi		387
GRAD	Gitel	Female			Hirsh		387
GRAD	Hirsh	Male			Atel		387
GRAD	Hirsh	Male			Gitel		387
GRAD	Shlomo	Male					387
GRAD	Sima	Female					387

GRAD		Male			Shlomo		387
GRAD KATZ	Leib	Male			Sara		387
GRAD KATZ	Sara	Female			Leib Aharon		387
GRAD KATZ	Simtzia		Leib	Sara			387
GRINBERG	Mala		Volf				387
GRINBERG	Sala		Volf				387
GRINBERG	Tebka		Volf				387
GRINBERG	Unia		Volf				387
GRINBERG		Male			Volf		387
GRINBERG		Male				Profession: Shoemaker	387
GRINBERG		Male					387
GRINBERG	Volf	Male					387
GRINBERG	Yulka						387
GROB	Fishel	Male			Khasia		387
GROB	Khasia	Female			Fishel		387
GROB	Lazar	Male	Fishel	Khasia			387
GROS	Gizia			Yehudit			387
GROS	Yehudit	Female	Yitzkhak				387
GROS NOIMAN	Poldetzio		Yitzkhak	Klara			399
GROSFELD	Rozia						387
GROSFELD		Male				From Potutory	387

GROSFELD		Male				From Potutory	387
GROSFELD		Male				From Potutory	387
GROSFELD		Male				From Potutory	387
GROSFELD		Male				From Potutory	387
GROSFELD		Male				From Potutory	387
GROSFELD	Zusia						387
GROSMAN	Karol	Male				Profession: Lawyer	387
GROSMAN		Male			Karol		387
GROSVAKS	Alter	Male					387
GROSVAKS	Hershel	Male					387
GROSVAKS		Male			Alter		387
GROSVAKS		Male	Hershel				387
GULDEN		Male				Profession: Coffee Shop	386
GULDEN		Male					386
GULDEN		Male					386
GUTENPLAN	Adolf	Male					386
GUTENPLAN	Aharon	Male					386
GUTENPLAN	Avraham	Male			Selka		386
GUTENPLAN	Basia	Female			Natan		386
GUTENPLAN	Lipa	Male	Natan	Basia			386
GUTENPLAN	Lipa	Male	Avraham	Selka			386

GUTENPLAN	Markal		Avraham	Selka			386
GUTENPLAN	Markus	Male	Natan	Basia			386
GUTENPLAN	Moshe	Male	Natan	Basia			386
GUTENPLAN	Naftali	Male	Natan	Basia			386
GUTENPLAN	Natan	Male			Basiah		386
GUTENPLAN	Selka	Female			Avraham		386
GUTENPLAN		Male			Yeshayahu		386
GUTENPLAN	Yehuda	Male	Natan	Basia			386
GUTENPLAN	Yeshayahu	Male					386
GUTENPLAN -	Manes						386
GUTENSHTEIN	Dreizi			Gitel			386
GUTENSHTEIN	Gitel	Female					386
GUTENSHTEIN	Nosia			Gitel			386
HABER	Leib	Male					388
HABER		Male			Leib		388
HABER		Male	Leib				388
HABER		Male	Leib				388
HABER		Male	Leib				388
HABER		Male	Leib				388
HAFTEL		Male				Profession: Seamstress	389
HALFTER		Male					388
HALFTER		Male					388

HALPERIN	Batia	Female	Moshe	Rakhel			389
HALPERIN	David	Male				From Lapszyn. In Berezhany during the war	389
HALPERIN	Ester	Female			Shimon		389
HALPERIN	Eti	Female			Yosef Barukh		389
HALPERIN	Eti	Female		Riva			389
HALPERIN	Feige		Yosef	Eti			389
HALPERIN	Heshi	Male			Rakhel		389
HALPERIN	Khaim	Male				Profession: Rabbi	389
HALPERIN	Khana	Female	Yosef	Eti			389
HALPERIN	Menakhem	Male				Profession: Rabbi	389
HALPERIN	Moshe	Male			Rakhel		389
HALPERIN	Rakhel	Female			Heschi Tzvi		389
HALPERIN	Rakhel	Female			Moshe		389
HALPERIN	Reizl	Female					389
HALPERIN	Riba	Female					389
HALPERIN	Roza	Female			Shraga Feibish		389
HALPERIN	Sara	Female	Yosef	Eti			389
HALPERIN	Sheindl		Yosef	Eti			389
HALPERIN	Shimon	Male	Yosef	Eti			389

HALPERIN	Shimon	Male			Ester		389
HALPERIN	Shimon	Male					389
HALPERIN	Shraga	Male	Yosef	Eti			389
HALPERIN	Shraga	Male			Roza	Profession: Rabbi	389
HALPERIN		Male			Menakhem Mendel		389
HALPERIN		Male			Reizl		389
HALPERIN		Male			Shimon		389
HALPERIN		Male			Riva		389
HALPERIN	Yenta	Female					389
HALPERIN	Yosef	Male			Eti		389
HALPERIN -		Male				From Lapszyn. In Berezhany during the war	389
HAMER	Dvora	Female					389
HANDESMAN	Avraham	Male					389
HANDESMAN	Ester	Female			Nakhman		389
HANDESMAN	Nakhman	Male			Ester		389
HANDESMAN	Shmuel	Male					389
HANDESMAN		Male			Avraham		389
HANDESMAN		Male	Avraham				389
HANDESMAN		Male	Avraham				389
HANDESMAN		Male	Nakhman	Ester			389

HAZELKORN	Khava	Female			Yekhiel		389
HAZELKORN	Saba	Female			Yaakov		389
HAZELKORN		Male	Yaakov	Saba			389
HAZELKORN	Yaakov	Male			Saba		389
HAZELKORN	Yekhiel	Male			Khava		389
HECHT	Breina	Female			Meir Khaim		389
HECHT	David	Male					389
HECHT	Ester	Female					389
HECHT	Meir	Male			Breina		389
HECHT		Male			David		389
HEIBIN	Ravitzuk						389
HELD		Male				Profession: Tailor	389
HELD		Male					389
HELER	Simkha	Male					389
HELER		Male			Simkha -		389
HELMAN	Genya	Female					389
HELMAN		Male				Profession: Lawyer	389
HELMAN		Male					389
HERTZ	Brunia		Menakhem	Sara			389
HERTZ	Etia		Menakhem	Sara			389
HERTZ	Gitel	Female			Yekhezkel		389

HERTZ	Menakhem	Male			Sara		389
HERTZ	Sara	Female			Menakhem Mendel		389
HERTZ		Male	Yekhezkel	Gitel			389
HERTZ	Yekhezkel	Male			Gitel		389
HERTZ	Yekhezkel	Male	Menakhem	Sara			389
HERTZOG		Male					389
HERTZOG		Male					389
HES	Adolf	Male			Ester		389
HES	Ester	Female			Adolf		389
HES	Leon	Male			Yehudit		389
HES	Meltza						389
HES	Mordekhai	Male					389
HES	More	Male					389
HES	Nekhemia	Male					389
HES		Male			Mordekhai		389
HES		Male			Mora		389
HES	Yehudit	Female			Leon		389
HES	Yoel	Male					389
HIBLER	Feige	Female			Moshe		389
HIBLER	Hertz	Male	Moshe	Feige			389
HIBLER	Moshe	Male			Feige		389
HIBLER	Rakhel	Female	Moshe	Feige			389

HIBLER	Sara	Female	Moshe	Feige			389
HIBLER	Sara	Female					389
HIBLER	Tzvia	Female	Moshe	Feige			389
HIBLER		Male					389
HIBLER		Male					389
HIBLER	Yitzkhak	Male					389
HIRSHBERG	Hirsh	Male	Khaim	Reiza			389
HIRSHBERG	Khaim	Male			Reiza		389
HIRSHBERG	Nonek		Khaim	Reiza			389
HIRSHBERG	Reiza	Female			Khaim		389
HIRSHHORN	Ester	Female					389
HIRSHHORN	Levi	Male					389
HIRSHHORN		Male		Ester			389
HIRSHHORN		Male		Ester			389
HOCHWEISS	Beniamin	Male			Roza		388
HOCHWEISS	Mila		Beniamin	Roza			388
HOCHWEISS	Roza	Female			Beniamin		388
HOKHBERG	Henka	Female	Yisrael				388
HOKHBERG	Khaia	Female					388
HOLANDER	Efraim	Male			Malka		389
HOLANDER	Malka	Female			Efraim		389
HOLANDER	Rakhel	Female			Yoel		389

HOLANDER	Yoel	Male			Rakhel		389
HOLTZMAN	Ruti	Female					389
HORN	Bashia	Female					389
HORN		Male			Bashia		389
HOROVITZ	Darne	Female			Shlomo		389
HOROVITZ	David	Male					389
HOROVITZ	Khaim	Male	Shlomo	Darne			389
HOROVITZ	Khana	Female	Shlomo	Darne			389
HOROVITZ	Lea	Female					389
HOROVITZ	Nonia	Female			Yidela		389
HOROVITZ	Shlomo	Male			Darne		389
HOROVITZ		Male	Shlomo	Darne			389
HOROVITZ		Male			David		389
HOROVITZ		Male	David				389
HOROVITZ		Male	Yidle	Nunia			389
HORSHOVSKI	David	Male			Pnina		389
HORSHOVSKI	Pnina	Female			David		389
HORSHOVSKI	Shmuel	Male	David	Pnina			389
HORSHOVSKI	Tova	Female	David	Pnina			389
IAGID	Berta	Female	Nakhum	Sushi			394
IAGID	Dzhunio		Nakhum	Sushi			394
IAGID	Nakhum	Male			Sushi		394

IAGID	Soshi	Female			Nakhum		394
IEGER	Hinda						394
IEGER	Kieltzia	Female			Yona		394
IEGER		Male					394
IEGER		Male					394
IEGER						From Saranczuki. In Berezhany during the war	394
IEGER	Yaakov	Male	Yona	Keiltza			394
IEGER	Yona	Male			Keiltzia		394
KAHANA	Ita	Female			Shlomo		394
KAHANA	Khaim	Male					394
KAHANA	Shlomo	Male			Ita		394
KAHANA		Female			Khaim	Maiden name ADLER	394
KAHANA		Male				From Konyokhi in Berezhany during the war	394
KAHANA		Male				From Konyokhi in Berezhany during the wa	394
KAHANA LAKS	Milcha	Female				Profession: Veterinarian	394
KALMAN	Khana	Female			Yisrael		404
KALMAN	Sara	Female	Yisrael	Khana			404

KAMINKER	Tzila	Female	Volf			404
KAMINKER		Female			Volf	404
KAMINKER	Volf	Male				404
KAMPEL	Sheindl	Female				403
KAMPEL		Male			Yitzkhak	403
KAMPEL		Male	Yitzkhak			403
KAMPEL	Yitzkhak	Male				403
KAMPEL	Yosef	Male		Sheindl		403
KANER	Rakhel	Female			Yaakov	404
KANER	Yaakov	Male			Rakhel	404
KARP						403
KARTEN	Somar					404
KASVIN	Fishel	Male				403
KATZ	Avraham	Male	Moshe			395
KATZ	Eli	Male			Miriam	395
KATZ	Ester	Female			Ioakhim	395
KATZ	Fania	Female	Natan	Pepa		395
KATZ	Fentzia		Moshe			395
KATZ	Frimtzia	Female			Yaakov	395
KATZ	Fritz	Male	Leib			395
KATZ	Hersh	Male				395
KATZ	Ioakhim	Male			Ester	395

KATZ	Khenia	Female					395
KATZ	Khulda	Female					395
KATZ	Lolek		Leib				395
KATZ	Lurke		Natan	Pepa			395
KATZ	Miriam	Female			Eli		395
KATZ	Moshe	Male					395
KATZ	Natan	Male			Pepe		395
KATZ	Pepa	Female			Natan		395
KATZ	Regina	Female	Yoel	Yeta			395
KATZ	Rozia		Natan	Pepa			395
KATZ	Rozia		Leib				395
KATZ	Shimon	Male	Leib				395
KATZ	Shmuel	Male					395
KATZ	Stela	Female					395
KATZ		Male			Moshe		395
KATZ		Male			Hersh Leib		395
KATZ		Male	Hersh				395
KATZ	Yaakov	Male		Khania	Frimtzia		395
KATZ	Yeta	Female			Yoel		395
KESLER	Hudel	Female					404
KESLER	Regina	Female				From Nadorozhniov in Berezhany during the war	404

KESLER		Male			Hudel		404
KESTEN	Pepka		Volf				404
KESTEN		Male			Volf Ber		404
KESTEN	Volf	Male					404
KESTEN	Yosef	Male	Volf				404
KESTEN	Zlata		Volf				404
KHAYUT	Dora	Female					392
KHAYUT	Fenka						392
KHAYUT	Mordekhai	Male					392
KHAYUT		Male					392
KIPNIS							404
KLARER	Beltzia	Female			Sender		403
KLARER	Danek		Sender	Rakhel			403
KLARER	Gita	Female			Nisan		403
KLARER	Herta		Nisan	Gita			403
KLARER	Lusia		Sender	Rakhel			403
KLARER	Nisan	Male			Gita		403
KLARER	Rakhel	Female			Sender		403
KLARER	Sender	Male			Beltzia		403
KLARER	Sender	Male			Rakhel	Profession: Clerk	403
KLARER	Tzesia		Nisan	Gita			403
KLARER		Male	Sender	Beltzia			403

KLARER	Yetka		Nisan	Gita			403
KLEID	Avraham	Male					403
KLEID		Male			Avraham		403
KLEIN	Moshe	Male			Yenta		403
KLEIN		Male	Moshe	Yenta			403
KLEIN		Male			Profession: ropemaker		403
KLEIN		Male					403
KLEIN		Male					403
KLEIN	Velvel	Male					403
KLEIN	Yenta	Female			Moshe		403
KLEIN	Yerakhmiel	Male					403
KLEIN	Yeshayahu	Male					404
KLEINRAUCH	Peretz	Male					404
KLEINRAUCH	Zysl						404
KNAUL	Adela	Female					404
KNAUL		Male					404
KNAUL	Yehuda	Male					404
KNOHL	Feiga	Female			Shimon		404
KNOHL	Golda	Female			Mordekhai		404
KNOHL	Mordekhai	Male			Golda		404
KNOHL	Rakhel	Female	Mordekhai	Golda			404
KNOHL	Shimon	Male			Feiga		404

KOHEN	Genya			Yetka		394
KOHEN		Male			Yetke	394
KOHEN		Male				394
KOHEN		Male			Lipa	394
KOHEN	Yetka	Female				394
KORN	Dvora	Female			Shlomo	403
KORN	Khaim	Male				403
KORN	Khana	Female			Yaakov	403
KORN	Leib	Male				403
KORN	Shlomo	Male			Dvora	403
KORN		Male	Yaakov	Khana		403
KORN		Male			Khaim	403
KORN		Male	Shlomo	Dvora		403
KORN	Yaakov	Male			Khana	403
KORNBAUM	Mordekhai	Male				403
KORNBAUM		Male			Velvel	403
KORNBAUM		Male			Yeshayahu	403
KORNBAUM		Male			Mordekhai	403
KORNBAUM		Male	Mordekhai			403
KORNBAUM	Velvel	Male				403
KORNBAUM	Yeshayahu	Male				403
KORNBERG		Male	Yitzkhak			403

KORNBERG	David	Male				403
KORNBERG		Male			David	403
KORNBERG		Male	David			403
KORNBERG		Male	David			403
KORNVEITZ	Dov	Male				403
KORNVEITZ	Dvora	Female	Khaim	Sara		403
KORNVEITZ	Fishel	Male	Khaim	Sara		403
KORNVEITZ	Khaim	Male			Sara	403
KORNVEITZ	Sara	Female			Khaim	403
KORNVEITZ	Yosef	Male	Khaim	Sara		403
KOSTAN						403
KRAUS	Mordekhai	Male	Pinkhas			404
KRAUS	Pinkhas	Male				404
KRAUS		Male			Pinkhas	404
KRAVITZ	Fruma	Female			Moshe	404
KRAVITZ	Hela		Moshe	Fruma		404
KRAVITZ	Mina	Female	Moshe	Fruma		404
KRAVITZ	Moshe	Male			Fruma	404
KREINDLER	Mikhael	Male				404
KREINDLER	Retza					404
KREINDLER		Male			Mikhael	404
KREINDLER		Male	Mikhael			404

KREINDLER		Male	Mikhael				404
KRESEL	Mordekhai	Male					404
KRESEL	Yaakov	Male					404
KRESEL	Yeta						404
KRONBERG							404
KRONTAL	Avraham	Male					404
KRONTAL	Herman	Male			Tzirel		404
KRONTAL	Hersh	Male					404
KRONTAL	Mordekhai	Male					404
KRONTAL	Tzirel	Female			Herman		404
KRONTAL		Male	Herman	Tzirel			404
KRONTAL		Male	Herman	Tzirel			404
KRONTAL		Male			Mordekhai		404
KRONTAL		Male			Hersh		404
KRONTAL	Yekhezkel	Male	Hersh				404
KURTZ	Regina	Female				Profession: Music Teacher	403
KURTZMAN		Male					403
KURTZMAN		Male				Profession: Pharmacist	403
KURTZMAN		Male					403
KURTZMAN		Male					403
KURTZROK	Helena	Female	Mark	Mania			403

KURTZROK	Ilana	Female	Mark	Mania			403
KURTZROK	Mania	Female			Mark		403
KURTZROK	Mark	Male			Mania		403
KVERTEL	Barukh	Male					403
KVERTEL	Betzalel	Male	Moshe				403
KVERTEL	Bezio		David	Miriam			403
KVERTEL	David	Male			Miriam		403
KVERTEL	Ester	Female	Moshe				403
KVERTEL	Khana	Female					403
KVERTEL	Mania	Female	Barukh				403
KVERTEL	Miriam	Female			David		403
KVERTEL	Moshe	Male					403
KVERTEL		Male			Barukh		403
KVERTEL		Male		Khana			403
KVERTEL		Male			Yitzkhak		403
KVERTEL	Yitzkhak	Male					403
LABER	Etia		Yosef	Genya			395
LABER	Genya	Female			Yosef		395
LABER	Klara	Female			Yaakov		395
LABER	Rakhel	Female			Yerukham		395
LABER	Yaakov	Male			Klara		395
LABER	Yerukham	Male			Rakhel		395

LABER	Yosef	Male			Genya	Profession: Lawyer	395
LAKHER	David	Male		Perla			396
LAKHER	Gitel						396
LAKHER	Itamar	Male		Perla			396
LAKHER	Lusia	Female			Monio		396
LAKHER	Miriam	Female			Mordekhai		396
LAKHER	Moniyo	Male			Lusia		396
LAKHER	Mordekhai	Male			Miriam		396
LAKHER	Perla	Female					396
LAKHER	Sofia	Female					396
LAKHER	Yetka			Sofia			396
LAKS	Anna		Moshe	Brunia			396
LAKS	Brunia	Female			Moshe		396
LAKS	Gusta	Female	Yaakov				396
LAKS	Moshe	Male			Bronia		396
LAKS	Shamai	Male					396
LAKS	Simkha						396
LAKS		Male			Shamai		396
LAKS		Male	Shamai				396
LAKS	Velvel	Male					396
LANDAU	Aharon	Male			Liba		396
LANDAU	Hersh	Male	Aharon	Liba			396

LANDAU	Liba	Female			Aharon		396
LANDENSBERG	Teodor	Male					396
LAUFGANG	Avraham	Male					395
LAUFGANG		Male			Avraham		395
LAZAR	Mikhael	Male					395
LEBEL	Moshe	Male					395
LEBEL		Male			Vevia		395
LEBEL		Male	Via				395
LEBEL		Male	Via				395
LEBEL		Male	Via				395
LEBEL		Male	Via				395
LEBEL		Male			Moshe		395
LEBEL		Male	Moshe				395
LEBEL		Male	Moshe				395
LEBEL	Via	Female					395
LEDER	Fania	Female					395
LEDER	Klara	Female		Fania			395
LEDER	Zusia			Fania			395
LEIBEL	Frania	Female			Natan		396
LEIBEL	Iya	Female			Natan		396
LEIBEL	Linka		Natan	Frania			396
LEIBEL	Natan	Male			Frania		396

LEIBEL	Natan	Male			Iya		396
LEIBEL	Olek		Natan	Iya			396
LEIBEL ZISKIND		Male					396
LEIBEL ZISKIND		Male					396
LEIBELE FIRER		Male					396
LEIBELE FIRER		Male					396
LEIBELE FIRER	Zeide	Male					396
LEIDER	Bernard	Male					396
LEIDER		Male			Bernard		396
LEIDER		Male	Bernard				396
LEIDER		Male	Bernard				396
LEITER	Dunia		Meir				396
LEITER	Lote		Meir				396
LEITER	Meir	Male					396
LEVI	Ester	Female					395
LEVI	Shlomo	Male					395
LEVI		Male			Ester	Profession: Shoemaker	395
LIBER		Male				Profession: Hairdresser	396
LIBER		Male					396
LIBER		Male					396
LIBERMAN	Sonia	Female					396

LIBERMAN		Male					396
LIBERMAN		Male					396
LIBLING	Genya		Moshe	Lusia			396
LIBLING	Khaitzia	Female	Yehuda				395
LIBLING	Lusia	Female			Moshe		396
LIBLING	Moshe	Male			Lusia		396
LIBLING	Shmuel	Male					396
LIBLING		Male			Shmuel		396
LIBLING	Yehuda	Male					395
LIBREIKH							396
LIBSTER	Shlomo	Male					396
LIBSTER		Male			Shlomo		396
LIBSTER		Male	Shlomo				396
LIFSHITZ	Leibish	Male			Zufia		396
LIFSHITZ	Shalom	Male			Orma		396
LIFSHITZ		Male	Shalom	Urma			396
LIFSHITZ		Male	Shalom	Urma			396
LIFSHITZ		Male				Profession: Inspector	396
LIFSHITZ		Male					396
LIFSHITZ		Male					396
LIFSHITZ		Male					396
LIFSHITZ		Male					396

LIFSHITZ	Urma	Female			Shalom		396
LIFSHITZ	Zufia	Female			Leibish		396
LIKHT	Hirsh	Male			Rakhel		396
LIKHT	Rakhel	Female			Hirsh		396
LIKHTMAN	Ester	Female	Yisrael	Rakhel			396
LIKHTMAN	Rivka	Female			Yisrael Yehuda		396
LIKHTMAN	Shlomit	Female	Yisrael	Rakhel			396
LIKHTMAN	Yisrael	Male			Rivka		396
LILE	David	Male					396
LILE	Dolek	Male					396
LILE		Male			Dolek		396
LILE		Male	Dolek				396
LILE	Yezi	Male					396
LINVAND	Kieltzia	Female			Yaakov		396
LINVAND	Shlomo	Male	Yaakov	Keiltza			396
LINVAND	Yaakov	Male			Keiltzia		396
LINVAND	Yitzkhak	Male	Yaakov	Keiltza			396
LIPMAN	Lazar	Male					396
LIPMAN		Male			Yosef		396
LIPMAN	Yosef	Male					396
LOKMAN	Avraham	Male			Gitel		395
LOKMAN	Bela	Female	Avraham	Gitel			395

LOKMAN	Brunia	Female	Avraham	Gitel			395
LOKMAN	Gitel	Female			Avraham		395
LOKMAN	Khana	Female	Avraham	Gitel			395
LOPATER	Beltzia	Female			Shalom		395
LOPATER	Berko		Shalom	Beltzia			395
LOPATER	Binka		Mikhael	Leitzi			395
LOPATER	Bruno	Male			Tontzia	Profession: Lawyer	395
LOPATER	Feibish	Male					395
LOPATER	Hentzia		Mikhael	Leitzi			395
LOPATER	Leitzi	Female			Mikhael		395
LOPATER	Leo	Male					395
LOPATER	Mikhael	Male			Leitzi		395
LOPATER	Moshe	Male	Mikhael	Leitzi			395
LOPATER	Roza	Female			Shmuel		395
LOPATER	Shabtai	Male	Mikhael	Leitzi			395
LOPATER	Shalom	Male			Beltzia		395
LOPATER	Shmuel	Male			Roza	Profession: Pharmacist	395
LOPATER	Tuntzia	Female			Bruno		395
LOPATER		Male	Shmuel	Roza			395
LOPATER		Male			Feibish		395
LOPATER		Male			Leo		395

LOPATER		Male			Yaakov		395
LOPATER		Male	Yaakov				395
LOPATER		Male	Yaakov				395
LOPATER		Male					395
LOPATER		Male					395
LOPATER		Male					395
LOPATER	Yaakov	Male					395
LOPATER	Yaakov	Male	Mikhael	Leitzi			395
LOPATER	Yehoshua	Male	Mikhael	Leitzi			395
LOPATER	Yosef	Male	Shalom	Beltzia			395
LUBINER	Charna	Female			Fishel Yerukham		395
LUBINER	Fishel	Male			Charna		395
LUBINER	Fridka		Fishel	Charna			395
LUBINER	Pesia	Female	Fishel	Charna			395
LUBINER	Sara	Female	Fishel	Charna			395
LUBINER	Shlomo	Male	Fishel	Charna			395
LUDMERER	Bernard	Male	Yokhanan	Elnura			395
LUDMERER	Elnora	Female			Yokhanan		395
LUDMERER	Emil	Male			Laura		395
LUDMERER	Gusta	Female			Izidor		395
LUDMERER	Izidor	Male			Gusta		395
LUDMERER	Koba		Nusia				395

LUDMERER	Laura	Female			Emil		395
LUDMERER	Nosia	Male					395
LUDMERER	Pnina	Female					395
LUDMERER	Shimon	Male	Nusia				395
LUDMERER	Yokhanan	Male			Alnora		395
MALER	Aharon	Male					398
MALER	Hirsh	Male	Mordekhai	Lea			398
MALER	Lea	Female			Mordekhai		398
MALER	Mordekhai	Male			Lea		398
MALER	Sara	Female	Mordekhai	Lea			398
MALER		Male			Aharon		398
MALER	Yitzkhak	Male					398
MANDELBERG	Meltzia	Female					398
MANDELBERG	Nakhum	Male					398
MANDELBERG	Rivka	Female		Meltzia			398
MANDELBERG	Yehoshua	Male		Meltzia			398
MARGULIES	Golda	Female			Zalman		398
MARGULIES	Khana	Female	Yaakov	Lea			398
MARGULIES	Lea	Female			Yaakov		398
MARGULIES		Male	Yaakov	Lea			398
MARGULIES	Yaakov	Male			Lea		398
MARGULIES	Yosef	Male	Yaakov	Lea			398

MARGULIES	Zalman	Male			Golda		398
MARIASH	Khaim	Male					397
MARIASH		Male			Khaim		397
MARIASH		Male	Khaim				397
MATES	Regina	Female					398
MATES		Male			Yisrael		398
MATES		Male			Regina	Profession: House Painter	398
MATES	Yisrael	Male					398
MAURER		Male					397
MAURER		Male					397
MAURER		Male					397
MEIBLUM	Avraham	Male			Rivka		397
MEIBLUM	David	Male			Sara		397
MEIBLUM	Khana	Female			Yehuda		397
MEIBLUM	Moshe	Male			Sheindl		397
MEIBLUM	Pnina	Female	David	Sara			397
MEIBLUM	Rakhel	Female			Yitzkhak		397
MEIBLUM	Rivka	Female			Avraham		397
MEIBLUM	Sara	Female			David		397
MEIBLUM	Sheindl	Female			Moshe		397
MEIBLUM	Silvia	Female	David	Sara			397
MEIBLUM	Tzila	Female	Yitzkhak	Rakhel			397

MEIBLUM	Tzipia		Avraham	Rivka			397
MEIBLUM		Male			Yosef		397
MEIBLUM	Yehuda	Male			Khana		397
MEIBLUM	Yitzkhak	Male			Rakhel		397
MEIBLUM	Yosef	Male	Avraham	Rivka			397
MEIBLUM	Yosef	Male					397
MEIBLUM	Yosef	Male	Moshe	Sheindl			397
MEIBLUM	Zalman	Male	Moshe	Sheindl			397
MEIBLUM	Zat		David	Sara			397
MEIBLUM	Zelig	Male					397
MEIER	Arie	Male	Shaul	Rakhel			397
MEIER	Berish		Shaul	Rakhel			397
MEIER	Rakhel	Female			Shaul		397
MEIER	Shaul	Male			Rakhel		397
MERKUR	Mania	Female					398
MERKUR SHERER	Aharon	Male			Yulia		398
MERKUR SHERER	Dina	Female			Yosef		398
MERKUR SHERER	Henia	Female			Leibele		398
MERKUR SHERER	Leibele	Male			Henia		398
MERKUR SHERER	Max	Male	Leibele	Henia			398

MERKUR SHERER	Mordekhai	Male	Yosef	Dina			398
MERKUR SHERER	Roza	Female	Leibele	Henia			398
MERKUR SHERER	Roza	Female	Aharon	Yulia			398
MERKUR SHERER	Yosef	Male			Dina		398
MERKUR SHERER	Yulia	Female			Aharon		398
MERZANT	Lazar	Male					398
MERZANT	Moshe	Male					398
MERZANT	Tzipe	Female					398
MERZANT		Male			Lazar		398
MERZANT		Male			Tzipe		398
MESER	Dina	Female	Sania	Malka			398
MESER	Ester	Female	Dudya				398
MESER	Feiga	Female	Dudya				398
MESER	Hirsh	Male	Dudya				398
MESER	Malka	Female			Sania		398
MESER	Sania	Male			Malka		398
MESER	Shai	Male	Sania	Malka			398
MESER	Sheindl	Female	Zeev				398
MESER	Yaakov	Male	Sania	Malka			398
MESER	Yeti		Sania	Malka			398

MESER	Yitzkhak	Male	Zeev				398
MESER	Zeev	Male					398
MESING	Avraham	Male			Sheindl		398
MESING	Etka						398
MESING	Sheindl	Female			Avraham		398
MIHLSHTOK	Dudile		Moshe	Lifsha			397
MIHLSHTOK	Eliezer	Male			Lea		397
MIHLSHTOK	Fishel	Male					397
MIHLSHTOK	Lea	Female			Eliezer		397
MIHLSHTOK	Lifsha	Female			Moshe		397
MIHLSHTOK	Moshe	Male			Lifsha		397
MIHLSHTOK		Male			Fishel		397
MILER	David	Male					397
MILER		Male			David		397
MILER		Male				Profession: Blacksmith	397
MILER		Male					397
MILER	Zigmund	Male					397
MILKH		Male					397
MILKH		Male					397
MILKH		Male					397
MILKH		Male					397

MILRAD		Male				From Saranczuki. In Berezhany during the war	397
MILRAD		Male				From Saranczuki. In Berezhany during the war	397
MIRBERG	Aharon	Male			Gitel		397
MIRBERG	Aharon	Male			Gitel		398
MIRBERG	Arie	Male	Tzvi				398
MIRBERG	Dora	Female			Moshe		398
MIRBERG	Feige	Female			Hirsh		397
MIRBERG	Frida	Female			Meir		397
MIRBERG	Gitel	Female			Aharon Moshe		397
MIRBERG	Gitel	Female			Aharon Moshe		398
MIRBERG	Hadasa	Female	Aharon	Gitel			397
MIRBERG	Hadasa	Female	Aharon	Gitel			398
MIRBERG	Hirsh	Male			Feige		397
MIRBERG	Khaim	Male			Malka		397
MIRBERG	Khaitze	Female			Zali		397
MIRBERG	Khana	Female	Zali	Khaitze			397
MIRBERG	Khanan	Male					397
MIRBERG	Lea	Female	Meir	Frida			397

MIRBERG	Leib	Male	Leizer	Rakhel		From Saranczuki. In Berezhany during the war	397
MIRBERG	Leizer	Male			Rakhel	From Saranczuki. In Berezhany during the war	397
MIRBERG	Lev	Male	Zali	Khaitze			397
MIRBERG	Lev	Male	Khaim	Malka			397
MIRBERG	Malka	Female			Khaim		397
MIRBERG	Mania		Meir	Frida			397
MIRBERG	Meir	Male	Leizer	Rakhel		From Saranczuki. In Berezhany during the war	397
MIRBERG	Meir	Male			Frida		397
MIRBERG	Mina	Female	Khaim	Malka			397
MIRBERG	Moshe	Male			Dora		398
MIRBERG	Rakhel	Female			Leizer	From Saranczuki. In Berezhany during the war	397
MIRBERG	Sara	Female	Zali	Khaitze			397
MIRBERG	Shalom	Male	Aharon	Gitel			397
MIRBERG	Shalom	Male	Aharon	Gitel			398
MIRBERG	Soniu		Hirsh	Feige			397
MIRBERG	Tzvi	Male					398
MIRBERG	Yeta		Leizer	Rakhel		From Saranczuki. In	397

						Berezhany during the war	
MIRBERG	Zali	Male			Kheitze		397
MITELMAN	Beniamin	Male					397
MITELMAN	Berta	Female			Yaakov		397
MITELMAN	Efraim	Male			Tzipa		397
MITELMAN	Etzia		Efraim	Tzipa			397
MITELMAN	Leib	Male					397
MITELMAN	Tzipa	Female			Efraim		397
MITELMAN		Male			Beniamin		397
MITELMAN		Male	Beniamin				397
MITELMAN		Male	Beniamin				397
MITELMAN		Male			Leib		397
MITELMAN		Male	Leib				397
MITELMAN	Yaakov	Male			Berta		397
MORGEN	Hirsh	Male					397
MOSHEL	Ester	Female	Shmuel				397
MOSHEL	Khaim	Male		Ester			397
MOSHEL	Mania			Ester			397
MOSHEL		Male					397
MOSHEL		Male					397
MOSHEL		Male					397
MOSHEL		Male					397

MOSHEL		Male					397
MUNDSHTEIN	Berta	Female			Raymond		397
MUNDSHTEIN	Raymond	Male			Berta		397
MUSKATENBLIT		Male					397
MUSKATENBLIT		Male					397
MUSKATENBLIT		Male					397
MUSKATENBLIT		Male					397
NABEL	Ira	Male					398
NABEL		Male			Ira		398
NADLER	Bernard	Male			Miriam		399
NADLER	Bina		Bernard	Miriam			399
NADLER	Golda	Female					399
NADLER	Mank			Ronia			399
NADLER	Miriam	Female			Bernard		399
NADLER	Ronia	Female					399
NAGELBERG	Aizik	Male			Charna		398
NAGELBERG	Charna	Female			Aizik		398
NAGELBERG	Klara	Female			Yaakov		398
NAGELBERG	Selka		Yaakov	Klara			398
NAGELBERG	Shimon	Male	Yaakov	Klara			398
NAGELBERG	Shimon	Male					399
NAGELBERG		Male					398

NAGELBERG	Yaakov	Male			Klara		398
NAGLER	Filip	Male					399
NAGLER		Male					399
NAROL	Arie	Male			Khana		398
NAROL	Asher	Male					398
NAROL	Khaia						398
NAROL	Khana	Female			Arie		398
NAROL		Male			Asher		398
NAROL		Male	Arie	Khana			398
NAROL		Male	Arie	Khana			398
NEBEL	Aba	Male			Sosia		398
NEBEL	Shmuel	Male					398
NEBEL	Sosia	Female			Aba		398
NEBEL		Male	Shmuel				398
NEMLIKH	Moniyo			Pnina			398
NEMLIKH	Pnina	Female					398
NEMLIKH	Tonka			Pnina			398
NEMLIKH		Male			Pnina		398
NIMAND	Heniu	Male				From Saranczuki. In Berezhany during the war	398
NIMAND		Male				From Saranczuki. In	398

						Berezhany during the war	
NIMAND		Male				From Saranczuki. In Berezhany during the war	398
NOIMAN	Beniamin	Male					399
NOIMAN	Blushia		Motel				399
NOIMAN	Dosiu			Gusta			399
NOIMAN	Gusta	Female					399
NOIMAN	Khana	Female					399
NOIMAN	Motl	Male					399
NOIMAN		Male			Khana	Profession: City Cantor	399
NOIMAN		Male		Khana			399
NOIMAN		Male			Beniamin		399
NOIMAN		Male	Beniamin				399
NOIMAN		Male	Beniamin				399
NOIMAN		Male			Leib		399
NOIMAN	Yenta		Leib				399
NOIMAN GROS	Klara	Female			Yitzkhak		399
NOIMAN GROS	Yitzkhak	Male			Klara		399
NOISHILER	Frederika	Female	Shimshon	Tzila			398
NOISHILER	Herman	Male	Shimshon	Tzila			398
NOISHILER	Heshi						398

NOISHILER	Moshe	Male					398
NOISHILER	Paula	Female	Shimshon	Tzila			398
NOISHILER	Shimshon	Male			Tzila		398
NOISHILER	Tzila	Female			Shimshon		398
NOISHILER		Male			Moshe		398
OBERLENDER	Iza		Natan				382
OBERLENDER	Natan	Male				Profession: Lawyer	382
OBERLENDER		Male			Natan		382
OBERLENDER	Vadia		Natan				382
OBERLENDER	Yosef	Male	Natan				382
OHRING	Avraham	Male			Ester		382
OHRING	Brintzia	Female			Khone		382
OHRING	Ester	Female			Avraham		382
OHRING	Golda	Female	Khune	Breintze			382
OHRING	Khone	Male			Breintzia		382
OHRING		Male	Avraham	Ester			382
OHRING		Male	Avraham	Ester			382
OIGENTZUKER	Feibish	Male					382
OIGENTZUKER		Male			Feibish Shalom		382
OIGENTZUKER		Male	Feibish				382
OKS	Fridl	Male			Rivka		382

OKS	Rivka	Female			Fridl	382
OKS		Male				382
ORENSHTEIN	Eugenia	Female				382
ORENSHTEIN	Mank					382
ORENSHTEIN	Yaakov	Male				382
ORGAL	Manio			Ruzia		382
ORGAL	Roiza	Female				382
ORGAL		Male			Rozia	382
OSTERMAN	Avraham	Male	Kopel	Sara		382
OSTERMAN	Kopel	Male			Sara	382
OSTERMAN	Leib	Male	Kopel	Sara		382
OSTERMAN	Sara	Female			Kopel	382
OSTROVER	Eidel	Female			Hirsh	382
OSTROVER	Hirsh	Male			Eidel	382
OSTROVER		Female			Yehuda Ber	382
OSTROVER		Male	Hirsh	Eidel		382
OSTROVER	Velvele	Male	Yehuda			382
OSTROVER	Yehuda	Male				382
OSTROVER FISHMAN	Moshe	Male			Sara Feiga	382
OSTROVER FISHMAN	Sara	Female			Moshe	382
PASTERNAK	Hinda	Female			Mordekhai	401

PASTERNAK	Mordekhai	Male			Hinda		401
PECHENIK	Ester	Female	Yaakov		Yona		401
PECHENIK	Fenka		Yona	Ester			401
PECHENIK	Moniyo		Yona	Ester			401
PECHENIK	Rozia		Yona	Ester			401
PECHENIK		Male				From Raj, Czechoslovakia	401
PECHENIK		Male				From Raj, Czechoslovakia	401
PECHENIK		Male				From Raj, Czechoslovakia	401
PECHENIK	Yona	Male			Ester		401
PELTZ	Sara	Female			Shimon		401
PELTZ	Shimon	Male			Sara		401
PELTZ		Male			Yekhiel		401
PELTZ		Male	Yekhiel				401
PELTZ		Male	Yekhiel				401
PELTZ		Male	Yekhiel				401
PELTZ	Yekhiel	Male					401
PENIAKER	Risa						401
PENIAKER		Male					401
PERLMUTER	Khaim	Male					402
PODHORTZER	Bluma	Female			Leib	From Kuropatniki	400

PODHORTZER	Leib	Male			Bluma	From Kuropatniki	400
PODHORTZER	Lina	Female			Monio		400
PODHORTZER	Moniyo	Male			Lina		400
PODHORTZER	Zuzia		Munio	Lina			400
PODOSHIN	Bela		Moshe				400
PODOSHIN	Boma						400
PODOSHIN	Boma		Yitzkhak	Keila			400
PODOSHIN	Feige	Female					400
PODOSHIN	Keila	Female			Yitzkhak		400
PODOSHIN	Moshe	Male					400
PODOSHIN		Male			Moshe		400
PODOSHIN	Yitzkhak	Male			Keila		400
POHORILES	Emanuel	Male			Roza		400
POHORILES	Khulda	Female	Emanuel	Roza			400
POHORILES	Roza	Female			Emanuel		400
POHORILES		Male				Profession: Pharmacist	400
POLBER		Male			Yosha		400
POLBER		Male	Yusha				400
POLBER		Male	Yusha				400
POLBER	Yosha	Male					400
POMERANTZ	Asher	Male					400

POMERANTZ	Filip	Male			Yosefina		400
POMERANTZ	Khantzia	Female			Yaakov		400
POMERANTZ	Miriam	Female	Filip	Yosefina			400
POMERANTZ	Shlomo	Male					400
POMERANTZ		Male	Yaakov	Khantzia			400
POMERANTZ		Male	Yaakov	Khantzia			400
POMERANTZ		Male	Filip	Yosefina			400
POMERANTZ	Yaakov	Male			Khantzia		400
POMERANTZ	Yosefina	Female			Filip		400
PREIS	Mordekhai	Male					402
PREIS		Male			Mordekhai Leib		402
PREIS		Male	Mordekhai				402
PREIS		Male	Mordekhai				402
PREIS	Yitzkhak	Male					402
PREIS	Zuzu		Mordekhai				402
PRIZAND	Feibish		Shlomo	Khava			402
PRIZAND	Khana	Female	Shlomo	Khava			402
PRIZAND	Khava	Female			Shlomo		402
PRIZAND	Mikhael	Male	Shlomo	Khava			402
PRIZAND	Shimon	Male	Shlomo	Khava			402
PRIZAND	Shlomo	Male			Khava		402
PRIZAND		Male					402

PTZENIK	Mala	Female			Vili		401
PTZENIK	Vili	Male			Mala		401
PUDER	Shaul	Male					400
PUDER		Male			Shaul		400
PUDER		Male	Shaul				400
PUDER		Male	Shaul				400
PUNDIK							400
PUTIKER	David	Male					400
PUTIKER		Male			David		400
PUTIKER		Male	David				400
RAVICH	Yaakov	Male					404
REDLIKH	Aidla	Female					404
REDLIKH	Avraham	Male					404
REDLIKH	Dvora	Female			Yaakov		404
REDLIKH	Herman	Male			Zuzi		404
REDLIKH	Hertz	Male	Yaakov	Dvora			404
REDLIKH	Mikhael	Male	Avraham				404
REDLIKH	Shlomo	Male	Yaakov				404
REDLIKH	Shlomo	Male				Profession: Hebrew Teacher	404
REDLIKH		Male			Avraham		404
REDLIKH		Male					404

REDLIKH	Yaakov	Male			Dvora		404
REDLIKH	Yezik		Avraham	·			404
REDLIKH	Yosef	Male	Avraham				404
REDLIKH	Zuzi	Female			Herman		404
REICHBAD	Naitschi	Female			Leib		405
REICHBAD	Shimon	Male	Leib	Naitshi			405
REICHBAD	Yaakov	Male	Leib	Naitshi			405
REIKH	Adela	Female			Bronia		405
REIKH	Batia	Female	Ioakhim				405
REIKH	Beniu		Adela	Brunia			405
REIKH	Bila		Ioakhim				405
REIKH	Brunia	Female			Adela		405
REIKH	Duzia		Adela	Brunia			405
REIKH	Ioakhim	Male					405
REIKH	Mats	Male					405
REIKH	Moshe	Male					405
REIKH	Tamar	Female	Adela	Brunia			405
REIKH		Male			Ioakhim		405
REIKH		Male			Moshe		405
REIKH		Male				Profession: Hairdresser	405
REIKH		Male					405
REIKH		Male					405

REIKH		Male					405
REIKH		Male					405
REIKH		Male					405
REIKH		Male			Mates		405
REIKHBAKH	Ezra	Male			Khana		406
REIKHBAKH	Khana	Female			Ezra		406
REIKHBAKH	Leib	Male			Naitshi		405
REIKHBAKH	Rivka	Female	Ezra	Khana			406
REIKHBAKH	Zunia		Ezra	Khana			406
REIKHMAN		Male					406
REIKHMAN		Male					406
REIKHMAN		Male					406
REIKHMAN		Male					406
REIKHMAN		Male					406
REIKHSHTEIN	Asher	Male	Mordekhai				406
REIKHSHTEIN	Hersh	Male	Mordekhai				406
REIKHSHTEIN	Mendel	Male					406
REIKHSHTEIN	Mordekhai	Male					406
REIKHSHTEIN		Male			Mendel		406
REIKHSHTEIN		Male	Mendel				406
REIKHSHTEIN		Male	Mendel				406
REIKHSHTEIN		Male			Mordekhai		406

REINER	Bela			Helena		406
REINER	Helena	Female				406
REINER	Khaim	Male			Rozia	406
REINER	Lipa	Male				406
REINER	Rozia	Female			Khaim	406
REINER		Male	Khaim	Ruzia		406
REITER		Male				405
REITER		Male				405
REITMAN	Adela		Nakhman	Tantzia		405
REITMAN	Fridka	Female			Lunk	405
REITMAN	Genya	Female			Noakh	405
REITMAN	Lunk	Male			Fridka	405
REITMAN	Lusia	Female			Salek	405
REITMAN	Malka	Female	Nakhman	Tantzia		405
REITMAN	Nakhman	Male			Tantzia	405
REITMAN	Nakhman	Male	Lunk	Fridka		405
REITMAN	Noakh	Male	Nakhman	Tantzia		405
REITMAN	Noakh	Male			Genya	405
REITMAN	Sala		Nakhman	Tantzia		405
REITMAN	Salek	Male			Lusia	405
REITMAN	Tantzia	Female			Nakhman	405
REITMAN	Yona		Lunk	Fridka		405

REIZER	Avraham	Male					405
REIZER	Avraham	Male			Klara		405
REIZER	Berta	Female	Avraham	Klara			405
REIZER	Dvora	Female			Khaim		405
REIZER	Feiga	Female					405
REIZER	Khaia	Female	Khaim	Dvora			405
REIZER	Khaim	Male			Dvora		405
REIZER	Khana	Female			Yehoshua		405
REIZER	Khanokh	Male					405
REIZER	Klara	Female			Avraham		405
REIZER	Leib	Male					405
REIZER	Moshe	Male	Yehoshua	Khana			405
REIZER	Shimon	Male	Khaim	Dvora			405
REIZER	Shoshana	Female	Yehoshua	Khana			405
REIZER		Male			Avraham		405
REIZER		Male			Itzia Yitzkhak		405
REIZER		Male			Khanokh		405
REIZER		Male			Leib		405
REIZER	Utzia	Male					405
REIZER	Yehoshua	Male			Khana		405
REIZMAN	Klara	Female					405
REIZMAN		Male		Klara			405

RENDELSHTEIN	Moshe	Male					406
RIGER	Khana	Female			Oskar		405
RIGER	Moshe	Male					405
RIGER	Oskar	Male			Khana		405
RIGER	Yaakov	Male					405
RINDER		Male				Profession: Electrical appliances	406
RINDER		Male					406
ROK	Anshel	Male			Feiga		405
ROK	Barukh	Male			Nashi		405
ROK	Beila	Female			Moshe Leib		405
ROK	David	Male					405
ROK	Feiga	Female			Anshel		405
ROK	Frida	Female			Volf		405
ROK	Moshe	Male			Beile		405
ROK	Neshi	Female			Barukh Yosef		405
ROK	Volf	Male			Frida		405
ROT	Frida	Female			Moshe		404
ROT	Moniyo		Moshe	Frida			404
ROT	Moshe	Male			Frida		404
ROTIN	Beltzia	Female			Bentzion		405
ROTIN	Khana	Female	Meir				406

ROTIN		Male			Beltzia		405
ROTSHTEIN	Hirsh	Male				From Koziany. In Berezhany during the war	405
ROTSHTEIN	Lea	Female					405
ROTSHTEIN	Meir	Male			Toibe		405
ROTSHTEIN	Shimon	Male					405
ROTSHTEIN	Toibe	Female			Meir Leib		405
ROTSHTEIN		Male	Meir	Toibe			405
ROTSHTEIN		Male	Meir	Toibe			405
ROTSHTEIN		Male		Lea			405
ROTSHTEIN		Male		Lea			405
ROTSHTEIN		Male			Shimon		405
ROZEN	Bila	Female			Binem		404
ROZEN	Binem	Male			Bila		404
ROZEN	Moshe	Male	Binem	Bila			404
ROZEN	Rivka	Female	Binem	Bila			404
ROZEN	Shlomo	Male	Binem	Bila			404
ROZEN	Yitzkhak	Male	Binem	Bila			404
ROZENBERG	Leibush						405
ROZENTZVEIG	Beila	Female			Gedalia		405
ROZENTZVEIG	Eliezer	Male	Gedalia	Beile			405
ROZENTZVEIG	Gedalia	Male			Beile		405

ROZENTZVEIG	Hirsh	Male	Gedalia	Beile			405
ROZENTZVEIG	Moshe	Male			Toibe		405
ROZENTZVEIG	Reiza						405
ROZENTZVEIG	Tilke		Gedalia	Beile			405
ROZENTZVEIG	Toibe	Female			Moshe		405
ROZENTZVEIG	Yekhiel	Male			Zysl		405
ROZENTZVEIG	Yetka		Gedalia	Beila			405
ROZENTZVEIG	Zysl	Female			Yekhiel		405
RUS	Asnat	Female			Moshe Meir		405
RUS	Etel	Female					405
RUS	Hersh	Male			Rivka		405
RUS	Khana	Female					405
RUS	Lea	Female	Hersh	Rivka			405
RUS	Liza		Yisrael	Zysl			405
RUS	Malka	Female	Hersh	Rivka			405
RUS	Moniyo						405
RUS	Moshe	Male			Asnat		405
RUS	Rivka	Female			Hersh		405
RUS		Male					405
RUS	Yisrael	Male			Zysl		405
RUS	Yula		Yisrael	Zysl			405
RUS	Zysl	Female			Yisrael		405

RUT	Bezio	Male		Rakhel			405
RUT	Dina	Female	Yosef				405
RUT	Eliahu	Male	Yosef				405
RUT	Ester	Female			Yosef		405
RUT	Fenka						405
RUT	Frimet	Female			Shlomo		405
RUT	Luntzia		Eliahu				405
RUT	Shlomo	Male			Frimet		405
RUT	Yenta						405
RUT	Yosef	Male			Ester Pinia		405
RUTENBERG	Tontzi	Male					405
RUTENBERG		Male			Tontzi		405
RUTENBERG		Male	Tontzi				405
SAFIR	David	Male	Shmuel	Miriam			399
SAFIR	Ester	Female	Shmuel	Miriam			399
SAFIR	Ita	Female			Moshe		399
SAFIR	Khaim	Male	Shmuel	Miriam			399
SAFIR	Miriam	Female			Shmuel		399
SAFIR	Moshe	Male			Ita		399
SAFIR	Shmuel	Male			Miriam		399
SAFIRSHTEIN	David	Male			Khana		399
SAFIRSHTEIN	Dina	Female					399

SAFIRSHTEIN	Etka			Dina		399
SAFIRSHTEIN	Khana	Female			David	399
SAFIRSHTEIN	Moshe	Male	David	Khana		399
SAFIRSHTEIN		Male			Dina	399
SAFIRSHTEIN	Volko			Dina		399
SAFIRSHTEIN	Yosef	Male	David	Khana		399
SALOMON	Berl	Male	Yosef	Golda		399
SALOMON	Betzalel	Male			Profession: Lawyer	399
SALOMON	Feibish	Male	Yosef	Golda		399
SALOMON	Golda	Female			Yosef	399
SALOMON		Male			Betzalel	399
SALOMON	Yosef	Male			Golda	399
SAMET	Shlomo	Male	Yitzkhak	Yenta		399
SAMET	Yenta	Female			Yitzkhak	399
SAMET	Yitzkhak	Male			Yenta	399
SAS	Fenka	Female			Shaul	399
SAS	Shaul	Male			Fanke	399
SAUBERBERG	Bela		Moshe			391
SAUBERBERG	Bela		Shlomo	Sara		391
SAUBERBERG	Brunia	Female			Shmuel	391
SAUBERBERG	Hinda	Female			Lazar	391
SAUBERBERG	Lazar	Male			Hinda	391

SAUBERBERG	Lidia	Female	Shmuel	Brunia			391
SAUBERBERG	Lusik		Shlomo	Sara			391
SAUBERBERG	Moshe	Male				Profession: Lawyer	391
SAUBERBERG	Sara	Female			Shlomo		391
SAUBERBERG	Shlomo	Male			Sara		391
SAUBERBERG	Shmuel	Male			Bronia		391
SAUBERBERG		Male			Moshe		391
SCHLICHER		Male			Yehoiakim		407
SCHLICHER		Male	Yoakhim				407
SCHLICHER	Yehoiakim	Male					407
SCHLICHER	Yezik		Yoakhim				407
SCHMIDT	Mikhael	Male			Sonia		407
SCHMIDT	Moniyo		Mikhael	Sonia			407
SCHMIDT	Sonia	Female			Mikhael		407
SEGAL	Dzunia		Lazar	Genya			399
SEGAL	Fenka		Leibish	Rakhel			399
SEGAL	Genya	Female			Lazar		399
SEGAL	Lazar	Male			Genya		399
SEGAL	Leibish	Male			Rakhel		399
SEGAL	Rakhel	Female			Leibish		399
SEGAL		Male			Zelig		399
SEGAL		Male	Zelig				399

SEGAL	Zelig	Male					399
SHAPIRA	Antshel	Male					407
SHAPIRA	Artek		Shlomo	Vitzia			407
SHAPIRA	Avraham	Male					407
SHAPIRA	Bilha	Female			Mikhael		407
SHAPIRA	Bunim	Male	Khaim	Sara			407
SHAPIRA	Bunim	Male			Reiza		407
SHAPIRA	Ester	Female			Yeshiyah		407
SHAPIRA	Ester	Female			Moshe		408
SHAPIRA	Ester	Female	Shlomo	Vitzia			407
SHAPIRA	Golda	Female	Yeshiyah	Ester			407
SHAPIRA	Khaia	Female	Bunim	Reiza			407
SHAPIRA	Khaim	Male			Sara		407
SHAPIRA	Liba		Shlomo	Vitzia			407
SHAPIRA	Ludvig	Male	Antschel				407
SHAPIRA	Mania	Female	Shlomo	Vitzia			407
SHAPIRA	Meir	Male					407
SHAPIRA	Mendel	Male	Shlomo	Vitzia			407
SHAPIRA	Mikhael	Male			Bilha		407
SHAPIRA	Mina	Female			Mordekhai Leib		407
SHAPIRA	Mira	Female					407
SHAPIRA	Miriam	Female	Bunim	Reiza			407

SHAPIRA	Montzi		Shlomo	Vitzia			407
SHAPIRA	Mordekhai	Male			Mina		407
SHAPIRA	Moshe	Male			Ester		408
SHAPIRA	Rakhel	Female	Mordekhai	Mina			407
SHAPIRA	Rakhel	Female	Bunim	Reiza			407
SHAPIRA	Reiza		Mordekhai	Mina			407
SHAPIRA	Reiza	Female			Bunim		407
SHAPIRA	Rivka	Female	Shlomo	Vitzia			407
SHAPIRA	Roza	Female					407
SHAPIRA	Sara	Female			Khaim		407
SHAPIRA	Tzvi	Male	Mordekhai	Mina			407
SHAPIRA		Male			Avraham		407
SHAPIRA		Male			Antschel Ira		407
SHAPIRA		Male			Yaakov		407
SHAPIRA		Male	Yaakov				407
SHAPIRA		Male	Mikhael	Bilha			407
SHAPIRA		Male	Mikhael	Bilha			407
SHAPIRA		Male	Moshe	Ester			408
SHAPIRA	Vitzia	Female			Shlomo		407
SHAPIRA	Yaakov	Male					407
SHAPIRA	Yehuda	Male					407
SHAPIRA	Yeshiyah	Male			Ester		407

SHEFER	Anna	Female			Antschel		408
SHEFER	Antshel	Male			Anna		408
SHEFER	Moniyo	Male					408
SHEFER		Male	Antschel	Anna			408
SHEFER		Male					408
SHEFER		Male					408
SHEFER		Male			Monio		408
SHEFER	Zeev	Male	Munio				408
SHEIN	Berish	Male					407
SHEIN		Male			Berish		407
SHEKHTER	Andzia		Yitzkhak	Yeta			407
SHEKHTER	Eliezer	Male					407
SHEKHTER	Heine	Female					407
SHEKHTER	Regina	Female					407
SHEKHTER		Male			Heine		407
SHEKHTER		Male			Eliezer		407
SHEKHTER		Male	Eliezer				407
SHEKHTER	Yeta	Female			Yitzkhak Meir		407
SHEKHTER	Yitzkhak	Male	Yitzkhak	Yeta			407
SHEKHTER	Zemlen		Yitzkhak	Yeta			407
SHERER	Khaim	Male					408
SHERER	Malka	Female			Mordekhai		408

SHERER	Mordekhai	Male			Malka		408
SHERER	Roza	Female	Mordekhai				408
SHERER	Shenka	Female					408
SHERER		Male				Profession: Goose Seller	408
SHERER		Male				Profession: Goose Seller	408
SHERER		Male				Profession: Goose Seller	408
SHERER		Male		Shenka			408
SHERER		Male		Shenka			408
SHITZ	Brakha	Female					407
SHLEZINGER	Mina	Female			Sheike		407
SHLEZINGER	Rakhela	Female					407
SHLEZINGER	Sheika	Male			Mina		407
SHMERTLING	David	Male	Yaakov	Serka Miriam			407
SHMERTLING	David	Male			Gitel		407
SHMERTLING	Gitel	Female			David		407
SHMERTLING	Hersh	Male	David	Gitel			407
SHMERTLING	Motel		David	Gitel			407
SHMERTLING	Serka	Female			Yaakov		407
SHMERTLING	Tzvi	Male	Yaakov	Serka Miriam			407

SHMERTLING	Yaakov	Male			Serka Miriam		407
SHNAPER	Hirsh	Male					407
SHNAPER	Moniyo		Hirsh				407
SHNAPER		Male			Hirsh		407
SHNEIDER	Avraham	Male					408
SHNEIDER	Ester	Female			Volf		407
SHNEIDER	Ira	Male					408
SHNEIDER	Lusia			Zisia			407
SHNEIDER		Male			Ira		408
SHNEIDER		Male	Ira				408
SHNEIDER		Male					384
SHNEIDER		Male			Avraham		408
SHNEIDER	Volf	Male			Ester		407
SHNEIDER	Yetka						407
SHNEIDER	Zisia						407
SHPAK		Male					408
SHPERLING	Lea	Female			Yosef		408
SHPERLING		Male	Yosef	Lea			408
SHPERLING		Male	Yosef	Lea			408
SHPERLING	Yosef	Male			Lea		408
SHPITZEN	Mania	Female			Aizik Yitzkhak		407

SHPITZEN	Moshe	Male			Rakhel		407
SHPITZEN	Rakhel	Female			Moshe		407
SHPITZEN	Yitzkhak	Male			Mania		407
SHREIBER	Khaia	Female			Levi Yitzkhak		408
SHREIBER	Levi	Male			Khaia		408
SHREIBER	Shlomo	Male	Levi	Khaia			408
SHREIBER		Male			Yehoshua		408
SHREIBER	Yehoshua	Male					408
SHREIBER	Zalman	Male	Levi	Khaia			408
SHTARK	Barukh	Male			Pesi		407
SHTARK	Dov	Male	Barukh	Pesi			407
SHTARK	Khaia	Female	Barukh	Pesi			407
SHTARK	Lea	Female	Barukh	Pesi			407
SHTARK	Mordekhai	Male	Barukh	Pesi			407
SHTARK	Moshe	Male	Barukh	Pesi			407
SHTARK	Pesia	Female			Barukh		407
SHTARK	Rafi	Male	Barukh	Pesi			407
SHTARK	Rivka	Female	Barukh	Pesi			407
SHTARK		Male			Yaakov		407
SHTARK	Yaakov	Male					407
SHTARK	Yekhiel	Male	Barukh	Pesi			407
SHTEIN	Bela		Khona	Henia			407

SHTEIN	Fredel	Female			Hersh Feigel		406
SHTEIN	Henia	Female			Khona		407
SHTEIN	Khona	Male			Henia		407
SHTEIN	Leizer	Male	Khona	Henia			407
SHTEIN	Naftali	Male					407
SHTEINBERG	Anna	Female			Yaakov		407
SHTEINBERG	Ester	Female					407
SHTEINBERG	Ester	Female					407
SHTEINBERG	Leon	Male					407
SHTEINBERG	Sokher	Male					407
SHTEINBERG		Male			Yosef		407
SHTEINBERG		Male			Sukher		407
SHTEINBERG		Male	Sukher				407
SHTEINBERG		Male	Sukher				407
SHTEINBERG	Yaakov	Male			Anna		407
SHTEINBERG	Yosef	Male					407
SHTEINFINK	Leon	Male					407
SHTEINFINK		Male			Leon		407
SHTEINFINK		Male	Leon				407
SHTERN	Avraham	Male			Ester		407
SHTERN	Bluma	Female			Zindel		407
SHTERN	Ester	Female			Avraham		407

SHTERN	Feiga	Female			Yaakov		407
SHTERN	Mala	Female	Avraham	Ester			407
SHTERN		Male	Zindel	Bluma			407
SHTERN		Male			Volf		407
SHTERN		Male			Zelig		407
SHTERN		Male	Zelig				407
SHTERN		Male	Zelig				407
SHTERN		Male	Zelig				407
SHTERN		Male			Yitzkhak		407
SHTERN		Male	Yitzkhak				407
SHTERN	Volf	Male					407
SHTERN	Yaakov	Male			Feiga		407
SHTERN	Yitzkhak	Male					407
SHTERN	Zelig	Male					407
SHTERN	Zindel	Male			Bluma		407
SHTERTZER	Avraham	Male			Matilda		407
SHTERTZER	Matilda	Female			Avraham		407
SHTERTZER	Moniyo		Avraham	Matilda			407
SHTREIZAND	Katriel	Male			Lea		407
SHTREIZAND	Lea	Female			Katriel		407
SHTREIZAND	Pepi		Katriel	Lea			407
SHTREIZAND	Uri	Male					407

SHTZAFNER	Leib	Male					408
SHUMER	Aba	Male					406
SHUMER	Ela	Female			Isser		406
SHUMER	Isser	Male			Ela		406
SHUMER		Male			Aba		406
SHUR	Aba	Male					406
SHVADRON		Male					406
SHVADRON		Male					406
SHVADRON		Male					406
SHVADRON		Male					406
SHVADRON		Male					406
SHVAGER	Liber	Male					406
SHVAGER		Male			Liber		406
SHVAGER		Male	Liber				406
SHVAM	Fruma	Female	Moshe	Rivka			406
SHVAM	Moshe	Male			Rivka		406
SHVAM	Neshia	Female			Yoel		406
SHVAM	Rakhel	Female	Moshe	Rivka			406
SHVAM	Rivka	Female			Moshe		406
SHVAM	Yehudit	Female	Moshe	Rivka			406
SHVAM	Yoel	Male			Nashia		406
SHVARTZ	Aizik	Male			Reizia		406

SHVARTZ	Beila		Feibish	Rivka			406
SHVARTZ	David	Male					406
SHVARTZ	David	Male	Yisrael	Dvora			406
SHVARTZ	Dvora	Female			Yisrael		406
SHVARTZ	Ester	Female					406
SHVARTZ	Hersh	Male	Feibish	Rivka			406
SHVARTZ	Ira	Male			Rivka		406
SHVARTZ	Khaim	Male			Rivka		406
SHVARTZ	Malka	Female	Ira	Rivka			406
SHVARTZ	Manes	Male					406
SHVARTZ	Mina	Female					406
SHVARTZ	Moshe	Male					406
SHVARTZ	Rakhel	Female					406
SHVARTZ	Reizia	Female			Aizik		406
SHVARTZ	Rivka	Female			Ira		406
SHVARTZ	Rivka	Female			Khaim		406
SHVARTZ	Rivka	Female			Feibish		406
SHVARTZ	Sara	Female			Yisrael	From Koziany	406
SHVARTZ	Simkha		Ira	Rivka			406
SHVARTZ	Tzipora	Female					406
SHVARTZ		Male	Khaim	Rivka			406
SHVARTZ		Male			Manes		406

SHVARTZ		Male	Manes				406
SHVARTZ		Male			Moshe		406
SHVARTZ		Male	Aizik	Reizia			406
SHVARTZ		Male	Aizik	Reizia			406
SHVARTZ		Male	Aizik	Reizia			406
SHVARTZ	Yekhiel	Male	Yisrael	Dvora			406
SHVARTZ	Yisrael	Male			Dvora		406
SHVARTZ	Yisrael	Male			Sara	From Koziany	406
SHVARTZ	Yona	Female					406
STAHL	Arie	Male					406
STAHL	Etil		Zelig	Tova			406
STAHL	Malka	Female					406
STAHL	Moshe	Male	Zelig	Tova			406
STAHL	Netka		Zelig	Tova			406
STAHL	Sara	Female					406
STAHL	Sheindl	Female					406
STAHL	Tova	Female			Zelig		406
STAHL	Yeta		Zelig	Tova			406
STAHL	Zelig	Male			Tova		406
STRETINER						From Mieczyzsczow. In Berezhany during the war	399
TADINIER		Male			Vilhelm		393

TADANIER	Vilhelm	Male					393
TAKSEL	Bila						394
TALER	Avraham	Male			Khana		394
TALER	Ber	Male	Lazar				394
TALER	Betzalel	Male	Avraham	Khana			394
TALER	David	Male					393
TALER	David	Male	Avraham	Khana			394
TALER	Heniu						394
TALER	Khana	Female			Avraham		394
TALER	Shprintza		Avraham	Khana			394
TALER		Male			Yitzkhak		393
TALER		Male					394
TALER		Male					394
TALER	Yeshayahu	Male					393
TALER	Yitzkhak	Male					393
TALER	Yitzkhak	Male	Avraham	Khana			394
TANENBAUM	Dina	Female					394
TANENBAUM	Frida	Female					394
TANENBAUM		Male			Frida		394
TANENBAUM	Yaakov	Male		Dina			394
TAUBER	Dov	Male	Moshe	Malka			393
TAUBER	Hirsh	Male			Khaia		393

TAUBER	Khaia	Female			Hirsh		393
TAUBER	Malka	Female			Moshe		393
TAUBER	Moshe	Male			Malka		393
TAUBER	Nakhum	Male	Moshe	Malka			393
TAUBER	Peril		Hirsh	Khaia			393
TAUBER	Rene	Female			Yitzkhak		393
TAUBER		Male	Yitzkhak	Rene			393
TAUBER		Male	Yitzkhak	Rene			393
TAUBER	Yitzkhak	Male			Rene		393
TEIDL	Henk	Male			Selka		393
TEIDL	Selka	Female			Hanek		393
TEIDL		Male					393
TEIDL		Male					393
TEITELBAUM	David	Male			Zahava		393
TEITELBAUM	Ema	Female		Yetka			393
TEITELBAUM	Etel	Female			Yaakov		393
TEITELBAUM	Shlomo	Male	David	Zahava			393
TEITELBAUM	Yaakov	Male			Etel		393
TEITELBAUM	Yetka	Female					393
TEITELBAUM	Zahava	Female			David		393
TEITELBAUM	Zigmund	Male	Yaakov	Etel			393
TEITELBAUM	Zufia		Yaakov	Etel			393

TEMPEL	Avromtze					394
TEMPEL	Brakha	Female			Yehoshua	394
TEMPEL	Dvora	Female			Hirsh	394
TEMPEL	Hirsh	Male			Dvora	394
TEMPEL	Ira		Hirsh	Dvora		394
TEMPEL	Khaia	Female	Yehoshua	Brakha		394
TEMPEL	Shulem	Male	Hirsh	Dvora		394
TEMPEL		Male			Profession: Tinsmith	394
TEMPEL	Yehoshua	Male			Brakha	394
TIHR	Khaim	Male				393
TIHR		Male			Khaim	393
TINTER	Malka	Female	Uziasch			393
TINTER	Nakhman	Male	Uziasch			393
TINTER	Osziasz	Male				393
TINTER		Male			Oziasch	393
TIR	Feiga	Female	Zalman	Frida		393
TIR	Frida	Female			Zalman	393
TIR	Moshe	Male	Zalman	Frida		393
TIR	Rivka	Female	Zalman	Frida		393
TIR	Shaul	Male	Zalman	Frida		393
TIR	Yaakov	Male	Zalman	Frida		393
TIR	Zalman	Male			Frida	393

TIRKFELD	Selka	Female			Yosef		393
TIRKFELD		Male	Yosef	Selka			393
TIRKFELD	Yosef	Male			Selka		393
TIRKISHER	Malka	Female			Shlomo		393
TIRKISHER	Shlomo	Male			Malka		393
TIRKISHER		Male	Shlomo	Malka			393
TIRKISHER		Male	Shlomo	Malka			393
TIRKISHER		Male	Shlomo	Malka			393
TOBIAS	Binem						393
TOBIAS	David	Male					393
TOBIAS	Dolek	Male	Zelig	Ester			393
TOBIAS	Ester	Female			Zelig		393
TOBIAS	Frimtze						393
TOBIAS	Mikhael	Male					393
TOBIAS	Rozia					Profession: Teacher	393
TOBIAS	Salo		Yitzkhak				393
TOBIAS		Male			David		393
TOBIAS		Male			Yitzkhak		393
TOBIAS		Male					393
TOBIAS		Male			Mikhael		393
TOBIAS		Male	Mikhael				393
TOBIAS		Male	Mikhael				393

TOBIAS		Male	Mikhael				393
TOBIAS		Male	Mikhael				393
TOBIAS		Male	Mikhael				393
TOBIAS	Yitzkhak	Male					393
TOBIAS	Zelig	Male			Ester		393
TOBIAS VEST		Male					393
TOBIAS VEST	Yakhit	Female					393
TOIB	Barukh	Male			Khana		393
TOIB	Beila		Kiva	Sara			393
TOIB	Khana	Female			Barukh		393
TOIB	Kive	Male			Sara		393
TOIB	Sara	Female			Kiva		393
TOIB	Yosi	Male	Barukh	Khana			393
TONIS	Asher	Male					393
TONIS	Avraham	Male			Lea		393
TONIS	Bela		Mendel	Tauba			393
TONIS	Feibish	Male	Avraham	Lea			393
TONIS	Hela		Avraham	Lea			393
TONIS	Hersh	Male					393
TONIS	Itzik	Male					393
TONIS	Lea	Female			Avraham		393
TONIS	Lea	Female	Asher				393

TONIS	Mendel	Male			Tauba		393
TONIS	Moniyo	Male					393
TONIS	Rakhel	Female	Avraham	Lea			393
TONIS	Rakhel	Female					393
TONIS	Suzi	Female	Itzik				393
TONIS	Tauba	Female			Mendel		393
TONIS	Zuzia						393
TRAUNER	Shimon	Male			Yula		394
TRAUNER	Yula	Female			Shimon		394
TUKH	Batia	Female	Zalman	Sara			393
TUKH	Etel		Zalman	Sara			393
TUKH	Fania	Female	Motke	Henia			393
TUKH	Heniá	Female			Motke		393
TUKH	Leib	Male	Zalman	Sara			393
TUKH	Motke	Male			Henia		393
TUKH	Sara	Female	Motke	Henia			393
TUKH	Sara	Female			Zalman		393
TUKH	Velvel	Male	Motke	Henia			393
TUKH	Zalman	Male			Sara		393
TURKTAUM		Male					393
TURKTAUM		Male					393
TZEIG	Ester	Female	Yaakov	Henia			402

TZEIG	Gershom	Male	Yisrael	Yenta			402
TZEIG	Gershon	Male					403
TZEIG	Henia	Female			Yaakov Volf		402
TZEIG	Hersh	Male	Shlomo	Khana			403
TZEIG	Khana	Female			Shlomo		403
TZEIG	Leib	Male					402
TZEIG	Mendel	Male					402
TZEIG	Mibel		Shlomo	Khana			403
TZEIG	Mordekhai	Male	Yaakov	Henia			402
TZEIG	Mordekhai	Male	Shlomo	Khana			403
TZEIG	Nakhum	Male					403
TZEIG	Sabina	Female	Tzvi	Sara			403
TZEIG	Sara	Female			Yoel		402
TZEIG	Sara	Female			Tzvi Hirsh		403
TZEIG	Sefka		Yisrael	Yenta			402
TZEIG	Shlomo	Male			Khana		403
TZEIG	Tzvi	Male			Sara		403
TZEIG		Male			Mendel		402
TZEIG		Male	Tzvi	Sara			403
TZEIG		Male			Nakhum		403
TZEIG		Male			Gershon		403
TZEIG	Yaakov	Male			Henia		402

TZEIG	Yenta	Female			Yisrael		402
TZEIG	Yisrael	Male			Yenta		402
TZEIG	Yoel	Male			Sara		402
TZIMER		Male		Zosia			403
TZIMER		Male		Zosia			403
TZIMER	Zosia	Female					403
TZITRON	Bashke	Female			Mikhael		402
TZITRON	Hinda	Female					402
TZITRON	Mikhael	Male			Bashke		402
TZITRON		Male	Mikhael	Bashke			402
TZIZER		Male			Zishia		402
TZIZER	Zishia	Male					402
TZUKERKANDEL	Etia	Female					402
TZUKERKANDEL	Roza	Female			Yitzkhak		402
TZUKERKANDEL	Yitzkhak	Male			Roza		402
TZVATLER	Gusta	Female					402
TZVATLER	u	Male			Gusta		402
UNGER	Aharon	Male			Dina		382
UNGER	Dina	Female			Aharon		382
UNGER	Golda	Female			Shmuel		382
UNGER	Khaim	Male					382
UNGER	Khaim	Male	Shmuel	Golda			382

UNGER	Shimie	Male	Shmuel	Golda		382
UNGER	Shmuel	Male			Golda	382
VAGNER	Gusta	Female				390
VANDERER	Ester	Female				391
VANDERER	Frimtze	Female			Moshe	391
VANDERER	Moshe	Male			Frimtza	391
VARSCHOVER	Feiga	Female				391
VARSCHOVER	Perla			Feiga		391
VASER	Khana	Female	Shlomo	Memtza		390
VASER	Memza	Female			Shlomo	390
VASER	Moshe	Male				390
VASER	Shlomo	Male			Memtze	390
VASER		Male			Moshe	390
VASER	Yaakov	Male	Shlomo	Memtza		390
VASHERTZBERG	Bronka					406
VASHERTZBERG	Dzhunio					406
VASHERTZBERG		Male				406
VASHERTZBERG		Male				406
VAVER	Sefi	Female				390
VAVER		Male			Safi	390
VAVER		Male	Sefi			390
VAVER		Male	Sefi			390

VEIDENFELD	Kreintzia	Female			Yaakov		390
VEIDENFELD	Leitzia		Yaakov	Kreintzia			390
VEIDENFELD	Lola		Yaakov	Kreintzia			390
VEIDENFELD	Reizl		Yaakov	Kreintzia			390
VEIDENFELD	Tzila	Female	Yaakov	Kreintzia			390
VEIDENFELD	Yaakov	Male			Kreintzia		390
VEINGARTEN		Male					390
VEINGARTEN		Male					390
VEINGARTEN		Male					390
VEINLAUB	Genya	Female					390
VEINLAUB	Yisrael	Male		Genya			390
VEINLOGER	Berish	Male					390
VEINLOGER	Moshe	Male					390
VEINLOGER	Reizl						390
VEINLOGER		Male			Berish		390
VEINSHTEIN	Henia	Female			Hirsh		390
VEINSHTEIN	Henia	Female	Yehoshua	Khaia			390
VEINSHTEIN	Hirsh	Male			Henia		390
VEINSHTEIN	Khaia	Female			Yehoshua		390
VEINSHTEIN	Khanla						390
VEINSHTEIN	Sara	Female	Yehoshua	Khaia			390
VEINSHTEIN	Shlomo	Male					390

VEINSHTEIN	Sonia	Female	Hirsh	Henia			390
VEINSHTEIN	Vitzia		Yehoshua	Khaia			390
VEINSHTEIN	Yaakov	Male	Yehoshua	Khaia			390
VEINSHTEIN	Yehoshua	Male			Khaia		390
VEINSHTEIN	Yoel	Male					390
VEINTRAUB	Herman	Male					391
VEINTRAUB	Liba	Female			Yosef		390
VEINTRAUB	Rozia		Yosef	Liba			390
VEINTRAUB	Yosef	Male			Liba		390
VEISBERG	Avraham	Male			Feiga Khava		390
VEISBERG	Babtzi	Female			Yitzkhak		390
VEISBERG	Feiga	Female			Avraham Yitzkhak		390
VEISBERG	Menakhem	Male	Avraham	Feiga Khava			390
VEISBERG		Male	Yitzkhak	Bebtzi			390
VEISBERG	Yitzkhak	Male			Babchi		390
VEITZ	Bernard	Male			Khaia		390
VEITZ	Khaia	Female			Bernard		390
VEITZ	Lurke		Bernard	Khaia			390
VEITZ	Moniyo		Bernard	Khaia			390
VEITZ	Yosef	Male	Bernard	Khaia			390

VEITZEN		Male				Profession: Metalworker	390
VELGER	Breina	Female			Nakhman		391
VELGER	Fenka	Female			Yosef		391
VELGER	Khava	Female			Yehoshua		391
VELGER	Meir	Male			Slova		391
VELGER	Naisko						391
VELGER	Nakhman	Male			Breina		391
VELGER	Nosia						391
VELGER	Slova	Female	Ioakhim		Meir		391
VELGER		Male			Yitzkhak		391
VELGER		Male	Yosef	Penka			391
VELGER	Yehoshua	Male			Khava		391
VELGER	Yosef	Male			Fanke		391
VIDERKER	Ester	Female	Moshe				390
VIDERKER	Feiga	Female	Hersh	Lea			390
VIDERKER	Hersh	Male			Lea		390
VIDERKER	Lea	Female			Hersh		390
VIDERKER	Moshe	Male					390
VIDERKER	Peril	Female	Hersh	Lea			390
VIDERKER		Male			Moshe		390
VIDHOF	Bluma	Female			Feivush		390
VIDHOF	Feivish	Male			Bluma		390

VIDHOF	Mendel	Male	Feivish	Bluma			390
VIDHOF		Male	Feivish	Bluma			390
VIDHOF	Yoel	Male					390
VILNER	Ada		Edmund				390
VILNER	Avraham	Male			Charna		390
VILNER	Charna	Female			Avraham Yehuda		390
VILNER	Edmund	Male					390
VILNER	Sara	Female					390
VILNER		Male			Edmund		390
VILNER	Yaakov	Male					390
VINLES	Neta	Male					390
VINLES		Male	Yosef				390
VINLES		Male	Neta				390
VINLES	Yosef	Male					390
VINTER	Babtzi		Natanel	Rivka			390
VINTER	Gedal	Male			Sheva Lea		390
VINTER	Khana	Female	Gadel	Sheva Lea			390
VINTER	Mikhael	Male			Pesel		390
VINTER	Moshe	Male			Roza		391
VINTER	Moshe	Male				Profession: Rabbinic Judge	391
VINTER	Natan	Male	Natanel	Rivka			390

VINTER	Natanel	Male			Roza		390
VINTER	Olga	Female					391
VINTER	Pesel	Female			Mikhael		390
VINTER	Rivka	Female			Natanel		390
VINTER	Roza	Female			Natanel		390
VINTER	Roza	Female			Moshe		391
VINTER	Sheva	Female			Gadel Getzle		390
VINTER	Shlomo	Male	Mordekhai				390
VINTER		Male				Profession: Engineer	391
VINTER		Male					391
VINTER		Male	Moshe				391
VINTER	Zufia						391
VISHBIANSKI	Genya	Female			Yezi		391
VISHBIANSKI		Male	Yezi	Genya			391
VISHBIANSKI	Yezi	Male			Genya		391
VITLIN	Faivel	Male			Klara		390
VITLIN	Klara	Female			Faivel		390
VITLIN	Miriam	Female	Faivel	Klara			390
VITLIN	Tzvi	Male	Faivel	Klara			390
VITMAN	Moshe	Male					391
VITMAN		Male			Moshe		391

VITMAN		Male	Moshe				391
VITMAN	Yoel	Male	Moshe				391
VITRIOL	Beltzia	Female					390
VITRIOL	Meir	Male			Mina		390
VITRIOL	Mina	Female			Meir		390
VITRIOL		Male			Velvel		390
VITRIOL	Velvel	Male					390
VIZENTAL	Bluma	Female					390
VIZENTAL		Male		Bluma			390
VOG		Male				Profession: Tailor	390
VOG		Male					390
VOG		Male					390
VOG		Male					390
VOGSHEL	Ester	Female			Hersh		390
VOGSHEL	Hersh	Male			Ester		390
VOHL	Avraham	Male			Etka		390
VOHL	Etka	Female			Avraham		390
VOHL	Mundek		Avraham	Etka			390
VOLF	Dolek						391
VOLF	Dora	Female			Leon		391
VOLF	Khana	Female			Yehoshua		391
VOLF	Leib	Male	Yehoshua	Khana			391

VOLF	Leon	Male			Dora		391
VOLF		Male	Leon	Dora			391
VOLF	Yehoshua	Male			Khana		391
VOLFER	Getzel	Male			Pepe		391
VOLFER	Pepa	Female			Getzel		391
VONDMEIR	Mark	Male					391
VONDMEIR		Male				Profession: Dentist	391
VONDMEIR		Male					391
VONDMEIR		Male			Mark		391
VORTZEL	Adolf	Male		Ruzia			391
VORTZEL	Gusta			Ruzia			391
VORTZEL	Rozia	Female					391
VORTZEL		Male			Rozia		391
YAKUBOVITZ							394
ZAKS	Aba						392
ZAKS	Eliezer	Male			Sushia		392
ZAKS	Gitel						392
ZAKS	Soshia	Female			Eliezer		392
ZAKS		Male	Eliezer	Sushia			392
ZALMAN	Golda	Female	Leizer	Sheindl			392
ZALMAN	Leizer	Male			Sheindl		392
ZALMAN	Sheindl	Female			Leizer		392

ZARVANITZER	Shalom	Male					392
ZEIF	Gizia	Female			Litman		392
ZEIF	Henia		Litman	Gizia			392
ZEIF	Litman	Male			Gizia		392
ZEIF	Manio		Litman	Gizia			392
ZEIFERT	David	Male			Lurke		392
ZEIFERT	Leitzia						392
ZEIFERT	Lurke	Female			David		392
ZEIFERT	Rosia	Female	Yisrael				392
ZEIFERT	Sala	Female			Yosef		392
ZEIFERT	Selka			Rusia			392
ZEIFERT	Yosef	Male			Sala		392
ZILBER	Barukh	Male			Tinka		392
ZILBER	Basia		Nakhman	Henia Rakhel			392
ZILBER	Bronka	Female					392
ZILBER	Etel	Female			Yaakov		392
ZILBER	Hela		Yaakov	Etel			392
ZILBER	Henia	Female			Nakhman		392
ZILBER	Khana	Female	Nakhman	Henia Rakhel			392
ZILBER	Klara	Female			Reuven		392
ZILBER	Leib	Male					392

ZILBER	Mania		Mordekhai	Sheindl			392
ZILBER	Miriam	Female	Yaakov	Etel			392
ZILBER	Monish	Male					392
ZILBER	Mordekhai	Male			Sheindl		392
ZILBER	Nakhman	Male			Henia Rakhel		392
ZILBER	Rakhel	Female					392
ZILBER	Regina	Female	Yaakov	Etel			392
ZILBER	Reuven	Male			Klara		392
ZILBER	Sheindl	Female			Mordekhai		392
ZILBER	Tauba		Munish				392
ZILBER	Tinka	Female			Barukh		392
ZILBER		Male			Leib		392
ZILBER		Male	Reuven	Klara			392
ZILBER	Yaakov	Male			Etel		392
ZILBER	Yisrael	Male	Yaakov	Etel			392
ZILBERFELD	Adela	Female			Tzvi		392
ZILBERFELD	Avraham	Male	Tzvi	Adela			392
ZILBERFELD	Malka	Female	Tzvi	Adela			392
ZILBERFELD	Nosia		Tzvi	Adela			392
ZILBERFELD	Pnina	Female	Tzvi	Adela			392
ZILBERFELD	Shantzia		Tzvi	Adela			392
ZILBERFELD	Tzvi	Male			Adela		392

ZILBERFELD	Unia		Tzvi	Adela		392
ZINGER	Ester	Female	Shmuel	Mania		392
ZINGER	Golda	Female	Shmuel	Mania		392
ZINGER	Hersh	Male			Mina	392
ZINGER	Khaim	Male			Mania	392
ZINGER	Mania	Female			Khaim	392
ZINGER	Mania	Female			Shmuel	392
ZINGER	Mina	Female			Hersh	392
ZINGER	Natan	Male	Hersh	Mina		392
ZINGER	Pepi		Hersh	Mina		392
ZINGER	Shmuel	Male			Mania	392
ZINGER	Yeshayahu	Male	Shmuel	Mania		392
ZLOTAKS	Asher	Male	Mordekhai	Klara		392
ZLOTAKS	Etka		Mordekhai	Klara		392
ZLOTAKS	Klara	Female			Mordekhai	392
ZLOTAKS	Mordekhai	Male			Klara	392
ZMOIRE	Emil	Male	Mark	Sofia		392
ZMOIRE	Henrik	Male	Mark	Sofia		392
ZMOIRE	Mark	Male			Sofia	392
ZMOIRE	Matilda	Female	Mark	Sofia		392
ZMOIRE	Sofia	Female			Mark	392
ZUSMAN	Hersh	Male				391

ZUSMAN	Lipman	Male				392
ZUSMAN	Manes	Male				391
ZUSMAN	Moshe	Male			Profession: Furrier	392
ZUSMAN	Shalom	Male				392
ZUSMAN		Male		Manes		391
ZUSMAN		Male	Manes			391
ZUSMAN		Male	Manes			391
ZUSMAN		Male	Manes			391
ZUSMAN		Male		Hersh		391
ZUSMAN		Male	Hersh			391
ZUSMAN		Male	Hersh			391
ZUSMAN		Male		Lipman		392
ZUSMAN		Male		Shalom Meir		392

[Pages 409]

The Names of Brzezany Natives Who Died in Israel

Translated by Moshe Kutten

Edited by Jane S. Gabin

Aharonson, Daniel	12.12.1912 5.17.1977	Native of Israel, a descended of fighters of the "Nili" underground in Zikhron Ya'akov. Married Khanka Dorfaman from Brzezany. A farmer in Hadera. Was known as a good person and a loyal friend to his friends and family. Died in Hadera.
Altshuler, Bunim. son of Barukh	7.10.1911 12.15.1977, 5 Tevet 5,738	Made Aliyah as a student in 1933. Due to the circumstances of the time, he did not continue his studies. He settled in Haifa, where he lived for the rest of his life and died there.
Eigen, Khaim	1907 1967	Made Aliyah as a pioneer in 1928. Settled in Rishon LeTzion, where he worked as a carpenter. He died there.
Ailyu, Israel-Ya'akov, son of Yeshayahu	1865, 5625 1945, 9 Tammuz 5,706 (5705?)	Made Aliyah in 1940. Lived in Haifa, where he died.
Ilan (Eilin), Moshe, son of Israel-Ya'akov	1895, 8 Shvat 5,655 1965,11 Sivan 5725	Made Aliyah from Vienna with his family in 1935. He was active in the Zionist Movement and assisted Brzezany's pioneers on their way to Israel. Served as a gabbai in the Great Synagogue in Haifa on Hertzel Street for 25 years. Was buried in Haifa.
Engel, Y.	1906 1979	Escaped to Russia during WW II. Made Aliyah after the War. Owned a dental office in Tel Aviv. Died in Tel Aviv.
Engel, Leah, daughter of Barukh Pechenik	1910 1972	Made Aliyah in 1935 and settled in Nahalal, where she died.
Ast, David (Dudileh)	1880 1938	A Torah scholar, made Aliyah in the 1920s thanks to his son, who was a member of the "Hebrew Battalion." Continued his Torah studies in Eretz Israel. Died in Tel Aviv.

Ekhoiz, Uri	3/24/1906 1968, 20 Kislev 5729	Made Aliyah as a pioneer in 1931. After leaving the *Kibbutz*, he settled in Tel Aviv, where he worked as a carpenter. He was successful in his work, helping anybody who turned to him.
Bomze (Vitlin), Berta	8/14/1913 7/23/1941	Made Aliyah with her husband Zeev in 1935. Having a friendly character, she was loved by all. Her home was always open for Brzezany people. She was a dedicated mother to her children, Ora and Amos. She died young. Was buried at *Kibbutz* Merkhavia.

[Pages 410]

Bergman, Dr. Yehuda	8.30.1874, Elul 5,633) 5634?) 11/22/1954, 26 Kheshvan 5,715	The Rabbi of Berlin. Energetic Zionist. The student of the MARSHA"M. Wrote many books and articles. Made Aliyah in 1934. Was buried in Jerusalem.
Bar-David (Zilber), Tova	12/14/1900 11.18.1974, 4 Kislev 5,735	Made Aliyah with her husband Moshe in 1935. Was active in the drama club in Brzezany. She nurtured the art collection of her family for years. Buried in *Kibbutz* Bar-Am, where the Institute for Jewish Studies, named after Bar-David, dedicated to the Brzezany community, is located.
Gutenshtein, Uri, son of Zelig	1901 1973	Made Aliyah as a pioneer in 1922. Settled in Jerusalem and worked at the Electrical Utility Company. Died in Jerusalem.
Goldman, Leib, son of Barukh	12/16/1890 1943, 5 Iyar 5,703	A wealthy merchant. Made Aliyah in 1939. Settled in Haifa. Buried in Givatayim.
Goldman, Ezra, son of Ya'akov	1912 7/22/1974	Was an activist in "HaShomer HaTzair" in Brzezany. Reached Israel through the USSR, where he served in Anders Army. After the War of Independence, he moved with his wife Tzipora to Moshav Be'er Tuvia, where he established a farm and raised three sons: Ilan, Tzvi, and Asher. Was active in the Moshav's affairs and was respected among the members as an honest man. Killed in a traffic accident and was buried in Be'er Tuvia.
Goldman, Dr. Shmuel, son of Avraham	3/16/1892 1/10/1977, 2 Tevet 5,737	Dermatologist. Was active in the Zionist institutions in Brzezany. Got married and moved to Ternov. He spent the Holocaust hell in Auschwitz, where he lost his entire family. Remarried and made Aliyah in 1950. Settled in Haifa and worked in the Histadrut's Kupat Kholim. Died and was buried in Haifa.
Glazer, Moshe, son of Ya'akov Bauer	5.26.1897, 24 Iyar 5,657 4.17.1973,	Made Aliyah as a pioneer, with the first group from Brzezany. He was forced to return to Poland due to an illness, where he survived the Holocaust. Made second Aliyah as an "illegal" immigrant on the ship "Yetziat Europa" [*Exodus*]. Settled in Hadera, where he worked as a teacher. He died in Hadera.

	13 Adar II 5,733	
Dorfman (Bleiberg), David	1887, Elul 5,647 12/12/1976, 12 Kislev 5,737	Made Aliyah with his family in 1935 as a wealthy merchant. Settled in Haifa and later moved to Zikhron Ya'akov. Was a philanthropist who donated to various charity organizations. In his last few years, he moved to Jerusalem, where he died.
Doron (Dorfman), Eliezer, son of David	8/21/1915 4/10/1976, 10 Nissan 5,736	Made Aliyah as a pioneer in 1935 as a member of *HaKibbutz* HaArtzi Gimel. Enlisted in the Jewish Brigade. Settled in Haifa, where he established a family. A father to three daughters: Ahuva, Tamar, and Einat. Died and was buried in Haifa.

[Pages 411]

Dukler, Moshe	1910 1966	Native of Jaslo. Married Rivka Halperin from Brzezany. Was an activist in the HaMizrakhi Movement. Worked in Tel Aviv at the TV dept. of the Communication Ministry. He died in Tel Aviv.
Holander (Segal), Leah	1907 1971, 5,732	Made Aliyah with her husband in 1935. Lived in Tel-Aviv, where she died.
Halbertal, Dr. Moshe	4/2/1895 10/31/1968, 9 Kheshvan 5729	Dr. of economics. Served as an officer in the Austrian Army. Worked in Vienna as an accountant until 1938. In 1938-39, he was imprisoned in the Dachau camp. Made Aliyah on the ship Patria.Settled in Hadera, where he worked at the "Tzarchan" Company and the Jewish Agency. Died in Hadera.
Helman, Shimon, son of David	1888 12/11/1947, 28 Kislev 5,708	In 1934, he liquidated his successful business in Brzezany and made Aliyah with his entire family. Settled in Haifa, where he was blessed with grandchildren. Buried on the Mount of Olives.
Helman, Rakhel, daughter of Tzvio Shraga Shtein	1896 9.20.1962, 21 Elul 5,722	Made Aliyah with her husband Shimon. Died and was buried in Haifa.
Vitalis-Yonati,Shmuel	1895 1977, 5,737	Native of Lviv. Made Aliyah in 1934 and married Rozia Shtark from Brzezany. Settled in Haifa and was a merchant. Died in Haifa.
Vilner, Dr. Khaim, son of Yehuda-Leib	1894 1950	A sharp and successful lawyer in Brzezany. Enthusiastic Zionist and dedicated to public needs and Aliyah. Chairman of "Ezra" and an energetic activist. Expelled to the USSR during the war and made Aliyah after the war. Died in Tel Aviv. Left part of his inheritance to the Hebrew University.

Vilner, Yitzkhak, son of Shmuel	2/11/1902 1/20/1974, 6 Tevet 5734	Native of Nadvirna. Married Sara Gros. One of the first workers of the Electrical Utility Company. Among the builders of the power station in Naharayim. With the evacuation of Naharayim in 1948, he moved to Haifa, where he continued to work in his position. Buried in Haifa.
Vilner, Sara	1/6/1907 12/25/1973, 1 Tevet 5,733	Student at the Teachers Seminary in Brzezany and a teacher in the Hebrew school there. Made Aliyah as a pioneer in 1934. Active in the "Working Mothers" and other charity organizations. Died in Haifa.
Veinlager, Yehuda-Hirsh	1908 1946	Made Aliyah as a pioneer. Settled in Tel Aviv, where he worked as a carpenter. Died in Tel Aviv.
Veisman, Moshe, son of Ben-Tzvi Arye	1901 12/31/1972 27 Tevet 5,732	Born in Radekhiv (Radziekhov). Married Nesia Shekhter from Brzezany. Made Aliyah after the Holocaust in 1948. Settled in Haifa, where he died.

[Pages 412]

Haber, Shimon	1874 1947	Made Aliyah in 1937. He worked as an agriculturalist in Rekhovot, where he died.
Vakhtel, Shlomo	1913 9/6/1976	Rzeszów's (Raysha) native. Married Selka Bezen from Brzezany. Settled in KiryatKhaim. Died in Haifa.
Zinger, Rivka, daughter of Moshe-Nathan Rok	1878 1954, I4 Iyar 5,714	Made Aliyah in 1936 as a mother who was a citizen of the British Mandate. Settled in Haifa, where she died.
Zakai (Klarer), Avner (Artek)	1911 October 1973	An activist in the Zionist Youth Movement. Made Aliyah as a pioneer in 1934. Among the founders of the educational institution "Neurim." Was a member of *Kibbutz* Tel Yitzkhak, where he died.
Za'it, Moshe	1898 1969	Born in Lithuania, Married Rakhel Hibler from Brzezany. Worked as a pioneer near Rekhovot. Moved to Haifa, where he worked in the municipality. Died in Haifa.
KhR"P Avraham, son of Aharon	7/10/1895 11/28/1967, 25 Kheshvan 5,728	Born in Kozliv. A laborer and person of Torah. Gifted Ba'al Tfila with pleasant manners. Made Aliyah in 1934 with his family & settled in Haifa. Was an activist in "HaPoel HaMizrakhi." Worked in "Shemen." Died in Haifa.

KhR'P Elka, daughter of Moshe Shpitzen	1895 5/3/1964, 21 Iyar 5,724	Learned. Worked in various jobs to enable children to attain proper education. Among the initiators of women's charities in Haifa. Died in Haifa.
Tukh, Pinkhas, son of Shlomo	2/21/1905 1/12/1974, 17 Kislev 5,729	An activist in the "Yad Kharutzim" organization in Brzezany. Made Aliyah w/family in 1936. Among the founders of the Brzezany Natives organization. Worked in "Solel Boneh." Settled in Haifa, where he died and was buried.
Taler, Mordekhai, son of Ya'akov Asher	1902 - ?	Made Aliyah as a pioneer in 1928. Worked in the National Library in Jerusalem, where he died.
Taksel, Mordekhai	1907 1958	Immigrated to Germany from Brzezany and made Aliyah from there in 1938. Worked in "Hamashir Latzarkhan." Settled in Khavatzelet, where he died.
Katz, Arye, son of Zelig	1908 1960	A modest laborer. Married Rakhel Redlik from Brzezany. Died in Tel Aviv.
Katz, Yehoshua (Ozio)	10/4/1908 4/13/1976	Born in Shchepaniv near Brzezany. Made Aliyah as a pioneer, and settled with his group in "Ein HaMifratz." Chaired many committees in his *kibbutz*. Acquired expertise in the cultivation of field crops. Was respected in the *kibbutz*. Established future generations in his field. Died in Ein HaMifratz.

[Pages 413]

Liberman, Hermina, daughter of Sh. Glazer	8/19/1924, 18 Av 5,684 8/30/1973×[a] 1 Av 5,733	Was raised in her Zionist father Sh. Glazer. Survived the Holocaust in Brzezany. Made Aliyah through Poland and Germany with the "HaNoar HaOved" on the ship *Exodus*. Settled in Hadera, where she worked as a social worker and where she died.
Libster, Izik	1885 1952	Was a successful merchant in Brzezany. Made Aliyah in 1933. Settled in Tel Aviv, where he died.
Libster, [?] Izik's wife	1892 1955	Made Aliyah with her husband. Lived and died in Tel Aviv.
Lakher, Kaim, son of Shalom	1904 1975, 1 Adar 5,735	Among the first pioneers who made Aliyah from Brzezany. An excellent builder. Constructed the YMCA building in Jerusalem and the Baha'i temple's dome in Haifa. Lived in Haifa from the 1940s, where he died.
Lakher, Sara	1906-1975	Khaim Lakher's wife. Died & was buried in Haifa.

Mitelman, Mordekhai, son of Ya'akov	5/5/1912 7/7/1976	Activist in Brezany's Beitar branch. Served in the Red Army in World War II. After the war was an activist of the Escape Movement in Poland. Made Aliyah in 1950, and settled in Be'er Sheva, where he died.
Mirberg, Hodel nee Teitelbaum	1885 1964	Made Aliyah in 1949, after the Holocaust when she lost her husband Tzvi (Hersh). Settled in Petah Tikva, where she died.
Mirberg, Tzvi, son of Yehuda	1909 1937	Made Aliyah as a pioneer in 1932. Settled in Hadera, where he died in a work accident.
Maler, Nathan	1905-?	Made Aliyah through the USSR. Settled in Tel Aviv, where he died.
Mun[?], Pepah, nee Feigenbaum	12/9/1909 8/18/1978	A pharmacist. Survived the Holocaust in a village in Galitsia. Made Aliyah in 1957. Settled in Haifa and managed a pharmacy there. Died in that city.
Mendelberg, Shlomo	1906 7/5/1978, 30 Sivan 5,736	Recruited to the Red Army in 1941. Stayed in Russia during the war, and from there through Poland – made Aliyah. He was an activist in the Labor Movement. Settled in Tel Aviv, where he died.
Mantzakh? Dr.	1891 1969, 5729	A physician born in Buchach and studied in Brzezany. Linked to our [?]with every vein of his heart. Enthusiastic Zionist who refused to speak a foreign language. Made Aliyah in the 1930s. Lived in Hadera and died in Haifa.

[Pages 414]

Mas, Khana, daughter of Barukh Yeger	1910 1972	Made Aliyah as a pioneer of HaShomer HaTzair. Settled in Haifa, where she died.
Nagelberg, Iziu, son of Izik	1914 1949	Fought in the ranks of the Red Army in WW II. Made Aliyah in 1948. Settled as an agriculturalist. Died a short while after that.
Noishiler, Shaul, son of Shimshon	1908 4/8/1978, 1 Nissan 5,738	A pharmacist. Made Aliyah in 1934. Activist in the Haganah. Was the head of a military hospital during the War of Independence. Worked in various jobs until he was accepted as the head pharmacist in the Haifa district. Died in Haifa and was buried in the Haganah plot there.
Neiman, Tzipora,	1/20/1914 3/14/1954	Made Aliyah as a pioneer. Married Y, Neiman. Settled in Tel Aviv. Died and was buried in Holon.

nee Bernshtein		
Segal, Asher (Antsel), son of Leibush	6/3/1898 8/18/1969, 4 Elul 5729	Enthusiàstic Zionist and an activist in Brzezany's Beitar & Drama Club. Made Aliyah in 1935. Settled in Tel Aviv and was an Etzel activist. Worked at the Hadassah Hospital in Tel Aviv. A good-hearted & pleasant person with a strong sense of humor. Helped anybody who turned to him for help, and was remembered as generous among his friends. Died in Tel Aviv. the words "friend of man – Asher Segal."
Sapir, Nakhum, son of Shmuel	6/8/1915 8/9/1971	Born in Ternopil, resided in Brzezany. Fought in the ranks of the Red Army in WW II and received a medal for his courage. Made Aliyah in 1948 and did not disclose his disability to be able to participate in the War of Independence. Later, he worked in the post office. Died in Haifa,
Fogel, Moshe, son of Benjamin	3/17/1902 1/21/1975, 10 Shvat 5,735	A Zionist activist involved in public affairs and drama club in Brzezany. Immigrated to Argentina in 1931. Educated his sons to make Aliyah. He fulfilled his aspiration and made Aliyah with his family. Settled in Rishon LeTzion, where he died.
Fogelman, Shimshon, son of Shimshon	5/16/1886 1973, 25 Tevet	Energetic Zionist. Gabbi in R' Yudel Synagogue. Made Aliyah after the Holocaust from Germany, where he worked to help the survivors. Settled in Tel Aviv and later in Natanya, where he was an activist in the synagogue affairs and studied Torah. He died and was buried in Natanya.

[Pages 415]

Fogelman, Hendel, nee Fenster	8/11/1886 5/25/1970, 19 Iyar 5,730	Shimshon Fogelman's wife. Made Aliyah with her family after the Holocaust. Settled in Tel Aviv. Lived in Natanya for the last few years of her life.
Fogelman, Ze'ev, son of Shimshon	11/9/1924 6/26/1978, 21 Sivan 5,738	Was a member of the Zionist Youth branches from his childhood. Survived the Holocaust in the ghetto and the forests around the city. Worked at Elco Co., where he served as a member of the workers' committee. Was loved and admired by all his friends. Energetic activist of the political left movement, and recently at "Sheli." Courageous fighter of the workers' class. Died in Ramat Gan.
Pohoriles-Priester, Nusya	12/18/1902 May 1974	A pharmacist. Settled In Tel Aviv, where she died.
Feigenbaum, Arye, son of Yosef	1872 1954	Made Aliyah in 1933 and settled in Haifa Near his son Benjamin Te'eni and two other daughters. In his last years lived in Kibbutz Ein HaMifratz with his son Yuzek.

Fuks, Tonka, nee Samet	1910 1973, Yom Kippur	Made Aliyah in 1936 and settled in Tel Aviv, where she died.
Fisher, Meir, son of Nakhum	1890 2/11/1972, 26 Shvat 5,732	Visit Eretz Israel in 1924, returned to Brzezany, and made Aliyah with his family in 1935. Was a merchant, and built a house on HeKhalutz Street in Haifa. Lived and died in Haifa.
Fisher, Fruma, nee Milrad	1891 12/8/1970	Meir Fisher's wife. Died and was buried in Haifa.
Froind-Katz, Nekha	1902 1972	Made Aliyah from Russia after the Holocaust. Settled in Moshav Khavatzelet, where she died.
Tzeig, Ze'ev (Valetzia?)	1902 1960	Made a living as a porter in Brzezany. During WW II he escaped to the USSR. Made Aliyah after the War through Cyprus. Settled in Tirat HaCarmel. Died in Haifa.
Tzimmeman, Ze'ev (Wolf)	1875 1958	Liquidated a successful business in Brzezany and made Aliyah in 1936. Built a house on HaTavor Street in Haifa, where he died and was buried in the city's old cemetery.
Tzimmerman, Cherna, nee Selba?	1880 1960	A talented merchant who accompanied her husband Ze'ev and served as his helpmate. Died and was buried in Haifa.

[Pages 416]

Tzimmerman, Dr. Ya'akov, son of Ze'ev	1899 1961 Independence Day	Was an enthusiastic Zionist. Completed medicine studies in Italy. Possessed a high intellectual level. Knew 8 languages fluently. The founder of Brzezany Natives Organization. Settled in Haifa and worked as a physician. Died in Haifa.
Tzimmerman, Shalom, son of Ze'ev	1/27/1906 2/28/1956, 28 Shvat 5,716	Made Aliyah as a pioneer. Joined *Kibbutz* Merkhavia, where he was a member most of his life. He later moved to Nahariya, where he managed a branch of Tnuva Company. Was buried in *Kibbutz* Merkhavia
Tzukerman, Sela, nee Feingenbaum	1899 1972	Made Aliyah in 1925. Settled in Haifa, where she worked as a teacher and crafts supervisor for 35 years, and where she died.
Kaufman, Tzipora, nee Goldwag	1906 1974, 28 Tammuz 5,734	Made Aliyah in about 1926. Married Aharon Kaufman. Died in Haifa.

Kaufman, Aharon	1902 1972, 20 Av 5,732	Born in Russia. Was among the founders of Kupat Kholim, where he worked. In his latest role, he managed the Megido Sanitorium in Haifa. Died in Haifa.
Kara-Kron, Michael, son of Oskar	1865 1964	Sculptor and painter who won many prizes abroad and in Israel. Studied in Budapest and lived in Italy. Made Aliyah in 1947. Sculpted many monuments in Israel and painted stamps. Died in Tel Aviv
Kikin, Yitzkhak, son of Moshe	2/28/1904 8/6/1974	Born in Shchyrets near Lviv. Made Aliyah in 1935. Married Belah Feld from Brzezany. Settled in Haifa. Volunteered to the "Haganah." Read the Bible extensively. Was a good-natured person who was respected by all. Died in Haifa.
Korev?-Likht, Seli	1898-?	Among the first pioneers. Made Aliyah in 1920. Member of the "Work battalion." Lived in Jerusalem, where he died.
Kipen, Elyakim	1898 1966	Made Aliyah in 1932. Worked as a proofreader in the "Tzur HaYom" newspaper in Jerusalem, where she died.
Kalman, Yosef, son of Israel	1898 8/14/1967 8 Av 5,727	Made Aliyah in 1920 and was among the first pioneers and the first people in the "Work Battalion" in Jezreel Valley. Worked as a pioneer in Jerusalem. Later, he settled in Haifa and then in Kiryat Motzkin, where he died.
Kalman, Zehava, nee Sirota	1900 1962	Kalman Yosef's stay-home wife. She accompanied him loyally in his hard life until she died in Kiryat Motzkin.

[Pages 417]

Kampel-Glazer, Yehuda	1906 1936	Made Aliyah as a pioneer in 1928. Worked in the south of the country. Died in Safed.
Kravitz, Zelig	1902 1968	Made Aliyah in 1925. Worked in the Dead Sea area for many years. Settled in Jerusalem and moved to Holon, where he died.
Krontal, Mania, nee Nusbaum	1902 1974	Ya'akov Krontal's wife. Made Aliyah from Vienna with her husband. Died in Tel Aviv.
Karni, Sara, nee Kampel	1902 1975	Made Aliyah in 1930. Died in Tel Aviv.
Kronberg, Litman, son of	1890 1967	Brzezany's native. As a Zionist made Aliyah from the USA. A pious man. Built a synagogue in the Bait VaGan neighborhood in Jerusalem. Died in Jerusalem. Left two daughters in the USA

Khaim-David		
Krontal, Ya'akov, son of Avraham	6/2/1906 9.11.1970 10 Elul 5,730	Made Aliyah at the age of 18 in 1924. Was an active member of the HaPoel Haifa and Tel Aviv soccer teams. Married Mania Nusbaum. Settled in Tel Aviv and established an open home for all friends. Joined the Haganah in 1930, and served as the commander of the intelligence unit in Tel Aviv. Served as a company commander in the War of Independence. Died in Tel Aviv. Left three sons, members, and activists in the agricultural labor force.
Roza, Yeshayahu, son of Khaim-David Kronberg	12/1988 10/1965	Escaped to the USSR in WW II, and made Aliyah from there. Activist of the JNF. Settled in Jerusalem. A pious Jew who used to serve as the Torah reader in Zion Mountain. Died and was buried in Jerusalem.
Rozan, Mordekhai (Motek), son of Gedalyahu	6/24/1914, 30 Sivan 5,674 1.16.1978, 18 Shvat 5,738	He was an activist in the Zionist Movement and the drama club in Brzezany. Made Aliyah in 1939. A 40-year member of *Kibbutz* HaMa'apil, where he served in various roles. Was liked by all of his friends and acquaintances. Died and was buried in the *kibbutz*.
Rot, Ozer, son of R' Nathan	1896, 11 Tevet 5,656 1962 28 Kislev 5,723	An enthusiastic Zionist and an activist in the HaMizrakhi institutions in Brzezany. Served as a representative to Zionist congresses. Made Aliyah with family in 1934. Settled in Haifa and continued his public service in the Haganah, HaPoel HaMizrakhi, Yad LeBanim, and other institutions. Died and was buried in Haifa.
Rot, Shifra, daughter of Israel Kalman	7/31/1892, 7 Av 5,652 [8/25] 1971, 4 Elul 5,731	Ozer's wife and his helpmate. Was an energetic woman. Died and was buried in Haifa.

[Pages 418]

Rot, Rozia, daughter of Mendel David	3/30/1900 12/4/1975 1 Iyar 5,735	She became Shimon Katz's widow at a young age. Remarried Aliyahu-David Rot. Most of the year handed assistance and contributed in secret to the needy, particularly during the Holocaust and in Israel. Made Aliyah through Cyprus in 1947 and settled in Haifa, where she died and was buried in Tiv'on
Rotshtein, son of Shimon	1910 1950	Made Aliyah after the Holocaust from the USSR. Settled in Jerusalem, where he died.

Ross, Dr. Nakhum, son of Yehuda-Wolf	1898 11/1969	Graduate of the college "The Rabbinical Seminary" in Germany, and served as a teacher in schools in Poland. Activist in the HeKhalutz Zionist movement. Immigrated to Argentina, from where he made Aliyah. Dedicated himself to cultural work for new immigrants. Died in Tel Aviv.
Riger, Arye-Adolf	1906 5/15/1961	He was a lawyer. Survived the Holocaust in a hideout located in Brzezany's municipal hospital. A Zionist at his core. Made Aliyah in 1952 from the USA. Settled in Jerusalem, where he died.
Reizer, Rivka, daughter of Uri Shtreizer	[Was not provided]	[Was not provided]
Reizer, Mordekhai, son of Khaim	11/12/1910 12/17/1968, 30 Kislev 5,729	Escaped to the USSR in WW II. Moved to Wrocław, where he was an activist in "Poalei Tzion Left." Made Aliyah in 1950 and settled in Moshav Gan-Sorek, where he died.
Reikhshtein, Zalman, son of Mordekhai	2/15/1912 5/10/1955	Made Aliyah after the Holocaust and settled in Haifa. Worked in the "Paz" Company. Died in Haifa.
Shumer, Dr. Moshe-Aharon, son of Aba	1/27/1890 5/10/1955	Was a physician and an energetic Zionist. He was recruited to the Red Army in WW II where he served with the rank of Major [Captain 3rd rank]. Made Aliyah after the War & settled in Hadera, where he died and was buried.
Shtreizand, Yosef, son of Meir-Yehuda	1877 7/7/1955, 24 Tammuz 5,715	He was a Zionist and an energetic activist in charity organizations in the R' Yudel Synagogue and "Khevra Kadisha" in Brzezany. The first professional who made Aliyah with his family in 1936. Settled in Kfar Saba, where he was an activist in the synagogue and Burial Society. He died and was buried in Kfar Saba.
Shtreizand, Rakhel, nee Shvam	1878 8/21/1969	R' Yosef's wife. A diligent housewife and helpmate. Died in Haifa and was buried in Kfar Saba.

[Pages 419]

Schmidt, Nina, daughter of Ya'akov Ogoshevitz	8/27/1927 5/14/1978, 7 Iyar 5,731	Born in Narewka. Survived the Holocaust's hell as a child in a concentration camp. On her way to Israel after the war. She married her husband, Moshe. Settled in Kiryat Frostig. Was buried in Haifa.

Shefer, Gizela, daughter of Ze'ev	1897 10/25/1965	Made Aliyah in 1953. Settled in Haifa near her sister. Died in Haifa.
Shefer-Idikos, Dr. Rakhel, daughter of Ze'ev	1892 3/24/1963	Made Aliyah in 1935. Was a dentist. Owned a private dental clinic in Haifa.
Idikos, Menakhem	1894 6/12/1978	Born in Drohobitz. Worked as a dental technician. Made Aliya with his wife, Dr. Rakhel Shefer. Died in Haifa.
Shneider, Yosef, son of Avraham	1/28/1914 2/3/1950	Made Aliyah as a pioneer in 1937. Was a member of *Kibbutz* Tel Yitzkhak. Later on, he moved to Haifa, where he worked as a scaffolding(?) erector. Died in Haifa.
Te'eni (Feigenbaum), Benjamin, son of Arye	5/14/1900 2/2/1948, 22 Shvat 5,708	Energetic Zionist. Made Aliyah in 1920 as a pioneering leader and joined the "Khavurat HaEmek" [literally the "Valley Group" of the "Work Battalion"]. In 1925, he was elected to Haifa's Hadar HaCarmel committee, where he modernized and managed the Water Works. Was active in several organizations in Haifa. Killed on a military mission on his way to Tel Aviv. Was buried in the military cemetery in Haifa

[Page 420]

Fallen Soldiers in Israel's Wars
In Memory of the Fallen

Translated by Moshe Kutten

Edited by Jane S. Gabin

Captain Arye Holander

Arye Holander was born in Tel Aviv on 11/20/1945 to Leah (z"l) and Dov Holander (may he live long). As a member of "HaShomer HaTzair," when the time came for his enlistment in the IDF, he hesitated whether he should join the [infantry] Nakha"l Brigade [stands for Fighting Pioneering Youth]. In the end, he decided to join the Armored Corps. He advanced in the corps and attained the rank of an officer. Despite his wish to establish an agricultural farm in a Moshav, in a border area, he gave up on his private plans, continued to serve in the standing army, and served in a fighting unit of the Armored Corps.

During the Six Days War, on 26 Iyar 5,726 (6/5/1967), he attacked the Rafah compound with a tank company for which he was a deputy commander. Exposed on the tank's turret, he was killed by a direct hit at Rafah junction. Captain Holander was one of the first fallen soldiers in the Six Days War. His life was cut short at the age of 21, at the beginning of his road.

We will remember him always - tall and smiling. His good-hearted nature was reflected in his dark eyes.

May his memory be blessed.

11.7.1913
ג' אייר תש"ח
13.5.1948

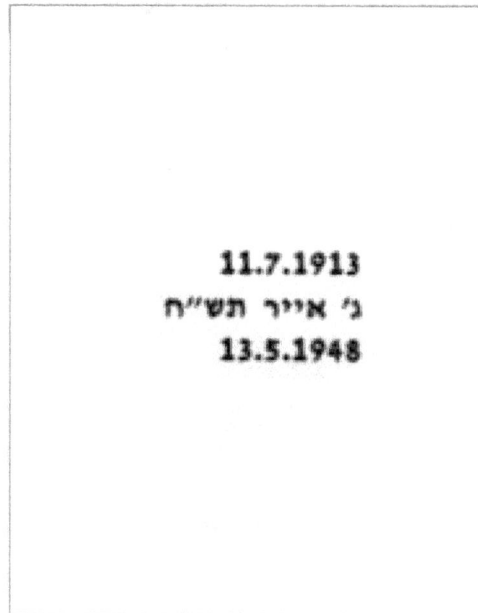

Holander Shimon
Born 7/11/1913 Died 5/13/1948, 3 Iyar 5,708

Shimon Holander made Aliyah as a pioneer in 1938. He joined a nucleus of ["Bnei Akiva" youth movement] who settled in Kfar Etzion. There, he married Yehudit, nee Shmeterling, from Brzezany. During the War of Independence, he took an active role in defending the kibbutz, where he was killed.

May his memory be blessed.

Tenenbaum Shmuel

Shmuel Tenenbaum, nicknamed "Shmulik" by his friends at the "Bnei Akiva" branch in Brzezany, was already industrious in work and Torah from early childhood. He was sharp and diligent in his studies. Despite the heavy burden imposed on him at a young age to support his mother and brother, did not abandon the Zionist idea and public Zionist activity. He dedicated all his vigor to the branch of "Bnei Akiva" in Brzezany, where he was one of the leaders. His work was also associated with Zionism, as he served as a teacher at the "HaMizrakhi" school in the city, and had also given private lessons in Hebrew. He did not associate his desire to make Aliyah with language studies. He used to say that "in Eretz Israel, there is a need for Hebrew workers," and "everybody is speaking Hebrew there." He, therefore, looked for a profession he could work after making Aliyah. For that purpose, he dedicated himself to bee-keeping.

After making Aliyah in the early 1930s, he joined *Kibbutz* Kfar Etzion, where he established a family. He was killed while defending the *kibbutz* in the War of Independence, on 5/15/1948, 3 Iyar 5,708.

May his memory be blessed.

[Page 421]

Heavy is the fate of parents who lose a son, but an indescribable calamity is to lose two sons on the same day. Such a cruel fate hit Leah and Meir Sapir. They lost Dan and his brother Yosi on the same day in the Yom Kippur War.

Lieutenant Colonel Dan Sapir

The older son, Dan Sapir, was born on 12 Tevet 5,699 (1/3/1939). He fell in the Sinai's blocking battle in the Yom Kippur War on 12 Tishrei 5,734 (10/8/1973) while serving in the senior position of Lieutenant Colonel.

Captain Dan Sapir

The younger brother, Yosi Sapir, a captain in the Armored Crop, fell as a hero in the blocking battle on the Golan [Heights] on the same day, 10/8/1973.

The paratrooper – Yoel Meir

Yoel, son of Moshe Meir from Narajow, enlisted in the Red Army in 1941 during the Soviet rule in Galitsia. After completing a paratrooper course, he took an active role in the war against the Nazis on various fronts. In his last letter to his brother in Israel in 1944, he wrote that he was in a faraway country. Since then, all traces of him were lost.

He was a good-looking and good-hearted person who fought bravely against the Nazis. His motto was "Blood for Death."

May his memory be blessed.

[Pages 423]

The Narajow Book
(Narayev, Ukraine)
49°32' 24°46'

[Pages 424]

Narajow My town

Zehava Shmushkin (Hertz)

Translated by Ruth Yoseffa Erez

Edited by Moshe Kutten and Jane S. Gabin

I like to tell you about my small town, Narajow. Jews lived in it for many centuries. They knew poverty, pogroms, humiliation, and… a few moments of happiness. A small town on the main road from Lwow to Brzezany, nestled between mountains, immersed in forests and groves, surrounded by valleys and abounding rivers.

It is a typical small town or village. There are many more like it in Galicia, in the Austro-Hungarian empire, which became part of Poland after WWI.

The village houses were like a circle within a circle. Stores were located at the center and around them, the Jewish houses. At the center lived the Jews, and around them lived the Ukrainians and Poles. Some of these Poles were brought from Western Poland after WWI to balance their number in the population. Around town, there were many farms; some of them belonged to Jewish families, especially before WWI and a few years after the war. These estate owners were respected Jews who added gist to the village life. I specifically remember the Bleyberg, Frash, and Nagelberg families.

I remember these estate owners well because one of them was my beloved grandfather, Isar Milshtok, whose farm was a little farther away. His farm was like the Garden of Eden, full of orchards and cultivated fields. It is known that after the war, antisemitism was on the rise, and it was difficult for a Jew to hold an isolated spot. Many Jews had to sell their land. My grandfather sold his farm as well for the same reasons.

[Pages 425]

The Polish settlers came and took their place after the Polish government divided the land among themselves. There were times of good neighboring relationships between Jewish and non-Jewish populations but starting with the 1920s and especially in the 1930s, the Nationalistic-Fascist feelings of the Poles and even more so of the Ukrainians grew bigger. They were inspired by the rise of Hitler and waited for the opportunity to destroy the Jewish community, murder them, and take over. Among the estates' owners were many Germans called "Volksdeutsche," who traded with Jews up to WW II and had decent relations with them. The truth was revealed only with the arrival of the Nazis. The "Volksdeutsches" were the most organized fifth column and helped the Germans tremendously. After the war, they fled to Germany.

Moshe Nadir

When trying to describe the distant past, we see only the beauty and the good, manifested in the songs of Isaac (Itzik) Reiss (Rayz) from Narajow, known by his pen name Moshe (Moyshe/Moishe) Nadir. This Yiddish author and poet, who emigrated to America as a young man, lived most of his life in America, and even when he visited Europe, he did not visit his hometown. He wanted to live with his memories – the good and the beauty of the distant town. "Reality is forever grey," he said. He dedicated a group of Yiddish songs to his hometown, two of which are presented in this book.

Different Livelihoods

Some earned a decent living, but many barely made it; that's why many emigrated, especially to America.

More than a few achieved respectable positions overseas, including many people in Narajow who survived due to money they received from their relatives who emigrated. Many shop owners, butchers, small craftsmen, and peddlers traveled during the week to neighboring towns to sell their merchandise.

Life was difficult despite help from charitable persons to the needy. They tried to ease the burden of many with *tzdaka* and secretly provided charity. There were institutes like the Jewish community and charity organizations but a support system like we have today in Israel did not exist. Nevertheless, there were no social problems like those we face in Israel today. People were ashamed to get support in the open and tried to work and earn a living in many ways. The people of Narajow did not lose their decency, and beggars were not among them. Educated and simple people lived next to each other. Some were even great Torah and Talmud scholars who, more than once, were asked to advise rabbis from far away on controversial issues in different disagreements. Yossia Neuman, Israel Ne'eman's grandfather, Eliezer Milshtok, Aryeh Goldschlag's grandfather, and my uncle (my grandfather's brother) were some of those scholars. I remember Narayevsky, a Catholic theologian and the Rector of the

[Pages 426]

University in Lwow, who was visiting his estate in town during his vacations. He used to sit in Eliezer Milshtok's house and argue with him on religious matters and different tractates of the Mishna.

Holidays and Happy Gatherings

Sabbaths and Holidays are engraved in my memory very well. The town became festive, and everyone, old and young took part, helped prepare and participated, and this atmosphere of togetherness filled the streets. How beautiful and fascinating were the holidays, each holiday with its unique character, whether we knew it or not. The Rosh Hashanah and Yom Kippur ambiance was felt already in the month of Elul: visiting the cemetery, the *Slichot* prayers, and the voice of the beadle (*Shamash*) before sunrise on fall days – "*Steit oif zu Slichot*" – echoes in my ears even today. The expiation (*Kaparot*) ceremonies on the eve of Yom Kippur and my good mom dividing the *Kaparot* chickens among the needy, like others probably did according to the custom. On the high holidays, the synagogues were completely full. Many lights, the white cloths, and the devotion made this unique atmosphere. On Simchat Torah, after the prayer, people walked in the streets, singing and dancing until they reached the Rabbi's house or one of the homeowners – and everyone was very cheerful. The celebrations of the Maccabees' holiday (Chanukah) were very meaningful, presenting the lighted candles in the window covered with frost flowers, the pleasant tune "*Hanerot Halalu*" (these candles), Chanukah songs, games, delicacies and later on there were balls whose revenues were dedicated to the Jewish National Fund ("Keren Kayemet Le'Israel") or to "Ezra" (Help) a special fund for the pioneers who were making *Aliyah* to Eretz Israel.

On Purim, there was a lot of activity as well. Different bands dressed in costumes from all the youth movements went from home to home with rich programs, dancing and singing during the feast, collecting money for Eretz Israel.

For Passover, preparation started on Hannukah, by preparing goose fat, and even before that, wheat for the *Matzah Shmurah* was collected and kept well and then baked under strict supervision. Only a few had the *Matzah Shmurah*. After Purim, the baking of *Matzah* for everyone started in Passover and a kosher *Seder* was performed in all the houses of Israel in town.

And so were all the other holidays. The mourning days, such as Tisha B'Av, were also observed, and you could feel the fasting, the Lamentations, and the saying of *Eichah*. I doubt if all these details can give a real picture of everything like it was. It is not surprising that due to this atmosphere, we stayed connected with our hearts and souls to everything national and Jewish.

Youth and Culture

The "Shomer Ha'tzair" branch

Such a tiny place raised between the two wars magnificent youth. A few left to continue their studies in the nearby city or in Lwow. Some youths were self-taught and educated, like the exceptional Aryeh Meir and more. It is hard to explain how, in a place where it wasn't a live language, the youth spoke such good Hebrew, saturated in a rich atmosphere of Zionism with a lot of Judaism. Before noon, children went to a Polish school, but they got more than just a general education. They studied the Torah and Bible with the *Melameds* in the Cheder. A few, like Shlomo Ne'eman, Yehezkel Herz, and Yaakov Weiss, learned Talmud with R' Yossia Neuman. A respectable place was reserved for the Hebrew school, which was founded

[Pages 427]

in the 1920s, by Shifra Marcus of Tarnopol (approx. 1925-6). That was a school like any other school: it taught Hebrew, literature, the Bible, History, Eretz Israel's studies, and more. There was a choir and plays – all in pure Hebrew. It is important to mention that the tuition for the *Kheders* and the maintenance of the Hebrew school and its funding were all the responsibility of the parents, according to their abilities.

A pretty chapter in the life of the town was the different youth movements representing all the sections: "Hashomer Hatzair" (The Young Guard), "HaKhalutz" (The Pioneer), "Betar," "The Zionist Youth" and "Bnei Akiva" (Akiva's children).

Life was beautiful and healthy. In spring and summer, activities were held outdoors. These activities, surrounded by nature, enriched the imagination. In the winter, activities were held in the Youth movement's building. The members paid for everything with their own money. The youth movements enriched the youth's life, they lived in "an en route state." Everyone expected to make *Aliyah* and fulfill these ideas in Israel Regretfully only a few had this privilege and we all know what the reasons were. The strict policy of the Polish government, which discriminated against Jews, caused unemployment and spread hopelessness among the youth.

Those who did not fulfill the Zionist dream dropped out of the youth movements and turned to the communist movement. Future days proved to be a tragic illusion.

The money collections for the Jewish National Fund ("Keren Kayemet Le'Israel") and to help the pioneers were organized by representatives of the youth movements in full cooperation. Just before it was time for the Zionist Congress, there was a lot of commotion in town. The election was accompanied by (sometimes ugly) typical vigorous publicity under strict supervision to prevent fraud. One distinctive character was Rabbi Zvi Grosswax, a representative of the Mizrachi movement who was also a member of the World Joint. He also served as the "Mizrachi" representative to the Congress.

All elections (electing a Rabbi or ending a term) were accompanied by deep quarrels and even violent forms of hatred between the different sides. Many were involved in what was happening in the larger world, and the Jewish world and had subscriptions to Polish newspapers. Mail would arrive from Brzezany in the evening. People used to gather near the post office where the mailman was handing out letters to those who were waiting. They would grab the papers and get carried away into enthusiastic arguments.

[Pages 428]

My Father - A Public Figure

I will sin if I do not mention my father, Mendel Herz, a lovely, heartwarming figure. A man who was knowledgeable in the ways of the Torah, in Polish, German, and Ukrainian, who was familiar with statutes and law, and who was a brilliant wood trader. He had a respectable place in the town's life. He was not born here; he was from the Carpathians, a descendant of the Stern-Shteg family, Tur Zahav.

He liked people, was charitable, and pious. He had a pleasant voice and served as "Baal Tefillah" at his *Kloiz* for many years, for the enjoyment of the praying audience.

He believed in G-d, the Jewish nation, and its redemption. He did not lose his faith even during the horrific days. I heard from the survivors – the brothers Beni and Aharon Weiss, that when the Jews were on the brink of destruction, my father would comfort them and strengthen their spirits by saying: "Netzakh Israel lo yeshaker" ["The eternity of the nation of Israel will not fail"].

The Road

This wide artery divided the town center in half. Besides its role in connecting the two major cities Lwow and Tarnopol, the road served as the hub of life in town and that's where many events took place for generations.

Here is where they all passed: army processions, princes, counts (grafs), estate owners, and simple people. This is where the parents of a noble Polishman fell on their knees in front of Kaiser Franz Joseph's wagon to get a pardon for their son who was held in Siberia, here is where Jews rejoiced, but from here they were also transported to the different extermination camps. Here, on Thursdays, the days of the weekly market, the many farmers' wagons passed, got situated in the center, and from there they sold their crops.

In the evenings, on Shabbat and during the holidays, the road served as kind of a promenade for pedestrians and bicyclists, and in the winter, in snow and frost, people would ice skate on it.

When motor cars were introduced, they too used that road, and so did the daily buses from Podhajce to Lwow.

This road witnessed happiness, but even more so – pogroms. The pogroms targeted the whole Jewish community because of the sins of single hot-tempered Jews. Especially on Sundays, the holy day for Christians, the incited Ukrainians were leaving the prayer house in a parade hurrying to complete their "holy work": breaking the windows of Jewish houses with all that's involved, causing fear and terror to spread among the peaceful Jews.

[Pages 429]

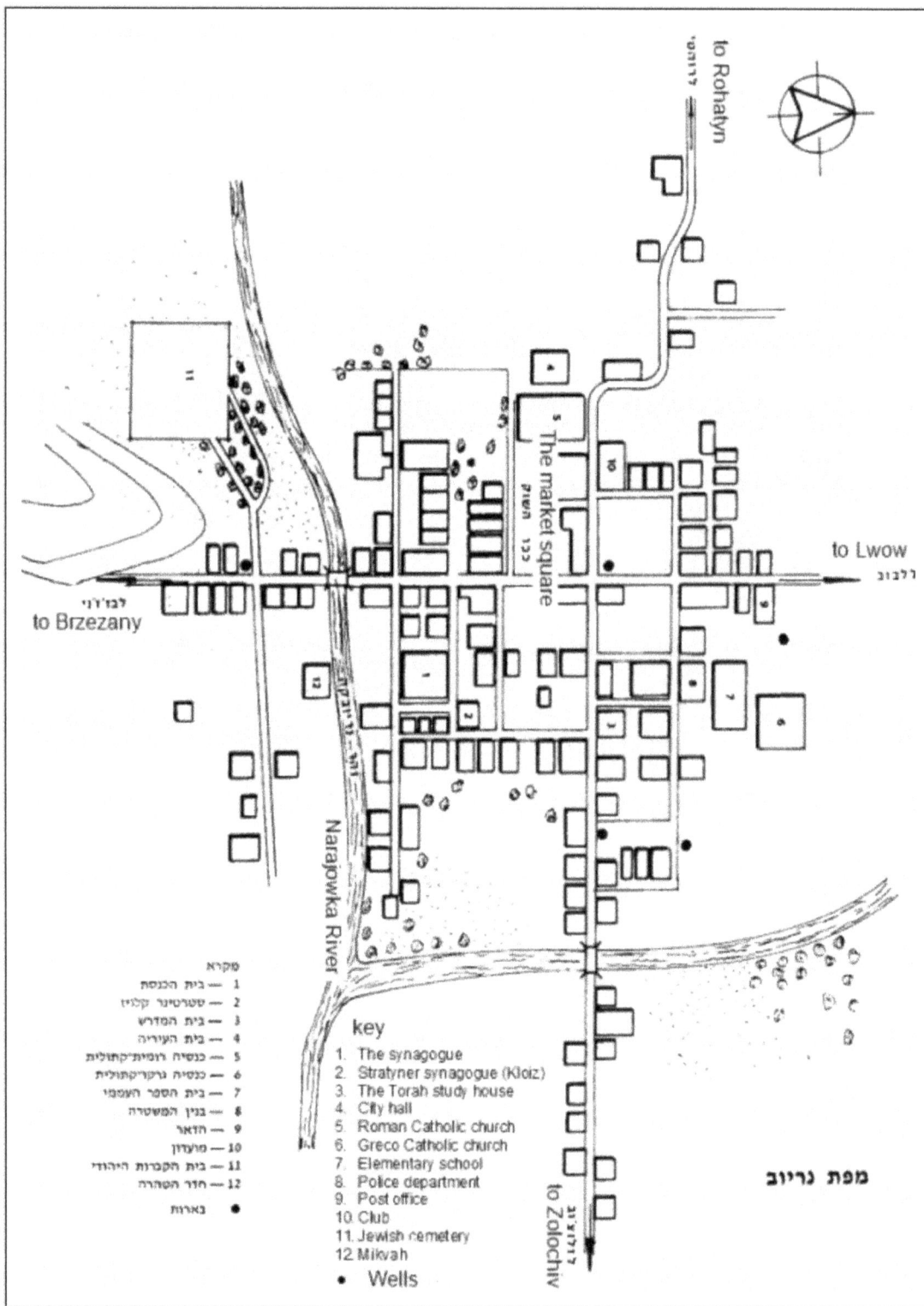

מקרא
1 — בית הכנסת
2 — סטרטינער קלויז
3 — בית המדרש
4 — בית העיריה
5 — כנסיה רומית-קתולית
6 — כנסיה גרקו-קתולית
7 — בית הספר העממי
8 — בנין המשטרה
9 — הדואר
10 — מועדון
11 — בית הקברות היהודי
12 — חדר הטהרה

● — בארות

key
1. The synagogue
2. Stratyner synagogue (Kloiz)
3. The Torah study house
4. City hall
5. Roman Catholic church
6. Greco Catholic church
7. Elementary school
8. Police department
9. Post office
10. Club
11. Jewish cemetery
12. Mikvah
● Wells

to Rohatyn

to Lwow

to Brzezany

to Zolochiv

The market square

Narajowka River

מפת נריוב

Narajow Map

[Pages 430]

Way of Life and Trade

Vast forests belonged to Count (graf) Potozky, and indeed, many wood traders came and bought portions of the forest. A diverse wood industry was established, and some products were exported to other countries.

Strange Yosale'

Throughout the day, most of the wagon traffic was to Brzezany, 16 kilometers away. A substantial part of the population spent many hours in Brzezany returning to town towards the evening: some to buy or sell something, some to the courts or district offices, and some to visit a tailor or a seamstress.

Some youth attended schools in Brzezany, but some preferred Jewish Hebrew schools in Lwow.

Trade, as well as social and cultural connections, brought the Jews in Narajow and Brzezany closer, both in times of Joy and during the Holocaust.

Trade life in the shops, stalls, and wagons was lively and full of charm, a mix of characters, colors, sounds, and movement. Among them, I can not forget the colorful coachmen: Shein, "the Red Moshe" ("Der Royter Moshe"), "Strong Not'e" ("Not'e Der Harb") and their wagons, which served the people of Narajow.

In the middle of town, there was a large, which supplied water to the residents. Well remembered is "Yekhezkel Der Wassertrener" which means: Yekhezkel the water carrier, a big pole on his shoulders with two buckets, with which he would deliver water in an orderly and concise manner to those who wanted it. Yekhezkel had a big family and later he emigrated to the US.

The carpet factory deserves to be mentioned as well. It supplied jobs to many young Jews and training personnel from "Bnei Akiva" (Akiva's children). This business was run by the Rabbi and his partner Yekhezkel Hertz.

And all this was going on during peaceful times, in summer and winter, in happy times, and during different pogroms, until the big Holocaust – when it all stopped. The murderous Nazi soldiers with their helpers, cleansed the town of its Jewish residents and took them through the aforementioned road to Brzezany, where they found their death.

May their memory be blessed.

[Page 431]

Memories from My Town – Narajow

Israel Ne'eman

Translated by Ruth Yoseffa Erez

Edited by Moshe Kutten and Jane S. Gabin

Narajow, a small town on the road from Brzezany to Lwow, is not too famous, without any distinguished people, except Moshe (Moyshe/Moishe) Nadir, the renowned Yiddish writer.

I heard from my grandfather, R' Yossef (Yossia) Neuman (Yosha Wawas), the city's Rabbinical judge, that Narajow's rabbinical chair was important and there were always famous Torah scholars occupying it. But while Jewish Galicia was influenced by the enormous wave of the Hassidic movement, and in every town and city, there was a "Righteous man" ("*Tzadik*") seated; Narajow did not take part in this Hassidic enthusiasm. In Narajow, there was no "Rabbi" and there was a reason for that.

Nearby Peremyshlyany (Premishlaner) had their famous Rabbi Meir'l (Meir), and neighboring Stratyn had a whole "dynasty": the Brandwein family, the righteous men of Stratyn, the first of which was Rabbi Yehuda Zvi who inherited this leadership from Rabbi Uril' (Uri) of Strzeliska. A branch from the Stratyn family made *Aliyah*about 70 years ago; one of their descendants served as the Histadrut's (Israeli Labor Federation) Rabbi, and he was Rabbi Zvi Yehuda Brandwein (z"l).

And again, I heard from my grandfather about his father R' Zeev (Wawa Neuman), a respected astute student, blessed with a large family, and seemingly had a big influence on the community. And Rabbi Wawa was a "*Misnaged*"[1] and did not "ascend" to Peremyshlyany or to Stratyn. It was important (most likely) for Rabbi Avramtche of Stratyn to draw Rabbi Wawa to Hassidism, and there was a personal correspondence between them. A few letters were kept in our house, and I read them (it's a pity that they were destroyed during the Holocaust and the destruction). The Rabbi from Stratyn couldto "convince" him and R' Wawa Neuman remained a "*Misnaged.*"

Most Jews in Narajow became Stratyner Hasidim, and they even built a synagogue (*Kloiz*) called the "Stratyner *Kloiz*." Rabbi Avramtche from Stratyn was surelyinvited to the dedication of the *Kloiz*. The Rabbi came to spend a Shabbat in Narajow and personally invited Rabbi Wawa to pray with him in the *Kloiz*. Rabbi Wawa refused and did not come, that's how deep he "sunk" into being a "*Misnaged*." In his last letter to Rabbi Wawa, Rabbi Avramtche writes: "It looks like you are beyond repair and you will never be a Hasid, but all your sons are destined to be Hasidim." Rabbi Wawa had seven sons and surely all became Hasidim, except for my grandfather, Rabbi Yosha, who stayed neutral. He understood and respected the Hasidism, but did not "ascend" to their Rabbi. He explained it to us: "The Mitzvah of respecting your father is very important!"

Other than the Stratyner *Kloiz*, there were three more synagogues in Narajow. The big synagogue was built with wide stone walls with small windows placed high close to the ceiling and a single entry with a heavy door. It was constructed in this manner for one apparent reason: to be used for protection and shelter during a pogrom.

At the entrance to the synagogue, there was a Torah study house nicknamed "the Small Torah study house," where the very early morning prayers took place. It was mostly used by commoners, as opposed to the big Torah Study house gloriously built and bordered the Rabbi's apartment.

[Page 432]

Actually, the "pulse" of the Jewish life in town was best felt in the *Kloiz*, which was very simple and lacked any signs of glory. It was a big hall with big windows around it. Simplicity and humbleness were characteristics of the Stratyner Hasidim. During the celebrations of Lag Ba'Omer, Purim, or a commemoration of a *Tzadik*'s death day, Hassidim would light many candles on all the surrounding windows and there was an "illumination" that lit the whole area. On the 20th of Tamuz, the date of Herzl's death, we would have the same lighting despite the objection by the anti-Zionists. We would have fierce arguments and symposiums between Hasidim and Hasidim, Zionists and Zionists, and Zionists and anti-Zionists, all in the same *Kloiz*. That's where we had election meetings for the Zionist Congress or, vastly different, election gatherings for the Polish Sejm, where we heard emissaries from Israel, preachers, and others who came to admonish or speakers from all the Zionist parties. Between the *Mincha* prayer and the Maariv prayer the *Kloiz* was packed with people, there was no need to announce the subject because there were always those who would listen and argue.

The *Kloiz* was buzzing with activity from early dawn until late at night, even when there was no praying going on, people would sit and study Torah and Gomorrah, divided into "classes" (two guys who were studying together were called a "class"). Booksellers would visit the town, every now and then; they would spread out their merchandise on the long tables in the *Kloiz*, and the youth would buy or read different *Bichalach* stories[2]. Wanderers and riff-raffs would be welcomed guests in the *Kloiz*; they would sleep behind the ever-burning big hearth. During the late-night hours, they would tell us "Arabian Nights" tales.

In the 1920s, a school was established to teach the Hebrew language. Shifra Marcus, a young intelligent, and full-of-energy woman, who happened to arrive in Narajow from Tarnopol, was able to establish the school and run it mostly by herself. Before she came, there were a few attempts to form a Hebrew school, but to no avail. Due to Mrs. Marcus (who is now in Israel) and her vigor, the school survived for a few years, the knowledge of the Hebrew language among the youth grew, and we were able to read Hebrew books and newspapers that arrived from Israel.

[Page 433]

The town's youth was affected by Shifra Marcus' Zionist passion, and it initiated the era of the Zionist organizations, the first of which was the "Hashomer Hatzair"[The Young Guard].

Rabbi Zvi Grosswax (z"l) and my brother Shlomo (z"l), who r the newspapers and were familiar with the "business" of the youth Zionist movements were strictly against the opening of the "Hashomer Hatzair" branch. They were very concerned that the youth will move away from the religion and the tradition. You must remember that at that time, even the communist "Hashomer Hatzair" members were amongst those who came to pray at the synagogue both in the morning (*Shacharith* prayer) and at night (Maariv prayer). Despite that, there were already signs of secularism and defilement of the Shabbat, but not in public. Rabbi Grosswax knew of a Zionist religious youth movement "Mizrachi" and personally knew Rabbi Dr. Federbush (z"l), who was the head of the center in Lwow. Dr. Federbush, who was a candidate for the Polish Sejm, came to Narajow to lecture and to promote his party, which was the radical party of Isaac (Itzhak) Greenbaum (Greenboim) as opposed to Dr. Reich's party. When he visited Narajow, Dr. Federbush was a guest at our house. Back in those days, there were no hotels in Narajow. When an envoy from Israel happened to come to town, he would stay with one of the respectable "homeowners." My grandfather debated some difficult questions in the Talmud with the Doctor, who was an astute scholar, and later that night they talked about Zionism and religious Zionism, and youths who desert their fathers' ways. Finally, he looked at me and said: "You will organize a group of youngsters for "HaMizrachi."I was only 15, at the time, too young for "HaMizrachi Youth," so the Doctor suggested calling it "HaMizrachi Flowers," and that's how it started. From that group grew a big and prosperous branch of Narajow's "Bnei Akiva."

A few years later, a "Mizrachi" activist from Eretz Israel came to Galicia, comrade Skortovski. He told us that in Eretz Israel, the religious youths call their movement "Bnei Akiva" (Akiva's children). This name captivated us, and we also called our movement "Bnei Akiva," unlike the centers in Warsaw and Krakow that called their religious Zionist youth movement "Hashomer Hadati" (The Religious Guard).

During the 1930s, the "Bnei Akiva" movement organized training groups to prepare its members for the pioneering realization in Eretz Israel. One of the first groups was in Kozowa on the Polish-Rumanian border. I joined this group in 1932.

In Kozowa, a new world opened to me. Kozowa was a center of the carpet industry, where the carpets were woven using simple manual looms. This industry supplied many jobs to all the Jewish youth and the training groups whose members learned the profession quickly and well. The local youth was well paid, well-dressed, and happy. That was in complete contrast to the so-called "home-owners" youth in Narajow, for whom manual labor or handicrafts were despised and did not match their pedigree, which is why extreme poverty and neglect ruled everywhere.

When I came back from Kozowa, I "sold" the idea of a carpet industry to Narajow. Rabbi Grosswax and Yehezkel Hertz liked the idea. We brought looms and instructors from Kozowa, and most youths busied themselves with it. The livelihood of the "Bnei Akiva" training group that was forming in Narajow, came mostly from cutting down trees and carpet weaving.

In 1935 I made *Aliyah* to Israel, before and after me a few more native Narajow pioneers made *Aliyah* and a few more who were able to flee the terrible Holocaust are in America.

May this chapter in the book serve as a tombstone to the small community where I spent my youthful years.

Mizrachi youth of Narajow - 1931

Translator Notes:

1. The term "misnagdim" (Mitnagdim) was used by European Jews to refer to Ashkenazi religious Jews who opposed the rise and spread of early Hasidic Judaism.

2. *Bichalach* is Yiddish for non-religious (forbidden?) books.

[Page 434]

The "Zionist Youth" Movement in Narajow

Chana Kvodi

Translated by Ruth Yoseffa Erez

Edited by Moshe Kutten and Jane S. Gabin

In 1933 the "Zionist Youth" movement was formed in Narajow (Today's "Israeli Scouts"). Its predecessors were "Hashomer Hatzair, "HaMizrachi," "Betar," and more.

Narajow was a small town with a few hundred Jews; the older ones had no particular affinity to Zionism. Many of the younger ones, on the other hand - who were members of youth movements and many of them members of "Hashomer Hatzair" and "HaChalutz" (the Pioneer) – made *Aliyah* to Eretz Israel towards the end of the 1920s. Narajow's Rabbi, an educated man, respectable and active in the "HaMizrachi" movement, was elected as a representative to the Zionist Congress.

Zehava Hertz (today Shmushkin), a young, pretty, energetic, and educated woman, took it upon herself to organize the "Zionist Youth" in Narajow.

I had the privilege of being one of the first members and the originators of this movement. Our group included 10-15 members, almost children, whose ages were between 12 and 15. We were mostly girls but there were two boys as well: Shmuel Weiss and Itzhak Hertz (Zehava's brother). They were the best youth in town, with great potential: full of energy, aspirations. and hope to fulfill their ideals. Zehava took them into her hands and, with enthusiasm and devotion, began to instill Zionism in them through "meetings" and "conversations."

We rented a room and started to handle the social, functional, and administrative aspects. We had a "money box" – to cover our financial expenses – with the monetary participation of each member, and immediately started a course to teach the Hebrew language. It was clear to us that knowing the language would help us to accomplish our goal and get us closer to achieving it. We used to get together twice or three times a week for "conversations" (today we call them "activities"[1]). Those conversations varied and covered different subjects such as the history of the Jewish settlement (Yishuv) in Eretz Israel, Jewish history, Eretz Israel's (then Palestine) geography, and the "Settlement's heroes." All those subjects were distant and foreign to us until that time. Suddenly we started to have interest in anything connected to Eretz Israel. The little library that we formed in our center helped us as well. We wanted to get older as fast as we could so we could join the *Hakhshara* [agricultural training] groups and fulfill our dream to make *Aliyah* to Eretz Israel, to be one of the "heroes," to join the pioneering movement and build the state of Israel.

I vividly remember one of the stirring conversations about the "Settlement's heroes," the conversation about Tel-Chai, and the heroism of Yosef Trumpeldor and his friends. We were excited and proud to have such personalities amongst the Jewish people; we identified with them, talked about them, and read a lot on this subject. I know that, I personally, was greatly influenced by these conversations and readings, and sure that they formed my identity and instructed me in later times, in major and crucial decisions in my life.

As time passed, our center evolved, another group of youngsters joined us and we, the adults, instructed them. Among other things, I organized a course to teach the Hebrew language, in which I shared with them the little knowledge that I already had. It must be noted that we worked vigorously and energetically and had a lot of activities. We decorated the hall as best as we could and purchased a Ping Pong table and equipment as part of our sports activities.

[Page 435]

We had excursions and inter-town meets to listen to lectures and exchange opinions and views; we had plays and parties and different games, as well as singing nights and *Hora* dancing on Saturdays. Everything of course was in Hebrew, whose words we did not always understand, but it was dear to us. We learned Hebrew literature, Bialik's poems, Tchernihovsky, and many more. We issued the movement's newspaper, in which any member who showed talent or interest in writing could participate, and there were those amongst us who were very talented. It is proper to mention here Rivka Halperin (z"l) who was blessed with such talent and many other wonderful traits, and who contributed a lot to our movement. Rivka perished in the Holocaust.

For a while, some of the members would go to a "summer camp" during the summer vacation – which was one of the happiest and most fun activities of the movement. Our center grew and earned more respect in town, which was apparent in the elections to the Zionist Congress. We would sell a respectable number of Shekels[2], and win many votes. A special experience for us was the Purim holiday. We would start practicing a few weeks before the performances and dances. During the holiday itself, a few groups or couples would pass among the houses and perform in each house, and all the donations were dedicated to the movement. I remember one Purim when I and my good friend Ester Zinger (z"l) wore Hungarian costumes and danced the *Chardash*, a performance that was a big success.

Since there was a lot of buzz around us and we had so many activities, we attracted members from other movements. From what we've heard, some didn't necessarily join us for ideological reasons; rather they did it because we had many girls in our center. One of these was Hersch Ehre (today, my husband – Zvi Kvodi) who left the "Hashomer Hatzair" for us.

The "Zionist Youth" group

[Page 436]

In 1937, Zehava Hertz the founder, instructor, and head of our center, started preparing to make *Aliyah* to Eretz Israel. When it was time, we naturally had a fancy party, we took photographs and departed from her with a lot of sorrow and jealousy – here she was about to realize her dream. We strongly hoped to meet her soon in Eretz Israel.

Our connection with Zehava was very tight, and we exchanged letters. Many times, she would mail us the "Hatzofe" newspaper, and then we would gather together - it was almost a festive occasion - and do our best to read the articles and decipher them, mainly to learn about what was going on in Eretz Israel. Zehava left us a substitute as the head of the center, a guy from Rivne [Rovno] named Lolek Rubinstein, who came to our town to teach Hebrew and was already back then, a member of the "Hagana" in Lwow (he lives in Israel now). After a while he left, and Shmuel Weiss who was a "graduate" of our group became the head of the center. In 1939, Shmuel decided to make "illegal" *Aliyah* to Eretz Israel, and on the eve of the war he left Narajow. After six months of trouble and hardship, he arrived in Eretz Israel. For a while, he was a member of *Kibbutz* Tel Yitzhak, and today he lives in Even Yehuda.

When the war erupted, our dreams were shuttered, but the Zionist spirit was with me throughout the war. Most of the members and our families perished in the Holocaust. My husband and I (we got married during the war) fled and tried to cross the border from Russia to Tehran to get to Eretz Israel from there, but unfortunately, we were unable to do so. Only after a long period of turmoil and suffering we finally arrived in Israel in 1949 when we were already a family with two daughters. They were born, by the way, on historical dates: one during the battle of Stalingrad and the beginning of the turning point of the war and the other on an even more important date, the day of the Declaration of Independence of the state of Israel on May 14, 1948.

Today, sitting in Haifa with my family, I rejoice in being fortunate to fulfill my youth dream.

Hebrew course - Narajow

Translator Notes:

1. "Pe'ulot" in Hebrew.

2. Shekels were bought as the memberships in the Zionist Movement.

[Page 437]

To Narajow's Character and Remembrance

Fridka Zlatkes-Rozenblat

Translated by Ruth Yoseffa Erez

Edited by Moshe Kutten and Jane S. Gabin

With excitement and sacred awe overcoming me I write a few anecdotes to describe the character and memory of my hometown, Narajow. I consider writing those memories down a humble contribution to this literary monument, whose purpose is to commemorate the memory of the Narajow community whose people were murdered in the Holocaust.

For different reasons, some of which are easily understood, it is not an easy task to put on paper, our town's life, even if just a small part of it. Things seem vague, absorbed with the vapors of forgetfulness. Only a few of the Narajow people survived, and there were no other sources from which one could get information or refresh the memory.

Little Narajow was a neighbor to the bigger city, Brzezany. Its population consisted of 4,000 people and was a peaceful combination of Jews, Poles, and Ukrainians. The people from these three origins lived together quietly and had lively commercial connections. The town was situated next to beautiful mountains and was surrounded by dense forests and fertile fields. Even now, many years after I left it for Eretz Israel, I remember very well how it looked. The memory of each stone, path, and house is inscribed in my remembrance forever.

It seems that the memory of the place where a person was born and which he left are most dear to him cannot be erased. These memories are stronger even than the teeth of time.

To me, the town had its own character even though Narajow was like thousands of other small towns, scattered around the vast open spaces of Poland and Russia. It wasn't a rich town, but it had a proud spirit. Her sons did not submerge in wealth but were attracted to knowledgeable matters. Only a few could afford to attend high school, but the majority, concentrated on self-learning to broaden their horizons.

That was the background to the prosperity of the different Zionist youth movements. The first was "HaShomer Hatzair," which many local youth joined. From this movement came the first Narajow'ers to make *Aliyah* to Eretz Israel, among which were Yoel Marcus and Berla Halperin. The last one left was in 1935 for Spain to fight in foreign fields, and that's where he found his death.

My Zionist activity started while I was still young when I started the "Betar" group in Narajow, which most of the youth joined. Some of those who joined came even from "HaMizrachi" and brought their library with them, saying that it belonged to them since they were the ones who brought it to "HaMizrachi" in the first place.

One morning, I remember this incident vividly, when the doors were opened to our "Betar" center, the person in charge was shocked to see the place was in complete chaos and the library disappeared. But worst of all was that the picture of the head of the "Betar" movement, Ze'ev Jabotinsky, was torn and thrown to the floor.

The guy came running to me, astounded, and in his mouth, there was one word: "Pogrom!" It took me a few minutes to get the story of what happened from him. I was badly hurt as well. I felt that this was something that I could not let go of in silence. I ran to the police and told them what happened. After a short investigation, the police arrested two "HaMizrachi" members.

[Page 438]

This story brings to mind my grandfather Israel (z"l), who was one of the most wonderful characters in our town. My son carries his name. Despite his older age, he was surprisingly involved in political life and was interested in what was happening in the world specifically what was going on with the Zionist movement.

Every morning, when he came to the *Kloiz* to pray, there were already youngsters there who made sure he was updated on everything in the political arena. He wanted to know especially the number of certificates[1] that were about to be approved, and who was waiting in line to make *Aliyah*.

And so, my grandfather Israel, whom I loved dearly, came to our house yelling "What have you done to me? You put Jewish boys in jail!" He pointed an accusing finger at me: "My eyes cannot stand this; we must release them immediately!" Of course, I was influenced by my grandfather's words, and I went to the police and asked to release them.

Understandably it wasn't so simple, but finally, we found a compromise and it all ended well.

There were a few other wonderful characters in Narajow. I remember, for example, Rabbi Grosswax who was a great scholar, with a liberal way of looking at things and served as a member of the world executive of the international "HaMizrachi" movement. I remember the Rabbi when the "Betar" movement had a regional conference in Narajow and how it ended with our beautiful march where we were greeted by the Rabbi, which served as a great attraction to all Narajow Jews.

However, the youth social life was not limited to the Zionist youth movements. There were also some more fun and romantic aspects, and to describe them Narajow's post office must be mentioned. This was the central gathering place for the entire town's youth.

How can I forget the long hours that I spent waiting next to this post office, not only for a letter that I yearned for but also to meet someone, to talk and to gossip, to set a date? This institution was almost part of us. Who can count the number of couples that originated next to it? Who can forget the pleasant recollections that go together with its memory? Narajow's post office.

On May 3rd, 1939 I made *Aliyah* to Eretz Israel and never saw my hometown again. I came to Israel as an enthusiastic pioneer, and it comes as no surprise that after a few days, I was part of the proud group of construction workers, who while singing both outwardly and inwardly, were building Tel Aviv. Back then, everyone was proud to belong to the construction workers group, the social elite of the soon-to-be state of Israel.

As far as I remember, representatives from all the youth movements in Narajow made *Aliyah* and had families in Israel.

"Betar" training group in Narajow - 1933

Translator Note:

1. Immigration certificates to Palestine.

[Page 439]

My Village Narajow

Aryeh Goldschlag

Translated by Ben Gilad

Edited by Moshe Kutten and Jane S. Gabin

Three wagons could pass through the big gate to our house and park overnight on their way to Brzezany, for the market day. Our village's whole existence was based on its being "on the road to Brzezany," and like any village located "on the road to," how would its Jews make their living? They opened pubs for the gentiles, offered a little beer, a bit of straw for the horses, and if the gentile so wished, a place to spend the night.

And the gentile? A gentile! At times drunk, at times arriving at midnight, knocking on the gate, and but for me, the boy, there were a widow and her three daughters at home; and my heart would shudder in fear.

Three such pubs were in Narajow, and all three were a thorn in our Mayor's side. More than the taxes he levied and the fear we felt of him (after all, we did open the pub on Sundays even though it was forbidden - but if not on Sunday, then when?!), he was constantly conspiring against us in every possible way. One day he decided to build a park where the wagons were parked so as to keep the drivers away from the Jews. That "park" which was never completed, turned into a puddle in winter and into perennial mud the rest of the year.

It was hard to make a good living in Narajow. It was a poor community that knew better days. The debts owed by the gentiles to my grandfather and his contemporaries were greatly diminished after World War I, and a big debt could be repaid with a single hen, a small pile of wheat, for pennies on the dollar. The village Jews lost everything; they made their livelihood by buying a duck, whose gentile owner they convinced was dying, and selling it for a slim margin over what they paid for it; How could they afford to pay for Jewish community institutions and the Jewish judge, *Dayyan*, my grandfather? Nevertheless, in times of trouble, their poverty notwithstanding, the Jews would stick by one another. I remember my father paying the milkman to give milk twice daily to an epileptic kid; On the days the leaven (*hametz*) was sold, just before Passover, they found an excuse to give the *Dayyan* a few pennies on which he survived until the next Passover or until there was an argument between Jews to settle or a dish bowl to pronounce kosher or not. I remember M. H who helped my widowed mother to decipher the account books left by my banker father. She knew nothing about finances, and the debts owed her by the gentiles; I remember the effort to feed the kids who had no families in the village. In times of trouble, the Jews stuck by one another.

A meeting place in the village was the Post Office. The postman himself – a drunken gentile - did not deliver letters to their addresses. The village people were forced to come to the Post office to collect them. Thus, the Post office became a default "community center" to which we would arrive an hour before the letters' delivery time and leave an hour later, and on the way announce to John Doe that he had a letter, and everyone in the village making sure he knew about it, so that he could run to the Post Office to collect it.

Another meeting place was the youth movements' houses: *Hashomer Hatzair, Tzionim Klaylim, Beitar,*

[Page 440]

and *Hapoel Hamizrachi*. There was little for the young people in the village to do. The young rabbi tried to introduce a few practical occupations knowing that after graduation from elementary school, most youths would turn to trade or involuntary unemployment, so he ordered looms from Kozowa to teach the youngsters spinning and weaving. The young people, however, turned to the more interesting challenges posed by the youth movements. There they learned Zionism. In my youth movement, *Hashomer Hatzair*, they learned socialism too, and social Zionism: a bit of Borochov, and a bit about Berl Katznelson, all preparing them toward *Alyia*. There they sang songs, played volleyball, and met girls; there they spent the best years of their lives. There lies my youth.

My memories have no chronological order, and no logical sequence. Now my mind's eye sees the teacher from the *Heder* (religious elementary school), to which we would walk at night carrying lamps carved with pumpkins and singing a song to ward off the darkness- born fear:

Hop hop, a gitte nacht	Good night, good night
Heyv meer on tzi nyen benacht	We are starting our march tonight
Ot azoy nisht azoy	Yes and no, yes and no / it does not matter
Ki leolam hasdo	Forever His mercy

…And the teacher, who would stretch a mischievous kid on the bench for flogging, but would spare me, an orphan, the only child of his widowed mother.

…Or the good smell of the cherry trees in the morning, their cherries large and juicy, none like them among all the fruits; you could eat them to no end…

…Or the vegetable garden by the house, where Mother would grow onion and red radishes, a bit of parsley to spice up the bread, to the benefit of us and the neighbors…

…Or the harsh winter days, when the M family would drive its wagon carrying a pile of slaughtered geese bought from the gentiles or even from the Jews who bought them from the gentiles, onward to Lvov. One night, one day, and one more night the wagon would travel, no matter the weather.

…Or the bridge in the village, on the way to the house of the youth movement, where the hooligans gathered, and the anxiety nagging inside: would they bother me? Beat me up? Let me pass in peace?

…And the river in the summer, and the wagon drivers leaving each day to Brzezany, same drivers that later would deliver potato latkes from mother to me, a student in Lvov.

And then, suddenly, one day in 1939, it all ceased to be.

[Page 441]

The author Moyshe Nadir

Pseudonym of Isaac (Itzik) Reiss (Rayz)

Bar-Dawid Moshe

Translated by Ruth Yoseffa Erez

Moshe (Moyshe) Nadir was born on 1885 in Narajow. His father came from Zloczow and taught German for one of the estate owners.

Up to the age of 12, Nadir studied Bible and Talmud in the Cheder[1] and his father taught him German and German literature. In 1898 he immigrated with his family to New York. He went to school until he was 16 and later worked in different jobs.

Nadir cherished the Yiddish language, without knowing that there is an extensive Yiddish literature, he aspired to display the significance of the Yiddish language. He lived in a gentile neighborhood, and when he found out there was a Yiddish newspaper he sent on 1902 some not so good poems, some prose and a few pretty good articles to the "Teglikhn Herold" (Daily Herald), since then he started publishing in various Yiddish newspapers and periodicals under his full name Isaac Reiss and under many other pseudonyms. He used to publish in the "Zukunft," "Neue Zeit," "Da Yidishe Wochenblatt," "Di Bokh," "Der Yiddisher Kemper," "Das neue Land" and more. He published short stories, humoresque poems and essays. He worked for a long time in the "Yiddisher Kundes," the humor magazine. A lot of his works, which were published in the press, were never published in any book. On 1915, a booklet was published with some strange and erotic poems, named "Vilde Royzn" under the pseudonym "Moshe Nadir". The book caused a lot of tumult among readers and writers alike (today this booklet cannot be found).

As he drew closer to the group of young writers, such as K. Tefer, Zisha Landau and others, his writing style changed.

Together with his friend Moyshe-Leyb Halpern, he edited the anthology "Fun Mentsh Tsu Mentsh," later he started writing his philosophical lyrical miniatures for "Tog" newspaper, and built his reputation as a great Yiddish writer. He also wrote articles and essays on current events, and reviews about books, theater and plays. Nadir wrote a few plays and some skits that were performed in the artistic Maurice Schwartz

Theater and on the marionettes stage of Zuni Maud and Cutler (Kotler) such as the plays "Kloyshterberg," "Sukses," "The last Jew," "The tragedy of nothing," "Hadishu" and "The Prophet Elijah" and the skits: "little people," "the crazy ones" and poems about life in the city and in the Shtetl.

He translated books by great writers such as Mark twain, Tolstoy, Anatole France, Kipling and others and he wrote in English as well, mostly essays. He used to say: "I am not writing in English because I want to, rather I write in English when I have nothing special to say, when I have something that comes from the heart I write in Yiddish. I think in Yiddish, it writes itself." On 1926, Nadir visited Europe; he was in Paris, Warsaw, Vilna and soviet Russia. He was greeted with enthusiasm everywhere, both by the educated and by the simple people.

Moshe Nadir was a special phenomenon in the Yiddish literature, one of the greatest most unique and creative writers in it. He had his own style. For many years he tried different formulas and types of literature, he wrote essays, humoresques, satire, poems, plays, children's songs and stories, and in all of these he expressed artistic individualism that was unknown in the world's literature.

He usually wrote about subjects taken from the life in the US, but his birth town Narajow, came along with him everywhere in his work, like a little loyal dog. A substantial part of his work is given to his warm peaceful home on the other side of the ocean, where he came from. In this matter he proves to have deep lyricism when his descriptions of the characters, events and scenery are full of beauty, without his usual cynicism. It's the deep warm sensitivity that he brought from the Galician town of Narajow.

Some of his writings were published in six books, and many are scattered in different periodicals around the world. His work was translated into many languages, German, French, Russian, Polish and more. He died in New York on 1943.

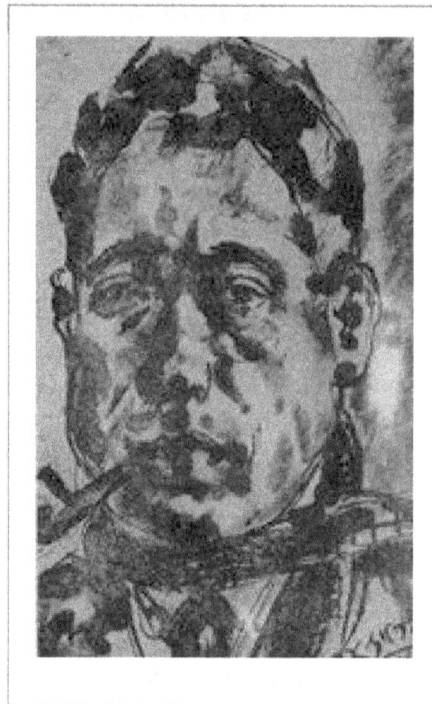

Moshe Nadir

Translator Notes:

1. Cheder was a traditional elementary school teaching the basics of Judaism and the Hebrew language, the lessons took place in the house of the teacher, known as a Melamed.

[Page 442]

Narayiv

Moyshe Nadir

Translated by Gloria Berkenstat Freund

Edited by Jane S. Gabin

I am Narayiv wherever I am,
Narayiv I am everywhere and eternally.
What does it matter to a person that the ground is dusty
What does it matter to the jug, which wine?

I have tried the east and the north, too,
In the south and in the west dwells my wind.
Who sees more than one who is blind
And drunk, who longs more than I?

Grief bleaches the night that it must become day.
The day – it grows dark toward the night.
I am Narayiv – in the final instance - though in pain.
Days: the last ones chased the first ones.

Migratory birds know you! Their lighter wings
Unlike those of a scavenger that hangs in the air.
I listen: something resounds, calls –
The Hand of God dips its black seal.

[Page 443]

Homeland, My Homeland

Moyshe Nadir

Translated by Gloria Berkenstat Freund

Edited by Jane S. Gabin

Homeland, you, my homeland, you have bound me
To you with ropes of love that never die,
I bless the light that you have lit in me,
I kiss the signs of your fine steps.

The seven silver-golden thrones of your week,
The thirty silvers of your golden month –
They ring and they rustle in my childlike heart
Like the curtain bells on the Torah ark.

I remember the diamond pillar of your bright dust
Your stems of hops, golden pear, damson plum
I remember the oak trees of your steadfast beliefs
The girls – like the matriarchs: Sarah, Rachel,
Rebecca.

Deep, cold wells, speckled sheep and cattle
Crescents of blossom branches – a golden bean,
The children scatter from the *khederim*[1] at noon,
The pig lies down slowly in the mud.

The morning – wet roses flushed and happy
The twilight – clean *talis*[2]. with a flaming crown
Your doves – aunts rich and thick,
The entire *shtetl* makes use of the evil eye.

Your Viennese turnpike goes in the distance
Through dogs and ears of corn; through trembling and
through rusting
And what your voice utters – the streams echo,
A village wedding from afar.

I see clearly and precisely through a tearful fog
My home – the green *shtetl*[3]. near the village;
My heart beats on the skins of the wedding drums,
I place on my shoulder the accusations of the years.

As if in a Roman toga, and my cape
I go facing you, Narayiv's *kloys*[4]. lantern,
I have searched, searched for you, I cannot find you.
In youth, you were my home, you are no longer here.

Oh, homeland, my homeland, you bound me
To you with ropes of fire, of satin and of silk.
Red wounds flame on oceans of rye –
And I climb up at the corner of heaven and of time.

Translator Notes:

1. *Khederim* – religious primary schools

2. *Talis* – prayer shawl

3. *Shtetl* – town

4. *Kloyz* – small one-room synagogue

[Page 444]

Narajow's Rabbis

Rabbi Meir Wonder

Translated by Ruth Yoseffa Erez

Rabbi Mordechai Pesches

Came from Russia to Galicia and was accepted as Narajow's rabbi. Of a distinguished lineage of Tzadikim (righteous men) and scholars all the way to Rabbi Yochanan the shoemaker and King David. The son of Rabbi Shmuel Zenvil, Zawalow's Rabbi who was also the father of Rabbi Yehuda Zvi Brandwein, the founder of the Stratyn Hassidism. More about him can be found in the book " Me'orey Galicia" Part 1 page 610.

Rabbi Yaakov Frenkel-Teomim

The son of Rabbi Yehoshua Heshel (Heschel) from Komarno who was in turn the oldest son of Rabbi Baruch, Chief of the Court of Lipniki, the author of the book "Baruch Ta'am." From around 1840, he served as Narajow's Rabbi, which was for him a springboard to positions in other communities: Miechow and Xions (Książ Wielkopolski) in Poland and Przeworsk and Cieszanów in Galicia. In his last position he served for 13 years, until he died in 1892.

Rabbi Yehoshua Heshel Frenkel-Teomim

The son of Rabbi Yaakov and his substitute in Narajow for around 10 years. He married Beile, the daughter of Elazar Horowitz Chief of the Court of Marijampole and Rohatyn. The son of Rabbi Meshulam Yissachar, Chief of the Court of Stanislawow. In 1878 he was called from Narajow to the Rabbinate of Lubaczow, he died there on 1894.

Rabbi Shraga Feivel Rohatyn

He was Narajow's Rabbi in the five years between 1878 and 1883. He then moved to Zloczow and was the Rabbi there by turns until he died on 15 of the month of Adar, 1910. He was an out of the ordinary and brilliant figure originating from a wealthy family in Lwow. With all his talents he was very successful in both Torah and science studies, and by himself graduated the Gymnasium and the University. He was a contractor and won the bid for building army barracks. He was discussing the Torah with the generation's geniuses and wrote a Halacha (Jewish Law) book. He promoted Zionism and the Hebrew language. There is a lot written about him in the Zloczow congregation book.

Rabbi Dov Berish Sim

His being very famous as a teacher, made Narajow's reputation rise up. He had a rare memory. Once when he travelled to Brody to visit Rabbi Itzhak Chayut, he heard 18 lengthy, in-depth studies from him. On his way back he visited the Maharasham[1] Rabbi in Brzezany and repeated all of them one by one to him. Later the Maharasham Rabbi said to Rabbi Yechiel Michel Lyter that he was impressed by the sharpness of the Brody Rabbi and by the memory of the Narajow Rabbi. After 20 years in town he fled to Budapest and there he died in the middle of WWI. His sons were not fitting to carry on the position after him and so his son in law was chosen as his successor.

Rabbi Zvi Yehoshua Grosswax

Son in law of Rabbi Dov Berish and his substitute between the two world wars. Was born on 1900 and before he turned 40 was offered the rabbinical chair in Zloczow. Was active in HaMizrachi movement and was a go-getter for religious institutes in his community. The Nazis cut off his life wick. His photo and life story can be found in the book " Me'orey Galicia" Part A, pages 741-742.

Narajow's synagogue

Translator Note:

1. According to Wikipedia, Rabbi Sholom Mordechai Schwadron of Brzezany, was known by his acronym Maharsham (translator)

[Page 446]

About the Rabbinate affair in Narajow

Israel Ne'eman

Translated by Ruth Yoseffa Erez

Narajow's Rabbi, Rabbi Dov Berish Sim, fled to Hungary with the wake of WWI. Before he left he engaged his young daughter, Feigale, to a young studious prodigy from Brzezany who was almost "Bar Mitzva," named Hershale Grosswax. The dowry that was promised to the youngster was the "rabbinical chair" of Narajow, as long as he persists with his studies and obtains rabbinical ordination.

When the town stayed with no rabbi, the community committee chose two Dayanim (rabbinical judges) from Narajow, both were very talented and excelled since they were young, and both were ordained as rabbis: Rabbi Eliezer (Leizer) Milshtock and Rabbi R' Yossef Neuman (Yosha Wawas, my grandfather *z"l*).

On 1921, Hershale Grosswax showed up after being ordained as a rabbi, and claimed the rabbinical chair that was promised to him by his father in law, Rabbi Sim. Like the rest of the Galician Jews who were deeply submerged in the fanatical Hasidism, the Narajow's community objected to appointing Rabbi Grosswax as the town's rabbi, for his leaning toward Zionism and his being an active member in "Hamizrachi."

The dispute that resulted caused arguments in the Torah study houses and in the *Kloiz*, even families squabbled over it. Only when the fear of army service was hovering above Hershale's head, did my grandfather, R' Yosha Neuman, tipped the scale and Rabbi Zvi Yehoshua Grosswax was accepted as Narajow's Rabbi.

The energetic young Rabbi was very active in promoting the Torah studies and the different charities as well as advancing youth employment. Soon even his most furious objectors reconciled with him and he was cherished by everyone.

The community committee continued to employ the two Dayanim who, together with the Rabbi, served as the rabbinical judges of the town. There were also three ritual slaughterers: R' Yehuda Zvi Mendelberg, R' Baruch Mendelberg and Rabbi Henik Shechter.

Why would such a small town need so many position holders? At that time, Narajow was doing the ritual Jewish slaughter not just for itself, it supplied Kosher meat to the Jewish community in Lwow. Lwow residents, Hassid and observant, knew that the meat with the seal of the Jewish slaughter house in Narajow was strictly Kosher.

Naturally, during the weekly fair on Thursdays, when horses, cattle, eggs and more were traded, disputes arose between the merchants, and they would turn to the rabbinical judges for arbitration and the Torah law.

The Rabbis and the town's elders served another role, a most important educational role. They taught the young ones who completed their studies in the Cheder[1] and those would continue their education by learning the six sdarim of the Mishnah and adjudicating for themselves.

The two Dayanim, Rabbi Leizer Milshtock and Rabbi Yosha Neuman (z"l) had the right to depart from this world before the Holocaust, before the destruction of the house of Israel in Poland.

Translator Note:

1. Cheder was a traditional elementary school teaching the basics of Judaism and the Hebrew language, the lessons took place in the house of the teacher, known as a Melamed.

[Page 447]

Rabbi Zvi Yehoshua Grosswax

Israel Ne'eman

Translated by Ben Gilad

Night after night the two sat close to each other studying a page of *Gemara* (part of the Talmud) by the lantern's light. The father, R' Alter, a trader who was a scholar, and his youngest boy, Hershale. And the boy who was both studios and gifted never tired, asking for more.

The mother, Hanna-Beyle of the Schlezinger-Neuman family of *Hassidim* (a pious religious sect), while basking in her son's successful studies, worried about his strength and urged him to go to bed to rest a bit before his father wakes him up for the morning lesson.

Every morning comes winter or summer his father would wake him up at 5am before dawn. The boy, sensing his parents went to sleep would go downstairs and move the clock's hands one hour ahead, making 5am a 4am. That way he would gain an extra hour of morning studies. That is how passionate he was about studying the Torah.

On one of his visits to his grandfather, the late R' Yosef Neuman, he realized that Hershale was doing well in his studies. He sent him to be tested with the genius R' Berish Dov Zon Abda"k[1] Narajow. The latter liked the boy and declared that he was ready to give him his daughter Feigale for a wife. The boy, not yet 13, refused, shamed to be a groom at his age, but the parents met and decided on the "terms" of the engagement, and the boy succumbed. (As he told me, he liked the idea of the journey from Brzezany to Narajow, about 9 mile of a ride in a wagon.)

Then WW1 started and the Jews escaped the towns in Galicia (Poland) to Czechoslovakia and Hungary. Hershale, who was 14-15 years old at the time (he was born in 1900) went all the way to Vienna, Austria's capital city. The years he spent in this big city left a strong impression on him. While continuing the religious studies he also began studying a secular curriculum, and when he retuned to Poland he passed the high school completion test (its equivalent test). He was welcome at the homes of the Rozyn admo"rs (title of a Hassidic Rabbis) and there he acquired his nationalistic education from the likes of Robert Shtriker and Anita Miller. When he returned to Brzezany in 1917 he became a full fledged Zionist. The time was that of Lord Balfour's Declaration – the national awakening time among the Jews.

Hershale looked for connections with the *Mizrachi* centre in Lwow, and opened a branch of *Mizrachi Youth* and *Mizrachi Pioneer* in town, and a place for agricultural training in the area.

Rabbi Grosswax

During the San Remo conference time (held at San Remo Italy at the end of WW1 to divide the control of former Ottoman areas), Hershale was the foremost organizer of the

Jewish youth. He arranged for parades and celebrations, leading young men like himself from the Hassidic courts who he swept with his Zionist enthusiasm, and demanding the local merchants closed their shops for the big national holiday for the Jews, the beginning of the redemption (*"geula"*).

In 1920 he married the Narajow Rabbi's daughter. The Rabbi died of Cholera during the war and none of his 4 sons was capable of inheriting his rabbinical chair. The people of the community regarded his son-in-law, the one who married his oldest daughter, to be the heir, but he, the son of the Rabbi from Burshtyn, migrated to the US and gave up his entitlement to his more talented brother-in-law. The majority of the Narajow Jews, however, objected to the "appointment" of Hershale, even though he was by then mature and ordained to rabbinical position by R' Shapiro, the head of the Rabbinical College and the Rabbi of Gliniany, who later became the head of Lublin Yeshiva. Narajow was a small town but its rabbinical appointment was held by highly gifted rabbis throughout the ages. It was a prestigious appointment and the young scholar, though talented, was also a Zionist. At that time in Galicia, few rabbis dared to voice national opinions in public, and here was this restless and energetic man, an organizer and member in the *Mizrachi* movement.

There was another aspect to the community's objection. At the time, two judges (*Dayanim*) served at the Narajow Jewish court, R' Leizer Milshtok and R' Yosef Neuman, my teacher and grandfather. Both were locals, clearly gifted scholars and were loved by the whole town and its environs. They properly fulfilled the rabbinical duties in the town, and the community leaders were worried the appointment of a young Rabbi as head of the Jewish court would be a sign of disrespect. So they postponed the appointment with vain excuses.

In the meantime, the young man was facing the "danger" of being drafted into the Polish army. The army service involved eating non kosher foods, violating the Sabbath, and so on, and it caused severe consternation to every religious Jewish household. Generally speaking, the young evaded the army service and moreover, an appointed Rabbi was exempted from the draft by law. And here was this perfect young man claiming the seat of the Rabbi.

My grandfather, who was a relative of Hershale's mother, could not watch her suffering, and convinced the majority of the community members that it was both a good deed and the young man were talented and perfectly suitable. And so it was decided and Hershale became R' Zvi Yehoshua Grosswax, head of the rabbinical court in Narajow. The minority did not accept this decision, and a conflict erupted as customary in those small towns on such occasions.

However, soon even his opponents were persuaded that no one was as talented and appropriate to the job. They became his devoted followers as they watched his dedication and youthful passion and implementation skill in raising the glory of Israel, spreading knowledge and changing the face of the community. He organized Torah studies, encouraged the youth to delve deeply into learning, and sustained a core circle of picked young men who held morning lectures in the Talmud.

We still remember his lectures and speeches to the *Mizrachi Youth* and *Bnei Akiva* branches. He was a great speaker, with a pleasing voice and a special sweetness in his prayers. He was a cantor in the big synagogue during High Holidays.

He was notable in the economic arena as well. He established a charity that operated on a budget of 40,000 Zahuv[2], a substantial amount for such a small town. The charity became a real leverage for all the town merchants and grocers.

He was active in the Jewish Colonization Association (a Baron de Hirsch's philanthropy organization) and was elected to the central committee in Lwow. With his influence, local Jewish farmers in the area received loans up to a 1000 Zahuv from a special trust. He built carpet weaving factories which employed 30 poor boys and girls, and many families made their living around these factories. Later, a training group from *Bnei Akiva* was also added to the workers, and upon making *Alyia*, its members joined the Abraham Group in Kfar Pines, Kfar Etzion (in Israel). R' Zvi Yehoshua participated in several Zionist congresses as a representative of the *Mizrachi Youth*.

He served as a candidate in the Zionist party to the Polish Sejm (parliament). Prior to the election to the Sejm, he made numerous trips to the towns in his area and campaigned for the Zionist party, especially since Dr. Sh. Federbush his friend headed the party in our district. It should be noted that all this activity was done against a vociferous argument and continuous struggle with the community leaders that were publicly supporting the government parties as this was the custom of Polish *hassidim* and especially the Belz *hassidic* dynasty (an infamous affair at that time).

One anecdote regarding his national pride is worth telling. The town's council used to levy mandatory service duties once a year, i.e., each resident was obliged to give a few days for working on road repair, carpet weaving, trench digging, etc. The Jews, of course, paid a ransom instead, and never actually did real work. The Rabbi succeeded in convincing a few youths not to evade the work so that they can prove to the town's gentiles that they were equal citizens with equal rights as well as equal duties.

One morning as the Rabbi was returning from the *Kloyz* (synagogue) he bumped into the police commander who was treating the Jewish workers badly. The Rabbi turned to him and asked: "Can you explain to me -- what's this work group to you? Are they your prisoners?" The question infuriated the police commander who was a young, proud and hot headed Pole and he retorted that he does not receive orders from the Rabbi and it's none of his business and he should stay out of it. The Rabbi did not budge and asked the commander to immediately cease his insults and when the commander ignored him the Rabbi called the district's head, who was respectful of the young Rabbi, and relayed the story to him. Moments later the young commander was called to the phone. The executive ordered him to immediately apologize to the Rabbi. Shamed and embarrassed, he did as told by his superior. The incident quickly gained wide publicity and even the gentiles in town treated the Rabbi with new respect.

His generosity was immense. He spent his money on the poor and used his meager salary to support charitable institutions.

He always aspired to serve in a bigger town, which will yield a bigger room for his boundless energy, but he always hesitated, reluctant to leave his small town and his beloved community.

A short time before the holocaust, he was a candidate for the rabbinical chair in the town of Zloczow.

In the huge storm that swept the Jewish communities in Poland during WW2, he died, R' Zvi Yehoshua Grosswax, together with his wife, his two daughters and his only son, Dov Berish, so named after his grandfather, the Rabbi from Narajow.

Bnei Akiva group in Narajow-Brzezany

Translator Notes:

1. Chief Justice, Jewish community court

2. Zahuv means golden which is the literal meaning of the word Zloty

[Page 450]

My happenings during the Nazi occupation

Chana Roten (Lushk)

Translated by Ruth Yoseffa Erez

When I was 14 years old, the Germans invaded our town. My family was one of the most affluent families in town. About two months later, the Germans, together with the local Militia, searched our house for so called hidden food. They didn't find food, but they filled two trucks with leather, textile and other valuables.

Everything that my parents worked for all those years was gone in an instant.

During the first year of the occupation, Jews had to pay ransom for each soul (contribution) as well as sweeping the streets, cleaning the offices and plowing the snow. In return we were beaten, as they wished.

When Yom Kippur approached on 1942, rumors spread that the Germans plan an "Aktion"[1] in town; I did not know the meaning of this word. My parents sent us - three children - to a Christian family, until things will quiet down. My parents hid in the basement.

The vicious rumors were true. The day after Yom Kippur the brutal German soldiers arrived from Brzezany and with the Ukrainians collaboration gathered the Jews who were not able to find a hideout and took them by trucks to Brzezany. From there to the death camp Belzec.

After about a month and a half, the town was declared "*Judenfrei*"[2]. We were ordered to leave and move to Brzezany. My mother and I with a few of our belongings left Narajow, leaving Dad and my two brothers at home. The evacuees from Narajow shared a big house in Brzezany, in which a few families shared each apartment. I remember vividly the second day in the new town; we were taken to plant trees. The soil was frozen and I wasn't able to dig. I had warts on my fingers from holding the hoe and I cried out of fear and pain, it was clear to me that if I don't finish my work, I'll have to stay there. Some people felt sorry for me and finished my work for me.

A month later another "Aktion" came upon us; it was on a Friday, the first day of Chanukah, 1942. I was still in bed when the Nazis broke into our apartment and took me and my mom outside. We were standing next to the Judenrat all that day. It was freezing. Towards the evening when hundreds of Jews were gathered, we were ordered to march in rows to the train.

They put us in cattle train cars, unbearably crowded. When the train began to move we all knew it was our last journey.

A few people had small tools hidden in their cloths. With great effort they were able to loosen one wooden plank. Despite the danger they started jumping out. Not everyone was lucky. More than one ended up falling under the train's wheels or getting shot by the Germans that were sitting on the train roof. My mom sat with a few neighbors in the corner of the train car and decided not to jump. She said she was tired of living this way. From where she was sitting she pleaded with me to jump, "Your life is still ahead of you" she said. I jumped and fell without a scratch on a snow pile. My mom was killed in Belzec and she is only 40 years old. I reached my father's house with the help of some adults that were miraculously saved as well.

My dad, my older brother and I left Narajow and made it again to Brzezany. My other brother stayed in Narajow with a few more Jews hoping to find a safer shelter there, despite the fact that Narajow was by that time "*Judenfrei.*" He really wanted to live and was afraid of the concentration camps, but the cruel fate wanted otherwise. On March of 1943 some Ukranians informed the Gestapo that there were still Jews in Narajow. It didn't take long for the Germans to come.

They were all gathered in the Herz home, killed and their bodies were thrown to the basement. My brother tried to run away but the murderers' bullet reached him when he was in the middle of the street and he is only 18.

Three weeks later there was another "Aktion" in Brzezany. My older brother who was 20 was captured. The next day it seemed like the "Aktion" was over. We went out of the bunkers and my dad went to the Judenrat hoping to save my brother. When he left, I knew I will never see him again. I asked him not to leave but he said "you can not understand me, in such a short time I lost both my sons" and he left.

A few minutes later my dad was caught and was sent with other men who were able to work to the concentration camp of Kamionka close to Tarnopol. The elderly, the women and the young ones were killed in the Brzezany cemetery.

A few weeks later, my dad met my brother in Kamionka. Every now and then I was able to send them some necessities trough the Judenrat.

Narajow natives in Yaar HaKdoshim

One day, a childless Christian came to the Ghetto looking to adopt a girl. He liked me and I joined him. On the wagon outside of the Ghetto, I felt an urge to go back, knowing I wouldn't be able to send my Dad and my brother those things any more. Without saying a word, I jumped out of the wagon and returned to the ghetto. Everyone was yelling at me for missing an opportunity to be saved.

Around the holiday of Shavuoth on 1943, the last "Aktion" in Brzezany was performed and Brzezany was declared "*Judenfrei.*" They did not discover our bunker.

On Sunday a few people from our bunker went out, some to bake some pita bread because of the hunger and some to fetch some drinking water. One woman, who gave all her belongings to a Christian lady, was waiting outside for that lady to come and take her with her. This Christian woman saw her and informed the Gestapo about it. Immediately the house was surrounded and 13 people including myself were caught. Three Germans put us all in one room and gathered our valuables. While they were busy dividing the plunder, I tried to hide under the bed but they saw me. When we went downstairs, I tested my luck again and slipped through an open door, this time successfully! I went back to the bunker. The rest were murdered in the cemetery.

That night I left the bunker together with my aunt and her three children and we escaped to the forest. I spent 14 months in the forest, life there was very harsh. We ate watery soup once a day from vegetables we gathered at night from the fields. More than once I drank filthy water. In winter, the snow served as drinking water but the frost was difficult to handle. Months passed with out washing my body, the lice were eating me and the sores hurt.

At the end of July 1944 we were rescued by the Russian army. I was the only one left from my family and from the whole town there were around 25 survivors. The rest of y dear ones and my towns people were murdered in the sanctification of God's name ("Kiddush Hashem"), may their memory be blessed.

Translator Notes:

1. Term used for any non-military campaign to further Nazi ideals of race, but most often referred to the assembly and deportation of Jews to concentration or death camps

2. In German: free of Jews, a Nazi term to designate an area free of Jewish presence during The Holocaust

[Page 452]

The Avenging Jew – Yankel (Yankale) Fenger

Rina Zlatkes (Rozenblat)

Translated by Ruth Yoseffa Erez

I would like to tell a story, in a few words, to try and contribute something to the commemoration of this figure, one of the Holocaust heroes. Yankel Fenger, who was known to all as Yanka'le was a Narajower, the son of Henya and Pinchas Fenger, from a village called Bile in the Peremyshlyany region,

18 year old Yankel turned during the world war into a hero surrounded with a radiating halo. The mention of his name alone would make the Jewish hating Ukrainians' hearts shiver with fear. Yankel Fenger didn't belong to any Partisan or military organization but he belonged to everyone.

Operating as a "lonely wolf," Yankel was supplying food to children, but his main attention was given to avenge the actions of those Ukrainians who collaborated with the Germans and murdered Jews.

With time, Yankel became the symbol for the "Avenging Jew" in the area. He was a mysterious figure who took revenge of the Goyim[1] for every act of hurting Jews. He had a pattern for his actions, every night he would get out to look for food (which in the partisan's language was called "skokim") in daring ways. He would bring back his "catch" in a sack on his back, or using a farmer's wagon.

Yankel Fenger, who had the complexion of a Ukrainian, would leave to his nightly operations wearing Ukrainian Police uniform and carrying a bag full of hand grenades. He acted mostly in the village of Narajow where the Ukrainians handed over to the Gestapo the Jews they helped hide in their homes, in return for money.

With these Ukrainians, Yankel was going to settle the blood account. In the middle of the night he would knock on the door of a collaborator. He would present himself as a Ukrainian underground member and say that he heard Jews were hiding in this house. He explained that the Jews hated the Ukrainian people and that if it's true, the owners will be punished.

If the farmer started justifying himself saying that he already handed over the Jews that he hid to the Gestapo – Yankel would reveal his real identity and kill him on the spot, him and his wife. He didn't harm the kids.

After he was done he would leave a note saying: "Here was Yankel Fenger, who killed the house owner and his wife in revenge for handing over Jews to the Nazis"

The stories about the avenging Jew passed from ear to mouth and the Ukrainian farmers dreaded him.

When Narajow was taken over by the Red Army, Yaakov Fenger volunteered to the Soviet militia, whose job was to destroy the Ukrainian underground. Yankel Fenger excelled in this mission and revealed many of the hiding places of the "Bendrovtzim." In one of those actions, he was killed.

Young Yankel Fenger became a legend while he was still alive. Even the Soviets considered him a hero and built a monument to commemorate him in Narajow.

I would like to note that I got the information about Yankel Fenger from Mr. Yunes who heads the Yiddish programming department in "Israel broadcasting Authority" during a meeting in Holy Land Hotel in Jerusalem with Yankel's step father who was visiting Israel from Montreal Canada.

Translator Note:

    1.   Gentiles

[Page 454]

Fragments from My Life Under the German Occupation

Ben Noyman and Chana Kvodi

Translated by Gloria Berkenstat Freund

Edited by Jane S. Gabin

In June 1942, when the Germans began to make "order" in Narayiv, their first mission was to harm the Jewish population, to break them morally, and force them into performing dirty and difficult labor, such as breaking stones on the roads, serving the *S.S.* men and various slavish work.

In order to make the [Germans'] work easier, the Germans organized people from the city who worked with lower elements and promised them that with this behavior they would save their lives. They created an *antinomium* [a place that rejects laws and moral, religious, and social norms], where one would lead another to his death. And finally, they also fell as victims. Thus, they created a *Judenrat* [Jewish council] and Jewish policemen who worked with the Germans.

I want to relate several fragments about what I lived through during that time. Walking early in the morning (this was *Shabbos* [Sabbath]) to my heavy labor in the area of the police house, I saw one of the Jewish policemen (he was named Dovid) beating my father with his whip. I immediately ran to him and threw off the policeman with my entire strength and asked what had happened. I was told that the *Judenrat* had given the order to take away the little bit of food from the people who had not gone to work on *Shabbos*. The food was about one baked good made of sugar beets that one could barely eat. As there was great hunger, these were also delicacies. My father had not permitted the food to be taken away from three girls and, therefore, he had been beaten.

I was assigned to work with the police, carrying out difficult tasks. At the time, German squads would come and surround the *shtetl* [town] and take Jews to be murdered. In such situations, I developed an instinct not to run in the streets, but to hide wherever possible close to where I was.

During one such *aktsia* [action, usually a deportation], I went up to the attic of the police station. A Ukrainian policeman (by chance, my neighbor) saw me there and wanted to remove me. A servant girl with the police (not a Jew) began to cry and did not let him take me out. Sitting in the attic, I heard the shouting and crying of the Jews who had been caught and led to their death. Thus

[Page 455]

a few days later, standing near the city council house, a Ukrainian acquaintance passed by. He warned me that I should escape. I immediately heard shooting and I ran into the forest. I found many of those from the city who worked there near the house of the forest watchman. I warned that there was a shooting and we began to escape, but the Ukrainian police surrounded us. There was an old Jew named Wajdman among us. He tried to escape, but the Ukrainians immediately pulled him back forcefully into the ranks. We were led under guard. I walked near a young man, Dovid Halpern. Not thinking a great deal, I grabbed him by the hand and dragged him from the ranks and we escaped together. We hid in straw, in a stall. The Ukrainians searched for us but to our good fortune, they did not find us. The Ukrainians told me that all of the people were taken to the camps and none of them returned.

And sometime later, going to work, we approached the school director, Calniuk, and he told me that I should quickly escape because the police commander wanted to give me to the Germans. Running, I saw they were taking out the woman, Ribtsia Glanc, and her daughter, Lurtsia. They were crying and screaming and begged the Germans to let them go. However, he [who?] only shouted that they should take off their clothes. When I was further away, I heard shooting and then a silence…

At that moment I decided I could no longer remain in the *shtetl*. I escaped to the forest at night and began wandering from one place to another. Once I encountered Sura Hochberg and her children and her brother, Hersh Luszak, and his son. We stayed in a bunker together. In difficult and almost inhuman conditions; we tried to live through the hard times.

The rifle butts were used to hit the heads of the victims in order to save bullets. People went out at night to look for something to eat. There were a few bunkers in the forest and approximately 70 Jews from Narayiv were hidden there. One beautiful day, the Ukrainians ended the bunkers. They attacked and murdered everyone except the 14 people in our bunker. This happened approximately three months before the liberation.

[Page 456]

Suddenly, we heard a shooting. First, we thought that this was from a distance. However, as soon as it grew quiet, I went out of my bunker to see what had happened. Entering the forest, I met a small boy, Moshe Kihn (he was then 7-8 years old). Today, he is at the *kibbutz* Messilot [communal settlement] in Beit She'an. He was then walking around in the forest crying and led me to see what had happened. A terrible scene was revealed to me. Still today I cannot free myself from the horrible murder and what my eyes saw. Shattered heads of adults and children whose brains came out. The murderers probably used the rifle butts to hit the heads of the victims in order to save bullets. It was shown that the murderous bandits were *Banderowces* [members of the Bandera faction of the Ukrainian Insurgent Army], our school friends – Ukrainians.

My cousins, still children, were in one of the bunkers. One of them was Dovid Arya. On the same day, half an hour earlier, he had been with me in the bunker and I had sent him to watch over the children and here I saw him dead with his sister, Bela. The smallest of them, Shimkha, who was eight years old, was missing. I immediately ran to look for him. While searching, a Pole neared me, the son of Heinish, who along with his entire family had greatly helped the Jews in the forest all that time. He [the Pole] called me to him to the place where there was snow (this was in the month of March). My smallest cousin, Shimkhale, shot through his face as well as his stomach and lay wrapped in a sheet. Covered in blood, he moaned like a kitten, not with a human voice. The Pole told me that he had brought him here because they were afraid to have him in their house. As he knew that there were other Jews in the forest and that I was his cousin, he went in search of me so I could take the child to the bunker.

Obviously, I immediately lifted him and took him into our bunker. Those living with me noticed me and said: "Why did you bring a dead child?" But I wanted to hope that God would help in showing miracles as I believe until today. I washed the child and covered the wounds, which began to show healing, with green leaves. I also found a few bandages in the abandoned bunkers and wrapped the wounded child in them. Slowly, the wounds began to heal. Every day was better and thus he survived. Today, he lives in Israel.

We had one interesting experience with a young man, Chaim Szuerer, from Narayiv, who was with us in the forest and today lives at *Kibbutz* Gazit in Israel.

This young man probably received a shock when he saw that his sister was dead and therefore became blind in both

[Page 457]

eyes. I helped him as much as I could. When we would go out to look for food, he would take a stick and hold on to me and go with me. Once walking with me, he said that he had dreamed of the Belzer Rebbe and he [the rebbe] had told him that he would be able to see in the morning. Chaim was very religious because during the Soviet times, he had studied with the Hasidim of the Belzer Rebbe who had settled in Narayiv at that time. Hearing his dream, I looked at him with pity and did not believe such a thing could happen. Two days later, in the middle of the night, he came running with joy and he said he could see again. To tell the truth, I accepted this as a great miracle; during the most difficult situations, a person wants to believe in miracles and interpret dreams.

Thus, we sat in the bunker and hoped. A short time after the great murder, we heard heavy fire in the area. We learned, more or less, from the Polish man that the front was approaching. At that time, we did not even leave the bunker to search for food. Suddenly, it became quiet. We did not know how to interpret the quiet. We were afraid to leave the bunker. We sat like this for a few days not knowing that the Germans were already far from us.

Yet, one day we decided to go outside and then learned that we were already free people. Now a new problem began: where to go?

We went to our *shtetl*, Narayiv. There, a fear of seeing what remained fell on us. We did not see a living soul, except the Russian soldiers. We went with them to Brzeżany. There we met a few Jews who had survived. We remained in Brzeżany for a short time and again wandered.

Of the 70 people from Narayiv who were hidden in the forest, alas, 14 remained and I was among them. Today, I live in America. Here, there are two sisters from Narayiv, Neshia, and Yehudus Lev, and our hope is to eventually settle in Israel.

[Pages 458-467]

Narajow's Martyrs List

Last name	First name	Maiden name	Gender	Father's first name	Mother's first name	Spouse's first name	Remarks	Page
	Feiga							467
	Gershon		Male			Zlata	Profession: Religious Teacher	467
	Khava		Female					467
	Lea		Female					467
	Roza		Female				Profession: Sexton	460
	Tzadikil		Male				Profession: Religious Teacher	467
			Male	Bertzi	Hentzia			462
			Male	Bertzi	Hentzia			462
			Male					462
	Zlata		Female			Gershon		467
ADLER	Avraham		Male	Yehuda	Bela			459
ADLER	Bela	PIZEM	Female			Yehuda		459
ADLER	Frida		Female					459
ADLER	Gusta			Yehuda	Bela			459
ADLER	Lea		Female	Yehuda	Bela			459
ADLER	Mikhael		Male			Sara		459

ADLER	Sara	ZLATKES	Female		Mikhael			459
ADLER	Yehuda		Male			Bela		459
AKERMAN	Buzio							459
AKERMAN	Fishel		Male	Motel	Perel			459
AKERMAN	Motl		Male			Perel		459
AKERMAN	Perel	SHAPIRA	Female			Motel		459
AKERMAN			Male					459
AKERMAN	Yekhezkel		Male	Motel	Perel			459
ANTZMAN	Avraham		Male	Nakhum		Beile		459
ANTZMAN	Beila	SHRAGA	Female			Avraham		459
ANTZMAN	David		Male	Avraham	Beile			459
ANTZMAN	Eidel		Female	Avraham	Beile			459
ANTZMAN	Nakhum		Male	Avraham	Beila			459
ANTZMAN	Shmiya		Male					459
ANTZMAN			Male			Shamia		459
BERGER	Henia	VEIS	Female			Yehuda		459
BERGER	Khana		Female	Yehuda	Henia			459
BERGER	Yehuda		Male			Henia		459
BIRNBOIM	Zlata	LEIB	Female					459
BLEIBERG	Gusta							459
BOGNER	Bushtze		Female			David		459
BOGNER	Bushtze			Leon	Rivka			459
BOGNER	David		Male			Bushche		459
BOGNER	Ester		Female				From Wierzbow	468

BOGNER	Leon		Male			Rivka		459
BOGNER	Rivka	GLAZER	Female			Leon		459
BOGNER			Male			Ester Gitel	From Wierzbow	468
BOIM	Lova	HOKHBERG	Female			Meir		459
BOIM	Meir		Male			Lova		459
BREITER	Lea	GABEL	Female			Moshe	From Wierzbow. In Narajow during the war	459
BREITER	Mania		Female			Yosef	From Wierzbow. In Narajow during the war	459
BREITER	Miriam		Female	Moshe	Lea		From Wierzbow. In Narajow during the war	459
BREITER	Moshe		Male			Lea	From Wierzbow. In Narajow during the war	459
BREITER	Yosef		Male	Moshe	Lea		From Wierzbow. In Narajow during the war	459
BREITER	Yosef		Male			Mania	From Wierzbow. In Narajow during the war	459
BUMZE	Matl						From Wierzbow	468
BUMZE	Meir		Male				From Wierzbow	468
BUMZE	Pesia		Female				From Wierzbow	468
BUMZE	Rivka		Female				From Wierzbow	468
BUMZE			Male			Meir	From Wierzbow	468
BUMZE			Male		Pesia		From Wierzbow	468
DELMAN	Eliezer		Male			Sheinel		460
DELMAN	Golda		Female	Eliezer	Sheinel			460
DELMAN	Sheindl	OHRING	Female			Eliezer		460
DELMAN	Yehuda		Male	Eliezer	Sheinel			460
DRUKER	Shimon		Male					460

DRUKER			Male			Yehuda		460
DRUKER			Male			Shimon		460
DRUKER	Yehuda		Male					460
EHRE	Avraham		Male	Natan	Gusta			464
EHRE	Etel	KIHN	Female			Moshe		464
EHRE	Gusta	KAHANA	Female			Natan		464
EHRE	Hentzi			Natan	Gusta			464
EHRE	Lea		Female	Moshe	Etel			464
EHRE	Mikhael		Male	Natan	Gusta			464
EHRE	Mikhael		Male	Moshe	Etel			464
EHRE	Moshe		Male			Etel		464
EHRE	Natan		Male			Gusta		464
EHRE	Rivka		Female	Moshe	Etel			464
EHRE	Rozia	VEITZMAN	Female			Yehuda		464
EHRE	Yehuda		Male			Rozia		464
EHRE	Yeshayahu		Male	Moshe	Etel			464
EHRE	Yisrael		Male	Moshe	Etel			464
FALES	Khaim		Male			Batsheva		465
FALES	Miriam	SAMUELG	Female			Yisrael		465
FALES			Male			Khaim Yosef		465
FALES	Yisrael		Male			Miriam		465
FANGER	Pinkhas		Male					465
FEFER	Khaim		Male	Yosef	Tova			465
FEFER	Khaim		Male				From Wierzbow	468

FEFER	Tova	TURNER	Female			Yosef		465
FEFER	Tova	TURNER	Female			Yosef	From Wierzbow	468
FEFER	Yosef		Male			Tova		465
FEFER	Yosef		Male			Tova	From Wierzbow	468
FEIRSTEIN ROITER	Bela		Female			Moshe		465
FEIRSTEIN ROITER	Moshe		Male			Bela		465
FIERSTEIN	Avraham		Male	Levi	Feiga			465
FIERSTEIN	Dov		Male	Hersh				465
FIERSTEIN	Eli		Male	Levi	Feiga			465
FIERSTEIN	Etel			Hersh				465
FIERSTEIN	Feiga	FERSHING	Female			Levi Yitzkhak		465
FIERSTEIN	Hersh		Male					465
FIERSTEIN	Khava		Female					465
FIERSTEIN	Leon		Male					465
FIERSTEIN	Levi		Male			Feiga		465
FIERSTEIN	Serl			Levi	Feiga			465
FIERSTEIN	Tzvi		Male	Hersh				465
FIERSTEIN	Tzvi		Male	Levi	Feiga			465
FIERSTEIN	Yehudit		Female	Hersh				465
FIERSTEIN	Yoel		Male					465
FIKHMAN	Gitel							465
FINGER	K							465
FINGER	Yaakov		Male					465
FRUKHT	Shlomo		Male			Tova		465

FRUKHT	Tova	HERMELIN	Female			Shlomo		465
FRUKHT			Male			Moshe		465
FUKS	Breina		Female	Meir	Khana			465
FUKS	Khana		Female			Meir		465
FUKS	Leib		Male	Meir	Khana			465
FUKS	Mania		Female	Meir	Khana			465
FUKS	Meir		Male			Khana		465
FUKS	Yisrael		Male	Meir	Khana			465
GABEL	Aba		Male			Sosia	From Wierzbow. In Narajow during the war	459
GABEL	Kaniel		Male	Aba	Sosia		From Wierzbow. In Narajow during the war	459
GABEL	Khaia		Female	Aba	Sosia			459
GABEL	Khana		Female	Aba	Sosia		From Wierzbow. In Narajow during the war	459
GABEL	Shraga		Male	Aba	Sosia		From Wierzbow. In Narajow during the war	459
GABEL	Sosia		Female			Aba	From Wierzbow. In Narajow during the war	459
GABEL	Zeev		Male	Aba	Sosia		From Wierzbow. In Narajow during the war	459
GALINER	Aizik		Male					460
GALINER	Gitel		Female	Aizik				460
GALINER			Male			Aizik		460
GEBOT	Avraham		Male					460
GEBOT	Sara	HIRSHHORN	Female			Yitzkhak		460
GEBOT	Sara		Female					460
GEBOT	Shaya		Male					460

GEBOT			Male			Shaya Halm		460
GEBOT			Male			Avraham		460
GEBOT			Male	Avraham				460
GEBOT			Male	Avraham				460
GEBOT	Yitzkhak		Male			Sara		460
GELBER								460
GELBER			Male					460
GIMPEL	Breintzi	KASHUVI	Female					459
GIMPEL			Male			Breintzi		459
GLANTZ	Bunio			Leizer	Rivka			459
GLANTZ	Gita	KROIS	Female			Shmuel		459
GLANTZ	Leizer		Male			Rivka		459
GLANTZ	Lurke			Leizer	Rivka			459
GLANTZ	Moshe		Male	Shmuel	Gita			459
GLANTZ	Pepka			Shmuel	Gita			459
GLANTZ	Rafael		Male	Leizer	Rivka			459
GLANTZ	Rivka	GOLDSHTEIN	Female			Leizer		459
GLANTZ	Shmuel		Male			Gita		459
GLANTZ	Zusia		Male	Shmuel	Gita			459
GLAZER	Lea		Female	Yisrael	Tzirel			460
GLAZER	Miriam		Female	Yisrael	Tzirel			460
GLAZER	Rivka		Female	Yisrael	Tzirel			460
GLAZER	Sara		Female	Yisrael	Tzirel			460
GLAZER	Tzirel	MEIER	Female			Yisrael		460

GLAZER	Yehudit		Female	Yisrael	Tzirel			460
GLAZER	Yisrael		Male			Tzirel		460
GOLOMB	Leopold		Male			Pepi		459
GOLOMB	Pepi	HERMELIN	Female			Leopold		459
GOLOMB	Tzvi		Male			Gusta		459
GOTSHTEIN	Lea		Female					459
GOTSHTEIN	Shimon		Male					459
GROSVAKS	Dov		Male	Tzvi	Feiga			460
GROSVAKS	Feiga	HERMELIN	Female			Hertzel		460
GROSVAKS	Feiga		Female			Tzvi Yehoshua		460
GROSVAKS	Frida		Female	Hertzel	Feiga			460
GROSVAKS	Frida		Female	Tzvi	Feiga			460
GROSVAKS	Hertzel		Male			Feiga		460
GROSVAKS	Itzik		Male	Hertzel	Feiga			460
GROSVAKS	Tova		Female	Hertzel	Feiga			460
GROSVAKS	Tzvi		Male			Feiga		460
GROSVAKS	Yona		Male	Tzvi	Feiga			460
HABER	Azriel		Male			Breina		460
HABER	Breina		Female			Azriel		460
HABER	Dvora		Female		Yeita			460
HABER	Hertzel		Male	Azriel	Breina			460
HABER	Mikhael		Male					460
HABER	Shaul		Male	Azriel	Breina			460
HABER	Tzipa			Azriel	Breina			460

HABER			Male			Velvel		460
HABER			Male			Mikhael		460
HABER	Velvel		Male					460
HABER	Yita		Female					460
HAFT	Shlomo		Male					461
HAFT			Male			Shlomo		461
HAFT			Male	Shlomo				461
HAFT			Male	Shlomo				461
HALPERIN	Ester	MANDELBERG	Female			Yosef		461
HALPERIN	Ester		Female			Yerakhmiel		461
HALPERIN	Khaia		Female			Natan Khaim		461
HALPERIN	Natan		Male			Khaia		461
HALPERIN	Rivka		Female	Natan	Khaia			461
HALPERIN			Male	Natan	Khaia			461
HALPERIN	Yosef		Male			Ester Rivka		461
HAND	Dunia				Khana			461
HAND	Dvora		Female		Khana			461
HAND	Khana		Female					461
HANDVEIL	Ester		Female					461
HASELKORN	Barukh		Male			Lea		461
HASELKORN	Lea		Female			Barukh		461
HASELKORN	Shmuel		Male					461
HASELKORN			Male			Shmuel		461
HASELKORN			Male	Shmuel				461

HASELKORN			Male	Shmuel				461
HEILVEIL	Avraham		Male			Rakhel		460
HEILVEIL	Elka			Meir	Sara			460
HEILVEIL	Ester		Female			Hersh		460
HEILVEIL	Gedalia		Male			Reizl	From Stryhance	468
HEILVEIL	Hersh		Male			Ester		460
HEILVEIL	Hirsh		Male	Gedalia	Reizl		From Stryhance	468
HEILVEIL	Mania		Female			Yisrael		460
HEILVEIL	Mania		Female					460
HEILVEIL	Meir		Male			Sara		460
HEILVEIL	Rakhel		Female			Avraham		460
HEILVEIL	Reizl		Female			Gedalia	From Stryhance	468
HEILVEIL	Sara		Female			Meir		460
HEILVEIL	Sheindl		Female	Meir	Sara			460
HEILVEIL			Male	Meir	Sara			460
HEILVEIL	Yisrael		Male			Mania		460
HERMELIN	Frida		Female	Shlomo	Khaia			461
HERMELIN	Khaia	REIZNER	Female			Shlomo		461
HERMELIN	Khana		Female	Shlomo	Khaia			461
HERMELIN	Roza	EHRE	Female					461
HERMELIN	Shlomo		Male			Khaia		461
HERMELIN	Tzvi		Male	Shlomo	Khaia			461
HERMELIN -	Batia	NOIMAN	Female			Lipa		461
HERMELIN -	Bela			Lipa	Batia			461

HERMELIN -	David		Male	Lipa	Batia			461
HERMELIN -	Lea		Female	Lipa	Batia			461
HERMELIN -	Lipa		Male			Batia		461
HERMELIN -	Moshe		Male	Lipa	Batia			461
HERMELIN -	Natan		Male	Lipa	Batia			461
HERTZ	Brunia			Menakhem	Sara			461
HERTZ	Etia			Menakhem	Sara			461
HERTZ	Gusta	ADLER	Female			Yekhezkel		461
HERTZ	Menakhem		Male			Sara		461
HERTZ	Sara	MILSHTOK	Female			Menakhem Mendel		461
HERTZ			Male	Yekhezkel	Gusta			461
HERTZ	Yekhezkel		Male			Gusta		461
HERTZOG	Dvora		Female	Mikhla	Gitzia			461
HERTZOG	Gitzia	HALPERIN	Female			Mikhla		461
HERTZOG	Mikhla		Male			Gitzia		461
HERTZOG	Reiza			Mikhla	Gitzia			461
HERTZOG	Sara	HAND	Female			Todros		461
HERTZOG	Tova		Female	Mikhla	Gitzia			461
HERTZOG	Tudrus		Male			Sara		461
HILFER	Gitel		Female			Hersh		460
HILFER	Hersh		Male			Gitel		460
HILFER	Lea	PELTZ	Female			Yerakhmiel		460
HILFER	Leib		Male			Miriam		460
HILFER	Miriam	GLAZER	Female			Leib		460

HILFER	Naftali		Male			Rosia		460
HILFER	Rosia	HOKHBERG	Female			Naftali		460
HILFER	Shmuel		Male					460
HILFER	Simkha							460
HILFER			Male	Leib	Miriam			460
HILFER			Male			Shmuel		460
HILFER	Yerakhmiel		Male			Lea		460
HOKHBERG	Avraham		Male					460
HOKHBERG	Khava		Female	Sana	Malka			460
HOKHBERG	Leibush		Male					460
HOKHBERG	Malka		Female			Sana		460
HOKHBERG	Nakhum		Male			Zlata		460
HOKHBERG	Sana		Male			Malka		460
HOKHBERG	Sara		Female	Sana	Malka			460
HOKHBERG	Zlata	REIZER	Female			Nakhum		460
HURB	Natan		Male					460
HURB			Male			Natan		460
IAGID	Aharon		Male			Bela		462
IAGID	Bela		Female			Aharon		462
IAGID	Berta		Female	Nakhum	Sushi			462
IAGID	Hersh		Male					462
IAGID	Itzi		Male	Aharon	Bela			462
IAGID	Kreindel		Female	Aharon	Bela			462
IAGID	Mendel		Male					462

IAGID			Male			Hersh		462
IAGID			Male			Mendel		462
IAGID			Male	Mendel				462
IAGID			Male	Mendel				462
IAGID			Male	Mendel				462
IEGER FUKS	Gitel		Female	Yaakov				462
IEGER FUKS			Male			Yaakov		462
IEGER FUKS	Yaakov		Male					462
KAHANA	Bunio			Yosef	Lea			462
KAHANA	Lea	NEIMAN	Female			Yosef		462
KAHANA	Liber			Yosef	Lea			462
KAHANA	Yosef		Male			Lea		462
KARTEN	Bluma	IAGID	Female			Zalman		466
KARTEN			Male	Zalman	Bluma			466
KARTEN			Male	Zalman	Bluma			466
KARTEN	Zalman		Male			Bluma		466
KATZ SZTROZAND	Itzik		Male			Lea		462
KATZ SZTROZAND	Lea		Female			Itzik		462
KENIGSBERG	Mala	VIDMAN	Female				From Podusilna. In Narajow during the war	466
KENIGSBERG			Male			Mala	From Podusilna. In Narajow during the war	466
KENIGSBERG			Male		Mala		From Podusilna. In Narajow during the war	466
KENIGSBERG			Male		Mala		From Podusilna. In Narajow during the war	466
KESLER	Avraham		Male			Pepke		466

KESLER	Pepka		Female			Avraham	466
KESLER			Male			Yitzkhak	466
KESLER			Male	Yitzkhak			466
KESLER	Yitzkhak		Male				466
KHOTINER	Aharon		Male				462
KHOTINER	Breina						462
KHOTINER	Liba						462
KHOTINER	Nesia						462
KHOTINER VAKHTEL							462
KIHN	Frida		Female				466
KIHN	Frida	KIHN	Female			Yehuda	466
KIHN	Getzel						466
KIHN	Matilda		Female			Zelig	466
KIHN	Mendel		Male				466
KIHN			Male				466
KIHN			Male				466
KIHN			Male				466
KIHN	Yehuda		Male			Frida	466
KIHN	Zelig		Male			Matilda	466
KIMEL	Beniamin		Male				466
KIMEL	Rozia		Female	Beniamin			466
KIMEL			Male			Beniamin	466
KORCHAN	Yosef		Male				465
KORCHER	Avraham		Male	Khanan	Miriam		466

KORCHER	Khanan		Male			Miriam		466
KORCHER	Mania		Female	Khanan	Miriam			466
KORCHER	Miriam		Female			Khanan Meir		466
KRAUS	Avraham		Male			Batia	From Rakosin, Czechoslovakia	468
KRAUS	Batia		Female			Avraham	From Rakosin, Czechoslovakia	468
KSHUVI	Rakhel	NOIMAN	Female	B		Todros		466
KSHUVI	Tudrus		Male			Rakhel		466
KUPFERSHMIDT	Mendel		Male					465
KUPFERSHMIDT	Reuven		Male					465
KUPFERSHMIDT	Sara		Female					465
KUPFERSHMIDT	Sosia							465
KUPFERSHMIDT			Male			Mendel		465
LAKHER	Fentza		Female			Yaakov	From Dworce	468
LAKHER	Henk			Munio	Ruzia		From Dworce	468
LAKHER	Litzi		Female			Shmuel	From Dworce	468
LAKHER	Merilka			Munio	Ruzia		From Dworce	468
LAKHER	Moniyo		Male			Rozia	From Dworce	468
LAKHER	Rozia		Female			Monio	From Dworce	468
LAKHER	Shmuel		Male			Litzi	From Dworce	468
LAKHER	Yaakov		Male			Fantze	From Dworce	468
LAKHER	Yehoshua		Male	Shmuel	Litzi		From Dworce	468
LAKS	Golda		Female				From Stryhance	468
LAKS	Meltzia						From Stryhance	468
LAKS	Mikhael		Male				From Stryhance	468

LAKS	Yitzkhak		Male				From Stryhance	468
LEITNER	Bela	MINTZ	Female			Nutzi		463
LEITNER	Hersh		Male					463
LEITNER	Leib		Male	Hersh				463
LEITNER	Miriam		Female			Yekhezkel		463
LEITNER	Notzi		Male			Bela		463
LEITNER			Male	Nutzi	Bela			463
LEITNER	Yekhezkel		Male			Miriam		463
LEV	Gnantzi	KOHN	Female			Itzik		463
LEV	Itzik		Male			Gnantzi		463
LEV			Male	Itzik	Gnantzi			463
LOSHAK	Avraham		Male	Yerakhmiel	Khaia Miriam			463
LOSHAK	Bela			Hersh	Reiza			463
LOSHAK	Dunia	SHLEZINGER	Female					463
LOSHAK	Hersh		Male			Reiza		463
LOSHAK	Keila		Female					463
LOSHAK	Khaia	KLETER	Female			Yerakhmiel		463
LOSHAK	Lea		Female			Yaakov		463
LOSHAK	Lea		Female	Yerakhmiel				463
LOSHAK	Leibush		Male	Yerakhmiel	Khaia Miriam			463
LOSHAK	Reiza	HILFER	Female			Hersh		463
LOSHAK	Shimon		Male	Yerakhmiel				463
LOSHAK			Male		Dunia			463
LOSHAK			Male			Keila		463

LOSHAK	Yaakov		Male			Lea		463
LOSHAK	Yerakhmiel		Male			Khaia Miriam		463
LOSHAK	Yerakhmiel		Male					463
MALER	Batke	BILET	Female			Leon	Died in Narajow.	463
MALER	Lemel		Male				Died in Narajow.	463
MALER	Leon		Male			Batke	Died in Narajow.	463
MALER			Male	Leon	Betka		Died in Narajow.	463
MALER			Male	Leon	Betka		Died in Narajow.	463
MALER			Male			Lemel	Died in Narajow.	463
MANDELBERG	Emil		Male					463
MANDELBERG	Fania	SHEKHTER	Female			Yoel		463
MANDELBERG	I		Male				Profession: Ritual Slaughterer	463
MANDELBERG	Rakhmiel		Male			Yehudit		463
MANDELBERG			Male	Yoel	Fania			463
MANDELBERG	Yehudit	FIERSTEIN	Female			Rakhmiel		463
MANDELBERG	Yoel		Male			Fania		463
MARKUS	Azriel		Male	Meir	Khaitzi		From Rakosin, Czechoslovakia	468
MARKUS	Dvora		Female				From Potoczany	468
MARKUS	Ita		Female	Meir	Khaitzi		From Rakosin, Czechoslovakia	468
MARKUS	Izio				Dvora		From Potoczany	468
MARKUS	Khaitzi		Female			Meir	From Rakosin, Czechoslovakia	468
MARKUS	Lunio				Dvora		From Potoczany	468
MARKUS	Meir		Male			Kheitzi	From Rakosin, Czechoslovakia	468
MARKUS	Pesia		Female				From Rakosin, Czechoslovakia	468

MEIER	Berish		Male			Sara		463
MEIER	Breina		Female			Shmuel	From Rakosin, Czechoslovakia	468
MEIER	Eliezer		Male	Moshe	Keila			463
MEIER	Hersh		Male	Moshe	Keila			463
MEIER	Keila	NOIMAN	Female			Moshe		463
MEIER	Khaim		Male	Moshe	Keila			463
MEIER	Lea		Female	Moshe	Keila			463
MEIER	Mira		Female	Moshe	Keila			463
MEIER	Moshe		Male			Keila		463
MEIER	Sara		Female			Berisch		463
MEIER	Shmuel		Male			Breina	From Rakosin, Czechoslovakia	468
MEIER	Yaakov		Male	Moshe	Keila			463
MEIER	Yoel		Male	Moshe	Keila			463
MELAMED			Male			Yisrael Yaakov		463
MELAMED	Yisrael		Male					463
MERKUR	Rivka		Female					467
MERKUR	Yehuda		Male					463
MERKUR	Yehuda		Male					467
MERTZES	Arie		Male	Berish	Khaia			463
MERTZES	Berish		Male			Khaia		463
MERTZES	Khaia	GOLDSHLAG	Female			Berisch		463
MERTZES	Moshe		Male	Berish	Khaia			463
MERTZES	Pepka			Berish	Khaia			463
MIHLSHTOK	Breina	EHRE	Female					463

MIHLSHTOK	David		Male	Yaakov	Rivka			463
MIHLSHTOK	Fruma	TZVERLING	Female			Moshe		463
MIHLSHTOK	Isser		Male			Rivka		463
MIHLSHTOK	Khaia	PELTA	Female			Yosef		463
MIHLSHTOK	Khana		Female	Isser	Rivka			463
MIHLSHTOK	Mina		Female	Isser	Rivka			463
MIHLSHTOK	Moshe		Male			Fruma		463
MIHLSHTOK	Rakhel		Female		Breina			463
MIHLSHTOK	Rivka		Female			Yaakov		463
MIHLSHTOK	Rivka	KUSHERSHMID	Female			Isser		463
MIHLSHTOK	Sara		Female	Isser	Rivka			463
MIHLSHTOK			Male	Yosef	Khaia Ester			463
MIHLSHTOK			Male	Yosef	Khaia Ester			463
MIHLSHTOK	Yaakov		Male			Rivka		463
MIHLSHTOK	Yosef		Male			Khaia Ester		463
MINTZ	Bela			Itzi	Gitel			463
MINTZ	Bela			David	Tova			463
MINTZ	Bentzion		Male	Itzi	Gitel			463
MINTZ	Brunia		Female	Itzi	Gitel			463
MINTZ	Bruria		Female	Efraim	Sara			463
MINTZ	Bruria		Female	David	Tova			463
MINTZ	David		Male			Tova		463
MINTZ	Efraim		Male			Sara		463
MINTZ	Feibish		Male					463

MINTZ	Gitel	SHLEIKHER	Female			Itzi		463
MINTZ	Gitel		Female					463
MINTZ	Hersh		Male					463
MINTZ	Itzi		Male			Gitel		463
MINTZ	Lea		Female					463
MINTZ	Mendel		Male					463
MINTZ	Rakhel		Female					463
MINTZ	Sara		Female	Itzi	Gitel			463
MINTZ	Sara	GABEL	Female			Efraim		463
MINTZ	Sara		Female	David	Tova			463
MINTZ	Shraga		Male	Efraim	Sara			463
MINTZ	Tova	SHLEIKHER	Female			David		463
MINTZ	Yona			Efraim	Sara			463
MIRBERG	Leib		Male			Reiza		463
MIRBERG	Reiza		Female			Leib		463
MUNDSHEIN	Berta	ADLER	Female			Raymond		463
MUNDSHEIN	Moshe		Male					463
MUNDSHEIN	Raymond		Male			Berta		463
MUNDSHEIN			Male			Moshe		463
NADEL	Hersh		Male			Khava		464
NADEL	Khava	VEINSHTEIN	Female			Hersh Yosef		464
NADEL	Mikhael		Male			Yokheved		464
NADEL			Male		Gela			464
NADEL			Male		Gela			464

NADEL	Yokheved	SHAMIR	Female			Mikhael Eliezer		464
NADEL	Yosef		Male		Gela			464
NAGELBERG	Bruno		Male				Died in Narajow.	464
NAGELBERG	Ditta		Female				Died in Narajow.	464
NAGELBERG	Leon		Male				Died in Narajow.	464
NAGELBERG	Parush						Died in Narajow.	464
NAGELBERG	Rafael		Male				Died in Narajow.	464
NAGELBERG	Rut		Female				Died in Narajow.	464
NAGELBERG	Shimon		Male	Leon			Died in Narajow.	464
NAGELBERG	Shmuel		Male	Leon			Died in Narajow.	464
NEMAN	Avraham		Male			Henia		464
NEMAN	Henia	SHIFMAN	Female			Avraham		464
NEMAN	Sara		Female	Avraham	Henia			464
NEMAN	Shlomo		Male	Avraham	Henia			464
NEMAN	Shmuel		Male	Avraham	Henia			464
NOIMAN	Dvora		Female	Mordekhai	Roza			464
NOIMAN	Eliezer		Male			Khana		464
NOIMAN	Eliezer		Male			Yona		464
NOIMAN	Eliezer		Male			Tova	From Wierzbow	468
NOIMAN	Khana	LIPA	Female			Eliezer		464
NOIMAN	Khava	EIGEN	Female			Meir		464
NOIMAN	Khava		Female			Meir	From Wierzbow	468
NOIMAN	Malka		Female	Yosef	Yehudit			464
NOIMAN	Meir		Male			Khava		464

NOIMAN	Meir		Male			Khava	From Wierzbow	468
NOIMAN	Mordekhai		Male			Roza		464
NOIMAN	Moshe		Male					464
NOIMAN	Rakhel		Female	Meir	Khava			464
NOIMAN	Rakhel		Female	Meir	Khava		From Wierzbow	468
NOIMAN	Rivka		Female	Yosef	Yehudit			464
NOIMAN	Roza	VEINSHTEIN	Female			Mordekhai		464
NOIMAN	Shaya							464
NOIMAN	Tova		Female					464
NOIMAN	Tova		Female			Eliezer	From Wierzbow	468
NOIMAN	Yaakov		Male	Mordekhai	Roza			464
NOIMAN	Yehudit	NOIMAN	Female			Yosef		464
NOIMAN	Yona		Female			Eliezer		464
NOIMAN	Yona			Mordekhai	Roza			464
NOIMAN	Yosef		Male			Yehudit		464
NOIMAN	Yosef	NOIMAN	Yosef		Male		From Wierzbow. In Narajow during the war	468
OHRING	Ester		Female					459
OHRING			Male			Motel		459
ORT	Brunia	KIHN	Female			Motel		459
ORT	Motl		Male			Bronia		459
OSTERMAN	Anshel		Male					459
OSTERMAN			Male			Anshel		459
OSTERMAN			Male	Anshel				459
OSTERMAN			Male	Anshel				459

PALTE	Avraham		Male			Tzila		465
PALTE	Henia		Female					465
PALTE	Khana		Female		Henia			465
PALTE	Sara		Female		Henia			465
PALTE	Tzila		Female			Avraham Yitzkhak		465
PARNES	Beril		Male			Breina		465
PARNES	Breina	LUSHAK	Female			Beril		465
PARNES	Hentzia	FROSH	Female			Moshe	From Podusilna. In Narajow during the war	465
PARNES	Khana		Female	Moshe	Hentzia		From Podusilna. In Narajow during the war	465
PARNES	Mizia		Female			Yaakov	From Podusilna. In Narajow during the war	465
PARNES	Moshe		Male			Hentzia	From Podusilna. In Narajow during the war	465
PARNES			Male	Yaakov	Mizia		From Podusilna. In Narajow during the war	465
PARNES			Male	Yaakov	Mizia		From Podusilna. In Narajow during the war	465
PARNES	Yaakov		Male			Mizia	From Podusilna. In Narajow during the war	465
PARNES	Yentzia			Moshe	Hentzia		From Podusilna. In Narajow during the war	465
PULVER	Khana	SHVERER	Female			Yehoshua Zelig		465
PULVER	Leib		Male					465
PULVER	Yaakov		Male				From Biala. In Narajow during the war	465
PULVER	Yehoshua		Male			Khana		465
REISHER	Miriam	FUKS	Female			Yisrael		466
REISHER	Yisrael		Male			Miriam		466

REIZER	Dunia				Perel			466
REIZER	Efraim		Male		Perel			466
REIZER	Perel		Female					466
REIZER	Shaya				Perel			466
ROIKH	Batia	LUSHAK	Female			Itzik Leib		466
ROIKH	Itzik		Male			Batia		466
ROITER	Golda		Female			Moshe		466
ROITER	Moshe		Male			Golda		466
ROL	Moshe		Male					466
ROZENBLAT	Leizer		Male			Miriam		466
ROZENBLAT	Miriam	LEIB	Female			Leizer		466
ROZENBLAT	Moshe		Male	Leizer	Miriam			466
ROZENBLAT	Nesia			Leizer	Miriam			466
ROZENBLAT	Pesia		Female	Leizer	Miriam			466
RUT	Shlomo		Male			Yenta	From Rakosin, Czechoslovakia	468
RUT	Yenta		Female			Shlomo	From Rakosin, Czechoslovakia	468
RUT	Bluma		Female	Shlomo	Yenta		From Rakosin, Czechoslovakia	468
RUT	Sara		Female	Shlomo	Yenta		From Rakosin, Czechoslovakia	468
RUTHEN	Berl		Male	Velvel	Tova			466
RUTHEN	Breina		Female	Velvel	Tova			466
RUTHEN	Sima		Female	Velvel	Tova			466
RUTHEN	Tova	HEIBER	Female			Velvel		466
RUTHEN	Velvel		Male			Tova		466
SAFRAN	Gershon		Male			Rosia		464

SAFRAN	Rosia	KIHN	Female			Gershon		464
SAMUELI	Pinkhas		Male					464
SAMUELI			Male			Pinkhas		464
SAMUELI			Male	Pinkhas				464
SHAMIR	Frida	EHRE	Female			Yosef		467
SHAMIR	Hersh		Male	Izik	Roza			467
SHAMIR	Izik		Male			Roza		467
SHAMIR	Roza	ROITER	Female			Izik		467
SHAMIR			Male	Yosef	Frida			467
SHAMIR	Yosef		Male			Frida		467
SHEFER	Moniyo							467
SHEFER	Volf		Male					467
SHEIN	Ester	MINTZ	Female			Yosef		467
SHEIN	Heni	MIHLSHTOK	Female			Moshe		467
SHEIN	Meir		Male			Selka		467
SHEIN	Moshe		Male			Heni		467
SHEIN	Rakhel		Female					467
SHEIN	Selka		Female			Meir		467
SHEIN	Selka		Female					467
SHEIN			Male	Meir	Selka			467
SHEIN			Male	Meir	Selka			467
SHEIN			Male	Meir	Selka			467
SHEIN	Yosef		Male			Ester		467
SHEKHTER	Adela			Moshe	Gusta			467

SHEKHTER	Dvora		Female			Herman	From Potoczany	468
SHEKHTER	Etka			Herman	Dvora		From Potoczany	468
SHEKHTER	Fania		Female	Henukh				467
SHEKHTER	Feiga		Female	Yehoshua	Khana		From Rakosin, Czechoslovakia	468
SHEKHTER	Gusta	ZLATKES	Female			Moshe		467
SHEKHTER	Henuch		Male				Profession: Ritual Slaughterer	467
SHEKHTER	Herman		Male			Dvora	From Potoczany	468
SHEKHTER	Khaim		Male	Moshe	Gusta			467
SHEKHTER	Khana		Female			Yehoshua	From Rakosin, Czechoslovakia	468
SHEKHTER	Leizer		Male	Yehoshua	Khana		From Rakosin, Czechoslovakia	468
SHEKHTER	Lunk			Herman	Dvora		From Potoczany	468
SHEKHTER	Moshe		Male			Gusta		467
SHEKHTER	Sonia		Female	Herman	Dvora		From Potoczany	468
SHEKHTER			Male	Henukh				467
SHEKHTER			Male			Henokh		467
SHEKHTER			Male	Henukh				467
SHEKHTER	Yehoshua		Male			Khana	From Rakosin, Czechoslovakia	468
SHEKHTER	Zeev		Male	Moshe	Gusta			467
SHEKHTER	Zuzu			Yehoshua	Khana		From Rakosin, Czechoslovakia	468
SHEPS	Batia		Female	Yaakov	Miriam			467
SHEPS	Miriam	TAKSEL	Female			Yaakov		467
SHEPS	Yaakov		Male			Miriam		467
SHIFMAN	Dvora	NOIMAN	Female			Max		467
SHIFMAN	Max		Male			Dvora		467

SHLEIKHER	Gitzi		Female			Uri	467
SHLEIKHER			Male	Uri	Gitzi		467
SHLEIKHER	Uri		Male			Gitzi	467
SHLEZINGER	Lea		Female	Velvel			467
SHLEZINGER	Leibush		Male	Velvel			467
SHLEZINGER	Velvel		Male				467
SHLEZINGER	Yehoshua		Male	Velvel			467
SHMETERLING	Khone		Male				467
SHMETERLING	Meir		Male		Khuna		467
SHMETERLING	Motl		Male		Khuna		467
SHMETERLING	Rivka		Female		Khuna		467
SHMETERLING			Male			Khone	467
SHTANDER	Avraham		Male			Bronia	467
SHTANDER	Brunia	MEIER	Female			Avraham	467
SHTANDER	Hersh		Male	Avraham	Brunia		467
SHTANDER	Sima		Female	Avraham	Brunia		467
SHTANDER	Uri		Male	Avraham	Brunia		467
SHTERN	Matilda		Female				466
SHTERN	Mikhael		Male			Tzivia	466
SHTERN	Tova		Female				466
SHTERN	Tzivia	SHAMIR	Female			Mikhael	466
SHTRASFELD	Lea	LOSHAK	Female			Yaakov	467
SHTRASFELD	Yaakov		Male			Lea	467
SHTREIZAND							467

SHUSBERG	Khana	SHEPS	Female			Motil		466
SHUSBERG	Mikhael		Male					466
SHUSBERG	Motil		Male			Khana Elka		466
SHUSBERG			Male			Mikhael		466
SHUSBERG	Yeta		Female					466
SHVARTZBERG	Lea	HERMELIN	Female			Moshe		466
SHVARTZBERG	Moshe		Male			Lea		466
SHVERER	Khana	SHEKHTER	Female			Shmuel		466
SHVERER	Nekhama		Female					466
SHVERER	Risia			Shmuel	Khana			466
SHVERER	Sara		Female	Shmuel	Khana			466
SHVERER	Shmuel		Male			Khana		466
SHVERER	Tzvi		Male	Shmuel	Khana			466
SHVERER			Male	Shmuel	Khana			466
SHVERER	Yisrael		Male					466
TABAK	Bela		Female			Mordekhai		462
TABAK	Khana		Female	Mordekhai	Bela			462
TABAK	Mordekhai		Male			Bela		462
TABAK	Rivka		Female	Mordekhai	Bela			462
TABAK	Shprintza			Mordekhai	Bela			462
TABAK	Yekhezkel		Male	Mordekhai	Bela			462
TAKSEL	Bertzi		Male			Hentzia		462
TAKSEL	Hentzia		Female			Bertzi		462
TANENBAUM	Tonka		Female				From Podusilna. In Narajow during the war	462

TANENBAUM			Male			Tonka	From Podusilna. In Narajow during the war	462
TEIKHER	Noakh		Male			Tzila		462
TEIKHER	Tzila	MOINIRA	Female			Noakh		462
TEIKHMAN	Lea		Female		Tova			462
TEIKHMAN	Shlomo		Male		Tova			462
TEIKHMAN	Tova	FUKS	Female					462
TOIBER	Perel		Female		Shuilkha			462
TOIBER	Shuilkha							462
TOIBER			Male			Volf		462
TOIBER	Volf		Male					462
TURNER	Elka		Female				From Wierzbow	468
TURNER	Khana	MILSHTOK	Female			Shmuel	From Wierzbow	468
TURNER	Khava		Female	Shmuel	Khana		From Wierzbow	468
TURNER	Moshe		Male	Shmuel	Khana		From Wierzbow	468
TURNER	Nakhum		Male				From Wierzbow	468
TURNER	Roza		Female				From Wierzbow	468
TURNER	Shmuel		Male			Khana	From Wierzbow	468
TURNER			Male			Roza	From Wierzbow	468
TURNER			Male			Yokhanan	From Wierzbow	468
TURNER			Male			Nakhum	From Wierzbow	468
TURNER			Male			Elka	From Wierzbow	468
TURNER	Yetka			Shmuel	Khana		From Wierzbow	468
TURNER	Yokhanan		Male				From Wierzbow	468
TZVEIG	Gershon		Male			Henia		465

TZVEIG	Henia	NES	Female			Gershon		465
TZVEIG			Male	Gershon	Henia			465
TZVEIG			Male	Gershon	Henia			465
VAGNER	Feiga		Female			Itzi		461
VAKHTEL	Frida		Female			Yerakhmiel		461
VAKHTEL	Itzi		Male			Feiga		461
VAKHTEL	Moniyo		Male	Itzi	Feiga			461
VAKHTEL			Male	Yerakhmiel	Frida			461
VAKHTEL			Male	Yerakhmiel	Frida			461
VAKHTEL			Male	Yerakhmiel	Frida			461
VAKHTEL			Male	Yerakhmiel	Frida			461
VAKHTEL	Yerakhmiel		Male			Frida		461
VARM	Batia		Female	Mordekhai	Roza		From Stryhance	468
VARM	David		Male	Mordekhai	Roza		From Stryhance	468
VARM	Mordekhai		Male			Roza	From Stryhance	468
VARM	Roza		Female			Mordekhai Asher	From Stryhance	468
VEIS	Aharon		Male			Bluma		461
VEIS	Beril		Male	Aharon	Bluma			461
VEIS	Bluma	DANZIGER	Female			Aharon		461
VEIS	Henia		Female	Aharon	Bluma			461
VEIS	Khaia		Female	Aharon	Bluma			461
VEIS	Matilda		Female	Aharon	Bluma			461
VEIS	Nekhemia		Male	Aharon	Bluma			461
VEIS	Yehoshua		Male	Aharon	Bluma			461

VEITZMAN	Charna		Female			Volf	From Podusilna. In Narajow during the war	461
VEITZMAN	Volf		Male			Charna	From Podusilna. In Narajow during the war	461
VEITZMAN	Yosef		Male	Volf	Charna		From Podusilna. In Narajow during the war	461
VIDERKER	Mikhael		Male			Suma		461
VIDERKER	Some		Male			Mikhael		461
VOHL	Rivka		Female			Shlomo		461
VOHL	Shlomo		Male			Rivka		461
VOHL	Shmuel		Male	Shlomo	Rivka			461
VOHL	Yitzkhak		Male	Shlomo	Rivka			461
ZELIG	Yehoshua		Male					461
ZILBERFELD	Rakhel		Female		Malka		From Potoczany	468
ZILBERFELD	Yitzkhak		Male		Malka		From Potoczany	468
ZINGER	Ester		Female	Shmuel	Mina			461
ZINGER	Golda		Female	Shmuel	Mina			461
ZINGER	Mina	MIHLSHTOK	Female			Shmuel		461
ZINGER	Shmuel		Male			Mina		461
ZINGER	Yekhezkel		Male	Shmuel	Mina			461
ZINGER	Yeshayahu		Male	Shmuel	Mina			461
ZLATKES	Breintza	SHVERER	Female			Leib		461
ZLATKES	Gitzia			Leib	Breitze			461
ZLATKES	Gusta		Female					461
ZLATKES	Leib		Male			Breintze		461
ZLATKES	Sara		Female					461

ZLATKES	Shlomo		Male	Leib	Breintze		461
ZLATKES	Shlomo		Male				461

[Page 469]

List of those who died in Israel

by Dr. Eliezer Shaklai

Translated by Moshe Kutten

Edited by Jane S. Gabin

Name	Dates	Notes
Blei Yosef, son of Adela Neiman	1902-1908	Made *Aliyah* from Germany in 1932. Settled in Petakh Tikva, where he worked in cultivation of citrus treed. He died in Petakh Tikva.
Gabel Mordekhai	1871-1967	Native of Wierzbow. Made *Aliyah* from Germany in 1938. Settled in Tel-Aviv where he died.
Gabel Miryam	1876-1967	Mordechai's wife who made *Aliyah* with him. Lived and died in Tel Aviv.
Goldschlag Sara, daughter of Eliezer Mihlshtok	1886-1951	Made *Aliyah* in 1934. Lived and died in Tel Aviv.
Goldschlag Mina	1907-1935	An activist in "HaShomer HaTzair." Lived and died in Tel Aviv.
Gurelnik Shoshana, nee Moshe Shapira	1904-1975	Made *Aliyah* in 1934. Lived and died in Haifa.
Gelber Moshe	1910-1974	Made *Aliyah* after the Holocaust in 1967 through Sweden. Settled in Netania where he died
Haber Zeev	1905-1956	Made *Aliyah* after the Holocaust. Settled in Netania where he died.
Hokhberg nee Loshak	1896-1975	A courageous woman who jumped from the train traveling to the extermination camp. Went through the Holocaust in the Ghetto and forests near Narajow.

		Made *Aliyah* in 1948. Settled with her children in Haifa where she died.
Hilfer Pesia nee Granovitter	1880-1960	Made *Aliyah* in 1930. Settled in Tel Aviv where she died.
Name?	1907-1936	The head of the "HaShomer HaTzair" branch in Narajow. Made *Aliyah* as a pioneer in 1928. Participated in the Spanish Civil War and was killed in Barcelona.
Hirschhorn Avraham (Toncho)	1920-1950	Made *Aliyah* in 1947 and settled in Kfar Saba. Was killed by a erroneous shell in his army reserve service. Left a wife and a baby.
Levi Zehava nee Fuchs	1912-1974	Member of "Bnei Akiva." Made *Aliyah* as a pioneer, settled in Netania where she died.
Shtern Mikhael-Eliezer	1900-1956	Among the first "General Zionists" in Narajow. Went through the Holocaust there and made *Aliyah* in 1951. Settled in Be'er Yaakov where he died.
Shlezinger (Kashuvi) Zisia	1910-1954	Made *Aliyah* as a pioneer in 1929 Worked as a construction worker and died at work by falling from a scaffolding.
Ravitz Luba, nee Goldschlag	1905-1968	Made *Aliyah* in 1929. Settled in Tel Aviv where she died

ENGLISH SECTION

[English Page 5]

Association of Former Brzezany Residents
Editor– Manachem Katz, Haifa, April 1978

Founding Committee
Dr. Zimerman Jakob – chairman
Roth Ozer – secretary
Charap abraham
Tuch Pinchas
Bar–Dawid (Bardowicz) Moshe
Segal antshel
Brik Jehoshua
Kleid Jehuda

Organizing Committee
Bleiberg Shimon
Bar–David (Bardowicz) Moshe
Brik Jehoshua
Bone–Prisand Batia
Danieli–Feld Bela
Dr. Fried Joseph
Ja'amin (Aufrichtig) Shimon
Nadler Itzhak
Ne'eman Israel
Kleid Jehuda
Rozenblat Rina
Sptizen Jehuda
Dr. Shaklai (wagshal) Eliezer

Organizing Committee in the United States
Goldwag Itzhak
Hammer–Gutenplan Rozia
Maiblum Shimon
Podoshin Moshe
Shneider Moshe
Zipper Mark
Zusman Mendel
Wanderer Itzhak

Members of the Editorial Board In Israel
Bar–David (Bardowicz) Moshe
Goldman Natan
Danieli–Feld Bela
Arch. Katz Menachem
Knohl Dow
Ne'eman Israel
Dr. Redlich Shimon
Dr. Shaktai (Wagshal) Eliezer

Private publication of the association of former Brzezany residents in Israel: April 1978

[English Page 6]

The last Jews of the city of Brzezany were murdered by the Nazi henchmen thirty–five years ago. Almost a generation's life – time had to lapse before the last will of some twelve thousand souls, men, women and children, who were put to death within the town's periphery or sent to outlying death–camps, could finally be fulfilled.

The names of the Jewish native population of Brzezany and Naraiow will now be committed to print for the sake of future generations. Along with them some nine thousand anonymous souls will be commemorated. They were Jewish refugees from various parts of western Poland who found their temporary and, as it happened, also terminal home here. They shared together with the local community four years of life and its tragic destiny.

The last survivors of Brzezany's Jewish community both in Israel and in the United States have decided to commemorate the martyrs. A committee of former citizens collected over years of unceasing effort a considerable documentation on which the present memorial book is based. I have contributed my own share to the effort of editing, design and printing. As a native of Brzezany and witness and survivor of the Nazi occupation period, I am not only acquainted with the history of my hometown and the martyrology of my community, but was constantly haunted since the end of the war by its tragic memory. I felt it a sacred obligation towards those who perished, a pledge we gave each other, in those dark days: "If you survive, remember those who did not. Report to the world. Tell the story of our annihilation and avenge our blood."

Now that these pages are brought to print, I trust that the little I am able to contribute to the commemoration of my community will materialize. I do not think there is further need for introductory notes, neither is it necessary to laud the past of my community and describe the illustrious men who lived in it

[English Page 7]

during its four hundred years of existence. All those interested in becoming acquainted with Brzezany and its people will be able to do so in these pages. The reading of it in itself will revive the memory of the past and commemorate all those who only wanted to live – to live as Jews.

To all those who helped me and supported my work and assisted in the materialization of this task– first and foremost Dr. Eliezer Szaklai–Wagszal my thanks and appreciation.

May this book serve as a memorial to the Jewish people and to the community of Brzezany, which fell victim to forces of darkness of Nazi Germany. May this book also serve as an eternal memory to the coming generation – a light to our youth which is renewing our existence as a free people in our homeland, and a warning to those of our people dispersed in the diaspora, who have not yet drawn the obvious conclusion from our tragic past.

[English Page 8]

Brzezany, the Town

In south–east Galicia, about 100 kilometers from the city of Lvov, in the triangle between the cities of Lvov, Stanislovov, and Tarnopol, hidden between trees and forests, close to the river Zlota–Lipa, at the edge of a lake, in a low valley, is situated the small town of Brzezany. The town is well known in the wide world thanks to its great Torah scholars whose fame went forth far from its boundaries.

Four roads, running in four different directions from the center connect it with the rest of the world. There is also another connection Brzezany boasts of – the railway. Thus Brzezany is the central town of an entire region. A number of villages with a population of one hundred thousand citizens are under its authority. The town itself is divided into five sections: the center and four suburbs. In the northwestern corner of the town rises the "Bernadine" mount. There, also stands the monastery, an ancient building, big and long. From there one has an unforgettable view of the entire town and its surroundings. One can see, stretching like a mirror, the long lake, framed east and west by mountains and hills. The lake was the source of sustenance and relaxation for the town's

[English Page 9]

The Potocki's palace in Rai

population. The height of the lake is about 100 meters above the level of the town. A high dam prevents the lake from shedding its waters into the town and flooding it. East of the town, between the two forks of the river stands a big stone structure, a remnant from the 16th century. Originally, this building served as a citadel for the Sieniavsky family, founders of the town. In this antiquated stronghold lived and were buried numerous generations of the Sieniavsky family. the citadel, together with an immense fortune, was handed down from generation to generation. The last member of this renowned family was the famous Graff Potocki, whose palace was in a nearby village Rai.

On the west side of the town was the park. Across the park stood the Polish community center "Sokol." At the back of the center stood an old, neglected building, called "Reitschule." Close to this forsaken building lay a wide open field which belonged to the fire brigade.

The center of the town ran symmetrically. Its central building was the "Town Hall." It was a big square building, surrounded by a spacious yard. It consisted of two floors with a tower in the center. In the tower was set a clock, visible from all four sides of the town. The tower also bore the crest of Graff Potocki, a five angled cross. Surrounding the base of the Town Hall, as well as in the courtyard, there were many stores. Most of them belonged to Jewish storekeepers. The second floor of the Town Hall served as a high school. Further west, between the houses stood the Greek Catholic church. Behind it was the Armenian's church and toward the south stood the Catholic church. Close to the south side of the Catholic church stood the statue of Jan Sobieski. On two sides, north and east were platforms which served as parking spaces for the horses and wagons, belonging to the farmers. Part of this plot was set for the local drivers and porters. All the houses in the center of the town, contained stores or bar rooms, owned mostly by Jews.

Further north, there was another market, the "Novi–Rynek." This market was much smaller and more neglected than the market in the center of town. Zbozova street connected both. On the east side of the street stood the two floor Jewish community center which was built after the First World Wr. Northeast and south of the commercial center extended a number of streets and alleys. On both sides of these streets stood small dilapidated houses. This was the residential section of the poorer Jewish population of the town. On the south side of this quarter stood the big synagogue, a beautiful well decorated structure which was constructed in the 18th century. On the way to this synagogue, there were two study houses, as well as a number of Hassidic houses of worship. Nearby stood the community bath house, the Jewish hospital, the dilapidated old–people's home and several other institutions owned by the Jewish community.

West of the business center was the most beautiful part of the town. Here stood magnificent homes, there were also a number of beautiful villas. Between the gardens and the homes, towards the southwest the street "Raiska" winds. Here, on this street were the cemeteries, the Jewish on right side of the street and the Christian on the left.

[English Page 10]

History

Brzezany was founded in the year 1530. The royal courtier Mikolai Sieniawa was given permission by the Polish King Sigmund the First, to change the village Brzezany into a township. The history of the Jewish community of Brzezany is tied to the history and development of the town. The town's population reached 260 souls in the year 1570, including four Jewish families who were engaged in trade. One hundred years later, in 1672, the town's population reached 500 families. Among these were one hundred Jewish families. Thus the number of Jews in our town continued to increase throughout the years.

In the seventeenth century Brzezany burned twice. These distressing events continued to plague the town until the first quarter of the eighteenth century. In the year 1772 Brzezany, together with the rest of Galicia, passed into the hands of the Austrian government. In the 19th century Brzezany became the center of the offices for the entire district, called the *"Starostwo."* The majority of the Polish section of the population were employees in government offices, the Ukrainians were farmers, while the commerce lay in the hands of the Jews. The respective occupation of these three people partly changed in the latter generation. Jews became doctors, lawyers, teachers, judges and officials, while commerce fell into the hands of the Polish and Ukrainians. The Poles and the Jews inhabited the town proper, while the Ukrainians lived in nearby villages. As a result of the first World War, the Ukrainians seized the rule of Galicia in the fall of 1918, however, in the spring of 1919, the Poles captured city after city, thus putting an end to the young Ukrainian state. Shortly thereafter, there was also a war between the Poles and Soviet Russia which lasted for a number of

The Main Square and the Greco Catholic Church

[English Page 11]

Statue of the Unknown Soldier

months and ended in a peace treaty. The Jewish population suffered most severely during that War. The town of Brzezany was burned twice, and the possessions of the Jewish population were plundered. Those years were decisively negative and tragic for the Jewish community.

The two decades after the First World War filled with chaotic and disorderly events which resulted in the Second World War which for us Jews brought destruction and annihilation.

This is a brief chronological review of the history of that time.

The Jewish Community

Jewish community organization was established according to the Magdeburg code of laws. At the head of the community stood the administrators. In addition to the administrators, three good persons were elected. They had their own court which was under the authority of religious judges (Dayanim) headed by the Rabbi, and their judgements and decisions had to be ratified by the community leaders. The life of the community was centered around the synagogue. The first synagogue was already in existence in the 17th century.

Near the synagogue were a school, a bathhouse, a hospital and a lodging house for poor transients. The Rabbi was chosen by the Jewish community and had to be authorized by the rulers of the town. The community administrators collected taxes from the citizens of the town. They cared for the poor, the education of the children and for the religious services. They had authority over the slaughter house, they supervised the burial society and the great synagogue.

The Habsburgs brought about cognizant changes in the lives of the Jews. They flooded them with instructions and enactments. First of all they levied high taxes. The government also limited the production of intoxicating drinks. In the cultural field it strove to Germanize the Jewish minority. First the Jews were given German family names, then they established government schools for the Jews. They also placed a head Rabbi of the entire district.

A decisive change took place in the days of the renewed Polish rule, following the First World War. The law decreed personal, secret and democratic elections. Every Jew in town who reached the age of 18 could participate. The last elections to the Jewish community Council were in 1936. Eight persons were elected with Dr. Klarer as its presiding officer. This administrative body became automatically active during the rule of the Nazis as the Council of the Jews, "Judenrat."

[English Page 12]

The Economic Situation

In Brzezany and surroundings there were no natural resources or industries of any kind. There were a handful of wealthy people such as owners of estates, possessors of flour mills and lumber dealers. The middle class was predominantly composed of physicians, lawyers and merchants. A lower class consisted of small traders, artisans and cart drivers who worked very hard from morning till night, but still needed financial aid. Quite a sizable portion of the Jewish community lived on welfare. It is therefore easy to understand the reason for the massive Jewish emigration in the late 19th and early 20th century. Multitudes left in order to find their fortunes in distant America. Of course, this emigration brought relief but it also caused many tragedies. A great number of emigrant husbands left their wives and children without any material aid and disappeared without leaving a trace.

The various wars which took place in the year 1914 – 1920 had an ill effect on the Jews of our town. Many Jews left Brzezany forever. Most of the Jewish homes were destroyed, the possessions of the Jewish community were robbed and the sources of livelihood were completely ruined. Merchants who returned after the wars reopened their stores, each one according to his ability. Soldiers who returned from the armies and youth that grew up during the war years and had no opportunity to acquire a trade, now turned their attention to business. The number of merchants grew more than this economy could support. The merchants organized themselves into a merchant's unions. Mr. Jacob Mittelman was elected as its president.

50ᵗʰ Anniversary Banquet of the Brzezaner Young Men's Association, New York – 1950

[English Page 13]

A very small number of Jews served as judges, and there were also a few high school teachers. Among the professionals of the town were six Jewish physicians. There were physicians who left our town to search of more suitable places of work. There were also doctors who completed their course of studies, but received no license to practice medicine.

There were about forty lawyers thanks to the district court. Some of these lawyers eked out a scant living from their profession. There were also a number of engineers who completed their course of studies but could not find any work in the field. Most of the druggists couldn't find any work either. A fair portion of them left the town. The same fate met the young teachers. All of them faced a hopeless future. The situation of the artisans and craftsmen failed to improve after the First World War, in many instances their lot became even worse. For the working youth there were no prospects of even finding employment in our town. They organized themselves in various youth movements and waited for "Aliyah" to Israel.

Members of the Brzezaner Committee in New York

Religion and Culture

Renowned Torah scholars lived in Brzezany. Rabbis went forth from here into all parts of the world. It is sufficient to mention – Rabbi Joseph Saul Nathanson, Rabbi Kluger, the magid (preacher) from Brod Rabbi Isaac Shmelkes and Rabbi Shulem Mordechai Hacohen Shwadron. Also Rabbis Margolis, Jehuda Bergman and rabbi Meirson studied and drank from the fountains of Torah in our town. The Hassidic movement captured many hearts. Various currents of Hassidim impressed their stamps on the Jews of our town, among them were the house of Rishin, Belz, Stratin, Zydachow. The second half of the 19th century witnessed the period of enlightening, the search for new ways and ideas. It caused a complete change in the cultural life of the Jewish community. Some of the local Jews started reading monthly and weekly literary publications in Hebrew, such as the "Halutz" (pioneer), the "Magid," the Mevaser" and others.

Part of the youth remained loyal to traditional Judaism, with the synagogue as their center, while others organized themselves into the various factions of the Zionist movement with the Hebrew school as their center.

Prior to the period of enlightenment and even after it, the Jewish town administrators attended to the cultural life of the community. They synagogue continued to serve as the center of all cultural and spiritual life. In the synagogue Jews gathered to study Torah, and to participate in prayer and worship. In the synagogue they celebrated their holy days, they preached their sermons, they exchanged informations and made decisions. Their joy or, God forbid, their sorrow found their expression in the synagogue. The Hassidim centered their spiritual activities around their "Klezlach" (small houses of worship). Architect Menachem Katz describes in this book the main synagogue of Brzezany, as well as the smaller prayer houses. I'll only mention their names.

[English Page 14]

Synagogues of the Town

Aron Hakodesh from the Large
Synagogue

The Large Synagogue

The large synagogue was built in 1718 and was renovated at the end of the 19th century. It was an imposing, beautiful edifice. This central building around which the life of the entire Jewish community was centered. Laws, judgements, decrees, fines, holidays, births, deaths – filled this holy place. So it was until the Soviet occupation of the town in 1939 when the synagogue was turned into a shelter for refugees. Afterwards it was turned by the Soviets into a grain storehouse. The Nazi oppressors who came afterwards did not change the functions of the structure. It continued to serve as a storage place even after the entry of the Red Army in 1944. The building is standing to this day. 2) The newly built Synagogue stood close to the left side of the big synagogue. Jews who worshipped in this synagogue were mostly from wealthy and middle class families. This house of worship was also undamaged from the wars and under the rule of the soviets it served as a grain storehouse.

"The Cantor's Synagogue"

"The Cantor's synagogue," in the corner of Zygmuntovska and Skoina streets, in which Rabbi Nathanson prayed and preached, remained completely desolate and forsaken.

"Reb Yudels Synagogue"

"Reb Yudels Synagogue" stood at the corner of Lvovska and Tarnopolska streets. This was a very popular synagogue. It was wide open for everyone. It never lacked a quorum for a prayer service. This house of worship was burned down and utterly destroyed.

The Tschortkower Klois

The "Chrotkover Klois" belonged to the Hassidim, followers of the Rabbi from Chortkow. This was a 2 floor building. The upper floor contained the section for women worshippers and stood near to the house of Rabbi Gaon Mordechai Hachohen Shwadron, the Rabbi of the town. The synagogue was completely destroyed in the First World War. Part of it was later reconstructed, but it was eventually destroyed.

[English Page 15]

The Jair Synagogue

The "Jair Synagogue" on Tarnopolska street was broken open and plundered and thus it remained.

"Rabbi Mendele Synagogue"

The "Rabbi Menele Synagogue" located on Strazacka street was burned down during the bombardment of the Nazis.

The "Old Stretiner Klois"

The "Old Streiner Klois" which was located near the renovated synagogue was turned into a grain storehouse during the rule of the Soviets.

The "Rozler Klois"

The "Rozler Klois" which was situated on the northwest side of the "Big Synagogue" became ruined and forsaken.

The "Potiker Kleizel"

The "Potiker Kleizel" which was housed in Reb Jidels Synagogue was destroyed. Destroyed and burned down during the Nazi bombardment, it was the Kleizel of the tailors, the porters worship place, the prayer quarters of Rabbi Seide Halperin, the prayer quarter of the Mizrachi and another synagogue called "Yad–Haruzim."

The People's Center – The National House

The People's Home was an important property of the Jewish community of Brzezany. Dr. Falk and his wealthy family provided the funds for the erection of this spacious structure on Zboshova street. The People's Home was more impressive than any other structure in the surroundings. This beautiful institution was dedicated in April 1930 to serve the needs of the community and was registered as the property of the Orphan Home. The building contained two halls. The large hall which could accommodate 500 persons

[English Page 16]

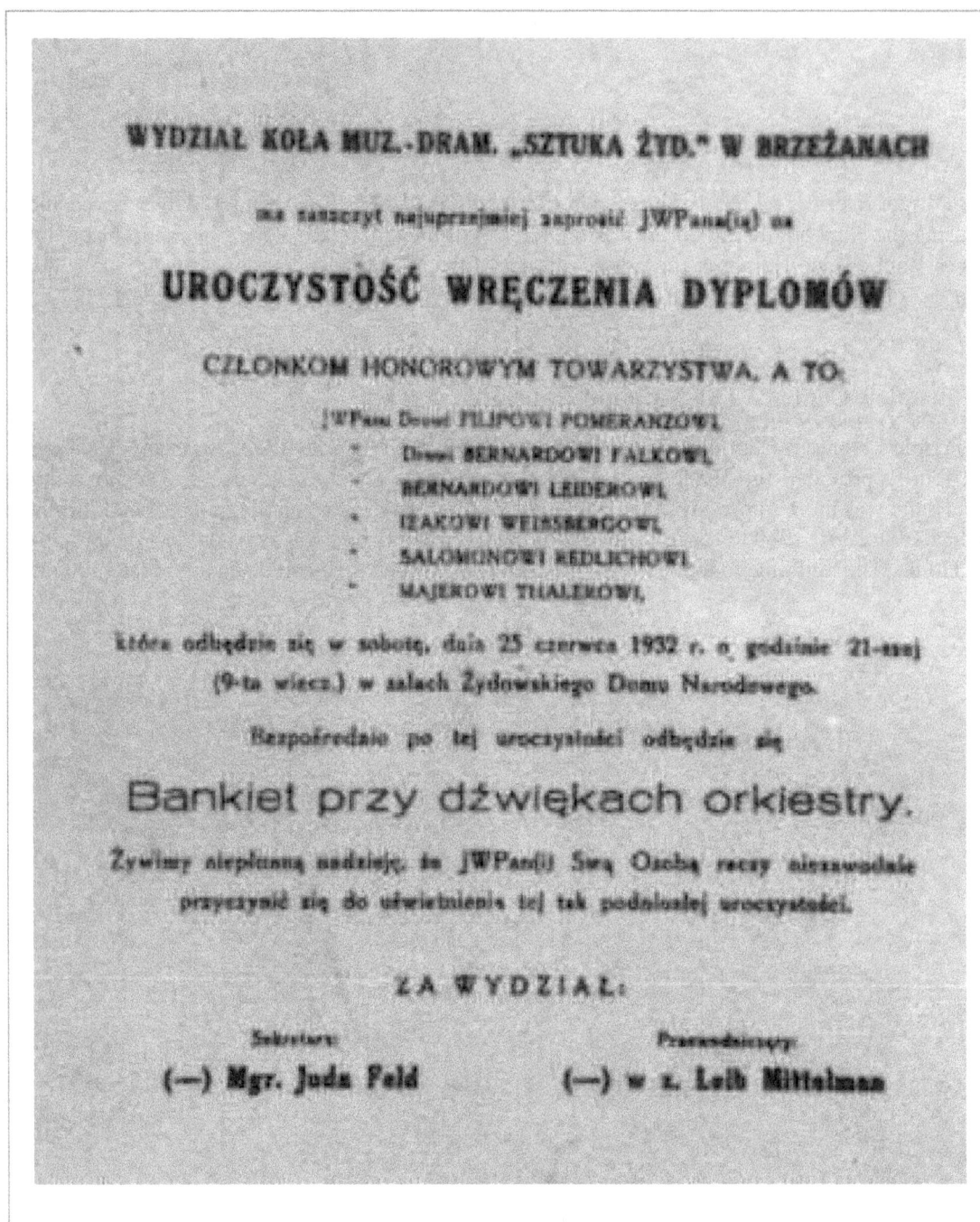

served mainly for important meetings and community events. The Dramatic circle staged its performances here. The Nazi oppressors made use of this hall as a detention place for the Jewish population before their deportation to concentration camps. During Soviet rule it was turned into a cinema. The People's Center is perhaps the only reminder of Jewish cultural life in our town. This lonely monument is a reminder that Jews lived here.

Z.K.S. The Jewish Sport Club

Jewish Sport Club was founded by a small group of youths in 1922. Its first activity was to organize a football team. They began without any financial means, but before long they were successful. In 1929 this team participated in regional games and advanced to league "A." Mr. Josef Maiblum was elected president of the Sport Club and Mr. Josef Lebers, vice president.

The Musical Dramatic Circle

In innovation, during the period of enlightenment was the appearance of theatrical groups in our town. There were performances in Hebrew as well as in Yiddish. The Yiddish spectacles were staged by local performers. Most active in these performances was Mr. Bialer, brother–in–law of Shlomo Redlich. Besides the performances staged by the local actors, there came to our town, professional theatrical groups, who staged dramas by Goldfaden, Gordin and others. Those active in the musical–dramatic circle after the First World War were S. Redlich, Bar–Dawid and Segal and the majority of the young people in our town were centered around it.

Alongside the Dramatic Circle was founded a library, the largest in our town. It contained books in three languages: Hebrew, Yiddish and Polish. There was also an orchestra. Two well–known families in our town appeared in musical performances on festive occasions – the Kurtzs and the Gutenplans. They also gave violin and clarinet lessons.

[English Page 17]

The Zionist Movement

This Zionist movement in our town existed since 1893. That year marked the founding of a Zionist organization, the "Beni Zion," who consisted mostly of the intelligentsia of our community and a number of property owners. Mr. Saul Maiblum was elected president of this organization. In 1897, Brzezany Zionists participated in electing a representative to the First Zionist Congress in Basel. S. Maiblum was elected as delegate. The teachers of Hebrew in town had a great influence in spreading the Hebrew word and the Zionist idea, which were closely tied with each other. The Zionist movement grew from year-to-year and there were a number of Zionist organizations in our town even before World War I.

In 1917, the youth movement "Hashomer" was founded in Brzezany. Its local head was M. Fried, followed by Mr. Bergman. The "Hashomer" movement was a national-Zionist movement attached to the world Scout movement. Two years later, the youth movement "Hehalutz" (the Pioneer) came into being. Many members of the "Hehalutz" movement went on "Aliyah" to "Eretz Israel." They were the first group to go on Aliyah, even before World War I. After World War I, these two Zionist movements were augmented by other Zionist movements such as: "Hashomer Hazair," "Mizrachi," "Zionist youth" and "Betar" movements. A considerable number of the members of these organizations also settled in Eretz Israel.

"Hechaluz" in Brzezany, 1926

[English Page 18]

Keren Kayemet – Keren HaYesod – Ezrah

In outstanding Zionist activity in our town was on behalf of the "Jewish National Fund." There were a great number of activists who dedicated their time and energy to this sacred work. Some of them were: Dr. Solomon Glaser, President, Mr. Thaler, secretary, E. Roth and M. Tunis were members of the committee. The names of these four devoted J.N.F. workers were inscribed in the Golden Book of the Jewish National Fund.

The "Keren HaYesod" in Brzezany was established in 1922. Dr. Nagler was elected President, M. Taub, treasurer and Mr. Bar-David, administrator.

The aim of "Ezra" was to render financial aid to those who wished to go on "Aliyah" to "Eretz Israel." The president of Zerah was Dr. Wilner. It is worthwhile to note that not one young person who wished to leave for Israel had to give up "Aliyah" because of lack of finances.

"Ezrah" in Brzezany

The Hebrew School

An important chapter in the history of the Jews of our town was the founding of a Hebrew school by the organization "Safa-Brura," (clear language) in May, 1903. The actual founders were: Mordechai Wolf Maiblum, Yehudah Zarvintzer, Zalman Zaper, Josef Finkelstein and Jacob Bauer. The teaching staff included: Abuhav, Cohen, Rachovski, Zigel, Dlugach and Zvi Scharfstein. Adolf Horn was elected president of the school. A club called "Ivriyah" with a library and a reading hall were established at the same time.

[English Page 19]

During World War I and even somewhat later, the teacher, Feld, served as principal of the school. He left our town in 1921. The Hebrew-School was opened again in 1926 with two teachers: Isaac Biterman and Abraham Halperin. At the end of 1927, they brought a new teacher, Mr. Komorovski, as principal. In 1929, a second Hebrew-School was founded by the "Tarbut" organization. Mr. Mansfeld was its principal. Shortly thereafter, yet another Hebrew-School was established by the Mizrachi organization.

Charity and Welfare Institutions

After World War I, many orphans without shelter and protection were left in the town. Thanks to the intervention of Mrs. R. Reich, Mrs. H. Goldenberg and Mrs. A. Milch and other Jewish women, a Jewish women's organization for the protection of these children was organized. In 1920, it changed its name from the Organization of Jewish Women for the Supervision of Orphans to the Society for the Protection of Jewish Orphans. This worthy cause was supported by Brzezany emigrants to the U.S.A. and particularly by the family of Isaac and Rosalie Feld from Philadelphia. Thanks to this aid, an Orphans'-home was built on Strazhacka Street. The majority of the 32 orphans of both sexes were taken in and brought up in this home. They received a thorough basic education and in addition, an occupational training so that they could later take care of themselves. This Orphans'-home ceased to function when World War II broke out. The destiny of these orphans was part and parcel of the destiny of the Jews in Brzezany.

The Holy Burial Society and the Coffin Bearers

This society was founded by Rabbi Naphtali Herz Halperin and Jakob Apel in 1837 and it was ratified in 1876 under the name of "Charity and Kindness." Every member of this holy society volunteered his services and took part in all its affairs without receiving anything in return. When World War II broke out, one member, David Ginsburg, took upon himself to conduct the affairs of this society. He devoted his time to this holy work to the very last day of his life. Other charitable and welfare institutions were: "The Diligent Hand of the Artisans," the "Society for Charity and Welfare," the "clothing of the Naked" and the "Mutual Assistance of the Academic Youth."

[English Page 20]

The Beginning of World War II

Both the Poles and the Ukrainians strove to seize the sources of livelihood from the Jewish population of the town. They were assisted in their evil deeds by the Polish Government. The Government levied heavy taxes upon the Jews and decreed harsh laws against them. The Polish and the Ukrainian mobs translated these laws into the force of the first. The Poles began by attacking and beating up their Jewish neighbours and the Ukrainians engaged in burning and pillaging Jewish homes and even murdering Jews who lived in villages. Anti-Semitism increased from day-to-day.

When World War II broke out, though we were aware that it could come, it was a heavy blow. We were not prepared for the war neither physically nor spiritually. Terror and confusion gripped us and fortunately, we didn't suffer human casualties in the brief initial period. From the Start, Polish officers and generals deserted the frontiers. The roads were jammed with refugees, soldiers and vehicles. There was confusion from constant bombardment by the German air force. The air attacks caused heavy losses. We helped the fleeing people with whatever we could. It is difficult to describe the prevailing confusion and despair. On Tuesday morning, September 17, 1939, we heard on the radio that the Soviets had crossed the Soviet-Polish border. We breathed relief. The great misfortune passed us by.

The Soviet Rule. 1939-1941.

When the soviets entered Brzezany, overnight, chaos broke loose though without bloodshed. The uppermost were made lowly and the lowly became uppermost. First of all, the Soviets released from jail all political prisoners and with their assistance, they established their rule. They helped themselves to whatever they needed and wanted. Every person's property was estimated and taxes were levied accordingly. "Counter-revolutionary" movements were checked and examined. Private property such as homes, merchandise and even furniture were confiscated. This condition lasted until the arrival of administrative personnel from Russia proper. All those who had served as officials before were dismissed. They newly arrived Russians bought out everything there was to buy. The stores were emptied and closed down. Farmers stopped bringing their produce to town. Before long, there was a shortage of foodstuffs and commodities.

The size of the population in town grew from day-to-day, due to the constant flow of refugees from the West and the arrival of the Soviet Government officials with their families from the East. In a short time, the Jewish population increased from 3,500 to over 12,000. The population of the town reached 35,000. To solve the problem of dwellings, the refugees used every vacant store, every synagogue and every hut and cabin. Local Jews did their utmost to render aid to the refugees,

[English Page 21]

but it was to no avail. The poverty and shortage grew from day-to-day, even if one had money, he couldn't obtain any food.

Towards the winter, the Soviet announced that the whole region was being added to the large family of the Soviet republics. Every person was obligated to obtain an identification certificate. However, prior to it, one had to sign that he was accepting Soviet citizenship. Those who were unwilling to assume Soviet citizenship were transported to Siberia. Other who received a special "paragraph" in their papers, which imposed all kinds of limitations particularly in the fields of employment and dwelling. Every person from the age of 18 and up had to work. If he was not employed, he was sent to the "Donbas" region. Those Jews of our town who had no specific occupation, or those who were superfluous in their trades, tried very hard to create places of work at their own expense so that they could remain in the town. The majority of the merchants became physical workers. Many professionals did likewise. The artisans organized themselves in "cooperatives." A Soviet official, called a "politrook" was assigned to each place of work. This official was responsible to the Government for his particular sector. Each person had a personal card issued to him by the N.K.V.D. (Soviet Ministry of Interior). This card bore all the particulars of the person's past and also of his present.

Our active life came to a standstill all of a sudden. The Library was closed down and the books disappeared. Not a vestige remained from the Dramatic Circle. The various Zionist movements were liquidated. A Hebrew word was considered (as a crime against the Government).

Everything one did was by order, according to a prepared plan. A man was only a tiny screw in a big machine. He was forbidden to think or, God forbid, to ask questions. We learned to keep silent. The Soviets forced us to spy on other people around us. Once a week, on a certain day and in the early hours after midnight, one had to appear before the N.K.V.D. and tell them what one had heard and saw. Closest friends became strangers to each other and shunned away from conversing with one another. Men of 18-50 years of age were subject to mobilization and a large portion of the youth served in the Soviet Army. In such a depressing atmosphere, we continued to live for almost 2 years.

On May 1, 1941, we heard rumours that the Germans were making preparations for war near the Russian borders. Worry and anxiety returned to us for we knew the meaning of these preparations! On the night of June 22, 1941, war broke out between the Nazi and the Russians. This time we suffered severely even before the Germans entered our town. German airplanes bombed Brzezany. Many houses were destroyed. Fires broke out in many parts of the town and there were a great number of casualties. Among the wrecked houses was the home of my parents. In the course of several minutes, we began to remove what we could out of the wreckage. We succeeded to extricate 8 living persons. After much effort, we pulled out another 30 persons and 25 dead bodies. Among them were 5 of my family. We dug graves with our own hands and performed for them the last kind deed. On July 1, 1941, the Germans entered our town.

[English Page 22]

The Holocaust

The Holocausts' meaning is the murder of six million Jews. Six million times – murder. Each individual and his specific and distinctive death, accompanied by fear and torture. Every human being represents an individual tragedy, a distinct story of his life and the days he lived saturated with tears, filled with rage and chagrin, agonized by hunger, by pain, by constant beatings and by the fear of death.

Suddenly we were attacked by an enemy who was strong, shrewd, corrupt, despicable and utterly cruel. An enemy who had only one aim – to exterminate all Jews without exception in the shortest way and by whatever possible means. To attain this goal, the Nazi mobilized learned professors, scientists, psychologists, medical doctors and simple scoundrels without any conscience or feeling. They had easy access to the most modern techniques and thus, they constructed a mass-murdering machine such as was never known in the annals of human history.

Against such a vicious, shrewd and powerful enemy, we stood helplessly believing naively in order, in law and justice. We thought, in our naivety, that the free world would not remain silent. The enemy exploited, on the one hand, his excessive strength and on the other hand, our naivety. Suddenly he hit us with savage cruelty until we lost sensibility. When we woke up, we found ourselves bruised physically and spiritually. We were starved, sick, feeble and depressed. We were shut up in ghettoes without any hope for the future. Hunger, epidemics and fright devoured us. All we were able to do was to reflect passively on the hope that the free world would emerge with its empathy and silence and would hasten to render us help. But the world continued in it's silence and help didn't come. Yet, in all these trying conditions, we were determined to endure and to survive. This is the secret of the eternal nation of the Jews – a stiff-necked nation that never despairs. People helped each other quietly without receiving any orders and sacrificed their lives to that others might live. They were the heroes.

The Germans entered our town on Tuesday and the following Wednesday night, a battle broke out between the German occupying forces and a detachment of the Soviet cavalry. The streets were full of dead soldiers and dead horses. The next day the German commander of the town issued an order that the streets had to be cleaned by the Jews in one day. Another German officer who supervised this work, picked out 3 Jews and shot them.

On Friday, a rumour spread that in the local prison, a locked cell containing 12 dead prisoners had been discovered. Right away, the Ukrainians spread a rumour that the Jews had killed these prisoners. The Sabbath passed by in relative quietness, however, on Sunday, mobs of peasants came from the countryside to pray in the church. There they received encouragement from their leaders

[English Page 23]

to attack the Jews. The peasants then scattered throughout the town and murdered and wounded, in bestial cruelty, hundred of Jews then robbed them of their possessions. At first, the dead were buried in the city park. Later, our people, guided by Ginsburg, transferred the dead from the public park to the Jewish cemetery. A total of 250 people were killed besides those who were killed in the Christian cemetery. The complaints of the local Jewish committee to the Nazi commandant of the town were answered by a number of announcements which informed us of a great number of anti-Jewish laws.

Two burning problems demanding immediate solution faces the Jewish community. The first one was the problem of hunger and the second was the need to provide work for all the Jews. The Ukrainian militia blocked all the roads leading to the town. No one could come in or leave, especially those with merchandise or commodities. The Ukrainians hoped to become the conquerors of the town and then confiscate all Jewish possessions. How strong was their disillusionment when the opposite happened. The Germans included the Lvov province in the general government. The attitude of the villages to towns changed completely. The Ukrainians began exploiting the food storage. In exchange for their products which were of very poor quality, they demanded valuable articles from the Jews.

The Germans demanded daily the Jews for different types of work. It was only the Jewish population that were obliged to fulfil all German demands on the very same day. The demands were not small. The German appetite grew from day-to-day. In those days, he who worked a day's work received, besides the beatings, one loaf of bread.

The health situation was frightful. There were hundreds of wounded and sick which hospitals would not admit. Dr. Falk and I, with the consent of the head of the Jewish community, opened a Jewish hospital in the community centre. Near it, we opened a clinic. We supplied all the necessary furnishings and equipment. Due to hunger and over-crowded living conditions, there appeared the first signs of an epidemic. We fought against this disaster with all our strength attempting to stop it, while there was time.

The military administration of the Germans ended after 6 weeks and a civil administration was established in its place. Easter Galicia was divided into 3 regions and our town belonged to the Tarnopol region in which was situated the headquarters of the Gestapo for the entire region. Kreishauptmann Asbach was put at the head of our town's administration and the Sonderdienst Police was put at his disposal. As soon as he arrived in town, he ordered Dr. Klarer to appear before him together with 23 men. I was one of them. I shall never forget this meeting. We entered as free men and left as the "Judenrat" (Jewish Council) responsible collectively for any disdain or opposition, punishable by death. We didn't know then what the task of the Judenrat meant but we had a feeling that a death sentence was put upon each one of us. Before the day was over, the Judenrat was already in full swing. The Kreishauptmann ordered the Judenrat

[English Page 24]

to collect 800,000 zloty from the Jews of the town within 6 days and then bring the collected money to him. After much crying and screaming, the Jews gave the demanded money and the Kreishautmann deposited it in his chest.

Rosh Hashanah arrived. We held services in private homes. We poured out our hearts before our Creator. In those moments, death sentences were decreed for many of us. Eight more days passed. On the day before Yom Kippur, an order from the Kreishautmann reached the Judenrat. Tomorrow, October 1, 1941 at 10 a.m., all Jews aged 20-30 headed by the Judenrat, had to appear at the "Targovica" square to register for work. The news spread in a second. We had the feeling that this order endangered our lives. We tried to clarify its real purpose but didn't succeed. No one knew whether he should advise the people to obey the order or to ignore it.

We finished the sacred prayer of "Kol-Nidrei." This service will never be forgotten by those who remained alive. The Yom Kippur morning service was completed at 9 a.m. Hand shaking tears and words of encouragement followed the service.

At 10 a.m. the Jews reported to the specified place. The Gestapo too was not late in coming. With weapons in their hands, they surrounded Targowice square. An order was issued: The Judenrat members would stand separately – workers would stand on the opposite side; the rest of the people such as lawyers, teachers, accountants and merchants would stand by themselves. After the assortment of the people was completed, they ordered the workers to go back to work and the members of the Judenrat were free to leave. The rest were surrounded by the Gestapo and led away to the prison. The following morning, after a meeting with the Kreishaputman, we rushed to collect golden items as ransom for the lives of those Jews who were put in jail. He took the gold and put it in his pocket dud did not release the people. Instead, they were loaded on trucks and transported to an unknown destination. They disappeared without leaving any trace. The peasants in the neighbourhood told, later, that these people had been murdered. The Germans claimed that they had been taken to a labour camp. We lived with the hope of seeing them alive again.

The German machine to finish off the Jews, worked without a halt. A new order came from the Kreishauptmann. He could not stand so many Jews in our town. He, therefore, decided to transport at least 100 of them weekly to nearby towns. The feeble, the old and the sick had to go first. Only those who were able to work and be useful were to be left in the town. The responsibility to carry out this scheme was placed on the Judenrat.

The Judenrat also had to report to the German authorities each time, the number of Jews deported to other towns. There was no alternative. The Judenrat had to comply with the order. To carry out this task, it was necessary to engage a force of men who would be subject to the authority of the Judenrat. An order was given by the German administration and the Judenrat organized a Jewish militia, the "Ordnungsdienst." In the time this militia became very helpful in

[English Page 25]

finishing off the Jews. The Kreishauptmann came with new demands each day. Thus, he demanded once that the Judenrat should place 40 men to his disposal for the purpose of clearing all the houses in the Jewish quarter, which were ruined by fire and bombardments.

The hunger and congestion affected the health of the Jewish population and epidemics began to spread. One day, I was called to the Judenrat. When I came there, I found the Gestapo waiting for me as I was responsible for reporting to them on the health conditions of the Jewish population. Right there and then, they gave me an order to inform them without delay on any case of a contagious disease. Of course, I promised to do so. I promised but did not carry it out. Yet, it didn't prevent the Gestapo from visiting our town each week and shooting a number of persons, justifying their action by claiming that they were clearing the town of typhoid. Actions such as these continued.

Eight days before Hanukkah, the Kreishauptmann called the Judenrat representatives to his office and told them, in anger, that he would not stand for the disregard of his command to transfer Jews from our town into neighbouring towns. He, therefore said: "You are given eight days in which to select and prepare 1,000 Jews (not one less) and deport them to the nearest town "Podhaica." The whole project was to be supervised by the "Sonderdienst" and by the Ukrainian militia. The march would take place during the night of December 15-16. The Jews would march by foot, 4 abreast. This news spread throughout the town with lightning speed. The Jewish inhabitants left their homes and scattered beyond their dwelling places. The town was left empty. After an exhaustive and costly effort by the Judenrat, Kriger, the assistant to the Kreishaupmann, was commanded to take it upon himself to investigate the whole project and to see to it personally that no harm should happen to anyone. He, himself, would see to it that the transfer of the 1,000 Jews should be orderly and that dwelling places would be prepared for these people. He also gave permission to take 20 wagons for the use of the elderly and the children. A great number of Jews were scattered outside the town and the Judenrat, together with the Jewish militia, could not collect the required number to be transferred. After midnight they were joined in the search for Jews by Germans. Altogether, they collected 600 men. At 3.a.m. the caravan moved in the direction of Podhaice. To this caravan were added the Judenrat officials who were helpful in collecting the Jews. The tragic end of this story was that the Gestapo was waiting for them. The whole caravan was brought into a forest and all of its members were killed.

One witness remained, as if by a miracle to tell what had transpired. Soon afterwards, we hastened to that spot. We found the massacred bodies buried in a mass grave.

The next day the Kreishauptmann was furious and, for the first time, he hit the Judenrat members and wounded Dr. Klarer because of the unsuccessful and disorderly project. At the same time, he gave another order – all Jews were to hand over, in the course of several days, their fur coats. To add more force to his order, he demanded 12 persons as hostages. We all felt responsible for the 12 hostages. Without delay, we brought the fur coats and the hostages were freed. This time the act was completed without bloodshed.

[English Page 26]

Labour and Concentration Camps

The Germans exploited the human strength of the Jews for rigorous labour. For this purpose, they concentrated them into labour camps. Near us were a number of such labour camps. All of them were not car from the city of Tarnopol. Such as the scamp in "Zborow," in "Kamionka," in "Hluboki Wielkie"and many others. In every such camps there were between 400 to 800 men. They worked in quarries and on highways. The Judenrat was obligated to supply the manpower according to the demands of the Gestapo. From the standpoint of actual work, there was only enough for several hundred men, but for the Gestapo and for the German labour offices, these camps turned into a sort of business. The German officials were interested in bringing into the camps not merely hundreds or thousands of Jews, but tens of thousands of Jewish slave labourers. To materialize this purpose, they used their energy in destroying and exterminating, by every possible means, the Jewish labourers who were already in the camps and bringing new ones in their place. With every new group of workers, they received a large sum of money from the Judenrat, besides robbing the workers of their belongings. The Nazi labour and concentration camps constituted one of the saddest, depressing and most painful chapters in the history of human brutality. It left the "mark of Cain" on everyone who had something to do with them. "Labour camp" – these two words spelt hunger, terror, torture, murderous beatings and degradation until redemption by the Angel of Death.

The labour camps as well as the ghettoes were a long legend of suffering. It was a Gehenna – a veritable inferno on earth. In camps and ghettoes, brother harassed brother and Jew battled his fellow Jew. This was the height of slavishness and degradation. The human being lost his hopes, stopped thinking and became a blind medium – a mere tool in the hands of his oppressors. There was no one to rouse him from his stupefying sleep. People were drugged, misled and went astray from the human path.

The winter itself caused many casualties, beside those who were murdered by the Nazi. Hundreds died from hunger and epidemics. The spring of 1942 that followed brought no relief for us. Day-after-day there came new commands and with them, new and fresh troubles. The Kreishauptmann was displeased with the Judenrat and reorganized it. He added another man, Bercio Feld. The Kreishauptmann saw in him the man who would carry out his orders to his fullest satisfaction. He also reduced the number of the Judenrat from 24 to 12 so it would be easier for him to deal with the Council. Feld's first activity was to reorganize the Jewish militia. He brought into it many of his trusted friends and appointed Bettinger as its commander. The Nazi order in those days was to concentrate in Brzezany these Jews who resided in nearby villages. It was forbidden for a Jew to live in a village without a special permit.

The holiday of Passover came. We spent the eight Passover days without agitating any incidents. The worrisome news about the plight of Jews in Western

[English Page 27]

Europe reached us. According to this news, which was brought to us by Polish neighbours who added a bit of poison to each story, the Germans were uprooting Jews from their places of residence and were being brought by train to the district of Lublin.

What were the Germans doing with those Jews? Everyone had his own comments. Finally, we learned the tragic truth about the final solution. The Nazi were transporting the Jews into special extermination camps. A place, or district where Jewish inhabitants had been exterminated became designated as free and clear of Jews – "*Judenrein*,"

Thus, the Jews began to look for ways and means to save themselves. There were some who attempted to cross the Hungarian border. Others tried to live as gentiles on "Aryan" papers. A good portion of Jews looked for hiding places among the neighborhood peasants. Some of them were lucky and survived, however, in most cases, the peasants themselves killed the Jews or handed them over to the Germans for a pot of "lentil-porridge." The simplest thing was to build a hiding place, each one in his own house and to use it as a shelter in time of trouble. Much planning, toil, effort and strength went into the construction of these hiding places, which were helpful but for a limited time.

During the month of July, 1942, the Germans, for the first time, instituted a search for young women to be sent to labour camps. They seized 60 girls and transported them to the Yagelnica camp near Chortkow. After several months of body-breaking work, the girls met their death.

The days were passing swiftly and each day brought new news. In those days we were informed about an extermination camp to be set up especially for us and constructed in the town of Belzec. Belzec, a small forsaken town, was suddenly marked on our map with the blood of innocent Jews. The uprooting of the Jewish population in our region began with the city of Lvov, and, according to Nazi plans, continued district-after-district and town-after-town. This is how the Germans operated. During darkness of night or close to dawn, they would surround the town, attack Jewish homes, make thorough searches, seize people and bring them to a central assembly place under a hail of shots, beatings, insults and shouts. They stood there for long hours and were then led away to the train railroad station under heavy guard. The train arrived, the people were brought into the coaches which were locked and sealed, and the train left. After travelling for hours in over crowded coaches, they arrived at their destination. The coaches were opened and the people led out. The Germans forced them to remove their clothing and they were then led away to the gas chambers. The gas jets were opened and the bodies were burned and even before this tragic scene ended, new transports arrived.

[English Page 28]

Finally, our town's turn also came. Yom Kippur, the day of Atonement, 1942, was approaching. We had not forgotten yet the last Atonement Day. The Gestapo, for a money bribe, promised to postpone the planned "action" for a later day but this time too, they deceived us as they had done many times before. Instead of starting their rounding up before dawn as we had expected them to do, they appeared suddenly at 7:30 a.m. and began their work with more cruelty than before. At the beginning they succeeded in gathering many Jews from the synagogues, but those Jews who were still at home succeeded in hiding or slipping away and evading the Gestapo. As a result, they were short of the number of Jews required by their plan. They continued the "action" the following day until the goal was attained. They took away from us more than 1,500 persons. The train made its way to the extermination camp in Belzec. On the way, some of our people succeeded in breaking down the doors of the wagons and those who had strength and luck jumped from the train and came back to town to start anew. On the morrow of this "action," the Germans collected the Jewish belongings what they "inherited" from the people they had murdered the previous day as though to fulfil the saying: "Thou has murdered and also taken possession!"

In order to make it easier for themselves in the future, the Gestapo confined us into a much smaller and closed-in ghetto. They brought us into half-ruined houses in the Jewish quarter. The living conditions in these ruins were unbearable. 20 persons were crowded into one room. It was no wonder that epidemics killed hundreds of us. The ghetto was closed and without a special permit, it was forbidden to leave it. This brought about the breakdown in the barter business with the peasants of the neighbourhood. We also lost at once most of our hiding places and the advantage of escaping from the town in time of danger.

The next "action" was not late in coming. By the month of January, 1943, 3 "actions" each one crueller than the other had taken place. We were only a small group of people left in the ghetto, a mere remnant of the Jews of our town. At the beginning of February, the Judenrat received an order from the Gestapo to bring back to town all of the Jews that had received special permission to live outside the ghetto. On 15th February, 1943, the validity of these special permits expired. This served as a sign that in the coming days, a complete and decisive purge of the remaining Jews would take place. We still do not know the reason which eventually caused the Germans to postpone the last "action" for a number of months.

On March 12, Jewish women received permission from the Gestapo to go and purchase whatever they needed in the market of Novi-Rinek. There, the German gendarmes were waiting for them. They arrested the women and brought them straight to the cemetery where they shot and killed them.

Prior to the final liquidation of the ghetto, there was one more "action" which lasted 3 days. It began several days before Passover. Unlike the previous "actions," this one was performed by local forces. It was done slowly, quietly and carefully. In a matter of 3 days, they succeeded in gathering 300 people, men, women and children into the prison yard. There, Herman of the Gestapo made a selection. Some were assigned to a labour camp while the rest were led away to the cemetery.

[English Page 29]

The Germans were making the last preparations necessary for the liquidation of the ghetto. Before our very eyes, they were digging in the cemetery mass graves for us. They were not hiding their intentions from s, on the contrary, with a smile on their lips, they told us of the approaching Judgment Day. Day-after-day, they organized our liquidation. Town-after-town was being finished off. We were counting the few remaining hours. Everyone was trying to utilize them. Some were trying to repair the hiding places, others were searching for ways and means to save themselves, even at the last moment. All of a sudden, we received encouraging news. The Gestapo informed our representatives that it had the authority to exempt 200 men with required skills. These men would have to reside in army barracks under a heavy German guard. They would work and would not be harmed. An admission card to these barracks could be obtained for an enormous sum of money and was given to men only. Two days went by and the number of persons who were ready and willing to pay the required sum of money for an admission card to the barracks were twice as many as the available card. After an effort by our emissaries, the Gestapo agreed to increase the number of admissions to 400.

During the month of May, 1943, the barracks were prepared for 400 men in the home of Dr. Falk. The Germans constructed high wire fence around the house so that no one could come in or leave without the guard's order. Everyone who had obtained a card had to come and reside there no later than the end of May. At dawn on Saturday June 12, the final "action" began, 3 days ahead of our expectations. On that day, the Gestapo finished off the ghetto as well as the people in the barracks. Once again, the Germans had succeeded in deceiving those who believed them. Under a heavy guard the barracks dwellers were brought to the cemetery. Only one witness of that event, Menachem Katz, survived and told us what had happened.

The Brzezaner synagogue in Brooklyn, N.Y.

[English Page 30]

The memorial table to the community of Brzezany and
Narajow in the Holocaust cellar on Mount Zion in
Jerusalem

    Several hundred Brzezany Jews succeeded in avoiding the brutal hand of the executioner and fled the town, but only a few returned in torn and rotten clothes, practically dressed in rags. They entered their hometown 13 months after they had left it. Altogether, 36 people survived. That was all that had been left out of 12,000 Jews who had resided in Brzezany when the German occupied the town. We, those who came back, lived like one family. All of us lived in one section, far from the ghetto and from those people and places where we dwelt during the Nazi rule. We had a strong desire to get away from the local population, a great majority of whom had given a helping hand to the murder of the Jews. We were looking forward to the day when we would be able to leave that terrifying place, where our lives and the lives of our dear ones were brought to a premature end. Our situation after the liberation by the Soviets became more difficult than before the Nazi occupation. The non-Jewish population as well as the Soviet government could not forgive the fact that we remained alive. They saw in us an unwanted remnant. They, as well as we, were waiting for the day when we could leave the place forever. Finally, that day arrived. According to an agreement between Poland and the Soviet Union, we were allowed to leave the town our fathers and forefathers had lived in. We left it with tears in our eyes to start our lives anew and to never forget all those who did not survive. We left behind a big empty synagogue, a desolate peoples' centre and a large cemetery, filled with mass graves.

Never, never shall we forget our dear ones ! !

Group of Brzezaner people around the memorial table in "Jaa'r Hakdoshim" in the forest hills near Jerusalem

NAME INDEX

Tauber, 28, 36, 519, 520
Te'eni, 165, 223, 545, 550
Teidl, 520
Teikher, 621
Teikhman, 621
Teitelbaum, 520
Tempel, 279, 521
Tenenbaum, 553
Thaler, 113, 114, 120, 122, 642
Tihr, 521
Tinter, 121, 521
Tir, 521
Tirkelfeld, 121
Tirkesher, 111
Tirkfeld, 522
Tirkisher, 39, 113, 522
Tishler, 39, 80
Tobias, 522, 523
Toib, 523
Toiber, 63, 142, 143, 283, 621
Toibish, 32
Tomarkin, 162
Tonis, 29, 33, 34, 36, 38, 98, 113, 121, 240, 380, 523, 524
Tontzio, 33, 111, 121
Trauner, 98, 145, 301, 394, 408, 524
Trumpeldor, 45, 56, 70, 76, 568
Tuch, 627
Tukh, 543, 524
Tulek, 58
Tunis, 642
Turktaum, 524
Turner, 597, 621
Tversky, 141
Tzeig, 48, 52, 117, 121, 283, 524, 525, 526, 546
Tzerbinski, 404, 407
Tzimer, 526
Tzimerman, 39, 53
Tzimmeman, 546
Tzitron, 526
Tzizer, 526
Tzukerkandel, 96, 526
Tzvatler, 526
Tzveig, 621, 622

U

Unger, 526, 527

V

Vagner, 527, 622
Vagshall, 97, 98, 301
Vakhtel, 542, 606, 622
Vanderer, 527
Vandmeir, 135
Varm, 622
Varschover, 527
Vaser, 527
Vashertzberg, 527
Vaver, 527
Veidenfeld, 528
Veingarten, 528
Veinlager, 542
Veinlaub, 528
Veinloger, 528
Veinshtein, 74, 97, 114, 528, 529, 612, 614
Veintraub, 40, 41, 138, 154, 529
Veis, 594, 622
Veisbeg, 77
Veisberg, 82, 113, 114, 529
Veisman, 542
Veitz, 529
Veitzen, 530
Veitzman, 596, 623
Veizer, 33
Velgar, 33
Velger, 530
Viderker, 530, 623
Vidhof, 111, 113, 121, 126, 530, 531
Vidman, 605
Viethof, 36
Vilner, 28, 37, 39, 50, 78, 82, 98, 102, 114, 126, 159, 207, 208, 300, 531, 541, 542
Viner, 67
Vinles, 531
Vinter, 33, 38, 97, 113, 114, 116, 120, 531, 532
Vishbianski, 532
Vitalis, 541
Vitlin, 532

www.ingramcontent.com/pod-product-compliance
Lightning Source LLC
Chambersburg PA
CBHW062020090426

42811CB00005B/910